Adolescence
Seventh Edition

Adolescence
Continuity, Change, and Diversity Seventh Edition

Nancy J. Cobb
California State University, Los Angeles

Sinauer Associates Inc. Publishers
Sunderland, Massachusetts U.S.A.

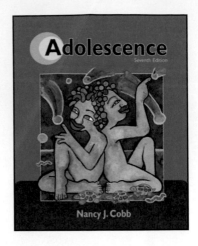

About the Cover

Adolescence   Watercolor by Joanne Delphia. This piece depicts one adolescent child in two different stages of development during these formative years. As the snakes represent the temptations of youth, the turtles represent how slowly time can seem to move by, even though change is in the air (depicted by shooting stars).

Adolescence, *Continuity, Change, and Diversity*, Seventh Edition
Copyright ©2010 by Sinauer Associates, Inc.
All rights reserved. This book may not be reproduced in whole or in part without permission from the publisher.
For information, address:
Sinauer Associates, Inc., 23 Plumtree Road, Sunderland, MA 01375 U.S.A.
FAX: 413-549-1118
E-mail: publish@sinauer.com
Internet: www.sinauer.com

Library of Congress Cataloging-in-Publication Data

Cobb, Nancy J.
 Adolescence: continuity, change, and diversity / Nancy J. Cobb. -- 7th ed.
   p. cm.
 ISBN 978-0-87893-338-9
 1. Adolescence. 2. Adolescent psychology. 3. Teenagers--United States. I. Title.
 HQ796.C596 2010
 305.235--dc22
                                                                       2010011440

For Michael,
as always

Brief Contents

Contents

3 The Biological and Physical Changes of Adolescence: Puberty, Health, and Well-Being 64

4 The Cognitive Changes of Adolescence 100

5 Defining the Self: *Identity and Intimacy* 138

6 Adolescents in the Family: *Changing Roles and Relationships* 176

9 Leisure, Work, and College 274

10 Sexuality 314

RESEARCH FOCUS BOXES

Research Focus Boxes in the Text

BOX 1.1 *An Experiment: "Who You Pushin', Buddy!" Perceptions of Aggressiveness   10*

BOX 2.1 *Erikson's Psychohistorical Approach: A Clinician's Notebook from the Dakota Prairies   44*

BOX 3.2 *Randomized Versus Quasi-Experimental Designs: What's in a Name? Communication across the Ages   95*

BOX 4.3 *Cross-Sectional and Sequential Designs: Does Intelligence Slip with Age?   120*

BOX 5.3 *Operationalizing Concepts: What Kind of Decision Maker Are You?   154*

BOX 6.1 *Sampling: How Emotional Are Adolescents?   180*

BOX 7.2 *Longitudinal Design: Friendship Patterns   224*

BOX 8.5 *Within-Subjects Design and Attention Deficit Disorder: "Can't I Stay Home? I Think I Don't Feel Well."   265*

BOX 9.1 *Correlational Research: Hangin' out on a Friday Night   290*

BOX 10.1 *Between-Subjects Design: Date Rape   317*

BOX 11.2 *Statistical Tests of Significance: What Do a Huai Haizi, a Warui Ko, and a Bad Kid Have in Common?   362*

BOX 12.4 *Bias and Blind Controls: Eating Disorders   401*

BOX 13.1 *Archival Research: Racial Socialization—Survival Tactics in a White Society?   419*

Research Focus Boxes on the Web Site
www.sinauer.com/cobb

Research Strategies

Case Studies: Educating the Gifted Adolescent

Factorial Designs: Interpreting Ambiguous Situations

Matched-Subjects Design: Sexual Orientation of Children Raised in Lesbian Families

Path Analysis: Too Young for Intimacy?

Research Issues

Coding Descriptive Responses: Gender Differences in Beliefs about Sexual Desire

Confidentiality: Troubled Relationships— "You Sound Just Like Your Mother!"

Dependent Variable: When Is a Stereotype Simply a Good Guess, and When Is It More?

Ethics: How Do Adolescents Feel When Making a Big Decision?

Internal and External Validity: Cholas and Gang Girls

Projective Measures: If Shakespeare Had Been a Woman, Romeo and Juliet Might Have Survived Romance

Questionnaires: Parenting Styles and Flow

Theory-Guided Research: How Sexist Is Our Language?

Preface

Writing the preface to the 7th edition of a text is something like making an entrance at your class reunion. You need to let old friends know that, despite some significant changes, you still retain the qualities that made them like you in the first place, all while introducing yourself to people you haven't met before. And so it is with this new edition of *Adolescence: Continuity, Change and Diversity*. While this revision contains some significant changes, the essential characteristics that distinguish it from other texts remain the same. Let me call your attention first to these, and then move to what has changed in this edition.

Features of this Text

Clear and Engaging Writing Style

It continues to be a source of pride to me that since this text first appeared in 1992 students have found it enjoyable to read as well as informative. This is largely because the stories and vignettes chosen to illustrate concepts are "slices of life," drawn from the personal experiences of adolescents. These stories have the same narrative qualities that make all genuinely human stories engaging, in what ever the context. They draw on adolescents differing in ethnicity, gender and life circumstances, enabling every reader to relate to what is being presented. Finally, I believe readers are engaged because concepts are presented in sufficient depth that they become easily understandable.

Strong Research Base

Scientific rigor needn't be *rigor mortis*. That is, good science doesn't have to be difficult to understand. What makes scientific research rigorous has little to do with difficulty, but rather with the validity of its theories and the strength of the evidence supporting these. For each of the topics covered in the text, I have presented the most current evidence available. In several places, regarding such pressing social issues as sex education, the prevention of adolescent drug abuse or improving high school graduation rates, I've contrasted programs that have been shown to be effective, based on scientifically rigorous research, with less effective, or even ineffective, programs and practices currently in place.

The research methods used by those who study adolescents are summarized in the second chapter, following a discussion of developmental theories. Additionally, every chapter contains a "Research Focus Box" which begins with a practical problem relevant to the topic of that chapter and illustrates the process researchers have undertaken to solve it. Taken together, the boxes present a range of issues important for students' understanding of research methodology in developmental psychology. In this way, methodological issues are explored in a context in which they provide answers to meaningful questions. Additional research boxes are available on the Website (www.sinauer.com/cobb).

Unifying Themes

Devoting an entire text to adolescence unavoidably suggests that somehow all adolescents are similar, in that what applies to one applies to all. Adolescents of course have many things in common or else they wouldn't constitute a category. But it's crucial that we not be captive to our categories; all adolescents are not the same, and there are systematic factors that make them different from each other. In this book, I focus on four important factors accounting for differences among adolescents: *gender, ethnicity, age,* and the *search for a stable identity*. These four themes run through all chapters.

GENDER   We are past assuming that the male experience is normative for both sexes, with just a few corrections to be made for females. Females definitely differ from males, there's no doubt about it. And this difference plays an enormous role in the lives of adolescents, as this text describes. But we are still struggling to distinguish which of the acknowledged differences are "built in" and which are "socially constructed." Or in other words, which differences are simply "our biological nature and can't be changed" and which are "the way we make them and might be changed"? This uncertainty concerning the most fundamental of human distinctions makes gender potentially problematic for every adolescent and a natural topic for scientific investigation.

ETHNICITY   Like gender, ethnic differences play a crucial role in understanding adolescent development. But unlike gender, which still sorts the population into two roughly equal halves, the ethnic composition of the United States is rapidly changing, with minority adolescents promising to supplant those who now constitute the majority. Minority versus majority status in society carries implications for many aspects of development, and these statuses are changing faster than we, or our theories, can comprehend. Theories of adolescent identity formation must address the tension between a changing self and an evolving society, yet most theories still presuppose a European American culture that no longer exists in much of the United States. While we still have no comprehensive account of the influence of ethnicity on adolescence, we do have a good deal of data and some "mini-theories" to account for them. I have incorporated these data and theories throughout the text so that even though we may not fully understand where we are, we are not deceived that we are still where we used to be.

EARLY AND LATE ADOLESCENCE AND EMERGING ADULTHOOD   Some differences are so obvious we don't take them seriously until we trip over them. We all too easily forget, at times, that there are immense differences between a 12-year-old and a 17-year-old because they are both "adolescents." However, the 12-year-old is just one step beyond the comfortable routine of grade school while the 17-year-old stands ready to exit high school and at the threshold of college or work. Similarly, the 12-year-old is just beginning to struggle with puberty and a new awareness of sexuality, while the 17-year-old is struggling to integrate sexuality into a meaningful relationship. In a word, the 12-year-old is in early adolescence and just leaving childhood, while the 17-year-old is a late adolescent and just entering adulthood. Additionally, emerging adults, though having resolved many of the identity issues adolescents wrestle with, don't necessarily see themselves as having reached adulthood. Throughout this text I have attempted to keep clear the unmistakable differences between these phases of development.

THE SEARCH FOR A STABLE PERSONAL IDENTITY   You might not think of the search for a stable personal identity as a source of difference, but it is—and a powerful one too. A person's identity is stable to the extent that it reconciles all the various influences converging on it. But since each adolescent has a different mix of these influences, each adolescent is led to a different reconciliation, and thereby to uniqueness. To put it slightly differently, the search for a personal identity is a quest to do justice to the profusion of claims made upon one. Each of the three factors that we have considered—gender, ethnicity and age—constitutes such a claim. An adolescent who finds it necessary to deny any one of these in coming to terms with the others is likely to have achieved only a tenuous and temporary adjustment that ultimately will require re-negotiation.

What Is New in this Edition

This new edition contains many changes; some of these take the form of expanded and updated content and research, and some are primarily pedagogical, making it easier for students to master the material being presented. Many of these changes were suggested by current users of the text as ways to improve what they already liked; other changes were made in response to the comments of reviewers who, although they had not adopted this text, indicated what it would take to convert them to users. First, let me highlight the expanded and updated content.

Expanded and Updated Content and Research

Current research articles from peer reviewed journals has been incorporated throughout the text, updating sections in every chapter. A number of topics receive special attention: health and well-being, a global focus on adolescent development, the influence of the Internet and the media, and effective programs for adolescents, families, and communities.

HEALTH AND WELL-BEING   Chapter 1 examines adolescents' generally positive outlook on life, in contrast to the more common stereotype of them as contrary and moody. Chapter 3 presents research on changing patterns of sleep in adolescence, and how sleepiness affects performance in school and introduces risks when driving. Sections on nutrition, physical activity, and the current epidemic of overweight have been updated. Also covered are adolescents' use of the Internet to obtain information they need, and the impact of poverty on adolescents' health, in particular with respect to increased exposure to air pollution and asthma-related allergens, poorer housing, inadequate health care, and the safety of their neighborhoods.

The effects of multitasking on attention and performance, whether this is doing homework in front of the television or using a cell phone while driving, are discussed in Chapter 4. A related section examines an increase in risk taking in adolescence, particularly when other adolescents are present, and policies that have been implemented to increase safety. Chapter 6 identifies and compares styles of parenting with respect to promoting healthy development. This chapter also treats the impact of divorce on adolescents, and reviews conditions that promote successfully coping with divorce. Chapter 8 looks at the resources available to students and their families through full-service schools, and Chapters 9 and 13 consider the benefits of organized activities for positive youth development. Chapter 13 also covers the contributions of parental monitoring, community resources, teachers, and personal strengths such as religious beliefs to adolescents' health and well-being.

GLOBAL FOCUS ON ADOLESCENT DEVELOPMENT   Chapter 1 compares the sense of self that adolescents develop in individualistic cultures, such as North American, Scandinavian, and Western European countries, with that of adolescents in collectivistic cultures, such as Latin American, Asian, or Middle-Eastern countries. Additionally, comparisons are made with respect to the developmental tasks of adolescence; we find that not all cultures place the same emphasis on the same tasks. For instance, although preparing for an occupation is expected of adolescents in all industrialized societies, the French emphasize this more than the Germans. Similarly, establishing mature relationships with peers, also expected of adolescents in both cultures, is given greater importance in Germany than in France. Likewise, although adolescents in all cultures face concerns related to body image and adult gender roles, these loom larger for those in traditional societies, in which gender roles are more clearly defined. Cultural differences exist as well with respect to emerging adulthood.

Chapter 4 compares risk taking among adolescents in different countries. Chapter 5 examines differences in cultural contributions to identity achievement, as well as similarities in the patterns of interaction and communication among different cultures. This chapter also looks at differences in the ways a sense of agency is expressed in individualistic and collectivistic cultures. Chapter 6 examines cultural differences in styles of parenting, and Chapter 7 compares friendship patterns and the meaning of friendship for adolescents in different cultures. Chapter 8 examines academic proficiency in basic subjects of adolescents from different countries, and different ways in teaching math. Chapter 9 looks at patterns of adolescents' work and leisure time across cultures. This chapter also presents figures for child labor in many regions of the world, and discusses the effectiveness of programs designed to curtail child labor. Factors that contribute to lower rates of pregnancy, birth, and abortion in many other countries than in the U.S. are examined in Chapter 10.

THE INFLUENCE OF THE INTERNET AND THE MEDIA   Adolescents comfortably move in a world their parents have entered only as adults—one of cell phones, smart phones, texting, the Internet, and social network sites. Chapter 5 examines the ways in which adolescents use the Internet as a way to experiment with their identities. The Internet offers a unique opportunity for such experimentation because of the anonymity it affords; those they meet online have no information as to their sex, age, the school they attend, where they live, or how attractive they might be. Chapter 7 looks at adolescents' use of social network sites to post information, stay in touch with friends they see on a regular basis, and to maintain contact with those they see infrequently. This chapter also discusses the risks of making friends through the Internet and the ways adolescents and parents protect against these.

Chapter 9 looks at adolescents' exposure to sexual themes and media violence through television, movies, video games, and the Internet, and examines research addressing the effect this exposure has on their sexual and aggressive behavior. Chapter 10 describes how adolescents use the Internet to get answers to questions regarding sexuality that they may be uncomfortable asking a parent or even a friend. Chapter 10 also looks at an innovative intervention program that involves the use of text messages; teenage mothers receive messages offering support, information on parenting, and even a message 'from the baby' each day.

EFFECTIVE PROGRAMS FOR ADOLESCENTS, FAMILIES, AND COMMUNITIES   Chapter 3 describes an intergenerational mentoring program for adolescents living in low-income, high-crime neighborhoods that helped them resist drugs, reduced absenteeism, and led to more positive attitudes toward school and their own futures. A critical interface where research on adolescence meets public policy concerns the effectiveness of sex education programs. Those that include a service option as well as information on the use of contraceptives have been found to be successful in delaying sexual initiation and protecting against adolescent pregnancy (Chapter 10). This chapter also includes research on the effectiveness and potential consequences of virginity pledges.

Chapter 8 summarizes conditions that contribute to the overall effectiveness of schools, and describes a program for reducing school bullying. This chapter also presents a way of teaching math, used in some Asian cultures, that engages students' interest and increases their understanding of concepts. The chapter highlights the effectiveness of early childhood intervention programs in improving academic achievement through adolescence and in increasing graduation rates. A program for getting students who drop out back on track is also spotlighted in this chapter. Chapter 9 examines the benefits of getting adolescents involved in organized activities and identifies intervention programs designed to prepare minority youth for a full range of occupational opportunities. Chapter 12 describes an innovative school lunch program that addresses the growing problem of obesity among adolescents. Chapter 13 includes a discussion of racial socialization, which explores the ways that minority parents prepare their children for life in the broader society, and a section on the conditions that foster positive youth development in all adolescents.

The problems of adolescents can not be neatly separated from problems facing the societies in which they live, with the consequence that many 'adolescent' problems can not be addressed adequately until societies confront issues such as the safety of neighborhoods, the availability of jobs, access to healthcare, and quality education for all. Adolescents, however, aren't waiting around for us to do something. In Chapter 13, we meet adolescents who volunteer time to work at community agencies and charitable organizations, and others who start their own charitable programs.

Pedagogical Features

CHAPTER OVERVIEWS   Information is easier to comprehend if you know what to expect. To help students anticipate what they will be reading, I have included Chapter Overviews at the beginning of each chapter that briefly summarize the main points of that chapter.

IN-CHAPTER GLOSSARIES   This is an improvement I should have made a long time ago. I have always been impatient with having to leave the page I'm reading to look up an unfamiliar term. I would have welcomed, as I believe students will in this edition, the definition of technical terms in the margin of the page on which they occur. Definitions for all glossary terms appear in the margins of the page next to the section in which they are introduced.

CHAPTER SUMMARIES   There's a useful adage common among journalists: Tell 'em what you're going to tell them, tell them the story, and then tell 'em what you've told them. The chapter overviews and chapter summaries for each chapter follow this advice. The summaries in this edition are even easier to follow when reviewing the chapter because they provide the chapter headings that identify each section as well as a summary of the material in that section.

Chapter by Chapter Changes

It is immensely helpful to have suggestions and comments from colleagues within the discipline when revising a textbook. I have been particularly fortunate in this regard in working on this revision. This section summarizes some of the more important changes that I've made in response to these.

Chapter 1 has been reorganized to present more clearly the themes of the text and prepare students for what will follow. Also, I have included information on the ways in which societal conditions, such as economic recession, affect individual adolescents' lives, looking at belt tightening and financial hardship among middle class as well as low-income families. I compare trends within the U.S., such as an aging population and changing patterns of ethnicity, with similar trends in other countries. A number of reviewers commented that Bronfenbrenner's theory needed to be presented in more detail. I have done this and added additional examples, making this easier to understand.

In response to suggestions from several reviewers, I have condensed the discussion of developmental theories in Chapter 2 in order to include a section on research methods in the second half of the chapter. As before, Research Focus Boxes in each chapter give a detailed view of some aspect of research by introducing a real-life problem relevant to the topic of that chapter and describing in detail an aspect of the research used in studying this. For instance, the box in Chapter 12 begins with a research assistant coding the behavior of adolescents with eating disorders to discuss problems of bias due to experimenter expectancy and the use of blind controls.

In Chapter 3, I detail the "trigger" for the feedback loop controlling the events of puberty, describing the role of Kisspeptin in releasing the action of the hypothalamic pulse generator. Chapter 3 also has an updated section on health and well-being with information on nutrition, physical activity, overweight, accessibility of health care, and the impact of poverty. This chapter also includes a discussion of changing sleep patterns and "sleepiness" in adolescents. Finally, I have included research showing that early maturation is not as advantageous for boys as previously believed.

Have you ever wondered why adolescents, who otherwise are charming and intelligent, can do things that, with even a moment's thought, they never otherwise would have attempted? Chapter 4 summarizes research on the relationship between brain maturation and impulsiveness. I also relate development of different areas within the prefrontal cortex to increasing flexibility in adolescent thinking. Emerging adults show even more flexibility in problem solving, and I compare approaches likely to be taken by them with those more characteristic of adolescents. Also in this chapter is a section on gender differences in intelligence. Controversy over gender differences seems never to subside for long. How many times has a casual remark by a friend or acquaintance revealed deep-seated beliefs about gender differences that surprise us? Chapter 4 includes a discussion of these beliefs and summarizes current research on gender differences in intellectual functioning, as well as on difficulties in assessing these. I also have included recent research on potential gender bias in culture fair tests of intelligence and on national achievement tests.

In Chapter 5, I discuss the development of autonomy in terms of self-determination, as discovering the activities that intrinsically motivate autonomous functioning, rather than becoming independent by emotionally separating from parents. Additionally, I have included cultural comparisons connectedness and discussed the development of agency in individualistic and collectivistic cultures. The already extensive coverage of the contributions of gender and ethnicity to identity have been updated, and I have added new research on changes in biracial identity as adolescents transition into adulthood, and adolescents' use of the Internet to experiment with identity issues.

Chapter 6 includes more examples drawn from adolescents' live to illustrate patterns of interaction within the family. The discussion of conflict with parents summarizes research showing the contribution of the attitudes adolescents bring to their interactions with parents as well as their respect for parents. Additional research on the ways adolescents attempt to avoid conflict is included, and on the way violating expectancies can contribute to conflict. Research comparing styles of parenting has been updated, specifically with respect to cultural differences in authoritative and authoritarian parenting.

Added to the discussion of adolescent friendships in Chapter 7 is a comparison of friendship patterns and the meaning of friendship in different cultures. The chapter includes a section on staying in touch with friends through the Internet and social network sites, and discusses rules and risks regarding online activity and sharing personal information. The chapter includes material on sociometric distinctions among popular, average, rejected, neglected, and controversial adolescents, and distinguishes between different types of popularity. Also included are sections summarizing research on friendships among sexual minority youth, and on youth cultures.

Chapter 8 includes information on learning styles and reviews research on the difficulties early adolescents experience in adjusting to secondary school. The chapter includes discussions of what makes schools effective, on the impact of poverty on academic achievement, and summarizes research describing effective intervention programs for low-income students. I also discuss ethnic differences in graduation rates and the use of faulty formulas that have masked the extent of these discrepancies, and include a description of alternative educational programs for students who drop out. A section on current educational reforms examines reasons for the difficulty of improving the quality of education for inner city students as this program presently exists.

Chapter 9 compares adolescents' leisure time in different countries and how they spend their free time. I have also included a section on child labor and on policies that have been effective in limiting this. I review research showing the various ways in which organized activities contribute to adolescents' development. Also included is a section on programs preparing minority youth for a full range of occupational opportunities. I also have updated material on the gender gap in pay.

The inclusion of gender roles, sexual identity, and sexual scripts at the beginning of Chapter 10 places the research on sexual decision making that follows in the broader contexts of self-definition and interpersonal relationships. Additionally, I discuss the importance of parents in adolescents' sexual decision making. Material has been added on prejudice and discrimination in a section on sexual orientation. Also, I review recent research comparing the effectiveness of abstinence-only and comprehensive sex education programs, showing the latter to be effective in both delaying sexual initiation and promoting responsible behavior. The chapter includes a comparison of rates of adolescent pregnancy, birth, and abortion in the U.S. with those in European countries, and relates lower rates for these in the latter to differences in attitudes toward adolescent sexuality and in availability of information and health care.

Chapter 11 reviews current research on the relationships between adolescents' values and those of their parents, and on the influence of gender, ethnicity, and religion on values. I have included social domain theory in discussing adolescents' approach to moral issues, and have expanded the coverage of religion in this chapter and throughout the text in response to reviewers' comments. Also in response to reviewers, I have included new research on cheating.

The discussion of runaway adolescents in Chapter 12 contains information on shelters and help lines. Problem behavior is discussed in terms of externalizing versus internalizing problems. Under the former, I distinguish among adolescents who are likely to persist in a pattern of life-course antisocial behavior from those whose antisocial behavior drops out as they enter adulthood, and review current statistics and research on gangs. The chapter also includes recent research on the effectiveness of antidepressants and types of psychotherapy in treating depression. Since relatively few adolescents experiment with drugs other than alcohol, cigarettes and marijuana, I have streamlined the discussion of drugs to reflect this, and have added material reviewing drug prevention programs that are effective and those that are not.

In Chapter 13, the discussion of positive adolescent development reviews research on the protective factors in adolescents' lives, such as responsive and supportive parenting and the importance of non-residential fathers to adolescents' development, the collective efficacy of communities, as seen in the willingness of neighbors to intervene, and the importance of teachers. The chapter stresses how one individual can make a difference in the life of an adolescent, and concludes with a section describing successful programs organized by adolescents to improve the lives of others.

It has been exciting incorporating new findings in the field of adolescence into the 7th edition of this text, and it is my hope that this text is not only informative and useful, but also communicates a sense of the immense richness of diversity in the lives of adolescents.

Acknowledgments

I am indebted to the many colleagues who reviewed the previous edition of this text for their insightful and helpful comments. It is easy to lose perspective when writing a text such as this, especially given the vast amount of research that has been published since the last edition. Incorporating their suggestions has substantially improved this edition. My thanks go to:

Todd C. Baird, Weber State University
Mildred Cordaro, Texas State University
Gary Creasey, Illinois State University
Parrilla de Kokal, Weber State University
Bradley L. Elison, Carroll College
Jaelyn Farris, University of Notre Dame
Sheryl Feinstein, Augustana College
Heather Henkell, City University of New York
Lisa Hensley, Texas Wesleyan University
Patricia Jarvis, Illinois State University
Jane Kroger, University of Tromsø
Michelle Meadows, Eastern Illinois University

Michael Meehan, Maryville University
Dagmar Moravec, Lansing Community College
Julie Osland, Wheeling Jesuit University
Rocio Rivandeneydra, Illinois State University
Wanda L. Ruffin, Hood College
Patricia Sawyer, Middlesex Community College
Jane P. Sheldon, University of Michigan-Dearborn
Jonathan Skalski, Brigham Young University
Judith Smetana, University of Rochester
Tina Williams, Tidewater Community College

I also wish to thank my editor Graig Donini for leading me through the process with a new publisher, Production Editor Chelsea Holabird who saw this revision through, Azelie Aquadro who ably assisted Chelsea, Kathie Gow for her copyediting prowess, David McIntyre for his keen photographic eye, and Joanne Delphia not only for the beautiful design of the book, but also the wonderful cover. Thank you.

Just as adolescents rely on the company of friends and family, I have as well. To all my friends at First Pres in Burbank, thank you for your prayers, and to Abba, Father God, thank you for the gracious ways You answered them. To Bill, thank you for the emails each day and the music to work by. To Michael, thank you for always being there and for simply being who you are. To Joshua and Jenny, who remain as amazing to me in adulthood as you did in adolescence—I celebrate your creativity and your courage.

Media and Supplements
to accompany Adolescence, *Seventh Edition*

eBook (ISBN 978-0-87893-426-3)
www.coursesmart.com

New for the Seventh Edition, *Adolescence* is also available as an eBook via CourseSmart, at a substantial discount off the price of the printed textbook. The CourseSmart eBook reproduces the look of the printed book exactly, and includes convenient tools for searching the text, highlighting, and notes.

For the Student

Companion Website
www.sinauer.com/cobb

For the Seventh Edition, the *Adolescence* Companion Website contains a wide range of study and review resources to help students master the material presented in the textbook. Access to the site is free and requires no access code. (Instructor registration is required in order for students to access the online quizzes.)

The Companion Website includes:
- Detailed chapter summaries
- Multiple-choice quizzes and essay quizzes
- Additional Research Focus Boxes
- Flashcard activities
- Complete glossary

For the Instructor

Instructor's Resource Library

The *Adolescence,* Seventh Edition Instructor's Resource Library includes a variety of resources to aid you in the planning of your course, the development of your lectures, and the assessment of your students. The Instructor's Resource Library includes:

- Figures & Tables: All of the line-art illustrations, photos, and tables from the textbook are provided as both high-resolution and low-resolution JPEGs, all optimized for use in presentation software (such as PowerPoint®).
- PowerPoint Resources: Two different types of PowerPoint presentations are provided for each chapter of the textbook:
  - All figures, photos, and tables
  - A complete lecture outline, including selected figures
- Test Bank in Word® format
- Computerized Test Bank: The entire Test Bank is provided in Diploma® format (software included), making it easy to quickly assemble exams using any combination of publisher-provided and custom questions. Includes the Companion Website quiz questions.

Online Quizzing

The Companion Website includes online quizzes that can be assigned by instructors or used as self-review exercises. Quizzes can be customized with any combination of the default questions and an instructor's own questions, and can be assigned as desired. Results of the quizzes are stored in the online gradebook. (Instructors must register in order for their students to be able to take the quizzes.)

Course Management System Support

e-Packs/Course Cartridges

Available for the Seventh Edition, *Adolescence* offers a complete e-pack/course cartridge for Blackboard® and WebCT®. This e-pack includes resources from the Companion Website and the Instructor's Resource Library, as well as the complete Test Bank, making it easy to quickly include a wide range of book-specific material in your Blackboard or WebCT course.

Assessment

Instructors using course management systems such as WebCT, Blackboard, and Angel® can easily create and export quizzes and exams (or the entire test bank) for integration into their online course. The entire test bank is provided in WebCT and Blackboard formats on the Instructor's Resource Library, and other formats can be easily generated from the included Diploma software.

Adolescence

Seventh Edition

Each culture has its stories. They offer a way of understanding ourselves and our lives. Most of us accept the stories our culture tells us— stories we've heard since childhood. It is daring to live lives that are too different from these stories. But in adolescence, one may dream the daring. Listen to the story told by a Chinese American girl who dares to dream for herself the exploits reserved for boys—initiation into the rites of a warrior:

After I returned from my survival test, the two old people trained me in

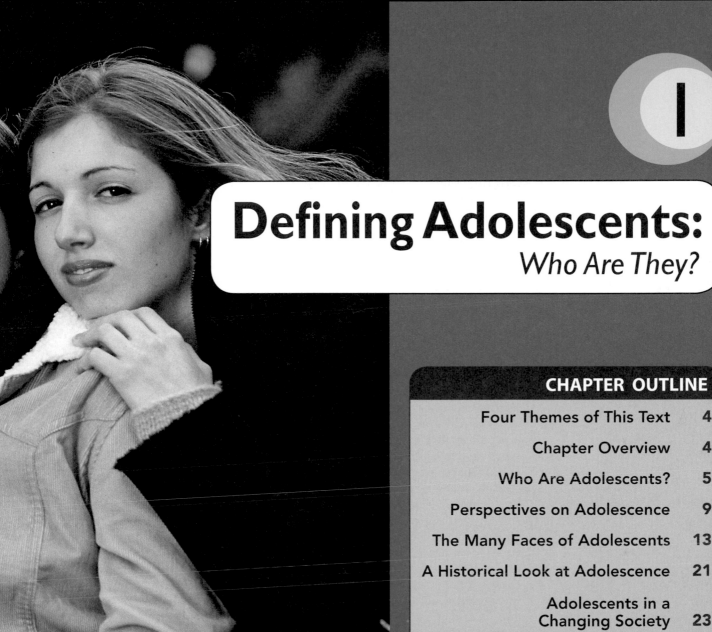

Defining Adolescents:
Who Are They?

1

So Maxine Hong Kingston describes the fantasies of a Chinese American girl who dreamed of avenging her people as a fierce and beloved warrior.

Adolescents still dream of dragons. Fantastic? Of course. But in another sense, dragons are made of common stuff. They are what looms large when one feels small. So, too, with dreams. This girl's dreams were not that different from those of other adolescents. The dragon was spun from remarks surrounding her youth: "Better to raise geese than girls." "When you raise girls, you're raising children for strangers." The dream, of course, was to slay the dragon— and prove them wrong.

Four Themes of This Text

Each culture offers up its dragons. The Chinese are no different in this respect. The trick is to recognize a dragon when one finds it. As Maxine Hong Kingston tells us, they are too large ever to be seen. In studying the youth who pursue them, though, we will have occasion to examine some of their parts. These are rarely the same from one culture to the next, or even within the same culture when it is as diverse as ours. Nor are they the same early in adolescence as they are later in adolescence.

All cultures have one part of the dragon in common. They hold up one set of stories for females and another for males, offering a different set of experiences to their youth depending on their sex. Adolescents of either sex, as a result, are likely to follow different developmental paths to maturity. We will trace the impact of gender on the developmental paths taken by adolescents.

Similarly, adolescents' lives reflect, in intimate ways, their cultural backgrounds. These cultures affect everything from which foods taste good to what language teenagers use when talking to their grandmothers. Cultures—like dragons—are too big to be seen by those who live within them, even though the very rituals, beliefs, and rhythms of one's culture provide the perspective from which one views the world. Members of a culture, because they share its rhythms and stories, share expectancies that give shape to the events they experience. Experience, you see, rather than being taken in raw, is interpreted; and culture, like a pair of eyeglasses, provides the interpretive lenses through which one looks. Just as with glasses, one sees *through* the lenses, missing the culture that makes that view of reality possible. The influence of ethnicity and culture on adolescents' development is a second theme of this text.

When looked at from a distance, adolescents all may appear to be facing similar challenges. If we step closer, however, we can see that, just as with childhood and adulthood, adolescence comprises several distinct periods. Early adolescence, from about 10 to 13 or 14, roughly corresponds to the years of middle school and junior high, and late adolescence, which ends at 17 or 18, to those of high school. Early adolescents are contending with puberty, changing sex roles, and developing more autonomous relationships with parents and more mature relationships with peers. Late adolescents face the need to pull all of these changes together into a coherent sense of themselves, while looking ahead to roles that have traditionally defined adulthood: those of work, marriage, and parenthood. More adolescents today than in the past continue their education beyond high school, thereby delaying commitment to an adult work role, and many similarly are postponing marriage and having children, thus creating a phase in life called emerging adulthood. Distinguishing early adolescence, late adolescence, and emerging adulthood is a third theme of this text.

Despite the many varying experiences of adolescents, all face the task of gaining a sense of themselves. Adolescents face a need to find out who they are, what distinguishes them from others, and what they have in common with others. Although adolescents go about this in somewhat different ways, all address the central question of adolescence: "Who am I?" The task of achieving an identity is a fourth theme of this text.

Chapter Overview

The chapter begins by defining adolescence. This task is not as easy as you might think. What is it, precisely, that makes someone an adolescent? Should we think of adolescence primarily in terms of biological development—that is, in terms of puberty and physical maturation? To what extent do we also need to consider social and emotional maturity? And does society have a say in when one finally reaches adulthood? In arriving at a definition, we will consider each of these questions, examining the biological, psychological, and sociological dimensions of adolescence.

Definitions are helpful in distinguishing adolescents as a group, but they can leave us in the dark when it comes to understanding individual differences. How can adolescents who grow up in similar circumstances or even in the same family be as different from each other as they are? Two perspectives, running throughout this text, offer useful insights. The constructive perspective describes the active, creative process by which adolescents, indeed individuals of all ages, perceive their world. This perspective assumes that adolescents actively put together, or construct what they see and hear, interpreting their experiences and making sense of the events to which they react. The contextual perspective examines the ways adolescents are affected by the numerous contexts of their lives. This perspective underscores the importance of knowing, for instance, how the relative presence or absence of community resources enables families to support healthy development; or whether an adolescent's ethnicity confers majority or minority status in the day-to-day contexts of school or neighborhood, and how that contributes to a developing sense of self.

We then turn to the many faces of adolescents, exploring the four areas highlighted earlier as themes for this text. We look first at differences between the sexes, and then turn to cultural and ethnic differences, followed by differences between early and late adolescents. Despite the tremendous diversity of experience among adolescents today, all face the task of gaining a sense of themselves, a fourth theme of the text; an examination of the process by which adolescents achieve an identity concludes this section of the chapter.

Viewed from a historical perspective, we will see that adolescence has not always existed as we know it today. Nor, for that matter, has childhood or adulthood. Two hundred years ago, most 16-year-olds worked alongside adults and saw little of the inside of a classroom. Today, 16-year-olds in industrialized countries spend most of the day in a classroom, an experience that clearly sets them apart from most adults and distinguishes them as a separate group within society.

Societies also change with time. We will look at some of the ways in which adolescents today are growing up in a world quite different from the one their parents knew. Finally, we will consider adolescence from the vantage point of the lifespan—as one developmental period of many in life. We will look at adolescents and parents, and *their* parents, noting similarities as well as differences in the developmental issues they face.

Who Are Adolescents?

Although youth all over the world enter their teens, not all become "teenagers." Much of what we consider typical of **adolescence** is, for the most part, characteristic of those living in Western industrialized countries. In **traditional cultures** in which customs have remained unchanged with the passage of time, and in recently industrialized **developing countries**, youth are not as likely to spend their days in school, for instance, or hang out with friends, or to go out on dates (Larson & Wilson, 2004; Verma & Saraswathi, 2002).

Similarly, adolescents in **individualistic cultures**, such as North American, Scandinavian, and Western European countries, have a different sense of themselves than do adolescents in **collectivistic cultures**, such as Latin American, Asian, or Middle-Eastern countries. Individualistic cultures encourage adolescents to define themselves in terms of their personal goals and accomplishments, whereas in collectivistic cultures adolescents tend more to gain a sense

adolescence A period in life that begins with biological maturation, during which individuals are expected to accomplish certain developmental tasks, and that ends when they achieve a self-sufficient state of adulthood as defined by society.

traditional cultures Cultures that have maintained their values and practices over long periods. These cultures often find themselves in conflict with other traditional or more rapidly changing cultures or with internal pressures for change.

developing countries Countries that have only recently begun to adopt modern technology, social forms, and means of production. Such countries were previously termed "third world" countries.

individualistic cultures Cultures that encourage a sense of self as independent, self-sufficient, and autonomous.

collectivistic cultures Cultures that encourage a sense of self in terms of one's rules or status vis-à-vis others.

TABLE 1.1	
Perceptions of the Self in Individualistic and Collectivistic Cultures	
INDIVIDUALISTIC CULTURE ONE SEES *SELF* AS:	COLLECTIVISTIC CULTURE ONE SEES *SELF* AS:
Independent	Interdependent
Autonomous, self-governing	Constrained by goals and values of the group
Behavior reflects personal motives and desires	Behavior is appropriate to one's status and role within the group
One works to achieve personal goals	One works to fulfill the goals of the group
Defined by one's unique traits, interests, and abilities	Defined by one's place within the group, by shared values and goals
Unique, different from others	Belonging, what one has in common with others
Asserting one's self	Fitting in with others

Source: Markus & Kitayama, 1991.

globalization The process by which expanding international trade, communication, and travel erases national and geographical boundaries.

puberty Growth processes, including the skeletal growth spurt and maturation of the reproductive system, that begin in early adolescence and transform children into physically and sexually mature adults.

of themselves through their roles or statuses vis-à-vis others and work in concert to promote each others' goals (**Table 1.1**) (Markus & Kitayama, 1991).

Despite differences such as these, increasing trends toward **globalization** are beginning to change the experiences of youth in both Western and non-Western cultures. Research comparing adolescents from various cultures differing in social and economic development, political systems, and regions of the world reveals considerable cross-cultural similarities (Dmitrieva et al., 2004; Vazsonyi et al., 2003).

Defining Adolescence

Adolescence is not easy to define. Think for a moment of a 17-year-old boy who has just graduated from high school. He's as tall as his dad and can beat him in arm wrestling. He has a driver's license but isn't allowed to drink alcoholic beverages in his state. He's old enough to enlist in the army—with parental consent—but can't vote for another year. It's clear that he is no longer a child, but is it just as clear that he is an adult? Even though he can drive a car and carry a gun, he is not old enough to vote or drink. Adolescence abounds with paradoxes such as these. To get a clearer picture of what adolescence is, we will look at a biological, psychological, and sociological definition of adolescence.

A BIOLOGICAL DEFINITION OF ADOLESCENCE   The biological and physical changes of puberty quite literally transform the bodies of children into those of sexually and physically mature adults. These changes occur in all adolescents, and in all cultures and are, in fact, the only universal changes of adolescence. They result from a heady hormonal cocktail served up by Mother Nature herself. Hormones, sometimes increasing by as much as twentyfold with the onset of puberty, account for puberty's dramatic events.

Puberty begins in early adolescence and can take anywhere from two to six years to complete. Several growth processes are involved; each of these is regulated by different hormones and all may occur at different rates, frequently leaving a teenager in doubt as to what to expect from one day to the next.

Some changes, such as growth of the testes or ovaries, go unnoticed. Other changes, such as the appearance of facial hair or breasts, though of less reproductive significance, are more dramatic. By age 10 or 11, nearly all preteens begin to look for signs of change in themselves. The events most closely associated with puberty—menstruation in girls and ejaculation in boys—actually occur fairly late in the process. Which changes an adolescent will notice first and just when they will happen is hard to say since variations from one adolescent to the next can be large. However, some general statements can be made about the most likely course of events.

The physical growth spurt, one of the first noticeable changes, is a period of accelerated growth beginning just after age 10 in girls and peaking at about age 12. Boys begin to grow approximately two years later, peaking at about age 14. During this period girls grow approximately 3½ inches a year and boys slightly more. Growth in height is accompanied by a corresponding gain in weight and an increase in the rate of muscular development. Body proportions also begin to change, as girls' hips widen and boys' shoulders become broader (Graber & Brooks-Gunn, 2002).

Changes in the reproductive system and the appearance of secondary sex characteristics can also be charted. For girls, the growth of breast buds and pubic hair typically coincides with growth of the uterus and vagina. Development of

Adolescence spans the years from 11 to 19, a time of dramatic physical, emotional, and intellectual changes. Some of these junior high students still look like children, and others seem nearly adult.

the external genitalia also typically occurs in the first year of puberty. Midway through puberty most girls begin to menstruate, usually coinciding with a peak in the growth spurt. For boys, changes in the testes and scrotum, and the appearance of pubic hair are among the first noticeable changes. Midway through puberty boys first experience ejaculation, which may or may not be accompanied by orgasm. Most adult males usually experience orgasm at the same time as ejaculation; however, these are independent processes and may occur separately. Boys, in fact, typically experience erections and sometimes orgasm well before the time they first ejaculate (Hyde, 1991).

Toward the end of puberty, secondary sex characteristics find full expression. Some are long awaited, such as breasts in girls and facial hair in boys; others less so, such as the development of sweat glands and oil glands, which can be responsible for embarrassing odors and acne. In addition to the visible changes of puberty, equally dramatic maturation of regions within the brain involved in reasoning and emotion enables adolescents to think and respond in ways that distinguish them from children.

Even though puberty serves as a convenient, if somewhat imprecise, marker for the onset of adolescence, the changes we have described typically are completed well before adolescence ends. The task of specifying an end to adolescence is more difficult, and for this we must turn to psychological and sociological definitions.

A PSYCHOLOGICAL DEFINITION OF ADOLESCENCE   Consider the world of a 15-year-old. Video games, comics, and friends fill after-school hours. Old toys and a skateboard are scattered about his room; two pet rats sleep in a cage on the bureau. A notice about a summer program in math for the college-bound is pinned to a bulletin board. He hates math, doesn't know if he wants to go to college, and can't imagine working. His childhood seems to be slipping away, and adulthood remains impossibly distant.

How do adolescents maintain a sense of themselves when faced with changes such as these? The answer gives us a psychological perspective on

developmental tasks
Age-related norms that reflect social expectations for normal development.

compulsory education laws
Legislation making school attendance mandatory for children and adolescents until they graduate or reach a minimum age.

adolescence. Each adolescent reaches a point when it is not possible to continue living out the same life patterns he or she did as a child. The task facing adolescents is to forge a stable identity, to achieve a sense of themselves that transcends the many changes in their experiences and roles. Only then will they be able to bridge the childhood they must leave and the adulthood they have yet to enter.

The task arises naturally from forces present in early adolescence: puberty, cognitive maturation, and changing social expectations. The first force to make itself felt is usually puberty. In addition to visible changes in height, weight, and body proportions, puberty brings an inner world of sexual stirrings. These bodily changes are accompanied by cognitive ones, giving adolescents a new awareness of themselves and others' reactions to them. Social expectations subtly change as well. Parents and others expect a new maturity from adolescents. They expect adolescents to begin planning for their lives and thinking for themselves. In short, they expect them to be more responsible—to be more adult.

The convergence of physical maturation with changing personal and social expectations confronts adolescents with new **developmental tasks** (Havighurst, 1972). These tasks represent a culture's definition of normal development at different points in life. Because our sense of ourselves comes in part from our awareness of how others see us, cultural norms give shape to personal standards. Biological maturation contributes more heavily to some tasks, such as adjusting to an adult body, whereas cultural norms contribute more to others, such as developing social skills. In general, adolescents evaluate themselves more positively as they experience increasing mastery of these tasks (Pinquart et al., 2004).

Not all cultures place the same emphasis on the same tasks. Preparing for an occupation, for instance, is expected of adolescents in all industrialized societies, however the French emphasize this more than the Germans. Similarly, establishing mature relationships with peers, also expected of adolescents in both cultures, is given greater importance in Germany than in France. Likewise, although adolescents in all cultures face concerns related to body image and adult gender roles, these loom larger for those in traditional societies, in which gender roles are more clearly defined (Schleyer-Lindenmann, 2006).

Although cultures may differ in the importance they place on any developmental task, each of the tasks that adolescents face can be thought of as a facet of one central task: achieving a continuing and stable sense of self as adolescents step into adulthood. Among teenagers in contemporary industrialized cultures, however, even those who master these steps find the gateway to adulthood locked, and must wait for someone to come along with the key. The lock is sprung not by biological or even psychological maturity. The final tumbler is keyed to a sociological definition of adolescence.

A SOCIOLOGICAL DEFINITION OF ADOLESCENCE   Sociologists define individuals in terms of their status within society, reflected in large measure by their self-sufficiency. From a sociological perspective, adolescents are individuals who are neither self-sufficient, and hence not adult, nor completely dependent, and thus not children. Adolescence becomes a transitional period whose end is marked by legislation specifying age limits for the legal protection of those not yet adult. In the U.S., complex social conditions surrounding industrialization required the prolongation of childhood or, rather, the delay of entrance into adulthood. Three resulting social movements contributed to the emergence of adolescence as a distinct new age group (Bakan, 1971).

Compulsory education laws were introduced for children between ages 5 and 18 on a widespread basis in the United States in the late nineteenth century. Previously, children either attended school or did not as their parents saw fit. Compulsory education laws ensured basic skills among future workers—and also protected the jobs of adults in the workforce.

Similarly, **child labor laws** specifying minimum ages for different types of work restricted the numbers of children who could hold full-time jobs. In 1832, 40% of the factory workers in New England were children. These young factory workers became a liability to the nation rather than an asset as industrialization solved what had previously been a labor-shortage problem. Child labor laws ensured humane working conditions for children, but at the same time they protected the jobs of adults in the workforce.

Additionally, laws instituting separate legal proceedings for juveniles, resulting in a separate **system of juvenile justice**, were introduced at about this time. These laws were intended to free the courts from punishing children as adults and to allow them to offer corrective measures instead. However, these laws also suspended important legal rights guaranteed to adults, such as due process and the presumption of innocence. This legislation, just as that governing child labor and education, targeted the population to which it applied in terms of age. Adolescence emerged as a period in life bounded at one end by puberty and at the other by legal age requirements.

Each of the three definitions of adolescence that we have considered is incomplete by itself, but together they give us a fairly well-rounded picture. What is adolescence? It is a period in life that begins with biological maturation, during which individuals must accomplish certain developmental tasks, and that ends when they achieve a self-sufficient state of adulthood as defined by society.

Perspectives on Adolescence

Having a definition of adolescence in hand, we can now examine this period in life more closely. We will look first at how adolescents perceive their world, a constructive perspective, and then at the contexts—families and friends, neighborhoods and cultures—that make up that world, a contextual perspective.

A Constructive Perspective

A **constructive perspective** assumes that we actively construct what we know of the world, interpreting our experiences, and composing or making sense of the events to which we react. Perceiving the world—whether it's reading a book, such as you're doing now, or listening to someone talk—is an active process. If you doubt that we actively "construct" the events to which we respond, take a moment to look at **Figure 1.1**. Did you notice that the very same lines that form the letter *B* in the top row also form the number *13* in the bottom row? Yet most likely you read the first line as "B – A – T" and the second line as "11 – 12 – 13". What determined whether you saw these lines as a letter or a number? The answer, obviously, is not in the lines themselves, because they are the same. Rather, it was your expectancy to see one thing or another that determined how the lines were perceived. This expectancy, in turn, was derived from the context in which the lines appear—that context being either a row of letters or a row of numbers.

This same active, constructive process occurs at each of many levels of human functioning, from the relatively micro-level of perceptual processing that we've just examined to the macro-level of social interactions. An adolescent, for instance, is likely to hear a casual remark such as "Whatcha doin'?" as meaning one thing if said by a friend, and as something entirely different if said by someone the adolescent had previously had a fight with—as a simple greeting in the first instance and a possible chal-

child labor laws Laws that specify minimum ages for various types of work.

system of juvenile justice Legislation instituting separate legal proceedings for juveniles and adults.

constructive perspective The view that perception is an active, constructive process in which individuals interpret and give meaning to their experiences.

● **Figure 1.1 What do you see here?** The same lines that form the letter B are the very same lines that form the number 13. Nothing has been changed except the way you see them!

Research Focus

An Experiment: "Who You Pushin', Buddy!" Perceptions of Aggressiveness

By Michael Wapner

People interpret experience by literally constructing or piecing together the events to which they respond. One of the most important manifestations of this interpretive construction occurs in determining the intentions of others. Even when an action is so obvious that it leaves little to interpretation, the motives behind the action still need to be understood, and this usually requires a good deal of cognitive construction. Observers may all agree that George bumped into Ira. But what the observers feel and do about it depends more on why they think George did it than the mere fact that he did. If George stumbled and could not keep from bumping Ira, that's one thing. But if George bumped Ira to get ahead of him in line, that's entirely different.

What is it that determines how observers interpret the intentions behind an act? Mary Lynne Courtney and Robert Cohen (1996) designed an experiment to investigate this question. In particular, they looked at the contribution of two variables to the interpretation of intention: (1) prior information and (2) the personality of the observer. These two variables, in addition to influencing an observer's interpretation of the intentions behind an action, illustrate, by their difference, something fundamental about the design of experiments in general.

Briefly, boys between 8 and 12 were shown a videotape of two boys playing tag on a playground. At a critical point in the middle of the tape, the boy being chased falls down after being tagged by the other boy. The fallen boy slowly gets up and resumes the game. The variables were introduced as follows:

(1) Prior Information: An Independent Variable

Previous research, and common sense, would suggest that observers' interpretation of the intention behind an act should depend on what else they know about the actors. Thus, one would guess that the subjects would more likely attribute hostile intent to the tag that caused the fall if they were told beforehand that the two boys were enemies and had just recently been fighting. Conversely, the likelihood of seeing the tag as accidental should increase if the observers believed the boys to be good friends. But what if the observers knew nothing about the boys? These three conditions—let us call them benign, hostile, and ambiguous—constitute the independent variable in the experiment.

In an *experiment*, each group of participants is treated differently than the others. In all other respects, the groups are equivalent. If the groups differ afterward, we can assume the difference is due to the way they were treated. In order to be confident about this assumption, however, we must be sure that the groups are the same at the outset. The simplest way to ensure this would be to start with identical groups. But because no two individuals are ever the same in all respects, such a tactic is impossible. An equally good approach is to make sure the groups don't differ in any *systematic* way. We can accomplish this by assigning individuals at random to each condition. If each person has the same chance of being assigned to each group, and if we assign enough people to each, the differences among the people would balance out among the groups. *Random assignment* will distribute any initial differences more or less evenly among the groups. Contrast this type of independent variable with a second variable these investigators studied.

(2) Aggressiveness of the Observer: A Classification Variable

Aggressive boys have been found to attribute hostile intentions to the actions of others more frequently than less aggressive boys. Courtney and Cohen incorporated the variable of aggressiveness by having classmates rate each boy for aggressiveness. Notice that unlike assignment to the prior knowledge variable, aggressiveness scores could not be assigned randomly. Rather, participants were *classified* based on judgments of a preexisting characteristic—that is, aggressiveness. Thus, if we find a difference between aggressive and unaggressive boys, we cannot be sure that the difference is due to something else that might be correlated with aggressiveness.

Now let's look at the results of the study. The participants (randomly assigned and classified as described above) were shown the videotape and asked to "segment" the action by pressing a button whenever one action stopped and another began. These points of segmentation are labeled

BOX 1.1 continued

"breakpoints." Of course, most natural behavior does not have discrete breakpoints. Rather, one activity flows into another. Thus, segmenting the flow of action is not simply marking what already objectively exists; rather, it is an act of cognitive construction and will vary from observer to observer.

A dramatic example of segmentation as a cognitive construction lies in the fact that we hear our native language spoken in discrete word segments, although the sound issuing from the speaker's mouth is continuous, as can be demonstrated by visualizing normal speech on the screen of an oscilloscope. It is our knowledge of the rhythms and sounds of our native language, as well as familiarity with the vocabulary and current context, that allows us to segment accurately. You can test this proposition. Rent a film in an unfamiliar foreign language. Then gather a few friends who are equally ignorant of the language and all try to count the number of words spoken in two minutes of dialogue. You will be surprised at the wildly different counts.

Segmenting the action in Courtney and Cohen's videotape is roughly the same kind of cognitive task. But unlike speech, there is no cultural consensus as to where the breakpoints belong. Because

the number of breakpoints should increase when an individual is seeking more information, it was expected that identifying breakpoints would be a function of how much information the boys had about the action. Recall, each boy got information from two sources: (1) from what he was told about the boys' friendship (the condition of prior information to which he had been assigned) and (2) from what he assumed (based on his level of aggressiveness). When participants were given information that the boys were enemies, aggressiveness did not predict the amount of segmentation. Everyone "knew," in other words, what was going on and didn't have to look for it. When participants were told the boys were friends, or were told nothing at all, participants who were more aggressive identified more breakpoints than less aggressive ones, suggesting that their perception of ongoing behavior differed from that of less aggressive boys. Aggressiveness relates not only to the motives one attributes to others, but also to the ways in which one organizes one's perception of ongoing events.

Source: Courtney & Cohen, 1996.

lenge in the second. In other words, one person's reality is not necessarily shared by another. In a very real sense, we make it up.

I remember frequently having difficulty understanding my mother-in-law, who spoke English with a heavy Yiddish accent. It's not that I couldn't ever understand her, but I had to know which language to "listen" in. If it were Yiddish, there was simply no hope of understanding. But even with English, if I *thought* it was Yiddish, I also didn't understand. Only when she was speaking English, and I expected to hear English, could I make out what she had said—knowing which sounds to listen for, knowing that "veh-dink" could be heard as "wedding," and that "voo-manh" could be "woman." **Box 1.1** provides an example of research on how school children read meaning into the behavior of others.

We interpret the behavior of others based on our own contextual perceptions. Some may perceive this teen as upset, while others may think he's concentrating.

A Contextual Perspective

contextual perspective
The view that development is influenced by one's ethnicity and culture.

microsystem One's immediate social contexts, involving firsthand experiences, such as interactions at home or in the classroom.

mesosystem Social contexts involving interactions of several microsystems, such as when parents meet teachers.

exosystem Contexts occurring at the level of the community, such as types of schools and housing.

Development takes place in real life contexts. "Development" may sound like an abstract concept, but it walks the corridors of schools and talks to parents over the dinner table. The **contextual perspective** looks at the ways in which development is influenced by the daily settings, or contexts, of adolescents' lives, in other words, by where they spend their time and who they spend it with. In a uniquely psychological twist, however, it is not so much the actual, physical contexts that affect development as it is how adolescents *perceive* these contexts that leaves its developmental footprint on their lives. Even adolescents who grow up in the same family, or go to the same school, or live in the same community can experience these as uniquely different developmental contexts (Bronfenbrenner, 1979a, 1994).

What aspects of our environment are we likely to perceive and incorporate into our reality? Urie Bronfenbrenner, a psychologist at Cornell University, identifies three features of one's environment, each of which, rather than being a static aspect of the physical setting, involves the person in a dynamic exchange with it. Bronfenbrenner points out that individuals are most likely to attend to and notice what they are doing, the ongoing *activity* they are engaged in at the time. Much of this activity involves us with others, in *interpersonal relations* that take the form of what we say and do when we are with other people. And last, being with others invariably implicates us in a *role*, with expectations for certain behaviors depending on the setting or the relationship.

At this point, it is important to highlight the interpersonal and very intimate nature of one's environment. The environment is not to be found in rooms, on streets, or in stores. Nor is it in books or clothes, or in the presence or absence of one resource or another. It is all of these, but also something more. The environment, in fact, is not that which is outside the person or separate from the person. Rather than being outside the self, the environment always *includes* the self, in the form of how we experience ourselves in relation to something else, usually another person. Bronfenbrenner (1990) emphasizes this point when he stresses the importance of a young person developing a meaningful relationship with an adult who finds that young person "somehow special, especially wonderful, and especially precious" (p. 31). Such a relationship becomes a springboard from which adolescents can step into other contexts, determining how they will be perceived.

Bronfenbrenner adds that the environment does not exist as a simple, unified context, but takes the form of multiple, overlapping spheres of influence (**Figure 1.2**). At the most immediate level of environmental influence, that of the **microsystem**, are the various settings in which the adolescent moves throughout the day: at home, at school, with friends, at work. A characteristic of the microsystem is that the activities, interpersonal relations, and roles involve the adolescent in face-to-face interactions with others. It's relatively easy to imagine how such interactions might affect an adolescent, whether they take the form of a verbal exchange with a parent or teacher, or supportive eye contact from a friend.

Bronfenbrenner maintains that adolescents are affected not only by face-to-face influences such as these, but also by various relations among the microsystems of daily life, influences at the level of the **mesosystem**. For example, a parent's involvement with school can significantly improve the adolescent's academic performance (Comer et al., 1996). In addition to the microsystem and mesosystem, adolescents can be affected by environments in which they are not present but that affect their immediate surroundings. Bronfenbrenner refers to such influences as the **exosystem**. Conditions in a parent's workplace, for instance, can affect the amount of time the parent has to spend with the family or the amount of stress introduced into family life, thereby affecting the adolescent.

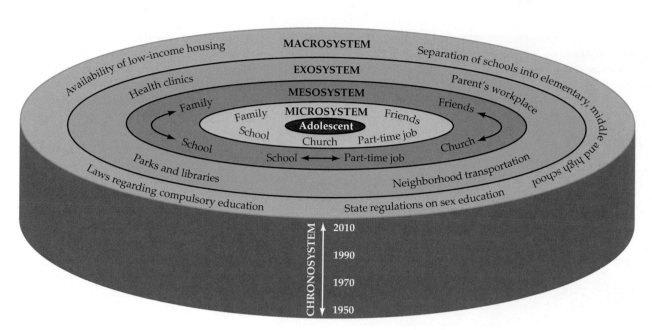

● **Figure 1.2**
Bronfenbrenner's
Contextual Theory
Adolescents' daily lives are
influenced by five over-
lapping systems, each of
which can affect conditions in
another sphere.

The **macrosystem**, which consists of the underlying social and political climate, is even further removed from adolescents' daily experiences, yet it impinges on their lives in very real ways. Laws concerning compulsory education, the mainstreaming of students with special needs, and the separation of grades into elementary school, middle school or junior high, and high school all illustrate the direct ways the macrosystem can affect the lives of adolescents. One way in which the macrosystem is affecting increasing numbers of adolescents is through geopolitical decisions that result in increased numbers of "triggers" for asthma, such as air pollution, exhaust fumes, or increased ozone levels. A national study of 9- to 17-year-olds in the United States found that 15.3% experienced recurrent attacks of asthma (Goodwin et al., 2003). In fact, asthma now affects approximately 6 million youth in the United States, making it the most common chronic illness for that age group (Centers for Disease Control and Prevention, 2008a).

Finally, development is affected by the **chronosystem**, which refers to the particular circumstances existing at any point in history within a culture that shape adolescents' experience of the various contexts of their lives. For instance, adolescents growing up in the United States prior to the industrial revolution were likely to attend schools in which classes were not graded by age, simply because there weren't enough students of the same age to constitute a separate class. Consequently, the microcosm of school did not confer on adolescents the same sense of themselves as a distinct age group as it presently does.

The Many Faces of Adolescents

We began this chapter by identifying four themes that will guide our study of adolescence throughout the chapters of this text: attention to issues of gender, ethnicity, distinct periods within adolescence, and identity. At this point, we will take a closer look at each of these.

Sex and Gender

Few differences are more important to adolescents than those associated with being male or female. Yet few are as likely to be misunderstood. Misunderstandings arise from a basic confusion—that of sex with **gender**. Sex refers to whether one is biologically female or male and is determined at the moment of conception. **Sex differences** are biologically based. Examples include differ-

macrosystem The underlying social and political climate at the level of society.

chronosystem The changing impact of the various environmental systems (micro-, meso-, exo-, macro) at different historical periods.

gender The cultural and psychological contributions to being female or male.

sex differences Biological and physiological differences distinguishing the sexes.

Why are so few girls in advanced science and math classes? Are boys naturally better at these subjects, or are they simply following gender stereotypes?

gender differences   Culturally determined differences in masculinity and femininity.

gender stereotypes   The cultural expectations concerning behaviors that are appropriate for each sex.

ences in the reproductive systems of males and females, or differences in the average height and body proportions of each sex. Gender refers to the distinctions a culture makes in what it considers masculine or feminine. **Gender differences** are socially determined. For example, most ethnic groups in our culture expect males to be strong and rational and females to be helpful and intuitive. One is *born* female or male, but one is *socialized* to be feminine or masculine.

A quick tour through a high school reveals many differences between students of either sex. It also reveals the difficulty we face in interpreting these differences. Walk into a math class, such as trigonometry or calculus, and you'll most likely see more males than females. Why? Is the male brain better suited to math than the female brain, or are males expected to be better in math and simply live up to that expectation? In other words, is this a sex difference or a gender difference? Continuing the tour, we'd probably find more females than males in an advanced-placement foreign language class. You might ask, is it in one's genes to be good at languages (a sex difference)? Or are females encouraged to develop these skills in ways that males are not (a gender difference)?

Gender stereotypes are the beliefs most people hold concerning what is typical for a male or female. These stereotypes encompass traits, roles, and occupations. For the most part, characteristics perceived as typically masculine are the opposites of those seen as feminine (Constantinople, 1973). Males, for example, are thought to be independent, active, and rational. Females, on the other hand, are perceived as dependent, passive, and emotional. As a result of this either/or approach, gender stereotypes can be problematic for adolescents, when being different from the stereotype for their own sex brings them closer to the stereotype for the other. Consider a girl who approaches situations rationally rather than intuitively. Not only is she seen as less feminine than girls who adopt intuitive approaches; she is also seen as more masculine (Lips, 2008).

On a more positive note, gender roles are more flexible today than in the past, allowing adolescents to express both feminine and masculine qualities. Adolescents of either sex can be sensitive and assertive, gentle and self-reliant. These adolescents are said to have androgynous traits ("andro" for male and "gyno" for female). However, fashioning one's own gender role in this way usually occurs in late adolescence because it requires a degree of self-knowledge and confidence beyond the reach of most early adolescents.

Whether based on sex, race, or even age, stereotypes usually reflect differences due to status as well. In our society, males frequently have positions of higher status than females. Behaviors of females and males that are attributed to their gender can often be explained by differences in their status. The masculine stereotype, for instance, includes qualities such as independence, decision-making skill, and risk taking. The confusion of status differences and gender differences becomes clear when we think of reversing the roles typically held by females and males. When status roles are reversed, as in the case of a male secretary and a female boss, the differences attributed to their gender often disappear. Who is more likely to make decisions, and who to be helpful? Or who will likely take risks, and who will be more dependent? Differences between the sexes exist in a social context, and this context will affect our interpretation of them (Lips, 2008).

Social context gives rise to another difference facing adolescents: their cultural backgrounds. Increasing numbers of adolescents in the United States belong to ethnic minorities. All adolescents—those in the majority as well as those in minorities—are affected by increasing cultural diversity.

Culture, Ethnicity, and Race

Melissa Herman (2004), a sociologist at Northwestern University, captures the issues raised for many adolescents in our ethnically diverse culture:

> Carlos Petterson (not his real name) was in his ninth-grade English class when he filled out a survey that asked him, among other things, about his race: "Select the major ethnic group that best describes you." This request posed a problem because Carlos' mother is part Filipino and part Mexican, and his father is White. Carlos marked the box to indicate that he was White, thus raising a number of questions: What factors motivate a biracial adolescent's self-definition? How does Carlos differ from other White-Filipino-Mexicans? From "pure" Mexicans, Filipinos, and Whites? (p. 730)

Ethnicity can affect adolescents in many ways. Adolescents who belong to a minority are more aware of the racial or ethnic differences that distinguish them than are those who belong to the majority (Bracey et al., 2004). Majority adolescents may even be unaware that they are also members of a racial group. Thomas Kochman (1987) found that whites distinguished each other in terms of ethnicity, but not race, referring to themselves, for example, as Irish or Polish, never as "white."

But what does it mean to belong to an ethnic group? Jean Phinney (1996), a psychologist at California State University, Los Angeles, points to the importance of examining ethnicity with respect to a number of dimensions that are critical in defining individuals' ethnicity: their cultural values and attitudes, their sense of belonging to the group, and their experience of being a member of a minority.

ethnicity The cultural group to which an individual belongs.

culture The values, beliefs, and customs that are shared by a group of people and passed from one generation to the next.

Although **culture**, the first dimension of ethnicity, is central to the identity of an ethnic group, there are such large differences in lifestyles and traditions within any group that culture alone is not enough to identify individuals as members of a group. The term Hispanic, for instance, includes not only Americans of Mexican descent but also people from more than a dozen South American countries, each with their own distinctive culture. Hispanic carries a different meaning for each of those cultures. What is important is that individuals belonging to the group are seen by others, and by themselves, as a separate group within society for whom their common heritage continues to be a significant part of their lives. Thus ethnicity is more than ancestry; it almost always involves culture, or the socially shared values, beliefs, and norms that determine one's way of life and that are passed on from one generation to the next (Betancourt & Lopez, 1993).

With schoolmates, dual-culture adolescents blend in with the mainstream teenage culture of their friends, but with their family, they engage in traditional customs and may even speak a different language.

ethnic identity An awareness of belonging to an ethnic group that shapes one's thoughts, feelings, and behavior.

minority A social group, distinguished by physical or cultural characteristics, that often receives differential treatment.

early adolescence That period of adolescence between the ages of about 11 to 15, marked by the onset of puberty, changing gender roles, more autonomous relationships with parents, and more mature relationships with peers.

Individuals within an ethnic group differ as well in the degree to which they identify with their group, or in their **ethnic identity**—the second dimension of ethnicity. Ethnic identity itself is multifaceted, including how one labels or identifies oneself, as well as one's sense of belonging to a group and the degree to which one values and participates in one's group (Ashmore et al., 2004). Furthermore, one's ethnic identity can be seen to change developmentally, from an initial stage in which ethnicity is simply taken for granted, through a period of exploration into the significance of belonging to a group, to a secure sense of oneself as a member of that group (Phinney, 1989, 1993).

Being a member of an ethnic group typically brings with it the experience of minority status, the third dimension of ethnicity, although not always. For instance, in Canada, English-speaking and French-speaking people are both members of dominant groups, yet each is a different ethnic group. At this point, the term **minority** deserves closer attention. It might seem, for example, that members of the majority would always outnumber those of a minority. Yet such is not always the case. Whites are actually in the minority throughout the world, though in the majority in the United States; however, white adolescents can experience minority status if they live in a community or attend a school in which some other ethnic or racial group predominates (Phinney, 1996). In certain areas of the United States, people of one race outnumber those of another yet are not considered part of the majority. In some counties of Mississippi, the ratio of African Americans to whites is three to one, yet the latter are considered the majority. It could be argued that the majority status of the whites is determined not by local ratios, but by those for the country as a whole. Yet a look at other countries suggests that qualifiers other than sheer numbers are involved in determining majority status. The British, for example, although vastly outnumbered in India, retained their majority status, as did whites in South Africa (Simpson & Yinger, 1985).

Minority status has less to do with numbers per se than it does with the distribution of power within a society, being associated, at least for those of color, with lower status and less power, whether in positions of leadership or, even when education is equated, in annual income (Dovidio & Gaertner, 1986; Huston et al., 1994). Stanley Sue (1991) argues that the very term *minority* connotes the unequal relationships that exist among various groups within a society, and that to fully understand the minority experience, one must understand the ways in which these relationships define patterns of exploitation.

Minority status also signifies, for one reason or another, a failure to be fully assimilated into the dominant culture. Louis Wirth (1945) defines a minority:

> as a group of people who, because of their physical or cultural characteristics, are singled out from the others in the society in which they live for differential and unequal treatment, and who therefore regard themselves as objects of collective discrimination. The existence of a minority in a society implies the existence of a corresponding dominant group with higher social status and greater privileges. Minority status carries with it the exclusion from full participation in the life of the society. (p. 347)

Minorities can be set apart by ethnic background, religion, nationality, or other defining features. (**Box 1.2** gives a personal account of minority socialization.) In fact, Wirth's definition of a minority could also include women, the elderly, those with disabilities, or adolescents themselves.

Early Adolescence, Late Adolescence, and Emerging Adulthood

The developmental issues and experiences confronting early adolescents differ markedly from those of late adolescents. Similarly, those of late adolescence differ from the experiences defining emerging adulthood. **Early adolescence**

BOX 1.2 In More Depth

Socializing African American Children

When strangers stop me on the street or at airports, often it is to comment on the essays I write about my family. Those about life in our old home in Brooklyn provide the most response. "It is obvious," a nun in a brown habit said one day, "that yours was a house of joy." I loved the phrase, but it troubled me.

It was not, I started to say to her, always so joyful. In fact, there were times that were painful, as there might be in any family. Some of our dinner-table discussions touched sensitive subjects. For example, our parents often struggled to help us understand and battle racial rejection. It was not always easy for them, proud immigrants in a new land.

One of the heroes of our family in the late 1940s was Dr. Ralph J. Bunche. He was then this nation's highest ranking black diplomat. He was also a leading academic. His field at Harvard had been international organization, a subject of special interest to our family. It was at the time of the formation of the United Nations. There must have been a dozen pictures of Dr. Bunche around our home. We owned at least one copy of everything published under his name.

The difficult time came the night of Dr. Bunche's public humiliation. He was denied entry to the Forest Hills Tennis Club [in New York], then the scene of the most prestigious matches in the world of tennis. Dr. Bunche's rejection became our own....

The idea that it would reject the hero of our family meant it had rejected each of us. ...

As one of my three sisters, a tennis player, began to put her troubled thoughts into words, tears welled up in her eyes, and she stopped talking. My mother's eyes met my father's. I could tell they had been discussing this between themselves.

"I want you children to understand what you are seeing here." He pointed across to a side table where the *New York Daily News* lay. The story of Dr. Bunche's rejection was prominently displayed. "I know you feel sorry about Dr. Bunche, but I tell you my prayers tonight are for those men who have humiliated him....

"People who create special rules of exclusiveness think they are showing the rest of us what great status they have achieved. In fact they are telling us the very opposite...."

"The very opposite." My mother repeated my father's last phrase for special emphasis. They often reinforced each other's points by repeating a few of the exact words.

"In fact," my father continued, "when people need racial exclusiveness in their social lives, it is usually to prove to others they have 'arrived.' But that's not how I read such men. I read them as socially insecure. Have you ever noticed that truly confident people walk and work among all with ease? The strong do not need that sort of status; the wealthy but weak do."

"Dr. Bunche," my mother said with a wry smile, "is fortunate he will not have to associate with such people." At last we laughed.

Source: Maynard, 1990.

---

is ushered in by the onset of puberty and the biological changes that transform the body of a child into that of an adult. Maturation of the reproductive system and a growth spurt put adolescents eye to eye and nose to nose with their parents. Early adolescents must integrate their changing bodies and new feelings into a new sense of themselves.

By **late adolescence**, the changes of puberty no longer dominate experience; instead, late adolescents feel a need to discover themselves and achieve mutuality and intimacy in their relationships. The social worlds of early and late adolescents mirror this change. Instead of congregating in circles of same-sex friends, common in early adolescence, late adolescents pair off in more intimate couples. In the intellectual realm as well, striking differences distinguish early from late adolescents. Early adolescents, for instance, are just beginning to think abstractly, whereas late adolescents use abstract thought to question not only their own values but also those of the society in which they live.

late adolescence That period of adolescence between the ages of about 16 to 19 that is organized around the central task of achieving an identity, in which adolescents integrate their sexuality into their relationships, prepare for a vocation, and fashion a personal set of beliefs.

emerging adulthood
A period between adolescence and adulthood characterized by demographic unpredictability and increased opportunity for identity exploration.

Finally, with respect to their daily routines, early adolescents are just one step beyond the comfortable routine of grade school, whereas late adolescents are on a path leading to the responsibilities of adult life. For early adolescents, a major psychosocial issue is achieving autonomy, primarily in their relationships with parents; in contrast, late adolescents are facing the need to consolidate the changes that accompany autonomy into a mature personality structure.

Significant as these differences are, equally significant differences distinguish late adolescence from the years of **emerging adulthood** (Arnett, 2000; Roisman et al., 2004). Jeffrey Arnett (2000) focuses on the years of 18 to 25 as a distinct period in life which he terms emerging adulthood. Characteristic of this period is a continued exploration of the direction one's life may take with respect to commitments that traditionally define adulthood: marriage, children, and occupation. Arnett distinguishes emerging adults in several ways: by their demographic unpredictability, their opportunity for identity exploration, and their subjective experiences.

Arnett points first to demographic differences distinguishing emerging adulthood from either adolescence or adulthood. Major demographics for adolescents, such as whether they're in school (95%), where and with whom they live (95% live with one or both parents), whether they're married (less than 2%) or have a child (less than 10%), are highly predictable. Nearly the same predictability exists for adults over the age of 30, though the trends are reversed, for instance, less than 10% are in school and 75% have a child. For 18- to 25-year-olds, however, it's almost impossible to say whether they're in school, where or with whom they might be living, and so forth.

The period of emerging adulthood also offers more opportunities for identity exploration than does adolescence. Even though identity traditionally has been regarded as a crisis of adolescence, nonetheless, emerging adults are able to more fully explore life options than are adolescents. Dating, for instance, can be recreational and fun but "few adolescents expect to remain with their 'high school sweetheart' much beyond high school" (Arnett, 2000). Until the years of emerging adulthood, marriage, and considerations of what would make it work or fail, remains safely in the future. Arnett suggests that the demographic unpredictability of emerging adulthood reflects opportunities for identity exploration, particularly with respect to intimate relationships, work, and beliefs and values. Support for this comes from findings that age-mates who do perceive themselves to be adult have a stronger sense of their identity than do emerging adults (Nelson & Barry, 2005).

A third way in which emerging adults can be distinguished is in terms of their subjective experience—they do not unambiguously see themselves as adults (**Figure 1.3**). They're clear that they are no longer adolescents, but they are not equally clear that they've reached adulthood. The criteria they use to mark this transition are relatively individualistic, such as being responsible for one's actions, making decisions independently, and being independent financially from their parents (Arnett, 2000; Nelson & Barry, 2005).

Once again, cultural differences exist in the expression of this period in life. For instance, with respect to demographic differences, emerging adults in Mediterranean countries are more likely to reside with their parents until they marry than those in Northern European countries, who characteristically live alone, with friends, or with a partner before marrying. Similarly, ages at which emerging adults typically marry and have their first child also differ by

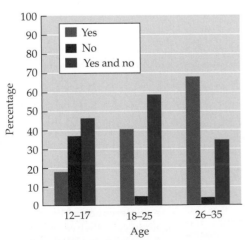

● **Figure 1.3 Emerging adults do not experience themselves as completely adult** When asked whether they think they have reached adulthood, they are likely to say "in some respects yes, in some respects no." (After Arnett, 2000.)

region. Nonetheless common features among Europeans distinguish this as a distinct developmental phase (Buhl & Lantz, 2009).

Who Am I? A Question of Identity

Children experience themselves in relation to their families. Ask them to tell you about themselves, and they will describe their families. They'll tell you what street they live on, who lives at home with them, how many sisters or brothers they have, and what they had for breakfast. Not so with adolescents. The once familiar answers no longer satisfy. They can tell you where they live, and who they live with, but this no longer informs them as to who they are.

Erik Erikson identified the central and most pressing question of adolescence as a search for personal **identity**. Adolescents are aware that they are not the children they once were, but they are equally sure they are not the adults they see around them. So who are they? Answers become organized around the developmental tasks confronting them (**Table 1.2**), tasks that arise as the physical changes of puberty and the changing expectations others hold for them determine the pace of their steps into adulthood.

identity The part of one's personality of which one is aware and is able to see as a meaningful and coherent whole.

TABLE 1.2
Developmental Tasks of Adolescence

Achieving More Mature Relations with Peers
Physical maturation plays an important role in this developmental task. Whether adolescents keep apace of peers in physical development or fall behind can influence the social circles they move in. Approval by their friends and by peers in general becomes especially important as adolescents experiment with new forms of social interaction.

Achieving a Masculine or Feminine Social Role
Although puberty provides the biological basis for this task, cultural expectations are equally important in determining which behaviors are regarded as masculine and feminine. Well-defined sex roles await adolescents, reflecting a culture's view of characteristic male and female behavior.

Coming to Terms with One's Body
Puberty again provides the biological basis for this task, as it transforms the bodies of adolescents into those of adults. The cultural basis for this task is given by well-defined stereotypes of the "perfect" body for females and males. The ease with which adolescents come to terms with their bodies will in part reflect the degree to which they match these images.

Achieving Emotional Independence from Parents and Other Adults
Puberty plays a less well-defined role in this task, although physical maturation is undoubtedly important. As adolescents become responsible for more areas of their lives, they experience new personal strengths. Redefining arenas of responsibility redefines their relationships with parents, leading to greater emotional independence.

Preparing for Marriage and Family Life
Although sexual maturation provides the biological basis for this developmental task, most individuals do not achieve a fusing of genuine intimacy with sexual feelings until late adolescence or early adulthood. Even though most adolescents will eventually marry and have children of their own, marriage today is more of an option than it has been in the past, and individuals are marrying later than previously.

Preparing to Support Oneself Economically
Perhaps nothing better signifies adult status than being able to support oneself. This developmental task has become increasingly problematic for adolescents today because of the many years of education that are necessary prior to entering many types of work.

Developing a Set of Values and an Ethical System to Guide Behavior
Thought undergoes profound changes in adolescence, enabling adolescents to consider abstract principles and hypothetical situations that are beyond the grasp of children. These changes make it possible for adolescents to evaluate their beliefs and values.

Achieving Socially Responsible Behavior
Whereas children view the world from the window of the family, adolescents and young adults do so from their places of work and new social roles. And just as children know themselves primarily through their relationships within the family, one's place within the community also contributes to adults' sense of self.

Puberty gradually transforms the bodies of early adolescents into those of adults. Wide variations in physical development are typical, both within and between individuals, giving puberty a special mystery for the adolescent, who is "the fascinated, charmed, or horrified spectator that watches the developments, or lack of developments, of adolescence" (Tanner, 1972, p. 1). Nonetheless, *coming to terms with one's body* is an important developmental task of adolescence. *Achieving more mature relations with peers* is a second developmental task, and one very much affected by the rate at which adolescents are developing physically. Those who fail to develop at the same pace as their peers can find themselves dropped from their social group. These groups are important since they serve as social laboratories in which adolescents try out more adult ways of interacting with others.

One of the more obviously adult ways in which individuals interact is through relatively well-defined gender roles. These reflect our culture's view of characteristic male and female behavior. Most adolescents will conform in large measure to these expectations, *achieving a masculine or feminine social role.* Most, too, will tailor their gender roles, taking a tuck here or there, to achieve the best fit. Our culture expects males to be strong, active, assertive, and independent, and females to be the weaker, passive, and dependent sex. Every Tarzan, in other words, needs a Jane. Fortunately for both Tarzan and Jane, as well as the rest of us, these roles have become more relaxed with time.

Adolescence is also the time when most of us redefine the sources of our personal strength; *achieving emotional independence from parents and other adults* is a developmental task confronting adolescents. As adolescents become responsible for more areas of their lives, they experience new personal strengths. Redefining responsibility, however, redefines their relationships with parents. Both parties are likely to greet these changes with mixed feelings. In return for self-reliance, adolescents must trade in a comfortable dependence. Parents must in turn trade a final say in things for trust in adolescents' judgment. The process is painful for both; it is difficult to shed familiar roles when new roles are not well defined or fully understood. These four tasks are primarily the concern of early adolescents, just as the next four primarily concern late adolescents and emerging adults.

Preparing for marriage and family life is a developmental task of late adolescence or emerging adulthood. Individuals are marrying somewhat later than they did a generation ago, and they are less likely to view marriage as marking their entrance to adulthood, although having a child remains a defining event. Equally important is *being able to support oneself*, although achievement of this developmental task is also delayed for many adolescents because of the increased years of schooling needed to prepare for careers. Late adolescents also are expected to think for themselves, to *develop a set of values and an ethical system to guide their behavior*, another developmental task of late adolescence. Related to this is the developmental task of *achieving socially responsible behavior* as adolescents assume new social roles. Each of these developmental tasks confronts adolescents with the larger task of achieving a sense of themselves. Each is a necessary step into adulthood.

Adolescents typically are torn between the desire for emotional and financial independence from their parents and the reluctance to give up the comforts of dependence.

A Historical Look at Adolescence

A brief look at history reveals that our conception of aging has expanded over the centuries, first distinguishing childhood as a distinct stage in life, then recognizing adolescence, and most recently distinguishing early and late adolescence, and emerging adulthood.

A Time Before Childhood?

Neil Postman (1982) argues that childhood became a recognizably distinct stage in life only when conditions prompted a redefinition of adulthood. Postman suggests that childhood was born in the mid-1400s, to strange parents: a goldsmith named Gutenberg and a converted winepress. If the invention of the printing press created childhood, it did so by default. What it really created, maintains Postman, was adulthood. Adults came to be defined as those who could read the new documents, maps, charts, manuals, and books that were quickly becoming available. The concept of adulthood was based on reading competence, and childhood on reading *in*competence. Before this time, adulthood directly followed infancy, which was considered to end at about age 7, when children mastered spoken language. Postman adds:

Adolescents develop a stable identity by trying out new roles and relationships, such as volunteering in a program to reintroduce Atlantic salmon to streams in New England.

> *In a literate world to be an adult implies having access to cultural secrets codified in unnatural symbols. In a literate world children must become adults. But in a nonliterate world there is no need to distinguish sharply between the child and the adult, for there are few secrets, and the culture does not need to provide training in how to understand itself. (p. 13)*

Printing brought about the concept of authorship and with it a new awareness of individuality. Postman believes this heightened sense of individual importance was critical in the development of childhood. "For as the idea of personal identity developed, it followed inexorably that it would be applied to the young as well" (Postman, 1982, p. 28). Prior to this point there was a striking lack of individuality, compellingly illustrated by the frequent practice of calling children within a family by the same name. Four sons might all be named John and distinguished only by order of birth.

The "knowledge gap" that developed with printing—something like 8 million books were printed in the first 50 years—created the need for schooling. Improving economic conditions made it possible for more families to send their children to school, and a new age group emerged in societies throughout Europe (Postman, 1982).

The Creation of Adolescence

In a similar way, adolescence emerged from childhood in the middle of the 19th century. This time industrialization gave birth to the new age group. As we read earlier in the chapter, adolescence emerged as a result of social conditions that required the prolongation of childhood. The machines of an industrialized society demanded new skills, and the entrance of young workers into the workforce was delayed until they had acquired these. Industrialization created a shift in the rural and urban population distribution. With this shift, large numbers of youth of the same age were concentrated in urban settings, a phenomenon unheard of in the days of the one-room schoolhouse. It became possible to have separate classes for youths of different ages. Industrialization also created a growing middle class, which meant that parents could send their children to school in order to secure the new jobs that were becoming available. The first high schools were formed in these urban centers in the early 1900s, and the youths who attended them became a noticeable new age group.

Stepping into the 21st century, we find ourselves in a postindustrial, postmodern society that continues to change rapidly. As in the past, we can expect our concept of adolescence to change as a result of social forces such as globalization, technological innovations, and increased immigration (Larson, 2002). In fact, globalization and the introduction of new technologies into many non-Western developing nations have resulted in the emergence of a stage of adolescence in these cultures where previously this had not existed. These non-Western experiences of adolescence bear their own cultural imprint, and in turn can be expected to contribute to the "reconstruction" of adolescence in developed nations as individuals immigrate to them from these cultures (Larson, 2002).

MEDIA CONTRIBUTIONS TO AGE DISTINCTIONS   Postman (1982) suggests that just as the printing press distinguished childhood from adulthood, the telegraph ushered in the age of electronic communication and, with this, a parallel revolution from print to images. Images, unlike books, are readily available to those of any age; they require no interpretation and no years of preparation for their mastery. The "knowledge monopoly" that previously separated children and adults was broken. Postman (1982) writes:

> The essential point is that TV presents information in a form that is undifferentiated in its accessibility, and this means that television does not need to make distinctions between categories of "child" and "adult."... This happens not only because the symbolic form of television poses no cognitive mysteries but also because a television set cannot be hidden in a drawer or placed on a high shelf, out of the reach of children; its physical form, no less than its symbolic form, does not lend itself to exclusivity. (pp. 79, 80)

Television, movies, and the Internet disclose secrets that were previously the domain of adults. For that matter, printed books did much the same thing 500 years ago when they broke the monopoly of the privileged few who could read and write. The difference is that literacy also established an obstacle that could be overcome only by years of preparation, as children learned to read and understand ever more complex forms of written expression. Television, however, tells all to anyone who may be watching; its images are self-explanatory. This point becomes important if one believes that groups are defined in significant ways by the exclusivity of the information available to their members. Lawyers are distinguished from doctors, students from teachers, or, in this case, children from adults by what they know. If the authority of adults derives, in part, from their ability to initiate children into their secrets, adult authority is diminished to the extent that there are no secrets (Postman, 1982).

The Internet provides an interesting twist on the power of secrets to confer—or diminish—adult authority. Teenagers can access information on nearly any subject simply by going online. But more than this, they can *step into* cyber worlds, entering chat rooms, visiting social networks, posting, texting, and blogging. And their parents need never know!

Emerging Adulthood

Similarly, social conditions have contributed to the period in life known as emerging adulthood. Jeffrey Arnett (2000) notes that emerging adulthood is found primarily in industrial and postindustrial cultures in which individuals typically continue their education beyond high school to prepare for a profession. The fact that many are not likely to complete their education until their early 20s makes it likely as well that they will postpone marriage and having children until they secure full-time employment.

Additional social conditions contribute to the emergence of this period in life as one characterized by continuing identity exploration. One of these simply has to do with age. Reaching the age of 18 confers legal status with respect to many things. Thus emerging adults can sign a rental agreement, be issued a credit card, open a bank account, purchase liquor, or vote. They can, in other words, function as adults in society without committing themselves to the defining tasks of adulthood. The second has to do with the lifting of societal sanctions against premarital sex, further freeing individuals from expected social roles and allowing them to explore relational life choices.

Adolescents in a Changing Society

Adolescents make up approximately 14% of the U.S. population. Nonetheless, they are a visible segment of society, perhaps because they highlight for us some of the ways in which societies are changing. For one thing, adolescents are living in an aging population. In the United States, as in most European and Asian countries, adolescents are coming of age in a population that has a few more gray hairs about its ears than in the past. **Figure 1.4** illustrates this trend (Jackson & Howe, 2008; U.S. Census Bureau, 2008a).

Adolescents highlight another aspect of our changing society—they have grown up in a technological world their parents entered only as adults, one of cell phones, personal computers, and the Internet. Over 90% of U.S. teenagers routinely access the Internet, 63% have a cell phone, and 72% have access to a personal computer. Uses of the Internet run from simply finding information to blogging, Twittering, social networking, emailing, instant messaging, downloading music, playing games, watching movies, or just "surfing." Adolescents, more than their parents, rely on the Internet and high-tech communication on a daily basis (Macgill, 2007; Wellman et al., 2008).

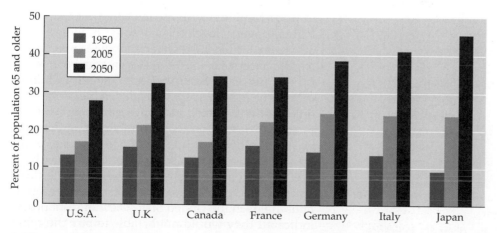

● **Figure 1.4   Aging populations**   The percent of the adult population that is aged 65 and over, 1950–2050. (After Jackson & Howe, 2008.)

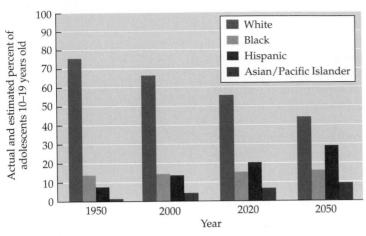

● **Figure 1.5** **Increasing ethnic diversity** Adolescents live in a society that is more diverse ethnically than the one in which their parents grew up. (After MacKay et al., 2000.)

low-income families Families with incomes no greater than twice the federal poverty level.

poor families Families with incomes that are below the federal poverty level.

There are other significant changes as well. The proportion of adolescents in the United States belonging to ethnic groups of color—including African Americans, Asian and Pacific Islander Americans, Hispanics, and Native Americans—has been steadily increasing. In 2000, 35% of adolescents in the United States belonged to an ethnic minority; by 2020, this figure will rise to 45%. By 2050, "minority" adolescents will become the majority, constituting 56% of adolescents in the United States. Additionally, increasing numbers of adolescents are multiracial, which means that one or both of their parents have parents claiming different racial or ethnic heritages. These trends mirror those in the general population, with those who previously had minority status making up the majority by 2050. Similar trends are occurring in other developed nations (**Figures 1.5** and **1.6**) (MacKay & Duran, 2007; Passel & Cohn, 2008).

Family characteristics are changing as well, with more families headed by a single parent. This change is due both to the number of marriages that end in divorce and to increasing numbers of children born to unmarried women. Approximately 30% of adolescents in the United States live with one parent. This figure varies with ethnicity, as can be seen in **Figure 1.7** (Kreider & Elliott, 2009). These figures contain a hidden dimension for many—poverty. Over a third of adolescents living in a female head-of-household live in poverty. The difficulty of making it on one's own while maintaining a family is one factor contributing to another change in family characteristics. Many single parents live with a relative, usually one or both of their parents, to make ends meet. As we begin the 21st century, more families than before are likely to have a grandparent at the wheel and mom and the kids in the backseat (**Figure 1.8**).

Poverty

Many adolescents in the United States experience poverty. Approximately 35% of U.S. adolescents live in **low-income families**, with incomes no greater than twice the federal poverty level. Another 15% live in **poor families**, with incomes that are below the federal poverty level; this latter figure increased by 21% from 2000 to 2007. Given that the U.S. economy entered a recession in 2007, this trend can be expected to continue (Falk, 2009; National Center for Children in Poverty, 2009). Poverty is related to the overall condition of the economy, and increases during economic recessions due to increasing numbers of parents who are unemployed. Those hardest hit by unemployment are those who already are disadvantaged, however even those who have felt safely "middle class" risk financial hardships. In a 2009 online survey of households in the United States, 50% of respondents indicated they would not be able to pay their bills for more than a month if they lost their job—this was true as well for 29% of those making over $100,000 a

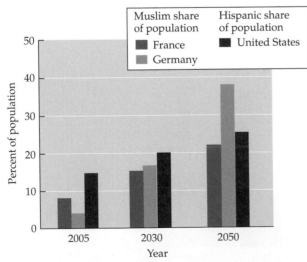

● **Figure 1.6** **Increasing ethnic diversity in France, Germany, and the United States, 2005–2050** (After Jackson & Howe, 2008.)

year (MetLife, 2009). **Figure 1.9** shows some of the ways families are likely to economize.

Perhaps because of statistics such as these, it's hard to get a handle on what poverty is (**Tables 1.3** and **1.4**). Existing stereotypes are largely false. Many associate poverty with chronic unemployment, dysfunctional families, and substance abuse. Assumptions such as these portray those living with economic hardships as somehow different from others, yet such is not the case:

> *Americans often talk about 'poor people' as if they are a distinct group with uniform characteristics and somehow unlike the rest of 'us.' In fact, there is great diversity among children and families who experience economic hardship. Research shows that many stereotypes just aren't accurate. About 40 percent of Americans will experience poverty at some point in their lives; only a small minority experience multi-generational poverty and chronic dysfunction. And more than 90 percent of low-income single mothers have only one, two, or three children. (Cauthen & Fass, 2008)*

What *is* true is that poverty affects the health and well-being of adolescents in multiple ways. Certainly, one of these ways can involve material hardships, such as not having adequate food, clothing, or housing. However, nonmaterial resources affect adolescents' well-being as well, and these, too, are in shorter supply for those who are economically disadvantaged. Examples of these resources include the safety of neighborhoods, the quality of schools, the availability of medical care, and community resources such as parks and libraries (Cauthen & Fass, 2008; Link et al., 2008).

Despite the challenges posed by social and personal change, adolescents by and large adopt a positive outlook on life. When asked who they look up to and admire, for instance, nearly twice as many mention someone they know rather than a media star or personality (Anderson & Cavallaro, 2002). And to the surprise of many parents, adolescents actually share their values. In other words, adolescents tend to view their world positively. This outlook is further

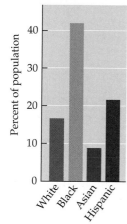

● **Figure 1.7   The percentage of adolescents in the United States who live with one parent varies with ethnicity**   (After Kreider & Elliott, 2009.)

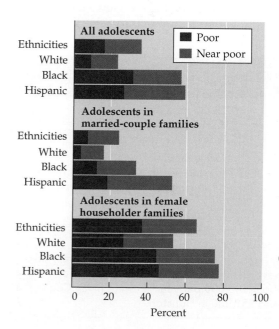

● **Figure 1.8   Poverty status among adolescents 10–17 years of age, by family structure and ethnicity: United States, 2005** (After MacKay & Duran, 2007.)

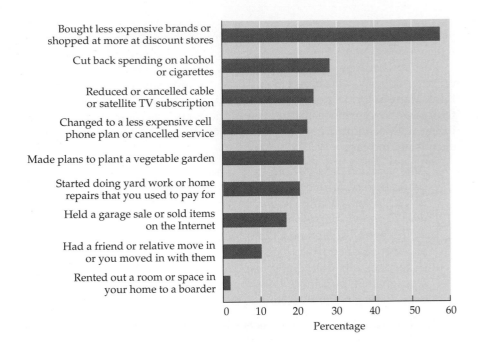

● **Figure 1.9 Belt-tightening in bad times** The percentage of individuals who said they had done one or more of the following because of the economic recession, responding to a survey conducted by the Pew Research Center. (After Morin & Taylor, 2009.)

reflected in the fact that a large proportion of youth volunteer for various types of community service (Frisco et al., 2004).

Adolescents Within the Life Span

The **life span perspective** enables us to see the ways in which adolescence, as one period in the life span, is related to other periods in life. For instance, the lives of an adolescent and a grandparent appear, and are, very different, yet beneath the surface each may be coping with similar issues. The adolescent, for example, may be trying to get the keys to the family car, whereas the grandparent may be facing the need to surrender them after a lifetime of use. The issue for both is the same—independence. If we were to study either of these ages apart from the other, we would miss important continuities to the experience of life.

The life span offers a unique perspective from which to view adolescence. Developmental issues that arise in adolescence can be traced back to child-

life span perspective
The view that development is characterized by continuity as well as change throughout life.

TABLE 1.3
The Federal Poverty Level in 2009 for Families of 2, 3, and 4 Persons

What is the federal poverty level (FPL) in 2009?	$22,050 for a family of 4 $18,310 for a family of 3 $14,570 for a family of 2

Is a poverty-level income enough to support a family?
Research suggests that, on average, families need an income of at least twice the federal poverty level to meet their most basic needs. Families with incomes below this level are referred to as low income.

$44,100 for a family of 4
$36,620 for a family of 3
$29,140 for a family of 2

These figures approximate the average minimum income families need to make ends meet, but actual expenses vary greatly by locality. For a family of four, the cost of basic family expenses is about $40,000 per year in rural Chelan County, Washington, $45,000 in Detroit, and $51,000 in Houston.

Source: Douglas-Hall & Chau, 2009.

TABLE 1.4
Basic Needs Budget: What A Family of Four Really Needs to Make Ends Meet

	URBAN NEW YORK, NY	URBAN HOUSTON, TX	SUBURBAN AURORA, IL	RURAL DECATUR COUNTY, IA
Rent and utilities	$15,816	$10,224	$11,328	$6,324
Food	$7,878	$7,878	$7,878	$7,878
Child care	$20,684	$15,422	$18,793	$11,682
Health insurance premiums	$2,609	$2,834	$2,265	$2,436
Out-of-pocket medical	$732	$732	$732	$732
Transportation	$1,824	$4,808	$4,808	$6,288
Other necessities	$6,397	$4,887	$5,185	$3,834
Payroll taxes	$5,113	$3,873	$4,437	$3,270
Income taxes (includes credits)	$5,787	–$34	$2,572	$304
Total	**$66,840**	**$50,624**	**$57,998**	**$42,748**
Percentage of 2008 Federal Poverty Level	315%	239%	274%	202%

Source: Cauthen, 2008.

hood and followed into adulthood. Issues of autonomy and competence, for example, are immensely important to adolescents. Both are also significant issues facing two other age groups: the elderly and toddlers. We can see continuities such as these and also note the more obvious changes that occur within the age category itself.

In the same way, similar developmental tasks are resolved and arise again at different periods in life. Just as early adolescents must come to terms with rapidly changing bodies and the resulting changes to their sense of themselves, so must their middle-age parents. An adolescent boy may notice a new "buffed" look; his father may be noticing a slight paunch around the middle and the tendency to become winded faster than he remembers. Parents may believe stress stalks in the form of adolescence, but it is just as likely to assume the form of middle age.

Interesting parallels exist between the tasks of both early and late adolescents and their parents. Early adolescents must revise their sense of self to accommodate the physical changes brought about by puberty, whereas their parents must come to accept and adjust to the physiological changes of middle age. Early adolescents also face the tasks of achieving emotional independence from parents and other adults; a parallel task for parents is assisting their teenage children to become responsible and happy adults, while simultaneously adjusting to the needs of their own aging parents. A task of late adolescence is to prepare for marriage and family life; that of middle age is to relate to one's husband or wife not only as a spouse but also as a partner or friend. Just as late adolescents face the task of preparing for an economic career, their parents face the task of reaching and maintaining satisfactory performance in their occupations. Similarly, late adolescents must achieve socially responsible behavior, whereas their parents face the need to achieve civic responsibility.

No cause for surprise, then, that relationships between adolescents and parents are occasionally tense. But despite sources of potential tension, most adolescents report surprising levels of satisfaction with their parents. Most agree with the way they have been parented and report that they hold many of the same values as their parents (Pratt et al., 2003; White & Matawie, 2004).

Parallels exist for both early and late adolescents and grandparents as well. Just as early adolescents must come to terms with rapidly changing bodies and the resulting changes to their sense of themselves, so must older adults. Similarly, late adolescents face the need to redefine the self in terms of an occupation, a task that requires commitment to a career. Conversely, grandparents face the need to maintain their sense of self once they have retired from a job that has been an important source of self-definition. The issue of economic independence also faces both of these age groups. Late adolescents may have to postpone work while they continue education; recently retired grandparents often face radically reduced incomes. In a similar fashion, most late adolescents are looking forward to marriage at a time when grandparents begin to worry about losing a spouse. Both face the task of adapting social roles to changing life circumstances. Finally, both face the need to establish satisfactory living arrangements, a problem for many late adolescents who continue to live at home while they pursue their education, as well as for grandparents who may not be able to maintain a separate residence of their own and face moving in with their children.

The many developmental tasks of adolescence confirm it to be a transitional period. However, to see adolescence just, or even primarily, as a transition is to miss the point—transition characterizes every age. It is, in fact, what allows us to distinguish each age from the preceding one. Middle age is no less a transition, nor is later maturity. To view adolescence simply as a transition is to fail to see adolescents as individuals in their own right. The lifespan perspective, then, draws our attention to similarities in the developmental issues facing adolescents and parents, and their parents, and encourages us to think of adolescence—like every other age—as a developmental lens that focuses the past onto the future.

Go to the **Adolescence** Companion Website at www.sinauer.com/cobb for quizzes, flashcards, summaries, and other study resources.

SUMMARY and KEY TERMS

Who Are Adolescents?

Defining Adolescence: To be complete, a definition of adolescence must consider biological, psychological and sociological changes. A biological definition emphasizes the events of puberty that transform the bodies of children into those of sexually and physically mature adults. A psychological definition distinguishes adolescence in terms of the developmental tasks to be accomplished, each of which relates to the central task of achieving a personal identity. A sociological definition defines adolescents in terms of their status within society, specifically, as a transitional period between childhood and adulthood.
adolescence, traditional cultures, developing countries, individualistic cultures, collectivistic cultures, globalization, puberty, developmental tasks, compulsory education laws, child labor laws, system of juvenile justice

Perspectives on Adolescence

A Constructive Perspective: A constructive perspective assumes that reality is not a given, that we each construct our own reality, actively interpreting experiences and reacting to them on the basis of our interpretation.
constructive perspective

A Contextual Perspective: From a contextual perspective we see that development is influenced by the daily settings, or contexts, of adolescents' lives—by where they spend their time and who they spend it with. It is not so much the actual, physical contexts that affect development, though, as it is how adolescents perceive these

SUMMARY and KEY TERMS

contexts, that leaves its developmental footprint. Bronfenbrenner describes these contexts as a set of five overlapping spheres of influence, each of which can affect conditions in another sphere.

contextual perspective, microsystem, mesosystem, exosystem, macrosystem, chronosystem

The Many Faces of Adolescents

Sex and Gender: Few differences are more important to adolescents, from either their perspective or that of their society, than those associated with being male or female. Both sex differences, which are biologically based, and gender differences, which are socially determined, influence adolescent development.

gender, sex differences, gender differences, gender stereotypes

Culture, Ethnicity, and Race: Today's adolescents are growing up in an ethnically diverse society. The strength of their identification as a member of a particular ethnic group depends on the extent to which they share the cultural values and attitudes of the group, feel they belong to the group, and experience being a member of a minority.

ethnicity, culture, ethnic identity, minority

Early Adolescence, Late Adolescence, and Emerging Adulthood: Adolescence can be distinguished by three stages, each with markedly different developmental issues and experiences. Early adolescence is ushered in by the onset of puberty and the changes that transform the body of a child into that of an adult. In late adolescence, the focus shifts to discovering themselves and achieving mutuality and intimacy in their relationships. The emerging adulthood stage finds them in continued exploration of the direction their life may take with respect to traditional adult commitments—marriage, children, and occupation.

early adolescence, late adolescence, emerging adulthood

Who Am I? A Question of Identity: Erik Erikson identified the central and most pressing question of adolescence as a search for personal identity. Adolescents are aware that they are not the children they once were, but they are equally sure they are not the adults they see around them. So who are they? Answers become organized around the developmental tasks confronting them.

identity

A Historical Look at Adolescence

A Time Before Childhood?: Neil Postman suggests that childhood became a recognizably distinct stage in life in the 15th century as a by-product of the printing press. What that innovation really created was adulthood—where adults came to be defined as those who could read the newly minted documents and books, and children were defined as those who could not.

The Creation of Adolescence: Similarly, industrialization in the mid-19th century prompted the emergence of adolescence from childhood, where several social conditions required the prolongation of childhood. The industrialized society demanded new skills and larger numbers of workers, prompting a population shift to the cities. With large numbers of youth of the same age concentrated in urban settings, it became possible to have separate classes and schools for youths of different ages, and a noticeable new age group was born.

(continued)

SUMMARY and KEY TERMS *continued*

Emerging Adulthood: Social conditions have contributed to the period in life known as emerging adulthood. Jeffrey Arnett notes that emerging adulthood is found primarily in industrial and postindustrial cultures in which individuals typically continue their education beyond high school to prepare for a profession.

Adolescents in a Changing Society

Although adolescents make up only 14% of the U.S. population, they are a visible group, perhaps because they highlight some of the ways in which our society is changing. By the year 2020, 45% of adolescents in the United States will belong to an ethnic minority, and many will be multiracial, with one or both of their parents having parents of different ethnic backgrounds.

Poverty: Family characteristics are changing as well, with more youth living in single-parent families and, with this, more experiencing economic hardship. Approximately 35% of adolescents live in low-income families, and another 15% live below the poverty line.
low-income families, poor families

Adolescents Within the Life Span

The life span perspective enables us to see continuities in the issues that arise at different points in life. Developmental issues that come up in adolescence can be traced back to childhood and followed into adulthood. Issues of autonomy and competence, for example, are immensely important to adolescents, but they are also significant issues facing two other age groups: the elderly and toddlers.
life span perspective

Sandra

Sandra had to talk to someone, or she'd explode! She tried Janie's number again. Still no answer… she couldn't believe he'd done that! Whatever was he thinking? She dialed again… come on, Janie, pick up! The phone seemed to ring forever, and then her friend answered.

"Janie, listen to this. You know how Harrison and I were working on the lip sync for the talent show? Yeah, that one. Well, you know how Elena was hanging around after rehearsal, all big eyes and smiles, and, like, talking to him? So you know what Harrison did? He said she could be in the act with us. How could he have done that! Doesn't he know…? I mean, he's the one who told me all the things she'd said about me. I feel so betrayed. Why would he ever do that? He seemed so… so sensitive. How could he be so cold!"

The Study of Adolescence:
Theory and Research

"Sandy, slow down. He's a guy, and you know how guys are. They don't think about things like that, I mean, not until we say something, and then it's... oh, I'm so sorry. It's a guy thing, believe me. It wasn't cold, it's just that... well, they aren't sensitive... I mean, not like us. Trust me, he didn't mean anything by it!"

Not to offend any male readers, or support any unwarranted conclusions among female readers, but Janie has just stated a theory concerning gender differences in interpersonal understanding. The field of adolescent development abounds with theories. Some haven't been much better than Janie's. But when they are good, theories help to explain events and make sense of our observations; they also enable us to anticipate related events.

Chapter Overview

Underlying every scientific theory are the beliefs we hold about the world we live in. Some people may think, for instance, that although adolescent males and females frequently see things differently, these differences would disappear if children of either sex were treated similarly. Others may believe that males and females are different—it's just in our natures—and that treating them the same will never change that. These assumptions represent very different beliefs about reality. When beliefs such as these produce a complete model of behavior, they are given a name. The contrasting beliefs stated above illustrate the environmental and the organismic models, respectively. The chapter begins by examining these models more closely and then looks at some of the theories concerning adolescent development that each has generated. The chapter closes by reviewing the methods researchers use in studying adolescent development.

Models and Theories

Models represent the implicit beliefs we hold about the world we live in. These beliefs can be so fundamental that they go unnoticed, yet they exert powerful influences on the theories they generate. For one thing, assumptions determine which questions appear reasonable and which seem foolish. If a researcher assumes that our behavior is primarily a reaction to events in the environment, then it makes sense to inquire what events immediately precede different behaviors. If another researcher assumes that behavior reflects goal-directed decisions, then it is reasonable to ask people about their goals and how they make their decisions. Notice that the first researcher is likely to observe what people do and what's going on around them when they do it. The second is likely to ask people why they do what they do. In each case, the beliefs that direct scientific investigation are collectively called a **model**.

model   A set of assumptions about reality in general and human nature in particular from which theories proceed.

theory   A set of testable statements derived from the assumptions of a model.

You might think that only researchers have models of human behavior. Actually, we all do. Do you think behavior is rational and goal-directed, or does it simply reflect past reinforcements? What motivates us? A succession of rewards and punishments? Inner goals? How much are we influenced by our biology? Do hormones and genes shape our interests and drives? Or do our interests and drives reflect acquired tastes and passions?

Although models are useful, they are too general to test. **Theories**, on the other hand, generate tentative explanations that can be verified or disconfirmed. Theories that derive from the same model bear a strong "family resemblance," reflecting assumptions characteristic of the model that generated them. The chapter begins with an examination of two contrasting models of human behavior and development and then looks at the theories they've generated.

How much do our personalities reflect inherited traits, and how much do they reflect environmental influences? Comparisons of the life course of twins have provided important information but no definitive answers about the relative influences of nature and nurture.

The Environmental Model

The **environmental model** traces our behavior to stimulating events in the environment. For instance, to explain how you are able to distinguish one word from another when you read, this model would focus on the amount and patterning of light stimulating receptors in the retina. This information is taken to be a copy of reality, meaning that you do not need to interpret what you are sensing; your sensory systems do this for you. You recognize the words in this sentence because receptors in the retina fire in patterns corresponding to the physical configuration of the letters. In a sense, the retina can be thought of as a film that retains the patterns of light to which it was exposed. Receptors carry the physical pattern of the letters through neural pathways to appropriate centers in the brain. All you need to do is simply keep your eyes open and make sure there's enough light to "expose the film."

This model is sometimes referred to as a mechanistic model because it attempts to reduce complex phenomena, such as reading, to simpler components that operate, in principle, as do those of a machine. Any piece of equipment, whether it's a simple vacuum cleaner or the latest computer, does not start on its own. Turning it on sets off a chained sequence of events that takes the identical form each time it unfolds. As long as the elements bear the same relationship to one another, tripping one will set the next in motion. Vacuum cleaners and computers do only what they are constructed to do: Vacuum cleaners don't process data, and computers don't suck up dirt. But if you know what type of device you have, and just what point in the sequence is unfolding, you should be able to predict what it will do next.

Is human behavior this predictable? The environmental model assumes it is—ideally. In actuality, it is difficult, if not impossible, to specify the myriad parts that make up the human machine. Even if one could, must our actions be prompted by events external to ourselves, or is behavior self-initiated?

If our actions are primarily reactions to forces external to us, the environment becomes a primary source of our behavior. Is an adolescent disruptive in class? Look for the events in the classroom that might cause this behavior. Is this student likely to get the teacher's attention, or that of classmates, only when acting out? Similarly, looking to the environment suggests ways of treating problems. Is a teenager anxious in social situations? Have the adolescent make a list of these, from those that produce the most anxiety (e.g. starting a conversation with someone from another crowd at school) to the least (talking to an aquaintance at lunch), then tackle the easiest first. Each success makes the next situation more approachable.

Although one might think it difficult to trace behaviors or emotions to the events that preceded them, it is infinitely easier than it would be if adolescents could, at any moment, choose to alter what they were doing just because they felt like it. Behavior is, at least in the abstract, predictable for those who hold to this model.

For those of you who think you take a more active role in defining your world, read on. The organismic model differs sharply from the environmentalist position.

The Organismic Model

In contrast to the environmental model, which looks to events outside the individual to explain what we do, the **organismic model** focuses on processes within the individual, assuming that individuals are active rather than passive, and that this activity is internally organized rather than structured by external events (**Table 2.1**).

environmental model
A set of assumptions in which the environment is taken to be the primary determinant of psychological development.

organismic model
A set of assumptions in which the unfolding of genetically organized processes is taken to be the primary determinant of psychological development.

What has readied these athletes to compete in this race? The unfolding of genetically programmed stages of maturation and growth? Or a continuous process of development shaped by their environments?

You have already met one organismic theorist, Urie Bronfenbrenner, whose ecological theory provided a framework in the first chapter for discussing the various contexts of development. Bronfenbrenner contends that the various contexts of adolescents' lives, such as their families, neighborhoods, or schools, are not significant in and of themselves. Instead, it is how adolescents perceive these that gives them developmental significance. One adolescent, coming home after school to her family's small apartment and hearing her mother and grandmother in the kitchen preparing dinner, can experience her home life as abundantly rich and secure. A sister, on the other hand, might notice the chipped paint and stained floors and feel the need to rise above what she experiences as her limited circumstances.

THE ACTIVE ORGANISM   Organismic theorists point out that environmental events become clear only when we respond to them. It takes an action from us to define the conditions that will then be perceived as events. Noam Chomsky (1957), a psycholinguist at MIT, has pressed this argument effectively. Chomsky argued that many sentences appearing to have a single meaning actually have many. They appear clear because we have already assumed a context in which they are unambiguous. Consider the sentence "They are eating apples." Seems clear enough. What are they doing? They are eating apples. Yet if you were asked "What kind of apples are those?" the meaning of the sentence changes. There are different kinds of apples. Some are for cooking and others for eating. And what are those? They are eating apples.

TABLE 2.1 Comparison of the Environmental and Organismic Models		
COMPARISON POINTS	**ENVIRONMENTAL MODEL**	**ORGANISMIC MODEL**
The human organism is:	Reactive	Active
Human activity is:	Structured by external events	Internally organized
Development occurs through:	Conditioning and learning	Environmental-genetic interactions
Developmental change is:	Continuous, quantitative change versus discrete stages	Discontinuous, as qualitatively distinct stages
The focus is on:	Observable behaviors	Thoughts, perceptions and feelings

ORGANIZED ACTIVITY   Perhaps the description of a simple experiment will illustrate the point best. Individuals participating in the experiment heard a click every 20 seconds for several minutes. With the first click, heart rate, brain-wave activity, sensory receptivity, and electrical conductance of the skin changed. These changes make up the orienting response, a general reaction to novel events. With each recurrence of the click, the orienting response decreased until it barely occurred at all (Sokolov, 1963). When habituation, or decreased response, had been pretty well established, the click was stopped, and everyone reacted with a full-scale orienting response. What was the stimulus for their reaction? Could it have been the absence of sound? The same silence, however, did not produce a reaction before the procedure began.

The phenomenon of **habituation** tells us that we detect regularities in our surroundings and anticipate them. Events that match or confirm, our anticipations provoke no further reaction. Those that do not match, prompt a reaction. Notice that our definition of a stimulus has changed. The stimulus is no longer an external event. Nor is it simply an internal event. It is a product of both. The stimulus is the match, or mismatch, of input with what is anticipated. As such, the original meaning of stimulus, as a goad or prod to action, is lost (Miller et al., 1960).

A final point before leaving this model concerns the way we know our world. Recall that the environmental model views perception as a copy of reality. The organismic model maintains, predictably enough, just the opposite—that perception is an active, constructive process. In order to perceive the letters that make up this sentence, we scan them to see whether certain features are present. We look for angles or curves, vertical or horizontal lines. Detecting certain of these leads us to "see" one letter or another. Recall the example given in Chapter 1, in which the very same physical configuration of lines can be read as either a B or a 13 in one context or another, depending on what the reader expects.

Is perception simply the stimulation of sensory receptors, as the environmental model asserts? If so, you should not be able to see the very same lines as either a B or a 13. Organismic theorists argue that context—whether a succession of clicks in a laboratory or a series of letters or numbers on a page—establishes an expectancy that directs the extraction of information. Put a slightly different way, they are saying that we actively "construct" the events to which we respond (Neisser, 1967, 1976).

Is the organismic model better because it offers sophisticated approaches to cognition and perception? Or perhaps the environmental model is more "scientific," because it focuses on behaviors that can be observed and precisely manipulated? Comparisons all too frequently lead to evaluations, and someone usually ends up holding the short end of the theoretical stick. Comparisons can also be misleading. Each model addresses different aspects of human functioning. We need both to begin unraveling the knotty problems of adolescence. The organismic model helps us understand motives and feelings that otherwise would never see the light of day. The environmental model gives us objective and readily testable theories of behavior. Unless we are willing to settle for theories about adolescents who act but don't think and feel, or those who think and feel but can't act, we need the insights each model offers.

But what about the developmental theories generated by these models? Remember, a single model can parent many theories. We will look at several theories for each. Examining more than one theory should help distinguish the assumptions of the model from the particular form they take in a theory. We will consider environmental theories first, then turn to organismic, or constructive, ones.

habituation   Decreased responsiveness to a stimulus with repeated exposure to it.

Radical behaviorist B. F. Skinner (1904–1990) contended that behavior is determined by external forces and can be explained only in terms of what can be actually observed. The subconscious urges described by Sigmund Freud have no place in Skinner's theories.

Environmental Theories

B. F. Skinner

B. F. Skinner's ideas have influenced countless psychologists and educators and infuriated others, both for the same reason: Skinner reduced the nuances and complexities of human behavior to the events that follow it rather than to what might have preceded it. His approach is a radical departure from the way most people understand their behavior. Most of us think that what we do is a response to inner states, to our feelings and thoughts. Skinner told us our behavior is under the control of external events.

Skinner's first subjects were rats. He constructed a small box with a metal lever protruding from one wall and selected a simple behavior—pressing the lever—for study. Because there was little for an animal to do in such a small space, its explorations soon brought it near the lever. Skinner waited until the animal touched the lever, then dropped a food pellet into a chute that ended in a dish beneath the lever. Each time the rat pressed the lever, a pellet of food (**reinforcement**) dropped into the dish. In no time the rat began to steadily press the lever. Skinner had brought a voluntary behavior—putting a paw on a metal lever and depressing it—under the control of its consequences. By making food contingent on lever pressing, he controlled the frequency with which the rat pressed the lever (Skinner, 1938).

Critics argue that humans are different from animals or, at the very least, different from rats. Our behavior reflects motives and intentions, not contingencies. Skinner's reply to these objections was that our intentions reflect our reinforcement histories. We can analyze many social interactions in terms of their reinforcing consequences. Sometimes such an analysis seems especially appropriate for problem adolescents in the classroom. Let's look at one such exchange between an adolescent and his teacher. She has just told him, once again, to stop rapping his pencil against his desk while she is presenting material at the board. He responds, "Sure thing, teach'," with a slightly sarcastic edge to his voice. She reacts quickly and sharply, calling out his name so loudly that everyone looks over at him. He casually puts the pencil down on the desk. Has she effectively put an end to this problem behavior? Or has she unwittingly reinforced the very behavior she finds disturbing?

Let's take a closer look at what has just taken place. By calling out his name when she allowed herself to become engaged by his sarcasm, the teacher actually reinforced this student with her attention (he received additional reinforcement in the brief moment following her reaction, when all eyes in the classroom were on him). Attention is a powerful reinforcer, even when, as in this example, it is not what most of us might regard as positive.

Also notice that the student reinforced the teacher. By putting the pencil down when she called out his name (stopping the activity that displeased her), he reinforced her scolding, making it more likely she will scold in the future, thus providing the attention that maintains his irritating behavior! We can analyze many parent–adolescent interactions in the same way. For instance,

reinforcement Any event that when contingent on a behavior increases the probability of that behavior occurring again.

have you ever noticed that adolescents frequently develop the very behaviors their parents find most objectionable? According to behaviorists such as Skinner, this is no accident. Those are the ones their parents are most likely to notice—and respond to.

Reinforcement is a powerful force in shaping and maintaining behavior. But must we actually do something, or actually receive reinforcement, in order to learn? Critics point out that we frequently know what to do before we ever do it. Many actions are novel, yet they unfold in smooth, successful sequences, not in the on-again, off-again manner one would expect if trial and error governed their performance.

Albert Bandura

Albert Bandura, a psychologist at Stanford University, agrees that learning accounts for much of our behavior; however, he stresses the social nature of learning. We needn't be directly

Young adolescents learn new skills by closely watching how other people behave and trying out those new behaviors themselves, either in fact or in their imagination. For social cognitive theorists, the most important element of learning is observation; for behaviorists, it is actually performing the behavior.

reinforced for doing something in order to acquire new forms of behavior. We simply need to observe others engaging in these activities and note what happens to them. In other words, important elements of the learning process for adolescents, indeed for all of us, are the context in which this occurs and the sense we make of what is taking place.

These three elements of the learning situation—context, action, and cognition—exert bi-directional effects in a process known as **reciprocal determinism**. Consider an adolescent who is teased by a classmate for a mistake she's just made, but instead of shooting back a curt remark, she responds with humor, earning the grudging admiration of the other girl. The environmental context (teasing by a classmate) certainly prompted this adolescent's behavior, but by reacting as she did, she effectively changed the environment.

Social cognitive theory has been put to effective use in the classroom by modifying adolescents' self-efficacy beliefs, in turn affecting their motivation to study and their resulting mastery of the material. Timothy Cleary and Barry Zimmerman (2004), at City University of New York, note that school-based programs are effective when they create self-motivating cycles of learning (Zimmerman, 2000). Students given training in the use of effective study skills can experience successes where previously they had failed, thereby changing their beliefs about their ability to master the material. Their beliefs, in turn, contribute to increased motivation and the ability to become more self-directed in their study habits.

Social cognitive theorists share with other environmental theorists a belief in the importance of the environment in explaining behavior. Also shared is the belief that learning is primarily the mechanism of change. Although social-cognitive theorists recognize the importance of many of the same processes as organismic theorists, e.g. thoughts and motives, they, just as other environmentalists, assume that one change builds on another in a quantitative fashion. They do not explain change as a succession of stages distinguished by qualitatively different features. Organismic theorists give us a very different view of things.

reciprocal determinism
The two-way influence between person and environment; not only does the environment influence behavior but behavior changes the environment.

Jean Piaget (1896–1980) developed his theory that we actively construct what we know of the world based on four stages of cognitive development.

Organismic Theories

Jean Piaget

Perhaps because Jean Piaget was first interested in biology, he approached human intelligence with questions a biologist might ask if discovering a new organism: How does a creature adapt to its surroundings? What does it do that allows it to survive? How is it changed by the processes that maintain it? For Piaget, intelligence was a means of adapting to one's environment, and only those forms of thought that promoted adaptation survived with increasing age.

Piaget traced the development of intelligence to maturation of the nervous system (Chapter 4). This emphasis on the biological and neurological underpinnings of intelligence did not prevent him from giving equal importance to environmental contributions. In fact, a singularly distinctive feature of his theory is the manner in which it accounts for the development of intelligence through the interaction of environmental and biological forces. Rather than viewing maturation as providing "ready-made knowledge" or "preformed structures," Piaget viewed it as "open[ing] up new possibilities... which still have to be actualized by collaboration with the environment" (**Table 2.2**) (1971, p. 21).

Robert Kegan

Building on the developmental process elaborated by Piaget, Robert Kegan (1982, 1994), a psychologist at Harvard University, argues that the most central human activity is that of "meaning making," of constructing from the moment a reality that makes sense given the balance one has already struck

TABLE 2.2
Piaget's Stages of Intellectual Development

STAGE	DESCRIPTION
Sensorimotor (Birth to 2 years)	Infants' awareness of their world is limited to their senses, and their reactions to general action patterns, such as sucking and grasping, through which they incorporate their experiences. This stage ends with the beginning of symbolic thought.
Preoperational (2 to 7 years)	Children can use symbols such as words and images to think about things, but confuse the way things appear with the way they must be (intuition). They may also fail to realize that the way things appear to them is not the way they may appear to others (egocentrism). When solving problems, they tend to focus on a single aspect of the problem to the exclusion of others (centration).
Concrete Operational (7 to 11 years)	Thinking becomes more flexible, allowing children to consider several dimensions of things simultaneously, realizing that though an object may look different, it has not necessarily changed (conservation). Piaget attributed this flexibility to mental operations, actions that children are able to carry out in their heads that can be reversed, or undone, enabling them to consider the same problem from several perspectives.
Formal Operational (11 years and older)	Thinking becomes abstract, embracing thought itself. Adolescents can consider things that are only possible, as well as those that are real, enabling them to think of themselves in terms of future possibilities as well as the present. Their thinking is also more systematic and logical.

with the world. Such a balance is the qualitatively different reality the individual achieves at different ages. This reality is shaped not only by increasingly mature ways of thinking (Chapter 4), but also by ways of feeling, of relating to others, and of relating to ourselves. These four dimensions—the cognitive, the affective, the interpersonal, and the intrapersonal—constitute the meaning-making arenas of the "self" (Kegan, personal communication).

Sigmund Freud

Freud began his professional life as a physician with a private practice in neurology. Were it not for some of his patients who complained of mysterious ailments, he might have remained an obscure but successful Viennese doctor. The mysterious symptoms were no different from those he saw daily, such as numbness and paralysis from damaged nerves. But the nerves in these patients were unaffected; he found only healthy neural tissue when he examined them. How could patients suffer neurological symptoms with no physical damage?

Freud formulated his theory of personality development while treating these unusual symptoms. He believed that they resulted from an inner war between conflicting aspects of the personality. Although Freud first noticed these aspects of the personality in his patients, he believed them to be present in all of us. For Freud, life is a battle, and we are all on the front lines. Two opposing forces, one within us and the other outside, fight for control. Because each is an integral aspect of our personalities, the victory of either one means a sure defeat to the individual. Instead, we must achieve a balance between internal biological drives and external social constraints. We achieve this balance only with time and at some personal cost. As in any war, there are casualties. True spontaneity may be the first to go. The second loss takes the form of compromise. We learn to make do with lesser delights to avoid the anxiety provoked by indulging our first instincts. There are victories as well. We gain control over primitive impulses that otherwise, he believed, could destroy us and our civilization (**Table 2.3**) (Freud, 1954).

Freud traced the source of the conflict to a human drama that he believed played itself out in the family. Freud believed that young boys fall in love with their mothers, the **Oedipus complex**, and girls with their fathers, the **Electra complex**. Since Freud framed his theory around the male experience, we'll consider how the conflict unfolds in boys. The boy's feelings for his mother

Sigmund Freud (1856–1939), the founder of psychoanalysis, defined five stages of psychosexual development. These particular stages have been subject to much debate, but many theorists have built on his general concept of developmental stages.

Oedipus complex   A Freudian concept in which the young boy is sexually attracted to his mother, and regards his father as his rival.

Electra complex   A Freudian concept in which the young girl is sexually attracted to her father and regards her mother as her rival.

TABLE 2.3	
Freud's Structure of the Personality	
STRUCTURE	**COMPONENT OF THE PERSONALITY**
Id	The primitive component of the personality, which seeks immediate gratification of biological impulses; the Id is amoral, operates according to the pleasure principle, and exists only in the unconscious.
Ego	The executive component of the personality, which seeks to satisfy the impulses of the Id in socially acceptable ways to avoid societal sanctions; the Ego operates according to the reality principle, and exists in both the conscious and unconscious.
Superego	The moral component of the personality, which represents the internalized standards and values of society, the Superego demands socially acceptable behavior and thus opposes demands of the Id, is the seat of the conscience, providing a sense of right and wrong, and of the ego-ideal, and exists in both the conscious and unconscious.

castration anxiety
In Freudian theory, a young boy's fear of being castrated by his father as punishment for the boy's sexual attraction to his mother.

superego   The aspect of the personality in Freudian theory that represents the internalized standards and values of society.

TABLE 2.4
Freud's Psychosexual Stages
Distinct structures of development unfold as psychic energy (the libido) is expressed through different zones of the body

STAGE	DESCRIPTION
Oral (Birth to 1½ years)	Infants derive pleasure through activities that stimulate the mouth, for instance, nursing, sucking, biting. Conflict occurs over weaning.
Anal (1½ to 3½ years)	Toddlers derive pleasure through expelling and retaining feces. Conflict occurs over toilet training.
Phallic (3½ to 6 years)	Preschool-age children become interested in their genitals and derive pleasure from their stimulation. Oedipus/ Electra conflicts involve relationships with parents.
Latency (6 years to puberty)	Sexual impulses are repressed in school-age children; there is little psychosexual conflict.
Genital (Puberty to adulthood)	With puberty, sexual impulses re-emerge; sexual gratification is sought with person(s) other than the parent. Conflict involves the competing demands of various aspects of the personality (Id, Ego, Superego).

---

transform his father into a rival. Given the sexual nature of these feelings, the boy fears castration as fitting punishment. Freud believed this fear (termed **castration anxiety**) motivated repression of the sexual nature of his feelings. In thus yielding to his father, the boy identifies with him and, in the process, takes on the father's values which, in turn, reflect those of the larger society. The resulting personality structure, or **superego**, emerging from this process reflects the power that the boy sees in his father (**Table 2.4**).

Erik Erikson

Erik Erikson built on Freud's analysis of the personality, yet he differed from Freud in his emphasis on the healthy personality. Erikson stressed the social functions of the ego that allow individuals to cope successfully. These functions assume central importance in adolescence, as adolescents question who they are and where they are going (Chapter 5). Identity is a central aspect of the healthy personality, reflecting both an inner sense of continuity and sameness over time and an ability to identify with others and share in common goals, to participate in one's culture. Erikson (1963) believed that identity develops as adolescents assume commitments to future occupations, adult sex roles, and personal belief systems. It is no accident that identity assumes importance as individuals step from childhood into adulthood and, with this, into their culture. **Box 2.1** offers a vivid look at group identity development.

PSYCHOSOCIAL STAGES OF DEVELOPMENT   Erikson (1963) believed that new aspects of the person emerge through inner growth, making new types of social encounters possible. As with other organismic theorists, he assumed that development occurs in the same set sequence for all, reflecting an internal ground plan in which each stage has its own period of ascendence, a time in which the individual is especially vulnerable to certain influences and insensitive to others. Society challenges us with new demands as we age. We experience these as crises. Each takes a slightly different form and gives each age its unique characteristics. **Table 2.5** describes each of Erikson's life stages.

Erik Erikson (1902–1994) built on Freud's theory of psychosexual development and formulated a psychosocial theory of development. According to his theory, people move from one stage to the next in response to social demands.

TABLE 2.5
Erikson's Eight Stages: Development Through Life

STAGE IN LIFE	PSYCHOSOCIAL CRISIS	CHALLENGE TO BE MET	RESULTING CHARACTER STRENGTH
BIRTH TO ADOLESCENCE			
Infancy	Trust versus mistrust	Trusting that others will take care of one	Hope
Toddlerhood	Autonomy versus shame and doubt	Becoming purposeful; doing things oneself	Will
Early Childhood	Initiative versus guilt	Exploring and trying out new things	Purpose
Middle Childhood	Industry versus inferiority	Mastering skills	Skill
ADOLESCENCE TO OLD AGE			
Adolescence	Identity versus identity confusion	Achieving a sense of oneself	Fidelity
Early Adulthood	Intimacy versus isolation	Forming emotionally intimate relationships	Love
Middle Adulthood	Generativity versus stagnation	Giving to the next generation	Care
Late Adulthood	Integrity versus despair	Accepting one's life as having meaning	Wisdom

Each of the first four crises equips adolescents to meet the central challenge of achieving an **identity**. Trust establishes the confidence in themselves and in others that is needed to begin the task. Autonomy gives self-direction and purpose, the ability to follow goals that one sets for oneself rather than those set by others. Initiative allows adolescents to explore the options that open up with adolescence, and industry allows them to realistically evaluate these options and select the ones they will commit themselves to (Erikson, 1963, 1968).

identity The part of one's personality of which one is aware and is able to see as a meaningful and coherent whole.

The establishment of identity involves the individual in a succession of commitments to life goals that serve to define the self. The young adult faces the crisis of sharing that self with another—of intimacy, first with a mate and then, for most, with children. Middle adulthood extends the adult's concerns beyond this intimate group to others in the community. Older adults face a final crisis of reviewing their lives and accepting the decisions they have made. Erikson calls this last crisis one of personal integrity.

Just as Freud before him, Erikson's theory reflects a male bias. He considered the achievement of identity to

A growing body of research can describe the differences in identity development for these two adolescents due to their gender. Fewer researchers, however, have explored differences in identity development for various racial or ethnic groups.

BOX
2.1 **Research Focus**

Erikson's Psychohistorical Approach: A Clinician's Notebook from the Dakota Prairies

By Michael Wapner

> When we neared the simple, clean homestead, the little sons were playing the small Indian boy's favorite game, roping a tree stump, while a little girl was lazily sitting on her father's knees, playing with his patient hands. Jim's wife was working in the house. We had brought some additional supplies, knowing that with Indians nothing can be settled in a few hours; our conversation would have to proceed in the slow, thoughtful, shy manner of the hosts. Jim's wife had asked some women relatives to attend our session. From time to time she went to the door to look out over the prairie which rolled away on every side, merging in the distance with the white processions of slow-moving clouds. As we sat and said little, I had time to consider what Jim's place among the living generations of his people might be. (Erikson, 1963, pp. 120–121)

So begins Erikson's description of the conversations that contributed to his understanding of the Sioux's early childhood experiences and their difficulty as adults in finding meaning to life. More generally, these observations led to his understanding of the ways in which one's society influences the course of each person's development.

Erik Erikson developed a unique style of research that combined the tools of clinical analysis with those of fieldwork. His insights into human development reflected the same psychoanalytic training that Freud and others practiced in urban European offices. Erikson took these skills to the rolling plains of the Dakotas, and later to the forested dwellings of the Yurok in the Northwest, and in doing so, opened new vistas in our understanding of human development.

His observations made him keenly aware that human development takes place within a social community. Each community raises its children to participate in the world as adults—but there are as many worlds as there are communities. Children are indulged or controlled, taught to give away or to hoard, and so on, depending on the wisdom of their group—a wisdom that reflects the peace their group has made with the realities of geography and the historical moment. The area in which one lives determines the form life takes, whether in the specifics of what one eats or wears or in abstractions such as notions of goodness and propriety (Coles, 1970).

The Sioux, for instance, value generosity and regard the accumulation of wealth as tantamount to evil. Erikson traces these attitudes to a nomadic life in which they followed the buffalo across the plains. The buffalo existed in great numbers and the Sioux rarely experienced need. As nomads, the Sioux learned to live lightly, without the encumbrances of possessions. Generosity, because it reflected a more basic harmony with their surroundings, was a virtue. Conversely, the Yurok value thrift and a meticulous management of resources. They live in settlements along the Klamath River. Once a year, when the salmon return to breed, they experience the abundance that the Sioux lived with in every season. For the rest of the year, they must cautiously manage that brief harvest to avoid hunger and need.

These particular differences are less important than the common function served by the communal practices of either group. Ritual ways of living provided each with a group identity. It is from this group identity that members of the community derived a sense of their own identity. Erikson arrived at this observation after noting what he referred to as a "cultural pathology" among the present-day Sioux Indians. He traced this problem to their inability to find "fitting images to connect the past with the future" (Erikson, 1963). The Sioux's lifestyle had been tied to the buffalo, the provider of meat for food; pelts for clothing and shelter; bones for needles, ornaments, and toys; and even dried droppings for fuel. The destruction of the buffalo herds by White settlers resulted in the destruction of the Sioux's way of life—and of the group identity from which new generations could derive a sense of themselves. Speaking of the present generation of Sioux, Erikson noted that "the majority of them have as little concept of the future as they are beginning to have of the past. This youngest generation, then, finds itself between the impressive dignity of its grandparents, who honestly refuse to believe that the white man is here to stay, and the white man himself,

BOX
2.1   *continued*

who feels that the Indian persists in being a rather impractical relic of a dead past" (1963, p. 121).

If Erikson's theory is correct, that without "fitting images to connect the past with the future" young people are lost, what are the images that performed this function for you? Is there any single or even small set of recurrent experiences that anchor you in your community and physical environment the way the buffalo anchored the Sioux? Is it possible that society in the United States at the beginning of the twenty-first century has no such single image? Perhaps these images belong to subgroups rather than the culture as a whole. For instance, is the gang for the East Los Angeles gang member in any way analogous to the buffalo for the Sioux? What functions would the gang have to fulfill for its members to qualify as an image? If it is an image in the Eriksonian sense, then what will it take to discourage gang membership in East Los Angeles and similar urban communities?

Sources: After Coles, 1970 and Erikson, 1963.

be the central crisis of adolescence, even though asserting that a different sequence exists for females. Most females resolve the crisis of intimacy, which Erikson places in early adulthood, before they complete identity issues. Their sense of themselves derives more from their relationships than from commitments to work and ideology. Although Erikson notes these differences, he does not change his sequence of life stages; that is, he equates the male experience with development in general (Gilligan, 1982, 2004).

Nancy Chodorow

Another theorist, also influenced by Freud, gives us a different view of development. Nancy Chodorow, offers an alternative to the universal developmental sequence charted by Erikson. Chodorow (1978) attributes psychological differences in the makeup of females and males to the social fact that for most children the first intimate relationship is with a woman—their mother. This initial relationship has different consequences for girls than it does for boys.

Chodorow asserts that infants experience themselves as continuous with the mother. They live within the boundless security of her presence, little caring which smile is theirs or whose hand reaches out to the other, all of it part of the same encircling awareness. Mothers, too, empathically relate to their infants and experience a continuity with them.

> In a society where mothers provide nearly exclusive care and certainly the most meaningful relationship to the infant, the infant develops its sense of self mainly in relation to her. Insofar as the relationship with its mother has continuity, the infant comes to define aspects of its self ... in relation to internalized representations of aspects of its mother. (Chodorow, 1978, p. 78)

Nancy Chodorow's research challenges Freud's and Erikson's assumptions of a universal developmental sequence. Because boys must define themselves outside their relationship with their mother but girls define themselves within that relationship, the course of identity development is fundamentally different for the two sexes.

Important to Chodorow are the necessary differences in the way children of either sex develop beyond this point. Girls can continue to define themselves within the context of this first relationship. Mothers, as well, can see their daughters as extensions of themselves. Girls can experience a continuing attachment to the mother while still defining themselves as females. None of this is possible for boys. They must separate themselves from the mother much earlier than girls in order to develop as males. Mothers, too, experience their sons as separate and different from themselves, unlike the way they experience their daughters. Thus, boys embark on a developmental path marked not by attachment but by separation and increasing individuation.

Chodorow argues that because the primary caregiver is the same sex for girls, there is less need for the girl to differentiate herself in terms of ego boundaries. Chodorow introduces a point made earlier by Freud and later by Erikson: The personalities of women are frequently less differentiated than those of men and are more closely tied to their relationships. But she sees this difference as an asset, as a strength rather than a weakness. Girls can experience continuity with others and relate to their feelings. Chodorow points to the heavy costs males pay for their greater individuation. In curtailing their emotional attachment to the mother, they also limit their ability in general to relate empathically to others. Thus, differences in ego boundaries lay a foundation for a greater capacity for empathy in females. In fact, Chodorow sees the capacity for empathy to be a core part of the feminine personality, giving them a sense of connectedness with others.

Carol Gilligan

Carol Gilligan, a psychologist at New York University, notes striking differences in the ways males and females think of themselves. These differences extend to the ways they resolve issues involving others (Chapter 11). Gilligan finds that males tend to see themselves as separate from others; females describe themselves in terms of their relationships with others. These themes of separation and connectedness appear over and over again in her writings and her research, whether she is studying morality and choice, descriptions of the self, or interpersonal dynamics (Gilligan, 1982, 2004).

Notice the way two of Gilligan's subjects, an 11-year-old boy and an 11-year-old girl, describe themselves, as shown in **Box 2.2**. Jake describes himself at length. He first identifies himself by his age and name and then his status within his community. We never know what his mother does, but this doesn't contribute to his sense of position as does his father's occupation. He then identifies his abilities and interests. He ends with a description of an important physical characteristic. We get the impression of a distinct personality from this description. Gilligan agrees. Jake has described himself in terms of the things that distinguish him from others. His self-description emphasizes his uniqueness and separateness.

Amy's description of herself is brief. We know only that she enjoys school and wants to be a scientist. Otherwise, she describes herself in terms of her relationships with others. We know nothing about Amy apart from the qualities she believes will allow her to help others. Short, tall, freckled, funny, well-off, or disadvantaged—things that set her apart from others receive little attention. Gilligan stresses that this sense of responsibility for and connectedness to others frequently appears in girls' and women's descriptions of themselves. It is, she notes, a very real difference between most women and men.

We see this difference clearly when Jake and Amy are asked how one should choose when responsibility to oneself and responsibility to others conflict (**Box 2.3**). Jake believes we are mostly responsible to ourselves. Being independent means taking care of ourselves and making sure that our actions don't hurt others. Jake starts with the assumption that individuals are separate and proceeds with the need for rules to protect each person's autonomy. Thus for Jake, responsibility is not doing certain things.

Amy's answer is much longer than the one she gave in describing herself. She puts her responsibility to others first. Not always, of course; but she differs in an important way from Jake. Amy sees responsibility as an action, as a positive response. She assumes a connectedness with others. She talks about people and caring, all on a personal level, whereas Jake mentions the community and seems to imply a need for rules to regulate the actions of its members.

Carol Gilligan, a psychologist at New York University, has focused her research on female development and challenged the definition of developmental stages by Lawrence Kohlberg and other developmentalists, whose theories are based primarily on the experiences of male subjects.

In More Depth

Self-Description of Two Adolescents

How would you describe yourself to yourself?

Jake: Perfect. That's my conceited side. What do you want—any way that I choose to describe myself?

Amy: You mean my character?

What do you think?

Amy: Well, I don't know. I'd describe myself as, well, what do you mean?

If you had to describe the person you are in a way that you yourself would know it was you, what would you say?

Jake: I'd start off with 11 years old. Jake [last name]. I'd have to add that I live in [town], because that is a big part of me, and also that my father is a doctor, because I think that does change me a little bit, and that I don't believe in crime, except for when your name is Heinz*; that I think school is boring, because I think that kind of changes your character a little bit. I don't sort of know how to describe myself, because I don't know how to read my personality.

If you had to describe the way you actually would describe yourself, what would you say?

Jake: I like corny jokes. I don't really like to get down to work, but I can do all the stuff in school. Every single problem that I have seen in school I have been able to do, except for ones that take knowledge, and after I do the reading, I have been able to do them, but sometimes I don't want to waste my time on easy homework. And also I'm crazy about sports. I think, unlike a lot of people, that the world still has hope. …Most people that I know I like, and I have the good life, pretty much as good as any I have seen, and I am tall for my age.

Amy: Well, I'd say that I was someone who likes school and studying, and that's what I want to do with my life. I want to be some kind of a scientist or something, and I want to do things, and I want to help people. And I think that's what kind of person I am, or what kind of person I try to be. And that's probably how I'd describe myself. And I want to do something to help other people.

Why is that?

Amy: Well, because I think that this world has a lot of problems, and I think that everybody should try to help somebody else in some way, and the way I'm choosing is through science.

Source: From Gilligan, 1982.
* Heinz is a character in one of Kohlberg's moral dilemmas who steals a drug to save his wife's life.

Amy and Jake have taken different paths through childhood. They are likely to follow different paths through adolescence and into adulthood. Amy experiences herself in terms of her connection with others, Jake through his separateness. Each is also developing different strengths: Amy in interpersonal relations, Jake in functioning autonomously. At this point, the strengths of one are the weaknesses of the other.

Gilligan suggests that because of the difference between females' and males' capacities for empathy, males should experience more problems with relationships and females with individuation. Because human development

In More Depth

Choosing between Responsibility to Self and Responsibility to Others

When responsibility to oneself and responsibility to others conflict, how should one choose?

Jake: You go about one-fourth to the others and three-fourths to yourself.

Amy: Well, it really depends on the situation. If you have a responsibility with somebody else, then you should keep it to a certain extent, but to the extent that it is really going to hurt you or stop you from doing something that you really, really want, then I think maybe you should put yourself first. But if it is your responsibility to somebody really close to you, you've just got to decide in that situation which is more important, yourself or that person, and like I said, it really depends on what kind of person you are and how you feel about the other person or persons involved.

Why?

Jake: Because the most important thing in your decision should be yourself, don't let yourself be guided totally by other people, but you have to take them into consideration. So, if what you want to do is blow yourself up with an atom bomb, you should maybe blow yourself up with a hand grenade because you are thinking about your neighbors who would die also.

Amy: Well, like some people put themselves and things for themselves before they put other people, and some people really care about other people. Like, I don't think your job is as important as somebody that you really love, like your husband or your parents or a very close friend. Somebody that you really care for—or if it's just your responsibility to your job or somebody that you barely know, then maybe you go first—but if it's somebody that you really love and love as much or even more than you love yourself, you've got to decide what you really love more, that person, or that thing, or yourself.

is charted, to date, in male terms—that is, in terms of increasing separation and individuation—when women have problems with individuation, these are seen as a sign of developmental immaturity. Men's problems with relationships, however, have not evoked a parallel interpretation. Gilligan pointedly notes that "women's failure to separate then becomes by definition a failure to develop" (Gilligan, 1982).

Gilligan points out that science has not been neutral. Our theories reflect "a consistent observational and evaluative bias." We tend to interpret "different" as either better or worse, because we have a tendency to work with a single scale. Because most scales are also standardized in terms of male development, male behavior is taken as the norm and female behavior as a departure from the norm. This approach has been perpetuated by the fact that most research was done by males, with many important studies using only males as subjects (Yoder & Kahn, 1993).

BOX
2.3   *continued*

And how do you do that?

Amy: Well, you've got to think about it, and you've got to think about both sides, and you've got to think which would be better for everybody or better for yourself, which is more important, and which will make everybody happier. Like if the other people can get somebody else to do it, whatever it is, or don't really need you specifically, maybe it's better to do what you want, because the other people will be just fine with somebody else so they'll still be happy, and then you'll be happy too because you'll do what you want.

What does responsibility mean?

Jake: It means pretty much thinking of others when I do something, and like if I want to throw a rock, not throwing it at a window, because I thought of the people who would have to pay for that window, not doing it just for yourself, because you have to live with other people and live with your community, and if you do something that hurts them all, a lot of people will end up suffering, and that is sort of the wrong thing to do.

Amy: That other people are counting on you to do something, and you can't just decide, "Well, I'd rather do this or that."

Are there other kinds of responsibility?

Amy: Well, to yourself. If something looks really fun but you might hurt yourself doing it because you don't really know how to do it and your friends say, "Well come on, you can do it, don't worry." If you're really scared to do it, it's your responsibility to yourself that if you think you might hurt yourself, you shouldn't do it, because you have to take care of yourself.

Source: From Gilligan, 1982.

Gilligan offers us a challenge: Can we see human behavior from other than this single perspective? She dares us to ask not only why women's feelings "get in the way" of their reasoning when thinking about others (a quality she does not regard as a weakness), but also why men's feelings do not. Instead of asking why more women than men have problems with individuation, we need also to ask why more men have problems with intimacy and relationships. Until we begin to ask and find answers to all of these questions, our psychology of human development will remain incomplete.

Gilligan brings a new awareness to the study of personality. She identifies two unique perspectives on human experience, each more dominant in one sex than the other. The first is individualistic, defining the self in terms of its uniqueness and separateness. Relationships with others are governed by a consideration of individual rights, rules, and the application of an impartial justice. Gilligan finds this approach more characteristic of males. The second perspective reflects a sensitivity to and connectedness with others. The self is defined through interpersonal relationships. Rather than rights and rules governing relationships, a sense of responsibility toward others arising out of one's connectedness with them shapes relationships. The extension of care dictates personal responsibility in dealings with others. This second approach is more characteristic of females.

Gilligan's theory has generated considerable interest and debate. Its strength lies in giving us a more complete picture of the human condition, one that gives equal attention to the experiences of adolescent girls and to a female perspective (Brown & Gilligan, 1992; Spinazzola et al., 2002).

A Scientific Approach to the Study of Adolescence

Throughout this text you'll read statements summarizing research on adolescents, statements such as "Adolescents experience more emotional highs and lows than do their parents," or "Adolescent boys have more positive body images than girls." These statements will be presented as trustworthy and factual. Social scientists aren't alone in presenting information this way, however. TV programs, blogs, and internet advertisements flood us daily with information, most of it presented as factual. But how are we to know what is reliable? What distinguishes the scientific approach from other ways of getting information, such as using common sense or relying on a known authority?

A distinctive feature of the scientific approach, or **scientific method**, is that it bases its conclusions on observation—it's empirical. Not all forms of inquiry are based on observation. In classical Western philosophy, for instance, Aristotle concluded that when objects are dropped, heavy ones fall faster than light ones. He based this conclusion on a theory about the qualities of objects (heavy objects were assumed to possess more "earthiness" and would thus be drawn more to the earth). This might or might not have been a reasonable theory—it turned out not to be—but the point is that Aristotle never thought it necessary to check it out. His conclusion was accepted as fact until Galileo actually timed the speed of falling objects that differed in weight and found that they fell at the same rate. The ultimate experiment on falling objects was conducted on the moon by the Apollo astronauts, who dropped a feather and a wrench and found that, in the absence of air resistance, both reached the ground at the same time.

Research Strategies

All research starts with a question (e.g., "I wonder if this heavy object will fall faster than a lighter one?"). In fact you might say that research is just a way of asking questions and getting answers to them, and that research strategies are the procedures scientists follow to safeguard against making faulty observations when getting their answers. As we'll see, each strategy carries a particular set of advantages and each has its own problems.

scientific method   A method of inquiry in which conclusions are verified empirically by checking them against observations; a methodology for making observations that will support or refute hypotheses.

archival research   The use of existing data, such as public records, to provide answers to research questions.

ARCHIVAL RESEARCH   **Archival research** uses data that already exist to answer questions posed by the investigator. Archival data exist in many forms, one of the most extensive sources being the U.S. Census. What percentage of adolescents live with a single parent? How many work at part-time jobs? What percentage of adolescents finish high school, go on to college, and so forth? To answer questions such as these, researchers can use census data and need not collect their own. Because census data are collected from large groups of individuals, they have the additional advantage of being representative of the population.

Other archival sources exist in the form of public records. Numerous public and private organizations maintain extensive archives; hospitals, housing and welfare agencies, newspapers, and

The U.S. Census Bureau is an extensive source of data for archival research on adolescents. Many of their data sets are available online at www.census.gov.

libraries are just a few examples. What diseases are most common among adolescents? Records maintained by local health agencies provide answers. Are males more prone to accidents than females? Hospital emergency-room records indicate that they are. Do more adolescents live in poverty today than 20 years ago? State and federal welfare agencies supply answers. For more on archival research, see Research Focus Box 13.1.

An obvious advantage to archival research is access to data that do not need to be collected by the current researcher. Additionally, some data sets, such as the U.S. Census data, are more complete than any that could be collected by an individual investigator. Frequently, too, the measures that are used to collect such data sets are unobtrusive, meaning that participants do not know they are being studied and therefore do not change their behavior or their answers to questions in order to appear more acceptable. There are disadvantages as well. Data may be lost with time, resulting in incomplete data sets. Additionally, the quality of record keeping can change over time, leading a researcher to infer trends where none exist.

NATURALISTIC OBSERVATION   Perhaps the purist form of research is to directly observe participants in their natural settings. Developmentalists using **naturalistic observation** as an approach do not disrupt the natural flow of events; they simply watch and record behavior. Dian Fossey's research on the mountain gorilla of central Africa is a well-known example of this type of research. Pure though it may be, this research is often extremely difficult to carry out. Fossey's research illustrates this point well. Mountain gorillas live in the rain forest, making it impossible to observe them from a distance. Yet, if she attempted to get closer, the gorillas would notice her and either flee or attack. Her solution was to become a participant observer, observing their behavior by moving among them as just another member of the group. How does one do this? For Fossey this meant acting like a gorilla until they accepted her as one. Fossey describes beating her chest, vocalizing like a gorilla, and sitting for hours chewing on wild celery. The gorillas eventually accepted her, making it possible for her to live among them and observe their behavior. Coming a little closer to home, Dexter Dunphy (1963) conducted a classic study of adolescent peer groups using naturalistic observation. He, like Dian Fossey, simply "hung out" with those he was studying. He documented the existence of two distinct types of social groups: the crowd and the clique. Crowd activities such as dances or beach parties provide relatively safe settings in which adolescents can experiment with new social behaviors; cliques, made up of an adolescent's closest friends, provide feedback about the success of these social moves (see Chapter 7).

Naturalistic observation is most helpful when the investigator does not know much about the domain being studied. As Fossey's and Dunphy's research illustrates, naturalistic observation allows one to discover patterns in the observed behavior. These patterns frequently suggest hypotheses that can be tested with other forms of research. Although this type of research gives richly detailed descriptions of behavior, naturalistic observation does not offer explanations for why the behavior occurs. Researchers arrive at explanations only when they can rule out competing alternatives. To do this, they must be able to control extraneous conditions that could affect the behavior.

QUASI-EXPERIMENTAL RESEARCH   **Quasi-experimental research** works with existing groups, introduces a treatment, and looks to see whether differences follow. This type of research differs from archival research and naturalistic observation in that the researcher intervenes in, or steps into, the flow of behavior. Quasi-experimental research differs as well from experiments,

naturalistic observation The observation and recording of participants' behavior in their natural setting.

quasi-experimental research   A research design in which participants are not randomly assigned to conditions, but in which preexisting groups are used, introducing possible confounding.

confounding The presence of additional factors other than the variable of interest that can account for observed differences.

maturation A potential confound resulting from systematic changes over time that are not due to the treatment being studied.

testing effect Knowledge and skills acquired by taking similar tests over the course of a research study; a potential source of confounding.

history effect Any event extraneous to a research project that can affect the results and jeopardize the internal validity of the research.

statistical regression A potential confound in quasi-experimental research in which extreme pretest scores drift toward the mean of the posttest distribution.

another form of research, in that investigators do not randomly assign participants to the groups. Instead they work with groups that are already in existence. Examples are groups of students in different academic tracks; social groups in high school such as the populars, the brains, the jocks, and so on. Quasi-experimental research is common in applied settings in which researchers may want to observe the effects of a treatment but don't have control over all the conditions that might affect their observations. An advantage of this type of research is that it enables researchers to study the outcome once a treatment is introduced; however, a disadvantage is that one can't rule out alternative explanations for the observed differences, that is, one can't be sure that the differences one observes actually reflect the treatment. The advantages and disadvantages are discussed in Research Focus Box 3.2 in Chapter 3.

The presence of alternative explanations for observed differences is known as **confounding**. A number of potential confounds exist in quasi-experimental research. One of these, **maturation**, refers to systematic changes over time apart from those due specifically to the treatment under study.

Another type of confound common to quasi-experimental research is a **testing effect**. The performance of adolescents enrolled in special programs, for instance, may improve simply because they have been tested so often that they are better at taking tests than others whose performance is not being monitored so closely. Testing effects include both specific and general knowledge. For instance, pretests might include the same types of questions, covering the same information, as those included on tests given at the conclusion of the program. Adolescents enrolled in such programs would then be more familiar with these items and do better on tests including them. Also, general test-taking skills are acquired with frequent test taking. Students learn, for instance, whether to guess, how to manage their time, and how to stay on top of anxiety that might otherwise interfere with their performance.

Similarly, a **history effect** refers to confounding resulting from events that occur during the time in which adolescents are being evaluated, which can affect the behavior being measured. For instance, a network channel might run a public service spot featuring a well-known athlete speaking against the use of drugs just when a school district is evaluating the effectiveness of their anti-drug program.

Statistical regression is yet another confound that can occur. This confound enters the picture when participants are selected because of their initial differences, because they are either behind or ahead of others in their group. For instance, students selected for a special program are more likely to have low scores on initial measures of their performance. When these students are retested at the conclusion of the program, the scores for most will be higher, but not necessarily because they have profited from the program. When they are tested at the end of the program, most scores will change somewhat simply because the two tests are not perfectly correlated. This change is to be expected because no tests ever are perfectly correlated. But for students who were initially at the bottom of the distribution, test scores can only go up. Because such a change is expected by those administering such programs, it is usually not questioned.

However, if one were to place another group of students who initially scored at the top of the distribution in such a program, their second test scores would drop, and for the same reason. Just as with the other students, there is only one direction in which their test scores could change, and for these students that would be down. In each case, scores on the second test drift toward the mean of the distribution, because this is where most of the scores are. In other words, to the extent that performance on the first test is unrelated to performance on the second test, chance influences the score a student gets. What score would a student be most likely to draw by chance? One of the scores that occurs most frequently in the distribution—in other words, a score that is close to the mean, where most of the scores lie.

CONDUCTING AN EXPERIMENT   Experiments start with equivalent groups of participants and treat each group differently. If the groups differ at the conclusion of the experiment, we can assume the difference is due to the way they were treated. Let's say we want to determine whether television can influence adolescents' preferences for products by advertising them as appropriate for their sex. Specifically, we want to see whether adolescent girls would be more likely to choose magazines that are described as "interesting for girls" over those that are described as "interesting for all adolescents."

To conduct an **experiment**, the researcher would have one group of girls view the first commercial and a second group view the other commercial. The type of commercial is the **independent variable**. The researcher would then compare the two groups on some measure of preference, the **dependent variable**, such as rating how likely they would be to subscribe to the magazine. If girls in the two groups rate the magazine differently, we can assume the difference is due to the commercial they viewed. To be confident of this, we need to be sure that the groups were comparable before the treatment was introduced. Given the many ways one adolescent differs from the next such an assumption might seem an impossible requirement. But is it? How can investigators be confident that the groups they're working with are comparable at the outset?

They can be reasonably confident of this by randomly assigning participants to the groups; the more participants assigned to each group, the higher their confidence that the groups are comparable. The important point here is that the groups need not be identical, only equivalent. Rather than requiring that participants be the same in each of the groups, an admittedly impossible requirement, we need only require that those in one group not differ in any *systematic* way from those in the other group. They will, of course, differ in countless respects, but if each participant has the same chance as any other of being assigned to either group, and if enough participants are assigned to each, differences among them will be balanced across the groups. **Random assignment** distributes individual differences evenly across the groups. The experimental approach was described in Research Focus Box 1.1. Finally, although it's not possible to have the same participants in each of the two groups, it *is* possible to have all of the participants experience each of the conditions (see Research Focus Box 8.5 for a discussion of within-subjects designs). More commonly, participants experience only a single condition (see Research Focus Box 10.1 for a discussion of between-subjects designs).

Conducting an experiment enables investigators to control extraneous variables that otherwise might influence the results, thus enabling them to unambiguously say that the independent variable caused the differences they observed between the groups. This experimenter could say, in other words, that television can influence what adolescent girls choose to read. Not all types of research yield answers that are this clear cut. However, there is a price to pay for clarity such as this. In order to control extraneous conditions that also might affect choice of reading materials, experiments are typically conducted in laboratory settings, which may bear little resemblance to real life circumstances. This approach is described in Research Focus Box 9.1.

CORRELATIONAL RESEARCH   Instead of working with an independent variable, one that can be assigned at random to different groups, **correlational research** works with **classification variables**. Developmentalists classify individuals according to characteristics of the participants, such as their age, or some other variable, and then see whether that variable is related to other differences.

experiment   A research procedure in which participants are randomly assigned to groups that are then treated differently.

independent variable
The variable that is manipulated in an experiment, by randomly assigning participants to different levels of the variable.

dependent variable
The measure used to determine the effect of the independent variable in an experiment.

random assignment
The assignment of participants to groups in such a way that each participant has an equal chance of being assigned to any condition.

correlational research
A procedure in which subjects are assigned to groups on the basis of preexisting characteristics.

classification variable
A variable, such as age, that cannot be manipulated by randomly assigning participants to levels of the variable.

Let's say we want to know whether adolescents become more conscious of the sex appropriateness of their behavior with age. We could show a group of 10-year-olds, a group of 15-year-olds, and a group of 20-year-olds video materials similar to those described above. Assume for the moment that we find that sex-appropriate choices of magazines increase with age. Is this because adolescents become more aware of the sex appropriateness of their behavior with age? They may, in fact, but this is just one of several alternative conclusions.

These adolescents already differ in at least one respect: their age. They probably differ in other ways, too. Their age may be related to another condition that is causing the relationship we noticed. Benton Underwood, an author of several books on methodology, tells of a teacher in a private boys' school who observed that the best students all had very good vocabularies. This teacher suggested to a colleague that the school should require all students to take a course in developing their vocabularies. After a moment's thought, the colleague answered that he had noticed a relationship between the height of these students and the length of their trousers, but he doubted whether the school could increase their height by lengthening their pants.

We also have no way of knowing, in this hypothetical study of ours, if the relationship we observed is due to age itself. All we observed was a difference that corresponded to age. This difference could be an age change, something we would see in any individuals the same age, regardless of their culture or the historical period in which they lived; or it could be either of two alternatives that are frequently confused with age in developmental research: cohort differences and time of measurement effects. Let's look at each of these more closely.

Age changes are the biological and experiential changes that always accompany aging; these occur in all cultures and all points in history. We assume that age changes have a biological basis (although we are not always able to identify it); therefore, these changes should be universal—that is, they should occur in all people no matter what their social or cultural background.

age changes Biological and experiential changes that accompany aging, irrespective of cultural or historical context.

cohort group People born during the same historical period or undergoing the same historical influences.

A good example of an age change is the loss of high-frequency tones in hearing. If we notice that adolescents in all cultures become more aware of the sex-appropriateness of their behavior with age, we might be willing to say this awareness is a genuine age change. Even so, the difference could reflect cohort differences and time of measurement differences.

The only way we can observe age changes is to observe individuals of different chronological ages. The problem is that people who differ in chronological age also differ in other ways, namely, in their social and historical backgrounds. These differences don't always have to affect the way they respond to the measures we are taking, but they might. People of the same age belong to the same **cohort group**. Cohorts are more likely to have similar cultural experiences than people of different ages. Adolescents today live

These adolescents differ in obvious ways, yet because they are the same age, they are members of the same cohort group and share many experiences in common.

in an information-rich society in which cell phones, the Internet, and instant messaging are commonplace, and contribute to rapidly changing fashions and attitudes. Adolescents born 30 years ago were less sophisticated technologically and society moved more slowly. Differences such as these appear in all sorts of attitudes and behaviors and can easily be confused with age changes; they are termed **cohort differences**.

If we return now to our hypothetical study, we can see how changing gender and work roles might lead to behavior that is less sex-stereotyped than before, with the consequence that older adolescents, who are further removed from these changes, may show more stereotyped behavior.

It is always possible, of course, to test a single group of 10-year-olds and then wait until they reach 15 and test them again, then wait and retest them again at 20. We wouldn't have any cohort differences, but we could have **time of measurement differences**. These differences reflect social conditions, currents of opinion, and historical events that are present when we make our observations and can affect attitudes and behavior. When we study age changes by repeatedly observing the same group of individuals over time, we can mistake time of measurement changes for age changes. It's always possible, for example, that researchers today are more aware of sexist attitudes and more likely to notice adolescents who label some things as appropriate only for one sex.

Researchers need to distinguish differences due to cohort effects and time of measurement from genuine age changes. We can evaluate the adequacy of three common developmental designs by their ability to do just this: cross-sectional, longitudinal, and sequential designs.

The **cross-sectional design** is one of the most common designs in developmental research. This design calls for testing several groups of individuals, each of a different age, at the same time. Going back to our hypothetical study, we would measure sex appropriate choices for adolescents at each of three ages: 10, 15, and 20. There is but a single time of measurement in this design, but several cohort groups (**Figure 2.1**).

It is difficult to interpret cross-sectional data, because differences between the groups can reflect either age changes or cohort differences. Until fairly recently, however, we were unaware of this weakness in the design and used it

cohort differences
Experiential differences between groups of people born at different periods in time; these differences can be confounded with age changes.

time of measurement differences Differences due to social conditions, currents of opinion, and historical events that can affect observations in longitudinal research; such differences are confounded with age changes.

cross-sectional design
A research design in which several age cohorts are compared at a single time of measurement.

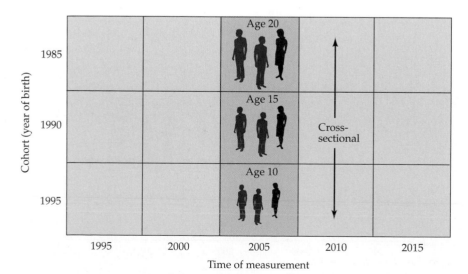

● **Figure 2.1 Cross-sectional design** (After Stevens-Long & Commons, 1992.)

How does intelligence change with age? Are personality traits constant over time? To answer these kinds of developmental questions, researchers use various methods, such as studying twins or using longitudinal studies of the same individuals over a number of years.

longitudinal design
A research design in which a single cohort group is followed over time, tested at several times of measurement.

subject mortality In longitudinal studies, the loss of participants over time.

regularly, mainly because it simplified data collection. We can obtain information about developmental differences relatively quickly, certainly in a matter of days as opposed to decades. The relative strengths and weaknesses of this design receive attention in Research Focus Box 4.3.

The **longitudinal design** studies a single cohort group of individuals over time, repeatedly observing its members as they age. Thus, we have a single cohort group but several times of measurement. We illustrated this design when we sampled a group of 10-year-olds, tested them, then retested them when they reached 15, and again at 20 (**Figure 2.2**). By following the same individuals over time, we can see patterns of development that we might miss with cross-sections. And because we are comparing individuals with themselves at each age, we minimize the problem of having equivalent samples.

This design, too, is flawed, however, because it confounds age changes and time of measurement differences. It is impossible, in other words, to separate the effects of age from those due to time of measurement. The design suffers from other problems as well. Longitudinal research is expensive because a large research staff is needed to maintain the elaborate records that must be kept to stay in touch with the individuals and maintain information about them over the years. Longitudinal research is also time consuming. We must wait while individuals age—and there is no guarantee that we'll outlive them.

A more serious problem than either of these is the nearly inevitable loss of individuals with time. People move away, lose interest, or for other reasons are not available for study. This loss is called **subject mortality** and is almost

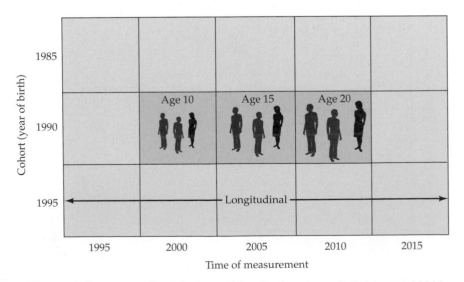

● **Figure 2.2 Longitudinal design** (After Stevens-Long & Commons, 1992.)

always systematically related to age. Thus, the individuals who remain are not representative of those their age in the population, because the less healthy and otherwise less fortunate are generally the first to leave the sample; see Research Focus Box 7.2.

Each of these designs has its own problems of interpretation, which we can see by looking at some of the research on age-related changes in intelligence. Cross-sectional studies for many years charted a marked decline in intellectual functioning after about age 30. It is likely, however, that most of this decline actually reflects cohort or generational differences. Our society changes significantly within our lifetimes, and individuals have different experiences than those born 20 or 30 years earlier. Longitudinal research shows that when we track the intellectual functioning of an individual over time, we fail to see real decline until advanced old age.

A third design, the **sequential design** is the most successful in isolating age changes from cohort and time of measurement differences. This design tests several different cohort groups at several different times. In a way, the sequential design is a number of longitudinal studies, each starting with a different age group, as shown in **Figure 2.3**.

Let's suppose we want to see whether intelligence changes with age. By looking at the blocks that form the diagonals in Figure 2.3, we can compare 10-year-olds with 15-year-olds and 20-year-olds. The means for each of those diagonals will reflect age differences in intellectual functioning as well as cohort differences and time of measurement differences.

By taking an average of the scores for the blocks in the top row, we get a mean for the 1990 cohort. By averaging the scores for the blocks in the middle row, we get a mean for the 1995 cohort. And by averaging the scores for the blocks in the bottom row, we get a mean for the 2000 cohort. Differences among these three means provide an estimate of the amount of variability in intellectual functioning that is contributed by cohorts.

We can also estimate the effect of time of measurement. We can compare performance measured in 2005 (the blocks in the second column), for example, with performance measured in 2010 and 2015 (the blocks in the third and fourth columns). Thus, by using appropriate statistical techniques, we can isolate cohort and time of measurement effects and subtract these out; differences that remain reflect age changes.

sequential design   A research design in which several age cohort groups are compared at several times of measurement; essentially, a number of longitudinal studies, each starting with a different age group.

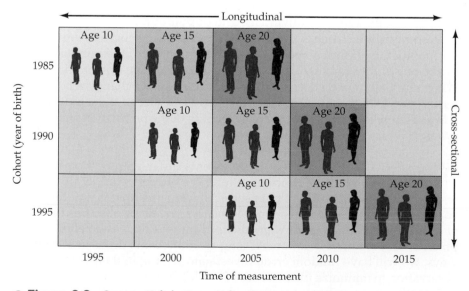

● **Figure 2.3 Sequential design** (After Stevens-Long & Commons, 1992.)

internal validity   The extent to which a research study unambiguously answers the questions it was designed to address.

external validity   The extent to which a research study's conclusions can be generalized to other populations and contexts.

population   The entire group of individuals in which an investigator is interested.

sample   A subgroup drawn from the population that is the subject of the research.

error   Unexplained and unsystematic variability.

Sequential designs signal an increasing sophistication in developmental research. Many problems of observation and data collection remain, of course, but we are still able to arrive at interesting observations about adolescents; see Research Focus Box 4.3.

Research Issues

INTERNAL AND EXTERNAL VALIDITY   Research is a way of asking and getting answers to questions. Thinking of it this way, we can evaluate how adequate research is by the quality of the answers it gives us. Are these answers clear and unambiguous? Or can they be interpreted more than one way? Research that provides unambiguous answers to the questions it was designed to address is said to have **internal validity**. Research in which competing explanations cannot be ruled out is confounded. Confounding exists when extraneous variables are not controlled.

A second criterion exists for evaluating any research study: How representative are its findings? Do they apply to other groups of adolescents than those who were studied? Research has **external validity** when its findings can be generalized to other populations and contexts. Frequently the conditions that are necessary to ensure internal validity conflict with those that promote external validity. Internal validity is easiest to achieve in laboratory experiments, in which the investigator has control over the conditions that can affect the observation. However, a laboratory setting is the very type of situation in which subjects are most likely to be on their best behavior—acting any way other than the way they normally would. On the other hand, external validity is virtually guaranteed for research conducted in natural settings, in which the investigator intervenes little in ongoing behavior. Yet these are the conditions that are rife with extraneous variables that can threaten the internal validity of one's observations. Look at the Research Focus Box "Internal and External Validity," which appears on the Web site, to see examples of this continuing tension in developmental research.

SAMPLING   Most studies actually work with relatively small numbers of adolescents; yet each generalizes its findings to all adolescents, or to subgroups—for example, early adolescent females, or college-bound late adolescents, or late adolescent minority males. How can an investigator who observes or interviews a limited number of adolescents hope to generalize the findings from that study to adolescents in general? The answer comes from the way the investigator samples the participants, who will be studied, from the larger population of individuals. The **population** is the entire group of adolescents in which one is interested. The **sample** is a subgroup drawn from this population. If the sample is drawn at random from the population, we can be reasonably confident that it will be representative of that population. When randomly sampled, each adolescent has the same chance of being chosen as every other adolescent. Consequently, as the size of the sample grows, it increasingly approximates the characteristics of the population from which it was drawn; see Research Focus Box 6.1.

BIAS AND BLIND CONTROLS   Adolescents differ among themselves in countless ways. These individual differences are reflected in all types of research. Specifically, variability in subjects' responses that is not due to the variable being investigated is termed *random error*. **Error** obscures the effect of a variable. Despite this unwanted effect, there is no way to eliminate its presence from an investigation. As long as adolescents differ in individual ways, we will have random error. Investigators arrange their conditions of observation to minimize the presence of random error.

Bias, like error, reflects variations in subjects' responses that are not due to the variable being investigated. However, the similarity between bias and error ends here. **Bias** occurs when the source of variation is *differentially* present in one condition and not the other. Unlike error, which simply makes the effect of a variable more difficult to detect, bias actually distorts the effect of a variable. Investigators have only one option when facing the possibility of bias: to eliminate it. Bias threatens an investigation's internal validity.

Bias exists in many forms. The extraneous conditions that threaten the internal validity of quasi-experimental designs reflect different types of bias. Another common source of bias that can influence observations can be traced to what the experimenter expects to see. **Double-blind controls** eliminate the possibility of this source of bias by controlling for the experimenter's knowledge of which condition a participant is experiencing. The experimenter is blind with respect to the condition each participant is in. As a result, expectations cannot bias observations; see Research Focus Box 12.4.

TESTS OF SIGNIFICANCE   Will adolescents get a better grade in a course if they keep a log of the date, hour, and time spent studying each time they read their textbook or study for the course? One could assign students at random to two groups within the course. The experimental group is told they are part of a study on how adolescents learn and is given instructions on how to keep the log. The other group, the control, is merely told that they are part of a study examining how adolescents learn. Will the simple act of keeping a log improve the grade of students in the experimental group? How can we tell? How much better would these students have to do in the course to support this conclusion? Remember, too, that each student is an individual, and each will learn at a slightly different rate due to individual differences. Individual differences contribute heavily to random error.

To determine whether a difference between groups is due to random error or whether it reflects the variable being studied, one uses a **test of significance** (see Research Focus Box 11.2). Common tests are chi-square, t-tests, and F-tests. If the value that is obtained is larger than a tabled value for the same number of participants, we can rule out random error as responsible for the difference and attribute it to the independent variable, in this case, whether students kept a log. The likelihood of random error being responsible for the difference decreases with increases in the number of participants in each group. The number of participants is reflected in the **degrees of freedom**, or the number of observations in a set that can vary without changing the value of the set. With larger degrees of freedom, one needs a smaller difference to reject the assumption that random error was responsible.

ETHICS   What ethical concerns guide research? Like most professional organizations, the American Psychological Association provides guidelines governing the ethical conduct of research with human participants. The overriding principle governing any research with human participants is to protect the *dignity and welfare* of those who participate in the research. Other considerations follow from this concern. Participants are told, for instance, that their participation is *voluntary* and that they are free to leave at any point. They are also informed of anything in the research that could affect their willingness to participate, meaning that when they agree to participate, they are giving their informed consent. Once participants agree to serve, investigators assume responsibility for protecting them from *physical or psychological distress*. After the data have been collected, the investigators *debrief* participants, informing them about the nature of the study and removing any misconceptions that may have arisen. If investigators suspect any undesirable consequences, they have the *responsibility for correcting* these. Any information gained about participants is confidential. Research Focus Boxes on "Ethics" and on "Confidentiality" appear on the Web site.

bias   Distortion of the effect of a variable due to research design or researcher expectations.

double-blind controls   A research procedure in which neither the researcher nor the participants know which individuals have been assigned to which experimental conditions.

test of significance   A statistical procedure for determining whether group differences are due to random error or can be attributed to the variable being studied.

degrees of freedom   The number of scores in a set that are free to vary given certain constraints, such as a known mean.

Go to the **Adolescence** Companion Website at www.sinauer.com/cobb for quizzes, flashcards, summaries, and other study resources.

SUMMARY and KEY TERMS

Models and Theories

Models reflect basic assumptions about the nature of reality, and although too general to test, are useful because they generate theories. Theories can be verified or disconfirmed. Theories that derive from the same model bear a family resemblance reflecting the assumptions characteristic of the model that generated them.
model, theory

The Environmental Model: The environmental model traces behavior to external, environmental antecedents.
environmental model

The Organismic Model: TThe organismic model focuses on processes within the individual, assuming that individuals are active rather than passive.
organismic model, habituation

Environmental Theories

B. F. Skinner: Skinner assumed that most behavior is learned, coming under the control of the events that follow it (reinforcers), rather than being controlled by preceding motives or intentions.
reinforcement

Albert Bandura: Bandura's social-cognitive theory emphasizes the importance of inner processes such as attention and memory for learning. Bandura assumes that most human learning occurs through observing others rather than through direct conditioning.
reciprocal determinism

Organismic Theories

Jean Piaget: Piaget viewed intelligence as biologically based. He assumed that knowledge, rather than being a simple copy of reality, is an active construction of what we know of the world.

Robert Kegan: Kegan assumes that the most central human activity is "meaning making," or constructing a reality that corresponds to our sense of self in relation to events and other people. Development is the cumulative process of differentiating our sense of "me" from "not me."

Sigmund Freud: Freud formulated his theory of personality development around sexually-based tensions that develop when children are attracted to the opposite-sex parent.
Oedipus complex, Electra complex, castration anxiety, superego

Erik Erikson: Erikson assumed that society challenges us with new demands as we age and that we experience these as psychosocial crises. Each crisis takes a slightly different form and gives each stage its unique characteristics. Achievement of a personal identity is the central crisis of adolescence.
identity

Nancy Chodorow: Chodorow attributes gender differences to the social fact that for almost all children the first intimate relationship is with a female—their mother. Girls can continue to define themselves within the context of this relationship, but boys must separate themselves in order to develop as males. As a consequence,

SUMMARY and KEY TERMS

girls' development is characterized by attachment, and boys' development by separation and individuation.

Carol Gilligan: Gilligan notes differences in the ways males and females define themselves, and finds these differences extend to the ways they resolve issues involving others. Males tend to see themselves as separate from others, whereas females are more likely to describe themselves in terms of their relationships with others.

A Scientific Approach to the Study of Adolescence

Research Strategies: Research strategies are the procedures scientists follow to safeguard against making faulty observations. Each strategy carries its own advantages and problems. Archival research, for instance, uses data that already exist, such as census data and public records. Its advantages include ease of access to data, large data sets (e.g., the U.S. Census), and use of unobtrusive measures. Disadvantages over time include loss of data and changes in quality of record keeping.

scientific method, archival research, naturalistic observation, quasi-experimental designs, confounding, maturation, testing effect, history effect, statistical regression, experiment, independent variable, dependent variable, random assignment, correlational research, classification variable, age changes, cohort group, cohort differences, time of measurement differences, cross-sectional design, longitudinal design, sequential design

Research Issues: Research quality can be evaluated by the answers it provides. Are answers clear and unambiguous? Or are they open to interpretation? A variety of factors affect research validity. For instance, internal validity is provided by research that gives unambiguous answers to the questions it was designed to address. External validity exists when the findings of a study can be generalized to other populations and contexts. A test of significance is a statistical procedure for determining whether group differences are due to random error or can be attributed to the variable being studied.

internal validity, confounding, external validity, population, sample, bias, double-blind controls, test of significance, degrees of freedom

Archival research uses data that already exist, such as census data and public records. Advantages to this type of research are ease of access to data, large data sets (e.g., U.S. Census), and use of unobtrusive measures. Disadvantages over time include loss of data and changes in quality of record keeping.

archival research

Naturalistic observation involves observation of behavior as it occurs in a natural setting. This research gives richly detailed descriptions of behavior, but does not allow researchers to rule out competing explanations for why behaviors occur.

naturalistic observation

Quasi-experimental designs work with existing, or intact, groups, introducing a treatment and observing any resulting changes. A disadvantage is that one can't be sure the differences observed actually reflect the treatment. Potential confounds include maturation, testing, history effects, and statistical regression.

quasi-experimental research, confounding, maturation, testing effect, history effect, statistical regression

(continued)

SUMMARY and KEY TERMS *continued*

Experiments offer the greatest control over possible confounds. In an experiment, the experimenter randomly assigns participants to groups, which are then exposed to different treatments. Random assignment ensures the groups are initially equivalent and allows the investigator to attribute observed differences to the way the groups are treated.
experiment, independent variable, dependent variable, random assignment

Correlational research works with variables in which individuals are classified according to existing characteristics—such as age, sex, and ethnicity. Age changes, the biological and experiential changes that accompany aging, can be confounded with cohort differences, differences among people born at different periods of time, and with time of measurement differences, which are due to conditions prevailing when measurements are taken.
correlational research, classification variable, age changes, cohort group, cohort differences, time of measurement differences

In cross-sectional designs, several age cohorts are tested at a single time of measurement. This method takes less time to complete but may miss developmental patterns and potentially confounds age changes with cohort differences.
cross-sectional design

In longitudinal designs, a single cohort group is followed over time and tested at several times of measurement.
longitudinal design, subject mortality

Sequential designs, in which several cohorts are tested at several times of measurement, allow investigators to estimate time of measurement and cohort effects and to isolate these from age changes.
sequential design

Research Issues: Internal validity is provided by research that gives unambiguous answers to the questions it was designed to address. External validity exists when the findings of a study can be generalized to other populations and contexts.
internal validity, external validity

A population is the entire group of adolescents in which one is interested. A sample is a subgroup drawn from this population. If a sample is drawn at random from a population, to the extent it is large enough, one can be confident that it is representative of that population.
population, sample, error, bias, double-blind controls

A test of significance is a statistical procedure for determining whether group differences are due to random error or can be attributed to the variable being studied.
test of significance, degrees of freedom

She checked herself in the mirror again. Maybe she'd wear the new shirt. Or maybe she'd put the bag it came in over her head, and go to school that way. Glasses… braces... and two more pimples! Wonder what Helen of Troy had looked like at 13? She had probably been cute—and short. This face wouldn't get a rowboat off the beach. And she was taller than everyone in her class—including the teacher. Being different was lonely at times. Sometimes she felt left out altogether.

3

The Biological and Physical Changes of Adolescence:
Puberty, Health, and Well-Being

Feeling left out and being rushed into changes too quickly are common for adolescents. Although both of these things happen to all teenagers, the process of change is faster for some than for others. In the space of a few years, adolescents exchange the bodies of children for those of adults—complete with a full set of emotions and fancy accessories. But none of the equipment is road tested as yet. And for most adolescents, it seems someone else must have the owner's manual.

Chapter Overview

This chapter maps the journey into maturity. The first stop takes us deep within the body, to the headquarters of an elaborate communications network, the neuroendocrine system. This network of neural centers, glands, and hormones plays a significant role in regulating the changes of puberty. A finely tuned feedback system triggers the onset of puberty, regulating delicate changes within the body that transform immature sexual organs into those capable of sexual reproduction. The neuroendocrine system is also responsible for everything from a remarkable growth in height to the nose becoming disproportionately large for one's face. Although it stays this way only briefly, it can leave a lasting fear of what surprises the body might bring next.

The second stop checks out the remarkable changes that take place in height, weight, and body contours. Puberty involves a surge of growth that brings adolescents eye to eye and nose to nose with their parents. Adolescents add inches in a single year at the peak of their growth. Sex differences become noticeable with changing body proportions and gains in weight; girls add more subcutaneous fat than boys do, and boys add more muscle mass than girls. Not all adolescents grow the same amount, or at the same rate. Nor do they start at the same age; some will begin years ahead of others. And to the confusion of all, different parts of the body mature at different rates. Yet trends exist, and we will review them.

Many factors affect the rate at which growth proceeds. Conditions as diverse as diet, amount of exercise, psychological stress, and even altitude can affect the rate of growth during puberty. And of course one's particular genetic inheritance plays a part as well. The growth spurt ends in sexual dimorphism, the characteristic physical differences between sexually mature females and males. We will explore these differences before moving to a discussion of the secular trend, a trend toward earlier and faster development that has occurred over the past several centuries.

Changes as significant as those of puberty can have far-reaching psychological and social effects, and these effects are discussed in the third part of the chapter. Puberty brings with it a heightened emotionality, along with changes not only in adolescents' experience of themselves, but also in their relationships with their parents. As one might expect, these relationships are among the first to be affected.

Pubertal changes themselves may not be as important as when they take place for a particular individual. Staying the same when all one's friends are changing can be every bit as stressful as going through the changes. The timing of puberty can be as significant as its end results. Early and late maturers face different advantages and different challenges.

The physical changes of puberty prompt adolescents to take a new look at themselves. Some like what they see and others are not so sure. We will examine changes in body image during adolescence before moving to a consideration of adolescents' health and well-being.

Adolescents stride into adulthood at the peak of fitness and health. Most give little thought to health issues or concerns, yet all are developing habits that shortly will begin to affect their health as adults as well as their present well-being. We will look at issues vital to the health of all adolescents: nutrition, getting enough sleep and exercise, maintaining proper weight, adequate health care, and healthy living conditions.

The Neuroendocrine System

The **neuroendocrine system** consists of glands within the body that produce hormones, and structures in the central nervous system that regulate their activity. It is part of a larger feedback system that controls the timing of puberty. The production of **hormones**, chemical messengers that travel

neuroendrocrine system
The system of the body that includes the glands that produce hormones and those parts of the nervous system that activate, inhibit, and control hormone production.

hormones Chemical messengers that are secreted directly into the bloodstream and regulated by the endocrine system.

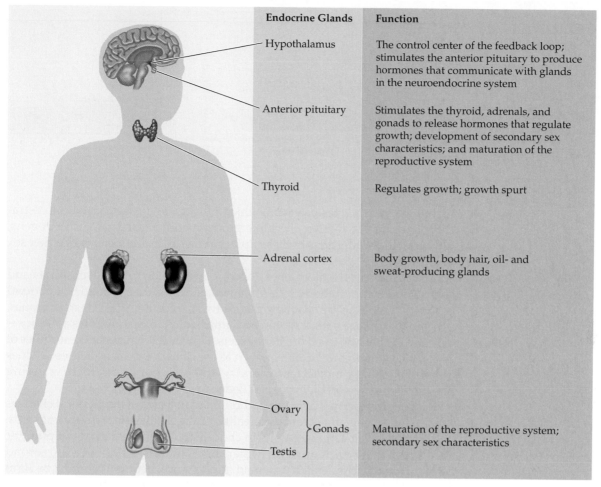

Endocrine Glands	Function
Hypothalamus	The control center of the feedback loop; stimulates the anterior pituitary to produce hormones that communicate with glands in the neuroendocrine system
Anterior pituitary	Stimulates the thyroid, adrenals, and gonads to release hormones that regulate growth; development of secondary sex characteristics; and maturation of the reproductive system
Thyroid	Regulates growth; growth spurt
Adrenal cortex	Body growth, body hair, oil- and sweat-producing glands
Ovary / Testis — Gonads	Maturation of the reproductive system; secondary sex characteristics

● **Figure 3.1**   **The major endocrine glands involved in puberty and their functions**   The endocrine glands producing the hormones that regulate pubertal change are shown within the body, together with a description of their general functions.

through the bloodstream, increases during late childhood. However, only with early adolescence is there a dramatic increase in the production of sex hormones (androgens in males and estrogens in females) and in the hormones that govern their release. The action of these hormones is part of a complex chain of events that triggers the onset of puberty (Plant, 2008). **Figure 3.1** shows the neural structures and glands related to the timing of puberty, and the hormones each one secretes.

Because hormones are secreted directly into the bloodstream and circulate throughout the body, they come into contact both with tissues that are sensitive to them and with those that are not. Tissues that form the male reproductive organs are most sensitive to **androgens**, the general class of male sex hormones. The most important of these is **testosterone**, which is associated with numerous changes in males such as skeletal growth, development of the genitals, and the appearance of facial hair. Similarly, tissues forming the female reproductive organs are most sensitive to **estrogens**, the class of female sex hormones. The most important of these is **estradiol**, which contributes to bone growth, development of the reproductive tract, the distribution of body fat and, in conjunction with progesterone, regulation of the menstrual cycle.

The chemical composition of both male and female sex hormones is similar, allowing the body to convert one hormone into another as needed. Thus **progesterone**, which plays an important role in the female menstrual cycle,

androgens   Male sex hormones.

testosterone   A sex hormone present in higher levels in males than in females.

estrogens   Female sex hormones.

estradiol   A sex hormone present in higher levels in females than in males; it contributes to breast development, distribution of body fat, and regulation of the menstrual cycle.

progesterone   A sex hormone present in higher levels in females than in males; it contributes to regulation of the menstrual cycle.

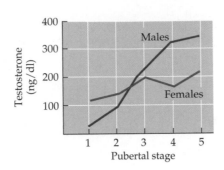
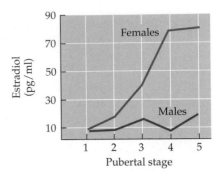

● **Figure 3.2** **Production of sex hormones by males and females** Males and females alike produce both androgens, such as testosterone, and estrogens, such as estradiol, though in different proportions. (After Levitt, 1981.)

forms the basis for testosterone, which in turn can be converted into estradiol. Thus, males and females alike produce both androgens and estrogens, although the proportions of these differ markedly in adolescents of either sex (**Figure 3.2**).

The effectiveness of hormones depends, in addition to tissue sensitivity and their blood concentration levels, on whether they exist in bound or unbound form. Hormones act by attaching themselves to receptor sites on target tissues. Hormones that are bound are already attached to other molecules and consequently are not free to act on their targets. However, at puberty, the number of molecules that might normally attach to the sex hormones decreases, as does the ability of these molecules to bond with the sex hormones, thereby freeing the latter to act on on their targets (Bedecarras et al., 1998).

Although puberty is commonly thought of in terms of the physical changes that occur during adolescence, in reality, changes take place in several steps, the first of which actually begins in childhood. This initial phase of puberty, or **adrenarche**, begins quite early, starting in middle childhood. The second phase, **gonadarche**, which ushers in adolescence, begins at about 9 or 10 in girls and approximately a year later in boys. We'll look first at adrenarche.

Prepuberty: Adrenarche

The adrenal glands, which are located right above the kidneys, increase their production of **adrenal androgens** starting at about the age of 7 in girls and 9 in boys. Levels of adrenal androgens continue to rise through adolescence for girls and boys alike (Matchock et al., 2007). The adrenal androgens are involved in a number of pubertal changes, such as skeletal growth, the growth of pubic and underarm hair, oil and sweat glands, and the external genitals in males, and may play a role in brain maturation in both females and males (Campbell, 2006; Ellis, 2004). They have also been found to affect daily moods in preadolescent girls (Archibald et al., 2003). However, relatively little research has examined these early hormonal influences on behavior.

Puberty: Gonadarche

The timing of the second phase of puberty is intimately connected to centers within the brain tucked beneath the cortex, a few inches behind the bridge of the nose. The most important of these is the **hypothalamus**. The hypothalamus has sometimes been called the body's master clock, because it serves as a control center for biological rhythms, including the ones of puberty. A second center is the pituitary, an endocrine gland, which hangs from the hypothalamus by a slender stalk (the infundibulum). The pituitary has two lobes, or sections. The one closer to the nose is the anterior (front) lobe; the farther one is the posterior (back) lobe.

The hypothalamus is actually very small, just one three-hundredth of the brain's total size. Yet it is involved in many aspects of bodily function-

adrenarche The initial phase of puberty, which involves activity of the adrenal androgens.

gonadarche The second stage of puberty, regulated by the neuroendocrine system.

adrenal androgens Hormones produced by the adrenal glands, which initiate the initial stage of puberty.

hypothalamus A center within the brain that governs hormonal activity and regulatory activities such as eating, drinking, and body temperature.

ing and plays a central role in regulating the events of puberty. Cells within the hypothalamus secrete a hormone called **gonadotropin-releasing hormone (GnRH)**. This hormone signals the **anterior pituitary** to manufacture gonadotropic hormones, which act directly on the gonads. The **gonads** are the sex glands—the ovaries in females and the testes in males. The gonadotropic hormones—**luteinizing hormone (LH)** and **follicle-stimulating hormone (FSH)**—stimulate the gonads to produce sex hormones, estrogens in females and androgens in males. The whole system acts sort of like a row of dominoes. Knocking the first one over trips the second, which affects the third, and so on (**Figure 3.3**).

A delicate feedback system controls the level at which hormones circulate in the bloodstream. When levels of circulating hormones drop too low, the hypothalamus signals the anterior pituitary to increase its production of LH and FSH, which then stimulates the gonads to produce more sex hormones. As levels of sex hormones increase, the hypothalamus decreases its signals to the anterior pituitary. Thus the activity of cells within the hypothalamus is both responsible for stimulating the production of hormones and, in turn, is regulated by the levels of circulating hormones that are produced.

During childhood, LH and FSH are present in the bloodstream only in low levels. By the beginning of puberty, however, these levels increase, prompted by pulses of GnRH from the hypothalamus. Both hormones are released primarily during sleep, particularly LH. **Figure 3.4** illustrates the marked difference in prepubertal and pubertal LH release in girls, with the sleep-associated release occurring only during puberty. By the end of puberty and throughout adulthood, LH is again released evenly over waking and sleep cycles (Archibald et al., 2003).

● **Figure 3.3   The feedback loop regulating pubertal change**   The feedback loop shows the path taken by hormones that regulate pubertal change.

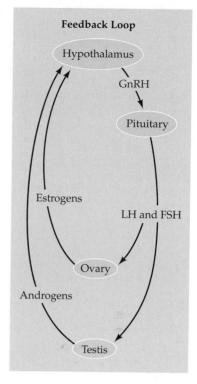

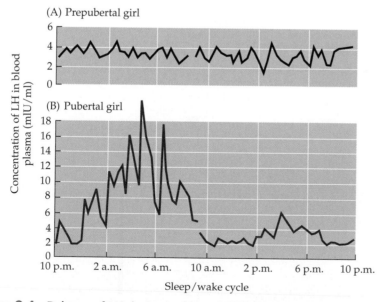

● **Figure 3.4   Release of LH during waking and sleep cycles in (A) a prepubertal girl and (B) a pubertal girl**   Sleep is important in adolescence, especially for the activity of many hormones. This graph shows that LH, a hormone that stimulates the sex glands to produce hormones that are responsible for many of the changes of puberty, is released primarily during sleep in adolescent girls; during waking hours, only small amounts of LH are released, no greater than in childhood. (After Warren, 1983.)

gonadotropin-releasing hormone (GnRH)   A hormone released by the hypothalamus and involved in regulating the timing of pubertal events.

anterior pituitary   A center within the brain that produces hormones that act on the gonads.

gonads   The sex glands; the ovaries in females and the testes in males.

luteinizing hormone (LH)   A gonadotropic hormone produced by the anterior pituitary that acts on the gonads.

follicle-stimulating hormone (FSH)   A gonadotropic hormone produced by the anterior pituitary that acts on the gonads.

GnRH pulse generator
Cells within the hypothalamus that pulse out bursts of GnRH.

kisspeptin A substance secreted by cells in the hypothalamus that activates the gene GPR54, triggering the pulse generator.

THE PULSE GENERATOR   The hypothalamus measures out its signals in rhythmic pulses much like a clock, sending bursts of GnRH to the anterior pituitary. If these pulses were not to occur, the anterior pituitary would fail to release its gonadotropins into the bloodstream, the gonads would fail to develop and to produce their sex hormones, and the familiar events of puberty would fail to occur.

But what knocks over that first domino that sets the whole thing in motion? That is, why weren't these hypothalamic cells emitting pulses of GnRH before? Thomas Plant (2008), at the University of Pittsburgh, notes that this question is particularly intriguing given that the **GnRH pulse generator** *was* active in infancy, but becomes dormant in childhood, suggesting that something like a "neurobiological brake" holds the pulse generator in check.

Clinical research with adolescents who have failed to undergo normal pubertal development has provided some answers. When given injections of GnRH, these adolescents developed normally, suggesting that the pulse generator had lacked the necessary instructions for manufacturing this hormone (deRoux et al., 2003; Seminara et al., 2003). Instructions for manufacturing anything within the body, from hip bones to hormones, are coded by genes. In each of these adolescents, mutations were found along a particular gene, known as GPR54, in their hypothalamic cells, the gene that provides the instructions for manufacturing GnRH (deRoux et al., 2003; Seminara et al., 2003). Answers to one question, however, only prompt another: What signals GPR54 to increase its activity, thereby activating the pulse generator?

A FIRST KISS: KISSPEPTIN   **Kisspeptin**, a substance secreted by neighboring cells has been found to be the signal that activates GPR54. Production of kisspeptin increases early in puberty, suggesting that kisspeptin serves as a gatekeeper for the events of puberty (Dumalska et al., 2008; Roa et al., 2008; Seminara, 2005; Shahab et al., 2005). The latch that causes the kisspeptin-GPR54 gate to swing open, however, lies *outside* the hypothalamus (**Figure 3.5**). This

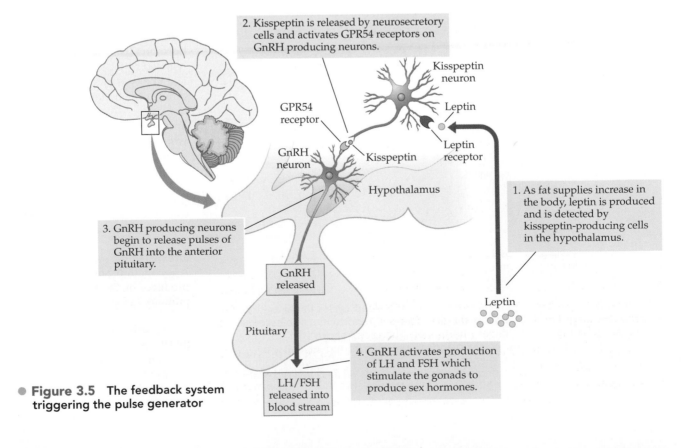

2. Kisspeptin is released by neurosecretory cells and activates GPR54 receptors on GnRH producing neurons.

Kisspeptin neuron

GPR54 receptor

Leptin

GnRH neuron

Kisspeptin

Leptin receptor

Hypothalamus

3. GnRH producing neurons begin to release pulses of GnRH into the anterior pituitary.

1. As fat supplies increase in the body, leptin is produced and is detected by kisspeptin-producing cells in the hypothalamus.

GnRH released

Leptin

Pituitary

4. GnRH activates production of LH and FSH which stimulate the gonads to produce sex hormones.

LH/FSH released into blood stream

● **Figure 3.5** **The feedback system triggering the pulse generator**

last link in the causal chain is found in fat cells distributed throughout the body. Pubertal development readies the body for reproduction; and reproductive readiness is dependent on the body's energy reserves (Lassek & Gaulin, 2008). These reserves are signaled by **leptin**, a hormone produced in fat cells. The cells that produce kisspeptin are equipped with receptors for leptin. As a consequence, as the level of leptin circulating in the blood increases, these cells increase their production of kisspeptin (Tena-Sempere, 2006; Roa et al., 2008).

Thus, increases in leptin trigger an increase in the production of kisspeptin, which in turn signals GPR54, activating the pulse generator and sending pulses of GnRH to the anterior pituitary, thereby leading to the cascade of events ushering in puberty.

The central role played by leptin also explains why adolescents who have a higher ratio of body fat to lean body mass—such as early maturing girls—enter puberty at an earlier age, and why a substantial loss of body fat, such as occurs with anorexia, delays pubertal development.

The timing of puberty is affected by other factors as well. Genetic factors have been found to significantly affect the activation of this feedback system (Banerjee & Clayton, 2007; van den Berg & Boomsma, 2007), as have lifestyle factors, such as underage drinking. Alcohol can interfere with the secretion of reproductive hormones (Dees et al., 2000; Hiller-Sturmhofel & Bartke, 1998), and can interfere as well with control mechanisms within the ovaries that help to regulate reproductive functioning (Dees et al., 2001). These findings take on added significance in the light of research indicating that early maturing girls are more likely to have friends who drink and more likely to engage in drinking themselves than are late maturing girls (Dick et al., 2001)

The Physical Changes of Puberty

Puberty brings about the physical differences that distinguish females and males. Differences in the reproductive system itself, such as growth of the ovaries in females and the testes in males, constitute **primary sex characteristics**. Other changes, such as the growth of pubic hair, the development of breasts in females and facial hair in males, represent **secondary sex characteristics**. Not all of these changes occur at once, of course, and not all are viewed as equally important by adolescents. The changes that occasion most fascination, such as menstruation in girls and facial hair in boys, are not however, the first to occur.

The sequence of changes varies less than their timing. One adolescent can be almost fully matured before another has begun to develop, yet each will experience the events of puberty in roughly the same order. These changes are easiest to follow if we chart them separately for each sex (**Figure 3.6**). Girls are generally a year or two ahead of boys. We will start with them first, as nature has done. An adolescent named Sarah will serve as our model.

Recollections of an Adolescent Girl

Sarah reports that the first change she noticed was in her breasts. She was in the fifth grade at the time, not quite 11 years old. It was such a small change that she almost didn't notice it at first. A slight mound had appeared just below each nipple. Sometime later the skin around the nipple darkened slightly. She couldn't see any difference when she was dressed, but by the time school let out for the summer, she felt a bit self-conscious in a bathing suit.

Sarah remembers the day she discovered a few wisps of pubic hair. It seemed as if they had appeared overnight. Actually, they had been growing for quite some time, but she hadn't noticed because they were unpigmented and very soft. Other changes were occurring within Sarah that she would

leptin A hormone secreted by fat cells that may play a role in menarche.

primary sex characteristics Differences between females and males in the reproductive system that develop during puberty.

secondary sex characteristics Differences between females and males in body structure and appearance, other than differences in the reproductive system, including differences in skeletal structure, hair distribution, and skin texture.

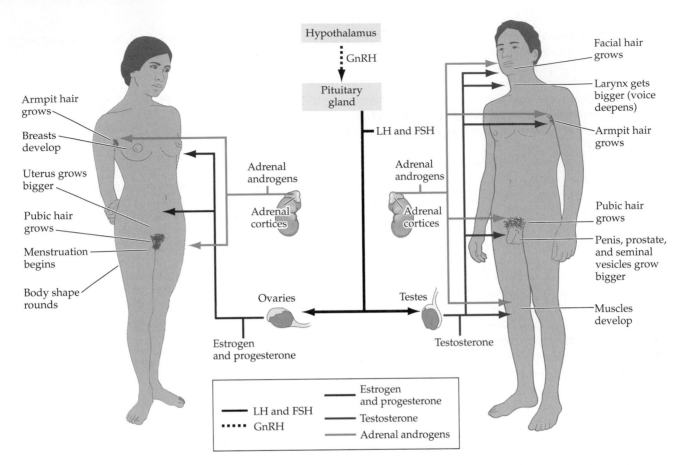

● **Figure 3.6** **Effects of hormones on physical development and sexual maturation at puberty**

never see. Her uterus and ovaries were enlarging and developing as the level of hormones circulating through her bloodstream increased.

She didn't notice anything else until the sixth grade. By then it became obvious how much faster she was growing, compared with before. By winter vacation, she was taller than most of the boys in her class, and most of her fall back-to-school clothes were too short. She spent a lot of time that vacation shopping for clothes. By the end of the sixth grade, she had grown several inches since the previous year.

Just before spring vacation, when she was in the seventh grade and 12 years old, Sarah had her first menstrual period. She had known for a while that it could happen at any time. A number of her classmates had begun menstruating this year, as had one or two the year before. She also knew girls in the ninth grade who had not begun to menstruate. Her mother told her that a girl could start as early as 10 or as late as 16.

Sarah stopped growing as quickly as she had started—a relief, because she'd started to identify with the giants in children's stories. She had also begun using an underarm deodorant and was shaving under her arms. Actually, she remembered thinking she looked pretty mature. Her figure had begun to fill out, and no one asked her age at PG-13 movies.

Recollections of an Adolescent Boy

Alfred will talk about his experiences of puberty. He is just as typical for boys as Sarah is for girls. Alfred recalls being very impatient for something to happen. With mixed emotions, he first noticed a change in his scrotum. It was slightly larger and a bit darker than it had been. This was in the seventh grade, just after he had turned 12. Very shortly after, wisps of pubic hair appeared at the base of his penis. Despite these early signs of his manhood, his penis remained the same size. He remembers having some problems with acne once he started the seventh grade. Other changes had begun within his body, but Alfred remained unaware of them. His testes were growing and secreting more androgen than before, and his seminal vesicles and prostate were developing. Maturation of the testes would be necessary for the ejaculation of seminal fluid—the wet dreams he had heard so much about.

By the end of the seventh grade, he had started to grow taller. It had begun slowly at first, but during the eighth grade, he grew 3 inches in a single year. His parents complained they couldn't keep him in clothes: As soon as they bought new ones, he outgrew them. It was also during the eighth grade that he noticed his penis had started to grow longer. What a relief. He remembers dreading gym class; he couldn't face the showers. A few of the guys in there looked as mature as his father. Of course, others still looked like kids.

Alfred recalls continuing to grow a lot in the ninth grade. By then he was 14 and his voice had started to change. He experienced his first ejaculation at about this time, too. He had the sexiest dream with it. His pubic hair was now thick and curly, and he had started to get some axillary (underarm) hair. He was still growing but says he started to slow down a bit after the ninth grade. He still didn't have any hair on his face. He was 15 before he noticed a few hairs growing in over his upper lip. His mom called it peach fuzz. He didn't have a real beard until he was 16. By then he also had a fair amount of hair on his body. Alfred says he didn't actually stop growing until his early twenties. He also developed more hair on his chest, back, and stomach all through his late teens.

The typical sequence of these events appears in **Table 3.1**, along with the age ranges for each. Sarah and Alfred are typical adolescents. However, other adolescents can pass through these changes at different ages and still be just as normal. You can see that for some events, such as menstruation in girls or body growth in boys, some adolescents can be as much as six years ahead of others and each will be within a range considered normal for development. With differences like these, the exception is almost the norm.

Hormones contribute to more than the physical changes of puberty. Exuberant, inexperienced, and self-centered thinking can lead to risk-taking behavior. This boy knows his behavior is risky, but he does not seem to understand that he could be seriously hurt.

The Growth Spurt

FEMALES   Growth is regulated by the growth hormone (secreted by the anterior pituitary) and the sex hormones (secreted by the gonads). The growth hormone affects the timing and amount of growth mostly by serving as a "gate crasher" for amino acids, the body's building blocks, helping them cross cell membranes and promoting cell multiplication. This results in a dramatic spurt of growth. The growth hormone also affects changes in the bones during puberty. Early in adolescence, bones begin to grow rapidly in size; this growth is followed, in mid-adolescence, by an increase in the mineralization, or hardening, of the bones. Approximately a third of the minerals eventually deposited in bones accumulates in a relatively brief period (three to four years) following the onset of puberty, a fact emphasizing the importance of nutrition and exercise in early and mid- adolescence (Hind & Burrows, 2007; Gunter et al., 2008).

Girls experience a period of rapid growth in height starting at about age 11. The **growth spurt** usually lasts a little over 2½ years. For some girls it can be as brief as 1½ years, and for others it can last up to four years. Girls gain about 8 to 10 inches in height from the start of the growth spurt until they have

growth spurt   A period of rapid growth that often occurs during puberty.

TABLE 3.1
Summary of Pubertal Changes and Their Sequence

CHARACTERISTIC	AGE OF FIRST APPEARANCE	MAJOR HORMONAL INFLUENCE
GIRLS		
Growth of breasts	8–13	Pituitary growth hormone, estrogen progesterone, thyroxine
Pubic hair	8–14	Adrenal androgen
Body growth	9½–14½	Pituitary growth hormone, adrenal androgen, estrogen
Menarche	10–16½	Leptin–Kisspeptin, FSH, LH, estrogen, progesterone
Underarm hair	About two years after pubic hair	Adrenal androgens
Oil- and sweat-producing glands (acne occurs when glands are clogged)	About the same time as underarm hair	Adrenal androgens
BOYS		
Growth of testes, scrotal sac	10–13	Pituitary growth hormone, testosterone
Pubic hair	10–15	Testosterone
Body growth	10½–16	Pituitary growth hormone, testosterone
Growth of penis	11–14½	Testosterone
Change in voice (growth of larynx)	About the same time as penis growth	Testosterone
Facial and underarm hair	About two years after pubic hair appears	Testosterone
Oil- and sweat-producing glands, acne	About the same time as underarm hair	Testosterone

Source: Goldstein, 1976.

Even though these adolescents are the same age, the girls appear older since they begin puberty a year or two earlier than boys.

finished growing. The most rapid growth occurs in the year before and the year after menarche, the beginning of the menstrual cycle.

Body proportions begin to change even earlier. About 1½ years before the growth spurt, girls' legs start to grow faster than their bodies, giving them a long, leggy look. Most of the early gain in height is due to a lengthening of the legs. The shoulders also widen before the actual growth spurt. Somewhat later, during puberty itself, the hips widen. These growth patterns give young adolescent girls a characteristic look: relatively long legs, slender bodies, wide shoulders, and narrow hips—our present standard of beauty. Puberty changes all this.

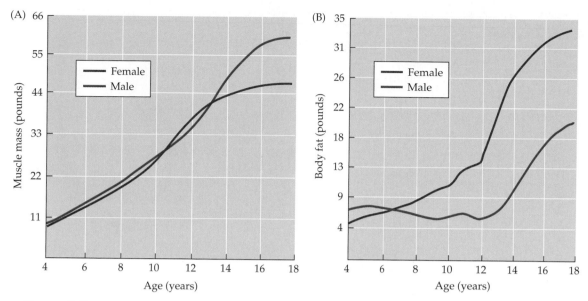

● **Figure 3.7**   **Development of muscle mass and body fat for females and males**
(A) A dramatic increase in muscle mass accompanies the height spurt in males,
starting at age 14. (B) An increase in body fat begins in late childhood in females,
prior to the height spurt. (After Cheek, 1974.)

MALES   The growth spurt can begin anywhere from age 10½ to age 16 in
boys. Boys grow for a longer time than girls, reaching their peak rate of growth
two years later than girls. The average height of boys prior to the height spurt
is 58 inches. They add another 12 or 13 inches during the growth spurt. Most
of this increase is due to a lengthening of the trunk, because the legs began
to grow earlier. Adequate diet and exercise need to be present before puberty
begins for these to optimally affect growth.

Striking sex differences begin to appear in muscle mass and body fat. By the
time they reach adulthood, males will have 1½ times more muscle mass than
females, and females will have twice as much body fat (**Figure 3.7**). In addition to these obvious differences, males also develop larger hearts and lungs;
they have higher systolic blood pressure, can carry more oxygen in their blood,
and can dispose of the chemical by-products of exercise more efficiently than
females. They also have more red blood cells. These differences, though genuine
sex differences, can also reflect variations in activity levels between females and
males that become more pronounced as they approach late adolescence. The
most obvious change, however, is in the shape of the body itself: In males, the
shoulders widen relative to the hips, whereas the opposite is true for females
(Fechner, 2003; Wells, 2007).

The Reproductive System

FEMALES   The **ovaries**, which flank either side of the uterus, grow in size
during adolescence and increase their production of female sex hormones.
These hormones, in conjunction with FSH and LH, stimulate the development of **ova**, or eggs. The uterus, ovaries, and vagina also increase in size. The
length of the **uterus** doubles, and the **vagina** grows to its adult length of 4 to
6 inches, becoming more flexible and developing a thick lining. Many girls
mistakenly think of the vagina as a hollow tube leading to an even larger space
inside. This misunderstanding can cause some teenage girls to be fearful of
losing tampons in some vast, unknown space within. In actuality, the vagina is
closed off at the inner end by a tight, muscular gate, the **cervix** (**Figure 3.8**).

ovaries   Structures within the
female reproductive system
flanking the uterus that house
the immature eggs and produce
female sex hormones.

ovum (plural ova)   The female
sex cell, also called the egg; the
male equivalent is sperm.

uterus   A muscular enclosure at
the top of the vagina that holds
the fetus during pregnancy.

vagina   The muscular tube in
females leading from the labia at
its opening to the uterus.

cervix   The opening to the
uterus.

● **Figure 3.8**
Female reproductive system

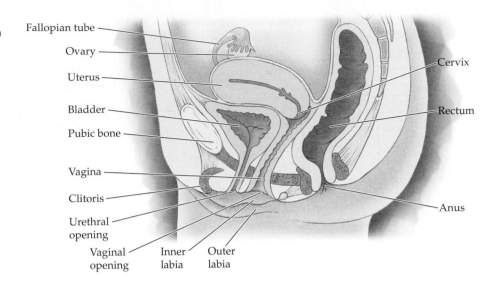

Fallopian tube
Ovary
Uterus
Bladder
Pubic bone
Vagina
Clitoris
Urethral opening
Vaginal opening
Inner labia
Outer labia
Cervix
Rectum
Anus

hymen   A fold of skin partially covering the opening to the vagina.

clitoris   That part of the external genitals in females that is the primary source of sexual stimulation.

glans   The part of the clitoris or penis that is most sensitive to stimulation.

shaft   The part of the clitoris or penis that becomes erect during sexual stimulation.

prepuce   A thin skin covering the glans of the clitoris or penis.

testes   Structures within the male reproductive system contained in the scrotum that produce sperm and male sex hormones.

sperm   The male sex cell; the female equivalent is the ovum.

The opening to the vagina is partially covered by a fold of skin called the **hymen**, sometimes referred to as the "cherry." This delicate membrane is frequently torn or stretched during childhood. Activities ranging from bicycle riding to using tampons can stretch the hymen. Folklore holds that first intercourse ruptures the hymen, and that an intact hymen is a sign of virginity. However, relatively few females today survive their active childhoods with the hymen intact.

The **clitoris**, not the vagina, is the primary source of sexual stimulation. The clitoris is similar to the penis; both develop from the same prenatal structures, and each has a glans, a shaft, and a prepuce. The **glans** is supplied by an extensive network of nerve endings, making it the most sensitive part of the clitoris. Hidden beneath the skin and connected to the glans is the **shaft**. Numerous blood vessels, which develop during puberty, feed into the shaft. During arousal, these become engorged with blood, causing the clitoris to become erect. A thin covering of skin, the **prepuce**, covers the glans.

MALES   The **testes** begin to develop at around 11 years of age. The very same hormones (LH and FSH) that stimulate the ovaries to develop and produce female sex hormones stimulate the testes to develop and produce male sex hormones. These, in combination with FSH, stimulate the testes to produce **sperm**, which can be found in the urine of boys by about the age of 14 (Fechner, 2003; Kulin, 1991b).

The testes themselves are about the same size, but the left testis frequently appears larger, perhaps because it hangs a bit lower than the right. The scrotal sac protects the testes from harm. One might argue that they would be even safer if tucked securely inside the body, as indeed they would. However, the temperature within the body is a few degrees too high for optimal production of sperm. The range of temperatures ideal for the breeding of sperm is relatively narrow. The scrotal sac accommodates to temperature fluctuations by contracting or relaxing, adjusting the distance of the testes from the warmth of the body cavity. Adolescent males may notice that the scrotum contracts in the cold, drawing the testes closer to the body. In hot weather, or after a hot shower, it hangs lower, keeping the testes farther from the body (**Figure 3.9**).

The penis doubles in length and thickness during puberty, growing to about 3 to 4 inches in length. Adolescent boys frequently express concerns about the size of their penis. These concerns almost surely reflect the considerable vari-

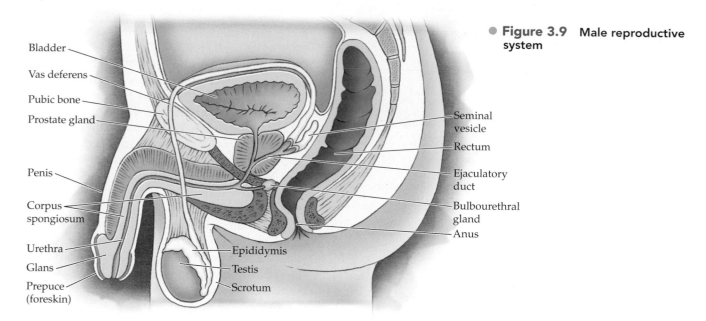

Figure 3.9 Male reproductive system

ability in size that exists from one boy to the next and the mistaken belief that the size of the penis is related to masculinity and sexual prowess.

The prepuce (or foreskin), is a thin fold of skin that covers the glans of the penis. The prepuce is frequently removed surgically, usually right after birth, in a procedure known as **circumcision**. Circumcision is widely practiced in the United States, for both hygienic and religious reasons.

Although female circumcision bears the same name, the procedure is in no way comparable; it is more accurately termed **female genital mutilation** (**FGM**). The World Health Organization distinguishes several forms of FGM, the most severe of which partially or totally remove the clitoris, a procedure that is comparable to cutting off the glans of the penis! Frequently the **outer labia** are sewn together, leaving only a small opening for the passage of urine and menstrual blood. These procedures are typically performed without anesthesia or antibiotics (World Health Organization, 2008). FGM can lead to numerous physical problems, such as recurrent infections and childbirth complications, and can even make simple acts, such as walking, sitting, or urinating, difficult. Additional emotional problems can result from this procedure (Abor, 2006; Behrendt & Moritz, 2005).

FGM is widely practiced in many non-Western nations, and has entered the United States and other Western countries as families emigrate from these nations (U.S. Department of Health and Human Services, 2005). Estimates based on the 2000 U.S. Census data, for instance, place approximately 62,000 girls in the United States at risk of FGM, despite federal and state legislation prohibiting this practice (African Women's Health Center, 2008). Legislation in the United States and other countries seeks to combat this practice both by imposing penalties for individual offenses and by instituting educational programs at community levels (Jones et al., 2004; Leye et al., 2006; Turillazzi & Fineschi, 2007).

Menarche

The term for a girl's first menstrual period is **menarche**. The average age for reaching menarche is presently about 12½ in the United States, though this varies considerably from one girl to the next (McDowell et al., 2007). Perhaps the best estimate as to when any girl is likely to experience menarche is given by knowing the age at which her mother had her first period, since individual differences reflect a strong genetic influence (Anderson et al., 2007; van den Berg & Boomsma, 2007). Ethnic differences exist as well, with African American and Mexican American girls reaching menarche somewhat earlier than

circumcision   Surgical removal of the prepuce (or foreskin) covering the glans of the penis.

female genital mutilation (FGM)   The World Health Organization recognizes several forms of FGM, the most severe of which involves cutting out the entire clitoris, along with sewing shut most of the outer labia.

outer labia   The outer folds of skin surrounding the opening of the vagina and the clitoris.

menarche   The occurrence of a girl's first menstrual period.

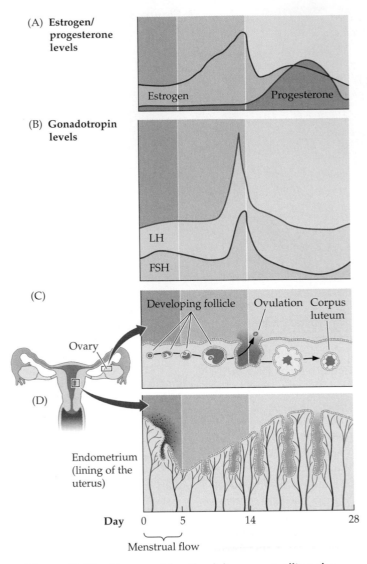

(A) **Estrogen/progesterone levels**

Estrogen   Progesterone

(B) **Gonadotropin levels**

LH

FSH

(C)

Ovary

Developing follicle   Ovulation   Corpus luteum

(D)

Endometrium (lining of the uterus)

Day   0   5   14   28

Menstrual flow

● **Figure 3.10** Hormonal feedback loop controlling the menstrual cycle

anovulatory Menstrual cycles that do not include the release of an egg.

European American adolescents (Casazza et al., 2008; McDowell et al., 2007).

The menstrual cycle is regulated by the feedback loop between the ovaries, the anterior pituitary, and the hypothalamus. **Figure 3.10** illustrates these relationships. At the beginning of the cycle (counting from the first day of the menstrual period), the level of circulating estrogen is low (**A**), prompting the release of FSH by the anterior pituitary (**B**). FSH stimulates the ovary to secrete more estrogen, and stimulates an egg within one of the ovaries to mature (**C**). FSH also stimulates the lining of the uterus (endometrium) to receive the egg if it is fertilized (**D**). A second hormone, LH, is subsequently produced by the anterior pituitary (B) which, once the egg is released, stimulates the empty follicle, now known as the corpus luteum (C), to produce progesterone (A), which inhibits further release of LH.

If the ovum is not fertilized, the follicle decreases its production of hormones, and the uterus, sensitive to the low levels of progesterone and estrogen, contracts, shaking loose the lining that has formed to receive a fertilized egg. The shedding of this lining by the uterus is the menstrual flow (D). The hypothalamus also reacts to low hormonal levels by signaling the anterior pituitary to release FSH, thus initiating the next monthly cycle.

Menstrual cycles sometimes occur without the release of an egg; such cycles are called **anovulatory**. They feel no different from those in which an egg is released and occur only because the hormonal feedback cycle is not sufficiently developed to release an egg each time. Up to half of a girl's cycles can be anovulatory for the first several years, but only about one-fifth will be by the end of her teens.

It is impossible to say with any certainty when a girl will ovulate. Ovulation usually occurs 14 days before the next period starts. If a girl's menstrual periods occur regularly every 28 days, she would ovulate on the 14th day of the cycle. Most adolescents do not have regular cycles, at least at first, and some evidence even suggests that a girl may occasionally ovulate several times during a cycle. What this variability in the timing and frequency of ovulation *means* is that it is not possible for the adolescent to identify a time during her cycle when she *cannot* become pregnant.

Reaching a certain proportion of body fat is critical for menarche to occur. Although age at menarche varies considerably from one girl to the next, all reach about the same percentage of body fat just prior to menarche. Additionally, the distribution of body fat appears to be at least as important as its percentage, with a higher ratio of hip circumference to waist circumference being associated with earlier menarche (Lassek & Gaulin, 2007). Body fat plays a role in converting androgens into estrogens, important to monthly cycles, and provides a supply of easily converted energy that the body could use, if necessary, to support a pregnancy. More importantly, fat cells secrete the hormone leptin, which triggers an increase in the production of kisspeptin, setting in motion the events of puberty (Bandini et al., 2008; Lassek & Gaulin, 2007).

Girls' reactions to menarche reflect the influence of many factors. In general, girls are more likely to have positive experiences when they have been prepared for menarche and know what to do (Marvan et al., 2006; Rembeck & Gunnarsson, 2004; Teitelman, 2004; Yeung et al., 2005). Similarly, those who view menarche as a natural and healthy bodily function have more positive reactions, as do those who have positive self-concepts (Hoerster et al., 2003; Teitelman, 2004; Yeungs et al., 2005). Of singular importance is a girl's relationship with her mother (Lee, 2008).

Janet Lee (2008), at Oregon State University, found that nearly 50% of the 18- to 21-year-olds she studied described menarche either very positively or as "no big deal." Of those who remembered the event positively, almost 90% had mothers who celebrated the event ("My mom was so excited that I'd started") or were emotionally engaged ("She was there the whole time and I knew she cared"). Conversely, daughters whose mothers were unsupportive reported more negative reactions to menarche.

Not only girls' mothers' attitudes but also those of their families affect their reactions to menarche. Anne Teitelman (2004) interviewed 14- to 18-year olds and found that family scripts played an important role in defining menarche for girls. As one girl said, "It was really celebrated in our family. Actually, I'm really glad I had that. A lot of people don't. Either it's just like, 'whatever,' or they're kind of happy, or some of them are upset about it. But, for me, it was really a rite of passage." Another said, "I was really happy about it…but we were so rushed that I didn't even get a chance to tell my mom. …Then we went over to my grandparents' house to have dinner that night, so I told my mom and my grandmother at the same time, and they were both really happy for me. My grandpa made me my favorite thing. He made his macaroni and cheese, which is my favorite food" (Teitelman, 2004).

Finally, to the extent that the reactions of families reflect ethnic or cultural differences, we might expect to see such differences in girls' reactions. A review of research examining ethnic differences notes that African American girls report more positive reactions from their mothers than do European American girls when informing them of their first period. Also, when asked what they might tell a younger sister about menarche, African American girls' remarks are more positive and reassuring. Finally, girls' depressive symptoms were related to pubertal status only in European American and not African American or Hispanic adolescents (Michael & Eccles, 2003).

Despite differences in their reactions to menarche, most girls tell their mothers right away, and most soon discuss their experiences with friends (Archibald et al., 2003; Brooks-Gunn & Ruble, 1982). Mothers also are the most frequent source of information (Costos et al., 2002). However, older sisters, teachers, and friends are also important. Fathers play a small role (Koff & Rierdan, 1995). It may be that girls are less willing than are their fathers to discuss menstruation. More than three-quarters say they would not report their menstrual status to their fathers, whereas a small sample of fathers who were interviewed said they would be comfortable talking with their daughters. It is interesting that girls who tell their fathers, or who know their mothers have told them, report fewer menstrual symptoms such as cramps or other discomfort. This inclusion of the father may reflect a more open, relaxed attitude about menstruation.

Spermarche

A boy's first ejaculation of seminal fluid, or **spermarche**, usually occurs early in his teens, by about 13 (Halpern et al., 2000; Stein & Reiser, 1994). For some boys, it will occur spontaneously in a **nocturnal emission** (also known as a wet dream), for others, through masturbation or intercourse. Relatively few

Some girls may feel ambivalent about menarche, whereas others accept it as a natural part of maturing. The difference is due in large part to how parents prepare their daughters for the physical changes of puberty.

spermarche A boy's first ejaculation of seminal fluid.

nocturnal emission A spontaneous ejaculation of seminal fluid during sleep; sometimes called a wet dream.

boys are likely to have anyone explain any of this to them (Frankel, 2002). Peers and books or magazines are the most likely sources of information; in fact, boys learn more about menarche than about ejaculation in their health classes. Despite the relative lack of preparation, most boys are not alarmed, although most do admit to being surprised. Generally, reactions are positive, boys reporting feeling excited, grown up, and glad (Gaddis & Brooks-Gunn, 1985; Stein & Reiser, 1994).

Boys are not likely to discuss their experience with friends or with their fathers. This reaction to ejaculation contrasts sharply with that of girls to menarche, most of whom tell their mothers immediately and share their new status with friends. The difference may reflect the closer association of first ejaculation with masturbation for boys. Among all experiences related to sex, boys are least willing to discuss masturbation (Halpern et al., 2000). For girls, the lack of association of menarche with masturbation may account for their greater willingness to discuss it. Or it may be that they have had discussion modeled for them by their mothers, because most are prepared for menarche, whereas most boys have not been prepared for first ejaculation by their fathers (Gaddis & Brooks-Gunn, 1985). In general, adolescent boys receive considerably less information than girls about pubertal changes. Few fathers explain nocturnal emissions to their sons, and neither parent is likely to explain menstruation to them. A survey of college males found that many had gotten much of their information about menstruation as young adults from female friends, once the security of early adulthood permitted such discussions (Brooks-Gunn & Ruble, 1986).

The Secular Trend

secular trend The earlier onset of puberty, faster growth, and larger size reached by adolescents today than in the past.

Puberty begins earlier today than it did in the past. This downward shift in age is called the **secular trend**. **Figure 3.11** shows a striking drop in age at menarche over a period of 130 years for a number of countries. The greatest changes occurred from the mid-1800's to the mid-1900's, in which age at menarche dropped by about three to four months every ten years (Tanner, 1991). More recent data find this rate of change to be declining. The age for menarche of 12½ years represents a drop of only three months over 20 years (McDowell et al., 2007).

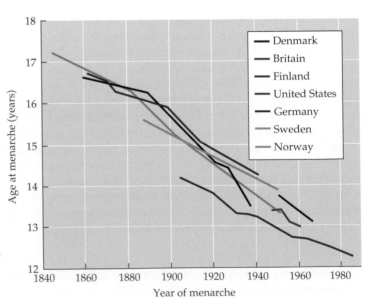

● **Figure 3.11** **Trends in the age of menarche** Puberty begins earlier than it has in previous years. This graph shows how the age of menarche has been steadily dropping. (After Tanner, 1968, and McDowell et al., 2007.)

Not only do adolescents begin puberty earlier than in previous generations, but they also grow faster. Although we have only scanty records from earlier centuries, the pieces fit a predictable pattern. In the 19th century in Britain, females reached their adult height at about 21. Adolescent girls stop growing today by 16 to 18. British men in the 19th century continued growing well into their mid-'20s, reaching their adult height at 23 to 25. Adolescent boys today reach their adult height by 20 to 21. Even after skeletal growth is completed, adolescents' bones continue to develop, increasing in density and in bone mineral content (Magarey et al., 1999; Cole, 2003).

Adolescents also grow to be larger than they once did, girls growing half an inch to an inch taller than their mothers and weighing about 2 pounds more. For boys these differences could be even greater. Generational differences are startling when we make comparisons across centuries. We know that American sailors during the War of 1812 were considerably shorter, because the decks of the USS *Constitution* were only 5 feet 6 inches high. Similar evidence from medieval armor, old clothing, and antique furniture all point to a dramatic increase in stature over the centuries. (Muuss, 1975; Tanner, 1991).

A number of conditions have contributed to the secular trend. Improved nutrition is almost surely an important cause of the accelerated growth patterns. One can reasonably ask, however, when this trend will level off. Some researchers suggest that it already has done so. They note that not all measures of puberty have continued to drop with age, particularly for boys (Euling et al., 2008), and point out that those that have are ones associated with increased body fat. Since obesity also is more common among adolescents today, there simply may be the appearance of a continuing trend where in actuality there is none (Kaplowitz, 2008; Shalitin & Phillip, 2003).

The Psychological and Social Implications of Puberty

Even experiences as close to a biological epicenter as those of puberty do not necessarily have the same significance from one adolescent to the next. Adolescents continually interpret the biological frontiers they are crossing, reading the reactions of friends and family for the meaning of the changes they are experiencing. Nor are they alone in doing so. Their parents, siblings, friends, and teachers also read significance into the biological script unfolding before them. Not surprisingly, puberty affects adolescents' closest relationships in intimate ways.

Reed Larson and Maryse Richards (1994) were able to document the details of adolescents' lives by having them wear beepers and paging them at random intervals throughout the day and evening, when they would report on their activities and feelings. These investigators remind us of what we too easily forget about our own lives—that even the simplest activities that make up a day, things such as having breakfast or hassling over kitchen responsibilities, are often suffused with emotion. They also remind us that such activities, when they involve more than one member of the family, are rarely experienced in the same way by each of them, that there are as many realities to be experienced as individuals to experience them. This reminder should strike a familiar note at this point, illustrating one of the central assumptions of the constructive approach taken in this text: namely, that we continually interpret our experiences, putting events together in ways that make sense to us, constructing the reality to which we respond.

Adolescents' emotions are often more extreme than they were when children, or will be as adults.

Heightened Emotionality

Larson and Richards point out that tensions are greatest in early adolescence, when puberty tips the psychosocial balance established throughout childhood. As adolescents' bodies assume more adult proportions, those around them, particularly parents and teachers, expect them to behave in more adult ways as well. Crowding in on the heels of puberty are additional stressors such as starting middle school or junior high, navigating problematic relationships with peers, redefining relationships with parents, and, for many, facing increasing pressures to experiment with sex and drugs. Because of the secular trend, adolescents as young as 10 or 11 begin to face these pressures of puberty, often before either they or their parents are ready for them (Larson & Richards, 1994).

How do early adolescents react to these changes? A common stereotype is that, with puberty, adolescents become moody, their emotions swinging from one extreme to another with little predictability. Larson and Richards indeed found some support for heightened emotionality in adolescence. **Figure 3.12** shows that adolescents more frequently report experiencing extreme states than do their parents. They also report a wider range of emotions. In addition to simply feeling happy, for instance, adolescents report feeling great, free, cheerful, proud, accepted, in love, friendly, and kindly. They also report a wider gamut of negative feelings, describing themselves as unsure, lonely, awkward, ignored, and nervous, or, as Larson and Richards put it, "a whole array of painful feelings that remind us adults why we never want to be adolescents again" (1994, p. 83). Even though they feel self-conscious and embarrassed two to three times as often as their parents, they are also bored more, perhaps because they feel less in control and less invested in the moment, often saying they would rather be doing something else. Furthermore, despite the advantage of youth, adolescents are more likely to say they feel tired, weak, and have little energy. These differing inner realities, as well as the more visible differences of their exterior lives, virtually ensure that misunderstandings with parents will arise.

● **Figure 3.12 Frequency with which family members feel gradations of happiness and unhappiness** Follow the black line to see how adolescents' emotions differ from those of their parents; although adolescents are frequently characterized as being more moody, they differ mostly in that they feel "very happy" more often than their parents. (After Larson & Richards, 1994.)

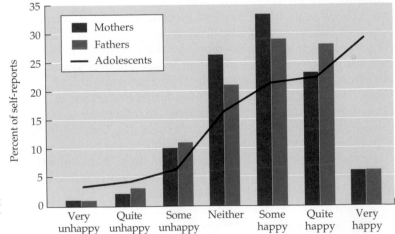

Relationships with Parents

Good relationships with parents can provide a powerful buffer against the stresses of life. Adolescents who see their parents as warm and loving, for instance, experience fewer emotional or behavioral problems (Wagner et al., 1996). Emotional harmony within the home may even affect the rate of physical development. In research following girls and their families from childhood into adolescence, warm and supportive relationships with parents, especially with fathers, were predictive of later, rather than earlier, pubertal development (Ellis et al., 1999). For most adolescents, however, closeness with parents temporarily decreases and the intensity of conflict increases with the onset of puberty (Laursen et al., 1998). Adolescents begin to demand a greater role in family decision making and more freedom in areas that their parents still believe require parental oversight, such as the adolescents' well-being (see Chapter 5). For their part, parents may see that the ways they have always parented are no longer appropriate, yet they have no ready substitutes for outmoded forms of discipline and guidance. The resulting scuffles, though often uncomfortable, lay the groundwork for renegotiated relationships. With few exceptions, however, studies of these changes have all involved white middle-class families.

Brooke Molina and Laurie Chassin (1996) compared parent–adolescent relationships in Hispanic and non-Hispanic families. These investigators found increased conflict and decreased closeness with pubertal onset only in white adolescent boys. For Hispanic boys, just the opposite occurred, with puberty actually bringing parents and sons closer together. Hispanic boys reported less conflict and greater emotional support from their parents once they began puberty. This increased closeness may reflect the value Hispanic families place on the traditional male role. Supporting this interpretation, Hispanic girls did not experience a comparable improvement in their relationships with parents.

The Timing of Change: Early and Late Maturers

Differences in the timing of pubertal change from one adolescent to the next, or within any adolescent, are collectively known as **asynchrony**. Asynchrony simply means that all changes do not occur at the same time. For adolescents who believe changes should occur together, the fact that they haven't, or that they occurred together but at the wrong time, can have enormous implications. Many changes receive cultural as well as personal interpretation. These interpretations affect the way adolescents feel and think about themselves. Change can be difficult enough when all goes according to schedule, but when adolescents develop faster or slower than their friends and classmates, or at obviously uneven rates within their own lives, differences can be hard to ignore.

Yet it is common for adolescents to experience asynchrony. In fact, our society seems to foster it. Most adolescents are biologically and intellectually mature by their mid- to late teens, yet many remain emotionally and socially dependent on parents while they obtain the education they need to succeed in increasingly technological jobs. Relatively little information exists on the possible effects of these asynchronies on personality development. Certainly, we need more research on this important topic and the ways in which it can affect the lives of adolescents and their parents.

Early and Late Maturing Boys

Initial studies comparing early and late maturers found that **early maturation** conferred distinct advantages for boys. Boys who matured earlier than their peers were more self confident, more popular, and achieved more recognition in activities ranging from captain of the football team to class president than did their **late maturing** peers (Jones, 1965; Jones & Bayley, 1950).

asynchrony Differences in the timing of pubertal changes within an adolescent or from one adolescent to the next.

early maturation Pubertal maturation occurring earlier in adolescents than the norm for their sex.

late maturation Pubertal maturation occurring later in adolescents than the norm for their sex.

Early maturing boys often show off their strength at the expense of smaller, later maturing boys. Will their different rates of maturation affect the development of self-image in these two boys?

Subsequent research, however, suggests that these advantages may come at a price. Early maturing boys have also been found to be more likely to engage in behaviors posing health risks, such as smoking or drinking (Susman et al., 2003), as well as in delinquent activities (Alsaker, 1995; Cota-Robles et al., 2002). Questions as to why they may do so are not that easily answered. It may simply be that early maturing boys take advantage of their physical maturation to associate with older boys. Their pubertal status, in other words, affords them access to an older crowd, and this increases the likelihood they will engage in behaviors more characteristic of older adolescents. Data from a four-year longitudinal study of Finnish adolescents support this interpretation (Dick et al., 2001).

Other research, however, suggests that early maturing boys may experience more adjustment problems independent of who they associate with (Alsaker, 1995; Ge et al., 2001a; Lam et al., 2004). Xiaojia Ge, Rand Conger, and Glen Elder (2001b), interviewing a sample of European American adolescents from rural areas and small towns in the Midwest, found that early maturing boys experienced more distress, such as feelings of sadness or anxiety, than other boys their age, as well as more hostility toward others. They also had more difficulty coping with other stressful events going on in their lives than did age-mates who had not yet entered puberty. Subsequent interviews with African American boys yielded similar findings (Ge et al., 2006).

A comparison of European American, Hispanic, and African American boys drawn from a national sample also found more problem behaviors among early maturing boys from each of the three ethnic groups (Cota-Robles et al., 2002). It is rare, however, when the findings of research are entirely consistent, and findings related to pubertal timing offer no exception, with some studies showing more adjustment problems for late maturing boys (Graber et al., 1997; Graber et al., 2004).

Early and Late Maturing Girls

The picture for girls is clearer. Early maturation confers few, if any, initial advantages and a number of problems. Recall that girls begin to develop approximately two years ahead of boys, which means that early maturing girls are not only ahead of all the other girls, but also ahead of all the boys their age as well. Many are self-conscious about their adult bodies, have lower **self-esteem**, and lack the poise of late maturing girls (Dusek & McIntyre, 2003; Susman et al., 2003). Their height, menarcheal status, and developing breasts can be sources of embarrassment among classmates who still have the bodies of children (Summers-Effler, 2004). The picture brightens with junior high, where early maturing girls are no longer set apart by their adult bodies and can enjoy a new prestige and, with this, frequent popularity.

Even so, a number of problems are associated with early maturation in girls. They, like early maturing boys, are more likely to associate with peers who are somewhat older and to engage in behaviors that pose health risks,

self-esteem The individual's overall positive or negative evaluation of herself or himself.

such as drinking, smoking, or disordered eating. They also are more likely to experience negative moods and depression (Ge et al., 2006; Ge et al., 2001a). Again, however, the findings of research are not entirely consistent. Research by Eccles and her associates finds that African American girls are not likely to experience distress due to early maturation. They appear to be less vulnerable than European American girls, protected by a more positive sense of self and a greater openness to their feelings (Michael & Eccles, 2003).

Perhaps not unexpectedly, early maturers of either sex are more likely to engage in early sexual behavior (Cavanagh, 2004; Susman et al., 2003). Shannon Cavanagh (2004), studying a nationally representative sample of adolescents, found earlier sexual activity to be associated with pubertal timing only for European American and Hispanic girls, and not for African American girls.

Why might being off-time in development affect adolescents? Most of us know from our own experiences how difficult it can be, at any point in life, to be out of step with those around us. This difficulty is compounded for adolescents because they go through many changes so quickly, and draw much of their support from peers. Being off-time sets adolescents apart from their age-mates and, with this, from the social supports to which they customarily turn. This explanation, known as the **maturational deviance hypothesis**, suggests that timing is important because it changes adolescents' status relative to their peers. Since girls generally mature several years ahead of boys, early maturing girls are the most deviant and should experience more disruption.

A second explanation, the **stage termination hypothesis**, suggests that early maturers simply don't have as much time to complete the developmental tasks of middle childhood. That is, they must cope with the experiences, expectations, and feelings attending puberty when they have not yet completely resolved the problems of middle childhood. Again, most difficulty would be expected for those facing the demands of adolescence first, that is, early maturing girls. A positive note for these adolescents is that they have more time to complete the tasks of adolescence.

A third explanation, the **adult status hypothesis**, suggests that the advantages or disadvantages of early and late maturation depend on the status that awaits adolescents when they become adults (Block, 1978). Adult males generally enjoy a higher status in society than females. They are frequently the decision makers within the family and have positions of greater power and influence in society. Movement toward adulthood for girls does not carry the clear advantages it does for boys, supporting the finding that when problems related to maturational timing occur, they tend to be greater for girls than boys.

In summary, then, research suggests that adolescents who develop off-time from their peers, either earlier or later, may experience more difficulty coping with the changes of puberty than their on-time age-mates. It is also the case that early maturation appears to be more of a problem for girls than for boys. It should be noted, however, that not all research finds a relationship between maturational timing and subsequent adjustment, and even when these are found to be related, research has not always found timing either to offer consistent advantages or disadvantages. Finally, although reported differences may be statistically significant, they may not be sufficiently large to account for much of the variability that actually exists from one adolescent to the next.

What does all this mean for individual adolescents and their families? Most adolescents can expect to travel the road to maturity with few, if any, missteps. This is also true for those who develop either earlier or later than their peers. Of course, this is not to say that pubertal changes do not present new challenges, or that there won't be problems that take time before yielding to adolescents' attempted solutions. But needing to cope with challenges in new

maturational deviance hypothesis   An explanation for the effects of asynchronous development that attributes the effects of timing to changing adolescents' status relative to their peers.

stage termination hypothesis   An explanation for the effects of early maturation that acknowledges not having as much time as needed to complete the developmental tasks of middle childhood.

adult status hypothesis   An explanation for the effects of asynchronous development that attributes the result of timing to the status that awaits adolescents of either sex when they become adults.

ways is not unique to adolescent development, and most adolescents by far cope effectively.

With this said, adolescents frequently have questions to which they need answers, often simply to know if what they are experiencing is normal. They also need to be able to talk to someone who is a good listener about what they are experiencing and feeling. Ideally, these needs would be met by discussions with a parent, or perhaps their physician. A national survey, however, found that 58% of adolescents had personal concerns they would not want to discuss with their parents, and 69% indicated concerns they would not want to discuss with friends (Cheng et al., 1993). Furthermore, confidentiality was an issue for 82% of youths in another national survey (Rideout, 2001). Frequently, the concerns early adolescents are embarrassed to talk about are seen as relatively commonplace by older adolescents and adults (such as menstruation or penis size), but they can be momentous to a young adolescent.

Problems related to embarrassment, confidentiality, and finding a good listener at 2 a.m. are addressed by increasing numbers of adolescents who turn to the Internet. Virtually all adolescents in the United States have access to the Internet either at home or at school, as do those in most other developed countries, making available sources such as web pages, chat rooms, and bulletin boards (Sun et al., 2005). The most frequent questions adolescents ask on the Internet clearly reflect the issues they face resulting from maturational changes, and are presumably the ones they are reluctant to discuss with parents, a doctor, or even their friends (Subrahmanyam & Greenfield, 2004; Suzuki & Calzo, 2004).

Lalita Suzuki and Jerel Calzo (2004) looked at questions posted on two bulletin boards, one on teen issues and one on teen sexual health (**Table 3.2**). Despite the potentially embarrassing nature of many of these, teens frequently responded by giving their personal opinions and by talking about their own experiences. Adolescents most likely feel less awkward due to the anonymity afforded by the Internet, something which is not possible in face-to-face conversations, yet still are able to feel a sense of connection to others (Gray et al., 2005; Suzuki & Calzo, 2004). Of course, use of the Internet in this way raises concerns about the accuracy of information adolescents are getting and whether teenagers who need medical attention are as likely to receive it. As Suzuki and Calzo suggest, participation by health professionals on sites such as these is one way of providing more accurate information.

body image An individual's satisfaction or dissatisfaction with the image of their body.

Body Image and Self-Esteem

How satisfied adolescents are with their bodies depends a lot on how others react to them. Adolescents' self-images reflect the attitudes of others, or their perceptions of these attitudes, as well as their own evaluations of how attractive a particular trait may be. **Body images** are reflected by social mirrors and always capture comparisons with others.

These images can get pretty distorted at times, especially in adolescence, when bodies change in so many ways. In early adolescence, physical changes contribute heavily to adolescents' sense of themselves. Adolescents' self-images are strongly tied to their body images; this is

Adolescents' self-images are tied to their body images, which always involve comparisons with others.

TABLE 3.2
Most Frequently Asked Types of Questions and Replies on General Teen Issues Bulletin Boards

TYPE OF QUESTION	RESPONSE PERCENT	EXAMPLE
Romantic relationships	36.9	"How do I ask a girl out, or at least talk to her?" "I feel awkward hugging and kissing my girlfriend with everyone around."
Physical health	14.6	"Will I get skin cancer if I only go tanning for two weeks?" "I have a problem with a lot of sweat coming from my underarms." "I have a hooked penis[a], do you know how to fix this?!?! PLEASE HELP ME!!!"
Body image/Exercise	10.7	"I would really like to drop 10 lbs. in the next 2 months." "I feel so fat compared to some of my friends who wear such small sizes."

TYPE OF REPLY	RESPONSE PERCENT	EXAMPLE
Personal opinion	63	"I don't think zits would turn me off. Lousy personality would." "I don't think weight matters just as long as you're a healthy person."
Advice	44	"You can put an anti-itch lotion very lightly there and see how that helps." "Just be yourself and express how you feel to him and you never know he might like you too."
Concrete information	37	"If your penis is truly bent then there is no home remedy for it. You will have to see a doctor." "A cold sore is Herpes, and the only things that will help it go away is a cream."
Personal experience	33	"I know what you mean… I didn't start wearing tampons until a couple of years after my period. But I realized how much more comfortable they are!"

Source: Suzuki & Calzo, 2004.

[a]Approximately 1 in 20 adult males suffer from this condition, known as Peyronie's disease. Until recently, this could be corrected only surgically, however treatment with the drug Xiaflex may become available, given FDA approval.

true for both sexes. Furthermore, just how satisfied adolescents are with their bodies roughly predicts their levels of self-esteem, especially for girls. Superficial or not, this relationship reflects something of a social reality.

Mainstream cultural messages on the importance of being thin are clear: To be considered attractive, females need to be thin (Field et al., 1999; Stice, 2002). For instance, three-quarters of the female characters on television sitcoms are actually underweight; most of the males, however, are of average weight (Fouts & Burggraf, 2000). Television is not unique in communicating to females the importance of being thin. Silverstein, Perdue, Peterson, and Kelly (1986) sampled advertisements in popular women's and men's magazines for messages about body shape. Ads for diet products in women's magazines outnumbered those in men's magazines 60 to 1. Despite the clear message to stay thin, women's

TABLE 3.3
Percentage of Body Satisfaction among Adolescent Girls Differing in Ethnicity

ETHNICITY	HIGH BODY SATISFACTION	LOW BODY SATISFACTION
Mixed Ethnicity	44.3	55.7
African American	40.1	59.9
European American	23.6	76.4
Asian American	20.0	80.0
Hispanic	19.8	80.2

Source: Kelly et al., 2005.

magazines contained more than 1,000 advertisements for food; only 10 food ads appeared in all the men's magazines.

Perhaps not surprisingly, boys have more positive body images than girls (Field et al., 1999; Rosenblum & Lewis, 1999). Girls tend to be critical of the way they look, believing themselves to be heavier than they are and wanting to be thinner, a trend that increases into late adolescence (Clark & Tiggemann, 2008; Clay et al., 2005; Lowry et al., 2005). This dissatisfaction is particularly true for those who have internalized the ideal body image presented in the mainstream media (Clark & Tiggemann, 2008; Schooler, 2008). Important exceptions exist, however, and these are related to ethnicity (Nishina et al., 2006). African American girls and girls of mixed ethnicity are more than twice as likely to be satisfied with their bodies than are Asian American, Caucasian, or Hispanic girls (**Table 3.3**). Additionally, girls who are satisfied with their bodies focus less on dieting than on eating in a healthy way and on exercising, attitudes they have in common with their parents and friends (Kelley et al., 2005).

Health and Well-Being

It is typically the case that bad news gets more press than good news, and this is true for news about adolescents' health as well. We hear alarming statistics about adolescent health problems, but few reports concerning their well-being. Yet the good news is that adolescents are at the peak of fitness and health. Muscles have increased in size and strength from childhood, fourteenfold in boys and tenfold in girls, bringing obvious increases in strength and agility, and the cardiovascular and respiratory systems reach their adult levels of efficiency. Chronic diseases are relatively rare, and those that eventually will occur following years of "wear and tear" have not yet had a chance to get a foothold. In short, adolescents are stronger, better coordinated, and healthier than they have ever been before.

Yet concerns about adolescents' health are legitimate for several reasons. For one thing, by far most of the causes of disease and death that occur among adolescents can be traced to their own behavior. For another, their behavior becomes progressively more under their own control, and less under their parents', as they age (Connell & Janevic, 2003). Lastly, many of their behaviors reflect lifestyle choices that eventually become habits. For some, these habits will give years of youthful energy; for others, they will prematurely impair the good health they presently enjoy.

Nutrition

Among the first health choices that adolescents make each day are what they will eat. Despite the increased nutritional needs introduced by rapid growth, many adolescents eat erratically. They are not alone. Poor eating habits are fast becoming part of the national character. Fast foods, frozen dinners, snacking, missed meals, and fad diets are common to all age groups. Nearly half of all the meals eaten in the United States are eaten in restaurants, most of which are fast-food chains. The nation is being fed by the Colonel, McDonald's, and assorted take-out stands.

Even though salads, milk, and juices are not at the top of the menu for most fast-food restaurants, adolescents can still eat at such places and meet nutritional needs. The biggest problem is not that they fail to get necessary nutrients, but that they get too many other things along with them. Fast foods taste good because of the excess fats, sugars, and salt in them; but these ingredients add calories—and with these, increased risk of becoming overweight. Healthy meals can still be selected from these menus with a few simple substitutions. For example, a 10-ounce carton of low-fat milk provides twice the recommended dietary allowance of calcium compared to a milkshake, and has less than half the calories. By adding a piece of fruit or a salad, burgers, wraps, and pizzas can add up to a nutritious meal.

Sleep

Not everything affecting adolescents' health reflects only lifestyle choices; some are closely tied to their developing bodies as well. Getting enough sleep is one of these. Patterns of sleep change as adolescents enter puberty; they fall asleep later and experience more difficulty waking up early (Jenni & Carskadon, 2004). Additionally, the amount of time they spend in deep sleep has been found to decrease by 40% (Carskadon et al., 2002). Since adolescents still need approximately nine hours of sleep a night, just as they did prior to puberty, feeling sleepy during the day is a common problem. A majority of adolescents fail to get enough sleep during the week on school days, catching up on missed sleep over the weekend when they can sleep in (Millman, 2005; Moore & Meltzer, 2008).

Sleepiness can affect adolescents in a number of ways. Perhaps the biggest challenge is staying awake at school, at least in early morning classes. Because of sleepiness, adolescents experience more difficulty paying attention, make more mistakes on tests, and find it harder staying awake when studying than do those just a few years younger. The amount of sleep adolescents get is also related to their moods throughout the day, with those getting less sleep reporting more negative moods (Fuligni & Hardway, 2006). Among those who drive, two-thirds say they have driven even when they found this difficult due to sleepiness. Not surprisingly, lack of sleep is related to increased risk of accidents while driving (Carskadon et al., 2004; Millman, 2005).

How much is sleepiness under adolescents' control? Couldn't they simply go to bed earlier? The answer to this is both "yes" and "no." Patterns of sleeping and waking are dependent on two interrelated processes, one of which is more closely tied to personal habits and the second to the circadian rhythm established by the 24-hour cycle of daylight and darkness. In the first of these processes, the need for sleep depends on how long one has been awake: the more hours awake, the greater the need for sleep; this is especially true for younger adolescents (Taylor et al., 2005). This cycle interacts with a second one that is independent of the amount of sleep one has had. Instead, it is regulated by the secretion of melatonin, a hormone released in greater amounts as it becomes dark; prepubertal children are able to fall asleep earlier than adolescents since their bodies release melatonin earlier in the evening. Additionally, the need for sleep builds faster during waking hours for prepubertal children than for adolescents (Crowley et al., 2006; Taylor et al., 2005).

Even though circadian rhythms can't be easily changed, a number of environmental factors affecting sleep merit closer attention. Parents, for instance, are less likely to set bedtimes for adolescents than they are for younger chil-

● Figure 3.13 **Distribution of school-night total sleep: Early- versus late-starting middle schools** Twice as many of the students who attended a late-starting school (8:37 a.m.) got 9 or more hours of sleep on school nights than those who attended an early-starting school (7:15 a.m.). (After Wolfson et al., 2007.)

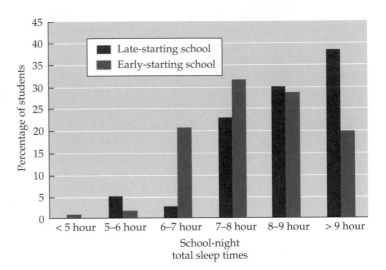

dren, being more likely to let adolescents stay up to finish homework, watch television or simply wait until they feel sleepy (Fuligni & Hardway, 2006; Millman, 2005). Additionally, adolescents who work 20 or more hours a week go to bed later, get less sleep, and report more sleepiness during the day. Not surprisingly, they also report using stimulants such as caffeine and cigarettes more (Millman, 2005).

Ironically, the school day starts earlier for most high school students than it does for younger middle-school and elementary students. Many schools start as early as 7:15 a.m., even though earlier starting times are associated with greater sleepiness during the day, difficulty concentrating on school work, increased likelihood of falling asleep in class, and poorer attendance (Crowley et al., 2006; Wahlstrom, 2002). Amy Wolfson (2007), at College of the Holy Cross, and her associates compared adolescents attending either of two middle schools, one starting at 7:15 a.m. and the other at 8:37 a.m., and found that students attending the school that started later got more hours of sleep on school nights, experienced less sleepiness during the school day, and were tardy much less often. Equally, if not more important, they found that starting time was related to how well students did academically. Eighth graders who started school at 8:37 a.m. had significantly higher grades than those attending the school that started at 7:15 a.m. (**Figure 3.13**).

Race and ethnicity are also associated with the amount of sleep adolescents get. Emma Adam, Emily Snell and Patricia Pendry (2007), at Northwestern University, asked a nationally representative sample of children and adolescents to keep a diary on randomly selected days, recording all that they had done that day, when they went to bed, and when they woke up. During weekdays, African American adolescents reported less time spent sleeping than European Americans, due in part to going to bed later, but also to longer travel times to school. For all adolescents, stricter family rules (e.g. watching television, eating sweets, after-school activities) were related to getting more sleep, as were eating meals

Being active during adolescence promotes physical health and contributes to psychological well-being.

together and the emotional warmth of adolescents' relationships with their parents, both of which suggest the importance of a supportive family structure.

Physical Activity

How much exercise adolescents get can profoundly affect their health and well-being. Regular physical activity not only contributes to adolescents' health through building and maintaining bones and muscles and controlling weight, but also is related to lower blood pressure and cholesterol levels. Being physically active also contributes to psychological well-being by reducing stress and anxiety, and improving adolescents' self-esteem (CDC, 2005d).

How active are adolescents? Most adolescents engage in some form of physical activity on a daily basis. However, only slightly over a third of those in high school are likely to meet the recommended level of physical activity (being active enough to raise their heart rate for at least an hour a day, and doing this five or more days a week). Additionally, the likelihood of being this active decreases with age, dropping from 38% of 9th graders to 30% of 12th graders, and differs with sex and ethnicity. Boys (44%) are more active than girls (26%); white adolescents are more active (37%) than either black (31%) or Hispanic (30%) adolescents (CDC, 2008b).

One might wonder why these figures for physical activity are not higher, since most schools require physical education classes, and many adolescents participate in team sports (a topic which we will look at in Chapter 13). Many schools, however, exempt students from PE for any number of reasons, such as participation in school or community sports or even in community service activities. Additionally, whereas nearly all schools require a physical education course in the 6th grade, this percentage drops to less than half by the 12th grade (**Figure 3.14**) (Brener et al., 2009).

Another factor that limits the extent of physical activity for some adolescents is their physical environment, namely living in a low-income—and for many, higher crime—neighborhood (Connell & Janevic, 2003; Krieger & Fee, 1994; Romero, 2005). In such neighborhoods, factors such as traffic, poor air quality, inadequate public transportation, or the presence of gangs can make it difficult getting to or being safe in recreational areas. Adolescents in such neighborhoods are likely to be more physically active when they can spend time in after-school programs where they feel safe with adults present (Romero, 2005). Although a majority of schools nationwide (71.6%) open their facilities for use before or after school hours and on weekends (CDC, 2005d), responsible adults may need to be present at these in order for adolescents to feel safe using them. Given the lifelong health benefits of physical activity, federal and state funding to ensure safe recreational centers in all communities, in addition to providing daily PE classes in middle and high schools, needs to be reexamined as a national priority.

Physical activity assumes added importance when we consider another aspect of adolescents' health and well-being, that of maintaining healthy weight.

Overweight

Adolescents are considered to be **overweight** if their weight is at or above the 95th percentile for their BMI-for-age (**body mass index**), and at *risk* of being overweight if they are between the 85th and 95th percentiles (CDC, 2005e). One's BMI is easy to compute; the formula for this is:

$$BMI = \frac{\text{weight in pounds}}{(\text{height in inches})^2} \times 703$$

and BMI-for-age charts can be found on the Internet at the Centers for Disease Control and Prevention Web site.

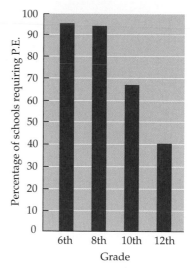

● **Figure 3.14   Percentage of schools requiring physical education**   Nearly all schools require students in the 6th grade to take a course in physical education, but fewer than half of the schools require 12th graders to take a physical education course. (After Brener et al., 2009.)

overweight   Individuals are considered to be overweight when their weight is at or above the 95th percentile for their body mass index.

body mass index (BMI)   One's weight in pounds divided by the square of one's height in inches times 703 ({weight in pounds/(height in inches)²} × 703). Since body fatness varies with age and sex, percentiles for BMI are specific to age and gender.

The number of adolescents who are overweight has tripled since the 1970's, with an estimated 17.6% of 12- to 19-year-olds currently overweight, and another 16.5% who are at risk of becoming overweight (Ogden et al., 2008). Adolescents who are overweight are more likely to be so as adults as well, thereby increasing their lifetime risk of a number of diseases such as hypertension, heart disease, diabetes, and certain forms of cancer (CDC, 2009a). The frequency of being overweight differs with ethnicity, being more common among Mexican American (21.1%) and African American (22.9%) adolescents than among European American adolescents (16%) (Ogden et al., 2008). For a creative approach to this problem, see **Box 3.1**.

Overweight adolescents tend to have somewhat different eating patterns than their average-weight peers. They are more likely to eat irregularly, miss meals, and snack—habits which make it difficult to maintain a balance between hunger and satiation. Overweight adolescents are also more likely to eat rapidly, to eat somewhat larger portions, and to eat food that is denser in calories (Lucas, 1988; Wadden et al., 2002). But perhaps the biggest difference is in how active they are, not how much they eat. Overweight adolescents are considerably less active than their peers of average weight and thus are less likely to burn off the excess calories they are taking in.

The relationship between overweight and inactivity highlights the importance of exercise in weight reduction programs. Exercise increases the body's metabolism, allowing the body to burn excess calories more rapidly, and in moderate amounts, exercise also depresses appetite. Dieting alone can have paradoxical effects, frequently causing a preoccupation with food, which in turn can prompt reactive overeating. Ellen Satter (1988) recommends programs that foster a reliance on internal cues rather than on external constraints, such as counting calories and diets. The latter force one to continually think about food and ways to avoid it, with some of the same difficulties experienced when trying not to think of a pink elephant!

Adolescents attempting to lose weight often have unrealistic expectations. Many view their weight as central to all of their problems and expect that once they lose weight, their problems will be solved—they will become popular, make the team, and so forth. When their problems do not roll away with the pounds, adolescents can become frustrated and fall off their diets. The most successful programs are multifaceted. The success of a weight control program for adolescents almost always depends on successfully integrating the family into the program (Epstein, 1994; McVey et al., 2002).

Health Care

How likely are adolescents to receive health care when they need it? A number of factors are important.

As an age group adolescents and young adults experience poorer access to health care than young children or older adults, although some of this may be a problem of *perceived* access. Adolescents report difficulty knowing where to go, finding transportation, anxiety as to what might be done, not wanting their parents to know, and not having insurance coverage (Samargia et al., 2006).

Most of these problems are intensified for adolescents living in rural communities or other non-urban settings. Barbara Elliott and Jean Larson (2004) found higher rates of foregone care for these adolescents than for those living in urban settings. The 10th graders in their study reported reasons similar to those given by other adolescents. But for small town and rural adolescents, costs of medical care can be more serious barriers, since adolescents in rural areas are less likely to be insured (Health Access Survey, 2003). Confidential-

BOX 3.1 In More Depth

The Edible Schoolyard

Two generations ago, when a presidential commission revealed that U.S. schoolchildren were physically unfit, schools and educators responded by building gymnasiums, adding courses in physical education to the curriculum, and hiring teachers trained to teach them (Waters, 2005a). Forty years later, the health of schoolchildren is again compromised. Nearly one-third of 12- to 19-year-olds are seriously overweight, placing them at risk for diseases such as hypertension, heart disease, and diabetes (CDC, 2005e; Hedley et al., 2004; Irwin, 2004; Muntner et al., 2004). Yet despite the seriousness of this problem, we have done little in our schools to address the situation.

The Edible Schoolyard, an innovative program located on the campus of Martin Luther King Jr. Middle School in Berkeley, California, may be a first step in changing that. The Edible Schoolyard is a nonprofit program that grew out of a conversation between chef and author Alice Waters and Neil Smith, former principal of the school. The student body at King Middle School had grown too large for the school cafeteria to accommodate them all, and the cafeteria had been closed. For lunch, students bought packaged food sold at the other end of a parking lot adjacent to the school. Rather than viewing this situation as just one more problem to be solved in the same old way, Waters and Smith saw an opportunity for a bold experiment—they turned the parking lot into a garden.

In The Edible Schoolyard, students learn how to plant, cultivate, harvest, and prepare their own food. Learning doesn't stop there, however. These experiences are integrated into the academic curriculum, transforming what otherwise might remain as bookish facts, such as the nitrogen cycle, into meaningful knowledge. Similarly, concepts taught in class provide information they will need in maintaining the garden. The Edible Schoolyard program is supported not only by students and teachers, but also by parents, volunteers, local farmers, and neighbors committed to the success of the project. An additional benefit of this support is that as students come into contact with others who share their interest in this project, they learn the importance of community and of their mutual dependence on each other and their environment.

So, what is lunch at King Middle School? It's not processed. It's not eaten alone. And it's not consumed mindlessly. In fact, at this middle school, lunch starts well before students ever sit down to eat. It's homegrown, in soil that's been mulched and cultivated until it's soft enough to hold the seeds students tuck beneath the surface. It's food that adolescents, working together, have planted and grown. And it's adolescents, sitting and talking together at tables, savoring their food—and their accomplishments.

As Alice Waters is ready to point out, "A school lunch curriculum is not a quick fix for the obesity epidemic. But by bringing kids into another kind of relationship with their food, we can bring about a deep and lasting change in the way they feel about themselves" (Waters, 2005b).

Information on The Edible Schoolyard is available at http://www.edibleschoolyard.org

ity is also a larger concern. In small towns, everyone's a neighbor—including the person scheduling your doctor's appointment and the pharmacist filling the prescription.

Another significant factor influencing the accessibility of health care is health care coverage. Presently, over 8 million children and adolescents in the United States do not have health insurance. Yet over half of these could receive

poor families   Families with incomes below the federal poverty level.

low-income families   Families with incomes no greater than twice the federal poverty level.

free health insurance either through Medicaid or the Children's Health Insurance Program (CHIP). CHIP provides health insurance to children in families whose annual incomes disqualify them from receiving Medicaid, yet are not high enough to purchase health insurance. In order for youth to be covered under Medicaid or CHIP, though, parents must apply for this coverage, and many parents are unaware that their children are eligible (Children's Defense Fund, 2008).

The Children's Defense Fund, established by Marion Edelman, has developed an outreach project, called SHOUT (Student Health Outreach), in which high school and college student volunteers help low-income families enroll children for free health care coverage (CDF, 2005). The Student Health Outreach Project is active in a number of states, and individuals interested in starting a local Project or joining one can get information on the Children's Defense Fund website.

Poverty

Perhaps the single most important factor affecting the health and well-being of adolescents in the United States is the presence of poverty—in their families and in their neighborhoods. These adolescents live with conditions over which they have no control, yet which constitute significant risks to their well-being. For a look at a program designed to increase the well-being of adolescents in low-income neighborhoods, see **Box 3.2**. Approximately 15% of U.S. adolescents live in **poor families**, with incomes below the federal poverty level, and another 35% in **low-income families** with incomes no greater than twice the federal poverty level (National Center for Children in Poverty, 2009).

Whether poor or low-income, these adolescents face many of the same health concerns. They experience greater exposure to toxins, more air pollution, inferior drinking water, more noise pollution, poorer housing, greater exposure to asthma-related allergens both inside and outside their homes, and live in more hazardous neighborhoods (Evans, 2004). Understandably, the conditions of poverty are strongly related to stress (Chen et al., 2004), and to elevated levels of risk-related injuries (Evans, 2004).

Solutions to the health concerns of these adolescents will require the nation's creative attention since the conditions contributing to their poverty do not necessarily reside within their families, but instead result from broader societal conditions (Ozawa, 2004). For instance, it is simply not the case that poverty can be explained away by suggesting that parents, or adolescents, are unwilling to work. In most poor or low-income families, either one parent, or frequently both parents, works a full-time job! It's also the case that most parents who are not employed full-time indicate this is because they are unable to find a job (NCCP, 2003).

A number of obvious policy implications arise from these data. As the U.S. Department of Health and Human Services points out, support for low-income families will necessitate institutional changes at the broadest levels of society (CDC, 2004b). One of the first of these changes would be to create more jobs. As Harvard sociologist William Wilson (1996) , points out, there is a new inner-city urban poverty. It is a jobless poverty. That is, poverty has always existed in poor neighborhoods—by definition. But in the past, a majority of the adults in these neighborhoods held jobs. This is no longer true. In Wilson's words, "the United States is hemorrhaging jobs." He suggests the establishment of a federal jobs program similar to the program that got our nation back on its feet following the Depression (Wilson, 1996).

Go to the Adolescence Companion Website at www.sinauer.com/cobb for quizzes, flashcards, summaries, and other study resources.

Research Focus

Randomized Versus Quasi-Experimental Designs: What's in a Name?
Communication across the Ages

Joey was beginning to like his name. He liked the soft way it sounded when Mrs. Thomas spoke to him, even though this was usually when they were talking about his homework. Funny, a year ago he would never have thought of doing homework, or going to a museum with his class or even to school basketball games. But he did now, and his mom did too, every now and then, when Mrs. Thomas called her. For that matter, a year ago he would never have thought he'd even know anyone as old as Mrs. Thomas. She must be at least 60, he thought, as he watched her coming into the room with a pencil and another piece of pie.

Joey lives in a low-income, high-crime neighborhood in Philadelphia. His sixth-grade class is part of an intergenerational mentoring program in which older members of the community, such as Mrs. Thomas, volunteer time with students, doing things such as helping with homework or school projects, going to games or cultural events, and taking part in community service activities. The purpose of the program is to increase the protective factors in the lives of high-risk children. By working with these students, mentors serve as friends and role models, as well as advocates and challengers, helping to build the students' self-esteem, confidence, and skills they need to stay drug-free.

In addition to mentoring, this unique program involves students in community service, offers classroom-based instruction in life skills, and includes a workshop for parents. The community service aspect of the program enables these students to see how they can help others, giving them a sense of personal and social responsibility and contributing to their self-esteem. In contrast, the classroom instruction teaches skills applicable to students' real life problems within their families and with their friends and with peer pressure. Finally, the workshop for parents helps the students' parents develop more effective parenting skills and more positive ways of interacting within the family. Essential to the success of the program are the teachers and school personnel who have been trained in its implementation and evaluation.

Programs like this are expensive—not only in money, but also in a community's investment of its

Carefully designed pretests and posttests are important components of randomized experiments designed to assess a program's effectiveness.

limited reserves of passion and hope. How might one determine whether an intergenerational mentoring program such as this one was effective?

A Randomized Design

Leonard LoSciuto, Amy Rajala, Tara Townsend, and Andrea Taylor (1996), at Temple University, employed a randomized pretest-posttest control group design. Three sixth-grade classes per school were randomly selected from all of the sixth-grade classes in schools that were willing to participate in the study (almost all of them). Within each school, each class was randomly assigned to one of three conditions:

1. Students received the complete program of mentoring, community service, instruction in life skills, and parent workshops.
2. Students received everything but mentoring.
3. Students received no intervention at all. They were the control condition.

At the beginning of the academic year, prior to starting the intervention program, all the students were pretested on a variety of measures assessing their knowledge, attitudes, and behavior related to the program goals. All students were tested again with a series of posttests at the end of the academic year. This type of experimental design, because it randomly assigns subjects to conditions and uses a separate control comparison (see Research Focus Box 1.1), in addition to the comparison between pretest and posttest performance, has high internal validity (see the Research Focus "Internal and External Validity"

(continued on next page)

BOX 3.2 *continued*

on the Web site). This internal validity enables the investigators to conclude that the changes they observe are actually due to the program and not to some other factor.

Because the students are randomly assigned to conditions and each student has the same chance as any other of being assigned to each group, one can be reasonably certain that the three groups do not differ in any systematic way at the outset of the program. Additionally, pretesting students before they begin the intervention program makes it possible to determine whether equivalence has, in fact, been achieved.

Pretesting offers other advantages as well. Pretests allow investigators to assess the extent to which individuals change over time. Thus, if some students are responsive to the treatment whereas others are not, pretesting may suggest clues, which can be followed up in subsequent research, as to why some are more responsive than others. Pretesting is also useful when subjects drop out of the program, as is common for lengthy programs. Loss of subjects in this manner is known as subject mortality and is a potential source of bias if it is systematically related to the experimental conditions. For instance, poorer students might be least responsive to the demands of mentoring and community service and most likely to drop out, leaving proportionately more of the better students in the intervention group. In this way, even interventions that have no effect may appear to result in improved performance. By inspecting the pretests of students who drop out, however, one can determine whether they differ from the students who remain in the program. Pretesting also has a disadvantage. It can sensitize subjects to the purpose of the investigation, making it possible for them to figure out what is expected of them and potentially affecting the way they respond to the experimental treatment.

Quasi-Experimental Design

Many intervention programs are not able to randomly assign subjects to experimental and control conditions. Research about such programs is termed quasi-experimental because it relies only on comparisons of pretest and posttest performance (see Chapter 2). A number of problems exist with quasi-experimental designs. Because there is no control condition, we don't know how to interpret the findings. Suppose, for instance, posttest scores are no better than pretest scores. Can we conclude that the program is ineffective? Not necessarily. It's always possible that performance could have declined during that time and that only because of the program did scores remain the same. Similarly,

increases in performance on the posttest do not lend themselves to a simple interpretation. Several potential confounds exist. These can be due to maturation, testing, history, instrument decay, or statistical regression.

Maturation reflects any systematic changes that occur over time. These can be long-term, such as the developmental changes in intelligence discussed in Chapters 4 and 10, or short-term, such as changes due to fatigue, boredom, or practice. A testing effect reflects any changes that occur due to familiarity with the tests. Because pretests usually involve the same type of questions as posttests and frequently measure knowledge about the same subject matter, testing effects are likely. A history effect refers to events that occur between testings that can affect the behavior being measured. For example, at the same time as the intervention program, television might run a series of public service spots featuring famous athletes who warn kids against the use of drugs. Instrument decay reflects changes in the measures used; these are especially likely when people are the "instruments"; for example, counselors or teachers can become more practiced over time, or they may change their standards in other ways. Statistical regression can occur when students are selected for a program because they are atypical, that is, because their scores are either especially low or high. Because no two tests can ever be perfectly correlated, most scores will change somewhat. Students who are selected because of especially low scores will look like they have improved due to the program, but because they were at the bottom of the distribution, their scores could only go up. By the same token, students with especially high scores on a pretest would show a drop in performance on the posttest. In each case scores "drift," or regress, toward the mean of the distribution, because that is where most scores are to be found.

None of these confounds, however, threaten the validity of the research of LoSciuto and his colleagues about the intergenerational mentoring program. These investigators found that students who received all four components of the program were likely to do best. They were more likely to react appropriately when offered drugs, were absent from school less, and had more positive attitudes toward school, community service, and their own futures. There is also some indication that mentoring resulted in increased feelings of self-worth and well-being and reduced sadness and loneliness.

Source: After LoSciuto et al. 1996.

SUMMARY and KEY TERMS

The Neuroendocrine System

The Neuroendocrine System: This system consists of glands within the body that produce hormones and structures within the central nervous system that regulate their activity. Neuroendocrine activity is regulated by a feedback system that controls the timing of puberty.
neuroendocrine system, hormones, androgens, testosterone, estrogens, estradiol, progesterone, adrenarche, gonadarche

Prepuberty: Adrenarche: Puberty occurs over two distinct phases, and the first, adrenarche, begins at 6 to 8 years of age and involves increased production of adrenal androgens that contribute to a number of pubertal changes—such as skeletal growth.
adrenal androgens

Puberty: Gonadarche: The second phase of puberty, gonadarche, begins several years later and involves increased production of hormones governing physical and sexual maturation.
hypothalamus, gonadotropin-releasing hormone (GnRH), anterior pituitary, gonads, luteinizing hormone (LH), follicle-stimulating hormone (FSH), GnRH pulse generator, kisspeptin, leptin

The Physical Changes of Puberty

Recollections of an Adolescent Girl: In girls, the appearance of pubic hair is one of the first visible signs of pubertal change. Breasts begin to develop at about the same time, along with the uterus, vagina, and ovaries.
primary sex characteristics, secondary sex characteristics

Recollections of an Adolescent Boy: For boys, who begin puberty an average of two years later than girls, the first sign of change is an enlargement of the scrotum, followed by the appearance of pubic hair. The penis starts to grow a year later. The height spurt precedes a change in voice and the appearance of facial and underarm hair.

The Growth Spurt: The growth spurt is a period of rapid growth in height, regulated by the growth hormone and the sex hormones. In girls, the most rapid growth occurs in the year preceding and the year following menarche. Boys reach their peak growth rate two years later than girls and grow for a longer period of time.
growth spurt

The Reproductive System: For girls, the uterus, the ovaries, and the vagina all increase in size. The ovaries increase their production of female sex hormones, and these hormones, with FSH and LH, stimulate the development of ova, or eggs. FSH and LH also stimulate the testes to develop in boys and produce male sex hormones. These, along with FSH, stimulate the testes to produce sperm. The penis doubles in length and thickness during puberty.
ovaries, ova, uterus, vagina, cervix, hymen, clitoris, glans, shaft, prepuce, testes, sperm, circumcision, female genital, mutilation, outer labia

Menarche: Menarche, the onset of menstrual periods, occurs midway through puberty. Most girls reach menarche in their 12th year. The menstrual cycle is regulated by a feedback loop involving the ovaries, the anterior pituitary, and the hypothalamus.
menarche, anovulatory

(continued)

SUMMARY and KEY TERMS *continued*

Spermarche: In boys, the presence of testosterone and other hormones stimulates the testes to produce sperm. Most boys experience spermarche, the first ejaculation of seminal fluid, by mid-adolescence.
spermarche, nocturnal emission

The Secular Trend: Puberty begins earlier today than in past generations. This downward shift in age is called the secular trend. Adolescents also grow faster and grow to be larger than in the past. Improved nutrition is almost certainly an important cause of the accelerated growth patterns.
secular trend

The Psychological and Social Implications of Puberty

Heightened Emotionality: Adolescence is a time of heightened emotionality. Adolescents experience more intense emotions than their parents and report a wider range of emotions.

Relationships with Parents: Adolescents who experience their parents as warm and loving experience fewer emotional or behavioral problems. For most adolescents, however, closeness with parents temporarily decreases and conflict increases. Ethnicity may be a factor, though, as research suggests puberty may involve less conflict with parents for Hispanic vs. European American males.

The Timing of Change: Early and Late Maturers

Early and Late Maturing Boys: Differences in the timing of pubertal change are referred to as asynchrony. Comparisons of early and late maturing boys find initial social advantages for early maturing boys, but also more adjustment problems.
asynchrony, early maturation, late maturation

Early and Late Maturing Girls: In contrast to boys, early maturation in girls carries few initial advantages. Like boys, however, early maturing girls experience more problems of adjustment. Ethnic differences suggest these are less likely among African Americans. Three explanations have been offered for the more disruptive effects of early timing, particularly with respect to girls: the maturational deviance hypothesis, the stage termination hypothesis, and the adult status hypothesis.
self-esteem, maturational deviance hypothesis, stage termination hypothesis, adult status hypothesis

Body Image and Self-Esteem: Pubertal changes bring about changes in adolescents' body images. How satisfied adolescents are with their bodies is also influenced by their perceptions of how they are evaluated by others. Females generally have less positive body images than males.
body image

Health and Well-Being

Nutrition: Despite the increased nutritional needs introduced by rapid growth, many adolescents eat erratically. Nearly half of all meals eaten in the U.S. are eaten in restaurants, most of which are fast-food chains. The biggest problem is not failing to get necessary nutrients, but getting too many other things along with them. Fast foods taste good because of excess fats, sugars, and salt; but these ingredients add calories—and with these, increased risk of becoming overweight.

Sleep: Patterns of sleep change as adolescents enter puberty. Adolescents fall asleep later and have difficulty waking up early—a pattern at odds with most high schools,

SUMMARY and KEY TERMS

which start earlier than middle or elementary schools. Consequently, a majority of adolescents fail to get enough sleep during the school week, and experience more difficulty paying attention and staying awake to study than do those just a few years younger.

Physical Activity: Regular physical activity contributes to adolescents' health through building and maintaining bones and muscles and controlling weight, and by reducing stress and improving self-esteem. Even so, older adolescents are less active than younger ones.

Overweight: The number of adolescents who are overweight has tripled since the 1970s, with an estimated 17.6% of 12- to 19-year-olds currently overweight, and another 16.5% who are at risk of becoming overweight. Overweight adolescents are more likely to eat irregularly and faster, and exercise less than adolescents who are not overweight. This relationship highlights the importance of exercise in weight reduction programs.
overweight and body mass index (BMI)

Health Care: As an age group adolescents and young adults report poorer access to health care than young children or older adults. Problems are magnified for those living in rural communities or non-urban settings who are less likely to have health care insurance. Presently, approximately 9 million children and adolescents in the U.S. do not have health insurance. Yet more than half of these could receive free health insurance either through Medicaid or the Children's Health Insurance Program (CHIP).

Poverty: Perhaps the single most important factor affecting the health and well-being of adolescents in the U.S. is poverty. Approximately 20% of U.S. adolescents live in poor families, with incomes below the federal poverty level, and another 12% in low-income families. These adolescents experience greater exposure to toxins, both inside and outside their homes, and live in more hazardous neighborhoods. The conditions of poverty are strongly related to stress, and to elevated levels of risk-related injuries. Solutions to their health needs will require the nation's creative attention, since the conditions contributing to their poverty do not necessarily reside within their families.
poor families, low-income families

Yuan-Pin

—Pete, to his friends—read alternatives "b" and "c" again. He knew this material. He had distinguished his family with good marks in this very subject before coming to this country. Yet he couldn't understand the question. The two choices seemed the same to him. He could feel the heat rising in his face as the words danced and mocked him. Blindly, he marked "c" and moved on. The bell would ring soon. So much depended on him. He would have to study his English again tonight after he and his father closed the shop. No time for hanging out, for video games or the sitcoms his friends watched each night. No wonder they thought he was a loner. Sometimes he thought he was crazy. How could he explain one world to the other? Or to himself?

Sehti's mind wandered as she stared at the quiz. She was still angry that she hadn't been able to study more last night. She'd had to help her mother

The Cognitive Changes of Adolescence

with dinner. Why had her uncle and aunt picked that night to visit? And why couldn't her brothers have helped? They didn't have half the homework she had, and they never had to help. Her mother said it was women's work, that she should leave her brothers alone. The bell—oh, no! She quickly marked alternative "b." Why couldn't she concentrate?

Joe looked at the quiz: 15 questions. He knew the answers to all of them—all but number 11. Actually, it was the way the question was worded. He could make an argument for either "b" or "c." Joe loved junior high. Math, social studies, drama, English lit.—each left him more excited than the last. By the end of the day, he was filled with ideas, ideas he framed easily in words that he spoke with quiet confidence. The bell! He chose "b" and wondered how successful he'd be in convincing Mr. Allen of his reasoning if his teacher had

Chapter Overview

You have just met three students, each competent, each standing on the threshold of a new world of thought and experience. All adolescents embark on the journey these three are beginning. Not all travel the same distance. Yuan-Pin, Sehti, and Joe probably will not either. They aren't likely to get the same grade on this quiz or to do equally well in junior high. Is this unfair? Differences in their grades will not necessarily reflect their capabilities. Yuan-Pin is still learning English; he doesn't have a chance to show what he knows. Sehti's concentration is scattered by conflicting demands at home and at school. Intellectual performance almost always reflects more than what one knows. Motives, interests, and even expectations held by others can affect performance.

The brain continues to develop in adolescence. Three related processes play a central role. Cell proliferation results in an excess of brain cells and their interconnections, synaptic pruning systematically eliminates those that are infrequently used, and myelination of remaining pathways results in more efficient and faster neural conduction. The prefrontal cortex continues to develop throughout adolescence, which makes new cognitive controls possible. The limbic system, involved in processing social and emotional information, develops earlier than the prefrontal cortex. Differences in the developmental trajectories of these two regions may explain adolescent risk taking, particularly when peers are present.

Brain development ushers in new forms of thought. Adolescents can plan for the future, imagine the impossible, catch multiple meanings to words and situations, understand nuance, follow a philosophical discussion, and respond to a simple question with an answer that would make the captain of a debating team proud. We will look at the nature of these changes and at explanations that have been offered for them, as well as consider conditions that affect intellectual performance in adolescents such as Yuan-Pin, Sehti, and Joe.

Piaget and Kegan assume that we actively construct what we know of the world, and that this understanding is organized in qualitatively different ways at different points in life. In adolescence, thought becomes abstract, enabling adolescents to consider a world of possibilities as well as their actual circumstances. Vygotsky and Rogoff also assume that children construct their understanding of the world, but emphasize the social nature of this process: Understanding increases by virtue of working alongside others who are more knowledgeable and more skilled.

The psychometric approach gives us a second way of understanding intellectual development. This approach views cognitive development as a continuous growth in the abilities, already present, that underlie general intelligence. We will look at how intelligence tests are constructed, what they measure, and at some of the problems they introduce when not interpreted correctly.

The greatest strength of intelligence tests is in predicting academic success. This strength is also a weakness. The paradox arises from our inability to distinguish precisely what success reflects: the general abilities presumed to be tapped by the tests? Or the degree of familiarity with the culture required to understand the questions? Just as Yuan-Pin experienced difficulty on his math quiz, he would have difficulty with many of the items on an intelligence test.

Robert Sternberg speaks of intelligence in terms of achieving life goals, and analyzes intellectual functioning into three components: one that organizes strategies for thinking, another that does the actual work, and a third that gathers new information when needed. Howard Gardner suggests intelligence takes a number of forms. He divides intelligence into areas as diverse as bodily-kinesthetic intelligence, logical-mathematical intelligence, and naturalist intelligence.

A final way of explaining intellectual development, an information processing approach, focuses on age-related changes in adolescents' use strategies for holding onto and retrieving information, and in their ability to monitor their thinking.

Throughout the chapter, we will look at the implications of intellectual development for everyday life. In the classroom, adolescents are better able to reason through problems, to think like scientists, and to develop more effective study skills. In their everyday relationships they can think about themselves in new ways, as well as imagine the thoughts of others, understand social nuance, experience new emotions, and even argue more effectively.

Development of the Brain in Adolescence

The brain of a 6-year-old is approximately the same size and shape as that of an adolescent, or of an adult for that matter. In fact, the brain changes relatively little, either in size or shape, from middle childhood to adolescence, reaching approximately 90% of adult size by the age of 5 (Purves et al., 2008). But to stop there would be like comparing an MG with a Ferrari simply because both are sports cars. Even without turning the key, differences become evident once you open the hood. What should we be looking for "under the hood" of the adolescent brain? What changes are taking place?

Cell Proliferation, Synaptic Pruning, and Myelination

The developmental changes that take place in the brain, other than in size and shape, are so significant that we can speak of an actual "remodeling" of the adolescent brain. Three related processes play a central role in re-forming the adolescent brain: cell proliferation, synaptic pruning, and myelination. As might be expected, these changes contribute substantially to the way adolescents think and act (Paus, 2005; Sisk & Zehr, 2005; Yurgelun-Todd, 2007).

Cell proliferation consists of the overproduction of both neurons and their interconnections. Simply put, more neurons are produced than are needed. The resulting mass of cell bodies, dendrites, and axons is referred to as gray matter. The increase in **cortical gray matter** follows an inverted-U function, reaching a peak in volume in adolescence and then declining. Cell proliferation occurs at different rates in different regions of the brain (**Figure 4.1**). Overall, this growth in brain volume peaks earlier in girls, at 11.5 years, than it does in boys, at 14.5 years (Lenroot et al., 2007).

Synaptic pruning consists of the selective elimination of the least used cells and their connections. The selective retention of frequently used cells and the elimination of relatively unused cells allow neural development to be "fine-tuned" by experience and, in this way, adapt the architecture of the brain to the life circumstances of the individual (Greenough et al., 1987; Sisk & Zehr, 2005).

An additional, related process that continues throughout adolescence is the **myelination** of the neural pathways that connect different areas within the brain. Myelinated pathways have a whitish appearance, giving the name of **white matter** to areas of the brain through which these tracts pass (**Figure 4.2**). Myelin, a fatty substance that coats the axons of neurons, functions much the way insulation around a wire does, by reducing interference from neighboring activity and enabling impulses to be conducted more rapidly (**Figure 4.3**). Myelination results in faster and

cell proliferation The overproduction of neurons and their interconnections.

cortical gray matter Regions within the brain consisting of cell bodies, dendrites, and primarily unmyelinated axons.

synaptic pruning The selective elimination of brain cells (neurons) and their connections.

myelination The formation of a fatty sheath surrounding a nerve fiber (axon), which increases the speed of neural conduction.

white matter Brain areas containing myelinated pathways.

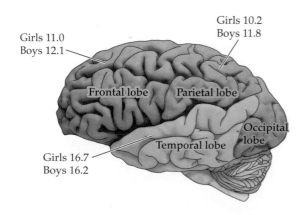

● **Figure 4.1 Changes in gray matter density in different regions of the brain** Cortical gray matter first increases, due to cell proliferation, and then decreases, due to synaptic pruning. These two processes occur at different rates in different areas of the brain. Overall, this growth peaks earlier in girls than it does in boys. (After Lenroot & Giedd, 2006.)

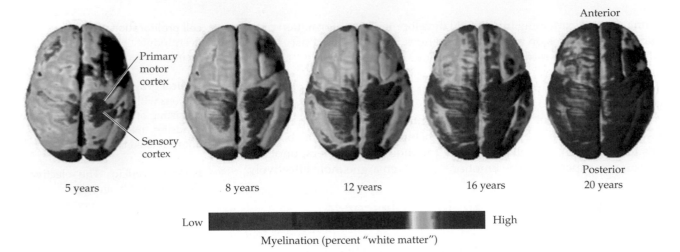

Low ——————————— High

Myelination (percent "white matter")

● **Figure 4.2** **Progressive myelination of cortex with age** Myelination of neural pathways results in more efficient communication among different regions of the brain. Myelination (purple areas) increases with age. (From Lenroot & Giedd, 2006.)

prefrontal cortex Region of the cortex located behind the forehead involved in abstract thought.

executive functions Mental activities, such as decision making, evaluating, and planning, that are regulated by the prefrontal cortex.

more efficient communication among different regions of the brain. Although most myelination is largely completed by about age 7, an age at which children show decided shifts in intellectual performance, myelination of some pathways continues well into adulthood (Lenroot et al., 2007).

The Prefrontal Cortex: Thinking Like an Executive

Synaptic pruning and myelination progress at different rates in different regions of the brain. One of the last areas of the brain to undergo these changes is the **prefrontal cortex**, an area which lies at the very front of the brain, right behind the forehead. This area of the brain is primarily responsible for what might be called "**executive functions**," such as decision making, evaluating, and planning. Development of this region of the brain enables adolescents to hold several choices in mind while evaluating the alternatives, to think of and

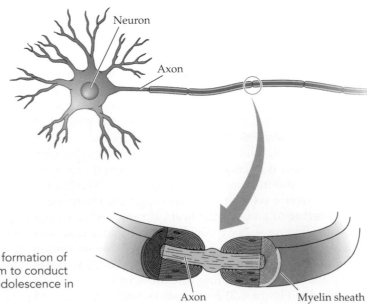

● **Figure 4.3** **Myelin sheath coating axon** The formation of a myelin sheath around neural fibers enables them to conduct impulses more rapidly. Myelination continues in adolescence in regions of the brain involved in abstract thought.

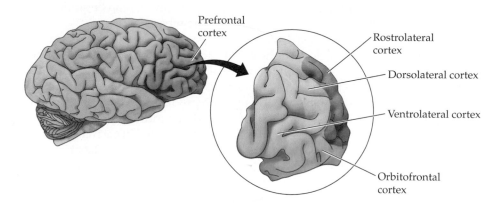

Prefrontal cortex

Rostrolateral cortex

Dorsolateral cortex

Ventrolateral cortex

Orbitofrontal cortex

● **Figure 4.4   Areas of the prefrontal cortex involved in the use of rules of increasing complexity**   Progressive maturation of areas within the prefrontal cortex enables adolescents to adapt their use of rules to fit current circumstances (ventrolateral and dorsolateral cortex) and to multitask (rostrolateral cortex).

then follow rules for guiding their behavior, to make plans and work toward long-range goals, and to stay at a task while ignoring distractions (Bunge & Zelazo, 2006; Purves et al., 2008).

The prefrontal cortex has a number of sub-regions, and as each develops with age, thinking becomes more flexible. An example of the increasing flexibility that occurs with age can be seen in the types of rules that become accessible for guiding behavior (Wright et al., 2008). Young children, in whom only the first of several regions has fully developed (i.e., orbitofrontal, see **Figure 4.4**) are able to follow *univalent* rules, which require them to give only one response to each of any events, for example, "If the light is red, stop" or "If the light is yellow, proceed with caution." However, they find it difficult to do what adolescents, as well as adults, can do with relative ease—to respond to an event in either of two ways depending on which of several other conditions is present. That is, adolescents can follow *bivalent* or *conditional* rules that require them to modulate their behavior depending upon the circumstances— for instance, "If the light is yellow *and no other cars are approaching the intersection*, proceed with caution" or "If the light is yellow *and other cars are approaching the intersection*, stop." This more complex behavior becomes possible when additional regions of the cortex have matured (ventrolateral and dorsolateral) (see Figure 4.4) (Bunge & Zelazo, 2006).

Even adolescents and adults, however, have difficulty maintaining their performance when switching from one type of task to another. Doing things well, in other words, requires not only knowing *how* to do each of them, but also *which* of them one is to do. Moving back and forth from one task to the next is another executive function. The region of the prefrontal cortex involved in this activity (rostrolateral) is at the very front of the cortex and is among the last to develop (Crone et al., 2006; Lenroot & Giedd, 2006).

Switching from one activity to another is termed **multitasking**. Adolescents are "old hands" at multitasking—checking email while talking on the phone, doing homework in front of the television, or texting a friend on the way to class. If the activities are simple, or ones that are familiar, the costs of multitasking aren't necessarily high. Even so, neither task can be done quite as well as when it is the only one attended to (Crone et al., 2006; Rubinstein et al., 2001). And under some circumstances, even activities that adolescents have

multitasking   Moving back and forth from one task to another.

come to regard as second nature, such as using a cell phone, can be sufficiently distracting as to be risky. This is particularly true when driving.

Adolescents' reactions when driving are slower and their judgments poorer—for instance, driving too close to the car ahead or cutting in front of another vehicle—when using a cell phone (Kass et al., 2007). In fact, the use of a cell phone has been found to affect driving as much as driving while legally drunk (Strayer et al., 2006). Additionally, the distraction produced by using a cell phone is no different if drivers are using a hands-free or a handheld phone, which is understandable when we realize that what is being diverted in each case is one's *attention*—not one's hands (Caird et al., 2008; Horrey & Wickens, 2006).

Using cell phones has been found to be risky for adolescent pedestrians as well as for adolescent drivers. Through the use of a virtual environment, preadolescents were monitored as they crossed a virtual street while either talking on a cell phone or not using a cell phone. Adolescents distracted by using their cell phones paid less attention to traffic—looking left or right fewer times—and were more likely to have a close call or be "hit" by oncoming traffic (Stavrinos et al., 2009).

The Limbic System: Risk Taking

By the time adolescents leave high school, most have taken a course in driver education and know the importance of using seat belts, leaving adequate space between cars when changing lanes and, above all, not drinking while driving or riding with someone who has been drinking. However, adolescents fail to put such information into practice. When they are asked how often they've engaged in various health-risk behaviors, approximately 11% of adolescents said they rarely or never wore a seat belt, 10% admitted to driving a car when they'd been drinking, and 30% indicated they had ridden with a driver who'd been drinking. Safety figures for those who ride motorcycles are even worse, with 34% indicating they rarely or never wore a motorcycle helmet (CDC, 2008c). Adolescents in other countries engage in similarly risky behavior; in Thailand, for instance, 12% admitted to driving after drinking, 19% to riding with a driver who'd been drinking, and 50% rarely or never wearing a helmet when riding a motorcycle (Ruangkanchanasetr et al., 2005).

Similarly, nearly all adolescents know the risks of unprotected sex, yet among those who were sexually active, 38% indicated that they had not used a condom when they last had intercourse (CDC, 2008b). And despite information concerning the dangers of smoking cigarettes, and the risk to even casual smokers of becoming addicted, 20% said they currently used cigarettes with some regularity, and among these, nearly 11% had smoked at least half a pack on the days in which they had smoked (CDC, 2008b). Given that adolescents are aware of these risks, how are we to understand their willingness to engage in risky behavior?

To appreciate why adolescents make risky choices, we need to look at a second important system within the brain, the **limbic system**. The limbic system, which consists of a set of structures located beneath the cortex, is involved in the way we process social and emotional information and evaluate rewards—the very type of information involved in many of the risky decisions adolescents make. As noted earlier, not all parts of the brain mature at the same rate. The limbic system develops earlier than the prefrontal cortex, the latter only gradually assuming cognitive control over behavior. Consequently, when the limbic system is activated, as it is in potentially rewarding social situations, its relative maturity enables it to dominate the executive controls of the prefrontal cortex (**Figure 4.5**) (Casey et al., 2008; Steinberg, 2008).

limbic system An area of the brain located beneath the cortex that is involved in processing social and emotional information and evaluating rewards.

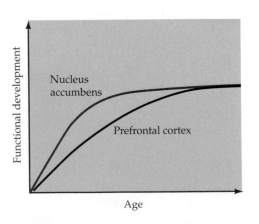

● **Figure 4.5 Not all parts of the brain mature at the same rate** The nucleus accumbens, an essential component of the limbic system, which is involved in the processing of social and emotional information and the evaluation of rewards, develops earlier than the prefrontal cortex, which is involved in executive functions and cognitive control over behavior. (After Casey et al., 2008.)

● **Figure 4.6** **Risky driving when playing the game "Chicken," either alone or with peers present** Younger adolescents are more likely to make risky choices when playing the game "Chicken" than are older adolescents or adults. For both younger and older adolescents, risk-taking is more likely when peers are present than when alone. (After Gardner & Steinberg, 2005.)

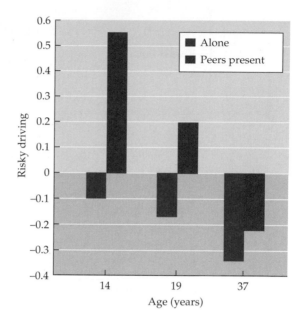

Since acceptance by peers is rewarding, we might expect that adolescents would be more likely to engage in risky behavior when other adolescents are present than when they are by themselves. Margo Gardner and Laurence Steinberg (2005), at Temple University, looked at the effect of peers on risk taking by comparing the risks adolescents took while playing a video game either by themselves or with several adolescents sitting next to them. Players got points for making it through an intersection once a light turned yellow, but lost points if they crashed (the game was called "Chicken"). Conversely, braking to the yellow light gave them fewer points, but they also didn't lose as many points as they would if they crashed. As these investigators had expected, adolescents took more risks when other adolescents were present (**Figure 4.6**). The influence of peers also was stronger for younger (mean age =14) than older (mean age =19) adolescents. Also, when it came to evaluating whether it was worth engaging in risky behavior, males focused more than females did on the benefits rather than the costs of taking risks.

Findings such as these might suggest that adolescents simply aren't aware of the possibilities of being injured or that they feel themselves to be invulnerable. In fact, however, adolescents are just as aware as adults of the potential for harm and, if anything, they are liable to overestimate the likelihood of risks to themselves (Fischhoff, 2008).

Statistics for adolescent drivers illustrate all too well that more is involved in making decisions than awareness of personal risk. Adolescents, particularly males, are more likely to be in an accident than any other age group (CDC, 2008c). Additionally, as we might expect, the risk increases if other adolescents are also in the car (Chen et al., 2000). Many states and countries have graduated driver licensing (GDL) laws that place restrictions on adolescent drivers, not only concerning the use of cell phones, but also the ages of passengers and the hours during which they can be on the road (CDC, 2008c).

When it comes to effective intervention programs, providing adolescents with information about the risks isn't always enough. They frequently know the risks. The most effective interventions combine educational programs with the use of external constraints, such as graduated driving laws, or raising the price of cigarettes in community-wide interventions to reduce smoking (Ronde et al., 2001).

How Adolescents Think

Thought takes interesting turns in early adolescence and carries teenagers places children can't easily go. Adolescents can think about things that don't exist and may never exist. They can think about what is possible as well as what actually is. Thinking becomes highly systematic and logical. This is not to say that adolescents are always logical and that children never are, or that children never consider possibilities as well as realities, or that adolescents always reason in the abstract. It is, rather, that adolescents do so more often and with greater ease. Each of these characteristics of adolescent thought—thinking abstractly, thinking hypothetically, and thinking logically—is discussed in the sections that follow.

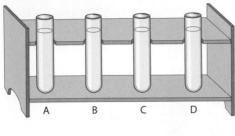

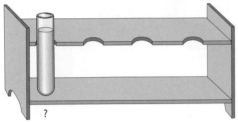

● **Figure 4.7** **Piaget's chemical solutions task** Adolescents are shown a rack with four test tubes, each containing a colorless liquid, and asked to determine which of these, when combined, will produce a yellow liquid. Can you think of which combinations to test? The answer is at the bottom of the page.

metacognition Awareness of one's thinking, cognitive abilities, and style.

Thinking Abstractly

"How is a horse like a goldfish?" If you ask adolescents this question, they are likely to come up with any number of answers. They might say, "Well, a horse and a fish are both animals," or "Both have to eat to live," or "Both take in oxygen and give off carbon dioxide." Children are more likely to stare you down. You can almost hear them think, "That was a stupid question!" In any event, they are not likely to think of any similarities. Why is their response so different from that of adolescents?

Children tend to think of things in terms of their physical properties. With horses and goldfish, this approach doesn't take them very far. If you had asked how a horse was like a dog, they would have had no problem: Both have four legs. They could tell you how a horse is like a cow: Both are large and eat grass. But as long as their thoughts are bound by the physical characteristics of things, fish remain worlds removed from horses. Adolescents can think of things as members of classes and can even think of ways to classify those classes (Drumm & Jackson, 1996). An adolescent can say, for example, "Both are animals, and animals can be either aquatic or terrestrial." **Box 4.1** hows how the tendency to think in terms of classes helps adolescents think through a science project.

Thinking Hypothetically

Adolescents are able to adopt a "what if…?" approach to problems, being able to see in a situation more than is presently before them. They're able to turn a problem around in their minds, in other words, generating hypothetical outcomes, and then test each of these out.

Thinking hypothetically, in terms of what *might* be, enables adolescents to come up with plans for solving problems. Following through with a plan requires the development of other capacities as well. Perhaps the first of these is simply to be able to stick with the plan. Continued development of the prefrontal cortex enables adolescents to inhibit impulsive actions, ones that aren't planned out, something that younger children have difficulty doing. Adolescents are able, as well, to monitor their own activity, keeping track of what steps they have already taken and which ones remain to be taken in solving a problem. This bird's eye view of their own thoughts and actions is termed **metacognition**.

In Piaget's chemical solutions task, adolescents are shown a rack containing four test tubes, each one containing a colorless liquid, and asked to determine which of these, when combined, will produce a yellow liquid (**Figure 4.7**). When presented with a problem such as this, most adolescents will ask for a pencil so they can write out all the different combinations. Once they've written all of these down, they start to test them out, systematically going through the list of combinations until they find the one, or ones, that give them a yellow liquid. Being able to imagine the possible, instead of thinking only of what is actually before them, allows adolescents to think hypothetically. Children, in contrast, focus on the actual liquids in the test tubes and have no plan of attack other than to jump in, mixing one liquid with another. Even if they succeed in solving the problem, they are not likely to have kept a record of what they did. There are 11 combinations that need to be tested. These are listed at the bottom of this page (upside down).

Answers to the chemical solutions task:
We can rule out the four liquids, which by themselves are colorless, and can also eliminate the possibility that no combination of the four would produce a yellow liquid since we've been told that at least one of them does. The remaining possibilities to be tested are: AB, AC, AD, BC, BD, CD, ABC, ABD, ACD, BCD, and ABCD.

BOX 4.1 **In More Depth**

Science Project

Ms. Jones has asked her seventh-grade class to consider the following problem: Imagine that scientists have just discovered a new planet. A research team has been given the task of determining all possible life forms that may exist on this planet. A space probe has returned with data suggesting that life could exist either in bodies of water (aquatic) or on land (terrestrial). The team suspects that life on this planet, as on ours, could either be vertebrate or invertebrate. What are all the possible forms that life might take?

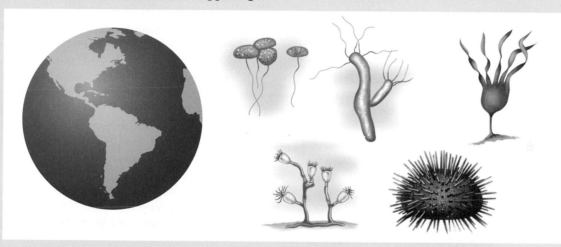

Children think of four types by combining the four separate forms: terrestrial vertebrates, aquatic vertebrates, terrestrial invertebrates, aquatic invertebrates. Adolescents come up with twelve more possibilities. They think not only to combine the separate forms of life but also to combine the combinations! The original four combinations, plus the separate life forms, give them a total of sixteen possibilities. One of these is the possibility of no life at all.

1. Terrestrial vertebrates (TV)
2. Aquatic vertebrates (AV)
3. Terrestrial invertebrates (TI)
4. Aquatic invertebrates (AI)
5. Only vertebrates (TV and AV)
6. Only invertebrates (TI and AI)
7. Only terrestrial animals (TV and TI)
8. Only aquatic animals (AV and AI)
9. TV and AI
10. AV and TI
11. TV, AV, and TI
12. TV, AV, and AI
13. TV, TI, and AI
14. AV, TI, and AI
15. TV, AV, TI, and AI
16. No animals at all

Sources: After Hunt, J. M., 1961, and Mosher & Hornsby, 1966.

John Flavell, a psychologist at Stanford University who has written widely on cognitive development, remarks that the school child's "speculations about other possibilities—that is, about other potential, as yet undetected realities—occur only with difficulty and as a last resort. An ivory-tower theorist the elementary school child is not" (Flavell et al., 1993).

Thinking Logically

As thought becomes abstract, adolescents are able to test different ideas against one another to establish their truth. They become aware of the logical relations that exist among ideas and can use logical consistency to determine whether a statement is true or false. Children check their ideas against hard facts; so do adolescents, but logical consistency is equally compelling for them.

This difference is dramatically illustrated in a simple experiment. Adolescents and children are shown poker chips and asked to judge whether statements about the chips are true or false. Sometimes the chips are hidden in the experimenter's hand; at other times they are clearly visible. The experimenter has just picked up a green chip and holds it in clear view. He says, "The chip in my hand is either green or it's not green." Both the adolescent and the child agree that the statement is true. Next the experimenter holds up a chip that is hidden in his hand and says, "The chip in my hand is either red or it's not red." The adolescent knows the statement must be true and agrees. The child says, "I can't tell," and asks to see the chip! Children evaluate statements such as these by comparing them to what they can see, not realizing that they could still evaluate their truth based on logical properties. Adolescents know that thoughts can be checked against themselves for logical consistency (Osherson & Markman, 1975).

One might assume, at this point, that adolescents are alike in the way they think through and solve problems. But thinking, like every other aspect of development, is highly individual. Quite large differences exist among early adolescents in the rate at which they acquire new reasoning abilities, and many adolescents do not reason in these ways even by the end of middle school or junior high. Instead, thinking changes with age throughout adolescence (Huizenga et al., 2007; Muller et al., 2001). For another look at logical thinking, and limitations to this in younger children, see **Box 4.2**.

Emerging Adulthood: Thinking Pragmatically and Tolerating Ambiguity

So far we have considered differences in the ways adolescents and younger children think. There are differences as well in the ways adolescents and emerging adults think. Perhaps the most noticeable of these is that emerging adults are more practical in the way they think (Labouvie-Vief, 1990). They realize that sometimes not all of the logical alternatives one can think of are available. Instead, when confronted with a problem, they consider the actual options available to them and adapt. Consider a problem in which a store keeper, who has given his employee the responsibility for opening the store in the morning, finds that the employee fre-

Models of atomic structures and other abstract concepts are meaningful only to students who have reached a level of cognitive development that enables them to use symbolic representations to evaluate the logical consistency of ideas.

**BOX
4.2**   **In More Depth**

Generative Interviews: "An Astronomical Joke"

By Michael Wapner

A famous astronomer is giving a public lecture. When he is finished regaling his very impressed audience with the state of the art on black holes, white dwarfs, and quarks, he asks for questions. Immediately a small, gray-haired man jumps up and furiously waves his hand for recognition. The astronomer calls on him.

"I want a straight answer and no evasions," challenges the little man.

"I'll do my best," replies the famous scientist, just a touch patronizingly.

"OK, then. What holds up the Earth?" Obviously pleased with himself for asking so fundamental a question, the man from the audience smiles knowingly at the people around him as he awaits his answer.

The scientist, having in his years of public lectures encountered flat-earthers, UFO abductees, and telepaths in direct thought contact with Mars, is not much surprised by the question. He attempts to get around it without offending.

"Well, you see, there is a problem with the way the question is put. Strictly speaking, nothing holds up…"

"Enough!" breaks in the little man, triumph in his voice and on his face. "I knew you would try to wiggle out. All you academic smarties dodge the hard ones. As a matter of fact, I know the answer to my own question. It's a turtle. A turtle holds up the Earth."

The scientist, condescension growing with impatience, responds, "And what holds up the turtle?"

The little man, gracious on the edge of victory: "Another turtle, of course."

The scientist, now in full sarcasm, "And what, pray tell, holds up that?"

The little man, not waiting for the end of the challenge, pounces for the coup de gras. "I got you now. It's another turtle. And then another turtle under that one. In fact, it's turtles all the way down."

However funny we find this story (and I hope you find it as funny as I did the first few times I heard it), there is more than humor here. Overlooking for the moment his turtle explanation, the little man's conceptual problem is quite understandable and not at all unusual. All of us, even small children, know that the Earth is round and moves in empty space around the sun. We have heard and read about it over and over. We have even seen pictures, taken from space, of the round Earth. But it is one thing to know this as an isolated fact. It is a deeper, and more difficult, thing to internalize the astronomical frame of reference into which this fact fits, and still more difficult to reason on the basis of this broader frame of reference. The man in the audience was having just this difficulty. He knew, as an isolated fact, that the Earth was an object in space. But his frame of reference had not caught up with that fact. He wanted to know how the Earth remained in space without falling. It was his, as it is everyone else's, common experience that heavy, unsupported objects "fall." And the direction in which they fall is "down." But everyone's common experience is from an earthbound perspective, in which Earth is not itself an object but the "floor of the world." When we take an astronomical perspective, then we no longer speak of "falling" and there is no meaning to the term "down." The man in the audience had confused these two perspectives.

Stella Vosniadou (1992) was particularly interested in how children and adolescents deal with this same problem, with how they reconcile what they have heard about the "roundness of Earth" with their more deeply internalized earthbound perspective. To investigate this question, she used what she terms a "generative" interview. A generative interview is one in which the interviewer does not stop with the answers to factual questions, but gives the subject problems that probe the reasoning behind the factual answers. Consider the following interview with Jamie, a third-grader.

Vosniadou: What is the shape of the Earth?

Child: Round.

Vosniadou: Can you draw a picture of the Earth?

Child: [Child draws a circle to depict the Earth.]

Vosniadou: If you walked for many days in a straight line, where would you end up?

Child: Probably in another planet.

Vosniadou: Could you ever reach the end or the edge of the Earth?

Child: Yes, if you walked long enough.

(continued on next page)

BOX *continued*
4.2

Vosniadou: Could you fall off that end?
Child: Yes, probably.

Clearly, had the interviewer stopped when Jamie said the Earth was round, she would have left with a seriously mistaken understanding of Jamie's view of the Earth. If one can "reach the end of the Earth by walking long enough" and then "probably" fall off, one is not walking on the surface of an Earth that is "round" as astronomers understand that term.

By posing astutely chosen questions (which are more like problems to be solved than questions to be answered), Vosniadou is able to infer the cognitive model of Earth the child must have constructed.

You may have noticed that the generative interview owes a great deal to the clinical interview of Jean Piaget. Piaget also posed "diagnostic" questions to children that allowed him to infer the way children think. The generative or clinical interview is to be contrasted with the survey interview discussed in Chapter 13. This latter form is designed to elicit facts or opinions of which the respondent is consciously aware. The generative interview, on the other hand, focuses more deeply on the cognitive structures that lie beneath conscious facts and opinions. To conduct a generative interview, the interviewer must be much more skilled, since each question must build on the child's last response and thus cannot be totally scripted beforehand. The standardized protocol of a survey interview is much too rigid to serve a generative function. On the other hand, the necessity of asking somewhat different questions of different subjects in the generative interview makes standardization, and hence data interpretation, more complicated. There is also a greater danger, in a generative interview, of the questions suggesting and hence contaminating the responses, since the material elicited is more complex and hence more vulnerable to suggestive influence.

Despite these dangers, the generative interview is wonderfully productive of insights on children's cognitive models. Here is Matthew, a first-grader.

Vosniadou: If you walked and walked for many days, where would you end up?
Child: If we walk for a very long time, we might end up at the end of the Earth.
Vosniadou: Would you ever reach the edge of the Earth?
Child: I don't think so.
Vosniadou: Say we kept on walking and walking and we had plenty of food with us?
Child: Probably.
Vosniadou: Could you fall off the edge of the Earth?
Child: No, because if we were outside the Earth we could probably fall off, but if we were inside the Earth we couldn't fall off.

Matthew has done pretty well in imagining the Earth to be round. Where his cognitive model seems to disagree with conventional science is that he has us living inside the sphere. That's why we don't fall off.

Source: After Vosniadou & Brewer, 1992.

quently has been arriving late. The store keeper tells the employee that he will be fired if he is late one more time, only to discover the following morning that the employee has once again been late.

When asked what the owner should do in this example, adolescents approach the situation logically. Noting (A) that the employee was told he'd be fired if he came in late again, and (B) that he once again was late, they're likely to respond that the owner should fire the employee. Logical as such an answer is, it may not be practical if the employer doesn't have anyone else to open the store! Emerging adults know that factors such as character and extenuating circumstances (e.g., a car in for repairs) could also be relevant, and are likely to suggest that the owner talk further with the employee to see if a solution can be reached. They're able, in other words, to bring personal experiences to bear on the problem rather than relying only on an impersonal logic.

A second difference is that emerging adults have more tolerance for ambiguity. They are able to see, for instance, that what they once may have accepted simply as facts are actually interpretations that reflect the perspective of their group; someone belonging to another group may view the situation from an entirely different perspective. Furthermore, they can see that each perspective can represent a legitimate point of view. Consequently, they are less likely to approach a problem by trying to find the "right" answer, that is, by trying to discover the "truth." Instead, they're able to take a number of perspectives into consideration, realizing that these can be inherently contradictory, and attempt to work toward some common ground.

Explaining Cognitive Development

In the classic horror movie *A Nightmare on Elm Street*, the villain, Freddy Krueger, reached his victims through their minds, appearing to them in their dreams. Unlike other dreams, these took on a chilling reality because they didn't end when the person woke up. The villain was able to step into one's waking life, through a door in one's mind, making the villain as close as a heartbeat and only a thought away. Children across the country didn't sleep for nights after watching this movie. Freddy Krueger had a power to terrorize that other villains lacked: Other monsters could more easily be separated from one's self.

A Constructive Perspective

The idea that thought gives substance to reality is a powerful one, taking different forms depending on one's age and even at different times in history. The ancient Hebrew alphabet, for instance, lacked symbols for vowels. These had to be supplied by the reader. Unlike consonants, which are formed as the tongue or teeth stop the flow of air, vowels are unstopped breaths. In reading, one had to breathe life into the message, fleshing it out with the thoughts that made one vowel more probable than another. Similarly, ancient texts, even up to medieval times, lacked punctuation, making it necessary for a reader to interpret the text in order to decipher it.

A constructive perspective assumes that individuals must continually interpret, or make sense of, all experience—whether deciphering printed words on a page, recognizing a familiar face, or listening to a conversation. In fact, this perspective argues that events remain ambiguous until we respond to them. Only by responding does the meaning of an event become explicit. Noam Chomsky (1957), a psycholinguist at MIT, illustrated this point by asking the meaning of the sentence "Flying planes can be dangerous." Does this mean that it is dangerous to fly a plane or that it is dangerous to be around planes that are flying? We rarely notice such ambiguities because we, just as the readers of ancient texts, breathe life into our experiences on a moment-by-moment basis. Pilots will hear Chomsky's sentence one way, and those living near airports will hear it another, the expectancies of each giving shape to their experience. Only when one is new to a task do expectancies fail, making it necessary to assemble understanding piece by piece. As any 5-year-old would tell you, reading is hardly automatic, even today.

PIAGET AND KEGAN   Jean Piaget adds a developmental twist to the constructive perspective. Fascinated by differences in the way children and adults understand their world, he assumed not only that we actively construct what we know of the world, but also that we organize this understanding in qualitatively different ways with age, each way resulting in a distinctly different stage of thought. These stages differ in the nature of the equilibrium that we

assimilation   Piaget's term for the process by which new events and experiences are adjusted to fit existing cognitive structures.

accommodation   Piaget's term for the process by which cognitive structures are altered to fit new events or experiences.

equilibration   Piaget's term for the process of balancing assimilation and accommodation that is responsible for the growth of thought.

differentiation   A process by which one distinguishes or perceives differences not previously recognized.

conservation   The realization that something remains the same despite changes in its appearance.

Because most middle school and junior high students are in transition from concrete operational thought to formal operational thought, they need a lot of hands-on activities.

maintain with our environment (Piaget, 1971). This equilibrium, or adaptive balance, is maintained through two complementary processes: assimilation and accommodation. Through **assimilation**, the individual is able to interpret new experiences in familiar ways, ways that are already a part of the self, fitting the new into what she or he already knows. Through **accommodation**, in order to understand something new, one must change the way one views things; one must work at understanding, "sounding" out the experience as a new reader does with a word, a process that also changes one ever so slightly, making the other familiar only by changing the self.

The processes of assimilation and accommodation must be complementary in order to maintain equilibrium. If assimilation predominates, the organism imposes its own order on the environment, and if accommodation predominates, the converse occurs. Neither one by itself represents the homeostatic balance between organism and environment that characterizes adaptation. Thus, with each assimilation, accommodation must occur. Piaget referred to the balance thus achieved as **equilibration**: the process responsible for the growth of thought.

Building on the constructive process elaborated by Piaget, Robert Kegan (1982, 1994) argues that intellectual growth takes place through a process of **differentiation** of self from other, a process that has the effect of simultaneously defining new aspects of one's surroundings and of one's self. In a manner similar to Isaac Newton's third law of motion, in which every action has an opposite and equal reaction, when one gives meaning to events in the world, one's sense of self in relation to these events also changes.

Kegan gives the example of two young boys, 5 and 9 years old, surveying a street scene from the observation deck of a skyscraper. They exclaim their wonderment in different ways. The younger one says, "Look at the people. They're tiny ants." The older one says, "Look at the people. They look like tiny ants." There is a complexity to the older boy's remark that is lacking in the younger boy's. We hear in his remark a comment that has to do as much with *how* he is perceiving as with *what* he has perceived. His awareness of people looking *like* ants, rather than simply being the size of ants, adds a reflective quality in which the percept, or object being perceived, is evaluated. In other words, he is aware both of the percept and of the evaluating self—both of what he is seeing and of himself seeing it.

In one of Piaget's most dramatic tests of **conservation**, which he used to demonstrate whether children knew that things remained unchanged even when they appeared to be different, he poured liquid from a short, wide glass into a tall, narrow one, causing the level of the liquid to rise, and asked if the amount of liquid was still the same (**Figure 4.8**). Younger children, such as the younger boy in our example, are unable to distinguish how the liquid *looks* from how much there *is* and say there is more in the taller glass. Older children, however, agree that the amount of liquid in either container must be the same. They say things such as, "I could pour the liquid back and it would look the same," a mental operation that Piaget referred to as "negation," or "This glass may be taller, but it's also narrower, and the one makes up for the other," which Piaget called "reciprocity." It is this ability to move from one perspective to another, and back again, using either of these operations, that enables older children to understand that the liquid is unchanged, giving their world stability, "concreteness."

To understand what takes place in adolescence, let's look at what enabled the older child in the preceding example to see that the people on the street below only looked as small as ants. He became aware not only of what he was seeing, but of how he was seeing it—of his

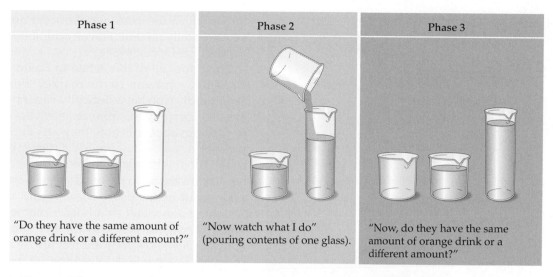

Phase 1	Phase 2	Phase 3
"Do they have the same amount of orange drink or a different amount?"	"Now watch what I do" (pouring contents of one glass).	"Now, do they have the same amount of orange drink or a different amount?"

● **Figure 4.8   Piaget's conservation of volume task**   The ability to mentally pour the liquid back into the first container (negation), or to consider the width as well as the height of the third container (reciprocity) enables school age children to master this test of conservation.

perceptions. The change allowed the boy to "own" his part in the tininess of the people. The ability to separate himself from his perceptions enabled him to see them for what they were—as ways of seeing or perspectives. When perspectives emerge for the child's inspection, the child can move from one perspective to another and back again, seeing that the object has not changed even though its appearance may. This understanding gives the child a new grasp of things. Things that previously expanded and shrank when seen from different vantage points, like reflections in a fun house mirror, now hold still and become concrete (Kegan, 1982).

Just as older children become aware of their perspectives, adolescents become aware of how these can be coordinated. They can see that the liquid is the same either because one could always pour it back or because the width of the second glass compensates for its height. They can also see that not only is the amount of liquid similar in the two glasses, but so are the *ways* by which they arrive at this understanding similar—that is, that negation and reciprocity are comparable. Note that each of these operations is a way of thinking, a point which illustrates a central characteristic of adolescent thought, namely that they are able to *think* about their thinking.

What enables adolescents to view the world differently than school children? What must they "own" in order to see the child's concrete world differently? Differentiation occurs when adolescents become aware of their part in creating this stability. When they distinguish what they do in coordinating different perspectives from the perspectives themselves, the concrete world of stable objects can be seen for what it is, as one of the many ways they might see their world.

The ability to think about thought allows adolescents to arrive at possibilities they could never reach otherwise. We can see this quality of thought at work in one of Piaget's tasks, a game in which balls are shot onto a game board using a spring launcher. The balls differ in size and in the smoothness of their surfaces. Eventually each stops rolling, the larger and rougher ones first. Piaget asks adolescents to explain why they stop. At first, adolescents identify wind resistance and friction as important. But they soon realize something else: that the balls would roll forever if neither of these were present. This conclusion can be reached only through thought, because the conditions

These adolescents contradict Piaget's assumption that once formal thought emerges, individuals think logically all the time. Even though these young women are certainly aware of the health risks of smoking, their behavior does not reflect their ability to reason logically or to envision the long-term consequences of their actions.

under which the event would occur are never actually present (Flavell et al., 1993; Ginsburg & Opper, 1988).

How does all of this relate to Freddy Krueger's power to terrorize? For 5-year-olds, who have difficulty separating their perceptions from themselves—how things appear is how they are. People are tiny ants—and Freddy Krueger is in the room with them. School children become aware not only of what they are seeing but of themselves seeing it, of watching a monster in a horror movie; Freddy Krueger is still scary for them, but at heart they know they are reacting to a character in a movie. Adolescents' awareness that the villain in the movie is simply one of any number of monsters that could be imagined, that Freddy Krueger is the product of someone's imagination, makes it possible, and even fun, for them to think of ways to make him scarier.

Piaget assumed that once adolescents entered the stage of formal thought, they would think logically—and do so all the time. Piaget traced the characteristic ways of thinking at any stage to underlying neural maturation. Consequently, one would not expect to see an adolescent using reasoning characteristic of an earlier stage. And yet adolescents often do, as do adults, particularly when thinking about situations that are unfamiliar or emotional (Blanchette, 2006; Pham, 2007).

A Contextual Perspective

VYGOTSKY AND ROGOFF   Lev Vygotsky and Barbara Rogoff believe culture gives shape to cognitive development. Vygotsky, just as Piaget, believed that individuals acquire knowledge of their world simply in the course of doing whatever they happen to be doing, without having to be formally instructed. But Vygotsky differed from Piaget in an important respect. For Vygotsky (1978), this knowledge is fundamentally social in nature, taking place under the tutelage of another, as a natural consequence of working alongside someone who has already discovered a better way of doing things. Vygotsky pointed out that as adolescents engage in day-to-day activities, they frequently do so in the presence of someone who is older—and more skilled in the very activity in which they are involved. The discoveries of others, what Vygotsky refers to as cultural tools, get passed on to them in this social context, without ever breaking the flow of the activity itself, or being labeled "learning" as such.

Take, as an example, a weekend project of painting a room. Everyone pitches in, the room finally gets painted, and the furniture moved back into place. Mom, a veteran of many painted rooms, heads over to the window with a single-edge razor blade in her hand, handing one to her son on the way. He watches her slide the blade under the dried paint on the pane, and does the same, until they have cleaned off all the panes. The use of a tool—*not* the razor blade, but the wisdom that it is easier to scrape paint off than to put masking tape on—has been acquired in a social context, without the need for direct instruction.

Although both Piaget and Vygotsky view the course of cognitive development in terms of progressive adaptations to one's environment, they differ in what they take as the proper unit of analysis. Piaget takes as this unit the solitary adolescent. Thinking, for Piaget, is a mental activity taking place *in the mind* as a person adapts to his or her environment. As such, thinking is a property of the individual.

Vygotsky takes as his unit of analysis not the solitary adolescent, but one who is working or playing alongside others, engaging in activities that are characteristic of the group, such as removing paint from a window, or programming the VCR. By observing individuals as they acquire the skills of those they live with, that is, of their culture, Vygotsky identifies thought in terms of the cultural tools that have enabled the members of that culture to "grasp" things more easily than they might otherwise. Thinking, for Vygotsky, develops as a person internalizes these tools through interacting with those who already use them. As such, thinking is fundamentally a social process that occurs as a result of living within a social group. The "mind" that Piaget observed within the individual exists for Vygotsky in the society in which that person lives, in the form of the cultural wisdoms that adolescents internalize through their interactions with those who are already skilled in their use. It is no accident that Vygotsky (1978) entitled the book in which he set forth this theory *Mind in Society.*

Vygotsky believed that, just as with tools, the mind of the apprentice learner grasps these cultural wisdoms. He assumed, as did Piaget, that their acquisition changes the way the mind apprehends reality, but unlike Piaget, he did not regard them as being forged anew by the individual, through her or his own interaction with the physical world. Instead, he saw them as handed down from those who are more skilled in their use.

For something to be passed on in this manner, the adolescent must be close enough to reach out for it. Vygotsky termed this closeness the **zone of proximal development**. This zone is the distance separating the adolescent's current performance from what their optimum performance might be. Proximal means "near" or "close to." Thus, in order for people to profit from working alongside those who are more skilled, their own performance must come close to, or approximate, the behavior of the other person. The zone represents the range of skills individuals must possess to profit from exposure to those who are more skilled. We see this zone illustrated in the example of removing paint from the windows. This adolescent was able to internalize the cultural wisdom that it's easier to scrape the paint off than to put tape on only because his own behavior was sufficiently close to the behavior he eventually acquired—that is, he could slide the blade along the glass without etching it or cutting himself.

Barbara Rogoff, a psychologist at the University of California a Santa Cruz, similarly regards the expertise of a culture as tools to be used by its members, and speaks of this appropriation as an apprenticeship in thinking (Rogoff, 1990; Rogoff et al., 2003). The term **apprenticeship** suggests that thinking, rather than a private event occurring in a person's head, is an activity that is shared with others, guiding practical action. Instead of regarding a particular context, such as one's home or culture, as an influence *on* behavior, Rogoff sees behavior as embedded *in* context, taking its particular shape and direction from context.

Rogoff points out that children's and adolescents' strategies for learning their culture are the same one would recommend to any visitor to a foreign culture: stay close to your guide, watch what the guide does, get involved whenever you can, and pay attention to what the guide may tell or show you. The guide complements the child's or adolescent's activity by adjusting the difficulty of the activity to match the other's abilities, modeling the behavior that is sought while the child or adolescent is watching, and accommodating his or her own behavior to what the other can grasp.

zone of proximal development Vygotsky's term for the range of skills which individuals must possess in order to profit from exposure to those who are more skilled.

apprenticeship Rogoff's term suggesting that thinking is an activity that is shared with others, guiding practical action.

psychometric approach
An approach that focuses on the measurement of individual differences in abilities contributing to intelligence.

intelligence The ability to profit from experience and adapt to one's surroundings; measured by intelligence tests.

Rogoff views development as multidirectional. Unlike Piaget, for instance, she does not see development as moving toward a single endpoint, toward a universal set of achievements, such as Piaget's formal thought. Instead, the course of development can take any of a number of forms, depending on the types of skills that are valued in the adolescent's culture. These skills, whether they be accounting or weaving, establish the developmental goals that are local to each culture. Thus, Piaget's developmental endpoint of logical, abstract thought reflects the value placed in our society on scientific reasoning. Formal thought, in other words, represents the "local" goals of Western societies.

Although research indicates that thinking changes dramatically with adolescence, it is equally clear that individual differences are large and that even adolescents who are skilled in the ways of thinking that their culture values do not do so in all situations. Critics of the constructive developmental approach have suggested that measures of abstract and hypothetical-deductive reasoning actually reflect the more general abilities that contribute to intelligence at *all* ages. This argument brings us to a second approach to intellectual development, one that comes out of the intellectual testing movement.

A Psychometric Approach to Intelligence

The **psychometric approach** focuses on individual differences in the general abilities that contribute to intelligence. Even though intelligence tests have been widely used to predict performance in a variety of settings, how they do this isn't clear. Explanations of "how" quickly reduce to questions of "what" when items included in standard measures of intelligence are used to test individuals from other cultures. Robert Sternberg, a psychologist at Tufts University, tells an amusing story that illustrates some of the difficulties in measuring whatever it is we call intelligence, let alone understanding what that is.

A team of psychologists had administered a number of tasks to people from a village in a traditional culture. One of the tasks involved sorting pictures. In our culture the best, or most "intelligent," approach to this task is to sort categorically, to put a picture of a robin under that of a bird, and so on. The people of this village did not adopt this approach. Instead of sorting the pictures categorically, they sorted them functionally. For instance, they placed the picture of the robin with that of a worm, explaining that robins eat worms. No amount of encouragement or hinting from the research team could get them to sort categorically. Finally, in exasperation, one of the psychologists told them to sort the pictures the way someone who wasn't intelligent would do it. Each person executed a perfect categorical sort! These people were clearly intelligent enough to sort categorically. They just thought that it wasn't very smart to do it that way (Baron & Sternberg, 1987).

Does practicing the guitar develop intelligence? The answer depends on whether intelligence is a single innate capacity or one of several specific abilities, such as musicality or numerical ability.

DEFINING INTELLIGENCE **Intelligence** is a term that most of us use almost daily. Out of sheer familiarity, one might think it would be easy to define. But it isn't. In fact, even experts in the field have come up with widely differing views of what it is. Yet most agree that intelligence allows us to profit from our experiences, adapt to our surroundings, and that it frequently involves abstract reasoning.

The measures that we have of this—intelligence tests—are simply collections of questions that reflect the information and abilities of the average person of a given age in our society. Depending on

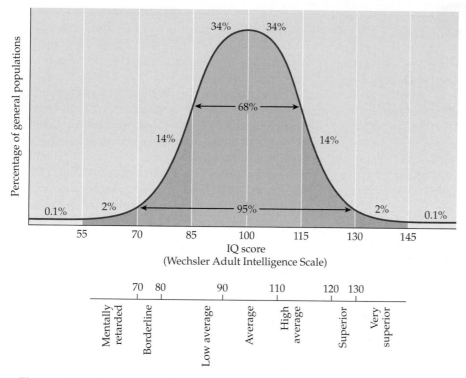

● **Figure 4.9   Percentage of individuals and intelligence classifications at different points from the mean IQ of 100**   Intelligence tests are constructed so that at any age the average person will score 100.

which questions are included, people with different experiences will do either better or worse on the tests.

One's score on an intelligence test, or one's IQ, reflects how one performs relative to others the same age. Comparisons with age-mates are important not only because they share similar cultural experiences, but also because, as noted earlier in the chapter, the brain continues to develop in adolescence, leading to changes in performance with age. Intelligence tests are constructed so that at any age the average person will score 100 (**Figure 4.9**). **Box 4.3** examines the issue of changes in intelligence with age.

A CLOSER LOOK: THE WISC–IV AND WAIS–III   One way of understanding intelligence is to take a look at what is measured by an intelligence test. The **WISC–IV** (Wechsler Intelligence Scale for Children–Fourth Edition) and **WAIS–III** (Wechsler Adult Intelligence Scale–Third Edition) are both commonly used measures of intelligence, the WISC primarily for children and adolescents up to the age of 16 and the WAIS for 16-year-olds and adults.

Rather than include questions that reflect academic knowledge, such as "What is the distance between the Earth and the sun," David Wechsler (1981) asked the type of information average people would be expected to pick up on their own. Examples of such questions are "What is the distance between London and San Francisco?" and "How tall is the average American man?" Notice that what can be considered general information in one culture is not necessarily so in another. Sehti, one of the adolescents in the introduction to this chapter, might be more familiar with the height of men in India than in the United States, for example. And Yuan-Pin might be able to estimate

WISC–IV   An intelligence scale for children and adolescents up to 16 years of age.

WAIS–III   An intelligence scale for adolescents and adults.

Research Focus

Cross-Sectional and Sequential Designs: Does Intelligence Slip with Age?

With Michael Wapner

Does intelligence decline with age? When can adolescents expect to peak intellectually? Putting it more bluntly, just how many good years do they have ahead of them? And why can't we give them any straight answers to questions such as these?

Straight, unambiguous answers are possible only with research that allows us to rule out alternatives. In such research, investigators manipulate variables by randomly assigning individuals to the conditions they are observing. Why can't we say for certain whether intelligence increases, decreases, or stays the same with age? Simply put, age cannot be manipulated. Individuals come to the laboratory with a certain age; they cannot be assigned one. People who differ in chronological age—that is, are of different cohort groups—also differ in other ways, namely, in their social and historical backgrounds. These differences don't always affect the way they respond to the measures we are taking, but they might. Cohorts are more likely to have similar cultural experiences than people of different ages. Adolescents today live in relatively plentiful times, and most grow up in urban or suburban settings. Adolescents born in 1930 grew up in the shadow of the Depression and were more likely to live in rural areas. Differences such as these appear in all sorts of attitudes and behaviors and can easily be confused with age changes. They are known as cohort differences.

Most of the studies finding that intelligence declines with age are cross-sectional. Cross-sectional research tests groups of individuals of different ages all at the same time. An obvious advantage to this approach is that one need not wait around while individuals grow older. A disadvantage is that differences between the groups can reflect either age changes or cohort differences. In contrast to longitudinal research, in which age is confounded with times of measurement, cross-sectional research confounds age with cohort differences.

Is there any way around the difficulties inherent in cross-sectional and longitudinal designs? Sequential designs provide a solution. These designs combine cross-sectional and longitudinal approaches. They test several cohort groups at several times of measurement. In a way, the sequential design can be thought of as a number of longitudinal studies, each starting with a different age group.

You might ask, "Won't both cohort and time of measurement effects be present?" Yes. But because they are, we can measure them and estimate their contribution. By subtracting these estimates from our estimates of age differences, we can statistically isolate these confounds from genuine age changes. The resulting design appears in the figure.

By looking at the cells that form the diagonals, we can compare 10-year-olds with 15-year-olds

the distance between Beijing and Bombay more accurately than the distance between London and San Francisco.

We began our discussion of intelligence with a warning that intelligence tests have an arbitrary quality to them. The questions they contain don't tap only the capacities with which one is born; they also tap a general knowledge gained by living in a culture. People from a different culture, though theoretically just as able, will not do quite as well as those from our own. If different questions were included, ones that reflected their particular cultural experiences, their performance would improve, whereas the performance of the average North American would drop slightly. These differences do not reflect ability so much as the nature of the questions themselves, as can be seen when adolescents from different cultures are tested in their own countries on equivalent tests of primary abilities (Li et al., 1996). Adolescents' cultural backgrounds, then, can be expected to affect their perspective on and approach to problems.

BOX 4.3 *continued*

and 20-year-olds. Cells 1, 7, and 13 are groups of 10-year-olds. Cells 2, 8, and 14 are 15-year-olds. And cells 3, 9, and 15 are 20-year-olds. "That's our age effect," you note. Not so fast. Even though the means of the diagonals reflect the performance of different ages, they can also contain cohort effects (e.g., any differences that might exist between 10-year-olds who were born in 1980 versus 1985 versus 1990) as well as differences due to time of measurement (depending on whether they were tested in 1990, 1995, or 2000). If all we had were the diagonals, we couldn't say anything about the relationship of intelligence to age.

But sequential designs give us more. We have vertical and horizontal means as well. The first of these, the column means, allow us to estimate differences due to time of measurement, and the second, the row means, the effect for cohorts. Comparing performance measured in 1995 (cells 2 and 7) with performance measured in 2000 (cells 3, 8, and 13), with that in 2005 (cells 9 and 14) provides an estimate of the amount of variability in intellectual functioning that is contributed by time of measurement. Differences among row means allow us to estimate the size of a cohort effect. By subtracting each of these estimates from the diagonals, we end up with an estimate of age effects.

So, does intelligence slip with age? Sequential designs find that age effects are minimal. Simply put, adolescents can expect to hold on to their smarts as they enter adulthood. But what shall we make of the cross-sectional data indicating (erro-

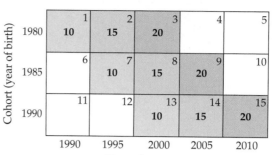

A sequential design The cells are numbered in the upper right-hand corner. The numbers in the centers of the cells indicate the participants' ages.

neously as it turns out) that intelligence declines in adulthood? Obviously, some measures of intelligence confound the period in which one lives, the historical context, with attributes of the individual. The result of that confusion is to stigmatize older people. Sound familiar? This problem is reminiscent of similar complaints that intelligence tests penalize ethnic and racial minorities because they confound cultural and economic conditions with attributes of the individual.

Source: After Anastasi, 1988.

INTELLIGENCE TESTS AND CULTURE   Imagine the following scene of a teenager taking a subtest in which she must rearrange a set of pictures to tell a story. The teenager is Korean American. The examiner places four cartoon drawings on the table in front of her and tells her to arrange them so that they tell a story. The drawings are of: (1) a man fishing by a river, (2) a woman pointing at a garden while the man looks on, (3) the man digging and discovering a worm, and (4) the   man getting out the gardening tools (**Figure 4.10**). The girl tries first one arrangement, then another. None seems right to her. Finally the time runs out. You are puzzled. Why was this difficult for her? You quickly arrange the pictures mentally, starting with 2, then 4, next 3, and then 1.The story? A "henpecked" husband has been told by his wife to garden, gets out the tools, discovers a worm as he works, and, reminded of more pleasant pursuits, goes off fishing. It's easy for most North Americans—unless they happen to be of Korean descent. In Korea, wives don't give chores to their husbands. This girl knew that, and the pictures made no sense to her (Cohen & Swerdlik, 2001).

● **Figure 4.10** **Example of a type of item in the picture arrangement subtest of the WAIS–R, a previous version of the WAIS–II** *Source*: Simulated items similar to those in the Wechsler Intelligence Scale for Adults. Copyright © 1991, 1997 by The Psychological Corporation, a Harcourt Assessment Company. "Wechsler Adult Intelligence Scale" and "WAIS" are registered trademarks of The Psychological Corporation.

Performance on measures such as the preceding can reflect not only an adolescent's ability but also the extent to which that adolescent's background is similar to that of the dominant culture. Minority adolescents with less exposure to the dominant culture are not as likely to do well as are adolescents whose daily experiences more closely mirror that culture. Similarly, socioeconomic level has also been found to be related to performance on intelligence tests, with adolescents from lower-income homes scoring below those from higher-income homes (Farah et al., 2006).

One last set of differences deserves our attention before we leave this approach to intelligence. These differences concern the sexes. It is only natural to ask whether males and females differ in their intellectual functioning.

Will standardized performance tests fully reveal this young woman's abilities? Many researchers believe that such tests may be weighted with questions based on experiences of the dominant culture and that the scores from such tests may not accurately represent the capabilities of adolescents from nondominant cultures.

ARE THERE GENDER DIFFERENCES IN INTELLIGENCE? Stereotypes abound in this area as in so many others. Before we go any further, however, keep in mind that females and males do not differ in overall intelligence (van der Sluis et al., 2006). Even so, several distinct patterns to performance can be noted. Females do somewhat better on measures of verbal reasoning and fluency, comprehending written passages, and understanding logical relations (Hedges & Nowell, 1995; Li et al., 1996). Males do better on the Information and Arithmetic subtests (van der Sluis et al., 2006).

A gender difference in spatial ability also exists. Males do better on tests that require one to mentally manipulate things or remember a visual figure in order to find it in a more complex figure. Whenever gender differences emerge, it is natural to ask whether these might be biologically based. Research exploring this question has found support for a relationship between spatial abilities and levels of circulating hormones, performance improving with higher levels of testosterone and, conversely, with lower levels of estradiol (Davison & Susman, 2001; Hausmann et al., 2000). However, not all research has confirmed these findings (Liben et al., 2002). Certainly, the relationship between spatial ability and hormonal influences is complex and, given the influence of hormones, is likely to reflect earlier organizational patterning as well as their subsequent effects (Newhouse et al., 2007; Sanders et al., 2002).

Gender differences in spatial ability assume added importance because of their potential contribution to a commonly used test of intelligence, the Raven Progressive Matrices Test. This measure was developed as a **culture-fair test**, eliminating cultural biases by asking individuals to match arrangements

Are males more logical and females more intuitive? Are males better at numbers and females better at language? Does any difference matter between males and females, or between any two adolescents, regardless of sex, when it comes to mastering the computer?

of symbols rather than answer questions verbally. Through mid-adolescence, females and males perform the same on the Raven; however, from about 16 years on, males perform appreciably better than females (Lynn & Irwing, 2004a, 2004b). When differences in spatial ability are statistically controlled for, this advantage disappears (Colom et al., 2004). However, if individuals' performance on the Raven is not evaluated in light of this difference, assessments of their intelligence may eliminate one type of bias, that due to culture, only to add another, that due to gender.

THE SAT   Gender differences are also evident in standardized achievement tests such as the **SAT**, the most widely used of the college entrance exams. Each year college-bound high school males outscore females by a wide margin on the math portion of this exam. However, the interpretation of this gender difference is problematic, since a comparison of grades in college mathematics courses for females and males with the same scores on the math section of the SAT, shows females get the higher grades (Lips, 2008). Obviously a number of factors contribute to mathematical performance, whether on the SAT or in actual coursework (Braswell et al., 2001; Lips, 2008). Given the importance of the SAT for students who plan to go to college, however, there's a pressing need to ensure that the questions comprising the exam adequately access mathematical ability (Hyde & Kling, 2001).

Males generally score higher than females on the verbal part of the SAT as well. Once again, this difference is difficult to interpret. An international program assessing performance of adolescents just a few years younger than those taking the SAT found that females typically scored higher than males on measures of reading and literacy in each of the 43 participating countries (Machin & Pekkarinen, 2008; OECD/UNESCO, 2003). Males' higher performance on the verbal portion of the SAT may result from a predominance of questions using analogies, the one measure of verbal ability in which males score higher than females. This type of question subsequently has been eliminated (Lips, 2008).

culture-fair test   A measure of intelligence that minimizes cultural bias by using materials or requiring skills not likely to be more familiar to one culture over another.

SAT   The Scholastic Aptitude Test, the most widely used college entrance exam.

metacomponents Higher-order cognitive functions that select and monitor lower-order cognitive functions, for example, metacomponents are employed to determine which performance components are required to perform a task.

performance components Cognitive mechanisms, selected by metacomponents, that operate directly on the information to be processed.

knowledge-acquisition components Cognitive mechanisms—for instance, perception and memory retrieval—that, under the direction of metacomponents, acquire new information as needed.

Sternberg's Componential Intelligence

Robert Sternberg, at Tufts University, takes a broader view of intelligence, defining it in terms of achieving life goals as well as success in school. Since life goals are highly individual, there's no common measure of intelligence that fits all. Different types of knowledge and different skill sets are needed depending on how one defines success (Sternberg, 2004).

Sternberg accounts for individual differences in problem solving and knowledge by analyzing intellectual functioning in terms of the processes, or components, that operate on information. He identifies three kinds of components: metacomponents, performance components, and knowledge-acquisition components. **Metacomponents** determine when more information is needed and whether a particular strategy should be used or another one constructed, and monitor one's progress. **Performance components** carry out the actual procedures selected by the metacomponents. If metacomponents are the supervisors, performance components are the actual workers. Performance components might decipher information in sensory memory, encoding this as names of letters. They might compare elements, inferring similarities or differences, or apply a procedure completed in one domain to another aspect of the problem. **Knowledge-acquisition components** acquire new information as it is needed. They sift through information, picking out that which is relevant to the problem and integrating it with what one already knows, giving it new meaning.

We can apply this analysis to the way people solve problems. Sternberg studied analogies because they reveal interesting age differences. An example of an analogy is the following: "Swift is to *Gulliver's Travels* as Pope is to: (a) the Baedeker, (b) 'The Rape of the Lock,' (c) the Vatican." To construct an analogy, one must choose the term that completes the second pair so that the two terms bear the same relationship to each other as the terms in the first pair.

To begin, one must encode each item: Does "Swift" refer to speed, or is it someone's name? (Encoding is a performance component.) The word "Travels" suggests the first alternative, and you know that the Baedeker is a travel guide. But then what is Pope? You may decide at this point that you need more information (a metacomponent) and search your memory for anything related to travel. You remember that *Gulliver's Travels* is the name of a book; then Swift could be the name of its author. Notice that one uses inference (another performance component) to determine the relationship between the first two terms. Encoding Swift as an author's name would mean that Pope is the name of an author. This last step has involved another performance component, mapping, or using the relationship between the first two terms to establish a relationship between the last two. Thus the fourth term must refer to something that Pope wrote. This extension rules out the Vatican, and because the Baedeker travel guide bears the name of its author, you are left with "The Rape of the Lock." You justify your selection by noting that the terms are all capitalized, as they would be in a title, and respond with alternative (b).

People of all ages use the same components to construct analogies, but spend different amounts of time on each (Sternberg & Rifkin, 1979). Adolescents and adults spend proportionately more time encoding the items than doing any of the other steps, whereas children spend relatively little time encoding. How does this fact relate to the characteristics of adolescent thought we reviewed earlier? Recall that adolescents tend to think of all the possible forms something might assume before they begin to work with any of them. They generate a world of possibilities, whereas children latch on to the first thing that comes to mind, their time for encoding being relatively brief. Sternberg (1981, 1984) also finds that with age, people spend much more time planning how to solve a problem than actually carrying out the steps. Once again, this difference reflects the tendency of adolescents to generate a strategy, and contrasts with the tendency of children to jump right in and move things about.

Notice, too, that analogies might be difficult for children because they require one to find the appropriate class for each term and then map the relationship between the classes of one set to those of the other. This higher-order, or abstract, form of thought awaits adolescence. Most children have as much success with analogies as they do in relating horses to goldfish (Sternberg, 1984).

Sternberg's componential analysis gives us an expanded view of intelligence. Rather than ranking one person relative to another in terms of a single number, such as IQ, we get a picture of intelligence at work: setting priorities, allocating resources, encoding information, monitoring feedback, and so on. But is it a single intelligence that works for us, or does intelligence take more than one form?

Gardner's Multiple Intelligences

Howard Gardner, a psychologist who has written extensively on the development of intellect and creativity, proposes not one but multiple forms of intelligence: logical-mathematical, linguistic, spatial, bodily-kinesthetic, musical, interpersonal, intrapersonal, and naturalist intelligence. Gardner (1999, 2006), like others, defines intelligence in terms of one's ability to solve problems as they arise, but the range of problems that he accepts as legitimate for the study of intelligence is much broader than it is for others. Gardner recognizes **multiple intelligences**.

Gardner points out that most measures of intelligence tap a limited range of abilities, which he identifies as logical-mathematical. Because these measures are also good at predicting success at school, they continue to be used. But what about problems that don't call for logical-mathematical analysis, such as finding one's way back to a parking lot in a new area of town or recognizing the composer of a piece of music? Do these tasks call upon intelligence? Do musicians, athletes, or surgeons have more of certain talents in common than the rest of us? Gardner would answer yes to both.

Of course, one could list endless problems or talents and claim a separate intelligence for each one. Gardner uses several criteria to isolate legitimate intellectual domains. He points out that a domain must be universal to all humans and should show development with age. Each intelligence should be capable of being expressed in its own symbol system, for example, words for language, equations for mathematics, or notes for music (Walters & Gardner, 1986).

Evidence for separate intellectual domains also comes from child prodigies, idiot savants, and people who have suffered brain damage. In each case we can see an uneven profile of abilities. Prodigies such as Mozart or Yehudi Menuhin showed musical genius at an early age, yet remained quite ordinary in other domains. Cases have been

multiple intelligences
The view that intelligence is comprised of a number of different capacities, each relevant to a different domain—for instance, music, linguistics, mathematics, interpersonal relations. One's ability in each domain is not necessarily highly correlated with ability in other domains.

This young woman searches her memory during a spelling competition. As adolescents grow older, they can retrieve items from memory more quickly, use memory strategies more effectively, and because of greater content knowledge, assimilate new information more readily.

TABLE 4.1
Gardner's Eight Forms of Intelligence

FORM OF INTELLIGENCE	POTENTIAL PROFESSIONS
Musical	Musician, music teacher
Bodily-kinesthetic	Dancer, athlete, actor
Logical-mathematical	Scientist, mathematician, teacher
Linguistic	Writer, lawyer, interpreter
Spatial	Artist, architect, landscape designer
Interpersonal (understanding others)	Teacher, counselor, salesperson
Intrapersonal (understanding oneself)	Writer, poet
Naturalist	Botanist, chef, forester

Source: Gardner, 1999.

reported of autistic children who could perform rapid mental calculations yet not be able to carry on a conversation or dress themselves. Similarly, people who have suffered brain trauma may have some areas of functioning spared. **Table 4.1** shows Gardner's eight forms of intelligence, with corresponding potential professions.

Gardner anticipates objections to labeling these domains as intelligence. But he replies that nothing is sacred about the word intelligence. His choice of the term over other equally suitable ones, in fact, is deliberate. It emphasizes his point that present measures of intelligence are limited because they place logical-mathematical and linguistic abilities on a pedestal above other abilities, such as musical and interpersonal ones. In doing so, our measures of intelligence reflect our culture's bias in favor of logical and verbal abilities over abilities such as kinesthetic or artistic ones. Gardner (1983, 1999) argues that to call one type of ability "intelligence" and another "talent" reflects this bias. He challenges us to consider them all talents or to consider them all intelligence.

PRACTICAL INTELLIGENCE   Gardner is not alone in viewing present measures of intelligence as overly narrow and related more to academic than real-life experiences. Many psychologists speak of a practical intelligence, which they distinguish from the academic intelligence tapped by intelligence tests (Sternberg et al., 2000). Neisser (1976) defines this type of intelligence as "responding appropriately in terms of one's long-range and short-range goals, given the actual facts of the situation as one discovers them," and points out that the problems one must solve on tests that tap academic intelligence share a number of features: They are designed by someone else, are usually not very interesting, and have nothing to do with daily experience. Also, most test problems are well defined; they have a single answer and only one way of arriving at it (Wagner & Sternberg, 1986). In contrast, **practical intelligence** applies when one must discover the problem, instead of having it defined by someone else. Another difference is that finding the solution is frequently pleasurable. Finally, usually a number of approaches will work, each leading to a slightly different solution.

The psychometric approach to intelligence has done much to further our understanding of intelligence. The approach to which we turn next has contributed considerably to our understanding of the processes that underlie intellectual functioning in all individuals, in all settings, whether in school, at work, or relaxing with a group of friends.

practical intelligence   To be distinguished from "academic intelligence" or intelligence measured by IQ tests, practical intelligence requires the individual, rather than a teacher or an examiner, to define the problem to be solved and decide what constitutes a solution.

An Information Processing Approach

Have you ever asked a person to repeat something they said that you missed, only to find you know what was said before hearing it again? Or caught yourself repeating a phone number until you can write it down? Some things are so second nature to us that we hardly pay them any mind, yet these examples illustrate two fundamental characteristics of cognition. Simply put, we are limited in just how much we can attend to at any point in time, and we are very good at adapting the way we think to the demands of the task or the moment.

Those who adopt an **information processing** approach to cognitive development focus on the specific processes involved in developmental change, rather than on the characteristics of any stage of thought, or on individual differences in measured intelligence. A number of such processes show progressive changes with age; these include automaticity, speed of processing, encoding, the use of strategies, and metamemory.

Automaticity enables this adolescent to easily scan the instructions for assembling this project, freeing him up to focus on precisely measuring and cutting the parts.

Automaticity refers to the increase with age in the efficiency with which individuals process information. For instance, adolescents can easily scan instructions for taking a test rather than have these read to them by a teacher, or effortlessly pronounce unfamiliar words that younger children would have to sound out letter by letter. As a consequence, these activities require less immediate attention, thereby freeing adolescents to focus on the next level, such as formulating the best strategy for taking the test or understanding the meaning of the passage they are reading (Siegler & Alibali, 2004).

Speed of processing also continues to develop into adolescence, reaching adult levels by mid-adolescence (Luna et al., 2004). How quickly information can be processed potentially affects a number of cognitive processes, and is closely related to the efficiency of our **working memory**, the brief memory, lasting less than a minute, that we use to hold on to information while working with it. An example of working memory would be remembering what one has just read in order to make sense of what one is presently reading, or knowing where one is within the sequence of steps in a long division problem, or simply remembering a phone number without writing it down. Working memory continues to improve in adolescence (Gathercole et al., 2004).

Encoding refers to the form in which experience is mentally represented. The features that one notices, or encodes, predictably change with age, with adolescents being better than younger children at recognizing which features of a problem are most important, as well as at processing these more efficiently. Related to this, adolescents are also able to attend to more features of a problem at once, and to organize information more systematically, thus giving them greater flexibility of thought, enabling them to shift their attention from one aspect of a problem to another, rather than getting stuck in outworn strategies (Keselman, 2003).

Another process contributing to developmental change concerns the use of strategies. **Strategies** are the activities that we consciously engage in to improve our performance, such as categorizing things in order to remember them, writing things down, or putting something needed for the next day in

information processing   An approach to cognition that focuses on the processes by which information is encoded, retrieved, and utilized.

automaticity   The ability to perform highly practiced cognitive operations without conscious attention.

speed of processing   The rate at which a cognitive operation (e.g., encoding, decoding, retrieval) or a combination of these can be performed.

working memory   A brief memory that holds information for less than a minute while further processing occurs.

encoding   The process by which information is transferred from one form to another in memory.

strategies   Activities that organize cognition so as to improve performance, such as repeating a phone number or categorizing a list of things to be remembered.

These dancers illustrate Howard Gardner's bodily-kinesthetic intelligence.

inductive reasoning
Reasoning from the particular to the general.

a place where it will be seen. Adolescents are more likely than children to recognize the need for strategies and to use strategies that are more efficient. One of the reasons they do so is that they are more aware of their thinking. This awareness is termed metacognition. Adolescents use their knowledge to monitor what they do. They know, for example, just how long a passage can be before they must reread it in order to remember it, or whether they are familiar with a name and hence likely to recall information about it. They know what strategies work best for them, are aware of using them, and realize how much they help (Siegler & Alibali, 2004).

In addition to developmental changes in these basic processes, how much knowledge one has also changes with age. Adolescents simply know more than younger children. This knowledge provides a context for assimilating new information, increasing the likelihood that relevant features will be processed and encoded. Because information can be related more easily to what one already knows, it has more meaning and is more easily used and remembered.

Implications for the Classroom

The intellectual developments we have talked about so far prepare adolescents for new challenges in the classroom. Courses in mathematics, science, and literature require increasingly abstract and logical thought. In algebra, for instance, when solving a problem in which x equals 5, they must know better than to assume that x really *is* 5 (Bjorklund, 1989). Literature courses ask them to discuss the nuances of motives and meaning in characters that live only in the pages of their books. In physical science, they must make observations, generate explanations for these, then systematically test each one out, controlling for extraneous conditions as they do.

Reasoning

Both inductive and deductive reasoning improve during adolescence (Muller et al., 2001). **Inductive reasoning** takes one from the particular to the general, from specific events to the class to which these belong, that is, to an explanation. For instance, to find that water in a closed container boils at several degrees below the point at which it boils in an uncovered container is a single observation resulting in a single fact—interesting, perhaps, but of limited value to science or the student. The logical thought process that enables a student to extrapolate from this single fact to a general rule (that there is an inverse relationship between the pressure exerted on a liquid and its boiling point) is an example of inductive reasoning.

Similarly, the adolescent who must write an essay analyzing why Hamlet was so slow to avenge his father's murder is also confronted with a task of induction. Shakespeare describes specific events in the life of Hamlet—conversations, thoughts, actions. To explain Hamlet's motives, the student must use induction to arrive at his character, that is, the source (class) of likely actions and the rules of their occurrence. The events Shakespeare actually shows us are analogous to the individual observations of a chemistry experiment such as the one above, and the step from these particulars to a general personality is as much an act of induction as formulating the rule relating pressure on a liquid to its boiling point. **Deductive reasoning** works the other way, going from the general to the particular, that is, checking a hypothesis by seeing what happens when conditions change. Thus, starting with the rule that the boiling point of water drops by a certain amount with every increase of pressure, one can deduce (predict) any particular boiling point for any given pressure. Likewise, given the diagnosis of Hamlet as indecisive but impulsive (the general personality or rule from which spring all of his actions), one can predict (deduce) that left to himself Hamlet will have difficulty formulating a plan of action but, once provoked, will act quickly and rashly.

deductive reasoning
Reasoning from the general to the particular.

The ability to think logically, abstractly, and hypothetically increases with age throughout adolescence. Even so, adolescents find it easier to reason about propositions that make sense ("If you are caught running in the halls, then you will be punished") than those that don't ("If you are caught running in the halls, then you are wearing sneakers") (Ward & Overton, 1990). At times, adolescents experience more difficulty than younger ones simply because they are able to think about aspects of problems not immediately relevant to their solution (Spiel et al., 2001).

Can Adolescents Think Like Scientists?

Adolescents can marshal facts to support or oppose principles, generate a realm of possible alternatives for any situation, think in abstractions, and test their thoughts against an inner logic. These abilities set them apart from children. They also make new forms of learning possible in the classroom. Adolescents' systematic approach to problems, for one thing, lends itself especially well to science.

Much of the excitement of science involves discovery. Often the first discovery is the nature of the problem itself. Alexander Fleming, for example, documents the discovery of penicillin by telling of a mold that had formed in one of his petri dishes. He noticed that the bacteria surrounding the mold had died. Instead of cleaning out the dish and starting a new culture, Fleming was puzzled (that is, he had discovered a problem). Why had only the bacteria around the mold died?

One could identify other, less interesting, problems, such as "What did I do wrong?" Perhaps Fleming did, too, but he chose to move on to why the bacteria surrounding the mold had died. What Fleming saw illustrates the first step in solving a problem. One must analyze a situation to discover its salient features (what a scientist would call the relevant variables). Only when these have been isolated can a strategy be formulated. Given a strategy, one can begin to test each of the features to see which produce a solution. Finally, one must be able to reach conclusions based on these tests (Ginsburg & Opper, 1988).

Notice that the success of the whole endeavor rests on the ability to think the situation through before starting to work

Science requires adolescents to put what they learn in class to the test, reasoning through complex processes and anticipating results.

Adolescents, more so than children, are aware of what they don't know, so they are better able to focus on filling the gaps in their knowledge and skimming over what they've already learned.

on it. Adolescents can do this. They can identify each of the possible variables, then generate combinations. Remember that a characteristic of adolescent thought is to think in terms of possibilities. In doing so, they are also generating a strategy, because each possibility must be tested.

A strategy makes for a systematic approach to problems. Adolescents know, for instance, that they must hold all the conditions constant except the one they are testing. Only then can they be sure their test reflects the possibility they have in mind instead of some other. They know, too, that frequently an effect can result from more than one combination of conditions. Even though they may discover that the bacteria die under one particular combination of conditions, they will continue with their tests, exhausting all the possibilities.

Study Skills and Knowing What You Don't Know

One of the factors contributing to better learning is that adolescents, more so than children, are aware of what they don't know and adjust the way they study to accommodate for the gaps in their knowledge. Children, on the other hand, often fail to realize when they have not learned what they have been studying. Campione and Brown (1978) observed fifth-graders through college students as they studied material in a textbook. Younger students focused on the same information each time they reviewed the material, whereas older students, realizing what they had missed, directed their attention to that material on subsequent readings. The development with age of metacognitive skills, and the consequent use of strategies, underlies this improvement.

Students who fail to monitor their performance can be taught to do so. Poor readers who were shown how to assess their reading comprehension by noting what they have missed climbed from the 20th percentile to the 56th percentile (Palinscar & Brown, 1984). Similarly, students taught to attend to cues such as chapter headings or to focus on cues embedded in the passages (such as "in comparison to" or "on the other hand") improved in their comprehension (Spires et al., 1992).

Metaphors and Meaning: When Is a Ship a State?

Children interpret remarks literally; adolescents can understand multiple levels of meaning. When asked to interpret an expression such as "His bark is worse than his bite," for example, children might answer that "you can't hear a dog bite" or that "some dogs bark a lot." Adolescents can understand the expression to mean that some individuals bluff their way through situations. Their ability to understand figurative uses of language makes many types of literature accessible that previously were not.

Adolescents can also appreciate *metaphor*; a metaphor makes an implicit comparison between ideas or objects to show some hidden similarity. They understand that when politicians refer to a government as a "ship of state," they are communicating that the fate of all citizens is bound together, just like the fate of passengers and crew on a ship at sea. Similarly, the phrase "evening of life" communicates that life is drawing to an end, just like the day at the approach of evening. Early adolescents easily understand expressions such as these; children do not.

Adolescents also begin to understand irony, sarcasm, and satire. Their ability to think in terms of hypothetical situations as distinct from actual ones makes an understanding of these concepts possible. Being able to consider the perspective of another and anticipate the other's intended effects by his or her remarks almost surely contributes to this new appreciation. Adolescents can appreciate the irony in passages from works such as *Pilgrim at Tinker Creek*, in which Annie Dillard (1974) writes the following:

> *Somewhere, and I can't find where, I read about an Eskimo hunter who asked the local missionary priest, "If I did not know about God and sin, would I go to hell?" "No," said the priest, "not if you did not know." "Then why," asked the Eskimo earnestly, "did you tell me?"*

The ability of adolescents to appreciate the irony in this story may be especially acute. They, like the Eskimo, face a challenge to change because of what they know.

Implications for Everyday Life

Many of the intellectual advances of early adolescent thought have their downside as well. For instance, the ability to hold a problem in mind and consider it from all possible perspectives occasionally leads teenagers to make things more complicated than they actually are (Elkind, 1978). Frequently teenagers fail to see the obvious not because the task is too hard for them, but because they consider every conceivable option. While a teenager is mentally ticking off all the oddball but nonetheless possible alternatives, someone else usually comes up with the answer. Teenagers can feel stupid, asking themselves, "Why didn't I think of that?"

This facility can also lead adolescents to read complex motives into situations where none exist. A simple request from a parent such as "Would you hand me the newspaper on your way out?" can be viewed with skeptical eyes. The teenager may wonder, "Is this just another attempt to control?" To avoid being controlled, the adolescent may consider refusing but may also suspect that the need to refuse is merely another response to control. Neither able to comply nor to refuse, the teenager shoots back an angry remark to the effect that the news isn't worth the ink it takes to print it and storms out, leaving the parent to wonder what would have been done with something as loaded as "How was your day?"

Adolescent Egocentrism

One of the hallmarks of adolescent thought is the ability to think in the abstract, and nothing is more abstract than thought itself. Adolescents can think about thinking, including the thoughts of others as well as their own. The ability to do so underlies a form of **egocentrism** in which adolescents fail to distinguish their own concerns from those of others. Because so much of what they think is about themselves, they can have the feeling that others, too, are thinking about them, thereby creating an **imaginary audience**. This gives them the feeling that every eye in the room is on them. The imaginary audience may explain adolescents' exaggerated feelings of self-consciousness, as well as their intense need for privacy.

The imaginary audience can do something else; it can confer a feeling of being special. This feeling goes hand in hand with a second mis-

egocentrism   The failure to realize that one's perspective is not shared by others.

imaginary audience   The experience of being the focus of attention that emerges with adolescents' ability to think about thinking in others and their confusion of the concerns of others with their own preoccupation with themselves.

Adolescents assume that everyone is as preoccupied with them as they are with themselves. This self-focused perception often leads to extreme self-consciousness, an intense need for privacy, and feelings of being unique and special.

personal fable   The feeling of being special; thought to derive from the imaginary audience.

social cognition   The ability to assume another's perspective and coordinate this with one's own.

understanding about themselves. In the **personal fable**, adolescents believe they are unique, that their experiences are unlike those of others. Confusion over this can lead adolescents to believe that no one else can understand their feelings, that they are the only ones to have ever felt this way. It's not unusual, for example, for a young teenager to tell her mother that she couldn't possibly understand how it feels to be in love! A danger in seeing themselves as unique, however, is that they may fail to see that what happens to others could happen to them as well.

The capacity of adolescents to catch glimpses of themselves in the eyes of others is important to gaining a sense of themselves. Erikson (1968) speaks of identity formation as a process by which adolescents come to see themselves as individuals and, at the same time, as members of a social group. Even while assessing their individual worth, adolescents use the standards and norms shared by members of their social group. How they see themselves will reflect the way they measure up in the eyes of others. The ability of adolescents to examine their thoughts and to imagine the thoughts of others underlies a new awareness of their own separateness from others and of what they have in common with others through shared values and behaviors.

Social Cognition: Understanding Others

Adolescents' awareness of others' thoughts contributes as well to social understanding, or **social cognition**, which develops as adolescents become better at assuming another's perspective and coordinating this with their own. Although preadolescents can put themselves in another's place and understand how that person might be feeling, they have difficulty relating this understanding to their own point of view and thus considering the situation from both perspectives. The ability to attend to multiple aspects of a problem at once, which develops in adolescence (discussed earlier in the chapter under "Thinking Hypothetically"), enables adolescents to move from one perspective to another. This, in turn, enables them to anticipate the outcome of adopting one course of action or another. Adolescents can infer how another might be thinking *and* anticipate how that person will react to their reactions to them. An adolescent, for example, might get angry with her friend upon hearing that the friend once again drank too much after promising he wouldn't, but may keep her anger to herself, guessing that her friend is also afraid, and angry with himself, and will not confide in her in the future if she loses her temper. Compare this type of understanding with that of a preadolescent, who might blurt out either her own feelings or those she suspects of her friend, with no ability to anticipate the consequences of doing either.

Despite significant developments in social understanding, adolescents often fail to consider the impact their remarks can have on others. Joan Newman (1985) describes a family conversation about where the Russian satellite *Cosmos* might fall. Neither parent had any idea where this might be, but the teenage son knew that it had already fallen, landing east-northeast of the tiniest island southwest of Madagascar. So impressed was he with his superior knowledge that he ridiculed the rest of the family saying, "You don't know anything, do you?" Yet this same teenager couldn't find his math homework or remember where he left his sneakers that morning.

Doubt and Skepticism

Children are likely to believe that knowledge comes simply with exposure to the facts, never considering that factual information can be interpreted in more than one way. As a consequence, differences of opinion are treated as one person being wrong and the other one right. Adolescents, however, can realize that what they have regarded as truth is simply one fix on reality and that other equally compelling interpretations are possible. The result can be a skepticism in which they come to doubt the possibility of knowing anything with certainty (Boyes & Chandler, 1992).

New Emotions

How one feels depends on the interpretations one gives to experience. "Did that person just brush me off, or simply fail to notice that I was going to say something?" Depending on which interpretation one gives, the encounter can occasion either feelings of irritation or no feelings in particular. Intellectual development in adolescence makes it possible for teenagers to react emotionally in new ways. Children focus on the immediate elements of the situation: To a compliment they react with pleasure; to a present, with happiness. Adolescents do all of this and more.

These girls may have been friends for years, but with early adolescence, they begin to relate to each other in new ways.

Adolescents can consider what a situation might mean as well as the way it appears. By being able to turn something around in their minds, they can assign more than the obvious meaning to social encounters. Adolescents do not always complicate life in this way, but they do so more than children and also more than most adults. A compliment can be the occasion for anger if seen as an attempt to win a favor. Or a present can cause depression if seen as an emotional bribe. Adolescents also experience emotions that are relatively foreign to children, such as feeling giddy, moody, depressed, or elated (Larson & Richards, 1994). Unlike children, adolescents relate their feelings to their experience of themselves as well as to the events that may prompt the feelings, adding an extra level of magnification to their view of the world.

Arguing

The ability of adolescents to consider the multiple possibilities in any situation affects more than their emotions. An immediate consequence is that adolescents can argue better than children can. To carry out an argument, whether in a debating class at school or with a parent in the kitchen, one must come up with ideas for or against something. Adolescents are not limited, as are children, to testing their ideas against facts; they can test them against other ideas. (Remember the experiment with the green and red poker chips?) This new ability makes it possible for adolescents to argue for or against an idea regardless of whether they actually believe in it. The test of the argument is whether it has an inner logic. Children are limited to arguing either for things they believe in or against those they do not. The only test they can apply is to

During some discussion, this father may realize that his son's arguments are better constructed and more difficult to refute. This adolescent's improved ability at argumentation may at times be frustrating, but it is also a sign of increasing maturity.

Go to the

Adolescence

Companion Website at

www.sinauer.com/cobb

for quizzes, flashcards, summaries, and other study resources.

compare what they say with how things really are for them—how they feel or what they believe.

Because of their literal approach, children cannot consider that a statement could mean something other than it says it does: It's simply taken at face value. A father's complaint, "If we had no dandelions, this would be a fine lawn," will bring a response of "But we have lots of dandelions, Dad," or "I like our lawn." Adolescents can consider statements about things that are contrary to the way they presently are or about things that don't exist. They can imagine a lawn that is free of dandelions or even a lawn of *nothing but* dandelions. Perhaps this ability to divorce thought from fact, to think in ideals, even when these are counter to fact, provides the basis for adolescents' increasing ability to plan and to gain new perspectives on themselves, their families, and their friends.

SUMMARY and KEY TERMS

Development of the Brain in Adolescence

Cell Proliferation, Synaptic Pruning, and Myelination: Brain development continues throughout adolescence, with different regions developing at different rates. Three related processes contribute to brain development in adolescence. Cell proliferation consists in the overproduction of neurons and their interconnections; synaptic pruning consists in the selective elimination of cells and their connections that are infrequently used; myelination consists in the formation of an insulating sheath along the length of a neuron's axon. Theories can be verified or disconfirmed. Theories that derive from the same model reflect the assumptions characteristic of the model that generated them.
cell proliferation, cortical gray matter, synaptic pruning, myelination, white matter

The Prefrontal Cortex: Thinking Like an Executive: The prefrontal cortex continues to develop during adolescence. This area of the brain is responsible for abstract thought, planning, and anticipating the consequences of one's actions.
prefrontal cortex, executive functions, multitasking

The Limbic System: Risk Taking: The limbic system is involved in the processing of social and emotional information. Because this region of the brain develops earlier than the prefrontal cortex, it dominates the executive controls of the prefrontal cortex in early adolescence, increasing the likelihood of risky decisions.
limbic system

How Adolescents Think

Thinking Abstractly: Going beyond what they were capable of thinking as children, adolescents can think of things in terms of class membership and can classify the classes. They can even think about thinking itself.

Thinking Hypothetically: Adolescents can think of things that are only possible but not necessarily real.
metacognition

Thinking Logically: Adolescents are able to test different ideas against one another to establish their truth.

SUMMARY and KEY TERMS

Emerging Adulthood: Thinking Pragmatically and Tolerating Ambiguity: There are differences as well in the ways adolescents and emerging adults think. Perhaps the most noticeable of these is that emerging adults are more practical, such as realizing that not all of the logical alternatives one can think of are available.

Explaining Cognitive Development

A *Constructive Perspective:* The constructive perspective assumes that individuals interpret experience. Piaget applies this perspective to development by suggesting that our understanding of the world is organized in qualitatively different ways with age. Kegan suggests that intellectual growth takes place through a process of differentiation of self from other.
assimilation, accommodation, equilibration, differentiation, conservation

A *Contextual Perspective:* Vygotsky views knowledge as social in nature, taking place under the tutelage of another, as a natural consequence of working alongside someone who has more experience. Rogoff views the acquisition of knowledge as an apprenticeship, in which individuals internalize cultural concepts and skills through association with more skilled members of their group.
zone of proximal development, apprenticeship

A *Psychometric Approach to Intelligence:* Although difficult to define, most agree that intelligence allows us to profit from our experiences and adapt to our surroundings and that it typically involves abstract reasoning. Common measures of intelligence reflect the knowledge and abilities of the average person in our society. Most intelligence tests, though, reflect one's familiarity with the culture. And while there is no gender difference in overall intelligence, several specific differences can be noted, such as females do somewhat better on measures of verbal reasoning and fluency, comprehending written passages, and understanding logical relations, and males do better on measures of spatial ability and score higher in math on standardized achievement tests such as the SAT.
psychometric approach, intelligence, WISC-IV, WAIS-III, culture-fair test, SAT

Sternberg's Componential Intelligence: Sternberg analyzes intellectual functioning in terms of components, or processes that operate on information.
metacomponents, performance components, knowledge-acquisition components

Gardner's multiple intelligences: Gardner defines intelligence as one's ability to solve problems as they arise, but includes problems from a broad domain, identifying eight types of intelligence. Practical intelligence requires that we define the problem to be solved and decide what constitutes a solution.
multiple intelligences, practical intelligence

An Information Processing Approach: The information processing approach to cognitive development focuses on the specific processes involved in developmental change, rather than on the characteristics of any stage or thought, or on individual differences in measured intelligence. A number of processes show progressive changes with age. For instance, adolescents get more efficient, and faster, at processing information, and are better able to address multiple problems at once, and use strategies to do so.
information processing, automaticity, speed of processing, working memory, encoding, strategies

(continued)

SUMMARY and KEY TERMS *continued*

Implications for the Classroom

Reasoning: Using inductive reasoning, adolescents are able to reason from the particular to the general; deductive reasoning enables them to reason from the general to the particular.
inductive reasoning, deductive reasoning

Can Adolescents Think Like Scientists?: Adolescents are able to think scientifically by formulating a strategy that enables them to systematically approach a problem, holding all conditions constant except the one they are testing.

Study Skills and Knowing What You Don't Know: Adolescents are able to study more effectively than younger children because they are better able to monitor their performance.

Metaphors and Meaning: When is a Ship a State?: Adolescents understand multiple levels of meaning, enabling them to understand figurative uses of language and appreciate metaphor.

Implications for Everyday Life

Adolescent Egocentrism: Adolescents frequently make problems more complex than they are and feel stupid when someone else comes up with the obvious solution. The ability of adolescents to think about thinking leads them to create an imaginary audience in which they feel themselves to be the center of everyone's attention. The personal fable is the complement of the imaginary audience; adolescents believe they are unique and invulnerable.
egocentrism, imaginary audience, personal fable

Social Cognition: Understanding Others: Adolescents' awareness of others' thoughts contributes to social understanding that is reflected in adolescents' ability to assume another's perspective and coordinate this with their own. Adolescents can infer how another might be thinking and anticipate how that person will react to their reactions to them.

Doubt and Skepticism: With the knowledge that "reality" and "truth" are often just one group's interpretation of the data comes a profound skepticism in which adolescents come to doubt the possibility of ever knowing anything for certain.

New Emotions: Intellectual development in adolescence makes it possible for teenagers to react emotionally in new ways, considering what a situation might mean as well as the way it appears.

Arguing: The ability of adolescents to consider the possibilities in any situation not only affects their emotions, but means they can argue better than children can, and can take either side of an issue, whether or not they believe in it.

Annie is 15 and standing in the dark on her aunt's doorstep. It's 2:30 in the morning. Only blocks away, Annie's frantic mother has called the police to say that her daughter has run away. That morning Annie's mother, looking for the medical card she had given Annie to use, found two joints in Annie's purse. When she confronted Annie about them, Annie accused her mother of spying on her, grabbed the purse and said that she was leaving. Annie's mother stood in the doorway and said they had to talk, but Annie pushed past her, nearly knocking her over. Later when the police, Annie's mother, and Annie all converge in her aunt's living room, Annie tells them she ran away because her mother is cold, selfish, demanding, and doesn't love her. Annie's mother describes Annie as bright and sweet, but immature, irresponsible, and thoughtless. Each has nothing to say that will reach the other.

If asked to describe herself, Annie's mother would never use words such as cold or selfish, nor would she say that she didn't love her daughter. Nor would

Defining the Self:
Identity and Intimacy

Annie describe herself as immature or thoughtless. How can the two of them
see things so differently? What has gone wrong? How much of their difficulty
is because of Annie? How much is because of her mother? And how much is
because Annie is 15?

*Eddie, 13, is sitting in his room waiting for his father to open the door.
His little sister went running to get him after she saw all the hair in the
bathroom and found her mother crying in the kitchen. It hasn't been all that
good around the house lately. Things came to a head, literally, when Eddie
shaved both sides of his, leaving a swath of hair down the middle, which he
dyed green and spiked with hair gel. His mother said she had never seen
anything like that. Who knows what his father will say. Or do. Eddie tells
himself he doesn't care. He has never felt so alone in all his life.*

How is it possible for Eddie to feel alone with his family all around him? And
what possessed him to give himself a green Mohawk?

Achieving an identity is not an easy process, and outward changes in dress or hairstyle enable adolescents to see themselves in fresh ways while they work on differentiating new aspects of themselves.

Chapter Overview

It's time to take a look at where we have been and where we are going. The preceding two chapters set the stage for what we will be discussing in this chapter: defining the self. The biological changes discussed in Chapter 3 have important implications for the way adolescents and their parents interact. As adolescents develop the bodies and feelings of mature adults, both their own and their parents' expectations change. Adolescents, for their part, expect to be treated in more adult ways, to be given more autonomy and a greater say in family decision making. Parents, in turn, expect adolescents to be more responsible and to act in more adult ways.

The intellectual changes discussed in the preceding chapter give adolescents new perspectives from which to view themselves and their relationships with others. The ability to think abstractly, for instance, enables adolescents to consider situations not only from their own point of view but also to understand how they might appear to someone else. Similarly, the ability to think hypothetically enables adolescents to imagine any number of possible future selves.

The first section of this chapter examines the way adolescents put together their experiences within the family to gain a new sense of self, one that is more autonomous yet still emotionally connected to the family. The next section of the chapter examines the psychosocial crisis of identity. We will look at differences among adolescents in the ways they explore and commit to life options, first examining these in terms of identity statuses, or self constructions, and then in terms of identity styles, or ways of processing information relevant to the self. Some adolescents also experiment with "online" versions of the self. Next we will consider the ways in which gender, ethnicity, and culture contribute to adolescents' resolution of identity issues.

The chapter moves to a consideration of changes in adolescents' self-concept and self-esteem. The sense of themselves that adolescents develop differs somewhat depending on how their culture views the self. Finally, the chapter closes with a look at adolescents' capacity for intimacy as a measure of maturity.

Constructing a Self

Robert Kegan (1982, 1994) argues that, at every age, individuals partition experience into two "rough cuts" of reality—that which is "me" and that which is "not me." Development occurs when aspects of the "me" become differentiated from that which has been regarded as "not me." This differentiation has the effect of simultaneously defining new aspects of our surroundings and of our self. When we give meaning to events out there, our sense of self in relation to these events also changes. For adolescents, this process of differentiation carries the promise of profound changes in their most significant relationships, changes that start within the family.

Going back to Annie and Eddie, despite other differences between them, both have one thing in common: Both have organized the way they have constructed the self, or the way they perceive themselves, in terms of their relationships with their parents. If asked to talk about herself, Annie would likely say something such as, "The problem's not me so much as it is my mother. She doesn't really care about me and just wants to control me." Annie has a hard time separating her feelings from how she sees her mother, her *self* from the *other*. One could say that she simply is not being honest. But the truth is, she is being honest. This is the way things are for her. In order for her to relate differently to her mother, she must be able to see *herself* differently, to differentiate the needs and feelings she has at the moment from her larger sense of who she is, from her sense of self (Kegan, 1982).

And what about Eddie? How are we to understand his feelings of loneliness? The differentiation that eventually leads to greater mutuality in relationships with parents takes years to achieve. Eddie didn't have years to spend on differentiation that afternoon. He knew he wasn't a child, like his sister, but he was not sure what it was that made him different from children her age or, for that matter, different from adults such as his parents. He didn't want to be seen as a kid anymore, nor did he want to be like his parents. At 13, scissors and paint, cutting and pasting, promised a quick fix to an identity. Why, then, was he feeling so lonely? Eddie had lost something. He had lost the self he had known himself to be, and he had not put together a way of being to step into when he stepped out of the other.

In life, one frequently finds oneself in the middle of something without knowing exactly what it is one is doing, or precisely what one wants to get out of it—not at all a new experience for adolescents as they attempt to understand themselves in new ways. Change at any age doesn't come easily, and the more people that are involved, the more difficult it is, for as adolescents define themselves in new ways, so, too, must those around them, most notably their parents.

Adolescents' search for the truth about themselves begins when the separate worlds in which they live begin to pull apart. Adolescents begin to see themselves as more than their parents' children, to question where the skills they are acquiring in school will take them, to ask who they will be living with in the future. Erik Erikson (1968) suggests that the search ultimately leads to a sense of "sameness and continuity" that allows adolescents to transcend the differences they experience in their many roles—full-time student, part-time employee, daughter, son, friend, neighbor, and more.

Gaining a sense of themselves almost seems to require the tools of a magician or an actor: mirrors, sleight of hand, impressive costumes. Adolescents frequently find themselves playing out roles that are just a bit too big for them or not quite right. They try on these roles because the comfortable ones of childhood no longer fit. Adolescents find themselves looking inward and outward all at once, one eye on the inner self and another on those around them. They are well aware others may be judging them in terms of the cultural images they share, but also in terms of how well the others have achieved precisely what they themselves are attempting to do (Erikson, 1968).

The drama of constructing a self unfolds on a well-known stage: at home as adolescents interact with parents.

Achieving Autonomy

One of the ways adolescents gain a sense of who they are is by making decisions for themselves and living with the consequences of these, by becoming more **autonomous**. The major decision is who is going to make the decisions, but because decisions take many different forms, this point is easily missed. Adolescents find themselves arguing with parents about how late they can stay up, how much is too much makeup, or who gets to say what courses they can take in school. Much of the process is repetitive. Decisions made one day must be renegotiated the next, as the same issues continue to come up in different forms.

autonomous The state of being self-governing and responsible for one's actions.

Perhaps the process is repetitive because it involves learning in a real-life situation instead of in a classroom. In the classroom, principles are stated explicitly, frequently apart from any context, and adolescents must relate these principles to real-life situations. Just the opposite occurs when learning outside the classroom. Outside their classes, adolescents learn by doing and by experiencing the consequences. No one is there to help identify which principles operate in that situation. As a result, it is often difficult to separate the elements that remain constant across situations from the situations themselves. Are adolescents really arguing about how loud their music can be, or about who gets to decide how loud is too loud?

There is another reason why adolescents tend to repeat the decision-making process: Frequently, what they learn from their decisions has very personal consequences, which they may not be ready to accept. Discovering how to solve an algebraic equation has little bearing on life outside math class; algebra is "safe" knowledge. But discovering that you are the only one who can make decisions for yourself, and that there is no one to blame or praise but yourself, is something else again. Understanding is rarely just an intellectual matter; it also reflects one's emotions and beliefs, and some things can be understood only when one is prepared to let go of old beliefs. Sometimes adolescents, or adults too for that matter, cannot allow themselves to understand until they can live with the consequences of that understanding. They may prefer to live with isolated actions, not seeing how one fits with another to form a larger picture (M. L. Wapner, personal communication).

Bids for greater autonomy can be expected to occasion some conflict with parents. Most conflicts are over everyday events, such as what clothes are appropriate for school or why they have to clean their room. Interestingly, conflicts occur not so much because adolescents contest their parents' right to set standards and make decisions as they do because of disagreements with parents over which areas of their lives they can do this *in*. Issues that parents believe require supervision are often those which adolescents see as personal issues that should be left to them. It's also the case that irrespective of the type of issue, parents believe that adolescents have a greater obligation to disclose their behaviors than adolescents do. With respect to activities that might involve some risk, such as being invited to a party where there could be drinking, adolescents, too, are likely to agree that they have an obligation to keep parents informed. In the end, how much adolescents disclose when talking with their parents depends on the mutual trust that exists between them. To the extent that trust isn't present, adolescents are likely to keep personal issues or those involving their friends secret from their parents (Smetana et al., 2004; Smetana et al., 2006). See **Box 5.1** for some parents' thoughts on raising adolescents.

Although disagreements between adolescents and parents will occur in every culture, these are likely to be resolved in different ways depending on the value a culture places on individual autonomy versus interdependence among family members. Individualistic cultures such as the United States, encourage individuals to state their opinions as a means of resolving a disagreement. Collectivistic cultures,

Keeping secrets from parents can contribute to adolescents' feelings of independence and their experience of autonomy.

In More Depth

Parents' Reflections About Adolescence

"…When you read about independence, it sounds like it's carefully planned out. When it actually happens, all of a sudden they want to do something that they have never done before and which you firmly believe they have no idea how to do. It can be driving for the first time or suddenly announcing they want to go somewhere with friends. I knew it was going to happen, but exactly how to handle it myself and handle it with them so they got a chance to do something new without it being dangerous has been a challenge to me." –Father

"I wish that I had got my children involved in more family activities. When they were mostly through adolescence, I heard a talk by a child psychiatrist who said that often when teenagers say they don't want to do something with the family, at times you have to insist because they do go along and enjoy the event. I wish I had known sooner, because I accepted their first 'No,' when I perhaps should have pushed more." –Mother

"I wish I had known to be more attentive, to really listen, because kids have a lot of worthwhile things to say and you come to find out they hold a lot of your viewpoints." –Father

"I wish I had known it was important to spend time with children individually. We did things as a family, but the children are so different, and I think I would have understood them better if I had spent time with them alone." –Mother

Source: From Brooks, 1999.

such as China, avoid direct conflict such as this, and encourage resolutions that maintain harmonious relations among individuals, such as compliance or negotiation. Even within the United States, adolescents and parents might be expected to handle disagreements differently depending on the cultural background of their families. Jean Phinney and her associates (2005) asked American adolescents from non-European collectivistic cultural backgrounds and European American adolescents to state how they would resolve a potential conflict with their parents (**Figure 5.1**). Just as these investigators had expected, adolescents from non-European backgrounds showed more compliance with their parents' wishes, stating concern for parents and importance of the family as reasons for doing so. Interestingly, though, they did not differ in autonomy from European American adolescents. Adolescents from all backgrounds were willing to assert themselves and express their desires; those from non-European backgrounds in which family interdependence is valued, however, showed concern for their parents while doing so.

The Role of Parents

We've been talking about adolescents becoming autonomous and making decisions for themselves, but to what extent do they do this without relying on others? Is it easier for adolescents to become autonomous when they are supported by significant others, such as parents? And if so, how are we to think of autonomy?

The process of achieving autonomy can be thought of in several ways. According to one of these, a psychoanalytic view, the development of autonomy involves a two-step process in which adolescents must first distance themselves emotionally from their parents (separation) before they can assume responsibility for their own thoughts and actions (individuation). This dual process is assumed to result in adolescents' ability to function independently of their parents' and others' expectations and support (Blos, 1979).

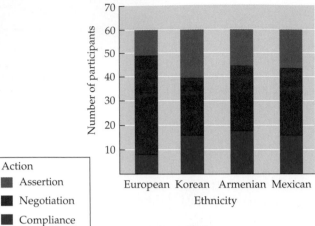

Chores. "You are living at home with your parents. When your parents come back from work, you are watching your favorite TV show. They notice that you have not done your usual chores and ask you to do them right away. You are in the middle of the show and want to finish watching it."

Action
- Assertion
- Negotiation
- Compliance

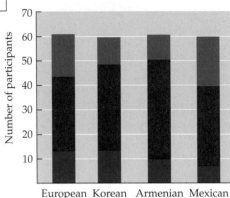

Concert. "A popular band that you like is giving a concert. You and your friends decide to attend the event. However, your parents do not want you to go to the concert."

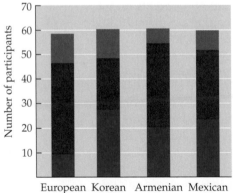

Family dinner. "A weekly family gathering is planned for the coming Friday night at your house. Everyone knows that Friday nights are family dinner nights. On Tuesday, some friends invite you to a big party that they are having on Friday. When you tell your parents about this, they say that it is important for the family to be together for the Friday dinner."

● **Figure 5.1 Differences in ways of resolving conflicts with parents in adolescents from individualistic and collectivistic cultures** (After Phinney et al., 2005.)

According to this view, parents need to promote independence in order for adolescents to become autonomous.

An alternative view stresses self-determination and assumes that adolescents become self-governing, or autonomous, as they discover what they are interested in and what they value, and start to base their decisions on personal goals reflecting these interests. Rather than having to separate from their parents in order to become autonomous, their parents support the development of autonomy by helping them discover the activities that will intrinsically motivate autonomous functioning (Deci & Ryan, 2000).

Bart Soenens and his associates (2007), at Catholic University of Leuven, in Belgium, assessed adolescents' perceptions of whether their parents promoted independence (e.g., "My mother/father encourage me to be independent from him/her") or self-determination (e.g., "My mother/father lets me make my own plans for things I want to do"), and asked them to complete measures of adjustment such as sense of self-esteem and well-being. They found that parenting that promoted self-governance uniquely predicted adjustment, whereas promoting independence did not. Additionally, adolescents' sense of self-determination mediated the relationship to adjustment. That is, encouraging adolescents to discover activities that are intrinsically motivating enables them to function more autonomously, which, in turn, contributes to their self-esteem and well-being.

Adolescents are most likely to perceive their parents as influential in their lives when they experience a warm and supportive relationship with them (McElhaney et al., 2008). In general, adolescents who have close emotional relationships with parents, who trust their parents and see them as available, and easy to talk with, have an easier time becoming autonomous and discovering their own individuality. Autonomy is less about separating from parents, in other words, than it is about finding oneself (Beyers et al., 2003; Joussemet et al., 2008; Wang et al., 2007).

The very conditions that foster healthy development at one age within the lifespan should be similar to those promoting development at other ages as well. This is true with respect to the conditions that promote the development of autonomy. Adolescents whose parents are emotionally open and supportive are those who feel free to explore life's possibilities. Similarly, Ainsworth (1973, 1993), who studied attachment in infants, found that infants whose caregivers are sensitive and responsive are more curious and more likely to explore their surroundings. The growth of autonomy, like attachment, reflects a healthy balance between a growing independence and continued closeness with parents. To the extent this balance is maintained, adolescents are able to assume increasing responsibility for their own individuality without fearing that doing so will distance them from their parents (Allen et al., 2004; MacKinnon & Marcia, 2002).

Connectedness with Parents

The sense of oneself that adolescents achieve as they come to distinguish their own attitudes and beliefs from those of their parents, and become more self-governing, is termed **individuation**. Harold Grotevant, at the University of Massachusetts, Amherst, and Catherine Cooper, at the University of California, Santa Cruz (1986), identified dimensions of family interaction that contribute to the development of individuation. They used a deceptively simple approach to study family interactions: They asked families to make plans for an imaginary vacation and analyzed the communication patterns that developed within the family. They looked for patterns that evidenced two qualities they believed to be critical for this development: individuality and connectedness. **Individuality** is the ability to have and express one's own ideas (*self-assertion*) and to say how one differs from others (*separateness*). **Connectedness** reflects one's openness to others' opinions (*permeability*) and one's respect for their ideas (*mutuality*). **Box 5.2** illustrates how these investigators analyzed patterns of interaction within a family.

Adolescents in an individuated relationship have a clear sense of themselves as distinct from other people yet feel emotionally connected with them. They have their own ideas, which they can express, and are open to the ideas of the person they are with. In a sense, individuation allows them to respect each person as an individual—including themselves. Equally important, individuated relationships allow adolescents to experience their connectedness with another person and still see how they are different. Research suggests that adolescents who achieve high levels of individuation can remain close to

individuation The process of distinguishing one's attitudes and beliefs from those of one's parents.

individuality A quality of family interactions reflecting the ability to express one's ideas and say how one differs from others.

connectedness A quality of family interactions reflecting openness to and respect for others' opinions.

In More Depth

Communication Patterns that Foster Individuation

Tanya: Why don't we visit Grandma and then go someplace exotic like the Everglades?

Willie: Do you know how hot it is in Florida in August? I vote to skip the family visit this year and go to Acapulco. That's a real vacation.

Dad: I could sure use some time on a beach.

Willie: Right, Dad, but you don't want to share it with a crocodile, do you?

Tanya: They're alligators, not crocodiles, Surfer Joe.

Mom: I'd like to see the pyramids in Mexico. We could stop off at Acapulco on the way.

Tanya: Hmm.

Dad: How far inland are they?

Mom: I don't know, but I could find that on the Internet.

Willie: Get real, Mom. Do you think you can get us to sweat a path through the jungle once we've seen the sands of Acapulco?

Tanya: Willie'd die in the heat there, too.

Dad: Maybe we should think of a winter vacation.

Tanya: All right, let's vote on this.

Willie: Okay, let's vote.

INDIVIDUALITY

Self-Assertion—The ability to have one's own ideas and express them. "I'd like to see the pyramids in Mexico."

Separateness—The ability to say how one differs from others.

1. Requests action
   "All right, let's vote on this."
2. Directly disagrees
   "Get real, Mom. Do you think you can get us to sweat a path through the jungle once we've seen the sands of Acapulco?"
3. Indirectly disagrees
   "Do you know how hot it is in Florida in August?"
4. Irrelevant comment
   "They're alligators, not crocodiles, Surfer Joe."

CONNECTEDNESS

Permeability—Openness and responsiveness to the opinions of others.
1. Acknowledges "Hmm."
2. Requests information or validation
   "How far inland are they?"
3. Agrees with another's ideas
   "I could sure use some time on a beach."
4. Relevant comment
   "Maybe we should think of a winter vacation."
5. Complies with a request "Okay, let's vote."

Mutuality—Sensitivity and respect for others' ideas.
1. Indirect suggestion of action
   "Why don't we visit Grandma and then go someplace exotic like the Everglades?"
2. Compromise
   "I'd like to see the pyramids in Mexico. We could stop off at Acapulco on the way."
3. States another's feelings
   "Willie'd die in the heat there, too."
4. Answers request for information/ validation
   "I don't know, but I could find that on the Internet."

Source: After Cooper et al., 1983.

their parents without feeling a loss of their own distinctiveness, and that parent-adolescent relationships continue to be close as they move toward greater mutuality (Pinquart & Silbereisen, 2002; White et al., 1983).

Just as adolescents resolve conflicts with their parents in ways that reflect the values of their different cultures, we might expect similar differences in the way they experience connectedness with their families. In other words, cultural backgrounds that emphasize the interdependence of family members might cause adolescents to experience a greater connectedness. Christina Hardway and Andrew Fuligni (2006), at the University of California, Los Angeles, examined connectedness in European American, Mexican Ameri-

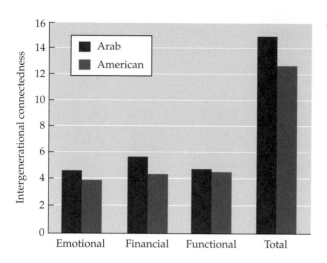

can and Chinese American adolescents. The latter two groups of adolescents share cultural traditions that emphasize the importance of the family over the individual. They found that although Mexican American and Chinese American adolescents felt a stronger sense of family obligation, in the form of providing support for and assistance to their families, European American adolescents were actually closer emotionally to their parents. Also, adolescents didn't differ in the extent to which their families contributed to their sense of themselves.

In general, the relatively greater emphasis placed on the family by collectivist cultures does not necessarily mean adolescents experience more connectedness with their families. Rather, the ways families express connectedness differs. An exception to this generalization occurs with Arab societies, which tend to be both collectivistic and authoritarian, and in which adolescents appear to experience more connectedness than do adolescents in the United States (**Figure 5.2**). However, comparisons among 16 independent and interdependent cultures reveal that although these differ with respect to the emotional distance among family members, the *pattern* for these differences is similar across cultures (**Figure 5.3**) (Dwairy et al., 2006a; Hardway & Fuligni, 2006; Georgas et al., 2001; Imamo lu & Karakitapo lu-Aygün, 2007).

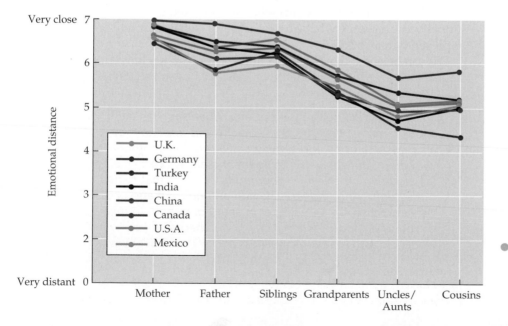

● **Figure 5.3** **Means of emotional distance with different relatives in 8 cultural groups** (After Georgas et al., 2001.)

Individuation gives adolescents a set of attitudes and ways of acting that are genuinely their own; however, they must still put these together into a working whole that reflects an inner sense of self. Although the process begins in early adolescence, adolescents do not consolidate these changes until late adolescence or even early adulthood when choices about jobs, college, and relationships force identity issues to a head. We turn to a consideration of identity next.

Identity as a Normative Crisis of Adolescence

"Normative crisis" sounds like an oxymoron, a combination of contradictory terms like "thunderous silence." Doesn't "normative" refer to a standard, a pattern, something that is predictable and regular? And doesn't "crisis" mean something *out* of the ordinary, something that violates the pattern, that doesn't happen every day?

In discussing the concept of "identity crisis," Erik Erikson (1968) noted that, although the phrase later acquired a distinctive meaning, at the time he first coined it, he considered himself to be naming something so familiar as to be taken for granted. He illustrated this point with a story about an old man who vomited each morning but refused to see a doctor. Finally, his family convinced him to get a checkup. After examining him, the doctor asked how he was feeling. "Fine, just fine" the old man replied. The doctor, impatient with what appeared to be denial of a serious problem, responded, "But your family tells me you vomit every morning!" The old man looked at the doctor in surprise. "Of course I do, doesn't everybody?" he asked.

Erikson's point to this story is that "identity crisis" describes something that all of us have experienced and have taken for granted, but would have no difficulty recognizing once it is labeled, something that is, despite the upset, quite normative (Erikson, 1968).

Similarly, Erikson used the word *crisis* to refer not to some imminent catastrophe but, rather, to a developmental turning point in which the individual must choose one course or another simply because it is no longer possible to continue as before.

Perhaps no term is more closely associated with the writing and thinking of Erik Erikson than *identity*. Erikson was, above all else, a clinician whose concepts reflected real-life experiences. In writing about the personality, Erikson noted that "old troubles" return when we are tired or otherwise defenseless, simply because we are what we *were* as well as what we might want to become or presently may be (Coles, 1970; Erikson, 1954).

Erikson believed that, like his patients, adolescents have to confront "old troubles" in arriving at an identity. Consider Erikson's (1968) description of Jill, a young woman he knew:

> I had known Jill before her puberty, when she was rather obese and showed many "oral" traits of voracity and dependency while she also was a tomboy and bitterly envious of her brothers and in rivalry with them. But she was intelligent and always had an air about her (as did her mother) which seemed to promise that things would turn out all right. And, indeed, she straightened out and up, became very attractive, an easy leader in any group, and, to many, a model of young girlhood. As a clinician, I watched and wondered what she would do with that voraciousness and with the rivalry which she had displayed earlier. Could it be that such things are simply absorbed in fortuitous growth?

Then one autumn in her late teens, Jill did not return to college from the ranch out West where she had spent the summer. She had asked her parents to let her stay. Simply out of liberality and confidence, they granted her this moratorium and returned East.

That winter Jill specialized in taking care of newborn colts, and would get up at any time during a winter night to bottle-feed the most needy animals. Having apparently acquired a certain satisfaction within herself, as well as astonished recognition from the cowboys, she returned home and reassumed her place. I felt that she had found and hung on to an opportunity to do actively and for others what she had once demonstrated by overeating: she had learned to feed needy young mouths. But she did so in a context which, in turning passive into active, also turned a former symptom into a social act.

One might say that she turned "maternal" but it was a maternalism such as cowboys must and do display; and, of course, she did it all in jeans. This brought recognition "from man to man" as well as from man to woman, and beyond that the confirmation of her optimism, that is, her feeling that something could be done that felt like her, was useful and worthwhile, and was in line with an ideological trend where it still made immediate practical sense. (pp. 130–131)

Jill fashioned her identity, as Erikson said we all do, out of old cloth, but she tailored it to the needs of the present. She translated what she *was*—an energetic, intelligent, but envious and dependent child—into a mature personality, capable of responding to her own and others' needs.

Identity, as Erikson used the term, refers to the sense of self that we achieve through examining and committing ourselves to the roles and pursuits that define an adult in our society in each of three domains: sexuality as expressed in an adult gender role; occupation; and ideology, or religious and political beliefs. Identity gives us a sense of who we are, of knowing what is "me" and what is "not me." As Jill's story demonstrated, the "me" includes more than the present. Identity allows us to experience a continuity of self over time. We can relate what we have done in the past to what we hope to do in the future, to our ambitions and dreams. Finally, our perception of self includes how others see us, and the importance they attach to our values and accomplishments.

Jill's story illustrates these aspects of identity. Her new maturity grew out of familiar issues—her "old troubles"—that she approached in new ways. Because the "me" that she had been as a child was still recognizable in her more adult concerns, there was a continuity to her experience over time. Lastly, her perception of herself, her confidence and self-esteem, resulted not only from becoming skilled in something she valued, but also from receiving the recognition of the society in which she achieved this, the cowboys she had worked with.

As Erikson illustrated in this case study, Jill experimented with a way of being, one of many possible ones, that incorporated much of what she already recognized in herself but enabled her to realize new strengths. Erikson (1959) suggested that adolescents imagine a number of **possible selves**, mentally trying them on to get a sense of who they might become, of what their lives might be like. Some of these versions of the self are positive, or hoped-for selves, whereas others represent feared outcomes that adolescents nonetheless believe could be possible as well. High school students, when asked to generate all the possible selves they can think of, think of quite a few, averaging about 13. The majority of these are positive, and also are seen as more likely than feared possible selves (Knox et al., 2000).

identity The aspect of one's personality of which one is aware and experiences as a meaningful and coherent whole.

possible selves Life options that adolescents imagine for themselves; some are positive, or hoped-for, and others are feared, or negative, possibilities.

exploration The process of exploring possibilities and life options in achieving an identity.

commitment The process of committing oneself to a definite course of action in achieving an identity.

identity statuses Resolutions to identity that differ in commitment and exploration of life options.

identity achievement The resolution of the psychosocial crisis of identity by exploring life options and then committing oneself to personally defined goals.

identity foreclosure The resolution of the psychosocial crisis of identity through the assumption of traditional, conventional, or parentally chosen goals and values without the experience of crisis or conflict over identity issues.

moratorium The experience of conflict over the issues of identity formation prior to the establishment of firm goals or long-term commitments.

identity diffusion The resolution of the psychosocial crisis without the experience of crisis or commitment over identity issues.

carefree diffusion The resolution of the psychosocial crisis by neither exploring nor committing oneself to life options primarily due to enjoyment of one's present circumstances.

In defining identity, Erikson considered the three domains noted earlier (sexuality, occupation, and ideology) to be of paramount importance. Each of these domains will be more closely examined in subsequent chapters: Sexuality and gender roles in Chapter 10, work and college in Chapter 9, and values and moral development in Chapter 11. But for now, we will examine the process of identity formation itself.

Identity Statuses

Although Erikson was the first to describe and elaborate the concept of identity as a normative crisis in adolescence, James Marcia (1966) has been largely responsible for generating research on identity formation, primarily by constructing a measure of identity that has made it possible to empirically test many implications of Erikson's writings.

Most of the work we do on our identity takes place in adolescence; however, as Marcia notes with a touch of humor, if identity formation were necessary by the end of adolescence, many of us would never become adults. His point is that achieving a personal identity is not an easy process. Adolescents must be willing to take risks and live with uncertainty.

Some of the uncertainty comes from exploring possibilities and options in life that differ from those chosen by one's parents or other members of one's family. Most adolescents expect this exploration to be risky. Few adolescents, however, expect the risks that occur when they make commitments based on their exploration. Adolescents form their identities both by taking on new ways of being *and* by excluding others. It is every bit as important to let go of their fantasies and commit themselves to a definite course of action as it is to challenge the familiar by exploring possibilities never even considered by their parents or families. Marcia (1966, 1980) refers to these two dimensions of the identity process as **exploration** and **commitment**.

Marcia distinguishes a number of ways by which adolescents arrive at the roles and values that define their identities. Each of these ways, or **identity statuses**, is defined in terms of the dimensions of commitment and exploration. Adolescents who are committed to life options arrive at them either by exploring and searching for what fits them best or by forgoing exploration and letting themselves be guided by the values of others. Adolescents who have searched for life options that fit them best are termed **identity achieved**; those who adopt their parents' values without question are termed **identity foreclosed** (Marcia, 1980, 2002).

Similarly, several paths lead to non-commitment. Some adolescents begin to evaluate life options but don't close off certain possibilities because the decisions are too momentous to risk making a mistake; as a result, they remain uncommitted to any path. These adolescents are in **moratorium**. Others remain uncommitted for the opposite reason, failing to see the importance of choosing one option over any other. They are termed **identity diffused**. Adolescents in a fifth identity status, **carefree diffusion**, also fail to explore or commit to life options, but appear not to because they enjoy their current state, rather than because of apathy or avoidance (Luyckx et al., 2005).

The process of reorganizing earlier identifications continues into late adolescence—and beyond. Self-definition in areas of occupational choice, religious and political beliefs, and gender roles continues into early adulthood. Jane Kroger (2007) notes that even among late adolescents, fewer than half are likely to have explored various options in life and then made commitments to these.

Given that individuals are expected to become more mature with age and, in Western cultures, to think things through for themselves before making commitments, there is an implicit developmental trend to these statuses. Identity-achieved adolescents who commit themselves to self-defined goals should be the most mature. Conversely, identity-diffused adolescents, who neither explore options nor commit themselves to personal goals, should be the least mature. Support for this trend comes from longitudinal studies showing the achieved status to become more frequent with age, and the diffusion status less frequent (Cramer, 1998; Kroger, 1995). Identity-achieved adolescents also score higher on measures of adjustment and well-being than identity-diffused adolescents (Luyckx et al., 2005; Cote & Schwartz, 2002). There is some support as well from attachment theory research, in which secure attachment to a caregiver in childhood has been found to be associated with a number of markers of maturity—such as increased resilience and social competence—later in development. (Sroufe, 1989). Identity-achieved adolescents are somewhat more likely to be securely attached, and identity-diffused adolescents to be insecurely attached (Arseth et al., 2009; Zimmermann & Becker-Stoll, 2002).

James Marcia's theory of identity statuses suggests that some of these young women are considering a military career because of a family military tradition, that others are motivated by a personal commitment to serve their country, and that still others see military service as a way to postpone deciding what they ultimately want to do with their lives.

Do adolescents simultaneously address identity issues in each of the different domains? That is, do they consider occupational, ideological, and sexual alternatives at the same point in time? Or do different domains become salient at different points in an adolescent's life? Can a 17-year-old male be identity-achieved in his occupational plans ("I'll work in construction with my uncle") but foreclosed in his gender role ("I want my wife to stay home with the kids the way Mom did"), diffused in his political beliefs ("I don't see the point in getting too worked up over political issues; after all, what can one person do?"), and in moratorium about his religious beliefs ("I don't think of God the way I did as a kid, but I can't dismiss the idea that God is interested in me personally")?

In a two-year follow-up study of late adolescents, Kroger (1988) found that only half the adolescents she studied had a common status in any two domains; another 9% had no domains in common. These data suggest that identity is not "a unitary structure, but…a sequence of distinct psychosocial resolutions involved in the definition of self" (1988, p. 60). Kroger's findings are comparable to those of other investigators in suggesting that adolescents do not work simultaneously on all identity domains (Archer, 1989; Goossens, 2001; Kroger, 2003).

Lea Pulkkinen and Katja Kokko (2000), at the University of Jyväskylä, in Finland, followed individuals into their mid-30s, assessing their identity status at the age of 27 and again at 36. These investigators found significant changes in the distribution of identity statuses across nearly all domains for both women and men. In general, the number of individuals in the diffusion and moratorium statuses decreased with age and those in foreclosure and achievement increased with age. In other words, as individuals aged, more of them moved into the achievement *and* foreclosure statuses.

These patterns of change in mid-adulthood stand in contrast to those found for college students who are more likely to move from foreclosure to moratorium (Kroger, 2000). If we assume, however, as did these investigators, that identity development in adulthood should reflect an increasing commitment to the values one holds in life, this progression makes sense. The individuals

Most, if not all, of these football players probably dream of sports scholarships or even going pro. But as they go through the process of identity formation, they will gradually let go of such fantasies and commit themselves to more realistic futures.

in this study were no longer in college, a setting designed to maximize students' exploration of options but, when last interviewed, were in their mid-30s. Movement into foreclosure, as opposed to moratorium, would reflect these adults' growing commitment to the life tasks of adulthood. Thus the relative maturity of an identity status must be considered within the larger context of the developmental tasks facing individuals at different points in their lives. What constitutes the most adaptive response to the developmental tasks of adolescence is not necessarily the most adaptive in adulthood.

Pulkkinen and Kokko are not alone in finding that individuals are not likely to remain in the moratorium status. In fact, Curt Dunkel (2000), at Illinois Central College, has suggested that moratorium is less an identity outcome than it is a transitory state. Dunkel points out that longitudinal studies may have shown us the *path* adolescents follow, but they have not identified the developmental *mechanisms* responsible for change (Josselson, 1987; Kroger, 1988; Marcia, 1976). Dunkel suggests that one such mechanism is at work during moratorium, and it takes the form of generating possible selves. That is, if identity formation involves the construction of a self, individuals need to explore the form this self might take, and they do so during moratorium. In support of this, Dunkel found that, when asked to think about all the selves they might be, college students who were in the moratorium status endorsed more possible selves than did those in any other status (**Figure 5.4**) (Dunkel, 2000; Dunkel & Anthis, 2001).

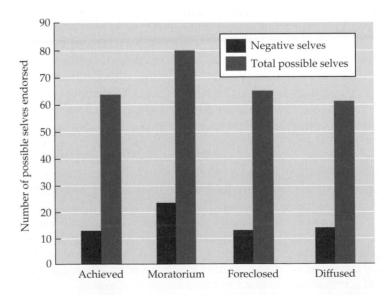

● **Figure 5.4   Identity status and possible selves**   When asked to think about all the possible selves, or alternatives in life, youth in the moratorium status are the most undecided; they also envision more negative possibilities than do youth in the other identity statuses. (After Dunkel, 2000.)

Identity Styles

Michael Berzonsky (1992; Berzonsky & Luyckx, 2008) has proposed an alternative way of thinking about identity statuses. To use Kroger's (1992) distinction, Berzonsky envisions identity statuses as "organizers" of experience, not as "organizations" of experience. In other words, Berzonsky views identity statuses as an input variable rather than an outcome variable, as a process rather than a structure.

Berzonsky suggests that individuals differ in the way they process information relevant to the self; these differences underlie Marcia's statuses. Some individuals, for instance, actively search for any information that might be relevant to the problems they face; then they carefully evaluate this information before making their decisions. This **information oriented** style characterizes identity-achieved and moratorium individuals. Others appear to do just the opposite, putting off decisions and avoiding problems by procrastinating. Berzonsky calls this style, which characterizes identity-diffused persons, **diffuse/ avoidant**. Finally, some individuals, when faced with problems, use social norms or the expectations of significant others, such as parents, as their guide. Berzonsky identifies this processing style as **normative oriented** and notes that it characterizes those who are foreclosed (Berzonsky, 2004). **Box 5.3** illustrates the relationships among identity styles and identity statuses.

Adolescents and the Internet

Approximately 93% of 12- to 17-year-olds in the United States use the Internet. They go online to communicate with friends—emailing, instant messaging, visiting social networking sites such as Facebook and MySpace—to download music, play games, find information for school projects, check on news and current events, and just to have "something to do" (Pew Internet & American Life Project, 2007).

If any one thing characterizes the way adolescents use the Internet it is multitasking. An adolescent who is downloading music may also be instant messaging a friend at the same time. The Internet makes it possible to simultaneously carry on activities such as these without appearing rude. As one adolescent put it, "I prefer to communicate with my friends online because that way, I can talk to them while doing other stuff online. When you're talking to them in person or on the phone, it seems rude to be doing something else because they notice and you get distracted" (Gross, 2004).

Adolescents of either sex spend about the same amount of time online, with the exception of those who are heavy game players, and these are primarily males. Otherwise, males and females alike spend most of their time on the Internet communicating with friends from school, primarily through instant messaging. In this sense, their use of the Internet is similar to the way adolescents have used the telephone in the past, to talk with friends from school, gossip, and just "hang out."

The Internet affords another opportunity to adolescents. At a time when adolescents are re-negotiating relationships within their families and exploring possible future selves, it makes sense to ask whether they also use the Internet as a way to experiment with their identities. The Internet offers a

For some young people, travel is a way to learn more about themselves and the world. For others, however, it is a way to put off making life decisions.

information oriented
A style of information processing characterized by actively searching for and evaluating information.

diffuse/avoidant oriented
A style of information processing characterized by procrastinating and avoiding decisions.

normative oriented
A style of information processing characterized by reliance on social norms and the expectations of relatives and friends.

BOX
5.3
Research Focus

Operationalizing Concepts: What Kind of Decision Maker Are You?

By Michael Wapner

Lucky for Henry there was a category for undeclared majors. It had let him postpone that decision for a year and a half. But here it was the end of the first semester of his sophomore year and he was still "undeclared." He had just about finished his general education requirements, and he had taken intro psych, intro soc, intro anthro, and intro poli sci. No way to keep going much longer without choosing a major. But how was a guy to know what he'd want to do three years from now? He'd pretty much narrowed it down to a social science. Or, really, it had been narrowed down for him. He wasn't much good at math or music. He didn't like chemistry or physics. And he couldn't paint or dance. So social science was about all that was left—but which one?

Really, to tell the truth, it wasn't just choosing a major. Henry hated choices in general. He never ate in the cafeteria. Barbara chose the movies they would see and even went shopping with him to pick out his clothes. (Come to think of it, he didn't really *choose* Barbara. They had been fixed up for a blind date and just kept going together.) In fact, he was even at this college because he had delayed so long in deciding that all the other colleges had withdrawn their acceptances.

Although Henry may be an extreme example, he is not unique. His style of dealing with decisions makes him a good candidate for what Michael Berzonsky, at the State University of New York, Cortland, calls a diffuse/avoidant identity orientation.

Berzonsky's social-cognitive model identifies three types of *identity orientation*, or ways an individual approaches (or avoids) the task of constructing and revising a self-identity. These three types are informational, normative, and diffuse/avoidant. The *informational orientation* is characteristic of individuals who are in an identity-achieved or moratorium identity status, and it is marked by deliberate self-exploration, a personally defined identity, an internal locus of control, problem-focused coping, and an openness to novel ideas, values, and actions. The *normative orientation* is associated with a foreclosed identity status, and it is distin-

guished by a tendency to be closed to information that would cause one to evaluate central aspects of the self and by conformity to the expectations of others. A *diffuse/avoidant orientation* is associated with a diffuse identity status, a greater likelihood of depression and neurosis, a less particular and pleasant interaction style than that of the other two categories, and a reluctance to deal with problems and decisions.

Berzonsky contends that each identity orientation is characterized by a different strategy of decision making. Information-orientated individuals are most likely to gather as much information as possible, by such means as talking to others or reading up on a subject, before they make a decision. Individuals with diffuse/avoidant orientations, such as Henry, are most likely to procrastinate and engage in defensive avoidance and other self-defeating approaches that are designed to escape decisions more than to make them. (In the research we are currently considering, Berzonsky made no particular predictions regarding the decisional strategies of normatively oriented individuals.)

Having hypothesized these relationships between identity orientation and decisional strategy, Berzonsky and his colleagues undertook extensive research to demonstrate them. However, before data on the question could be gathered, an essential step had to be taken. The concepts under consideration (identity orientation and decisional strategy) had to be *operationally defined*. Because concepts are, by definition, abstract, there are usually a number of different ways of interpreting them. Operationally defining a concept pins it down by expressing it in terms of the methods used to measure it. Operationalizing is a very fundamental process employed in all empirical science. Even a seemingly simple concept like "friendliness," in order to be studied, must be operationally defined in terms of a score on a friendliness scale or a questionnaire filled out by an individual's acquaintances. By operationalizing a concept, investigators define it in a way that others can use and follow and be sure they are studying the same concept.

But not all operational definitions are equally adequate. Suppose, in studying friendliness, we operationally defined a "friendly" person as "anyone who is smiling the first time that person is observed." Although that does fulfill the minimum requirement for an operational definition—that is,

BOX 5.3 continued

it specifies what operation to perform to determine if someone is friendly (observe the person and see if that person is smiling)—it is not likely to be a satisfactory definition. It is likely to be deficient with respect to the two most important criteria for any measure—*reliability* and *validity*—that is, its consistency and the degree to which it measures what we assume it is measuring.

To assess, or operationally define, identity orientation, Michael Berzonsky and Joseph Ferrari employed a questionnaire—the Identity Style Inventory (ISI)—constructed and revised just for this purpose (Berzonsky, 1992). The ISI contains a 10-item informational-style scale with items such as "I've spent a great deal of time thinking seriously about what I should do with my life"; a 10-item diffuse/avoidant scale with items such as "I'm not really thinking about my future now; it's still a long way off"; and a 9-item normative-style scale with items such as "I prefer to deal with situations where I can rely on social norms and standards." Subjects were asked to rate the degree to which statements applied to them.

To asses decisional strategies, Berzonsky and Ferrari used a decision-making questionnaire, in which participants were asked to rate the extent to which they engage in various decision-making practices. The subscales include vigilance ("When making decisions I like to collect lots of information"); panic ("I feel as if I'm under tremendous time pressure when making decisions"); and decisional avoidance ("I avoid making decisions").

Were these measures reliable? One way of determining reliability is to give the measure to the same individuals on two separate occasions. The *test–retest reliability*, or consistency in responding to questions from one time to the next, was relatively high. Of equal, if not greater, interest is whether the measure is a valid one. One way to determine a measure's validity is to see how well the measure relates to other measures of the construct. This assessment of validity is known as *construct validity*. In originally constructing the Identity Style Inventory, Berzonsky (1989) selected a number of measures that were known to distinguish individuals in each of the identity statuses themselves, and administered these to another group of individuals, together with his measure of decision styles. Would the decision-making scores correspond in a meaningful way with those on the other measures? Berzonsky found that they did.

Berzonsky and Ferrari administered the Identity Style Inventory and the decision-making questionnaire to college students. They also administered two scales of procrastination. Are different identity orientations characterized by different strategies of decision making? As expected, students who could be classified as information oriented were likely to use decisional practices in which they gather information, and individuals who could be classified as diffuse/avoidant oriented were more likely to procrastinate and engage in avoidance, excuse making, and other maladaptive behaviors.

Sources: Berzonsky, 1989, and Berzonsky & Ferrari, 1996.

---

unique opportunity for such experimentation because of the anonymity it affords. Unlike the people that adolescents might meet at school or at a party, those whom adolescents meet online have no information as to their sex or age, what school they attend, where they live, or how attractive they might be.

A substantial percentage of adolescents indicate they have pretended to be other than who they are when they are online. This is truer for early adolescents than for older ones. In fact, one of the most common alterations is for adolescents to say they are older than they are. Many report doing this, but just as a joke and usually when a friend is there. Others, more of whom are shy or lonely, alter their online identity as a form of self-exploration, to see how others will react to them. Experimenting online with their identity for these adolescents can contribute to their social competence by increasing the number of social interactions in which they can practice their social skills (Gross, 2004; Valkenburg & Peter, 2008; Valkenburg et al., 2005).

Identity: Gender and Ethnicity

Adolescents look for answers to questions concerning their identity by examining the societal roles they see around them, roles they will soon assume. Erikson considered one's occupation to be the most central question to be resolved, followed closely by one's political and religious beliefs, and the expression of an adult gender role (Erikson, 1968). Occupation, political stance, and ideology—all of these characterized males more than females at the time Erikson formulated this concept. Is this still true for adolescents today? A number of studies supply us with answers to these questions.

Gender Differences in Identity Formation

Research has found few differences among male and female adolescents in identity development with respect to Marcia's identity statuses (Cramer, 2000; Dunkel & Anthis, 2001; Goossens, 2001; Kroger, 2003; Pulkkinen & Kokko, 2000; Schwartz & Montgomery, 2002). When gender differences emerge, these most frequently show interpersonal concerns to figure more centrally in females' than males' identities (Archer, 1989; Cramer, 2000; Pulkkinen & Kokko, 2000; Schwartz & Montgomery, 2002). Even then, research that finds interpersonal issues to be more salient for females than males does not find occupational concerns to be of less importance than they are for males (Archer, 1989; Goossens, 2001; Pulkkinen & Kokko, 2000). Additionally, interpersonal issues have been found to be more important for males than earlier assumed (Kroger, 2000). With respect to the timing of identity formation, however, issues of identity and intimacy are more apt to be resolved concurrently in females than males (Patterson et al., 1992).

Serena Patterson, Ingrid Sochting, and James Marcia (1992) have suggested that, in addition to exploration and commitment, a third dimension, relatedness, is important in defining identity statuses for females. Is this suggestion contrary to research finding that the process of identity formation is more similar than different between adolescents of either sex? Sally Archer (1992) offers a tentative resolution to this apparent contradiction. She points to a remarkable tunnel vision that she noticed in her interviews with adolescents when it came to seeing the implications that commitments in one domain have for another domain. For instance, an adolescent boy might describe his vocational plans in detail as well as his plans for marriage and children, and yet not connect the two. Thus, potential conflicts, such as who would care for the children if his wife also chose a career, or whose career would determine where they would live, simply are not anticipated. Those interviewed by Archer who were most likely to make connections between domains were late-adolescent females. A sense of relatedness for females, an awareness of themselves in relation to others, may prompt them to integrate identity domains.

Taken together, the research on gender differences reveals more similarities than differences. Adolescents of either sex who allow themselves to question, explore, and experience the uncertainty of not knowing—to experience a period of crisis—mature in this process.

Because our sense of self reflects an awareness of how others see us, cultural values as

Identity-achieved females appear to focus on achieving a balance between self-assertion and relatedness. They use strengths drawn from their relationships to fuel their solo efforts.

well as individual experiences contribute to the development of identity. We turn to a consideration of ethnicity and identity next.

Contributions of Ethnicity to Identity Development

As adolescents look to the culture in which they live to gain a glimpse of themselves, European Americans will see themselves more easily in the face of the mainstream U.S. culture than will adolescents who are members of an ethnic minority. For these latter adolescents, the process of identity formation includes an additional step, one of resolving issues related to an ethnic identity.

Ethnic identity is an awareness of belonging to an ethnic group that shapes one's thoughts, feelings, and behavior. Simply put, it is a way of understanding oneself in terms of the values and traditions of one's group (Phinney, 1996, 2005). The boundaries that define one's group provide members with a feeling of belonging. When boundaries are clear, they allow adolescents to distinguish between their own and other groups, and result in stronger ethnic identity. Some boundaries are maintained from within by the group, others are imposed on the group by the dominant culture. Internal boundaries come about through identifying with others in one's group. Adolescents adopt the values, attitudes, and perspectives of their group. Interactions with those outside the group provide a second type of boundary, through which minority adolescents experience the social opportunities and constraints that exist for members of their group— the relative status and value given them by others. The status of one's group within society is an important component of ethnic identity (Phinney, 1996).

As might be expected, adolescents' consciousness of their ethnic identity varies with the situations they are in (Harris & Sim, 2002; Herman, 2004). Rosenthal and Hrynevich (1985) found that adolescents experience a strong ethnic identity when they are with their family or speaking their parents' native language, but feel part of the dominant culture when with others from that culture, such as when they are at school. They also found that the strength of the inner boundary of the ethnic group relates to adolescents' pride in their ethnic identity. This strength is reflected in the institutional completeness of the community, the extent to which it provides its own schools, markets, churches, and other institutions.

In the process of **acculturation**, the outward behaviors of minority adolescents frequently become less distinct from those of the majority culture; however, attitudes and values are more likely to remain unchanged because they are more central to their sense of belonging to their group. Thus, minority adolescents whose behavior closely resembles that of peers from the dominant culture may still have strong ethnic identities in other respects. Doreen Rosenthal and Shirley Feldman (1992), comparing ethnic identity in first- and second-generation Chinese American and Chinese Australian adolescents, found that despite differences in knowledge about their culture and in observable behavior between first- and second-generation minorities, the core aspects to their ethnic identities differed little; both first- and second-generation adolescents ascribed the same importance to their ethnic group membership and evaluated their ethnicity equally positively.

ethnic identity An awareness of belonging to an ethnic group that shapes one's thoughts, feelings, and behavior.

acculturation A socialization process by which members of a minority adopt the customs of the dominant group, while maintaining a separate cultural identity.

Adolescents with an achieved ethnic identity have a clear sense of their ethnicity that reflects feelings of belonging and emotional identification.

unexamined ethnic identity
An initial stage in ethnic identity formation that involves a lack of awareness of the issues related to one's ethnicity and a simple internalization of the values of the dominant culture.

ethnic identity search
An intermediate stage in ethnic identity formation involving exploration of the meaning of one's ethnicity.

achieved ethnic identity
A stage in ethnic identity formation in which one has a clear sense of one's ethnicity that reflects feelings of belonging and emotional identification.

bicultural identity The process by which minority adolescents identify themselves with respect to the two cultures to which they belong.

STAGES OF ETHNIC IDENTITY DEVELOPMENT   Jean Phinney (1989) points out that the progression toward an ethnic identity parallels differences among Marcia's identity statuses. Just as with Marcia's identity statuses, it is possible for minority adolescents to avoid exploring the implications of their ethnicity and to remain committed to the values of the dominant culture. Adolescents with an **unexamined ethnic identity** have simply internalized the values and attitudes of the dominant culture, in a way similar to that of foreclosed adolescents, and have little understanding of issues related to their ethnicity. Those in an **ethnic identity search**, or moratorium stage, are involved in exploring the meaning of their ethnicity and may experience a growing conflict between the values of the dominant culture and those of their ethnic group. Adolescents with an **achieved ethnic identity** have a clear sense of their ethnicity that reflects feelings of belonging and emotional identification. They show little defensiveness and experience pride in their ethnicity (Phinney, 1989). These stages correlate positively with measures of psychological well-being, such as sense of mastery and positive relations with peers and family, and parallel stages of racial identity formation (Cross, 1980, 2005).

The stages themselves are independent of any particular minority. As shown in **Table 5.1**, just about the same percentages of adolescents from the three minority groups were in each of the three stages of ethnic identity formation. This latter finding suggests that adolescents from different minority groups have the same need to come to terms with the personal implications of minority membership. The important element appears not to be the particular minority group the adolescent is from, but the adolescent's stage of development of an ethnic identity. An exception to this finding comes from European American adolescents, who had little sense of their own ethnicity and saw themselves only as "American." This ethnocentrism has continued despite an increasingly pluralistic society in which ethnic minority adolescents constitute just under a third of all adolescents in the United States (Phinney et al., 2007; Syed & Azmitia, 2008).

Although different procedures and the use of somewhat different definitions make it difficult to compare findings from one study of ethnic identity development to those of the next, research suggests that exploration of one's ethnicity peaks in mid-adolescence and that psychosocial adjustment is associated with an achieved, or internalized, ethnic identity (Bracey et al., 2004; Newman, 2005, Phinney & Kohatsu, 1997; Pahl & Way, 2006; Yasui et al., 2004).

MULTICULTURAL AND MULTIRACIAL ADOLESCENTS   How do minority adolescents identify themselves with respect to the several cultures to which they belong? Do they arrive at a **bicultural identity** by keeping the two cultures separate? By combining them? Or do they deemphasize the whole issue of ethnicity and culture? Jean Phinney and Mona Devich-Navarro (1997) interviewed African American and Mexican American adolescents, asking them questions similar to those just mentioned.

TABLE 5.1
Percentage of Minority Adolescents in Stages of Ethnic Identity Formation

	UNEXAMINED	SEARCH (MORATORIUM)	ACHIEVED
Asian Americans	57.1	21.4	21.4
Blacks	56.5	21.7	21.7
Hispanics	52.1	26.9	21.7
Total	**55.7**	**22.9**	**21.3**

Source: Phinney, 1989.

Approximately 90% of those who were interviewed thought of themselves as bicultural. However, there were differences in the ways in which they integrated the two cultures. Many consider themselves to be members equally of their ethnic group and of the wider culture, expressing a strong sense of being American without denying their ethnicity, and resolving issues raised by culture either by combining elements of both cultures or by deemphasizing differences. Those who regard their ethnicity as more central to their sense of themselves are likely to think of themselves differently depending on where they are or who they are with—such as feeling more American at school and more ethnic at home. Bicultural adolescents differ among themselves not so much in the importance of their ethnicity as in their identification with the U.S. culture. Those who think of themselves as equally members of their ethnic group and of the general culture are more likely to see the U.S. culture as inclusive and diverse, thus making it possible to see themselves as fitting in, whereas those whose identity is more situational have less sense of connection with being American.

Not until the 2000 census were individuals able to indicate their race by marking more than one racial group. One might think this change would bring clarity to a previously ambiguous statistic, however racial identity isn't easily reduced to a number. Achieving a racial identity introduces a complexity not necessarily present in ethnic identity. Racial distinctions are based on differences in physical appearance, rather than the less visible qualities that distinguish ethnic groups. Adolescents' construction of their racial identities, then, reflect not just the pride they have in membership in their group, but also their awareness of their appearance and how others will respond to them based on this (Phinney, 2005).

Perhaps nothing better reflects the difficulties involved in achieving a racial identity than the way multiracial adolescents identify themselves in different situations. When asked to provide information about themselves at school, adolescents are likely to respond differently than when they are surveyed at home, suggesting that racial identity for many adolescents is fluid. For instance, three-quarters of adolescents who identify themselves as multiracial at school do not do so at home (Harris & Sim, 2002).

Racial identities are more fluid for some adolescents than others, most likely reflecting differences both in internal and external constraints on the construction of their racial identity. Jamie Doyle and Grace Kao (2007), at the University of Pennsylvania, examined racial identification among biracial and mono-racial adolescents as they transitioned into adulthood. They found that changes in racial identity among biracial adolescents were extremely high. Only slightly more than half of African American-European American adolescents (57%) and Asian American-European American adolescents (53%) identified themselves the same way as they did as young adults. Individuals in each of these groups were more likely to identify themselves in terms of their minority race as young adults than they had been as adolescents. The direction of this change most likely reflects both a strong internal sense of pride in their racial group and the mediating effect of physical appearance, serving as an external constraint. However, the adolescents most likely to change the way they identified themselves as they transitioned to adulthood were those of Native American-European American heritage, with more identifying themselves as European American. In contrast to biracial adolescents, single-race European American, African American and Asian American adolescents almost always identified themselves in the same way as young adults (**Figure 5.5**). In general, for adolescents of all races, physical appearance either increases or sets limits on the fluidity of constructing a racial identity; and biracial individuals continue to work on their racial identity into adulthood despite having identified themselves as one race or another in adolescence.

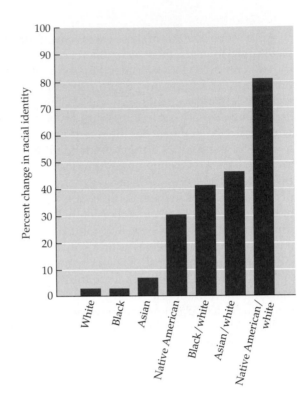

● **Figure 5.5** Percent change in racial identity from adolescence to early adulthood for single race and biracial individuals (After Doyle & Kao, 2007.)

In the section that follows we will look at how adolescents' cultures contribute to their understanding of the self. As we shall see, cultures teach us who we are.

Understanding the Self: Cultural Contributions

A fundamental dimension running through the socialization process is a culture's understanding of "self" in relation to others. **Individualistic cultures**, such as the United States and many Western European countries, view the self as independent and self-contained, and expect a person's actions to reflect his or her unique preferences and goals. **Collectivistic cultures**, such as China, Japan, and Latin American cultures view the self as interdependent, and completed in one's relationships with others. Rather than one's behavior being directed by personal desires or goals, a person's actions are constrained by the expectations of others, and guided by an awareness of interpersonal responsibilities. The self is defined as much, if not more, through relationships with others than through reference to internally organizing forces such as an individual's own thoughts and feelings.

A sense of **agency**, of asserting one's thoughts and feelings through one's actions, is at the core of the independent self. Given differences in how the self is experienced in collectivistic cultures, how might something like agency be expressed? Instead of experiencing the self in terms of one's needs and prerogatives, the self is experienced interdependently, in the context of relationships with others. One's behavior is motivated less by personal goals than by attentiveness to others, voluntarily controlling emotions and actions so as to maintain harmonious relations (Markus & Kitayama, 1991). To see how one's view of the self can shape even the simplest of interactions, consider two adolescents, Jenny and Kim, who have met to work on a school project. Jenny, whose house they're meeting at, offers Kim lunch before they start. In an individualistic culture, this exchange might be as follows: "Kim, how about a sandwich? I have bologna, tuna, and egg salad." Kim quickly answers "Sure, I'll take bologna!"

individualistic cultures
Cultures that encourage a sense of self as independent, self-sufficient, and autonomous.

collectivistic cultures
Cultures that encourage a sense of self in terms of one's roles or status vis-à-vis others.

agency An aspect of mature functioning characterized in independent cultures by asserting one's thoughts and feelings, and in interdependent cultures by self-restraint and maintaining harmonious relationships.

What does this interaction reveal about the self-concepts of adolescents in an individualistic culture? Jenny offers her friend a choice because she knows that people have personal preferences and assumes that Kim would prefer one type of sandwich to another; she also assumes that Kim has a right to express her preference. Kim, who lives in the same culture, believes, just as Jenny, that she is entitled to say what she wants and promptly lets her know. If Kim were an exchange student from China, however, she would most likely be surprised by the question, and respond with something like, "Um, I don't know." An interdependent self assumes that it would be Jenny's responsibility as host to know what would please her friend and simply to offer that to her. Conversely, it's the friend's responsibility to accept with pleasure what she has been given, thus affirming the host's choice (**Table 5.2**) (Markus & Kitayama, 1991).

Self-Concept: Who Am I?

The capacity for self-reflection that comes with adolescence brings with it a concern about personality in general and thoughts about oneself in particular. The beliefs adolescents have about themselves determine many of their emotional reactions. Which of these beliefs are central to their sense of self, or **self-concept**? Adolescents can easily know which are most central by the way they react when these ideas are challenged. An adolescent who values her independence, for example, will find herself in frequent arguments whenever someone tells her that she cannot do something, and one who values his competence will resent having anyone tell him he is not able to manage a task.

Because so many of the beliefs about the self in adolescence are recently formulated, they lack experiential support. Perhaps because of this, adolescents spend a lot of time and energy gathering evidence in support of their theories of the self. Events that otherwise might be commonplace take on significance if they support adolescents' beliefs about themselves. Getting a driver's license and going out on a first date are examples of experiences

Adolescents' sense of self includes who they have been as well as who they hope to be. Formulating their self-identity requires them to discover what they like, what they are good at, and what they believe in.

self-concept The individual's awareness of the self as a person; a theory about the self that explains personal experience.

TABLE 5.2		
Comparison of the Independent and the Interdependent Sense of Self		
FEATURE COMPARED	**INDEPENDENT**	**INTERDEPENDENT**
Definition	Separate from social context	Connected with social context
Structure	Bounded, unitary, stable	Flexible, variable
Important features	Internal, private (abilities, thoughts, feelings)	External, public (statuses, roles, relationships)
Tasks	Be unique, express self, realize internal attributes, promote own goals, be direct; "say what's on your mind"	Belong, fit-in, occupy one's proper place, engage in appropriate action, promote others' goals, be indirect; "read other's mind"
Role of others	*Self-evaluation:* others important for social comparison, reflected appraisal	*Self-definition:* relationships with others in specific context define the self
Basis of self-esteem[a]	Ability to express self, validate internal attributes	Ability to adjust, restrain self, maintain harmony with social context

Source: Markus & Kitayama, 1991.

[a]Esteeming the self may be primarily a Western phenomenon, and the concept of self-esteem should perhaps be replaced by self-satisfaction, or by a term that reflects the realization that one is fulfilling the culturally mandated task.

self-esteem The individual's overall positive or negative evaluation of herself or himself.

that assume this kind of significance, because they validate important beliefs, such as "I'm adult" or "I'm attractive" (Okun & Sasfy, 1977). Many of the "self" statements adolescents include in their self-concepts reflect potential more than actual accomplishments. These discrepancies also explain why the theory of self is at first so vulnerable to disconfirming evidence.

To be healthy, self-concepts need to be self-correcting. When they are, adolescents can face new information about themselves openly. When teenagers feel threatened, they tend to close themselves off to defend their beliefs, incapable of seeing the ways in which their experiences fail to confirm these beliefs. But adolescents who feel secure about themselves are able to revise their beliefs in light of their experiences. Remaining open to new views of the self is especially difficult in adolescence because so much changes, and the need to explain these changes is so great.

The self-concept becomes more abstract, more differentiated, and more adaptive during adolescence. Children derive their sense of themselves from concrete, physical characteristics. Adolescents think of themselves in terms of psychological characteristics such as being impulsive, shy, loud, or witty. Children draw their characters in bold strokes—as either good or bad, right or wrong, strong or weak. Adolescents make finer distinctions; they see subtleties and nuance. They understand how a characteristic can be both a strength and a weakness. A 15-year-old might pride himself on his reflectiveness in social situations and his sensitivity with his friends, yet realize that these very same qualities can be his downfall when faced with a taunting classmate, knowing that a less-reflective friend would simply swing a punch at the offender. Self-concepts also become more adaptive as adolescents accumulate more years of decision making. These decisions provide a history of successes and failures. Most have learned that they usually make good decisions and that, even when they make mistakes, these are not devastating. See **Box 5.4** for parents' reactions to adolescents' increasing maturity.

Self Esteem: Do I Like Myself?

If the self-concept is a set of beliefs about the self, then **self-esteem** is a measure of how good one feels about these beliefs. A girl who describes herself as athletic, a social leader, witty, short, and friendly does not stop there. She evaluates each of these qualities. "Is it really okay to be as athletic as I am? So I'm witty, but is that as good as being a brain? Am I too short or just tall enough?" The answers she comes up with contribute to her feelings of adequacy and self-worth. Self-esteem is the adolescents' overall positive or negative evaluation of herself or himself (Simmons & Blyth, 1987).

Self-esteem is the overall positive or negative evaluation of oneself. Opportunities for responsible work help to build positive self-esteem.

FOUNDATIONS OF SELF-ESTEEM Relationships with parents provide the foundation for self-esteem. When parents are loving, children feel lovable and develop feelings of self-worth. These feelings become established early in life. Infants quickly learn whether the world in which they live will meet their needs; when those around them are responsive, they develop a sense of trust. The establishment of trust in these first, basic relationships permeates all later ones. Self-esteem among adolescents still reflects their interactions with parents

In More Depth

The Joys of Parenting Early Adolescents

"He is a talented athlete, and his soccer team got to a championship game. He scored the winning goal, and when he took off with the ball down the field, I was very proud of him. It was a unique feeling of being proud that someone I had helped to create was doing that. He had felt a lot of pressure in the game, so to see how incredibly pleased he was gave me great joy."
—Father

"It's nice to see her being able to analyze situations with friends or with her teachers and come to conclusions. She said about one of her teachers, 'Well, she gets excited and she never follows through with what she says, so you know you don't have to take her seriously.'" —Mother

"I was so impressed and pleased that after the earthquake, he and a friend decided to go door-to-door and offer to sell drawings they made of

Teenage Mutant Ninja Turtles. He raised $150 that he gave for earthquake relief. I was very proud that he thought this up all by himself."
—Father

"I was very happy one day when I found this note she left on my desk. It said, 'Hello!!! Have a happy day! Don't worry about home, every-one's fine! Do your work the very best you can. But most important, have a fruitful life!!' I saved that note because it made me feel so good."
—Mother

"He's very sensitive, and his cousins two years older than he ask his advice about boys. They may not take it, but they ask him even though he's younger." —Father

Source: After Brooks, 1999.

(Bolognini et al., 1996; Turnage, 2004). Adolescents with authoritative parents, who stress self-reliance, shared decision making, and willingness to listen, have higher feelings of self-worth (Bartle et al., 1989; Garber et al., 1997).

Two especially important sources of self-esteem in adolescence come from interactions with peers and from satisfaction with one's body (DuBois et al., 1996; Klomsten et al., 2004; Williams & Currie, 2002). David DuBois, at the University of Missouri, and his associates (1996) assessed the contribution of five domains of experience to self-esteem in early adolescents: peers, school, family, body image, and sports/athletics. As can be seen in **Figure 5.6**, peers and body image are the two largest contributors to global self-esteem. In general, males tend to have somewhat higher self-esteem than females (Baldwin & Hoffmann, 2002; Kling et al., 1999).

ETHNICITY AND SELF-ESTEEM   In general, black adolescents have significantly higher self-esteem than any other group of adolescents, including whites (Herman, 2004; Twenge & Crocker, 2002). Minority membership,

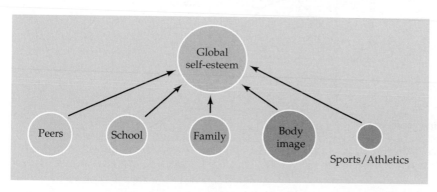

● **Figure 5.6   Sources of global self-esteem, indicated by their relative importance**   Many things contribute to adolescents' feelings of self-esteem; two of the most important are friends and having a positive body image. (After DuBois et al., 1996.)

however, does not confer the same advantage for other ethnic groups. In the same meta-analysis, white adolescents were found to have significantly higher self-esteem than Asian Americans, Hispanics, or Native Americans (Twenge & Crocker, 2002). The advantage enjoyed by blacks relative to whites is most likely due to a more positive racial identity (Phinney et al., 1997).

The ways in which minority adolescents resolve their relationship with the majority culture, confronting and coping with issues such as racism and discrimination, have been found to be associated with differences in self-esteem. Different ways of resolving this relationship, recall, are represented by the various stages of ethnic identity discussed earlier in the chapter. Thus, pre-encounter adolescents, who have a white cultural orientation, have been found to have lower self-concept scores and generally show poorer psychological adjustment than bicultural or internalized adolescents who have a strong sense of their ethnicity as well as a sense of belonging to the larger culture (Phinney & Kohatsu, 1997).

Gender is an important variable mediating self-esteem in minorities. The difference in self-esteem between black and white adolescents, for instance, is even greater among females than it is among males. For Asian Americans and Hispanics also, self-esteem relative to that experienced by whites is lower for males than for females (Twenge & Crocker, 2002).

GENDER AND SELF-ESTEEM   Self-esteem tends to be higher in boys than in girls (Baldwin & Hoffman, 2002; Khanlou, 2004). As can be seen in **Figure 5.7**, this difference increases dramatically with age during high school. Roberta Simmons and Dale Blyth (1987) noticed that girls are more likely to evaluate negatively the characteristics about themselves that they consider to be most important. In mid-adolescence, for example, nearly one-third of all girls who care either "a great deal" or "pretty much" about their appearance are not satisfied with the way they look. Similarly, more than 50% of all ninth-grade girls who are not satisfied with their weight nonetheless care about it very much. Also, when asked to list all the possible selves they can think of, both positive and feared, girls have been found to rate feared possible selves as somewhat more likely to occur than boys (Knox et al., 2000). Self-esteem has nowhere to go but down under conditions such as these.

The greater resilience of boys' self-esteem during adolescence shows up in another respect as well. Their self-esteem is less vulnerable in the face of change than is that of girls. All adolescents face some transitions in common:

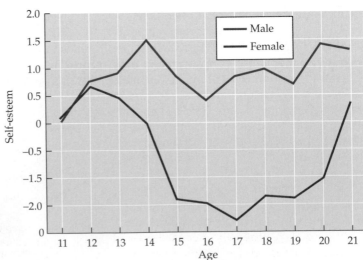

● **Figure 5.7   Changes in boys' and girls' self-esteem with age**   Self-esteem is higher in boys than it is in girls throughout adolescence. (After Baldwin & Hoffmann, 2002.)

puberty, a change in schools, and, with dating, a reordering of their social world. Some adolescents must also cope with geographic relocations and with family disruption when parents change jobs or divorce. Having time to gradually get used to one change before having to cope with another makes it easier to adjust to such transitions.

The more changes adolescents must cope with simultaneously, the more likely they are to show the effects of related stress. As the number of changes increases, self-esteem also drops, especially in girls (Baldwin & Hoffmann, 2002; Simmons & Blyth, 1987). However, the more stability adolescents have in any one area, the better they can cope with changes in others.

Consider a hypothetical 14-year-old girl who is midway through puberty and just beginning to date. Her parents are recently divorced, and she lives in a new neighborhood. She has so many things to talk about with her friends, but she never gets to see them. She doesn't know which of the physical changes she's experiencing are normal and which are weird. She feels angry all the time—except when she's depressed. When she tells her counselor at school, he tells her it's because of her hormones. The last person she can talk to is her mother, who feels even worse than she does. Her grades have fallen, and she's lost interest in doing things at school. When asked how she feels about herself, she has a hard time thinking of any qualities that she likes.

This adolescent's experiences are extreme, yet the situation she faces is increasingly common for many. Under conditions such as these, self-esteem understandably suffers in adolescence.

How do adolescents come up with a sense of themselves that they can live with and like? Puberty forces the issue, but it also sets the stage for new answers. Because of pubertal changes, adolescents find it difficult to think of themselves as they did as children. But they also develop ways of thinking that give them the means to combine aspects of the old self with newly developing ones. Many of these aspects involve others; we turn to intimate relationships next.

intimacy The ability to share oneself with another, characterized by self-disclosure and mutuality.

Intimacy: Discovering the Self Through Relationships

Intimacy is often misunderstood. Like many adults, most adolescents associate it with romance, passion, being together, or being so close one can finish the other's sentences. Yet arguments, like romance, can provide the ground for intimate encounters, passion can involve little sharing of feelings, and always being together may signal a relationship that provides little room for being oneself. As for being able to finish another's sentences, this may mean the other has said nothing new for some time. What is **intimacy**, then? It is a sharing of one's feelings and thoughts in an atmosphere of caring, trust, and acceptance. Intimacy begins with oneself and only then can it be extended to others.

Knowing Oneself

In order to develop intimate relationships with others, adolescents need to be in touch with their own feelings and needs. That is, adolescents' capacity for intimacy should

Adolescents have to learn to accept themselves before they are ready for an intimate relationship, which requires having the self-confidence to let someone else know them as they really are.

BOX
5.5

In More Depth

Intimacy

By Michael Wapner

Gregory Bateson once said, "It takes two to know one." What he meant is that to know yourself, you must let someone else know you. This suggests that intimacy is not simply letting someone else know what you already know about yourself, but letting someone else get close enough to you to help you discover what you don't yet know about yourself.

It is commonly believed that to be intimate with someone is to let that person see parts of ourselves that we ordinarily hide, but which we ourselves are fully familiar with. Thus in moments of intimacy, we may confess a weakness that we usually keep secret, or admit to a fear that we usually try to cover, or relate a shameful experience that we have told no one else. But in all these cases, the assumption is that we already know all about those aspects of ourselves. It is just this other person, this confidant—the intimate—who will learn something new. In this view of intimacy we control the image of ourselves that we present to the other person. Even though what we are sharing may be something we are not terribly proud of, we still are the one who determines whether, and in what way, it will be shared.

But if it really takes two to know one, then keeping control over what the other discovers about us by selecting what is confided is not the deepest form of intimacy, nor does it foster self-knowledge. Deeper forms of intimacy require a relaxation of our guard so that when others come close they may discover things about us that we don't already know, things about ourselves that we had never noticed before. Not having had the opportunity to review and edit these before they are expressed, we have no control over what the other witnesses about us. But once they are witnessed, the other person may inform us of, or even confront us with, what they have discovered, so that we discover it too.

Learning about ourselves in this way can be truly disturbing, even frightening, unless it occurs within a safe and trusting relationship. When this safety and trust are absent we must remain guarded in our relationships, maintaining control over how we are seen, even when we are sharing "intimacies." But when safety and trust are present we can risk being spontaneous and unguarded in ways that may display things about ourselves that we didn't plan to show because we didn't know about them in the first place.

This way of viewing intimacy implies that people who are alone, or maintain only superficial relationships, not only do not know others very well, but don't know themselves very well either, even if they spend all of their alone time thinking about themselves.

develop under the conditions that make it safe for them to know themselves. We discussed some of these conditions in the context of individuation. Families that allow members to express their ideas, even when they differ from those of others, communicate that it is safe to disagree. Once adolescents have this safety, they are able to examine how they really feel (Grotevant & Cooper, 1986).

Self-acceptance is also important for intimacy (**Box 5.5**). Adolescents who like themselves are free to be themselves without trying to change anything. Self-acceptance and self-awareness go hand in hand. Those who have accepted themselves can be aware of desires and feelings that they otherwise might feel a need to deny or distort. Because a common way of distorting needs is to attribute them to others (that is, projection), self-awareness makes it possible for adolescents to perceive others more accurately as well. In appreciating the complexity of their own feelings, they can realize that the feelings of others are similarly complex and can validate those emotions. Self-acceptance creates a self-perpetuating cycle; having been validated, others are able to hear what these adolescents are saying and, in turn, validate them (Bell & Bell, 1983).

An important ingredient to self-acceptance is liking oneself. Adolescents who like themselves can let others get close enough to see them as they really are. People who don't like themselves frequently feel ashamed and are unwilling to let others get close. Often they feel it necessary to put up a front to look better or to use their relationships to prove to themselves that they are acceptable (Masters et al., 1988). These approaches block intimacy, either by not being open with the other person or by using that person for one's own needs. Adolescents who feel negative about themselves are likely to handle their feelings of depression and anxiety in ways that block self-knowledge, by escaping into alcoholism or drug abuse, seeking distractions such as television, or finding substitutes such as eating. None of these behaviors lends itself to intimacy. Of course, adolescents need not be happy with themselves all the time. As William Masters, Virginia Johnson, and Robert Kolodny (1988) note:

> Generally, we separate what we like from what we don't like and use this process to try to change. If we are honest in our self-appraisals, the intimate knowledge we develop helps us relate to others. At the same time, a person who **never** looks inward has such distorted self-perceptions that it is unlikely he or she can contribute fully to a relationship with someone else. (p. 318)

Intimacy with Others

Self-disclosure is important to intimacy—adolescents who are intimates share their thoughts and feelings with each other. Not everything they share is personal (often it's just gossip), but much of it is. Intimacy takes time to develop, as adolescents learn to trust one another with increasingly personal aspects of themselves. Self-disclosure has to be mutual to be comfortable; one adolescent cannot tell all and have the other tell nothing. Actually, we tend to shy away from people who tell us everything about themselves the moment we meet them. Choosing to disclose things about oneself is a bit like taking off one's clothes. How undressed one appears depends on how much others are wearing. Someone in a bathing suit has enough on when lounging poolside, but at a dance would look nearly naked.

Adolescents are willing to share their personal experiences when they can trust that others will respect their confidence. Trust takes time to develop and usually requires some testing of the waters. An adolescent may start by sharing things she would not be devastated to hear repeated, such as what she thinks of a particular teacher, and work her way up to her most private thoughts and feelings, for example, what she really thinks of her stepfather or the details of her relationship with her boyfriend. This kind of trust requires a commitment to a relationship (Montgomery, 2005).

Intimacy and Identity: Different Paths to Maturity?

To what extent are intimacy and identity related? Can adolescents be close to others without knowing themselves well? Can they develop a sense of themselves apart from their intimate relationships with others? Erikson believed that identity is a necessary precursor to intimacy. He wrote that "true engagement with others is the result and the test of firm self-delineation" (1968, p. 167). Intimacy assumes developmental significance for Erikson only after identity has been achieved.

This developmental progression, however, is not typical of females. Josselson (1988) writes that development in females takes place on an "interpersonal track" that is not represented in Erikson's scheme. Erikson wrote, for example, about industry (the crisis preceding that of identity) as the development of competence by learning how things are made and how they work. Competence for females is more likely to take the form of increasingly complex interpersonal skills (Marcia, 1980). These two types of skills set a different stage for the drama that unfolds during adolescence than that envisioned by Erikson. Prior developments prepare females to define themselves *interpersonally* through skills that bring them into relationships with others, whereas the same developments pre-

Some theorists believe that females define themselves primarily in the course of their relationships but that males must define themselves *before* they are capable of close relationships. If they hope to build a lasting relationship, young couples need to be willing to accept changes in their partner's self-definition.

pare males to define themselves *impersonally* through skills that result in products. As girls move into adolescence, their social networks relate to their self-esteem and to their perceived self-competence across a variety of areas, in ways that boys' relationships do not (DuBois et al., 1996; Feiring & Lewis, 1991). In early adulthood, girls' relationships continue to contribute more heavily to identity than does school or occupation (Meeus & Dekovic, 1995).

Erikson viewed intimacy as a characteristic of relationships with others. For females, it is also a process by which they define themselves. Rather than postponing identity consolidation until they find a mate, as Erikson suggested, female adolescents *achieve* self-definition through intimacy, through their relationships with others (Gilligan, 1982; Josselson, 1988; Marcia, 1980). Josselson (1988) states:

Intimacy, or interpersonal development, among women is identity and resides not in the choice of a heterosexual partner, but in the development, differentiation, and mastery of ways of being with others (not just men) that meet her standards for taking care, that connect her meaningfully to others, and that locate her in an interpersonal network. (p. 99)

If relationships assume a different developmental significance for females, we should expect to see gender differences in levels of intimacy during adolescence, and we do (Montgomery, 2005). Don Schiedel and James Marcia (1985), at Simon Fraser University, classified late adolescents into intimacy statuses that reflected commitment to and depth of relationships, as shown in **Table 5.3**. They found significantly more females in the higher intimacy statuses than males. In fact, females were nearly twice as likely as males to be in the highest two statuses. Perhaps because the individuals they studied were in late adolescence or early adulthood, the proportion of females high in intimacy did not increase with age. This proportion did increase for males, however, suggesting that males, as Josselson and Gilligan imply, are not as prepared for relationships as are females. This pattern may be changing, however. When 15- to 18-year-old high school students were asked to respond to dilemmas involving identity and intimacy choices, females as well as males assigned

TABLE 5.3	
Intimacy Statuses in Late Adolescence	
Isolate	Relationships consist only of casual acquaintances.
Stereotyped	Relationships are shallow and conventional.
Pseudointimate	Relationships are similar to those of Stereotyped but have commitment to long-term sexual relationship; these defined through conventional roles rather than self-disclosure.
Preintimate	Close, open relationships characterized by mutuality; ambivalence regarding commitment to long-term sexual relationship.
Intimate	Relationships are similar to those of Preintimate but also have commitment to long-term sexual relationship.

Source: Schiedel & Marcia, 1985.

greater importance to identity choices, and males were as likely as females to mention intimacy considerations, either by themselves or fused with identity issues (Lacombe & Gay, 1998).

But what about the relationship between intimacy and identity mentioned earlier? A number of studies support Erikson's belief that intimacy is contingent on achieving identity but find this relationship to be more characteristic of males than females (Dyk & Adams, 1990; Schiedel & Marcia, 1985). These findings support Josselson's contention that for females intimacy *is* a means by which identity is resolved.

Does development take the form of increasing autonomy and separation? Most personality theorists have answered yes. Every now and again a few voices raise alternatives, and some of these have been incorporated into mainstream developmental theory (Gilligan, 1982; Gilligan et al., 1989; Josselson, 1987, 1988).

David Bakan (1966) distinguishes two aspects of mature functioning. Agency captures qualities of assertiveness, mastery, and distinctiveness; and communion reflects qualities of cooperation and union. Bakan considers these two facets of personal functioning to be balanced in the mature person. Developmentalists have traditionally translated these aspects of maturity into a developmental progression moving *from* communion *to* agency, thereby assigning greater maturity to agency. An alternative interpretation of Bakan's view of maturity, but one that equally distorts it, has assigned agency to the masculine personality and communion to the feminine. This approach easily reduces to the first because development in females often falls short of that in males when comparisons use measures that have been standardized with males (for example, Kohlberg's measure of moral development or the use of rules in games). Most Western cultures implicitly confirm either of these translations through the greater value they place on agentic over communional behaviors. Our society, for example, defines success in terms of individual accomplishment and achievements rather than the quality of a person's relationships.

But is development most accurately thought of as increasing separation and individuation? Josselson (1988) notes that research in two areas within psychology—adolescent development and the psychology of women—reveals difficulties in viewing development this way.

Developmental Issues in Adolescence

Development during adolescence does not require an end to, but rather a modification of, significant relationships with parents. Adolescents achieve a sense of themselves *within* their relationships, not in spite of them (Josselson, 1988). Research with adolescents and their parents such as that of Harold Grotevant and Catherine Cooper (1986) finds that attachment and separation are not opposites but are different aspects of the same process. If the task of adolescence is to break ties with parents, then adolescents who accomplish this cannot also also remain attached. However, if the task is to renegotiate these relationships in order to achieve greater mutuality and equality, they can separate as persons *and* remain emotionally connected or attached (Josselson, 1988). Any theory that emphasizes separation as developmentally more advanced gives a distorted view of development in which an autonomous self is accepted as the pinnacle of maturity (Josselson, 1988).

Although differences among individuals of the same sex can be greater than those between the sexes, men and women do characteristically differ in the way they relate to other people. Females pay more attention to relationships and expect them to change over time.

A second challenge to the prevailing view of development as progressive separation and individuation comes from attempts to chart female development. These attempts bring a new awareness of the male bias in much developmental theory. Developmentalists have assumed their theories to be universal, that is, to cover issues fundamental to the whole of human experience. Yet theories are not totally objective representations of human nature; they are interpretations that often reflect the personal experiences of the theorists. And most personality theorists have been males. There is a growing recognition that theories address experiences that are more common among, or even unique to, males (Adelson & Doehrman, 1980; Bettelheim, 1961; Gilligan, 1982, 1986; Josselson, 1988).

Erikson, for instance, thought of identity as an exploration of issues related to vocation, political views, and religion. When females are interviewed about their identity concerns, one hears about their relationships—not about industry, autonomy, or ideology. Autonomy may well serve the function of a developmental organizer for most males in our society, but relationships serve this function for most females. Josselson (1988) adds, "Because women define themselves in a context of relationship, a developmental orientation that equates growth with autonomy will automatically relegate women to lower rungs of development" (p. 99). She notes in support of this point that the cultural myths that exist in our society make it difficult to view the "achievement of adult commitment, fidelity, intimacy, and care [as] meaningful and heroic" (p. 99).

Gilligan (1986) comments that the adolescent girl especially faces a problem in that, as she affirms her connection with her mother, she sees how disconnected they both are from a society in which the male experience defines reality. Gilligan (1986) writes:

> The ability to establish connection with others hinges on the ability to render one's story coherent. Given the failure of interpretive schemes to reflect female experience and given the distortion of this experience in common understandings of care and attachment, development for girls in adolescence hinges...on the courage to challenge two equations: the equation of human with male and the equation of care with self-sacrifice. Together these equations create a self-perpetuating system that sustains a limited conception of human development and a problematic representation of human relationships. (p. 296)

Dimensions of Relatedness

Josselson points out that social scientists have developed a rich vocabulary for talking about the self, distinguishing among terms such as *self-consciousness*, *self-awareness*, *self- control*, *self-concept*, and *self-esteem*, yet have few words to describe the self in relation to others. A single term, *relationship*, serves to describe the many, varied ways we have of interrelating. The paucity of our language has, in turn, contributed to a cultural blindness in which "when we wish to know people, we are therefore more likely to ask about what they do than about how they love. But in fact we would know them better if we knew how they are with others and what they want from them" (Josselson, 1992, p. 2).

Josselson (1992) gives us a multifaceted theory of human connection, describing eight dimensions of relatedness. Each of these follows a developmental course, being expressed initially in concrete and literal ways, and only with time symbolically. The dimensions themselves are independent of one another, one not being reducible to the other, and develop more or less simultaneously rather than as stepwise stages. Also, either the relative absence of each form of relatedness in a person's life or the excessive indulgence of it is unhealthy. **Table 5.4** shows the dimensions and these two poles. The first

TABLE 5.4
Josselson's Eight Dimensions of Relatedness

INSUFFICIENT PRESENCE	HEALTHY EXPRESSION OF RELATEDNESS	EXCESSIVE DEPENDENCE
Falling	*Holding*: Gives a sense of being contained and bounded; provides sense of security. Later takes the form of feeling "supported" by others, of having others who are "there" for us.	Suffocation
Aloneness, loss	*Attachment*: The need to be close to those who are important to us, which the infant expresses by crying in protest when its mother leaves; an essential ingredient of human connection.	Fearful clinging
Inhibition, emotional deadening	*Passionate Experience*: Others become the objects of our desires; ranges from the need to suck in infancy to sexual desire in adolescence and adulthood.	Obsessive love
Annihilation, rejection	*Eye-to-Eye Validation*: Lets us see ourselves through the eyes of others and gives us a sense of ourselves in relation to them.	Transparency
Disillusionment, purposelessness	*Idealization and Identification*: Expansion of our sense of ourself by reaching out to and embracing those who are bigger, stronger, grander.	Slavish devotion
Loneliness	*Mutuality and Resonance*: By sharing our experiences with another, we arrive at something jointly created; an expression of our social nature.	Merging
Alienation	*Embeddedness*: A sense of belonging, having a place in the group, experiencing communality.	Overconformity
Indifference	*Tending and Care*: Nurturance that is intentional and deliberate; our capacity to care for others reflects our own need to be needed.	Compulsive caregiving

Source: Josselson, 1992.

four dimensions—holding, attachment, passionate experience, and eye-to-eye validation—are present either from birth or shortly thereafter. The second four do not develop until later. Idealization and embeddedness require that one experience the self apart from others as well as see that self in relation to those others, both of which require a certain cognitive maturity Similarly, mutuality and tending require the capacity to be responsive to others, which can develop only when the child moves beyond egocentrism.

Gender Differences in Relatedness

Josselson (1992) cautions against overstating gender differences in relatedness, pointing out that considerable variability exists among individuals of the same sex in their expressions of relatedness, but she notes several important differences as well.

Females describe greater complexity to their relationships, catching more nuance to experience and being able to incorporate contradictory elements, whereas males approach their relationships in more straightforward and simpler terms. Females tend to view relationships as evolving over time. In contrast, males see them as more static than dynamic, more as products that, once arrived at, will remain that way. And, finally, individuals of either sex emphasize different dimensions of relatedness.

Males, more than females, tend to define relationships according to fixed categories and to assume that they'll always remain the same. The difference in the genders' view of relationships may be partly due to differences in identity formation: Males are defined more in terms of what they can do, and females are defined more in terms of how they relate to others.

Josselson traces these differences to several underlying factors. First, males tend to fit their relationships into an abstract conceptual system, whereas for females relationships are more immediate and experiential. For instance, in their interviews, males would frequently mention being influenced and moved by the works of men whom they had never met, such as artists and philosophers, yet with whom they had carried on passionate inner dialogues. These intellectual exchanges felt relational to them. Females, in contrast, needed some measure of "affective coloring" before they experienced an exchange as relational.

Josselson locates this abstractness in males within a second factor, one concerning gender definition. If, as Nancy Chodorow points out, a boy needs to separate himself from his mother in order to develop as a male, he achieves masculinity at the *expense* of that emotional closeness (see Chapter 2). This distancing has implications for all future relationships, in which "he learns to relate to others across a gulf that both separates him and guards his masculinity" (Josselson, 1992, p. 225). In contrast to the boy, the little girl need not distance herself from her mother, but instead learns what it is to be herself within the context of relatedness, comfortable with "the paradox that she is both merged and distinct, both connected and separate" (p. 225).

Having to define oneself as a male this way requires action on the boy's part, that is, separating from the mother, whereas defining oneself as a female does not. A third factor, then, is that males gain a sense of themselves through their actions, through doing, and females through their relationships, through being. Males evaluate themselves in terms of what they can do, their skills and accomplishments, how far they can kick a soccer ball or how many space aliens they can knock out in a video game. Conversely, observes Josselson (1992),

> Girls are not liked for being smart or good at soccer, as boys are, but for ill-defined qualities, such as responsiveness to others, self-confidence, playfulness, and charm. And the girl understands, quickly and deeply, that she, too, will be labeled and located in this slippery interpersonal universe. She will be responded to for how she is deemed to be, not for what she wills or for her skills. (pp. 226–227)

Because of these factors, gender differences in relatedness are to be expected. For instance, females are more comfortable experiencing mutuality than are males. "For women," says Josselson (1992), "the regulation of closeness and distance, and the shared experience of emotion is the essence of relating" (p. 232). Eye-to-eye validation is also a more significant dimension of relatedness for females, because their sense of self is rooted more deeply in others' responses to them. Passionate experience that is expressly sexual, on the other hand, is more of a driving force in males' relationships. Also, because the way males know themselves is more closely tied to action and doing, identification and idealization are more salient to their relationships than to those of females. Males' ambitions are personalized through identification with figures who are bigger than life, heroes to be idealized and modeled. Females are more apt to draw their strength from those who are close at hand (Josselson, 1992).

A New Definition of Maturity

Josselson (1988) asserts that gender differences in individuals' sense of self are sufficiently great that we need to redefine identity to include the concept of self in relation to others. Presently, our definition of identity views separation as contributing to the mature individual's experience of self; Josselson argues that our approach to identity must give equivalent weight to a person's relatedness to others. Maturity involves movement toward a greater capacity for relationships. Contributing to this capacity are assertion and autonomy. Josselson turns the tables and makes self-in-relationship the more embracing concept of which autonomy and separateness are components.

Does development move from dependence to autonomy, as traditional theory asserts? Does it involve increasingly articulated ways of relating to others? Adolescents of both genders work out their identities in the context of continuing significant relationships with others, and males as well as females face intimacy as a central issue leading to adulthood. Josselson maintains that each person has a need for separateness *and* attachment, for inclusion *and* exclusion. Each of these creates tensions, but to give in to one and not strive for balance is to forfeit some degree of maturity (Josselson, 1988).

Go to the **Adolescence** Companion Website at www.sinauer.com/cobb for quizzes, flashcards, summaries, and other study resources.

SUMMARY and KEY TERMS

Constructing a Self

Achieving Autonomy: The process of defining the self leads to a renegotiation of the parent-child relationship during adolescence. This renegotiation initially is prompted by the biological changes of puberty and changes in the way adolescents think. Adolescents become more autonomous as they choose to be part of the decision-making process, asking to be treated as more adult and taking responsibility for the consequences of the decisions they make.
autonomous

The Role of Parents: The role parents play in the development of autonomy can be thought of (1) as promoting independence, in which adolescents must first distance themselves emotionally from their parents, or (2) as promoting self-determination by helping adolescents discover their interests and values. Self-determination contributes to self-esteem and well-being.

Connectedness with Parents: The sense of oneself that adolescents achieve as they distinguish their own attitudes and beliefs from those of their parents and become more self-governing is termed individuation. Family characteristics of individuality and connectedness facilitate the process of identity achievement. These qualities of family life help adolescents explore options while feeling emotionally supported even when family disagreements arise.
individuation, individuality, connectedness

Identity as a Normative Crisis of Adolescence

Achieving an identity is a central task facing adolescents. Resolving the psychosocial crisis of identity gives one a coherent, purposeful sense of self. Erikson used the word *crisis* to refer to a developmental turning point in which adolescents must choose one course or another simply because it is no longer possible for them to continue as before.
identity, possible selves

(continued)

SUMMARY and KEY TERMS *continued*

Identity Statuses: James Marcia, largely responsible for generating research on identity formation by constructing a measure of identity for empirically testing adolescents, notes that achieving a personal identity is not an easy process. Adolescents must be willing to take risks and live with uncertainty. According to Marcia, a number of identity statuses can be distinguished based on the presence or absence of exploration of life options and commitment to self-chosen alternatives.
exploration, commitment, identity statuses, identity achievement, identity foreclosure, moratorium, identity diffusion, carefree diffusion

Identity Styles: Michael Berzonsky offers an alternative way of thinking about identity statuses, envisioning them as "organizers" of experience, versus "organizations" of experience. He suggests individuals differ in the way they process information relevant to the self. For instance, some individuals actively search for information that might be relevant to their problems, then carefully evaluate that information before making decisions. He terms this style an information orientation.
information oriented, diffuse/avoidant oriented, normative oriented

Adolescents and the Internet: Most American adolescents today use the Internet, and individuals of either sex spend about the same amount of time online, with the exception of heavy game players who tend to be male. A substantial percentage of adolescents indicate they have pretended to be other than who they are when online: This experimentation with their identity can contribute to their social competence by increasing the number of interactions in which they can practice their social skills.

Identity: Gender and Ethnicity

Gender Differences in Identity Formation: Research finds few gender differences in identity development. When gender differences emerge, they most frequently show interpersonal concerns to figure more centrally in females' than males' identities, as well as differences in timing. For instance, issues of identity and intimacy are more apt to be resolved concurrently in females than in males.

Contributions of Ethnicity to Identity Development: For adolescents who are members of an ethnic minority, the process of identity formation includes an additional step, one of resolving issues related to their ethnic identity. Ethnic identity is a way of understanding oneself in terms of the values and traditions of one's group, and its development progresses through several stages that correlate with ego identity statuses.
ethnic identity, acculturation, unexamined ethnic identity, ethnic identity search, achieved ethnic identity, bicultural identity

Understanding the Self: Cultural Contributions

A fundamental dimension running through the socialization process is a culture's understanding of "self" in relation to others. Whether one belongs to an individualistic culture or a collectivist culture cannot help but color an adolescent's view of their rights and responsibilities in the world.
individualistic cultures, collectivist cultures, agency

SUMMARY and KEY TERMS

Self-Concept: Who Am I?: The beliefs adolescents have about themselves determine many of their emotional reactions, and these self-concepts become more abstract, differentiated, and adaptive during adolescence. In fact, many of the "self" statements adolescents include in their self-concepts reflect potential more than actual accomplishments.
self-concept

Self-Esteem: Do I Like Myself? Self-esteem reflects the overall positive or negative attitude adolescents have about the self. Relationships with parents and peers and satisfaction with one's body provide the foundations for self-esteem.
self-esteem

Intimacy: Discovering the Self Through Relationships

Knowing Oneself: Intimacy is the sharing of innermost feelings and thoughts in an atmosphere of caring, trust, and acceptance. To be intimate with others, adolescents must first know and accept themselves.
intimacy

Intimacy with Others: Self disclosure may provide a vehicle for intimacy with others. Intimacy is often contingent on achieving identity, at least for males. For females, intimacy is often the means by which identity is resolved.

Intimacy and Identity: Different Paths to Maturity?

Developmental Issues in Adolescence: Development has traditionally been viewed in terms of increasing autonomy and separation from others. Research on adolescent-parent relationships and on female development questions this view.

Dimensions of Relatedness: Relationships between adolescents and parents show that continuing emotional attachment and increasing autonomy coexist and are different aspects of the same process.

Gender Differences in Relatedness: For females, relationships with others contribute importantly to their sense of self. Males, on the other hand, gain a sense of themselves through their actions, through doing, according to Josselson.

A New Definition of Maturity: Because these gender differences in individuals' sense of self are sufficiently great, we need to redefine identity to include the concept of self in relation to others. New definitions of maturity should also include increasing autonomy and separateness.

Neena's mother knocked on the half-closed door and stepped in when she heard the soft "Come in," careful to avoid the pile of clothes in her path and whatever lay beneath them. Surveying the room, she couldn't help but comment on the mess.

"Look, Mom, I know where everything is, honest," her daughter answered. What Neena really wanted to say was, "It's my room and I can keep it any way I like!" But she knew what her mom would say to that. Her mother, not to be dissuaded by pragmatic appeals to reason, pointed out that she had told Neena several times already to straighten up her room.

Adolescents in the Family:
Changing Roles and Relationships

Looking at her mother's back, rigid with irritation as she left, Neena sighed inwardly. It seemed lately that the two of them couldn't agree on much of anything, even things Neena thought were rightfully hers to decide, such as what clothes she wore, what music she listened to, or the friends she had. Her little brother Joey, still in the fourth grade, got along great with Mom. Being an adolescent wasn't all that easy.

Chapter Overview

We can learn more about the relationship between Neena and her mother from what they *don't* say to each other than from what they do say. Both are aware of changes in their relationship, and step around each other as carefully as Neena's mother stepped around the clothes in her room.

Relationships change within the family as adolescents make bids for greater autonomy and question parental authority. The first section of this chapter examines these changes. The time adolescents spend with their families changes, as does the emotional tone of their interactions. Although conflict increases, adolescents and parents renegotiate relationships in ways that enable them to maintain connectedness and increase mutuality.

The success families have in navigating these changes depends in part on how responsive and demanding parents are, that is, on their style of parenting, and on knowing what adolescents are doing when they're *not* with them. Adding an additional wrinkle to changing relationships, parents face their own identity crisis, as they confront their feelings about aging.

Interactions within the family vary somewhat with parents' roles, particularly whether both parents work outside the home, as well as with the presence of siblings, and may vary as well with ethnicity. We will look at each of these in turn, and then consider changes in family structure through divorce, single parenting, and remarriage.

Changing Relationships within the Family: Adolescents

Relationships within the family change in a number of ways. Adolescents spend less time together with their families, their relationships are not as warm, and they experience more conflict with their parents.

Time Spent with Family

Adolescents spend up to 40% less time with their families by their senior year in high school than they did in the fifth grade as early adolescents. On any day, early adolescents spend over a third of their waking hours in the company of others in the family; this figure drops to 14% for late adolescents (**Figure 6.1**). Despite a dramatic decrease in the time adolescents spend doing things together with their families, such as watching television or eating meals, adolescents still spend about the same amount of time talking with others in their family, particularly with their mothers (Larson et al., 1996; Nomaguchi, 2008).

By the time adolescents reach high school, decreases in the time they spend with their families can be explained in terms of their involvement in activities occurring outside the home. For early adolescents, however, when they're not with their families, they're likely to be in their rooms by themselves, all the more so if there's a television or a phone in there as well.

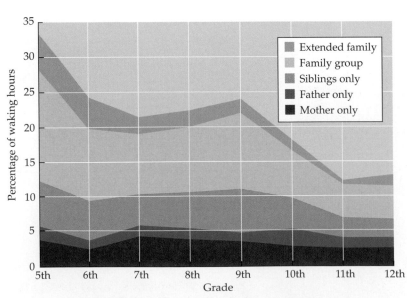

● **Figure 6.1 How much time adolescents of different ages spend with family members** (After Larson et al., 1996.)

Adolescents' ethnic background needs to be taken into consideration when talking about the amount of time early adolescents spend by themselves or with their families. By the eighth grade, for instance, African American adolescents may spend upwards of 60% more time with their families than European American adolescents. Furthermore, they are more likely to spend time as well with their extended family than are European American adolescents, even when the families of either live equally near. Differences such as these point to strong kinship ties in the African American community (Hatchett & Jackson, 1993; Larson et al., 2001).

Warmth of Family Interactions

Adolescents' emotional experiences when they are with their families also change with age. The positive feelings most had upon entering adolescence become more negative by junior high, becoming more positive again toward the end of high school (**Figure 6.2**). Adolescents are less affectionate with their parents, and are less spontaneously helpful than they had been as children, even though they continue to believe that it's just as important for them to be helpful as it is for their parents to help them. Adolescents' perceptions of their parents change as well. They see parents as less supportive, and believe their parents view them less positively, which should not be surprising given the changes just mentioned (Fuligni, 1998; Furman & Buhrmester, 1985; McGue et al., 2005; Smetana et al., 2009). These trends are similar across cultures and ethnic groups, although adolescents from ethnic minorities whose families have immigrated from cultures that value family interdependence report a stronger sense of family obligation (**Figure 6.3**) (Hardway & Fuligni, 2006; Kiang & Fuligni, 2009; Yau & Smetana, 2003; Zhang & Fuligni, 2006). See **Box 6.1** for a study of the emotional experiences of adolescents.

Even though older adolescents participate less in family activities, they spend about the same amount of time in conversations with individual family members, and as much time alone with their parents as early adolescents

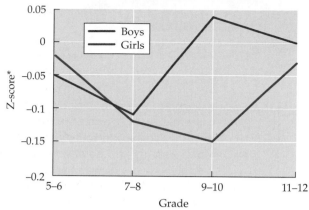

● **Figure 6.2   How younger and older adolescents feel when with family members**   *A Z-score converts a raw score to standard units above or below the mean. (After Larson et al., 1996.)

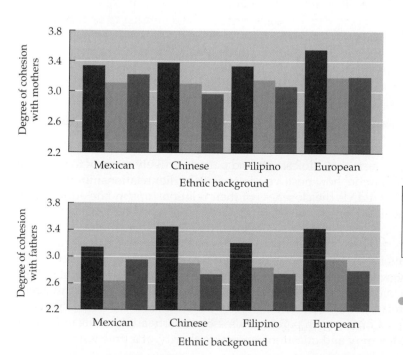

● **Figure 6.3   Similarities across cultures in sixth-, eighth-, and tenth-grade adolescents' feelings of cohesion (i.e., closeness and supportiveness)**   (After Fuligni, 1998.)

BOX 6.1 Research Focus

Sampling: How Emotional Are Adolescents?

Do words such as impulsive, moody, and intense capture something special about adolescence as a time of life? Are adolescents more emotional than their parents? Parents and educators have come to expect emotional turmoil with the onset of adolescence, but what evidence is there that the daily emotional states of adolescents are different from those of children or adults?

Reed Larson and Maryse Richards (1994) tackled this difficult question in an unusual way. They asked fifth- to ninth-graders and their parents to wear beepers for one week. Each time they were beeped, they filled out a one-page form indicating their emotional state. You might ask, "How can we be sure these investigators caught all the emotional states adolescents and parents experience? If they beep each person only a few times each day, they will catch only a few emotional states and perhaps reach the wrong conclusions. How do we know the emotions they recorded are representative of all adolescents' and parents' feelings?"

"Beeping" adolescents and their parents is a way of sampling emotional states. Larson and Richards could not ask individuals to record each and every feeling every moment of the day. Instead, they sampled from this larger population of emotions. The population consists of the entire group of people or events, or, in this case, emotional states, in which one is interested. The sample is a subgroup drawn from this population. If the sample is drawn at random from the population, we can be reasonably certain that it will be representative of that population. This is because in random sampling, each person or event has an equal chance

of being chosen. How might this procedure apply to emotional states?

Larson and Richards first limited the population to waking states between the hours of 7:30 a.m. and 9:30 p.m. They organized these into four two-hour blocks of time from 7:30 a.m. to 3:30 p.m. and four 90-minute blocks between 3:30 p.m. and 9:30 p.m. (The more frequent sampling during later afternoon and evening hours provided better sampling of family time together.) They randomly beeped each adolescent once within each of the eight blocks of time. This procedure ensures that each of the 120, or 90, minutes within each block has an equal chance of being sampled. To imagine how this might work, think of a hat containing 120, or 90, slips of paper, one for each minute in the block of time. The time written on the slip you pull would be the time the adolescent is beeped.

What did the samples show? Are adolescents more emotional than their parents? These investigators found that adolescents are in fact more emotional than their parents. When sampled, adolescents reported extremes of highs and lows much more frequently. Adolescents reported feeling "very happy," for instance, five times more often than their parents did. Similarly, they reported more intense lows than their parents, their beepers catching them as "very unhappy" three times more often than their parents. Larson and Richards conclude that the inner life of adolescents differs significantly from that of their parents, adolescents "ascending higher peaks of rapture and tumbling into deeper crevasses of dejection" (p. 83). Differences such as these make it easier to understand how misunderstandings can so easily arise between adolescents and parents. As Larson and Richards put it, "They are on different wavelengths."

Source: After Larson & Richards, 1994.

do, which suggests that adolescents and parents actively attempt to maintain closeness. In the end, how positive adolescents' earlier relationships were with their parents predicts the closeness of their relationships in late adolescence (Smetana et al., 2004).

Increased Conflict with Parents

Adolescents become conscious that they live in two very different social worlds: one with friends, in which they participate on an equal footing, share in decision making, and negotiate differences; the other with parents, in which they have relatively little power, make few decisions, and conform to parental expectations. Conflict with parents increases as early adolescents make bids for more autonomy and question parental authority, at a time when changes due to maturation blur lines that once clearly distinguished areas of responsibility and authority (Youniss, 1980).

NEGOTIATING FAMILY CONFLICTS   Perhaps at no time are their changing roles more evident than when parents and adolescents discuss their perceptions of family conflicts. Judith Smetana and Rusti Berent (1993), at the University of Rochester, asked adolescents and their mothers how they would respond to typical conflicts that occur at home, such as those involving household chores, keeping one's room clean, or personal appearance. **Table 6.1** shows differences in the types of justifications each might use in appealing to the other.

It should come as no surprise that, given their responsibility for maintaining family ways, mothers considered conventional justifications to be more adequate in resolving

Are disagreements between adolescents and their parents an inevitable part of growing up? Research says they are, but also says that most adolescents and parents stay close despite conflict.

conflict than did adolescents. Adolescents, on the other hand, saw this type of reasoning as a source of conflict. This was especially true of mid-adolescents, for whom family conflict is likely to have reached a peak as gains in autonomy are won by questioning parental authority.

Mothers also considered appeals to authority and threats of punishment to be more effective in getting adolescents to comply with their wishes than

TABLE 6.1
Differences in the Parent's and the Adolescent's Attempts to Resolve Conflict[a]

	TYPE OF JUSTIFICATION	EXAMPLE
Parent	Conventional	Reference to behavior standards, arbitrarily arrived at by family members (e.g., "I'd be embarrassed if any of my friends saw you looking like that.")
	Pragmatic	Consideration of practical needs or consequences (e.g., "You'll catch a cold.")
	Authoritarian	Reference to authority and punishment (e.g., "I'm your parent, and I say you can't dress like that.")
Adolescent	Conventional	Reference to standards of behavior shared with peers (e.g., "My friends would think I'm weird.")
	Pragmatic	Consideration of practical needs or consequences (e.g., "I'm comfortable in these clothes.")
	Personal	Portraying the issue as one of maintaining personal jurisdiction in an area (e.g., "The way I dress is an expression of me and my personality.")

Source: Smetana & Berent, 1993.

[a]The examples below are responses to a typical conflict: Mother wants Anne to change what she is wearing, but Anne doesn't want to.

did adolescents, a difference that increased with adolescents' age. Adolescents, on the other hand, appealed to practical considerations, perhaps because such arguments are less likely to be challenged by parents. Smetana has found that, although adolescents may believe their position can be justified by appeals to personal jurisdiction ("It's my room and I can keep it as I like"), they will use pragmatic reasons ("It doesn't matter if it's messy; I can find whatever I need") when arguing with a parent. Parents are not as likely as adolescents to view the behaviors in question as rightfully within the adolescents' purview. Adolescent appeals to social convention in resolving family conflict are likely to generate more conflict than they settle, usually because the conventions referred to are those of their peers, perhaps already a sore point for many parents.

DOMAINS OF AUTHORITY   One might think that adolescents would be wise to pick their battles carefully given their unequal footing. But most conflicts between adolescents and their parents aren't real battles. Adolescents *agree* with their parents on the big issues; most adolescents believe it's important to have a good family life and to be successful in their work, just as their parents did when they were adolescents. Values such as these haven't changed much from their parents' generation (Jodl et al., 2001; ter Bogt et al., 2005).

Instead, it's the little things they argue about, such as what clothes they can wear or the music they listen to. Adolescents consider decisions such as these to be questions of personal choice which, since they affect no one other than themselves, should be theirs to make. With respect to issues where someone's well-being is involved, they agree that parents have the right to make the rules. Similarly, most adolescents consider conventional issues, such as doing chores or "watching their language," to be the legitimate province of parental decision making. These perceptions, by the way, do not change with age, suggesting that parents are seen as rightfully the ones to establish and maintain the social as well as the moral order and adolescents as the ones seeking greater autonomy within this (Smetana & Asquith, 1994). Thus, adolescents still believe their parents have the right to make rules, and parents believe adolescents should have a say, agreeing with adolescents that they have the right to make decisions about personal issues.

So where's the conflict? Conflicts between adolescents and their parents are not so much about whether adolescents have authority in some domains and parents in others, as they are about *which* domain any decision falls within. For instance, although both adolescents and their parents believe that adolescents have a right to make decisions about personal issues, disagreements arise when issues that adolescents consider to be personal are not seen as such by parents (**Table 6.2**). Adolescents consider their friends, for example, to be a matter of personal choice. Parents, on the other hand, are likely to consider the choice of friends to fall more legitimately within their domain, and feel obligated to step in when they disapprove of certain friends. Similarly, even though parents and adolescents agree that parents have the authority, and even the obligation, to set down rules concerning prudential, or safety, issues, disagreements are likely to arise as to whether a particular issue falls

A messy room and a busy phone may be signs of a young adolescent moving toward autonomy rather than of innate sloppiness or irresponsibility.

TABLE 6.2
Differences in Adolescents' and Parent's Perceptions of Domains of Authority

Moral (well-being) issues
Agreement that parents have authority to make decisions
Examples:
> Taking money from parents without permission
> Hitting brothers and sisters
> Lying to parents

Conventional issues
Agreement that parents have authority to make decisions
Examples:
> Not doing chores
> Calling parents or teachers by their first names
> Cursing

Prudential (safety) issues
Agreement that parents have authority to make decisions, but disagreement over what constitute prudential issues
Examples:
> Smoking cigarettes
> Drinking alcohol
> Driving with friends who are new drivers

Personal issues
Agreement that adolescents have authority to make decisions, but disagreement over what constitute personal issues
Examples:
> Watching cartoons on TV
> Choosing own clothes
> Spending allowance money on games

Friendship issues
Agreement that adolescents have authority to make decisions, but disagreement over what constitute friendship issues
Examples:
> Seeing a friend whom parents do not like
> Going to a movie alone with a boyfriend or girlfriend
> Inviting a boyfriend or girlfriend over when parents are not home

Source: Smetana & Asquith, 1994.

within this domain. Again, parents see themselves as having more authority to govern adolescents' behavior than do adolescents. Differences in parents' and adolescents' perceptions of issues indicate where the struggle for autonomy is fought—not on moral or even conventional grounds, but on what constitutes the personal prerogatives of adolescents (Daddis, 2008; Smetana, 2005; Smetana & Daddis, 2002).

The issues adolescents and parents disagree about vary little from one culture to the next; most conflicts are about everyday issues (e.g., doing homework, how late they can stay up). This is as true for adolescents growing up in Madrid or the People's Republic of China as it is for adolescents in Boston or Los Angeles (Yau & Smetana, 2003). Most of the conflicts are resolved by adolescents giving in to parents, with parents having the final say. This, too, is true across cultures, although European American adolescents are somewhat less compliant than those whose families have emigrated from interdependent cultures (Table 6.3) (Phinney et al., 2005; Smetana et al., 2003; Yau & Smetana, 2003).

TABLE 6.3
Adolescents Comply and Negotiate Conflicts with Parents

	MIDDLE ADOLESCENTS	LATE ADOLESCENTS	EMERGING ADULTS
Reasons for compliance, involving parents/family			
European Americans	My parents feel it would be best for me. My parents don't want me to go.	My parents are usually right. I listen to my parents.	My parents generally have good reasons. I put first commitments first.
Korean Americans	I honor my parents' decision. I would do what is best for my family.	I must obey my parents with respect. I don't want to upset my parents.	Friends come and go but families are forever. Family dinners are important to them.
Armenian Americans	I love and respect my parents. I don't want to lose their trust in me.	I love my family and want their satisfaction. I should listen to them and not disobey them.	I love and respect my parents; I would honor their reasons. Family gatherings are important; it brings the family closer.
Mexican Americans	I would do anything for my family. I wouldn't want them to suffer; I would rather they be happier than me.	I like my family. I respect my guardian—my aunt; she comes home tired from work.	I have the most respect for my family. My mom needs to come home and relax in a nice, clean home.
Reasons for negotiation			
European Americans	To convince my parents to let me go.	So I may understand their argument and debate the situation.	Talking with them works, they'd understand.
Korean Americans	So that they might reconsider. I can be content as well as my parents. I hate arguing, so I always find the way to peace.	Both my parents and I would be happy.	So they would understand it's important. I don't want to argue with my parents. If my parents don't like that person, I won't get married to him.
Armenian Americans	So everyone would be happy. I won't get them angry, and we will both get what we want.	That way you'll be satisfied and you'll satisfy your parents.	To be both places and not disappoint my parents. That way my parents won't be upset.
Mexican Americans	That way we'll know how much we trust each other.	To please everyone at the same time. To compromise and not get them upset.	I want to respect the family but also go to the party.

Source: After Phinney et al., 2005.

The realm of issues that parents and adolescents consider to be the domain of adolescents increases with age, with more of these being regarded as personal issues both by adolescents and their parents, thus expanding the sphere of adolescent autonomy. This sphere, however, remains narrower for parents than it does for adolescents. Parents continue to see themselves as legitimately setting rules that might affect adolescents' well-being. Thus, although parents are more likely to regard older adolescents than younger ones as having a right to privacy in personal matters, they balance this right with what they see as adolescents' entitlement to proper care, even when this might entail a violation of privacy (Smetana & Asquith, 1994). As one mother said, when asked whether her tenth-grade daughter had the right to have a private diary, "Yes, she should have that privacy, but it is also the parents' right to know what's going on in a child's life. She has the right to privacy but [some] secrets in there, mom has the right to know" (Ruck et al., 2002, p. 392).

Some families routinely seem to handle conflict better than others, staying cooler, expressing less anger, finding ways to resolve differences, and even finding some humor in the process. Much of this depends on what adolescents bring to the situation; differences in temperament among adolescents play a large role in determining the intensity of conflicts with parents and how successfully they are resolved. In fact, these differences are more likely than any others to determine the course of any conflict, strongly influencing how parents respond, rather than the reverse. Adolescents' temperaments, in other words, trump differences in how they've been parented when it comes to negotiating conflicts. Adolescents whose first response is likely to be negative, or who have difficulty controlling their emotions, are the ones for whom relatively minor conflicts blossom into big ones. Conversely, adolescents who enter situations with a more positive attitude negotiate conflict more successfully (Eisenberg et al., 2008; Darling, 2008).

Finally, the respect that adolescents communicate for their parents when disagreeing with them is important in successfully negotiating conflicts. This is particularly true in African American and Hispanic families, both of which place a high value on respect for elders, not only for parents but for elders in the community as well (**Figure 6.4**) (Dixon et al., 2008).

ALTERNATIVES TO CONFLICT   A good number of potential conflicts never arise because adolescents simply don't tell their parents what they intend to do. Most of the time, this takes the form of leaving out important information when they're talking about what they're planning, although avoiding the issue and lying are not uncommon (**Figure 6.5**). When adolescents do disclose their plans to their parents, they do so for the most part out of feelings of respect and obligation ("they're my parents, so I should") or because they hope to change their parents' minds, rather than simply thinking they can't get away with not telling them (**Figure 6.6**) (Darling et al., 2006; Tasopoulos-Chan et al., 2009).

You may recall from Chapter 5 that, in the end, how much adolescents disclose when talking with their parents depends on the trust that exists between them. To the extent that trust isn't present, adolescents are likely to keep personal issues or those involving their friends secret from their parents (Smetana et al., 2004; Smetana et al., 2006).

VIOLATING EXPECTANCIES   Many conflicts are not as much a test of wills between adolescents and parents as they are something of a surprise to each of the parties involved. Early adolescents can change more rapidly than parents realize, and parental expectations that are based on earlier behavior may not always apply.

When parents and adolescents agree on domains of parental authority, adolescents are able to better communicate with their parents about issues that come up in their lives because they don't feel that their autonomy is threatened.

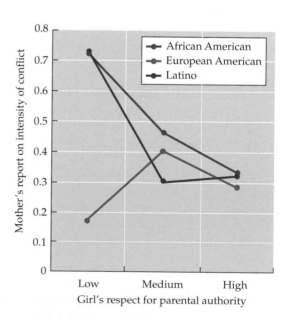

● **Figure 6.4   Conflicts are less intense and more likely to be successfully resolved when adolescents show respect, especially in African American and Latino families** (After Dixon et al., 2008.)

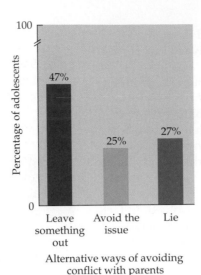

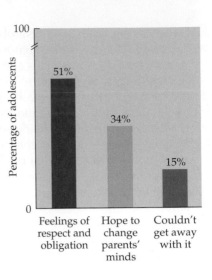

● **Figure 6.5 Adolescents frequently choose alternatives to open conflict with parents** (After Darling et al., 2006.)

● **Figure 6.6 Adolescents' reasons for disclosing their plans to parents** (After Darling et al., 2006.)

Consider a scenario in which a young adolescent, about to leave for school in the morning is stopped by her mother, who asks to see what clothes she's wearing under her coat. The mother, knowing her daughter just purchased a T-shirt that would not be appropriate for school, is concerned that her daughter might be wearing it. The daughter, proud of her restraint this morning in choosing to wear a more conventional top, is offended and hurt that her mother doesn't expect her to show good judgment.

The mother, recalling the difficulties her daughter has had in the past due to poor judgment, didn't expect the maturity revealed in her choice of tops. The words they most likely exchanged following this incident probably sounded, on the surface, as just one more argument about who has a say over what the daughter wears to school. On another level, and perhaps never put into words as such, is the mother's awareness of a new maturity in her daughter, which most likely prompts the mother to reexamine her expectations. Violations of expectancies such as this occur frequently in early adolescence, requiring those who are involved to adapt and revise their interpersonal expectancies. These revisions contribute to the way parents and adolescents renegotiate their respective domains of responsibility (Collins & Luebker, 1994).

Emotional Climate of Families

In general, it is not so much adolescents as their parents who are responsible for changes in the emotional climate within the family. Reed Larson and David Almeida (1999) point out that this climate changes as emotions are transmitted from one person to another through daily interactions. In fact, one can actually follow the path of an emotion as it moves through a family. A parent, for instance, might come home after work tense and irritable, yell at a child, who then fights with a sibling.

Research on such **emotional transmission** reveals a number of characteristic patterns. First, negative emotions are more easily transmitted than positive ones. It is easier to pass on anger, anxiety, or depression, for instance, than joy or peacefulness; however, families with greater psychological resources are less likely to experience the transmission of negative emotions than those with fewer resources.

emotional transmission
The transmission of emotions from one person to another within a family.

Second, some members of the family are more likely than others to transmit emotions. The flow of emotions from one person to another is often unidirectional rather than reciprocal. Specifically, the emotions of men are more likely to affect their wives and children than vice versa. It is unclear whether this pattern reflects individuals' relative power within the family or, with respect to women, a greater sensitivity to the emotional states of others as well as a greater responsiveness to these. Emotions are also more likely to flow from parents to children than vice versa (Larson & Gilman, 1999). And when they do, these are more likely to be the father's emotions than the mother's. This is not to say that mothers do not pass on their emotional states at the moment to their children; they are just less likely to do so than fathers.

Some of the negative emotions fathers pass on can be traced to stresses they experience at work. This has been found for mothers as well, though less consistently (Larson & Richards, 1994; Matjasko & Feldman, 2006). Marital tensions, on the other hand, are likely to be transmitted by mothers and fathers alike (Almeida et al., 1999).

Finally, it is common for an emotion that is passed from one person to assume a different form in the next person. Thus the transmission of anger on the part of a parent may result not in anger in an adolescent, but in anxiety. In this way, the effects "of "secondhand" emotions on children can include physiological symptoms and patterns of behavior as well as emotional states. Thus, adolescents can experience nervous stomachs or headaches, form "defensive alliances" within the family, or simply experience anxiety.

The way adolescents react to the emotions of others depends in large measure on the way in which they interpret these emotions. Adolescents actively construct, or make sense of, the emotional states of others just as they do other aspects of their world. Simply because an emotion is expressed does not mean that it will be experienced in the same way by different individuals. Geraldine Downey, Valerie Purdie, and Rebecca Schaffer-Neitz (1999) compared anger transmission from mother to child in mothers who experienced chronic pain and those who did not. They found that anger in the latter was likely to result in consequent anger in the child, but not in families in which the mother experienced chronic pain. This appeared due in part to the way in which children of these mothers interpreted their mothers' anger. These children simply did not interpret the anger the same way as they would were it not for the pain—that is, as a statement about themselves.

Changing Relationships within the Family: Parents and Parenting

Parents themselves initiate many of the changes that occur in relating to their adolescent children. They expect adolescents to be more assertive and independent than when they were younger. They think teenagers should get around more on their own, whether going to the library or to a part-time job, and have ideas of their own, from what to wear to how to study for a test. Even so, many parents react with ambivalence to adolescents' bids for independence. For some adults, their sense of themselves is strongly tied to their parenting roles, and to include adolescents in more family decisions, they must redefine those roles.

Styles of Parenting

Parents differ in any number of ways when interacting with their children, but two characteristics are particularly useful in distinguishing among these. Diana Baumrind (1967, 1971, 1991b), at the University of California, Berkeley, has identified two dimensions, or characteristic ways of responding to chil-

responsiveness The degree to which parents are sensitive, supportive and involved.

demandingness The degree to which parents expect adolescents to act responsibly, and supervise and monitor their activities.

authoritative parenting Parents who stress self-reliance and independence, establish clear standards for behavior and give reasons when disciplining.

authoritarian parenting Parents who stress obedience, respect for authority, and traditional values.

TABLE 6.4
Parenting Styles

PARENTING STYLE	CHARACTERISTICS
Authoritative	High in demandingness: expect adolescents to act responsibly, consistently enforce standards High in responsiveness: warm and nurturing, discipline with explanation, maintain open dialogue, encourage independence
Authoritarian	High in demandingness: expect responsible behavior, consistent in enforcing standards Low in responsiveness: less openly affectionate, expect adolescents to do as they are told, encourage obedience
Indulgent	Low in demandingness: make few demands for responsible behavior, discipline inconsistently, exercise little control over adolescents' behavior High in responsiveness: warm and nurturing, openly affectionate, enjoy spending time with their children
Disengaged	Low in demandingness: make few demands for responsible behavior, discipline inconsistently, exercise little control over adolescents' behavior Low in responsiveness: provide little warmth or support, relatively uninvolved in adolescents' activities or interests

Authoritative parents, in contrast to authoritarian and permissive ones, try to balance tradition with innovation, cooperation with autonomy, and tolerance with firmness. The children of such parents tend to be socially competent and responsible.

dren, that are present in all parents' behavior. **Responsiveness** refers to how sensitive, warm, and supportive parents are, and **demandingness** refers to the degree to which parents expect their children to behave in responsible ways and supervise their children's activities, monitoring them in terms of where they are going and who they are with.

These dimensions of parenting are independent of each other, that is, parents can be responsive without being demanding, and vice versa. For example, a parent can be warm and supportive (high in responsiveness) without having high expectations for mature and responsible behavior (low in demandingness). Because parents can be responsive without being demanding, and vice versa, it is possible to identify four styles of parenting in terms of these dimensions (**Table 6.4**).

Authoritative parents are both responsive and demanding. Or put another way, just because they are warm and supportive, doesn't mean they are "pushovers." They know what children are capable of doing at any age and expect theirs to act in mature and responsible ways. These parents establish clear standards as to what is acceptable and unacceptable behavior, and consistently enforce these standards; instead of obedience, however, they value self-reliance. When communicating with their children, they encourage discussion, and maintain an open dialogue, listening to their children and expecting their children to listen to them. They give explanations and reasons as well when disciplining.

Authoritarian parents are equally demanding but less responsive than authoritative ones. They, too, establish clear standards as to what behaviors are acceptable and what are unacceptable, and are consistent in enforcing their standards. They value obedience over self-reliance, and expect children to do as they are told, believing that they know what is best and that children should accept the rules established by their parents. Rather than backing up their discipline with reasons, they are more likely to use force.

Indulgent parents are more responsive than they are demanding. These parents are affectionate and friendly, and enjoy spending time with their children. They're supportive of their children and proud of their accomplishments; however, they make few demands for responsible behavior. They punish infrequently and inconsistently, and they exercise little control over their children's behavior.

Disengaged parents are neither responsive nor demanding. These parents provide little warmth or support, and little supervision. They typically do not involve themselves in their children's interests or activities, focusing more on themselves and their own needs, and so have little knowledge of what their children might be doing or who their friends may be.

Authoritative parenting carries clear advantages. Adolescents raised in authoritative families have been found to be more mature, self-reliant, confident, have higher self-esteem, and be more successful academically than those raised under other styles (Martinez & Garcia, 2008; Steinberg et al., 1994). Why is authoritative parenting as effective as it is?

Authoritative parenting provides a balanced approach to parents' expectations for responsible behavior and adolescents' bids for autonomy. Parents provide standards and set limits for their children, but within these they give children the opportunity to make choices, and in this way promote self-reliance and self-control. Authoritative parents promote intellectual development by engaging children in verbal give-and-take, inviting discussion, and stressing the importance of coming up with reasons to support one's position. By giving reasons and expecting children to do the same, they encourage adolescents to think for themselves. Authoritative parents explain why family rules are important, and give reasons when disciplining, which helps adolescents, in turn, to understand social relationships better and develop empathy for others. Over and above these characteristics, the closeness of the relationship fostered by authoritative parenting is important. Their warmth and acceptance promotes trust and openness on the part of adolescents, and increases their effectiveness as parents (Steinberg, 2001). Even with optimal family relationships such as these, parents can still wish at times that they had known more about adolescence (**Box 6.2**).

Cultural Contexts of Parenting

Research with European American adolescents clearly links authoritative parenting to measures of adjustment and school success (McKinney & Renk, 2008; Milevsky et al., 2008; Simons & Conger, 2007). One might ask, however, whether this is equally true for ethnic minority adolescents. A first point to note is that when comparisons are made, authoritative parenting is found to be less common in ethnic minority families than in families with European American backgrounds. Even though ethnic minority adolescents are less likely to *have* authoritative parents, they are with few exceptions still likely to profit from this style of parenting (Driscoll et al., 2008; Lamborn et al., 1996; Smetana & Chuang, 2001).

Ruth Chao (1994, 2001) argues, however, that parenting styles cannot be separated in any simple way from their cultural contexts. She points out that Chinese American parents, though often referred to as controlling or strict, are not similar to European American parents for whom strictness translates into being authoritarian. For instance, control, instead of taking the form of a

indulgent parenting
Parents who are warm and supportive but provide little supervision.

disengaged parenting
Parents who provide little support or supervision.

In More Depth

What Parents Wish They Had Known About Adolescence

"They seem to get caught up in fads in junior high. They do certain things ... to be part of the crowd. I wish I'd known how to handle that. At what point are these fads okay, because it's important to identify with your peer group, and at what point do you say no? If they are really dangerous, then it's easy; but with a lot of them, it's a gray area, and I wish I'd known what to do better."—Father

"I wish I had realized that she needed more structure and control. Because she had always been a good student and done her work, I thought I could trust her to manage the school tasks without my checking. But she lost interest in school, and I learned only very gradually that I had to be more of a monitor with her work than I had been in the past."—Mother

"I wish I had known more about the mood swings. When the girls became 13, they each got moody for a while, and I stopped taking it personally. I just relaxed. The youngest one said, 'Do I have to go through that? Can't I just skip that?' Sure enough, when she became 13, she was moody too."—Mother

"I wish I'd known how to help the boys get along a little better. They have real fights at times, and while they have a lot of fun together and help each other out, I wish I knew how to cut down on the fighting."—Father

Source: After Brooks, 1999.

---

unidirectional exercise of power by parents over the child, in Asian cultures is bidirectional, carrying with it an obligation to nurture and support the child, making parents, in other words, high in responsiveness.

In individualistic cultures such as the United States, authoritative parenting confers distinct advantages, contributing to self-reliance. But in collectivist cultures that place greater importance on respect for elders and less importance on self-reliance, authoritarian parenting should actually reflect the values of the culture better than authoritative parenting and be more adaptive than it is in individualistic cultures. Marwan Dwairy (2006, 2008) found this to be true for Arab adolescents, raised in an authoritarian culture. Authoritarian parenting was associated with fewer negative outcomes than for adolescents in more liberal cultures. Dwairy suggests that it is not the parenting style per se that promotes psychosocial adjustment as much as it is its consistency with the culture. In non-Western cultures, which are more authoritarian and collective, authoritarian parenting frequently is associated either with positive outcomes, or at least with ones that are not negative.

parental monitoring
A practice in which parents monitor their children's behavior when they are not physically present to supervise their activities.

Chinese American parents may appear to be controlling or strict, but they differ from authoritarian parents in that control is bidirectional.

Knowing What Your Kids Are Doing

An important aspect to parenting is knowing what your children are doing. Parents can monitor adolescent's activities even when they're not there to see what's going on in person. **Parental monitoring** refers to parents' awareness of where their children are, who they are with, and what they are doing. For instance, a mother may require her ninth-grade son to call her whenever he will be staying after school for an activity, and to tell her whose parent will be driving him home, and when. This only works, of course, if his mother knows the friend and has met the parent. But if this mother is good at monitoring, she will know both of these, and may touch base with the mother who drove him home as well.

How much parents actually know of their adolescents' activities depends on a number of things. Asking adolescents to keep them informed is only one of these, and not necessarily the most reliable. Adolescents are less likely to get into trouble when parents are involved in their lives, but also when parents exercise some control over their behavior, such as specifying how late they can stay out or who they can be with (Fletcher et al., 2004; Soenens et al., 2006).

In nearly all cultures, parenting isn't limited to mothers and fathers. Many ethnic minority, as well as majority, families include a grandparent or other relative living in the home.

Warm and loving relationships within the family help adolescents individuate and develop self-esteem. Without family members who believe in them and stand by them, teenagers may lose faith in themselves and drop out of school long before graduation day.

Adolescents who have contact with grandparents, aunts, and uncles, whether under the same roof or close enough to visit, typically benefit from their support. Adolescents who have an extended family network of relatives on whom they can count for advice and support, are more self-reliant and successful in school, and have fewer problem behaviors (Taylor, 1996).

Whose Identity Crisis? Parents and Middle Age

Middle-aged parents face the downward slope of the developmental curve their adolescents are climbing, meaning that the developmental tasks confronting adolescents come up for review again at midlife, precisely when parents may be facing identity issues of their own (Table 6.5).

Just as the physical changes of puberty mark the beginning of adolescence, physical changes alert their parents that they are entering middle age, and many find these changes difficult to accept. Perhaps the first sign of aging for most adults appears when they step on the bathroom scale. Middle age brings an increase in body weight and a change in its distribution. The face becomes thinner, as do legs and arms. But what is lost in the extremities is gained through the middle. Bob Hope once quipped that "middle age is when your age begins to show around your middle." Changes such as these are difficult at any age, but the kicker for most parents is the timing: Most adults begin to experience these changes just when their children are developing bodies that reflect the prime of youth.

How might these and other physical changes affect the willingness of parents to listen to or share responsibility for decision making with adolescents? An everyday example such as buying clothes can provide some insights. Bathing suits may be only swimwear to parents with young children, but to parents of adolescents they can raise issues of sexuality or even competition. Adolescents' arguments that suits of the same style are worn by young children can go unheard if parents are alarmed by their adolescent's obvious physical maturity or their own feelings about their sexual attractiveness.

Middle-aged parents face another assault on their egos. The functioning of the reproductive system changes, marking a period of life known as the

TABLE 6.5
Developmental Tasks of Adolescents and Their Middle-Aged Parents

ADOLESCENTS	PARENTS
Achieving new and more mature relations with peers	Finding a congenial social group[a]
Achieving a masculine or feminine social role	Developing adult leisure-time activities
Accepting one's physique and using the body effectively	Accepting and adjusting to the physical changes of middle age
Achieving emotional independence from parents and other adults	Adjusting to aging parents
	Assisting teenage children to become happy and responsible adults
Preparing for marriage and family life	Relating to one's spouse as a person
Preparing for an economic career	Reaching and maintaining satisfactory performance in one's career
Acquiring a set of values and an ethical system as a guide to behavior	Taking on civic responsibility[a]
Desiring and achieving socially responsible behavior	Achieving adult social and civic responsibility

[a]A task begun in early adulthood.

climacteric The gradual decline in functioning of the reproductive organs in middle age.

menopause Cessation of menstrual period in middle age.

climacteric. As the body decreases its production of sex hormones, menstrual periods cease in women (**menopause**). The climacteric affects men as well. Erections and orgasms take longer to achieve, and some men begin to experience erectile dysfunction. For both sexes, orgasms are likely to diminish in intensity. Just when their children reach sexual maturity, parents may be questioning their own sexuality and themselves as sexually desirable partners. For increasing numbers of parents, these changes come at a time when they face the loss of a marriage partner through divorce, and doubts and anxieties raised by dating. As a consequence, parents may view their adolescents' dates and romantic involvements with more concern than they would if their own sexuality were not as salient to them.

Similarly, as adolescents start to think about future careers, their parents review their own careers and may question the jobs they have pursued for the past several decades; many also will realize that they are not likely to advance beyond their present position. Listening to their children's plans about the future can be difficult as parents face hard facts about their own present realities and share concern about an uncertain future for their children.

Each of these areas of change is a source of potential stress in the lives of parents and adolescents. The fact that the changes experienced by one generation complement those experienced by the other can introduce additional tensions into relationships already stressed by changing family roles.

Families in Context

So far, in looking at relationships within the family we have focused on those between adolescents and their parents. Here, we consider some additional factors that affect adolescent development.

Ethnic Minority Membership

Ethnicity is an important factor contributing to the impact of the family on adolescent development. Over recent decades, the number of ethnic families in the United States has increased dramatically, from just over 10% of the population in 1950 to over 40% estimated by 2020, with over 50% of all children being minorities by 2023 (U.S. Census Bureau, 2008a).

AFRICAN AMERICAN FAMILIES   Approximately 14% of adolescents in the United States are African American (U.S. Census Bureau, 2008a). Family roles tend to be more flexible and less gender specific than in the dominant culture, with parents assuming responsibilities within the household according to work hours and type of task. Parents also show less differentiation in the roles and tasks they assign to children of either sex. Support from extended family members is also more common than in majority families (Levitt et al., 1993).

Parents influence their adolescents in multiple ways. Do these adolescents enjoy roller blading because they have shared other activities like this with their parents? Or do they share similar activities with their parents because they also share a gene pool?

Among African Americans, considerable diversity exists in income levels, and in associated educational attainment and other indices of well-being. Despite the massive inroads made against discrimination in jobs, schooling, and housing in the 1960s, many forms of covert discrimination still exist. Rates of unemployment are higher and median earnings are lower, for instance, than for white workers (Douglas-Hall & Chau, 2009).

Despite Erik Erikson's (1959) concern that black adolescents would have difficulty developing a positive identity due to negative images of blacks in the dominant culture, the self-esteem of black adolescents is higher than that of adolescents from other ethnic backgrounds, including that of whites (Twenge & Crocker, 2002).

ASIAN AMERICAN FAMILIES   Approximately 9% of adolescents in the United States are of Asian and Pacific Islander descent (U.S. Census Bureau, 2008a). Asian traditions emphasize the importance of the group rather than the individual, and Asian American adolescents feel strong loyalties to their families. Roles in Asian American families tend to be more rigidly defined than in Western families, and relationships are vertically, or hierarchically, arranged, with the father in a position of authority at the top. Family relationships are likely to reflect the roles of members more than in individualistic, Western cultures. An aspect of the children's role is to care for their parents. This sense of responsibility to the family characterizes Asian American adolescents (Fuligni et al., 2002). Socialization practices emphasize duty, maintaining control over one's emotions and thoughts, and obedience to authority figures within the family. Chinese American adolescents, for example, responded that they would meet parental expectations rather than satisfy their own desires when these conflicted. However, many of those responding to such questions cited practical reasons for doing so in addition to respect for cultural traditions, saying it would increase the likelihood that they would be given permission to do something else they might want to do (Yau & Smetana, 1993). As with African American families, more Asian American families are low-income than are nonminority families (Douglas-Hall & Chau, 2009).

HISPANIC FAMILIES   Approximately 15% of U.S. adolescents are Hispanic (U.S. Census Bureau, 2008a). For adolescents from Spanish-speaking homes, the sense of being between two cultures is especially strong. Traditionally, Hispanic families tend to be patriarchal; however, roles have changed as more Hispanic women find work outside the home. Employment is associated with higher status for the wife and greater decision making in the family (Herrera

For bilingual adolescents, intergenerational conflicts over differences between their native culture and the majority culture of their peers are underscored by the different languages spoken in each sphere.

& DelCampo, 1995). Nonetheless, adolescents tend to be socialized into well-differentiated gender roles (Casas et al., 1994; Ramirez, 1989). As do African American families, Hispanic families enjoy greater extended family support than do majority families. Also, as with African American and Asian American families, more Hispanic families are low-income than are nonminority families (Douglas-Hall & Chau, 2009).

Siblings

Another aspect of the family system that affects adolescent development is its size. Adolescents growing up with sisters and brothers experience a different family life, and are affected differently by it, than those without siblings. Over three-quarters of adolescents have at least one sibling. Most adolescents find that despite the conflicts that inevitably arise, they develop close bonds of affection with siblings, and these increase with age (Buist et al., 2002). Gene Brody, Zolinda Stoneman, and Kelly McCoy (1994), at the University of Georgia, followed 70 families over a four-year period, assessing the quality of sibling relationships. In general, siblings reported that their relationships with each other improved over time. However, as siblings reached early adolescence, they reported relationships with other children in the family as being more negative, a finding that corroborates that of other researchers, who also found adolescents' emotional experiences, when they were with their families, to become more negative by junior high (Larson et al., 1996; McGue et al., 2005).

Older siblings tend to serve as models for younger ones. Through their interactions with parents and others, they illustrate expected forms of behavior and family standards. Their achievements influence younger siblings' aspirations and interests. An adolescent girl's interest in sports, for example, will be influenced by having an older sister on the varsity field hockey team. She sees the interest her parents take in her sister's activities and the pride her sister has in her team role. The girl takes it for granted that girls participate in sports and intends to try out for the swimming team herself when she reaches junior high.

Older siblings are also likely to serve as caretakers for younger children in the family. Having to watch out for a younger sister or brother can increase an adolescent's sense of responsibility, usefulness, and competence. If these caretaking activities are too demanding and take time away from schoolwork or friends, however, they can result in frustration, anger, and lowered self-esteem (Hetherington, 1989). Adolescents in single-parent homes are more likely than those from intact families to be given responsibility for watching over younger siblings.

Siblings provide emotional support, friendship, and company for each other (Seginer, 1998; Tucker et al., 1999). Because they are closer in age to each other than to a parent, they are often more in touch with the problems each face and can frequently offer better advice than a parent. An older brother can advise a 12-year-old girl that the hazing she is experiencing in the first weeks of junior high will soon end. He knows, because that was his experience a year ago when he started junior high. A parent would be less likely to have this information.

Siblings in blended families may experience somewhat more conflict than those in intact families. However, relationships frequently improve with time and may reach the level of accord found in intact families (Hetherington & Kelly, 2002).

Dual-Earner Families

In most families with children under the age of 18, both parents are employed (U.S. Census Bureau, 2005a). Despite the fact that having two working parents in the home is normative for adolescents, most research on dual-earner families has focused on the effects of maternal employment.

What effect *does* maternal employment have on adolescents? Research addressing this question suggests that *whether* mom works is not as important as the *conditions* that are present when she does (Gottfried et al., 2002; Joebgen & Richards, 1990). Joebgen and Richards (1990), for example, periodically contacted adolescents and parents throughout the day (via beepers) to sample their activities and their moods. They found that maternal employment per se was not important; what mattered in terms of both her well-being and the adolescent's emotional adjustment was the match between the mother's interests and abilities and the work she did during the day, whether inside or outside the home.

Studies of working mothers and their children find few consistent relationships between maternal employment and indicators of adjustment in adolescents, such as academic achievement, emotional development, or social competence (Armistead et al., 1990; Bird & Kemerait, 1990; Keith et al., 1990). Problems, when they arise, are related more to the lack of parental monitoring than to maternal employment per se (Jacobson, 2000). Similarly, parent-adolescent relations are most likely to be affected when *both* parents experience work-related stress (Galambos & Maggs, 1990; Galambos et al., 1995). Job-related stresses of employed mothers do not seem to spill over to their relationships with their adolescent children as much as do those of fathers, or to affect children's psychosocial adjustment (Matjasko & Feldman, 2006).

GENDER ROLES   Maternal employment has a liberalizing effect on gender roles in the household. In single-earner families, with the traditional model of fathers as "breadwinners" and mothers as "homemakers," fathers spend more time with their sons than their daughters, while in dual-earner families they spend equivalent amounts of time with each (Crouter & Crowley, 1990). Even though traditional, single-earner families expect daughters and sons to spend equal amounts of time doing household chores, they assign work in gender-stereotypic ways. Girls, for example, might be expected to clear the table, do dishes, or watch younger siblings; boys might mow the lawn, wash the car, and take out the garbage. In other respects, dual-earner families mirror for daughters the social realities facing employed mothers. Just as the workload of employed mothers increases when they work outside the home (because they continue to be responsible for work within the home), daughters actually do 25% more work in dual-earner homes than in the traditional, single-earner families (Benin & Edwards, 1990).

MATERNAL WELL-BEING   Maternal employment may affect the mother's sense of well-being more than the children's during adolescence. A study of over 100 families with adolescents between ages 10 and 15 found that parents who were positively invested in their jobs weathered the stresses of parenting adolescents better than those who were not (Silverberg & Steinberg, 1990). As adolescents enter puberty, begin dating, and engage in more activities outside the home, parents face midlife identity issues and frequently a drop in self-esteem and life satisfaction. Parents who are involved in their work roles, however, show increases in self-esteem and life satisfaction and have fewer midlife concerns when their children start to date.

Maternal employment can relate to well-being in yet another way. As adolescent autonomy increases, conflicts with parents increase, especially with mothers. The stability of work roles outside the home, in which established patterns of authority and decision making are not questioned, can buttress parental self-esteem in the face of changing relationships at home (Gottfried et al., 2002).

Families in Transition

Several major social trends exert significant influence on the lives of adolescents. Increasing numbers experience divorce, single parenting, and stepparenting.

Divorce

What impact does divorce have on adolescents? Simple answers do not exist. The effect divorce has on adolescents depends on a host of conditions. E. Mavis Hetherington, a developmentalist who has followed numerous families through divorce, remarks that one of the most notable things she has observed is how differently families respond (Hetherington & Kelly, 2002).

Even relatively amicable divorces can be emotionally charged and stressful. As a consequence, researchers have not been surprised to find a number of negative effects associated with its occurrence. Adolescents from divorced homes frequently have lower academic self-concepts than those from intact homes; as a group, they are more likely to use substances such as cigarettes, alcohol, or marijuana, and to engage in sexual intercourse at an earlier age. Other, more global measures such as self-concept, self-esteem, social competence, happiness, and maturity have been found to differ for those from divorced homes (Hetherington & Kelly, 2002; Ge et al., 2006; Sun, 2001; Wallerstein & Lewis, 2004).

How extensive are these problems? Hetherington, who has studied almost 1,400 families, many of them for more than three decades, has found that 25% of children whose parents are divorced experience one or more of the above problems, in comparison to 10% of those from intact families. Looked at another way, however, one can say that 75% of adolescents do not experience serious problems, and a small minority actually come through their parents' divorce even stronger than they had been before (Hetherington & Kelly, 2002).

CONDITIONS CONTRIBUTING TO STRESS   Perhaps because negative findings support popular stereotypes of adolescents with divorced parents, researchers have been relatively slow to look beneath the surface to determine what factors other than *not* living with a father in the home (the usual custodial arrangement) might have contributed to them. One of the first studies to follow children of divorce over time discovered a number of conditions contributing to stress, not the least of which is divorce's effects on the parents (Hetherington et al., 1982). Subsequent research by Hetherington has supported these earlier observations (Hetherington & Kelly, 2002). Recently divorced parents, for example, report more depression and have poorer parenting skills than those not divorced. Difficulties in adjusting among their children can be traced, in part, to the *parents'* reactions to the divorce. Divorce can be highly damaging to a parent's self-esteem and sense of worth. Many leave a divorce with a sense of failure, not just in the relationship, but as individuals. Most experience depression and increased tension as they adjust to their changed life circumstances. Parents can become preoccupied with their own problems and consequently less responsive to the needs of adolescents who are also adjusting to the divorce (Hetherington & Kelly, 2002). Adolescents whose parents remain as caring and supportive as they were previously are less likely to be affected by marital discord or divorce (Davies & Windle, 2001; Dunlop et al., 2001).

However, divorce is frequently accompanied by less intimate relationships between parents and children (Sun, 2001). Fathers in particular are perceived as less caring (Dunlop et al., 2001), and adolescents' relationships with noncustodial fathers are likely to further deteriorate over time (Gunnoe & Hetherington, 2004; Burns & Dunlop, 2001).Two years following a divorce, for instance, only 25% of noncustodial fathers saw their children once a week, with most seeing them biweekly or even monthly (Hetherington & Kelly, 2002).

Parenting changes following a divorce. This father is likely to be less consistent and effective than he was previously, or will be again.

Not only is the quality of relationships with parents likely to suffer, but initially so is the effectiveness of parenting. Fathers become more permissive, perhaps reluctant to spoil their available time on a dispute over discipline, and mothers become more inconsistent, at times ignoring infractions and at other times reacting more severely. Each of these changes adds to the level of stress. Parents who are consistent and firm in their discipline, while maintaining warm and supportive relationships with their children, are the most successful in helping adolescents adjust to a divorce (Hetherington & Kelly, 2002).

As a rule, life evens out within a two- to three-year period following the divorce. Parents and adolescents regain much of their earlier emotional stability, and each is better able to "be there" for the other. Interviews with over 500 adolescents four years following their parents' divorce found that the most important predictors of adolescents' adjustment were how close they were with the parent they were living with and how well that parent monitored their activities, such as knowing where they were after school, how they spent their time and money, and who their friends were (Buchanan et al., 1992).

Additionally, because divorce is more common today than in previous generations, adolescents are less likely to experience stigma associated with it. Many of their friends have gone through a similar experience, and natural support groups exist in which adolescents can air their feelings and gain perspective on their situation.

HOLDING ON, LETTING GO, AND STAYING IN PLACE   Divorce can be difficult because it introduces changes in the family just at the time adolescents themselves are in the process of changing. It's hard to push off from something, in other words, when it is moving away from you. Robert Kegan (1982) speaks of three functions that the environment must serve, at any age. The first is *holding on*; the environment needs to support, nourish, and sustain the adolescent. Individuals—such as parents, siblings, and teachers, who make up the adolescent's environment—must "be present" for the adolescent, recognizing and accepting what the adolescent is going through. The second

Adolescents in single-parent families must often take on new roles and responsibilities, such as part-time jobs and additional chores around the house. In return for greater responsibility, however, they gain in autonomy and independence.

function is *letting go*, or assisting the adolescent in establishing the ways in which she or he differs from others, helping the adolescent find her or his own way. These two functions parallel the dimensions of family interaction referred to earlier as individuality and connectedness. A final function of the environment is *remaining in place*, thereby permitting the adolescent to reintegrate aspects of the self that have become differentiated. Kegan notes that "it takes a special wisdom for the family of an adolescent to understand that by remaining in place so that the adolescent can have the family there to ignore and reject, the family is providing something very important, and is still, in a new way, intimately and importantly involved in the child's development" (1982, p. 129). Were the family to "move away," as opposed to remain in place, those aspects of the self that the adolescent has thrown off can become lost to the adolescent and be more difficult to reintegrate into new ways of relating to others.

MARITAL CONFLICT   Marital conflict rather than divorce per se contributes heavily to the stress adolescents experience (Amato & Afifi, 2006; Turner & Kopiec, 2006). Conflict is most likely to affect adolescents by affecting the quality of relationships within the family (Fauber et al., 1990; Sun, 2001). A three-year longitudinal study of over 1,000 seventh-, ninth-, and eleventh-graders found that conflict within the family, not divorce, was associated with negative effects such as depression, anxiety, and physical symptoms. In fact, adolescents from intact homes with high levels of conflict showed lower levels of well-being than those in low-conflict divorced homes on all measures that were used (Mechanic & Hansell, 1989).

Single-Parent Families

About half of the adolescents who live in single-parent families do so because of divorce; most of them (80%) live with their mothers (U.S. Census Bureau, 2002). One of the most noticeable differences between these adolescents and those from intact homes is their economic status. Close to 30% of families headed by a single female parent live at the poverty level, compared to approximately 5% of two-parent families (U.S. Census Bureau, 2008b). For many adolescents, this income level is a dramatic change. One year following a divorce, a single mother's income is likely to have dropped to 67% of the total household income before divorce, whereas the father's income is likely to drop only to 90% (**Figure 6.7**). The initially lower earning capacity of most women, along with frequent lack of child support and little state support, contributes to this pattern. Economic hardship can contribute to adolescents' distress in intact families as well.

Adolescents in single-parent families face the need—some for the first time—to take on part-time jobs to pay for things they previously took for granted. There are advantages and disadvantages in this situation, as in almost any other. On the positive side, adolescents stand to gain in autonomy and independence through being more responsible. Hetherington finds that adolescents are

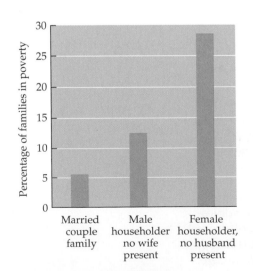

● **Figure 6.7   Current population survey of poverty rates in two-parent families and single-parent families**   (After Bishaw & Stern, 2006.)

given greater responsibility, have a greater role in family decision making, and are given more independence than in intact families. Potential disadvantages can result when responsibilities exceed adolescents' capabilities or keep them from normal activities, such as schoolwork and social participation.

Many adolescents face additional changes immediately after a divorce. Thirty percent of adolescents move within the first year following a divorce; for many this means adjusting to a new neighborhood and a new school and making new friends. Less frequent contact with old friends is an additional loss. Frequently, divorced mothers will change their employment within the same time period, adding to the general level of stress within the family. Divorced mothers report lower levels of psychological well-being and more concerns than mothers in two-parent families. Adolescents living with divorced mothers are likely to enjoy the same family support as before, yet they typically have less contact with their neighbors than those living in two-parent families. Most divorced mothers, however, are relatively successful in establishing the social supports they need, and those who maintain discipline and family routines have adolescents who adjust positively to their new circumstances (Hetherington & Kelly, 2002; Larson et al., 2001).

On the positive side, relationships between adolescents and mothers often become stronger in the process of coping with these conditions; relationships become closer and less hierarchical. Mothers and daughters especially are likely to find these relationships satisfying, with the exception of early maturing girls, for whom family conflict increases. Adolescents living with their mothers may also develop more liberal attitudes regarding work and gender roles. Daughters living with their divorced mothers report high expectations from their mothers for them to attend college. Divorced mothers may see a need for their daughters to be economically and socially independent, in case they find themselves in similar circumstances (McLanahan et al., 1988; Sessa & Steinberg, 1991).

Although most adolescents live with their mothers following a divorce, some live with their fathers. Most fathers are comfortable in their custodial role, particularly the longer they have been doing this.

PATERNAL CUSTODY   An increasing number of divorced fathers receive custody of their children, although this arrangement is still relatively uncommon. Of all children living with a single parent because of divorce, only 20% live with their fathers (U.S. Census Bureau, 2002). Perhaps because of the special circumstances under which fathers are likely to be awarded custody, more fathers experienced difficulty. For instance, hostility between parents remained higher when fathers had custody; fathers with custody also worked more hours per week than did mothers with custody, and residential arrangements changed more frequently following the divorce than with mothers with custody or shared custody arrangements.

Other things being equal, however, fathers have been found to adjust to their custodial role well. A survey of over 1,000 single fathers found them to be relatively comfortable in their roles. Those who were most comfortable were the ones who had been at it the longest; presumably they had worked out the kinks and developed their own successful routines over the years. Those who were satisfied with their social lives also reported more satisfaction with their roles, as did those who had higher incomes and rated themselves high as a parent (Greif & DeMaris, 1990).

Remarriage and Blended Families

role clarity Clear understanding among family members concerning the nature and responsibilities of each person's role.

Parents who divorce are likely to remarry and to introduce a stepparent into their children's lives. Close to 20% of U.S. children under the age of 18 live with a stepparent, who in most cases is a stepfather. Adolescents do best, understandably, when they can maintain close relationships with both their resident and non-resident parents (Scott et al., 2007), but also having a close relationship with a stepfather is important. Closeness to stepmothers, though, is less strongly related to adjustment (King, 2006, 2007). Remarriage usually occurs soon on the heels of the divorce, typically within three years. Many stepparents bring a stepsibling or two (residential or weekend) in the process. For adolescents, this series of events comes on top of the changes introduced by puberty, moving to a new type of school, and rapidly changing social relations. Fewer changes would be enough to disrupt anyone's equilibrium. Yet many families weather the stresses of these new relationships, and some even thrive. Success cannot be rushed, though, and more typically than not comes only after years of relationship building.

What makes the difference between success and failure after remarriage? A number of general statements can be made.

ROLE CLARITY   Perhaps the first thing to emphasize is the importance of **role clarity**, the understanding among family members regarding each person's role and how it affects the others (Hetherington & Kelly, 2002). Agreement as to what these roles are is often difficult, since roles that are acceptable to a parent or stepparent may not be acceptable to the children, who, as Hetherington notes, may not even view the stepparent as a member of the family. Adolescence introduces its own confusions into roles and the issues that surround them, such as being a child versus an adult, being dependent versus independent, being autonomous versus emotionally connected. The addition of stepparents to this confusing mix creates the potential for real drama. An adolescent who bridles at suggestions from his mother may find it even harder to listen to a stepfather. If a 6-foot tall, strapping 15-year-old is confused about his role as a child to a biological parent, magnify that confusion by an order of 10 when you add a stepfather who is 3 inches shorter, 20 pounds lighter—and an emotional rival.

Things may be no clearer to the stepparent. As one stepfather remarked, "I have no idea how I'm supposed to behave, or what the rules are. Can I kiss my wife in front of my stepchildren? Do I tell my stepson to do his homework, or is that exceeding my authority? Can I have my own kids over for the weekend, or is that going to be an imposition? It's hard living in a family where there are no clear rules or lines of authority" (Hetherington & Kelly, 2002, p. 181). Families with the most ambiguity in roles are those with a stepmother and at least one child in common. The difficulties facing stepmothers are especially acute, because they are likely to oversee the management of the household, a role that can bring them into direct conflict with stepchildren who may resent their presence.

Ordinary family problems are magnified in blended families. The most successful families establish clear guidelines for parenting. The same type of parenting that works best in intact families, authoritative parenting, is also best in blended families. The catch is that it's harder to be authoritative if you're a stepparent. Hetherington and Kelly (2002) estimate that only a third of stepfathers, and even fewer stepmothers, become authoritative. Rather than a direct hands-on approach, it is better for stepparents to support the biological parent's use of discipline and to work on building trust and friendship with the stepchild (Moore & Cartwright, 2005).

TIMING OF REMARRIAGE   Another factor contributing to the success of remarriage and building successful relationships is the age of children when the stepparent arrives on the scene. Remarriages are most likely to be successful when they take place either before children reach the age of 10 or after 15. With younger children, roles are easier to define. Similarly, older adolescents can appreciate having a stepparent as an emotional support for the biological parent as they begin to think about leaving home, either to go to college or to start work and live on their own. However, early adolescents are attempting to establish their autonomy and may feel threatened by the presence of another adult with whom they may need to negotiate the decisions they make. Also, early adolescents who have been living with a single parent are likely to have enjoyed a greater role in family decision making than age-mates from intact families and may resent losing this role to a new stepparent (Hetherington & Kelly, 2002).

On the positive side, younger and older adolescents alike can appreciate the benefits of having a parent remarry when this is successful. Not only are financial problems likely to be lessened, but the biological parent is likely to be happier. As one child put it, "Mother's not worrying so much and working so hard now. I've never seen her really happy before. She's a different person. I realize now how tough things were for her" (Hetherington & Kelly, 2002, p. 191). Many adolescents also appreciate having a stepparent fill what previously had been a void in their lives. As one boy said, "I love Mom, but it's different having a dad in the family. Nick throws a football around with me and he's teaching me to fly-fish and we go to basketball games together. We do guy things I couldn't do with Mom. I talk about different things with Nick" (Hetherington & Kelly, 2002, p. 191).

RITUALS   In addition to role clarity and the timing of a remarriage, a third factor contributes to the success of blended families. Successful families are those that establish their own rituals. These can range from everyday routines, such as sitting down for breakfast together or taking a walk with the dog each night, to family traditions, such as piñatas at birthday parties, backpacking on weekends, or barbecues on the Fourth of July. Rituals provide a family with shared experiences and foster a sense of belonging (Hetherington & Kelly, 2002).

SUMMARY and KEY TERMS

Changing Relationships Within the Family: Adolescents

Time Spent with Family: Relationships within the family change in a number of ways during adolescence. With age, adolescents spend less time with their families, becoming more involved in activities outside the home, though maintaining about the same amount of time spent talking with family members.

Warmth of Family Interactions: Adolescents' emotions when with their families become less positive by junior high, becoming more positive again toward the end of high school. Also, conflict with parents increases as adolescents make bids for more autonomy.

Increased Conflict with Parents: Although adolescents agree that parents have the right to set rules governing the social and moral order in the family, disagreements arise as to which of their behaviors fall within these domains and which are matters of personal choice. The nature of adolescent-parent conflict differs little from one culture to the next, although European American adolescents are somewhat less

(continued)

SUMMARY and KEY TERMS *continued*

compliant than those whose families have emigrated from interdependent cultures. Differences in temperament among adolescents are more important in determining the intensity of conflict than differences in parenting. Adolescents avoid many potential conflicts by not fully disclosing their plans to parents.

Emotional Climate of Families: Negative emotions are more easily transmitted within the family than are positive ones, and emotions are more likely to flow from parents to children than vice versa.
emotional transmission

Changing Relationships Within the Family: Parents and Parenting

Styles of Parenting: Two dimensions, or characteristic ways of responding to children, are present in all parents' behavior: demandingness and responsiveness. These dimensions of parenting are independent of each other, and the combinations yield four styles of parenting, each of which fosters different behaviors.
responsiveness, demandingness, authoritative parenting, authoritarian parenting, indulgent parenting, disengaged parenting

Cultural Contexts of Parenting: Styles of parenting must be considered within the context of ethnicity. Authoritative parenting has been shown to be an effective style of parenting for African American, Asian American, and Hispanic adolescents, as well as for European American adolescents.

Knowing What Your Kids Are Doing: Parents can monitor adolescents' activities even when not physically present, by keeping tabs on who they are with and whether or not another adult is present. Adolescents are less likely to get into trouble when parents are involved in their lives, but also when parents exercise some control over their behavior.
parental monitoring

Whose Identity Crisis? Parents and Middle Age: Most parents face middle age just when adolescents reach puberty. This particular combination of developmental changes and identity crises can heighten the tensions within families with adolescents.
climacteric

Families in Context

Ethnic Minority Membership: Ethnicity contributes to the impact of the family on development in varied ways. Adolescent-parent relationships assume somewhat different forms in families with differing cultural backgrounds.

Siblings: Over three-quarters of adolescents have at least one sibling. Most develop close bonds of affection despite the inevitable conflicts. Older siblings serve as models for younger ones; they are also likely to serve as caretakers.

Dual-Earner Families: In most families with children under 18, both parents are employed. The effects of maternal employment on adolescents are mediated by several factors, one of the most important being the mother's satisfaction with her work. Maternal employment may liberalize gender roles in the family and increase a parent's sense of well-being.

SUMMARY and KEY TERMS

Families in Transition

Divorce: Increasing numbers of adolescents experience divorce. The impact of divorce depends on conditions in the adolescent's life, such as age, gender, amount of marital conflict, support from family and friends, and economic stability. Marital conflict, rather than divorce itself, contributes heavily to the stress adolescents experience, but exposure to conflict need not always be negative.

Single-Parent Families: About half of the adolescents who live in single-parent families do so because of divorce, and about 80% of them live with their mothers. One of the biggest differences between these adolescents and those from intact homes is their economic status, with close to a third of families headed by a single female parent living at or below the poverty level.

Remarriage and Blended Families: Most parents who divorce will remarry. Role clarity facilitates interaction in blended families. Factors contributing to successful blended family relationships include authoritative parenting by the biological parent, supported by the stepparent; the age of the children (remarriages are more successful if the children are under 10 or over 15); and family rituals.

role clarity

"**Hey,** Jenny!" Alisa tossed her books on the table and perched on the chair beside her friend. "I saw Sylvan today. Think he'll ask you to the rally Friday night?"

"What if he did?" asked Jenny. "I wouldn't be able to go. My parents won't let me date until…"

"Sure, I know—until you're 15. That's what mine said."

"If only! They won't even say. Dad just says 'When we marry off your older sister.' Too bad I don't have an older sister, it might make things easier."

"I do. It doesn't…just makes them nervous."

Adolescents and Their Friends

"Uh-huh," agreed Alisa.

"Anyway, Sylvan's not that hot."

"Forget you!" exclaimed Alisa. "You were so distracted yesterday you put your clothes on over your gym shorts."

"Yeah," smiled Jenny, "but, you know what I mean... It's just like he's, well..."

"Yeah, I understand."

"I know you do. That's what's so great."

Chapter Overview

Friends are important at any age, but especially in adolescence when so many things are new. Friends are emotional supports to whom adolescents turn with their concerns, triumphs, secrets, and plans. In larger numbers, they are socialization agents, guiding adolescents into new, more adult roles. And one-on-one, they are mirrors into whom adolescents look to glimpse the future within.

Dramatic neurological, hormonal, and physiological changes literally transform the emotional and social arenas of adolescents' lives. Ironically, adolescents are least able to turn to their parents in the face of these changes, because relationships with parents are part of the changes. Peers step in to bridge the gap. Changing relationships with parents, together with their need for belonging, underlie the psychosocial task of forming a group identity in early adolescence. Distinctive themes distinguish friendships in early adolescence from those in preadolescence. These themes reflect the concerns of each age. Preadolescents are concerned with being accepted by others; adolescents with discovering—and accepting—themselves. The first section of this chapter addresses these aspects of friendships and ends with a discussion of their contribution to self-esteem.

The next section examines the varying patterns to adolescent friendships. Early adolescents, for instance, have friends who are almost exclusively the same sex as they, whereas late adolescents are likely to have friends of both sexes. Adolescents who are considered popular by their peers can say and do things that other adolescents would be shunned for. Friendship patterns, then, can be seen to differ with age and social status; they also differ with gender, ethnicity, and sexual orientation.

The chapter then moves to peer groups: their organization and the functions they serve. Small groups bridge adolescents' first steps outside the family. Larger groups provide a social setting in which adolescents try out more adult social roles. One of the functions of the larger peer group is to facilitate the transition to mixed-sex interactions and dating. This section closes with a discussion of dating.

The culture in which adolescents move throughout the day, though similar in many respects to that of their parents, younger siblings, and neighbors, is also different in many ways. Their experiences at school or after school, in informal groups or structured activities, or just with friends define them as a distinct group. We look at the attitudes and behaviors adolescents share with their friends, and consider whether these conflict with those shared with parents.

Many parents voice concerns over peer pressure. Even though we are influenced by our friends at every age, parents of adolescents seem particularly distrustful of their influence. Although peers exert more influence than parents do in some areas of adolescents' lives, parents continue to influence their children more than friends do in other areas.

The Importance of Friendships

Adolescents gain a sense of who they are and what their lives are about through seemingly small and insignificant daily encounters with friends and members of their families (Erikson, 1968). They try out new aspects of themselves in the relative safety of close relationships. As a consequence, adolescents are often just as interested in what they discover about themselves as in what they find out about each other. This is especially true for friendships during early adolescence.

Adolescents experiment with new behaviors as they face a pressing need to discover what is acceptable and what is not. They know, for example, that they cannot be as dependent as before, but neither are they totally self-reliant. And what about their emotions? Sentimentality is "uncool," but do they have to put a cap on all emotion? Friends provide essential feedback. Adolescents try on new behaviors much as they do clothes on a shopping spree. Which ones fit? Which make them look better? Friends become mirrors in which they can see themselves as they imagine they must look to others. The ability of adolescents to consider the thoughts of others gives early friendships this special reflective quality.

Group Identity

Barbara Newman and Philip Newman (2001), at the University of Rhode Island, argue that early adolescents experience a heightened need for connection and belonging, and that they seek to affiliate themselves with, not distinguish themselves from, others. The psychosocial task facing early adolescents, they note, is one of forming a **group identity**, not one of achieving a personal identity. Only when issues related to affiliation and belonging have been resolved will they be ready, in mid-adolescence, to address the differences in interests, values, and skills that distinguish them from others—that is, to address issues related to an individual identity.

Early adolescents come to see themselves in terms of what they share with other members of their group, making possible a new kind of identity.

group identity
A psychosocial task of early adolescence that entails the resolution of issues related to affiliation and belonging.

Seeing the self as a member of a group is not peculiar to early adolescence, of course; belonging to a family has been central to children's experience of themselves. What is different, however, is the group to which they see themselves belonging and, with this, what belonging means. Unlike one's family, in which parents remain, in some ways, larger than life, and in which siblings' ages and interests only imperfectly match one's own, the peer group is composed of others whom one sees to be very much like oneself, making possible a new kind of identity. Early adolescents come to see themselves in terms of what they share with other members of the group. Only later will they begin to see how they are different from, as well as similar to, others in their group and, with this, be ready to address issues related to a personal, as opposed to a group, identity (Newman & Newman, 2001).

Seeing the self in relation to the group can also lead to feelings of alienation. Most obviously, these can come from seeing others as part of something to which one does not belong. However, belonging to the group does not in itself protect against alienation. It is still possible for adolescents to feel cut off, or alienated, from themselves while a member of the group. Adolescents must learn, for instance, how to be a member of a group without losing themselves to the group, and how to enjoy shared interests without succumbing to pressures to conform. Failure to master these skills also can lead to alienation, with adolescents feeling themselves forced into roles or positions they do not support or that are counter to their values.

Gossip and Self-Disclosure

Friendships change with age, taking on themes that characterize the concerns of each age group. Preadolescents want to be understood and accepted by others; adolescents want to understand themselves—and different processes facilitate both of these concerns. Gossip helps preadolescents establish norms and avoid being rejected; self-disclosure helps adolescents define themselves.

Gossip is a favorite pastime of preadolescents, and it has a developmental purpose. From discussions of other people's behavior, they learn social norms to guide their own behavior.

Friendships reflect these themes in characteristic patterns of interacting.

PREADOLESCENCE   Preadolescents spend a lot of time comparing themselves to others. In fact, being accepted by others is one of their central concerns. Peer reactions figure heavily in determining preadolescents' levels of self-esteem and self-definition. The cognitive changes discussed in Chapter 4, especially being able to assume the perspective of another, contribute to their awareness of the importance of socially appropriate behavior and the need for "impression management." Fear of rejection and ridicule, and jockeying for position in friendships, characterize relationships among this age group (Parker & Gottman, 1989). Keller and Wood (1989) found that most of the preadolescents they interviewed mentioned trust as the most important issue in their friendships.

gossip   A process by which preadolescents establish group norms.

Insecurity regarding one's social position is perhaps best reflected in a characteristic mode of interaction: gossiping. Even though **gossip** is an unreliable source of information and is generally considered inappropriate, almost all preadolescents gossip (Kuttler et al., 2002). Gossiping is important to preadolescents with good reason: It discloses the attitudes and beliefs that are central to the peer group (Parker & Gottman, 1989). This function is vital when we realize that these behaviors are the basis for being accepted or rejected by the group. Listen in on the following conversation as two friends discuss telling lies, something friends are not supposed to do with each other:

> Dari: Barb said that her mom gave her $300 to buy a dress and shoes for the dance, and that the dress, the yellow one she showed us, remember? Well, that this dress cost over $200.
>
> Tracey: That yellow dress she took out of the closet? It was ripped. I saw it!
>
> Dari: Yeah. Under the arm. I saw it too.
>
> Tracey: That wasn't a new dress. There was a stain on it.
>
> Dari: She told us she bought it for $200. But I think her sister gave it to her, the one who's married.
>
> Tracey: Yeah. She gives her a lot of clothes.

Notice that in gossiping about Barb, Dari and Tracey affirm the norms of the group; that is, friends don't lie to each other. They also communicate to each other that they adhere to these norms.

Mutual disclosure and affirmation of group norms through gossip allows preadolescents to reaffirm their membership in the group. This is especially important because preadolescents are often insecure about their social status and their general acceptability. Much of the energy that goes into friendship is devoted to solidifying their position and protecting themselves against rejection (Parker & Gottman, 1989).

Gossip serves another important function. It allows preadolescents to explore peer attitudes in areas where they lack clear norms, without actually committing themselves to a position. Because many of the behaviors in question are not common among their peers, gossip frequently involves well-known older adolescents, as in the following example, or even popular figures such as rock musicians and movie stars:

> Jim: They say Dale [captain of the varsity football team] uses steroids every football season.
>
> Artie: A lot of athletes do. It helps them build up muscle.
>
> Jim: Steroids are really drugs, you know.
>
> Artie: You think the coach knows?
>
> Jim: Nah. How could he and still let Dale do it? He might lose his job.
>
> Artie: Yeah.

Neither Jim nor Artie directly stated an opinion about using steroids or drugs in general. Yet by the end of the conversation, they had established that athletes who use them have to hide that fact from others and consequently it must be wrong to use them. As demonstrated in this example, gossiping is a low-risk way of determining the attitudes of one's peer group. Neither boy had to reveal a view of his own in order to discover the position taken by the other. Their conversation affords them a way of sampling the reactions and attitudes of peers regarding behaviors that are not yet common to their group (Parker & Gottman, 1989).

Preadolescents are still learning which emotions are appropriate for them and what rules exist for displaying these. By monitoring feedback from peers in social situations, they gain invaluable information regarding each of these aspects of social competence. Even so, their rules for emotional expression are rough at first. Perhaps their most salient guideline is to avoid sentimentality at all costs, especially when with one's friends. The rule of thumb is to be rational, cool, and in control.

ADOLESCENCE   Adolescents' friendships reflect different concerns, which at this stage take the form of defining who they are and what they are going to be in life. Friends get together to discuss the mix of experiences offered up each day. The remarks of classmates, teachers, and parents and the successes and failures of the day are expressed, taken apart, analyzed, and reanalyzed. Friends provide the support—and sometimes the challenge—that adolescents need to meet the new and untried, as the following conversation illustrates:

> Rob: So we're watching the game last night and my dad says, "You need to think about your future." Like, I don't know what I want to do but it doesn't really bother me. [Laughs.]
>
> Matt: [Returns laughter.]
>
> Rob: [Laughs again.] It's my life and it bothers my dad more than me that I haven't got my future planned.

Whereas younger children derive much of their sense of self-worth from their parents, adolescents receive validation primarily from their friends.

Matt: My dad's the same. I tell him: "I know I'll be doing something."

Rob: Right, something! [Laughs nervously.]

Matt: "Que sera," you know?

Exploring uncharted territories in one's life is never easy, as the nervous laughs of these two adolescents suggest. Yet adolescents are peculiarly well equipped for the task. In many ways, they have reached the pinnacle of thought and can think easily in the abstract, reasoning about the possibilities in their lives and those of their friends (see Chapter 4). Rather than seeing themselves as limited to their present circumstances, they can see their present realities as reflecting a limited sample of the many possible alternatives that exist. Parker and Gottman (1989) note that adolescents are uniquely qualified to help each other through indecisions such as these, and do so with genuine concern, even seeing this as one of the obligations of friendship.

They take this obligation seriously. When adolescents are with their friends, they are most likely to talk about themselves rather than gossip about others. Just as gossip serves the very real needs of preadolescents—affirming group norms and group membership—self-disclosure serves the needs of adolescents. It is one of the primary means by which they discover themselves. **Self-disclosure** is an intimate sharing or exchange of thoughts, feelings, and otherwise undisclosed aspects of the self with another person. It takes a very different form in adolescence than in childhood or preadolescence. Adolescents respond to disclosures with an honest, almost confrontational examination of the issues raised. They accept these offerings of the self in the spirit in which they are given—as problems to be addressed and solved—whereas self-disclosures among preadolescents are more likely to evoke feelings of solidarity, such as "Me, too." With age, adolescents get increasingly better at establishing intimacy this way (McNelles & Connolly, 1999; Parker & Gottman, 1989).

Adolescent friendships reflect considerable emotional development beyond those of preadolescents. Adolescents begin to master the rules for emotional display and feeling that so mystify preadolescents. Adolescents are comfortable expressing a range of emotions, which preadolescents would likely deny. They have moved beyond cool to compassion or any of the many other emotions that might be called for in a situation. They understand that actions can be motivated by several emotions. What remains to be refined is an understanding of the potential impact of emotion on their relationships. Many of their conversations are about losing control of an emotion—exploding at someone or just "blowing it"—and the effects this can have (Parker & Gottman, 1989).

Friends and Self-Esteem

Friendships bear a special burden at first, as significant sources of adolescents' feelings about themselves. Children derive feelings of self-worth from the simple fact that their parents love them; adults additionally derive much of theirs from their work. Adolescents can neither turn to their parents with the simple needs of children nor feel the strength they will later experience through their work and families of their own. Friends help them bridge this difficult passage and enable them to feel good about themselves. In this respect, having close friends, even if only a few, is better than being popular. The latter, although not to be slighted, may make adolescents feel socially competent, but it does not contribute to **self-esteem** as do friends (Keefe & Berndt, 1996; Rubin et al., 2004). Friends, especially same-sex friends, affirm adolescents' sense of self. They do this simply by enjoying each other's company and by "being real" with each other (Impett et al., 2008).

Just as individuals pull in their stomachs and stand a bit straighter when passing a mirror, adolescents see more than their present selves reflected

self-disclosure A process by which adolescents understand and define themselves through an intimate sharing of thoughts and feelings.

self-esteem The individual's overall positive or negative evaluation of herself or himself.

by their friends. By imagining themselves as other than they are, adolescents can rehearse new roles, set goals, and plan ways of attaining them. They can envision ways they would like to be—their **ideal self-image**. This image includes more than the roles they are refining; it anticipates the adult roles they will assume (Bybee et al., 1990; Dunkel & Anthis, 2001). We see the importance of an ideal self-image in studies relating it to other measures of adjustment. Adolescents with high ideal self-images are better adjusted: They are more reflective, do better in school, tolerate frustration better, and are more resilient to stress.

For girls in their early and middle teens, friends are reflections of themselves. They tend to pick friends primarily on the basis of obvious similarities, especially of style and status.

How positive adolescents feel about themselves affects the quality of their relationships with others. As the quality of their relationships improves, these improved relationships contribute to even more positive feelings about themselves (Berndt et al., 1999). Adolescents who feel inadequate and are unsure of themselves find it difficult to believe that others will like them any better than they like themselves, which in turn can contribute to feelings of jealousy and loneliness (Parker et al., 2005). Conversely, adolescents who have positive self-attitudes anticipate positive reactions from others. Not surprisingly, knowing about an adolescent's level of self-esteem tells us a lot about the quality of that person's relationships with others. Adolescents with high self-esteem report having friendships that are more intimate and satisfying than those with low self-esteem (Buhrmester, 1990).

ideal self-image
The individual's idealized image of the self, including anticipated as well as actual ways of being.

Parents and Self-Esteem

Relationships with parents contribute in important ways to adolescents' self-esteem. Interactions that communicate support, affection, and encouragement promote self-esteem (Colarossi & Eccles, 2000; Quatman & Watson, 2001). Families in which these qualities exist support each other, even when they disagree. In fact, the way families handle negative emotions may be particularly important in contributing to adolescents' competence and self-esteem. Talking about a shared negative experience, such as the loss of a job or the death of a grandparent, can be helpful in a number of ways (**Box 7.1**). In guiding discussions of these, parents can help adolescents identify the emotions they experienced, enabling them to better understand what prompted these, as well as the likely consequences of responding in certain ways. Over and above this, discussion of negative experiences establishes an emotional climate that communicates that it's safe to express one's feelings, even when they're negative. Adolescents, in turn, are better equipped to be emotionally authentic with their friends, as well as to better understand their friends' feelings (Marin et al., 2008).

Adolescents see their parents as major sources of support (Levitt et al., 1993). In fact, relationships with parents become closer with age, with high school seniors reporting greater intimacy with each of their parents than eighth-graders report (Rice & Mulkeen, 1995). Adolescents who are close to their parents report being more satisfied with themselves and having closer relationships with friends than those who are not close to their parents (Hodges et al., 1999; Raja et al., 1992). They are more likely to go to their friends for support as well, perhaps because they have learned from their families that others can be helpful in solving problems.

BOX 7.1   In More Depth

Talking About Unpleasant Experiences Can Be Helpful

Notice how the parents of this adolescent (Rachel) pick up on, and affirm, the emotions she experienced when she attended her great-grandfather's funeral. Notice, too, how her parents provide a safe and supportive emotional context for talking about negative emotions. Families who confirm the thoughts and feelings expressed by family members help adolescents understand their feelings.

Dad: And we had to go up at Christmastime for Grandpa's funeral, didn't we?

Rachel: mmm hmm

Dad: mmm hmm, and, what do you remember about that?

Rachel: It was very sad and...

Dad: Especially that it was right at Christmas time and Grandma had just passed away about a year before that, which made it really hard for everyone. And I had to get out of work early and mom had to get out of work and you had to get out of school and we all had to go up to Michigan and it was sad 'cause it was around the holidays.

Mom: Yeah...I thought it was especially sad for um Grandpa, you-your dad.

Dad: mmm hmm

Mom: You know, having to deal with that.

Dad: Yeah, it was sad for me "cause it was my last grandparent too.

Mom: Yeah

Dad: How did it effect you Rachel?

Rachel: I thought it was sad even though I didn't spend a whole lot of time with Grandpa, our Great Grandpa, but it was still sad, you know, a member of the family had passed away.

Dad: mmm hmmm

Mom: Why was it scary? You just said a minute ago it was kind of scary.

Rachel: Well because I mean...

Mom: John! (talking to younger sibling)

Rachel: It was just seeing him lay in the casket

Mom: I'm sorry I didn't hear you Rachel, what?

Rachel: Just seeing him lay in the casket kind of scared me.

Mom: mmm hmm

Rachel: ...that I didn't really wanna... but and it was just sad and it was scary because of those...

Mom: Yeah, are you still scared of stuff like that?

Source: After Marin et al., 2008.

Friendship Patterns

What do adolescents want from their friends? Emotional support, intimacy, and advice. They get these in somewhat different ways depending on their sex. The major activity in girls' friendships is talking. Girls develop close friendships primarily by sharing their feelings. Self-disclosure contributes to emotional closeness in boys as well, but they also develop emotional closeness through sharing experiences, such as sports and other activities (Camarena et al., 1990; Gummerum & Keller, 2008).

Same-sex friendships become more intimate and affectionate with age and become increasingly important as sources of emotional support. Whereas parents are the primary source of support for children, mid-adolescents are as likely to confide in their same-sex friends as in their parents, and late adolescents indicate that friends are more important in this respect than their parents (Furman & Buhrmester, 1992; Levitt et al., 1993). Not surprisingly, adolescents spend a lot more time with friends than they did as children.

The number of friends also increases in adolescence, especially for girls. The percentage of these friends whom mothers know (40%) remains about the same as in childhood; however, because the circle of friends widens in adolescence, the actual number of friends whom mothers do not know increases substantially (Feiring & Lewis, 1993).

Age Differences in Friendship Patterns

When adolescents are asked what friendship means to them and why friends are important, they give characteristically different answers depending on their age. These differences, however, are strikingly similar across cultures and even generations. Michaela Gummerum and Monika Keller (2008), interviewing adolescents in China, the former East Germany, Iceland, and Russia, found age differences in reasoning about friendships to be similar to those found by Elizabeth Douvan and Joseph Adelson (1966), who interviewed adolescents in the United States several generations ago. Both research teams distinguished three stages to adolescent friendships. Furthermore, adolescents at any stage talked about their friendships in similar ways, differing for the most part only in the ages corresponding to these stages. In the first stage, friends are valued for the ways they help meet self-interests, and close friends are those who enjoy doing the things one enjoys doing. In the second stage, friends are valued for their companionship, and close friends are those with whom one gets along and who can be trusted. The third stage is characterized by mutual understanding and support, and closeness is experienced in terms of sharing intimate concerns (**Figure 7.1**).

Disclosure to a close friend is one of the most important ways that older adolescents learn about themselves.

The ages reported by Gummerum and Keller in which adolescents moved through these stages are younger than those for Douvan and Adelson, most likely reflecting the earlier onset of puberty than in the past (see a discussion of the secular trend in Chapter 3). Otherwise, the sequencing of friendship patterns described by Douvan and Adelson (1966) and Gummerum and Keller (2008) are the same today as they were more than a generation ago.

In early adolescence, friendships focus on the activities that bring friends together. Early adolescent friendships are more intimate than they were in childhood, but less so than they will be in middle or late adolescence (Berndt, 1982; Douvan & Adelson, 1966; Gummerum & Keller, 2008). When asked to say what is important in friends, early adolescent girls say less about the personalities of their friends than about the things they do together. When listening to girls talk about their friends, one has the feeling that friendships are not emotionally relevant at this age; if anything, distinct personalities of friends appear to be a disadvantage to the extent that they might interfere with activities. These early friendships are almost always with someone of the same sex (Camarena et al., 1990; Lempers & Clark-Lempers, 1993).

Early adolescent boys' friendships, just as those of girls, are almost exclusively with others of the same sex. Boys report feeling close emotionally with their friends, although they achieve closeness in somewhat different ways, spending less time talking about their feelings than do girls and more time sharing activities that cement friendships (Camarena et al., 1990).

In middle adolescence, girls' friendships focus on security; girls want friends they can trust. Friendships lose their earlier superficial quality and involve companionship, emotional sharing, and mutuality. Mid-

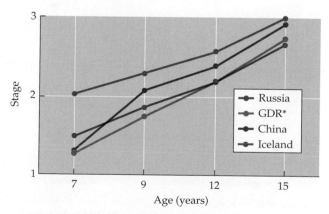

● **Figure 7.1 Stages of reasoning about friendships across ages and cultures** (After Gummerum & Keller, 2008.) *Former East Germany

adolescent girls are more aware of their friends' concerns than they were just a few years earlier. There is also more concern with personal qualities of friends. Girls are particularly concerned with having a friend in whom they can trust and confide. It is especially important that their friends not disclose their secrets to others or talk about them behind their backs (Berndt, 1982; Frankel, 1990; Gummerum & Keller, 2008).

These concerns fall into place when we consider the changes that occur with puberty, and adolescents' need to understand these by sharing their feelings and observations with their friends. Finding out that others are going through the same things assures them that they are normal, and nothing is wrong with the way they feel. In disclosing their feelings, however, they are turning over a part of themselves to their friends, perhaps the part about which they are least secure. Naturally they don't want their confidences divulged to others.

Most girls start to date in mid-adolescence, and friends become especially important in making sense of the emotions they encounter (Dating is discussed in more detail later in the chapter). Dating can also be a source of tension among friends. Girls experience more conflict with their friends than boys do when moving into opposite-sex relationships, conflicts frequently centering on fears of disloyalty and competition. Relatively few girls develop close friendships with boys at this age, friendships with other girls remaining more important for the majority (Hogue & Steinberg, 1995; Lempers & Clark-Lempers, 1993).

Anxieties about friendships peak in mid-adolescence. The most common anxieties reflect more general insecurities about the changes adolescents are experiencing. They are midway through puberty, renegotiating relationships with their parents, facing a more impersonal and challenging school setting, and beginning to date. These teenagers need the emotional support of friends, and anything that appears to threaten that support causes anxiety.

Boys' friendships in mid-adolescence have many of the same characteristics as do those of girls in early adolescence. Friendships increase in intimacy and affection for boys, as they do for girls, although increases are less pronounced (Furman & Buhrmester, 1992). Boys are looking for someone with whom they can do things. Like girls in early adolescence, they appear to have little interest in the personal characteristics of their friends as long as these do not interfere with the activities they are enjoying together. They have less concern than girls for sharing feelings or being understood. They want someone who is easy to get along with and who enjoys doing the same things they do. Perhaps because they do not self-disclose as much as girls, mid-adolescent boys are not as concerned that friends not betray their confidences. However, they expect their friends not to "squeal" about things they have done together (Douvan & Adelson, 1966; McNelles & Connolly, 1999).

During late adolescence, girls report that the quality of their friendships is better than previously. Their friendships focus more on personalities than they did before. Some of the earlier intensity is gone, but intimacy continues to grow. Late adolescent girls have more stable identities and better social skills. Being more secure both with themselves and others may make them better able to tolerate individuality in their friends. They no longer need friends

In early and middle adolescence, boys achieve closeness by sharing activities, such as scouting or sports, rather than talking about their feelings, as girls do.

TABLE 7.1
How Teens Communicate with Friends Using Social Networking Sites

THE PERCENTAGE OF TEEN SNS USERS WHO...	
Post messages to a friend's page or wall	84
Send private messages to a friend within the social networking system	82
Post comments to a friend's blog	76
Send a bulletin or group message to all of their friends	61
Wink, poke, give "e-props" or kudos to their friends	33

Source: Lenhart & Madden, 2007, and Pew Internet & American Life Project, 2007.

---

to reflect themselves as they did in mid-adolescence. Instead, friends can be appreciated for who they are. Self-disclosure is still important, but each friend is able to appreciate the unique qualities the other brings to the relationship (Douvan & Adelson, 1966; Thomas & Daubman, 2001; Way & Greene, 2006).

In late adolescence, same-sex friendships continue to be important for boys and they, just as late adolescent girls, report the quality of these friendships to improve. Older adolescent males also report rewarding friendships with female friends. (Thomas & Daubman, 2001; Way & Greene, 2006).

Gender and Friendships

Close friendships for most adolescents are with peers of the same gender, especially in early adolescence. This being said, there are few differences in the quality of friendships that adolescents of either sex have, in the number of friends, how intimate they are, or in the amount of conflict experienced in their friendships. Although gender differences are frequently reported in research on adolescents' peer relationships, these differences, though significant statistically, do not account for much of the variability that exists from one adolescent to the next. Adolescent girls and boys, in other words, are more alike than they are different in the ways they relate to their friends (Hyde, 2005).

Adolescents and the Internet

The most frequent way adolescents stay close to their friends is still by talking on the phone, or simply by getting together. However, increasing numbers of teenagers stay in touch with each other through email, cell phones, text messaging, and social networking sites (**Tables 7.1** and **7.2**) (Lenhart et al., 2007).

Over 90% of adolescents use the Internet, and for those who do, communicating typically involves more than conversations. Nearly two-thirds use the Internet to post videos or photos online, original artwork, stories, or for maintaining an online journal or a personal webpage. Additionally, over half of online adolescents have a personal profile on a social networking site such as Facebook or MySpace on which they can

---

TABLE 7.2
Adolescents and Text Messaging: Can U Read This? "J2LYK 9 CFN"[a]

2G2B4G	Too Good To Be Forgotten
2BZ4UQT	Too Busy For You Cutie
4COL	For Crying Out Loud
CFN	Ciao For Now
9	Parent Is Watching
99	Parent Is No Longer Watching
?	I Have A Question
!	I Have A Comment
411	Information [e.g., "Do you have any 411 on this?"]
831	I Love You [8 letters, 3 words, 1 meaning]
459	I Love You ("I" "L" "Y" correspond to 4, 5, and 9 on keypad)
J2LYK	Just To Let You Know
J/W	Just Wondering
JOOTT	Just One Of Those Things
N-A-Y-L	In A While
NE2H	Need To Have
NE1ER	Anyone Here
WAEF	When All Else Fails
WAG	Wild Ass Guess
WAFM	What A F***ing Mess
WAYD	What Are You Doing?
WAYN	Where Are You Now?

Source: www.netlingo.com/dictionary.
[a]"Just to let you know, parent is watching. Ciao for now!"

TABLE 7.3
What Teens Post on Their Personal Profiles

82% of profile creators have included their first name in their profiles

79% have included photos of themselves

66% have included photos of their friends

61% have included the name of their city or town

49% have included the name of their school

40% have included their instant message screen name

40% have streamed audio to their profile

39% have linked to their blog

29% have included their email address

29% have included their last name

29% have included videos

2% have included their cell phone number

6% of online teens and 11% of profile-owning teens post their first and last names on publicly-accessible profiles

3% of online teens and 5% of profile-owning teens disclose their full name, photos of themselves, and the town where they live in publicly-viewable profiles

Source: Lenhart & Madden, 2007, and Pew Internet & American Life Project, 2007.

post photos and information about themselves, receive messages, play games, and stay current with other friends who visit this page (Table 7.3). Although most adolescents (91%) use these sites to stay in touch with the friends they see on a regular basis, such as at school, many also use them to maintain contact with those they see only infrequently, and a sizeable percentage (49%) visit social networking sites to make new friends (Lenhart et al., 2007).

Making new friends through social networking sites can entail some risk. Among adolescents who use social networking sites, 31% indicate they have "friends" whom they've never met in person, and 43% report having had total strangers contact them online. Adolescents protect themselves in a number of ways. Two-thirds of those with personal profiles limit access to these, and nearly half include false information, both as a way of protecting themselves and also, some say, just to be silly (Lenhart & Madden, 2007).

A majority of parents either have filters on computers at home that are used by teenagers or are able to monitor what they do when they're online, and 65% say they check up on their teenagers' online activity once they've left their computers. Most parents (85%) also have rules concerning which sites adolescents can visit, as well as how much, and what type of, information their adolescent can share with others when communicating online (Lenhart & Madden, 2007).

Social Competence

As with so many of their activities, adolescents' ability to make and keep friends involves a number of skills. These skills involve the way they assess situations, how they respond to them, and how they approach relationships.

The first component of **social competence**, assessing the situation, is to see what's going on and adapt one's behavior accordingly. In a sense, joining a social group involves some of the same skills adolescents learn when driving. One has to judge the speed of the ongoing activity, accelerate, then move into the thick of things. Pulling onto a turnpike at 10 miles per hour requires everyone else to slow down to your speed: It doesn't work.

When adolescents "pull into the fast lane" with a remark such as, "What are you doing?" they're asking others to stop for them, an unlikely response if they are enjoying themselves. Entry remarks that call attention away from the ongoing activity are likely to be rebuffed. Similarly, remarks about oneself are usually unsuccessful ways of getting a group's attention. Instead, fitting into a group appears to be a matter of figuring out what the group is doing. Those who are better at this are more popular. In short, one needs to be able to know what the group is doing in order to join in (Dodge, 1983; Putallaz, 1983).

The second component of social competence involves how adolescents respond to others' behavior. Prosocial behaviors, such as fairness, being willing to listen, or ready to help someone who's in trouble, and speaking up for others, are characteristic of adolescents who are well-liked. These adolescents are also more fun to be around. They're better at keeping things going, and

social competence
Skills enabling individuals to accurately assess social situations and respond adaptively.

others appear to have a better time with them (Dodge, 1983; Pakaslahti et al., 2002; Rose & Asher, 2004).

The third component of social competence involves how adolescents approach relationships. Those who are well-liked recognize that relationships take time to develop. They understand that the best way to reach a goal is sometimes an indirect one, such as striking up a conversation about the food in the cafeteria or a popular television show.

Social Status: Who's In and Who's Not

One might think that adolescents who are liked most by their classmates would also be the most **popular** ones at school. But such is not always the case. Simply put, there's more than one way to be popular. Popularity can refer to **social preference**, how much others like you, or to **social prestige**, how much others look up to you. Social preference is assessed by asking adolescents to list the classmates they "like the most." Adolescents who emerge as popular using this measure are characterized by **prosocial behaviors**, such as being cooperative, kind, trustworthy, and friendly. Measures of social prestige, on the other hand, ask adolescents who "the most popular" classmates are. Using this measure, the popular adolescents tend to be athletic, attractive, influential—and frequently aggressive.

Aggression is relatively easy to recognize when it's physical; examples of **physical aggression** would be actions such as pushing or starting fights. **Relational aggression** is more subtle. Adolescents who engage in this type of aggression affect peers by manipulating their relationships, such as excluding them from a group, divulging their secrets, or spreading rumors. In a longitudinal study that followed adolescents from the ages of 10 to 14, adolescents who were perceived as popular were found to use both types of aggression, especially relational aggression (Cillessen & Mayeux, 2004). These adolescents apparently use aggression as a way of maintaining their privileged status as well as a means of achieving this in the first place (Cillessen & Mayeux, 2004; Rose et al., 2004; Xie et al., 2002).

At the other end of the social spectrum are **rejected adolescents**. These adolescents are rarely mentioned by classmates as someone they "like the most" and are frequently mentioned as someone they "like least." Rejected adolescents engage in relatively few prosocial behaviors and also appear to lack the social skills that would enable them to get along better with peers. Although not all rejected adolescents are aggressive, many are (Friman et al., 2004; Pakaslahti et al., 2002).

Controversial adolescents are both highly liked and highly disliked by their peers, frequently being mentioned as a best friend and just as frequently by others as someone they "like the least." They tend to be confident, sociable, and socially skilled (Pakaslahti et al., 2002). However, they can also be aggressive and are more likely than popular adolescents to engage in problem behaviors (Miller-Johnson et al., 2003).

Average adolescents, as the term suggests, are moderately popular with their classmates and moderately disliked as well. They are more friendly and cooperative than rejected or neglected peers, but less so than popular or controversial peers. In terms of social skills, they are similar to popular adolescents (Pakaslahti et al., 2002).

Neglected adolescents are neither highly liked nor disliked, rarely being identified as someone that others "like the most" or as "disliked." Some neglected adolescents have difficulty making and maintaining friends due to their poor social skills. However, others may have adequate skills, yet fail to approach others because of their negative self-image and fears of rejection. The status of these adolescents is more dependent on their social context than

popular Adolescents nominated by their classmates as those they most like.

social preference An index of popularity measuring how much an adolescent is liked by others.

social prestige An index of popularity measuring how much an adolescent is looked up to by others.

prosocial behaviors Positive behaviors such as cooperativeness, kindness, and trustworthiness.

physical aggression Aggressive actions involving physical contact, such as pushing or hitting.

relational aggression Aggression achieved by manipulating relationships, such as by excluding someone from a group or spreading rumors.

rejected adolescents Adolescents frequently mentioned by classmates as someone they least like and rarely mentioned as someone they most like.

controversial adolescents Adolescents frequently mentioned by classmates as someone they least like and by others as a best friend.

average adolescents Adolescents who are moderately popular with their classmates and moderately disliked as well.

neglected adolescents Adolescents who are rarely mentioned by their classmates as someone they most like or as someone they least like.

social skills training
A component of social-cognitive intervention programs.

social-cognitive intervention
An intervention program based on social-cognitive learning principles.

that of other adolescents. In a supportive peer environment, their behavior is closer to that of average adolescents. However, when challenged by peers, they tend to withdraw; this, in turn, creates a self-fulfilling prophecy in which others, by not spending time with them, reinforce their initial self-perceptions (Caldwell et al., 2004; Gazelle & Rudolph, 2004).

INTERVENTION PROGRAMS   Failure to fit in with peers can be especially painful for adolescents. As we have seen, a number of factors can cause problems in peer relationships, such as having poor social skills, being overly aggressive, or having a negative self-image. Although interventions can be tailored to particular problems such as these, approaches that are multifaceted are generally most successful (Spence, 2003; Sukhodolsky et al., 2004).

Social skills training is part of many interventions since poor social skills contribute to a number of social and emotional problems. Social skills training uses a variety of techniques, including direct instructions on how to do something (e.g., initiate a conversation), the use of others to model how it's done, role-playing the behavior in question, and getting feedback (Spence, 2003). **Social-cognitive intervention** programs address how accurately adolescents perceive the intentions and behaviors of others. An example would be training in which adolescents are asked to identify situations or emotions that have been problematic for them, and then asked to think of all the ways they could have responded to these and to predict how others would react to each of these alternatives. Interventions such as this have been found to be effective in reducing subjective anger and aggressive behavior (Sukhodolsky et al., 2004; van Manen et al., 2004).

Reputation may also be more important than previously thought. For instance, similar behaviors in popular and rejected youth can be responded to differently, adolescents reacting more positively to those who are popular, even when they are aggressive, than to others. Although it is certainly possible that adolescents' reactions can be traced to subtle differences in the behaviors themselves, it is also possible that they are reacting not just to the momentary exchange, but also to a history of interactions. The status of neglected adolescents, for example, frequently changes when they enter a different peer setting, such as a new school, or even a different home room within the same school as they begin a new academic year.

Interethnic Friendships

As with gender, most friendships among adolescents are with peers of the same ethnic and cultural backgrounds (Hamm, 2000; Hartup, 1993). As a consequence, the sheer number of adolescents at school who share one's ethnic background is likely to be important in forming friendships. When African Americans are a minority within a school, for instance, they are less likely to be members of cliques, or small groups of close friends; similarly, when European Americans are a minority within a school, they are the ones less likely to belong to cliques (Urberg et al., 1995). This is particularly true of European American and African American adolescents. Jill Hamm (2000), at the University of North Carolina at Chapel Hill, studied friendship patterns among adolescents from a number of ethnically diverse high schools in California and Wisconsin. She found that 80% of European American and African American adolescents indicated someone from the same ethnic group as themselves as their best friend at school; in contrast, only 60% of Asian American adolescents did so.

Even so, Andrea Smith (2000), at the University of Toronto, found that, with respect to ethnicity, adolescents are more inclusive than exclusive in their choice of friends. Similarly, Jean Phinney and Nancy Cobb (1996) found that nearly 75% of the adolescents they interviewed indicated they would favor including a peer from an ethnic group other than their own in a club, even if that club were made up exclusively of students from their own background. However, even though the number of adolescents in favor of including such a student did not differ for Hispanic and European American adolescents, the reasons given for refusing membership—for those who thought the student should not be included—did differ. Hispanic students more frequently mentioned cultural barriers to friendship, whereas European Americans cited rights and rules. It is likely that Hispanics, because of their experience as members of a minority group, were more aware of cultural differences than European Americans, who, for the most part, need only be familiar with their own, the dominant, culture.

Friendships among members of different ethnic or cultural groups are most likely among those who go to the same school and live in the same neighborhood. Adolescents usually form their closest friendships with people of the same ethnicity and socioeconomic status.

Generally, adolescents are likely to have friends who live in the same neighborhood, go to the same school, and share other things—like ethnicity—in common. Of those who live in ethnically mixed neighborhoods and have classes together, many form friendships with those from other ethnic groups. Adolescents report these friendships to be close, although they may not see these friends with the same frequency outside of school as they do friends of the same ethnic group (DuBois & Hirsch, 1990; Hallinan & Teixeira, 1987).

Several conditions affect the formation of friendships between adolescents from different ethnic backgrounds. Classroom climates have been found to affect the sociability of white adolescents toward black peers. Classrooms where students work together, such as those in which teachers assign students to small working groups, have more interethnic friendships. These friendships are most likely to develop when academic competition is deemphasized and learning per se is emphasized (Hallinan & Teixeira, 1987).

In general, it appears that the more positively adolescents regard their own ethnic group, the more positive are their attitudes toward those who belong to other groups. Jean Phinney, Debra Ferguson, and Jerry Tate (1997) found this relationship to be mediated by adolescents' ethnic identity. Adolescents who were secure in their own ethnicity, in other words, were likely to regard other members of their group positively. These positive in-group attitudes, in turn, were related to more positive attitudes toward classmates who were members of other groups. These investigators also found that each of the ethnic minorities they studied tended to perceive their own group more favorably than the other groups. They point out that this bias, commonly referred to as ethnocentrism, rather than contributing to

Adolescents who are secure in their own ethnic identity are able to have close friends who are members of other ethnic groups, particularly if they live in the same neighborhoods.

enculturation Acquiring the norms of one's social group.

negative attitudes toward other groups, actually appeared to support their development of positive intergroup attitudes.

How favorably adolescents viewed students from other ethnic minorities is also related to how much contact they have with them outside of school (Phinney et al., 1997). Neighborhood conditions affect the likelihood of such friendships as well. Most adolescents who attend integrated schools report having at least one close friend at school who belongs to another group, but less than one-third of these see the friend outside school. Those who do are more likely to live in integrated neighborhoods and are also less likely to be white. Black adolescents are almost twice as likely as whites to maintain school friendships with those from another group outside of school. Blacks have more close neighborhood friends in general than whites (DuBois & Hirsch, 1990).

Interethnic friendships face special challenges, not the least of which are differences in the enculturation experiences of adolescents from different backgrounds. **Enculturation** is the acquisition of the norms of one's ethnic group. It differs from acculturation, which is the acquisition of the norms of the larger society. The norms of their group shape adolescents' expectations and reactions to others. The Mexican American culture, for example, stresses group affiliation, interdependence, and cooperation. The African American culture, in contrast, places greater emphasis on individualism and independence. Mexican American adolescents tend to be brought up in homes with clear hierarchical family relationships and are expected to accept and show respect for authority figures. African American adolescents grow up in more egalitarian homes that permit questioning of authority (Rotheram & Phinney, 1987). We might expect these enculturation experiences to affect the way adolescents from either culture react to social situations, and they do. Mary Jane Rotheram-Borus and Jean Phinney (1990) showed videotapes of social encounters to African American and Mexican American children and adolescents. The videotapes were of everyday scenes. In one, a student asked a peer for lunch money; in another, a student witnessed a fight; and in another, a student needed materials that a classmate had in order to complete a class assignment.

Clear ethnic differences emerged in reactions to these scenes. The responses of Mexican American adolescents reflected the emphasis their culture places on the group. They were more likely, for example, to say that a peer should share lunch money with someone who had lost theirs, even when the latter was disliked. They also expected others to anticipate their needs (as they would the needs of others) and would wait for others to notice what those needs were. In response to the video in which two peers working at the same table with the supplies that both needed beyond the reach of one and close to the other, Mexican American adolescents saw no problem with the situation, expecting the other person to hand over the supplies. African American adolescents indicated they would be upset and were likely to reach over and get what they needed for themselves. A small difference? Not really. These are just the types of situations that create misunderstandings and lead to hurt feelings among friends.

Another sequence showed a boy being rejected for a team. African American students reported they would get angry or leave; not one of them said they would feel badly. Two-thirds of the Mexican American adolescents said they would feel hurt, but almost none of them would leave, and relatively few said they would be angry. These differences translate easily into the failures of understanding that test friendships. Consider an example in which Eddie, a Hispanic, tries out for football but gets cut early in the tryouts. He doesn't seem especially angry and doesn't say much about it. His friend Joe, who is African American, thinks Eddie must not care and offers no consolation. Eddie, who has been waiting for his friend to say something, doesn't understand Joe's ostensibly callous attitude and begins to question whether he's really his friend. Joe, assuming that Eddie would react as he would if he minded being cut (by being angry, not silently hurt) has no way to anticipate his friend's growing resentment toward him.

Friendships and Sexual-Minority Youth

Sexual-minority youth are adolescents whose sexual orientation is not exclusively heterosexual. These adolescents share the same friendship concerns as heterosexual youth, with some additional ones thrown in. Lisa Diamond and Sarah Lucas (2004), at the University of Utah, found sexual-minority adolescents, when questioned about their friendships, to have more fears and concerns about relationships with their peers, to have experienced a greater loss of friends, and to have smaller peer networks. By late adolescence, however, sexual-minority adolescents actually had more close friends than heterosexual youth. Furthermore, they did not differ from heterosexual adolescents in how connected they felt to their friends or in how much control they had over their relationships.

These investigators also found that sexual-minority youth who were "out," that is, who openly disclosed their sexual orientation to heterosexual peers, had more friends, but had also lost more friends. Overall, however, these investigators found that it was the quality of adolescents' relationships with their friends, rather than their sexual identity per se, that contributed to their sense of well-being (Diamond & Lucas, 2004).

The Peer Group

A Malayan proverb counsels that one should trumpet in a herd of elephants, crow in the company of cocks, and bleat in a flock of goats. This pretty much sums up the behavior of adolescents with their peers. The **peer group** is one of the most important socializing forces in the lives of adolescents, regulating the pace as well as the particulars of the socialization process. Adolescents who fall behind their friends in social skills are dropped from the group, just as are those who move ahead too quickly. Similarly, those whose tastes and attitudes fail to match the group's are likely to be considered nerdy, geeks, or just "out of it." The cost of bleating when others are crowing can be high.

The peer group assumes special importance in adolescence for a number of reasons. Adolescents are moving toward greater autonomy and independence, and peers provide much-needed emotional and social support. Adolescents also learn many social skills with peers that they would not learn from parents or teachers. Peers reward each other with potent reinforcers: acceptance, popularity, and status (Muuss, 1990).

Cliques and Crowds

Most adolescents move in two types of groups: the clique and the crowd. A **clique** consists of the close friends with whom adolescents spend most of their time. Cliques can be as large as 10 or as small as three. These friends are usually the same sex and age, are in the same class in school, share the same ethnic background, and live relatively close to each other. Similarities in the composition of boys' and girls' cliques are striking. Aaron Hogue and Laurence Steinberg

These two girls are likely to belong to the same clique, and are not likely to include an outsider in their intimate conversation.

sexual-minority youth
Adolescents whose sexual orientation is not exclusively heterosexual.

peer group   A group of individuals of the same age; a social group that regulates the pace of socialization.

clique   A peer group made up of one's best friends, usually including no more than five or six members.

liaison Adolescents who have friends in several cliques but do not themselves belong to any particular clique.

isolate Adolescents who have few friends, either within a clique or outside it, and who have few links to other adolescents in the social network.

crowd A peer group formed from several cliques of the same age group.

(1995), at Temple University, asked over 6,000 high school students to name their closest friends at school. Sixty-five percent of boys' cliques and 63% of girls' cliques were made up exclusively of same-sex friends, and 85% of boys' and 86% of girls' cliques had no more than one friend of the opposite sex.

Even though cliques are the most common type of social grouping, only about half of students belong to a clique. What about the other half? Two other types of peer relationships, liaisons and isolates, are also common. **Liaisons** are socially active adolescents who have friends in a number of cliques but do not themselves belong to any particular clique. These students actually bring together groups of adolescents who otherwise would have few channels of communication—in a sense, plugging these cliques into the larger social network within the school. As an example, one of an adolescent's best friends may have been in several school plays with him and another may be on the baseball team. When he gets together with these friends, each of them may occasionally bring one of their friends along, with the result that members of the baseball team and the class play now give each other "high fives" when they meet, whereas previously they would not have known each other. **Isolates**, like liaisons, also are not members of cliques but have few links to other adolescents in the social network (**Figure 7.2**) (Ennett & Bauman, 1996).

A **crowd** is larger than a clique and more impersonal. Crowds usually number about 20. Not all the members of a crowd are close friends, but each is someone other members feel relatively comfortable with. Crowds usually consist of several of the friends in one's clique along with adolescents from several other cliques. For about half of the adolescents, their best friend is also in the same crowd. It is relatively unlikely for an adolescent to be a member of a crowd without belonging to one of these cliques; however, many adolescents belong to a clique and not to a crowd (Urberg et al., 1995).

The functions of cliques and crowds differ. Crowd events provide the settings in which adolescents try out new social skills. Clique activities provide feedback about the success of these skills and advice when skills fall short. If the crowd has a single purpose, it is to help adolescents move from same-sex to mixed-sex interactions (Dunphy, 1963). Many adolescents need all the help they can get.

Adolescents spend most of their time talking about crowd activities when they are with members of their clique, either planning the next event or rehashing the last one, gathering valuable information from such "pregame" and "postgame" analyses. The feedback comes from specialists—other ado-

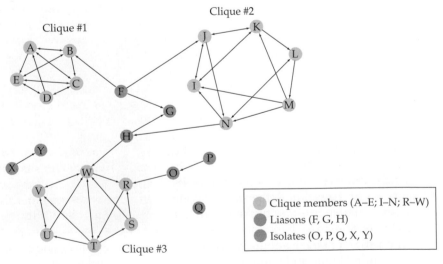

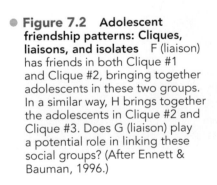

● **Figure 7.2 Adolescent friendship patterns: Cliques, liaisons, and isolates** F (liaison) has friends in both Clique #1 and Clique #2, bringing together adolescents in these two groups. In a similar way, H brings together the adolescents in Clique #2 and Clique #3. Does G (liaison) play a potential role in linking these social groups? (After Ennett & Bauman, 1996.)

lescents who know just how difficult a social maneuver can be and who can recommend something that has worked for them in similar situations.

If clique activities are coaching sessions, crowd events are the game itself. Adolescents enter the field ready to try out new social moves. Reflecting their specialized nature, crowd and clique activities take place at different times during the week. Crowd events, just like actual games, occur on weekends, and clique activities, like other coaching sessions, take place throughout the week.

Developmental changes occur in the structure of peer groups just as they do with friendships. Both cliques and crowds evolve as adolescents face different issues; so does the importance of being in a group. Belonging to groups is most important to early and middle adolescents, and less so for preadolescents, for whom they are not yet needed, or late adoles-

At crowd events, such as high school football games, where various cliques mingle, adolescents can practice new social skills and new roles with new people.

cents, who no longer need them. Initially adolescents move in isolated same-sex cliques. The first movement toward heterosexual encounters occurs with the emergence of the crowd. Members of unisex cliques get together in crowds made up of cliques of both genders. Adolescents consider these initial interactions to be daring and engage in them only in the safety of groups. The author can attest to the accuracy of this observation. At a party given by her sixth-grade daughter, one of the girls hung some mistletoe. Within minutes the boys had fled the house and milled about in the yard in the dark, returning only after the mistletoe had been removed. Yet reports that filtered back over the week indicated the boys had had a great time and wanted to know when there would be another party.

Late adolescents are comfortable with others of the opposite sex, and the crowd disintegrates into loosely grouped cliques of couples who are "going together." Cliques also become less important with age. The number of adolescents belonging to a clique declines from the sixth to the 12th grades. As **Box 7.2** discusses, however, membership in a clique tends to be stable over time.

All crowds are not created equal. Ask any adolescent. Some are more prestigious than others. A "leading crowd" exists at most schools. Students in this crowd are held in high regard by others, sometimes even to the point of envy. Almost always the members of this crowd feel good about themselves as well, having higher levels of self-esteem than students in less-prestigious crowds (Brown & Lohr, 1987). All the students at any school know what it takes to be a member of the leading crowd. In addition to academic performance, for boys, being good at sports is important; for girls, it is being a social leader. Students in the leading crowd are also likely to be leaders in the school and even have teachers look to them for help with extracurricular activities. (Stone et al., 2008).

Other crowds form a loose status hierarchy below the leading crowd. Adolescents receive constant reminders at school of their status. Who sits with them in the cafeteria, who can cut in front of whom in line, which clubs and activities are open or closed to them—all confirm the loose pecking order that reflects the relative prestige of their particular crowd. One might think that the only ones to escape with their self-esteem intact would be those from the leading crowd. However, adolescents from other crowds appear to fare just as

Research Focus

Longitudinal Design: Friendship Patterns

How stable are adolescents' friendships? Are the kids that make up an adolescent's closest circle of friends likely to be in that same circle a year later? For that matter, how common is it for adolescents to have a group of intimate friends instead of, say, a single best friend or few close friends at all?

Studies of adolescents' friendships have identified a number of friendship patterns, but until recently we have not known how common or stable each of these patterns was. One friendship pattern is the *clique*. A clique is a small group of intimate friends who are similar in sex, age, ethnicity, and social status. Friends who belong to the same clique spend much of their time together. A second type of friendship pattern is that of the *liaison*. Adolescents who are liaisons have a number of close friendships, but these are with adolescents who belong to several different cliques. Thus, liaisons open channels of communication between cliques, increasing the likelihood that adolescents from different cliques will do things together. A third friendship pattern, that of *isolates*, characterizes adolescents who are not members of a clique and, unlike liaisons, have few friendships in general.

Susan Ennett and Karl Bauman (1996) asked adolescents to name their best friends—first when they were in the ninth grade and a year later when they were in the 10th grade. These investigators used a *longitudinal design*. In this type of research, one studies a single cohort, a group of individuals all the same age, and takes a number of measurements at different ages.

By following the same individuals over time, we can see patterns to development that we might otherwise miss. And because we are comparing the adolescents with themselves at each age, we minimize the problem of having equivalent samples. Are there any problems with this type of research? Unfortunately, the answer is yes. To understand what these problems are, we must define three terms: age changes, time of measurement differences, and confounding.

Age changes are the biological and experiential changes that always accompany aging. They occur in all cultures and at all points in history. We assume that age changes have a biological basis (although we are not always able to identify them) and should therefore be universal; that is, they should occur in all people no matter what their social or cultural background. A good example of an age change is development of the prefrontal cortex, which continues into adolescence and underlies the development of increasingly abstract thought (see Chapter 4).

Time of measurement differences reflect social conditions, currents of opinion, and historical

well if they like the crowd to which they belong. This suggests that although peer group membership is important for adolescents, it is a sense of belonging rather than the status of the group itself that is critical.

Crushes and Dating

Even before dating begins, adolescents go through a stage in which they develop crushes. A **crush** involves an idealized fantasy about another person, and it is rarely reciprocated. The other person remains distant, even if it's someone just two seats away in the same class. The absence of reciprocity and the distance factor in crushes are important features, because they allow adolescents to explore new role possibilities at a safe distance (Erikson, 1950, 1968).

Even so, it is common for early adolescents to get together in various types of mixed-sex activities. In one study, fifth- through eighth-graders were questioned at the beginning and again at the end of each school year concerning the extent to which they participated in various types of mixed-sex activities. These could range from simply hanging out together, to dating, to having a girlfriend or boyfriend. By the sixth grade, the amount of time students spent in mixed-sex activities had increased, and for seventh- and eighth-graders, **dating** had increased by the end of the school year (Connolly et al., 2004).

crush An idealized fantasy about another person that is rarely reciprocated.

dating A social activity that typically begins in mid-adolescence.

events that are present when we make our observations and can therefore affect attitudes and behavior. When we study age changes by repeatedly observing the same group of individuals over time, we can mistake time of measurement changes for age changes. It's always possible, for example, that transition from a middle school to a high school setting could disrupt existing friendship patterns.

Confounding occurs when observations reflect systematic differences in more than one variable, with the result that we cannot separate the effects of one from the effects of the other. Longitudinal research frequently confounds age changes with time of measurement differences, making it impossible to conclusively separate the effects of age from those due to time of measurement. Do changes in friendship patterns over adolescence reflect differences due to age or to disruptions due to transitions from one school setting to another?

Longitudinal research can suffer from other problems as well (see Chapter 2), with the most important being the loss of subjects over time. This loss is called *subject mortality* and is almost always systematically related to age. In other words, the individuals who remain in the study are not necessarily representative of those their age in the general population, because the less healthy and otherwise less fortunate are the first to leave the sample. (Perhaps adolescents with few friends, for

instance, do not want to be reminded of this and drop out of the study.)

With these cautions in mind, let's go back to Ennett and Bauman's study and see what they found about adolescents' friendships. Consistent with the findings of other studies of friendships, these investigators found that the most frequent type of friendship pattern was the clique, with 44% of adolescents belonging to a clique. Additionally, significant numbers of adolescents were isolates (27%) and liaisons (29%).

What about the stability of these friendship patterns over time? These investigators found that both adolescents who were clique members and those who were isolates at the first time of measurement were more likely to have the same status one year later than were those who were liaisons. These findings may not be that surprising, especially when we learn that clique membership itself tends to be stable over a year's time. Also, adolescents who have already experienced difficulty integrating themselves into a social group may not find it any easier to do so a year later. Liaisons, on the other hand, have already had close friendships in one or more social groups and can more easily move into any one of them, changing their characteristic friendship pattern to that of a clique member.

Source: From Ennett & Bauman, 1996.

Dating is so much a part of the cultural scene one might assume it has always been practiced. Yet it is a relatively recent phenomenon. Prior to the early 1900s, couples dated primarily to determine their suitability for marriage. Before that, girls were given in marriage by their families to suitable partners; young couples had little say over the choices of their prospective mates.

Dating today serves a number of functions, of which the selection of marriage partners is only one. A very important function for adolescents when they first begin to date is simply recreation: Dating is fun—or at least it's supposed to be. Adolescents also report feeling nervous and apprehensive. Dates can have awkward moments. Many adolescents fear rejection and are uncertain about how to act on a date. Should the boy or the girl open the car door? One girl explained, "You just sort of walk along and if he walks the other way, you know you have to open it yourself." Should the boy help the girl on with her coat? "I act like I'm having problems, and if he doesn't notice, I forget it," suggested one teenager (Place, 1975). Yet despite the uncertainties, most adolescents find dating enjoyable.

Related to these uncertainties is another important function of dating: Dating enables adolescents to explore a new role, namely, the adult sexual role they will assume. When adolescents date, in other words, they find them-

When they are just beginning to date, most adolescents worry about awkward moments and fear rejection. Once they do date someone regularly, however, the self-consciousness diminishes and they can relax and have fun.

selves in a role that is significantly different from that of any other they have previously assumed, whether as child, friend, student, or employee (Dowdy & Kliewer, 1998). As a consequence, dating is fraught with uncertainty and excitement.

WHEN DATING BEGINS   Dating typically starts in mid-adolescence, although age itself is not the only indicator. One can better predict whether an adolescent may be dating by knowing whether friends have begun to date than by knowing the adolescent's age or even sexual maturity (Dornbusch et al., 1981). Parents seem especially subject to a form of peer pressure all their own in this respect. As one adolescent girl remarked when she explained how she got her parents to consent to letting her go on a date, "If your girlfriends are not going out, forget it. I just gave examples of who was going out." Another ice-breaker was a strategy learned from childhood:

Daughter: Dad, can I go to the movies with Eddie?

Father: I don't know; ask Mom.

Daughter: Mom, Dad said Eddie and I can go to the movies if you say it's okay.

Mother: Okay, then, you can go.

Daughter: Dad, Mom said it's okay.

Most parents establish rules with respect to dating behavior, and most are more likely to do so for daughters than for sons. As with other behaviors, mothers tend to be more involved than fathers in using rules for dating, though the rules are likely to be established by both parents (Madsen, 2008).

The peer group regulates the pace of socialization into more adult roles. Adolescents who don't begin dating when their friends do may be dropped from their peer groups. However, those who become involved in a serious relationship are also likely to have relationships with their friends change. For adolescent girls who date casually, best friends continue to be sources of support and companionship. This changes for those involved in a serious relationship; their boyfriend rather than their best friends is more likely to be their source of companionship and support, occasionally resulting in friends feeling overlooked and the adolescent herself feeling disloyal and guilty (Kuttler & La Greca, 2004; Roth & Parker, 2001).

A Youth Culture

In many respects, adolescents are no different from individuals of any age. Most of us spend our free time with those who enjoy the things we do, laugh at the same jokes, and share similar beliefs as to what's important in life. When you think of it, this is also how we've talked about culture—in terms of the shared customs and beliefs among members of a group. How, then, do peers influence adolescents, and does their influence create cultural barriers that parents and others find difficult to cross?

School

A concern among some parents and educators is that adolescents place less importance on academic achievement than they should, presumably due to competing values held by their peers. In a classic study, students at 10 different high schools were asked to identify which of their classmates they most admired (Coleman, 1961). For boys at every school, the best athletes were also considered to be the most popular. Athletes were twice as likely to be in the leading crowd as were those who did well in school. Perhaps not surprisingly, when boys were asked how they would like to be remembered, 44% of them said as an athletic star. For girls, being a leader in school activities contributed most to popularity and was the way they wanted to be remembered.

This picture appears to have changed little over the years. However, one noticeable change is that girls value good grades more than they did a generation ago, even though they do not see these as valued by peers any more than in previous years (Hopmeyer Gorman et al., 2002; Quatman et al., 2000; U.S. Department of Health and Human Services, 2002c).

Even though adolescents think good looks are important, physical attractiveness probably contributes to popularity only for those adolescents at either extreme. For those in between—and this would include most adolescents—other factors are more important. Conversely, academic achievement is probably more important than most research has suggested. Part of the difficulty in interpreting the findings on academic achievement may be due to the way questions have been worded. When asked, "How would you like to be remembered?" boys say as an athletic star and girls as a leader in activities. But when asked, "How would you rank the following in importance to you?" most adolescents will put getting good grades above being good in sports or being a social leader (Quatman et al., 2000).

The importance of athletic ability, school activities, and academic achievement also varies from one school to another. Athletic ability tends to have more importance, for example, in rural communities and in schools drawing from lower socioeconomic levels, whereas this ability is valued less in urban settings or in communities with more highly educated parents.

conformity The tendency to go along with the norms and standards of one's group.

Conformity and Peer Pressure

Friends draw adolescents into realms beyond the family that highlight differences between themselves and their parents. These differences become important ways of organizing their individuality; however, they can leave adolescents with feelings of loneliness. Peers provide the emotional support that contributes to feelings of self-worth. Peer expectations for well-defined standards of speech and dress also establish outward behaviors that define the group and establish a sense of belonging among its members. Adolescents consider it a bargain to give up some of their individuality for the security that comes with belonging to a group.

Conformity peaks in early adolescence when young teens begin to experience their separateness from their parents. Studies of conformity show that early adolescents are influenced by others' judgments, sometimes even changing answers that are obviously right to conform

Every generation of adolescents creates a culture that seems wholly foreign to older generations. And yet, despite their untraditional tastes, adolescents' values remain surprisingly similar to those of their parents' and grandparents' generations.

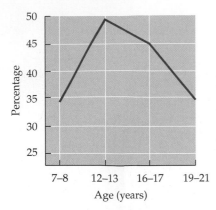

● **Figure 7.3 Changes in conformity with age** (After Costanzo, 1970.)

to those of the group. By mid-adolescence, conformity has already begun to decrease, and by late adolescence it has decreased even more (**Figure 7.3**) (Gavin & Furman, 1989). With respect to age-linked behaviors such as smoking and drinking, however, adolescents' concerns about what their friends might think peak somewhat later (Hendry et al., 1996).

Conformity isn't limited to adolescence; it characterizes behavior at every age. Nor is conformity necessarily bad. It is simply a tendency to go along with the standards and norms of one's group. Trends in fashion, food, and recreation are as apparent among 50-year-olds as among 15-year-olds. We notice conformity, however, when the norms for one group run counter to those of another, as sometimes occurs with adolescents and their parents. Different behaviors and skills contribute to acceptance more by peers than by adults. These differences increase with age in early adolescence.

Not all adolescents are equally likely to conform to the opinions of others. Those who have high status in their peer group, and those who have a well-developed sense of themselves are less likely to show conformity. The same has been found to be true for adults (Harvey & Rutherford, 1980; Marcia, 1980).

These strengths can be traced, in part, to adolescents' relationships with their parents. Parents who have encouraged adolescents to take part in responsible decision making within the family, who provide reasons when disciplining, and who encourage a verbal give-and-take with their children—authoritative parents—have adolescents who show the least conformity (see Chapter 6). Adolescents from these homes have more positive self-concepts and a better developed sense of self. Further, they have learned from childhood to live with the consequences of their decisions, even when these have been as simple as deciding not to clean their rooms and choosing to be grounded instead. They have also learned that even when their parents disagree with them, they still have their emotional support.

However, even authoritative parents can worry that peers will have more influence than they have on their children's values and activities. Adolescents are beginning to spend more time with their friends than with their families. Perhaps, too, parents realize that the decisions adolescents make can affect their futures in ways decisions rarely do for children, such as the type of friends they spend time with, or the grades they work for in school. Even so, adolescents report that parents are the best all-around source of support, whether emotional or informational, in the form of advice (Reid et al., 1989).

Fashion fads such as pierced eyebrows, spiked hair, and baggy jeans do little to alleviate parents' fears that they have lost their children to an alien culture. But even flagrant differences such as these do not mean that parents no longer influence their children's values. If they did not, adolescents would not have to go to such extremes to assert their individuality. Nor do obvious differences in taste, as in music and clothes, reflect a shift in underlying values. This is not to say that adolescents are not influenced by their peers. They are. But the extent to which they are and the way this occurs cannot be thought of simply as an either-or contest between the values of parents and those of peers.

Adolescents experience **peer pressure** as a pressure to think and act like their friends. The price of belonging to a group is to maintain the ways of the group. This pressure changes with age. One of the primary functions of the peer group is to help adolescents gain their footing as they step outside the family. As adolescents become more sure of themselves, pressures to maintain the norms of the group lessen. Peer pressure is strongest in early ado-

peer pressure Experienced pressure to think and act like one's friends.

lescence, when adolescents most need the support of a well-defined group. Conformity is also greatest then. As adolescents become more sure of themselves, the peer group becomes less important. As a result, the need to define group membership through rigidly prescribed standards of dress, speech, and so on lessens (Clasen & Brown, 1985).

With age, too, adolescents become more comfortable in thinking for themselves and arriving at their own decisions. They are less likely to look to their parents or their friends for advice, and when they do seek advice, they are better able to weigh the opinions of others and arrive at their own decisions. This confidence reflects a new level of security in their values and how they arrived at them.

Values

If anything, the values of peers and parents are likely to complement each other rather than conflict. Friends typically share similar experiences; they live nearby, come from families of about the same income level, and are likely to share the same ethnic background. Friends' parents are also important in maintaining the values established by an adolescent's parents, primarily, it seems, by influencing the behavior of the adolescent's friends. Socially and academically competent adolescents are likely to seek the company of similar adolescents. These interactions, in turn, often amplify the initial advantages of each. Anne Fletcher, Nancy Darling, and Laurence Steinberg, at Temple University, and Sanford Dornbusch, at Stanford University (1995), studied a large sample of 14- to 18-year-olds, looking in particular at the way adolescents' friends described their parents. In general, adolescents whose friends described their parents as authoritative had more positive attitudes toward school and were less likely to use substances such as alcohol or cigarettes. For boys, authoritative parenting among their friends' parents was also associated with behavioral measures, such as greater resistance to conformity and lower levels of misconduct, and for girls, this parenting style was associated with measures of psychosocial adjustment, such as higher levels of self-reliance and self-esteem.

Most adolescents spend more time talking with their friends than with their parents and are more influenced by their friends about day-to-day decisions. But the background and the values of an adolescent's friends tend to be similar to those of the adolescent's parents.

Of course, some differences between parents and peers can be expected. And when they occur, the reference group that adolescents turn to will depend on a number of factors, one of which is the type of decision to be made. Adolescents generally look to their friends for short-term decisions, such as whether to go to a party or what clothes to buy. They turn to their parents for decisions about their futures: plans for education, marriage, or choosing an occupation. Thus, parents have more influence over the larger decisions of life, and friends over the day-to-day particulars of living it.

Important life decisions reflect values, and adolescents are likely to share these with their parents—values about education, relationships, and work. But values as broad as these do not translate easily into the language of daily affairs. They say little about how one spends an afternoon or which movie to see. With respect to actual behaviors such as these, friends have more influence.

Peers and Parents: When Values Conflict

The support of friends becomes important when adolescents engage in behavior they know their parents would disapprove of. Adolescents seek out friends who engage in similar activities and, in turn, are influenced by the activities of their friends. Adolescents who smoke, for instance, are more likely to have friends who smoke than those who don't (Ali & Dwyer, 2009; Kristjansson et al., 2010; Urberg, 1992). The same can be said for the use of other substances such as alcohol and marijuana (Cleveland et al., 2010; Wang et al., 2009). Kimberly Henry and her associates (2005, 2009) followed adolescents and their friends over a two-year period, and found that not only did adolescents' use of alcohol reflect the number of their friends who drank, but that changes over time in their drinking corresponded to similar changes in their friends' use of alcohol over time.

Before wrongfully concluding that adolescents are likely to do whatever their friends are doing, it should be pointed out that the influence of peers is moderated by adolescents' beliefs and personalities. Thus, those who view drinking as harmful are less influenced by drinking among their friends. Similarly, more general aspects of adolescents' personalities, such as level of autonomy or willingness to take risks, moderate peer influence (Allen et al., 2006; Henry et al., 2005). Gender is also related to adolescents' experience of peer pressure. Boys are more likely to consider the anticipated outcome, and say "no" if they think they might get in trouble. For girls, peer approval and friendship are important sources of pressure, which they often cite as reasons for going along with something, even when they anticipate a negative outcome (Pearl et al., 1990; Treboux & Busch-Rossnagel, 1990).

How much influence parents retain with their teenagers when conflicting values arise depends in large measure on the quality of the relationships they have with them. Parents who are overly permissive or authoritarian are least effective when it comes to influencing the choices of their children. Andrew Fuligni and Jacquelynne Eccles (1993), studying a sample of over 1,700 sixth- and seventh-graders, found that adolescents who perceived themselves as having little opportunity to make decisions on their own, and who believed their parents to be overly strict, were less likely than other adolescents to seek advice from their parents and more likely to turn to their peers. They were also more likely to give up important aspects of their lives, such as doing well in school or developing their talents, in order to be popular with friends.

Adolescents are most likely to listen to parents who have involved them since childhood in decision-making in the family, holding them responsible for their actions, disciplining consistently, and monitoring their activities. Family relationships such as these contribute to a strong sense of self, making it less likely for adolescents to be pressured by peers to misbehave. The protective effect of parenting, however, has been found to vary with the larger school and neighborhood context, with families being able to offer less protection in high risk surroundings such as, for example, schools in which most students do not come from families that are similarly cohesive and supportive (Cleveland et al., 2010).

It is easier for adolescents to listen to their parents' views when they are sure of their own autonomy. The quality of the relationship between adolescents and their parents, not the existence of another reference group, determines whether adolescents will remain close to their parents and seek them out for advice in decisions about their lives.

It should be clear at this point that the relative influence of parents and peers cannot be thought of as a simple tug-of-war with the adolescent in the middle (Kandel, 1996). The values of friends frequently overlap with those of parents, minimizing conflict when it occurs. Parents may occasionally even look to an adolescent's friends to determine what is normative when they are uncertain about what adolescent behaviors are appropriate—for example, when to wear lipstick, or when to get a part-time job. Also, the values of parents and peers influence different types of decisions, leading to less conflict than many parents anticipate. Finally, adolescents vary considerably among themselves in the extent to which they are influenced by the attitudes and behaviors of others, whether these be parents or peers.

Are adolescents and their parents likely to experience conflict? Probably. Does conflict weaken the relationship? Not necessarily. Conflict can help adolescents restructure and strengthen relationships with parents. Parents are likely to participate in this restructuring process as well. Even as they attempt to get teenagers to agree with them, parents also encourage adolescents to think for themselves and to speak their own minds. Honest exchanges such as these frequently lead to the evolution of joint views shared by both (Youniss & Smollar, 1989).

Youth Organizations

In addition to informal get-togethers with peers and the more formal world of school, many adolescents devote their time to another aspect of youth culture: youth organizations. Adolescents belong to clubs, are members of teams, and participate in volunteer work in their communities. **Structured voluntary activities**, such as sports, the creative arts, or volunteer work, are part of most adolescents' worlds and contribute substantially to their well-being. Reed Larson (2000), at the University of Illinois, argues that because such activities are intrinsically motivating and challenging, and because they demand adolescents' concentrated attention, they build skills and develop initiative. They also have a spillover effect, promoting other positive qualities such as self-control, assertiveness, and even improved grades (Hattie et al., 1997).

Sizable numbers of adolescents participate in after-school activities. Some, but not all, of these activities are school-related. For instance, approximately 25–40% of high school seniors indicate being involved in sports, the creative arts, academic clubs, or other school activities (Youth Indicators, 2005). Additionally, many adolescents belong to national youth organizations such as the Scouts or 4-H and to local community organizations, and a substantial number of adolescents are involved in religious activities. Over 30% of high school seniors attend religious services weekly, and many of these also attend weekly youth groups (Bachman et al., 2009; Huebner & Mancini, 2003; Youth Indicators, 2005). Additionally, many adolescents are involved in various types of community volunteer work, with approximately a third of high school seniors doing so at least once or twice a month (Youth Indicators, 2005).

Activities such as these also fill the hours after school lets out but before working parents typically return home. Sara Goldstein, Pamela Davis-Kean, and Jacquelynne Eccles (2005), at the University of Michigan, followed adolescents from the seventh to the 11th grade, determining, among other things, how they spent this time. These investigators found evidence that by the eighth grade, unsupervised and unstructured time spent with peers was associated with problem behavior in the 11th grade.

Despite the increasing importance of friends in adolescents' lives, parents continue to remain significant sources of strength and influence. Both parents and peers contribute to adolescents' ability to face changes in yet another area of their lives—school. We will look at these changes in the next chapter.

structured voluntary activities
Activities that are intrinsically motivating and challenging that build skills and foster initiative.

Go to the
Adolescence
Companion Website at
www.sinauer.com/cobb
for quizzes, flashcards, summaries, and other study resources.

Youth organizations, like 4-H, contribute to an adolescent's sense of well-being by building skills and developing initiative.

SUMMARY and KEY TERMS

The Importance of Friendships

Group Identity: Adolescents experiment with new behaviors with their friends and, in doing so, discover new things about themselves. The psychosocial task in early adolescence may be more one of forming a group identity than of achieving a personal identity. The latter task assumes salience in mid-adolescence when issues related to affiliation and belonging have been resolved, and adolescents are ready to address the differences that distinguish them from others.
group identity

Gossip and Self-Disclosure: Friendships change with age. Those of preadolescents reflect a concern with being accepted. Preadolescents use gossip as a way of affirming group norms and their membership in the group. Adolescent friendships reflect a concern with self-discovery, and self-disclosure becomes important to this process.
gossip, self-disclosure

Friends and Self-Esteem: Friends contribute to adolescents' well-being; they facilitate the formation of an ideal self-image and are important sources of self-esteem.
self-esteem, ideal self-image

Parents and Self-Esteem: Parents also contribute to well-being. Interactions that communicate support, affection, and encouragement promote self-esteem.

Friendship Patterns

Age Differences in Friendship Patterns: Patterns of friendship differ with the age and sex of adolescents. Early adolescent girls' friendships focus on the activities that bring friends together. Mid-adolescent girls' friendships are concerned with the personal qualities of friends more than before. Girls want friends they can confide in and trust. Friendships in late adolescence focus more on personalities. Intimacy continues to grow and more friends are of the opposite sex. Boys' friendships in early adolescence are also centered on shared activities. By middle adolescence, their friendships are as close emotionally as girls' friendships, but involve less discussion of feelings.

Gender and Friendships: Close friendships for most adolescents are with peers of the same gender, especially in early adolescence. But beyond this, there are few differences between girls and boys in the ways they relate to their friends.

Adolescents and the Internet: Increasing numbers of teenagers stay in touch with each other through the Internet, with email, instant messaging, and social networking sites, and through cell phones and text messaging. Of those who communicate this way, their activities typically involve more than conversations. Nearly two-thirds use the Internet to post videos or photos online, original artwork, stories, or for maintaining an online journal or a personal webpage.

Social Competence: There are several dimensions to social competence: assessing a situation, responding to it, and knowing that relationships take time to develop. Competent adolescents are better able to see what is going on in a social situation and adapt their behavior accordingly. They also realize that developing friendships takes time.
social competence

SUMMARY and KEY TERMS

Social Status: Who's In and Who's Not: Popularity can refer to social preference, how much others like you, or to social prestige, how much others look up to you. Popular adolescents who enjoy social prestige often use either physical or relational aggression to both achieve and maintain their status within the group. Adolescents can be categorized into five social statuses based on the frequency with which classmates nominate them as someone they "like the most" or "like the least:" popular, rejected, controversial, average, and neglected. Intervention programs address problems in peer relationships, such as having poor social skills, being overly aggressive, or having a negative self-image.

popular, social preference, social prestige, prosocial behaviors, physical aggression, relational aggression, rejected adolescents, controversial adolescents, average adolescents, neglected adolescents, social skills training, social-cognitive intervention

Interethnic Friendships: Interethnic friendships form when adolescents live in integrated neighborhoods and attend integrated schools. Classroom climates affect the formation of such friendships, which are likely to develop when students are assigned to small groups to work together in a noncompetitive atmosphere. Interethnic friendships face challenges posed by different enculturation experiences. Adolescents of different backgrounds can perceive and react to the same situation differently, and misinterpretations and hurt feelings can result.

enculturation

Friendships and Sexual-Minority Youth: Sexual-minority youth have more fears and concerns about relationships with their peers and experience more friendship loss than heterosexual youth. However, by late adolescence, they have more close friends than heterosexual youth.

sexual-minority youth

The Peer Group

The peer group regulates the pace of socialization. Adolescents who either fall too far behind or move too far ahead of their friends are dropped from the group.

peer group

Cliques and Crowds: The most common type of peer group is the clique, though only about half of students belong to one. Adolescents not in cliques may be liaisons, who have friends in several cliques, or isolates, who are not part of the social network. The larger peer group, crowds, let adolescents try out new social skills. The crowd is primarily important in helping adolescents move into mixed-sex interactions, whereas clique activities provide feedback about the success of new social skills. Cliques and crowds change in importance as adolescents age. They are most important in mid-adolescence and become less so as adolescents begin to form couples who are "going together."

clique, liaison, isolate, crowd

Crushes and Dating: Before dating begins, adolescents go through a stage in which they develop crushes. Dating tends to begin anywhere between the ages of 12 and 16. Girls start somewhat earlier than boys. The most important determinant of when they start to date is whether their friends are dating.

crush, dating   *(continued)*

SUMMARY and KEY TERMS *continued*

A Youth Culture

School: School provides adolescents with a society of their peers. Adolescents may value academic achievement less than athletic achievement or being involved in many school activities.

Conformity and Peer Pressure: Conformity peaks in early adolescence. Adolescents with high social status and a well-developed sense of self are less likely to feel the need to conform. Authoritative parenting also gives adolescents skills that help them make decisions for themselves.
conformity, peer pressure

Values: The values of peers and parents more frequently complement each other than conflict, and most adolescents have friends with values similar to theirs. When adolescents seek advice from parents and friends, they are more likely to seek parental advice concerning long-term life decisions and the advice of friends in daily matters. With age, adolescents become more comfortable in making their own decisions.

Peers and Parents: When Values Conflict: Peers have an important influence on deviant behaviors. Gender differences exist in response to peer pressure; boys consider the anticipated outcome more, and girls consider peer approval and friendship more. Despite the importance of the peer culture, adolescents and parents share many basic values.

Youth Organizations: Many adolescents participate in structured voluntary activities such as sports, the creative arts, or volunteer work. These activities build skills and develop initiative because they are intrinsically motivating and challenging, and because they demand adolescents' concentrated attention.
structured voluntary activities

"**Oh**, no! Here he comes," I nodded.

"Move over, slime ball. Thanks for the place in line."

The kid was huge and his breath was fogging up my glasses. No food was worth this. I stepped out, and he stepped in line. From what I could see of the steam table, I was ahead on this one.

"Aren't you going to fight him?" nudged Erin.

"Sure, Erin. You want me to end up in the tossed salad?"

"This is too much!" she sighed. "The morning has gone from bad to awful—I want out!"

Adolescents in the Schools

"Me too," I muttered. "But I don't think I could find my way. I got lost three times already today. If I'm late to another class, I'll have detention—and it's still the first week! Four minutes to get to classes! What are they training us for, the track team? I can't even open my locker that fast."

"Some ninth-grader slammed mine shut this morning—just as I popped the combination."

"Welcome to scrubs-ville, Erin."

"If this is what it's going to be like, I'm out of here!" she vowed.

Chapter Overview

Secondary school is a new experience for early adolescents, one that most will never forget. Once adolescents leave elementary school, the pace of learning will quicken. How well adolescents keep up will depend on many things. We will look at what adolescents bring to the classroom and at the learning environments they are entering.

We turn next to the characteristics that distinguish effective schools. These schools have skilled teachers and small classes, and are designed to meet the needs of early versus late adolescents. They also offer a variety of programs in addition to academic coursework, serving as a base for services ranging from health care to parent education.

We look next at school safety and ways of maintaining this by addressing violence and bullying, and we will look as well at the characteristics of bullies and victims. We then turn our attention to intervention programs that are effective in reducing bullying in schools, and at conflict-resolution programs designed for all adolescents.

Not all students have the same interests and not all learn at the same rate. We will look at ways for meeting the needs of diverse groups of students, such as mixed-ability grouping, tracking, and parental involvement in the schools. We will also turn our attention to how well schools are meeting the needs of female and male students, and the needs of adolescents from ethnically and culturally diverse backgrounds.

In the next section of the chapter, adolescents themselves step into the spotlight. Some rise to the occasion, meeting their own and others' expectations, while others lag behind. We will look first at proficiency in basic subjects and then at patterns of achievement among different groups of students. We then move to a consideration of students at the edge—those who are gifted, those who have learning disabilities, and those who drop out of school.

In the last section of the chapter, we consider ways of measuring the success of schools. Research into effective schools raises the question of whether or not changes that are necessary in order to reach alienated minorities are also necessary to effectively teach mainstream adolescents.

secondary education
Middle schools, junior high schools, and high schools.

direct instruction
Instruction directed toward the mastery of basic skills; all students are involved in the same activities at any given time.

Classroom learning can be structured in different ways. In this classroom, students work individually at their desks and the teacher offers direct instruction, providing them with necessary information and help when needed.

Educating Adolescents

The growth of **secondary education** in this country, that is, of middle schools, junior high schools, and high schools, has been nothing short of phenomenal given that fewer than 5% of the population completed high school in the early 1900s. Yet the successes of secondary education have been punctuated by crises as well, and by questions as to how best to educate adolescents.

Structuring the Learning Environment

School districts and teachers face choices as to how best to structure classroom learning. We can distinguish two broad approaches to instruction. **Direct instruction** has as its goal the mastery of basic skills. Teachers work with the class as a whole, involving all students in the same activities at any given time during the class. Students spend class time working on tasks assigned by the teacher, covering basic disciplines such as math, literature, and science. Students typically work individually at their desks, while the teacher circulates around the room giving feedback or answering questions. Teachers offer direct instruction, providing students with necessary facts and illustrating solutions to problems. A basic assumption is that by having students work an all aspects of each lesson, each student will be given the opportunity to master all the elements of the assignment.

Differentiated instruction assumes that learning is not so much getting the facts straight as knowing what they mean; in that sense, this approach reflects the constructivist perspective described in this text. Since no two students are assumed to share the same learning profile of abilities and interests, classrooms are structured so that students have multiple ways of gaining information and of making sense of what they are learning—that is, classroom structure is flexible. At any one time, various groups of

The structure of this classroom reflects the assumption that students differ in their interests and abilities; consequently students are given multiple ways of gaining information and of making sense of what they are learning.

students can be working on a number of different projects; at other times, teachers may use whole-class discussions to relate the different projects to a common theme (Hall, 2002). Learning is seen as an active process, discovering solutions rather than being shown them. Consequently, students are encouraged to help plan the learning tasks they will study, set goals, and define the ways they will approach these.

A central assumption of differentiated instruction is that students have different learning styles. **Learning styles** can be distinguished in terms of students' preferences for various elements of the learning situation. For instance, some students prefer to work for extended periods of time and others need frequent breaks. Some students prefer to work alone and others in groups; groups can be further distinguished by whether students work in pairs or as part of a team. Yet another difference concerns the modality in which information is presented. Some students learn best when information is presented visually, as in reading, whereas others do better if they can listen to a lecture (Dunn & Dunn, 1993; Lovelace, 2005).

Preparing for High School: Middle School or Junior High

In some communities, students make the transition from elementary school into high school through a **middle school**, which they typically enter in the sixth grade and graduate in the eighth grade. An alternative transition is through a **junior high school**, which adolescents typically enter in the seventh grade and graduate in the eighth or ninth grade. Two events highlight the significance of entering either a middle school or junior high. Adolescents enter puberty during these years, and they experience intellectual, emotional, and psychological changes as well as biological ones. Additionally, moving to a middle school or a junior high confronts adolescents with a larger, more impersonal environment than the one to which they've become accustomed in elementary school.

Even though junior high schools and middle schools are designed specifically to meet the needs of early adolescents, the transition from elementary school still can be difficult. Adolescents leave behind the comfortable familiar-

differentiated instruction
Flexible classroom structure providing multiple formats for gaining information.

learning styles   Students' preferences concerning various aspects of the learning situation, for example, working individually or in groups, getting information by reading or listening to a class presentation.

middle school   A secondary school that includes the fifth or sixth through the eighth grades.

junior high school
A secondary school that typically includes the seventh through the ninth grades.

Whether they graduate to a junior high or a middle school, the transition from elementary school is a big step for young adolescents. No longer do they stay in the same classroom with the same teacher; now they have to find their way around campus and manage their time so that they can carry out assignments from several teachers.

ity of a classroom they knew as well as their living room and a teacher they spent more hours with during the day than either of their parents. And instead of being the oldest and biggest kids at school, they are once again the youngest and smallest, just when the intellectual and physical changes they're undergoing prompt them to see themselves as more adult.

Perhaps we shouldn't be surprised, then, by research showing that students' grades drop when they leave elementary school for either a middle school or a junior high. It's unclear what may be responsible for this drop since their achievement test scores do not show a comparable drop in knowledge (Eccles, 2004). There is some evidence that performance is more disrupted in white students than in black or Latino students; however, the reasons for this are unclear since grades for the latter were already significantly lower than for the white students, indicating that for minority students, problems affecting their performance are already present in elementary school (Kuperminc et al., 2004).

Problems adjusting to secondary school may reflect students' response to the more impersonal classroom environment they enter when they leave elementary school. Secondary schools typically are larger and classroom environments less supportive than in elementary schools (Barber & Olsen, 2004). Also, teachers involve students less in classroom decision making, which collides with young adolescents' need for greater autonomy. Perhaps because of this, Kuperminc et al. (2004) found students' sense of efficacy to drop with the transition, despite no change in feelings of self-worth. Finally, recall that this transition coincides with the onset of puberty which, like toppling a row of dominoes, has a cascading effect extending to all areas of adolescents' lives.

Parents can help by being involved in their adolescent's education. The ways in which they can be most helpful, however, change as adolescents leave elementary school for a secondary school. In the former, parents can actually assist in the classroom, whereas in the latter involvement is more indirect, taking the form of helping teachers with fundraising for special projects, attending school activities, and by communicating their expectations for achievement and the importance of a good education. The latter are especially important in helping adolescents maintain an interest in their classes in junior high (**Figure 8.1**). Both their fathers' education and their mothers' expectations for their academic achievement are related to adolescents' interest in their studies (Dotterer et al., 2009; Hill & Tyson, 2009).

What Makes Schools Effective?

What types of learning environments are likely to be most effective for young adolescents? Effective schools have skilled teachers, are smaller or establish small learning communities within larger schools, provide a supportive school climate, and involve parents and the community in the services they offer.

● Figure 8.1 Drop in academic interest with the transition to junior high as a function of mothers' academic interest (After Dotterer et al., 2009.)

Skilled Teachers

One factor consistently distinguishes effective schools: the beliefs of the teaching staff that all students are capable of learning. Teachers at effective schools have high expectations. They interact with students more, reward them more, and have friendlier classrooms. They have an infectious enthusiasm for what they teach, engaging even those students that other teachers consider "troublemakers" (**Box 8.1**) (Teddlie et al., 1989). Research constantly underscores the potent effect that individual teachers can have on their students (Crosnoe & Needham, 2004; Schoon et al., 2004). Expecting the most from students and letting them know when they have succeeded are every bit as important as the latest in software and the number of books on the shelves.

Students in classrooms where progress is monitored and feedback is given as to how well they are doing adjust better academically, and have higher achievement levels (Wentzel, 2002). In fact, the characteristics of effective teachers are similar to those of effective parents. Effective teachers are supportive and encourage their students, have organized classrooms in which students know what is expected of them, and make frequent use of feedback in guiding students' activities. Such environments, whether in the classroom or at home, facilitate adjustment by enabling adolescents to regulate their own behavior (Brody et al., 2002; Wentzel, 2002).

Skilled teachers are also able to present material in ways that can be understood by all of their students. Consider a science class in which, to solve a problem, students must hold each of the conditions constant except the one they are considering. The development of hypothetical thought enables adolescents to do this. Because not all students develop at the same rate, skilled teachers are likely to combine abstract approaches that illustrate isolating variables with concrete examples to bring their points home to less advanced thinkers as well. The example in **Box 8.2** illustrates this point. Notice how the discussion revolves around common objects such as a Frisbee, a shoebox

The most important characteristic of an effective school is teachers who care about their students and have high expectations for them.

BOX 8.2   In More Depth

Science in the Classroom: Analysis of a Frisbee

The teacher in this science class has told students to bring in something that flies. One student brought in a Frisbee.

Teacher: Okay, let's consider some explanations now. Why is the Frisbee built this way? Look back at our list of structural features on the blackboard... Why is the Frisbee designed the way it is? I'd like to see almost everyone's hand up with one idea.

Student 1: Well, it's round so you can spin it.

Teacher: Okay. Now let's take this a little bit further. Could you spin it if it weren't round?

Student 1: No. Well, I guess you could. But it wouldn't work very well. It would flop around; it wouldn't sail smoothly.

Teacher: Can anyone think of an example of something shaped like a Frisbee...? What has a rim like a Frisbee but isn't round?

Student 2: Maybe the lid of a shoe box. You know, it's shaped like a rectangle but it has sides like a Frisbee.

Teacher: And what would happen if you spun it like a Frisbee?

Student 2: Well, it wouldn't go very far. The air slows it down maybe.

Teacher: Good. Anyone else have some ideas about why it slows down?

Student 3: It doesn't spin well because the sides of the box lid hit the air.

Teacher: Good point. When it's not round, the sides hit the air and slow it down. That's a reason for a Frisbee being round. But that leads to another question: Why is spin so important? What happens if you throw a Frisbee without spinning it, versus throwing the Frisbee with a spin?

Student 4: It flops if you don't spin it. So I guess the spinning keeps it straight.

Teacher: Very good. So a Frisbee is round so it can spin fast without slowing down when its edges hit the air. And it needs to spin to keep it from tumbling. What about some other feature on the structure list? Who has an explanation for something else?...

Student 5: It's rounded on top. I mean it isn't perfectly flat. That maybe helps it to fly.

Teacher: A very interesting idea. So a Frisbee is a kind of spinning wing. The spinning keeps it straight and the wing shape helps it to stay up. Can anyone think of other things you can throw?...

Student 6: A discus.

Student 7: A tin-can lid. You can throw those by spinning them.

Teacher: Interesting examples. I wonder if we can see whether the rounded shape of a Frisbee really gives it more lift than something that's flat.

Student 8: But a discus is pretty heavy; so are tin-can lids.

Teacher: That's a good point... When you're making a comparison, you want it to be fair. If you're comparing how much the rounded top helps, you don't want the comparison messed up by other differences, like weight. Is there any way we could make a fairer comparison? Could we test the Frisbee against itself somehow?

Student 9: How about throwing it upside down? If the rounded top really helps it to stay up, it shouldn't fly as well upside down.

Teacher: That's a good idea. Is it a fair comparison?

Student 9: Sure, because it weighs the same right-side up and upside down.

Teacher: Okay, so we have a good idea for controlling the variables. It's a fair test because everything is the same except what we're interested in—the rounded top. We have a Frisbee here, so let's try the experiment.

Source: From Perkins, 1987.

lid, and a tin can lid. Even concrete thinkers can wrap their minds around these examples.

Smaller Schools and Smaller Communities for Learning

The size of schools is known to affect behavior at school—inside and outside class. Adolescents from smaller schools have more positive interactions with each other, fewer discipline problems, less absenteeism, and fewer dropouts. The critical size for a school is about 500 students. Once that number is passed, the benefits of a smaller school are lost (Garbarino, 1980).

Small schools can be more flexible in responding to the needs of adolescents. Anthony Bryk and Stephen Raudenbush (1988) analyzed data from a national survey of over 1,000 schools. They found that smaller schools can overcome differences related to social class, academic background, and personal factors more readily than large schools. Programs on drug use, multicultural education, and cooperative learning are easier to set in motion and to change in response to student needs. Students in small schools have more opportunity to participate in activities. The particular type of activity is not important—yearbook staffing, hall monitoring, cheerleading, or peer counseling. Each one gives students a sense of belonging and a way of identifying with school.

Although it is not practical, or sometimes even possible to eliminate large schools, it *is* possible to create smaller "communities for learning" within them. These smaller environments can be just as responsive to students' needs as small schools (Herlihy & Kemple, 2005). Small classes, in particular, may be especially important in facilitating learning. A comparison of ninth-grade students who had been randomly assigned to one of several class sizes for the first four years of their schooling (K–3) found that those assigned to smaller classes performed significantly better in mathematics—six years later. Those who benefited most from smaller classes were minority students (Nye et al., 2001).

School Climate

Unique characteristics of schools may be at least as important as their size. The relationship between school input variables—number of students per classroom, computers per student, or books in the library, for example—and school output, in the form of student achievement, is not a simple one. Schools with similar resources can differ markedly in their effectiveness. Process variables that reflect the qualities of a school, such as differences in social and academic climates among schools or differences in their teaching staffs, must also be entered into the equation. Achievement is as much a function of how effectively a school's resources are integrated into the instruction as it is of the resources themselves. In this respect, the relationships teachers have with their students are of vital importance. Teachers who are supportive and fair and have clearly defined expectations for their students contribute substantially to a school's climate (Barber & Olsen, 2004; Gottfredson et al., 2005). Relationships among students, such as perceived friendliness and noncompetitiveness, also contribute to a school's climate (Loukas & Robinson, 2004). Additionally, schools that involve parents, either as classroom aides or tutors or as members of governing committees making schoolwide decisions, are more effective, especially in low-income districts where continuity between the home and the classroom needs bridging (Hill et al., 2004).

Schools that place as much value in educating students in music or drama as in college algebra or literature promote higher levels of achievement among all students. Often this requires a redefinition of values among teachers, staff, and parents. Our society has come to define intelligence in terms of verbal and mathematical abilities (see Chapter 4). In emphasizing these abilities, though, we have slighted others such as mechanical, interpersonal, or musical, in which students can also excel.

full-service schools
Schools that provide a variety of health and social services to students and their families in collaboration with the community.

Full-Service Schools

Full-service schools collaborate with community agencies to provide a variety of health and social services for students and their families (Dryfoos & Maguire, 2002; Smith, 2004). Some of these services are offered on the school campus and others are available through referrals. Examples of these services are health clinics, ESL (English as a Second Language) classes, and family welfare services. Such "one-stop" schools support students by supporting their families. They also strengthen ties between the school, parents, and the community, and are one of the policy recommendations made by the Carnegie Council on Adolescent Development (1989) as a way of improving education.

Parental Involvement

Effective schools also work to involve parents in their children's education. Adolescents whose parents are involved have more positive attitudes toward school, higher achievement scores, and higher educational aspirations (Fan & Chen, 2001; Hill et al., 2004). Parental involvement at school can take many forms, from volunteering in the classroom or cafeteria, to sitting down with teachers and administrators to discuss educational issues, to participating in parent-teacher organizations.

James Comer (2008), a physician and educator at Yale University, argues that parental involvement begins before their children ever enter school, and consists of providing the experiences that *prepare* children for learning—giving them a sense of worth, a belief in themselves, exposure to the wider world, and social skills for entering it. When the connections that bridge families with the community haven't been established, students find it difficult to experience education as meaningful.

Comer points out that too many intervention programs start with the assumption that students themselves are the source of the problem, pointing to their disruptive behavior in class, chronic absenteeism, and poor test performance as evidence. These beliefs only contribute to the problem, in that "expectations are internalized by the students and contribute to low levels of achievement and school failure. Parental hope that the school will make a difference for their children is lost, and a climate of distrust, anger, and alienation often replaces it" (Comer, 2008, p. 308). Comer's successful School Development Program brings parents and students into the decision-making process, involving them in various aspects of school governance in order to break the downward spiral of low expectations, anger, and alienation and foster genuine achievement.

School Safety

More important than a school's size or climate or the attitudes of its teachers is its ability to provide an environment in which students feel safe. In the past, safety was simply taken for granted. No longer. Among the top disciplinary problems listed by teachers in the 1940s were chewing gum and running in the halls. More recently, teachers have to be concerned about assault, rape, drug abuse, and robbery.

Teachers' concerns reflect students' realities. Nearly half of ninth-grade males in the United States report having been in physical fights at school, over 10% said they had been threatened or injured with a weapon, and nearly 6% reported that they sometimes felt too unsafe to go to school (CDC, 2008b) (Table 8.1). Differences among ethnic groups and between sexes are large. Myriad factors contribute to school violence, ranging from domestic violence, witnessing community violence, the presence of gangs, and the very real

TABLE 8.1
Percentage of Adolescents Experiencing Violence While at School, 2007

	9TH GRADE		12TH GRADE	
	FEMALE	MALE	FEMALE	MALE
Felt too unsafe to go to school	7.4	5.8	4.3	5.3
Carried a gun at least 1 day in last 30 days[a]	1.4	8.9	0.9	9.2
Carried a weapon such as a gun, knife, or club on school property	3.1	8.7	2.3	9.8
Been threatened or injured with a weapon on school property	6.8	11.4	4.5	8.1
Been in a physical fight at school	31.8	49.6	21.8	34.3
Had property stolen or damaged on school property	28.8	32.2	18.8	27.2

Source: CDC, 2008.

[a]Not necessarily on school property.

threats to personal safety—both at home and at school—for many adolescents. Additionally, seventy-eight percent of youth homicides involve firearms (CDC, 2005c). Nevertheless, explanations for school violence, especially school shootings, are elusive (see In More Depth Box 12.2).

Bullies and Victims

For some students, violence, or the threat of it, takes the form of bullying. Bullying is a fact of life for a significant number of adolescents. A nationally representative sample of over 15,000 sixth- through 10th-grade students in schools throughout the United States found that 16.9% of those sampled had experienced moderate or frequent bullying (Nansel et al., 2001). Olweus (2001) distinguishes bullying from teasing, which is done in a friendly or playful way, and from actual fights or arguments, which take place between students of about the same strength or power.

What is bullying? Dan Olweus (1978, 1993, 2001), a pioneer researcher in this field, defines **bullying** as repeated aggressive behaviors or remarks directed against a student by one or more others over a period of time, and against which the victim finds it difficult to defend himself or herself. There are three things to note in this definition of bullying: The actions are hurtful, they are repeated over time, and there's an imbalance of power between the aggressor and the victim. The import of being bullied, in other words, is not simply that one has been hurt in some way by another. Rather, it is that one can expect this to occur again and that there is little one can do to prevent it. As a consequence, victims of bullying never feel completely "safe" at school.

Among adolescents, middle schoolers are much more likely to be bullied than are high schoolers (Craig et al., 2001; Nansel et al., 2001; Pellegrini & Long, 2002). Nansel and her associates (2001) found that 13.3% of sixth-graders reported being bullied on a weekly basis and another 10.9% reported occasional bullying. Given figures such as these, it should come as no surprise

bullying Repeated aggressive behaviors or remarks occurring over an extended period of time that the victim finds difficult to defend against.

that middle schoolers list bullying as one of their major concerns. In contrast, the corresponding percentages for tenth-graders were 4.8% and 4.6%, respectively.

Bullying is likely to take a different form among boys than among girls. With boys, acts of direct physical aggression are common. Examples can range from knocking a book or cafeteria tray out of a victim's hands to pushing, tripping, hitting, or even locking a victim in a room. Direct verbal aggression, such as name-calling or teasing, is also common. Among girls, indirect forms of aggression are more typical, such as spreading rumors, excluding another girl from a group, or completely ignoring the victim. Girls also are just as likely as boys to experience verbal bullying (Nansel et al., 2001, Olweus, 2001).

Given the importance to early adolescents of connection with one's peers and of belonging to the group—that is, of establishing a group identity (see Chapter 7)—bullying can have genuinely harmful effects. Students who are bullied report experiencing anxiety, depression, feelings of loneliness, and a loss of self-esteem (Graham & Juvonen, 2002; Nansel et al., 2001; Olweus, 2001). They find it harder to make friends, and they do more poorly in school (Nansel et al., 2001).

Some adolescents are more likely to be bullied than others. The classic profile of a victim is an adolescent who is anxious and insecure and has low self-esteem (Olweus, 1978). Conversely, adolescents who are easygoing and friendly are less likely to be victimized (Jensen-Campbell et al., 2002). Also, bullying is somewhat more common among males than among females. Adolescent males typically react to bullying in one of two ways: passively or provocatively. Passive victims tend to be sensitive and quiet boys who are somewhat depressed and anxious, don't feel that they are liked by their peers, and have low self-esteem. All of these characteristics make them "easy marks." They are not likely to retaliate on their own or to rally support among their peers. But not all boys who are bullied are passively submissive.

Some victims are actually aggressive, being easily provoked by others and reacting angrily, their outbursts apparently targeting them for retaliation. These provocative victims, who make up a much smaller percentage of victims, share many of the characteristics of passive victims but differ from them in being hyperactive and more likely to engage in aggressive behavior. Their aggression differs from that of those who bully them, however, taking the form of unwitting emotional outbursts rather than being used intentionally to dominate others (Olweus, 1999, 2001; Salmivalli, 2001).

One might think that bullies would be rejected by their peers due to their aggressive behavior, but that typically is not the case (Olweus, 2001). Bullies do not stand out from their classmates in terms of popularity, but they do stand out in other ways. They tend to be more impulsive and aggressive than their peers and, at least among boys, to be somewhat bigger and stronger than their victims. Bullies and victims alike tend to score lower on measures of psychosocial adjustment, such as ease of getting along with others, social problem solving, and managing feelings of depression. The similarities don't end there. Many bullies are themselves victims of other bullies (Haynie et al., 2001; Nansel et al., 2001).

INTERVENTION PROGRAMS For an intervention program to be effective, teachers, staff, and parents, as well as students, must be aware of what is going on and be involved. Intervention programs typically entail actions at several levels. One of these programs, implemented by Olweus in the Norwegian school system, has been highly effective, reducing bullying by as much as 50% to 70% in some schools (Olweus, 2001). The program identifies actions at three levels: the school, the classroom, and the individual.

At the school level, the first step in reducing bullying is to provide individuals with information about the frequency with which this occurs. Many teachers and staff are unaware of the extent of victimization among students. Questionnaires filled out anonymously by teachers, students, parents, and staff can give accurate information about the frequency of bullying, and about where and when this is most likely to occur, as well as who is most likely to be involved.

Also important are measures that enable teachers and staff to identify bullying when they see it. This step entails coming up with a definition of bullying that everyone can understand and then engaging in a dialogue. The objective of such a dialogue is to incorporate this knowledge into school policies that promote healthy relationships among students, specifically addressing ways of preventing bullying and victimization.

To be effective, intervention programs need to be schoolwide. These programs work not just by changing the behavior of individual students or teachers, but by "restructuring" the school environment: At the end of the day everyone on campus knows that it is each student's right to feel safe at school, and that the school will not tolerate bullying.

Once teachers and staff are more informed about bullying, they're in a position to better supervise interactions among students, especially during unstructured times, such as lunch breaks, free periods, and before and after school.

At the class level, Olweus recommends the use of materials such as videos that show everyday occurrences of bullying. Videos can serve as a format for class discussions, both by helping students recognize bullying and by enabling them to identify with the effects of bullying. Students can react to bullying in a number of ways, from taking an active part themselves in the bullying to actively trying to help the victim. Olweus conceptualizes these roles in terms of their position within a "bullying circle" (**Figure 8.2**), which he uses in classes to stimulate discussions of ways of getting students to move from the left in the circle (the role of an aggressor) to the right (the role of a defender). Through discussions such as these, students are encouraged to speak up and to assume responsibility to try to stop bullying when they see instances of it.

Finally, at the individual level, talking with bullies is most effective when they do not have their support group present, that is, by meeting with them one-on-one. Once alone with a teacher or counselor, bullies are more likely to accept responsibility for their actions, especially if they are invited to think of ways to change the situation rather than being blamed for what they have done. Issues related to bullying, just as in parenting, are resolved best when approached in an authoritative, rather than an authoritarian, way (Pikas, 2002; Rigby, 2001). It's also helpful to speak with the victim as well as the bully, and then bring the concerns of each to the other, before having the students themselves meet to formally agree to what has been worked out. Typically, some training is needed for teachers or counselors to learn effective mediation procedures.

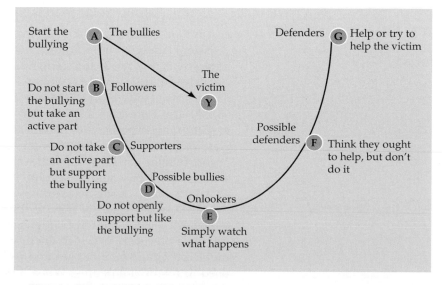

● **Figure 8.2   The bullying circle: Possible student responses to bullying**   (After Olweus, 2001.)

cooperative learning
Placing students of different ability levels together in small working groups.

conflict resolution training
Programs designed to teach students to view conflict as a problem to be solved mutually, with a win-win outcome.

constructive controversy
A technique using controversy to stimulate solutions to problems by having students alternately argue their own and the opposing side of a conflict.

male generic language
Use of the pronoun "he" to refer to an individual of either sex, and use of words such as "man" or "mankind" to refer to all people.

Teaching Peace

Conflicts will occur at school, of course, even in the absence of bullies. Morton Deutsch (1993) suggests several ways in which schools can "teach peace," by providing a variety of experiences that help students arrive at constructive ways to resolve conflict. Classrooms that are structured as **cooperative learning** environments or jigsaw classrooms help students develop interpersonal skills, since goals are shared by members of a group and competition is reduced. Students have more frequent opportunities to be helpful and cooperative in these learning environments than in the more traditional, individualistic, and competitive ones.

Also, some schools offer **conflict resolution training**, programs in which both teachers and students are trained in listening skills and conflict resolution. Programs in conflict resolution help students perceive conflicts as problems to be solved mutually by all involved, increasing the likelihood that all participants will leave satisfied, instead of solved competitively, with some winning and others losing.

Controversy, in itself, is not undesirable. Teachers can use classroom disagreements to stimulate students to think about problems in new ways and come up with creative solutions. An effective classroom technique, called **constructive controversy**, is to have students work in small groups in which pairs alternately argue for opposing positions and then reverse their arguments, taking their opponents' position and arguing as earnestly as they can for that. Finally, all work toward reaching a consensus.

Education for All

One of the challenges facing secondary schools today is to reach students with differing interests, backgrounds, and abilities using methods and materials that capture their interest and fire their imaginations. For this to occur, the materials schools use must be equally accessible to all their students.

Gender in the Classroom

Materials that show women and men in nontraditional roles or filling roles in proportion to their actual numbers in the workforce lead to greater flexibility in sex-role attitudes among students. Thus, students who read about females who are doctors or postal carriers and males who are telephone operators or daycare directors are less sex-typed in their approach to occupations in general and in their personal interest in these professions.

From Hamlet to Harry Potter, however, a majority of the central characters adolescents read about and see in films are males. Although females appear as frequently as males in illustrations for school materials, characters of either sex are portrayed differently. Males are shown in a greater variety of occupations as well as in more adventurous roles. The majority of a student's time in school is spent with various types of educational materials such as books, films, or class handouts. Even though many states have introduced regulations to ensure that the portrayal of females and males in textbooks is balanced, many schools do not buy new books until the old ones need replacing.

Another form of bias occurs through the gender characteristics of language itself. Many languages designate different words as either feminine or masculine. Although the English language does not, the use of **male generic language** is prevalent, in which the pronoun "he" is used to refer to an anonymous individual of either sex and words such as "'man" or "mankind" are used to refer to all people. When individuals are identified as female, it is often to call attention to the fact that they are not male, such as in terms like "woman doctor" or "actress." These usages suggest not only that doctors and actors ordinarily are males, but also that when they are females, they are different enough from "regular" doctors and actors to require different labels (Lips, 2008).

A formidable array of research shows that male generic language causes people to think of males, rather than people in general (Kennison & Trofe, 2003; Lenton et al., 2009; Liben et al., 2002). In one study, seventh-graders completed a story about a student's first day in their class. Some students read a story referring to the new student as "he"; others read stories in which the student could be of either sex. When the subject was referred to as "he," all the males and 80% of the females wrote stories describing the student as a male. When "he or she" or "they" were used, significantly fewer students referred to the new student as a male. Those most affected by the use of inclusive language were females; when the subject was referred to as "he or she" or "they," only 21% and 12%, respectively, wrote about a male student (Switzer, 1990). When we realize that teachers are just as susceptible to the influence of male generic language as students, the implications of these findings assume even larger proportions.

Male generic language also affects adolescents' judgments of how competent a woman is in different types of jobs. When students are asked to consider how well a woman might perform a fictional job (for example, a "surmaker"), their evaluations are influenced by the sex of the pronouns used to describe the characters performing the job. Women are thought to be least competent for the job when the surmaker is referred to as "he" and most competent when referred to as "she." Referring to doctors, mechanics, scientists, or artists as "he" has clear implications not only for adolescent females' ability to see themselves in those professions, but also for all students' evaluation of the relative competence of the men and women in those occupations (Hyde, 1984; Lips, 2008).

Multicultural Education

LaRue glanced briefly at his group as Mr. Brooks, his physical science teacher, finished giving the assignment: to study the activity of gases. That shouldn't be too difficult, he thought. But what would he do for his part? He had to think of common examples illustrating the properties of gases. Paulo had an easy part to present to the group; all he had to do was describe their chemical properties. Becky's part would be interesting: identifying the gases that are present in different substances. He could imagine the fun Yinpeng would have with that one. He liked his group. They worked well together, and it was more interesting than working on their own. But what could he contribute? Then he remembered the canned drinks he had put in the freezer— the juices had burst open but the soda hadn't. Of course, gases constrict and liquids expand when cold.

LaRue's physical science class is organized as a **jigsaw classroom**, in which students work in small groups that are balanced for ethnic background and ability. Each student in the group contributes a different part of the lesson. The parts fit together, much like the pieces of a jigsaw puzzle: One needs each part to see the whole picture. This approach to classroom learning fosters cooperation among students and promotes better relations among adolescents from different ethnic and cultural backgrounds (Aronson, 2002, 2004).

Even in classes that foster cooperative and friendly relations, minority adolescents often face problems that don't exist for those from the dominant culture. They do not always share the cultural perspective, for instance, that is assumed by much of their class material; many textbooks reflect a Eurocentric

jigsaw classroom   A classroom organized into small, ethnically balanced working groups in which each student contributes a different part of the lesson.

Minority students from cultures that value the group more than the individual may pay as much attention to the feelings of others as to the task at hand. This orientation can frustrate teachers, but serves the students well in group-learning situations and in the world outside the classroom.

bias in their portrayal of minorities, often omitting their contributions or presenting them negatively (Garcia, 1993; Hu-DeHart, 1993). African American comedian and social activist Dick Gregory once remarked that he and his friends used to root for the Indians against the cavalry, because they didn't think it was fair for textbooks to characterize the cavalry's winning as a great victory and the Indians' winning as a massacre. Many minority adolescents would agree. For them, life experiences frequently run counter to what they learn at school.

Seeing things from a different point of view can make otherwise easy material difficult to understand. Carpetbaggers, for instance, have traditionally been portrayed as low-life opportunists who turned the chaos following the American Civil War to personal advantage. Yet if one believes that members of the white majority at that time (or the present) have opportunistically taken advantage of minorities, this portrayal does not raise meaningful distinctions, or at least does not evoke the same sensitivities as it would for those whose views reflect the dominant culture. Similarly, does the westward expansion on the North American continent have the same implications for Native Americans, Hispanics, and African Americans as it does for European American students (Seixas, 1993)? Probably not. Classes that introduce multicultural perspectives surmount this difficulty. Asking students to describe the experiences of the pioneers, the Native Americans, and the Mexicans turns this problem into an advantage. The introduction of a multicultural perspective enriches all students' understanding of the issues surrounding westward expansion.

Textbooks used in courses such as U.S. history and literature frequently present a narrative account that evolves from a single frame of reference—a European American perspective. Many teachers uncritically adopt this same perspective. Students who do not share this view of history, as many minorities do not, will fail to experience these courses as "making sense." Yet teachers and textbooks are seen as authoritative sources, and students who cannot remember the facts as presented by them will be seen as the problem, not what they're asked to learn.

In the classroom, unfamiliar patterns of communication can complicate learning for minority students. The simple matter of asking questions can be a case in point for many students. Teachers ask questions in the classroom in a different way than do adults in their communities (Brice-Heath, 1982). Teachers use questions to stimulate classroom discussions and to focus ongoing behavior. It's common to ask about things the class has already discussed. Adults in the community, however, typically ask questions only when they want information they do *not* have. They rarely ask questions as a way of discussing issues or of channeling ongoing behavior into more desirable forms (as a teacher might, by asking a question of a student who is talking with a classmate to get that student to pay attention). Consequently, students may misunderstand questions regarding material the class has already covered ("What is she asking this for? We've gone over that."). Effective intervention depends on discovering differences such as these. The solution in this instance is for everyone—teachers, parents, and students—to be made aware of the different rules that regulate language in class and at home (Slaughter-Defoe et al., 1990).

Other problems can arise from lack of familiarity in using standard English, the language used in the classroom. Minority students may understand what's being said well enough but still not be at ease speaking in front of classmates if they speak a dialect at home. Using different languages at home and in school limits opportunities to practice the way they're expected to speak at school, and can cause students to be silent for fear of embarrassing themselves. Even written schoolwork can become problematic for students who have difficulty translating the ideas they frame easily in the intimate language of their home into standard English (Feldman et al., 1990).

In school, adolescents not only learn to master subjects such as math and biology, they are also taking steps toward becoming members of a larger society, one that awaits them outside the intimate confines of their homes. To the extent that this society, as mirrored in their schooling, does not reflect the comfort and safety they have known within their families, the step is a difficult one to take. In *Hunger of Memory*, Richard Rodriguez (1982) writes of his reluctance to take this step, by adopting English, the public language used in school:

> *Without question, it would have pleased me to hear my teachers address me in Spanish when I entered the classroom. I would have felt much less afraid. I would have trusted them and responded with ease. But I would have delayed—for how long postponed?—having to learn the language of public society. I would have evaded—and for how long could I have afforded to delay?—learning the great lesson of school, that I had a public identity.*

> *Fortunately, my teachers were unsentimental about their responsibility. What they understood was that I needed to speak a public language. So their voices would search me out, asking me questions. Each time I'd hear them, I'd look up in surprise to see a nun's face frowning at me. I'd mumble, not really meaning to answer. The nun would persist, "Richard, stand up. Don't look at the floor. Speak up. Speak to the entire class, not just to me!" But I couldn't believe that the English language was mine to use. (In part, I did not want to believe it.) I continued to mumble. I resisted the teacher's demands. (Did I somehow suspect that once I learned public language my pleasing family life would be changed?)*

Urie Bronfenbrenner (1979b) has described the experiences that make up an individual's reality in terms of overlapping spheres of influence (see Figure 1.2). At the most immediate of these, the microsystem, are an adolescent's first-hand experiences—interactions at home, in the classroom, and with friends. Interactions among the different microsystems of which one is a part constitute the mesosystem; it is at this level that minority adolescents frequently experience problems. They may see, for instance, that their parents distrust the system, or that teachers communicate less respect for their parents than for those of other students.

Adolescents experience the exosystem at the level of their communities. Available housing and the types of schools they attend reflect decisions made at the community level but which influence their lives directly. The macrosystem, which consists of the underlying social and political climate, is even further removed from adolescents' daily experiences, yet can impinge on their realities in very real ways. Laws concerning compulsory education, the mainstreaming of students with special needs, and the separation of grades into elementary, junior high, and high schools all illustrate the direct ways the macrosystem can affect the lives of adolescents. A less observable, but no less real, effect of the macrosystem is experienced in the form of beliefs, biases, and stereotypes. The values of the macrosystem can be at odds with those of the home microsystem for adolescents from some minority groups.

John Ogbu (1981, 1992) notes that educational programs have assumed that the problems evidenced by many minority students, such as poor attendance, high dropout rates, and low achievement, should be addressed at the level of the microsystem—by improving the home environment or enriching educational experiences. Ogbu suggests, however, that the problem is generated at the macrosystem level and can be solved only by changes introduced at that level. He attributes poor academic performance and high dropout rates among minorities to a "job ceiling," or discrimination in job opportunities, and to their perception that members of their own families have not been rewarded for their achievements.

If all adolescents progressed through the same social mobility system, one in which mobility, or social class, reflected their abilities, then the most effective method of intervention for minorities who are failing would be at the microsystem level, reaching into the home or classroom to bring their abilities and skills up to the level of the others. But do all members of our society move through the same mobility system? Is there more than one system, similar to academic tracking, in which students are assigned to one of several courses of study, but with respect to economic rather than educational opportunities?

If there is more than one mobility system, what factors other than ability and skill determine the system in which individuals participate? Notice that if we have more than one social mobility system, social class is an effect rather than a cause, and the problems of minorities must be addressed at another level. Social status among minorities, argues Ogbu, reflects the realities of a job ceiling: a consistent set of social and economic obstacles preventing equal selection based on ability imposed on certain minorities at birth—that is, a society stratified by ethnic and racial castes as well as by class. The problems of minority groups need to be addressed at multiple levels—at the macrosystem level as well as that of the microsystem level.

Academic Achievement

In this section, we will look at some of the factors that affect students' achievement. One of the single most important factors contributing to differences in achievement is socioeconomic level. As we will see, proficiency in basic subjects also differs from one country to the next. Within the United States, differences in achievement correspond to students' beliefs as well as their study habits.

Socioeconomic Status

Family income is consistently related to academic achievement. Students from low-income families score lower on achievement tests, get lower grades, and are less likely to finish high school (Felner et al., 1995; McLoyd, 1998). The reasons for these differences are many and varied. Low-income students are likely to have poorer nutrition and less adequate health care. Living spaces are more crowded, making it more difficult to find quiet places to study, and other obligations (such as caring for a younger sibling) compete with schoolwork. More frequent residential moves disrupt schooling and decrease the likelihood of parental involvement with their adolescent's school.

Additionally, low-income students have access to fewer resources such as books, computers, transportation for school events, or help with homework. They also are less likely to have role models in either their families or neighborhoods who have completed high school and gone on to college. Moreover, higher rates of unemployment in low-income neighborhoods offer less incentive for getting an education.

The quality of schools serving low-income versus middle- or high-income neighborhoods also differs, in both teaching staff and physical facilities. Schools in low-income neighborhoods are more likely to have teachers who are less experienced and less well trained in the subjects they are teaching. For instance, there are fewer teachers with master's degrees in low-income schools than in middle- or high-income schools. Also, substantially more teachers teach subjects in which they have not majored or for which they are not certified. These disparities are even greater in high-poverty schools, in which classes in math and science are two to three times more likely to be taught by someone not trained in the field. Schools in low-income neighborhoods are more likely to be overcrowded and have larger classes and fewer resources, even basic ones such as textbooks and supplies, not to mention computers or science labs. Furthermore, differences such as these in the quality of schools are likely to have been present for low-income students in the elementary grades as well, result-ing in lower scores in basic skills even before

Students attending schools in low-income neighborhoods are likely to have overcrowded classrooms, fewer resources such as computers, and teachers who are less well trained in the subjects they are teaching.

they enter secondary schools (National Center for Education Statistics, 2003). See **Box 8.3** for a description of one such school that turned itself around.

Existing public programs, however, can be effective in countering the effects of economic adversity on academic achievement. "Wraparound" early child-hood intervention programs that continue into the second or third grade, as opposed to ending in kindergarten, are particularly effective. Arthur Reynolds and Judy Temple (1998) found that students who had been in such programs had higher achievement scores in the seventh grade in reading and math and were less likely to have repeated a grade. Students in such programs are also less likely to need special education and more likely to finish high school (Reynolds et al., 2004; Reynolds et al., 2001).

academic tracking
The assignment of students to one of several courses of study in high school on the basis of criteria such as academic interests and goals, past achievement, and ability.

Addressing Diversity

Academic tracking is a common solution to problems created by the diverse interests and abilities of students. **Academic tracking** is the practice of offer-

---

BOX 8.3 **In More Depth**

Turning a School Around: Miami Central High

Miami Central High was about to be shut down. It had received five consecutive F grades for the past five years on the Florida Comprehensive Assess-ment Test (FCAT), the worst academic record in Florida. Teachers had difficulty maintaining disci-pline, students loitered in the halls, absenteeism was chronic, the physical campus was in disrepair, 14% of the students attended special education classes, and the school regularly flooded each sea-son, earning as its nickname "The Fishbowl." One more failing grade and the school would close.

Tests were two months away when Doug Rodriguez accepted the job as principal at Miami

Central, leaving his previous position at one of the top schools in the state. Over the next two months, Rodriguez got little sleep, teachers took special classes, students came to school on Satur-days, troubled students were routed to alternative schools—and there was no loitering in the halls.

Students and teachers alike bought into the changes, transformed by hard work, discipline and pride. The morning that the preliminary test results came out, no one knew which grade they'd finally achieved—but they all knew it wasn't an F!

Source: From McGrory, 2009.

Secondary school students are often divided into vocational and college-bound tracks. The mere assignment to one track or the other can profoundly affect students' performance and teachers' expectations.

parental involvement
The involvement of parents in classroom instruction, homework, school governance, and community service.

ing students several programs of study, with assignment to these based on prior achievement, stated goals, and the evaluations of counselors.

Most high schools offer at least two tracks—college preparatory and non-college—and many offer other options as well. Students in different tracks frequently do not take classes together even for the same course. Educators assume that multiple tracks allow students to work at different paces and teachers to adjust the content of their courses to match differing abilities and interests.

However, tracking may also contribute to the problems it was designed to correct. Adolescents from minority groups and low-income families are more likely to be placed in non-college than in college tracks. Of the students in non-college tracks, more lose interest in school and drop out than those in college preparatory tracks. Some research suggests that assignment to a lower track makes it more likely that students will work toward lower goals, proceed at a slower pace, have fewer opportunities to learn, and achieve less than students in higher tracks (Raudenbush et al., 1993; Snow, 1986).

Not all data support this conclusion. A nationwide study comparing students of similar ability levels attending schools in which tracking was either practiced or not practiced suggests that tracking may actually benefit students by enabling them to more favorably compare themselves with those of similar interests and abilities (Catsambis et al., 2001). And when tracking is restricted to a particular subject, such as math, neither students' academic self-concept nor their general self-esteem may be affected (Chiu et al., 2008).

An alternative to tracking for dealing with diversity is to place students of different ability levels together in small working groups. As identified earlier, cooperative learning gives students recognition for both their individual performance and that of the group. Power relationships subtly shift, placing the responsibility for learning on students rather than on the teacher. Cooperative learning increases achievement in many students and has eased tensions in multicultural classrooms as students learn to work together (Slavin, 1985; Slavin et al., 2003).

Another powerful alternative in the educational process is **parental involvement**. Parents can be involved in a number of ways: instructing students in the classroom, helping them at home, participating in school governance, and becoming involved in community service. James Comer and his colleagues (1985, 1996, 2006), at Yale University, have created a program in which parents, along with teachers, administrators, and staff, are responsible for administering the activities of the school. This program addresses the social and developmental, as well as the educational, needs of students. Comer believes, for instance, that social skills and ties to the community are as important as academic subjects, especially for

Learning in a group can be more interesting than learning on one's own. Students work in small groups that are balanced for ability, gender, and ethnic or racial background.

lower income students, who often lack these assets. In two inner-city schools using Comer's model, student performance so improved that the schools tied for third and fourth place in the district, with the students testing up to a year above the average for their grade! Attendance also improved dramatically, and behavior problems practically disappeared.

It is easy to understand why such a program could work: Teaching becomes more relevant when academic subjects are translated into the daily concerns of students and their families. In turn, what is learned in the classroom receives the support of parents who are committed to educational programs they help plan.

Despite their proven success, though, alternatives such as cooperative learning and Comer's model will not be beneficial unless teachers and staff are trained to use them effectively. Cooperative learning, for example, is a relatively complex technique to implement, requiring in-service training. Similarly, parental involvement can be cumbersome and can even increase conflict if parents' and teachers' views of education conflict.

Another alternative combines assignment to non-college tracks with actual **work experience** for which students receive academic credit. This approach also addresses the financial difficulties many low-income students face.

work experience   Receiving academic credit for work done on a job.

Academic Success

In general, mastery of basic skills such as reading (**Figure 8.3A**) and mathematics (**Figure 8.3B**) by adolescents in the U.S. has changed little over the last several generations, with the exception of African American and Hispanic adolescents, whose performance has improved significantly (Planty et al., 2009). With respect to international comparisons of basic skills, adolescents in the U.S. score below the international average in both mathematics and

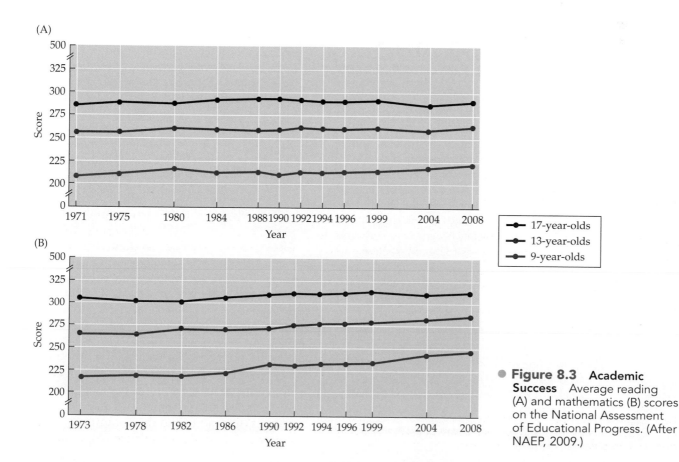

Figure 8.3   Academic Success   Average reading (A) and mathematics (B) scores on the National Assessment of Educational Progress. (After NAEP, 2009.)

● **Figure 8.4** Average scores on mathematics and science literacy assessments among 15-year-old students in selected countries (From OECD, 2008.)

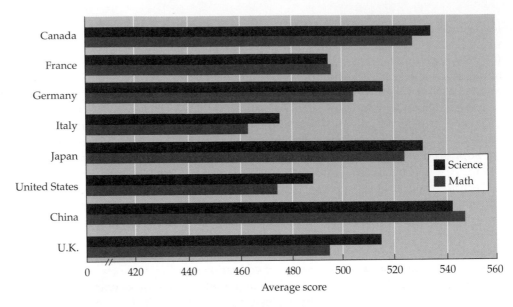

science (**Figure 8.4**) (OECD, 2008). Different approaches to teaching subjects such as mathematics adopted by other countries can significantly improve students' mastery of the subject. For one such approach, see **Box 8.4**.

Why do so many high school students fail to do better? Laurence Steinberg, Bradford Brown, and Sanford Dornbusch (1996) studied over 20,000 adolescents, talking as well with parents and teachers, in an effort to discover why some adolescents succeed in school and others do not. These investigators worked with an ethnically diverse sample, with nearly 40% of the adolescents from African American, Asian American, and Hispanic families, approxi-

BOX 8.4 | **In More Depth**

Teaching Mathematics for Understanding

Although "two plus two" will always equal four, there's more than one way to teach mathematics. James Stigler and Harold Stevenson (1991), intrigued by cultural differences in achievement in math, looked at the way mathematics is taught to North American and Asian students. They found a number of differences: In Asian classrooms, students spend more time interacting with each other and with the teacher than they do working alone at their desks. Lessons typically begin with a concrete problem, enabling students to become active participants in a process of discovery, rather than passive recipients of information. Additionally, up to eight times as much time is devoted to reviewing and summarizing what they have learned than in American classrooms. Let's take a look at a typical lesson in a fifth-grade class in Japan:

> The teacher walks in carrying a large paper bag full of clinking glass. Entering the classroom with a large paper bag is highly unusual, and by the time she has placed the

bag on her desk the students are regarding her with rapt attention. What's in the bag? She begins to pull items out of the bag, placing them, one-by-one, on her desk. She removes a pitcher and a vase. A beer bottle evokes laughter and surprise. She soon has six containers lined up on her desk. The children continue to watch intently, glancing back and forth at each other as they seek to understand the purpose of this display.

> The teacher, looking thoughtfully at the containers, poses a question: "I wonder which one would hold the most water?" (p. 14)

After getting a number of different answers, she asks how they can discover which answer is correct. The class agrees on a way of measuring each and is divided into familiar working groups, each assigned to measure one of the containers. Students move about the classroom, each group carrying out the procedures agreed on by the class and recording their observations in a notebook. When they are finished, the teacher stands at the blackboard and asks a child from each group to report what that group has found:

BOX 8.4 *continued*

She has written the names of the containers in a column on the left and a scale from 1 to 6 along the bottom. Pitcher, 4.5 cups; vase, 3 cups; beer bottle, 1.5 cups; and so on. As each group makes its report, the teacher draws a bar representing the amount, in cups, the container holds.

Finally, the teacher returns to the question she posed at the beginning of the lesson: Which container holds the most water? She reviews how they were able to solve the problem and points out that the answer is now contained in the bar graph on the board. She then arranges the containers on the table in order according to how much they hold and writes a rank order on each container, from 1 to 6. She ends the class with a brief review of what they have done. No definitions of ordinate and abscissa, no discussion of how to make a graph preceded the example—these all became obvious in the course of the lesson. And only at the end did the teacher mention the terms that describe the horizontal and vertical axes of the graph they had made. (pp.14–15)

Stigler and Stevenson liken such lessons to a good story. They are organized around a central drama and capture students' interest. Like a story, they have a beginning in which a problem is intro-duced, a middle that is characterized by a search for a solution, and an end in which the problem is mastered. They also, like good stories, maintain students' interest and capture their imaginations. Furthermore, lessons are not interrupted by extraneous activities that would break students' interest or lessen the experience of discovery and mastery at their conclusion. Nearly 50% of American fifth-grade math lessons, for instance, experienced some interruption, whereas fewer than 10% of classes were interrupted in Asian classrooms.

Finally, the amount of time devoted to actual instruction is greater in Asian classrooms. American lessons are more likely to have students working on problems at their seats, with the teacher walking around answering questions. In the fifth grade, teacher-led instruction accounts for only 46% of class time in U.S. classrooms, in contrast to 90% of class time in Taiwan and 74% in Japan (see **Figure**). Put another way, there was no one guiding the instructional period for only 9% of the time in Taiwan and 26% in Japan, but this was true for 51% of the time in U.S. classrooms, leaving U.S. children to work by themselves for relatively long periods of time during which they may have had difficulty focusing on their work or understanding how it was relevant.

Source: From Stigler & Stevenson, 1991.

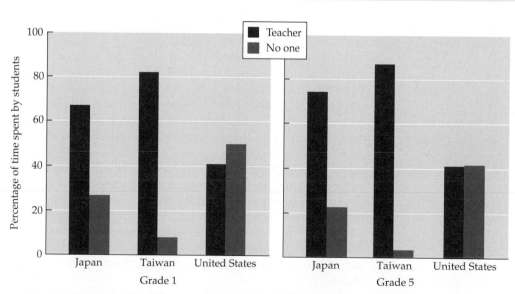

Percentage of time students in Japan, Taiwan, and the United States spend in teacher-led instruction versus instruction led by no one. (Stigler & Stevenson, 1991.)

Why are some students engaged in school and others unmotivated? One of the key contextual factors is beliefs about the future consequences of success or failure in school.

mately the percentage that will soon characterize the general U.S. population. A number of their findings are disturbing; others are equally encouraging.

One of the more unsettling findings is that many high school students are disengaged from school. Over a third said they spend much of their time during the school day "goofing off with their friends," and many admitted to cheating on their schoolwork. On average, these students spent only four hours a week doing homework, a figure that is roughly equivalent to the number of hours per *day* spent by students in other industrialized nations. In addition to spending time with friends outside of school, two-thirds of high school students had part-time jobs, many working more than 15 hours a week, and many intentionally taking easier classes to reduce their workload while maintaining their grades.

These investigators suggest that the problems in secondary education are due not so much to what is taking place in the classroom as to what is going on outside the classroom—at home, with friends, and in the community. This is not to say that the quality of schooling does not matter; rather, it points to the importance of the larger context in contributing to the influence schools can have. What contextual factors might be supporting this disengagement from school?

One factor appears to be students' beliefs about how important it is for them to do well in school in order to be successful once they graduate. In a nationwide survey, only about 40% of European American high school seniors indicated that good grades were of great importance to them. In contrast, about 60% of African American students believed this to be of importance (U.S. Department of Health and Human Services, 2002c). These investigators found that although students believe that future success is related to graduating from high school, they do not relate success to how well they did in their classes. In other words, they believe that having a diploma is important, rather than what they have learned. Given this belief, it is not surprising that many put so little work into their classes. These students appear to be motivated more by the need to avoid failing, or the fear of not graduating, than by the need to get something out of their classes.

How might one change this motivational pattern? Several answers were suggested, interestingly, by differences in achievement among adolescents from different ethnic backgrounds. Specifically, Asian American adolescents consistently outperformed European American adolescents, who performed better than African American or Hispanic adolescents. These differences existed even after other factors that are known to relate to academic success, such as family income or parental education, had been controlled for. In fact, ethnicity was more importantly related to academic achievement than any other factor, including affluence. As these investigators note, mention of ethnic differences in academic achievement is a sensitive subject, leading as it does to questions of differences in native ability. A more probable explanation than native ability, however, is that Asian American students simply work harder and have more adaptive attitudes toward school; if they really were superior, they would not be likely to put in twice as many hours on homework as other students.

So, what is it that contributes to the academic success of Asian American students? We've mentioned one factor—effort. They spend more time on schoolwork than their peers. Differences in their beliefs, however, are also important. Steinberg and his associates found that students from different ethnic backgrounds differed little in their beliefs about school success or the importance of getting a good education, but they did differ in their beliefs about failing in school. When asked, for instance, if they thought that not doing well in school would interfere with their ability to get a good job, striking differences emerged. Asian American students, more so than any others, believed that not doing well would hurt their chances for later success. These investigators point out that it is excessive optimism, not pessimism, that is the problem for many African American and Hispanic students: They do not believe that doing poorly in their classes will affect their later success.

Asian American adolescents have also been found to report more positive feelings when engaged in activities they perceive as "work-like," indicating they feel happier, enjoy themselves more, and feel better about themselves when doing these than do European American adolescents. Over 60% of the time these activities were related to school, taking place either in the classroom or outside it, such as with homework. Their feelings, however, were no more positive than those of other adolescents when the activities they were engaged in were unrelated to work. Such findings suggest that, in part, the greater academic success of Asian Americans reflects having internalized cultural values concerning the importance of hard work and academic achievement (Asakawa & Csikszentmihalyi, 1998). Other research, as well, underscores the importance of hard work and self-discipline for academic success. Angela Duckworth and Martin Seligman (2005) found that self-discipline, rather than measured intelligence, was the best predictor of how well students would do in school. In other words, work habits, and not ethnicity, are key to academic success.

What are the encouraging findings from this research? Perhaps the most important is the power for change that lies within the reach of parents (Sorkhabi, 2005; Steinberg et al., 1996). Most parents value education and want their adolescents to succeed in school. However, not all ways of parenting are equally effective in promoting academic achievement. The most effective parents are accepting (versus rejecting), are firm (versus lenient), and encourage autonomy in their children (versus controlling them). This type of parenting is known as authoritative parenting (see Chapter 6). Authoritative parenting, in addition to promoting competence, maturity, and academic success, can also offset negative peer influences. Parental expectations, and adolescents' perceptions of these, contribute significantly to academic achievement. When parents become engaged, their children become engaged as well, and academic achievement improves (Comer et al., 1996; Hill et al., 2004).

The Power of Positive Thinking: Patterns of Achievement

The power of positive thinking is getting some scientific backing. The attitude adolescents take toward their successes and failures is an important determinant of future success. It's not so much whether they fail or succeed—we all experience our share of both; it's what adolescents attribute their failure or success to that determines whether they will persist and eventually achieve. Research distinguishes two quite different patterns of achievement behavior: one defined by a focus on the task and what it takes to master it, a **task-mastery orientation**, and the other by a focus on one's performance or ability, a **performance-ability orientation**. The first approach is adaptive; the second is not (Dweck, 2002; Midgley et al., 1996). We saw these two patterns earlier in this chapter in the discussion of school climate; schools also define success and achievement in these ways.

Adolescents who are task, or mastery, oriented enjoy situations that challenge them, and they work at them even when they are difficult. They even take pride in how much effort they have to put into mastering something

task-mastery orientation
A motivational pattern in which students focus on the task they are learning and work to increase their mastery and competence.

performance-ability orientation   A motivational pattern in which students focus on their own performance, using it as a way to assess their ability.

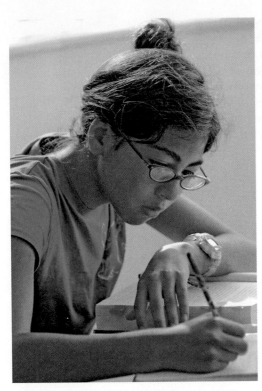

Task-oriented students, who focus on the task to be learned and work to increase their mastery and competence, are more likely to succeed than are students who are primarily concerned with the performance aspects of learning.

self-handicapping strategies
The adoption of behaviors to account for poor performance in lieu of ability.

new. Adolescents who are performance, or ability, oriented avoid challenging situations and show little persistence in the face of difficulty.

Performance-oriented adolescents tend not to pursue challenging material unless they're sure they will succeed. They choose situations that will not reveal what they regard as their lack of ability. These students are likely to prefer tasks that are either very easy or very difficult; failure at the first is unlikely, and failure at the second cannot be taken as a measure of their ability. Even above-average students who are performance oriented will avoid situations that involve risk in preference to situations where they can perform effortlessly and thereby feel smart. In doing so, however, they can miss situations that promote further understanding (Grant & Dweck, 2003).

Carol Dweck (1999; Dweck & Molden, 2005) focuses on students' beliefs about the nature of intelligence in explaining different patterns of achievement. Differences between students who allow themselves to be challenged by difficult tasks and those who shy away from these can be traced to underlying beliefs about intelligence. Those who believe that their intellectual skills can actually be developed by working through difficult tasks are likely to be mastery oriented. Conversely, those who view intelligence as something one is born with, that's fixed and can't be changed, are more likely to be performance oriented. These adolescents are likely to be disrupted by failure, frequently to the point of giving up. Because they interpret failure to mean that they lack the ability for what they have attempted, they defensively withdraw in the face of it. To believe this is also to believe that trying harder isn't going to help. Rather than trying harder, these students are more likely to explain their failure as bad luck or the task as being too difficult. For them, having to work hard to achieve is dangerous; it's just another way of calling their ability into question.

Carol Midgley, Revathy Arunkumar, and Timothy Urdan (1996) examined the use of **self-handicapping strategies** among African American and European American early adolescents. Such strategies are behaviors—such as not studying until the last minute or partying the night before a test—that could be seen as a cause of poor performance when students do not do well. Like achievement attributions, students may use strategies such as these to explain their performance in achievement situations; however, self-handicapping strategies are put into play before, rather than after, a student experiences success or failure. Thus, instead of explaining why one failed a test that one had actually studied for by saying that one hadn't studied hard enough (achievement attribution), one might intentionally not study until the night before (self-handicapping strategy), using inadequate time to study as an excuse for failing. Self-handicapping strategies hold the allure of a win-win situation: If one does poorly, those strategies provide an excuse, and if one does well, they make one appear even smarter. The disadvantages to their use are two-edged: Not only do they actually handicap students, making failure more likely; they also interfere with the use of adaptive ways of coping with achievement demands.

Given what we know of the ways adolescents interpret failure, we might suspect that some are more likely to self-handicap than others. Midgley and associates found, as suspected, that adolescents who adopt a performance-ability orientation to achievement situations more frequently report using these strategies. Additionally, even though the grade-point averages for African American and European American students did not differ, African

American students who adopted a performance-ability orientation were more likely to self-handicap than were European American students. This difference is particularly surprising because African American adolescents were more positive in their self-esteem and certain attitudes toward school than European American adolescents were. Claude Steele (1992; Steele & Aronson, 1995) suggests a possible explanation. Steele argues that African American students face an additional challenge to their ability, which he terms stereotype threat. **Stereotype threat** is the risk of confirming a negative stereotype about one's ethnic group, and hence about oneself, a threat that may increase the use of self-handicapping strategies as a self-defense.

stereotype threat
The perceived risk of confirming a negative stereotype.

Gender Differences and Achievement

Gender, as well, is related to perceptions of academic competence (Johns et al., 2005; Ryan & Ryan, 2005). With regard to late adolescents, Jennifer Steele, Jacquelyn James, and Rosalind Barnett (2002) found that female college students also experienced stereotype threat when taking courses in traditionally male-dominated fields such as math, science, and engineering. Beliefs about competency in different domains are established early (Hyde & Durik, 2005; Tenenbaum & Leaper, 2003). David Cole and his associates (1999), at Notre Dame, followed children and early adolescents over a three-year period, starting in the third and sixth grades, periodically obtaining estimates of their competency beliefs. By the fourth or fifth grade, differences associated with gender emerged, with boys overestimating their abilities and girls underestimating theirs. These differences increased with age through early adolescence. Similarly, Jennifer Herbert and Deborah Stipek (2005) found that by the third grade, girls evaluated their competency in math lower than did boys even though they performed at the same level.

Dweck (2002) points out that teachers and parents can help male and female students alike adopt more adaptive achievement motives by focusing on their efforts and not on their successes. Students who are praised for sticking with a challenging task until they eventually master it, learn to value the effort that's often needed to solve new tasks. Giving them feedback about the strategies they're using is important since this focuses them on the process of learning and what they can do to improve it. Students who are praised for the strategies they come up with when faced with challenging tasks, and not for how smart they are when they solve problems quickly, will actually enjoy having to work at something until they discover an approach that is successful.

Females frequently respond to success and failure in different ways than do males. Males are likely to attribute their successes to their ability and their failures to lack of effort. What this means, of course, is that males will persist at a problem until, more likely than not, they get it right. Females are more likely to attribute their successes to hard work, luck, or the ease of the task, and their failures to lack of ability, thereby discounting their successes and taking responsibility only for their failures. This interpretation can make females helpless in the face of success; they're not sure how they did it and unsure whether they could do it again. Females can be equally helpless in the face of failure. Because they attribute it to their inability, they have little recourse but to give up and try something new (Dweck, 1986, 2002).

These motivational patterns frequently become evident only when adolescents enter junior high. Prior to this point, course material may not be sufficiently challenging to prompt defensive withdrawal. Mathematics represents a case in point. Girls and boys perform equally in math throughout elementary school. Dweck (1986, 2002) notes that achievement in math takes a new turn in junior high, one that is likely to call into play the gender differences in motivational patterns that we have been discussing. Dweck points out that math, unlike verbal tasks, often requires students to determine which solutions are

Female students, even gifted ones, are more likely than male students to attribute initial confusion about a task to their own inability, rather than to the nature of the task itself, and consequently to withdraw in the face of failure.

gifted Description of students who place above a predetermined cutoff point on intelligence scales or who demonstrate special talents in diverse areas.

appropriate to which problems. In verbal tasks they can follow the same approach with new material as with the old. Whether a word is dog or dogmatic, if it is unfamiliar, the solution is the same: Look it up in the dictionary. New problems in math often require students to adopt a different approach, and they are likely to make errors at first. The initial confusion that results is more likely to interfere with the performance of girls than with that of boys.

Dweck (2002) cautions that maladaptive motivational approaches can have cumulative effects. They can lead female adolescents to take fewer math courses and consequently to become less skilled than males in math. As math is a "gateway" subject, opening up possibilities in fields such as medicine, engineering, and most branches of science, this poses a very real stumbling block.

Adolescents at the Edge

Three quite different groups of students have special needs and frequently find themselves out of step with the rest of the class. These adolescents come from all backgrounds. They are the gifted, those with learning disabilities, and those who drop out.

Gifted Adolescents

In 1925 Lewis Terman, of Stanford University, defined the gifted as those who place among the top 2% on a test of intelligence. Today, as well, the most common criterion for placing students in special educational programs is still a score on an intelligence test: 130 or higher. The following descriptions come close to what the average person is likely to think of as gifted: the super smart, the ones who ace school, the kids behind the books. But does giftedness embrace more than this?

In 1981 Congress passed the Education Consolidation and Improvement Act, which defines giftedness more broadly. The **gifted** and talented are those "who give evidence of high-performance capability in areas such as intellectual, creative, artistic, leadership capacity, or specific academic fields, and who require services or activities not ordinarily provided by the school in order to fully develop such capabilities" (Sec. 582).

Howard Gardner (2006) also includes more than traditional measures of intelligence in defining giftedness. Gardner considers multiple domains of intelligence: musical, bodily-kinesthetic, logical-mathematical, linguistic, spatial, interpersonal, intrapersonal, and naturalist (Table 4.1). Adolescents can be creative in any of these different domains, and for Gardner, creativity is the highest form of functioning. Creativity and giftedness, however, are not neatly related. Many gifted individuals are also highly creative, but many are not. Also, many creative people are not intellectually gifted.

IDENTIFYING GIFTED STUDENTS   Perhaps because intelligence reflects our personalities, gifted adolescents fail to fit any stereotype. It is easy to identify those who have large vocabularies or who top out on standard tests of achievement. But what about the ones who never see things the way others do, have zany senses of humor or vivid imaginations, those who get bored easily or who, when they can't do things perfectly, fail to do them at all? Gifted adolescents are likely to fit any of these descriptions as well.

Barbara Clark (1988), an educator at California State University, Los Angeles, offers nearly two dozen characteristics (**Table 8.2**) as indices of cognitive giftedness. Many of these characteristics would not be taken as signs of unusual talent or intelligence by most of us. Some, in fact, seem to signal just the opposite.

TABLE 8.2
Some Characteristics of Gifted Students

Asks many questions	Completes part of an assignment and leaves it unfinished for something else
Has much information on many topics	Continues to work on an assignment when the rest of the class moves on to something else
Adopts a questioning attitude	
Becomes unusually upset at injustices	Is restless
Is interested in social or political problems	Daydreams
Has better reasons than you do for not doing what you want done	Understands easily
	Likes to solve problems
Refuses to drill on repetitive tasks	Has own ideas as to how things should be done
Becomes impatient when can't do an assignment perfectly	
Is a loner	Talks a lot
Is bored and frequently has nothing to do	Enjoys debate
	Enjoys abstract ideas

Source: Clark, 1988.

Most gifted adolescents not only excel academically, they typically apply their intelligence to advantage in other areas of their lives as well. They tend to be more mature, have better social skills, and be more self-confident, responsible, and self-controlled. So much for the negative stereotypes of the gifted as bookworms and wimps.

Being gifted does not offer immunity to social and emotional setbacks, though. In fact, it may make them harder to take. Social injustices can be especially difficult for those concerned with social or political problems, and slights can easily be exaggerated by those who react to life intensely and with passion. Adolescents who sailed through grade school with nothing lower than an A can be devastated when they get their first B. And gifted adolescents—just like others—must cope with emotions and concerns magnified by the changes of puberty.

EDUCATING GIFTED STUDENTS   Educational programs follow one of two alternatives: enrichment or acceleration. The goal of **enrichment** is to provide gifted students with more opportunities and experiences than they would normally get, without moving them to a higher grade. An example would be offering special courses in literature, math, science, or the arts, along with their normal course of studies. **Acceleration** allows gifted students to advance beyond their grade level at a faster than normal rate—that is, skipping grades. Advocates of enrichment point to the social and emotional needs of gifted students, arguing that these are best met by keeping them with others their age. Although many gifted adolescents are socially and emotionally more advanced than their peers, this argument is especially compelling for late maturers, especially boys.

On the other hand, failure to advance the highly gifted can present as many problems as acceleration. Adolescents who experience little or no intellectual challenge in their classes and feel they are simply "marking time" can face intellectual stagnation, loneliness, and apathy—difficulties as serious as any introduced by moving ahead of their age-mates.

enrichment   Providing gifted adolescents with additional opportunities and experiences.

acceleration   Allowing gifted adolescents to advance beyond their grade level at a faster than normal rate.

Adolescents with Learning Disabilities

For some students, marking time takes a very different form. They, too, have difficulty maintaining interest in their classes but for reasons very different from those of gifted students. These students have experienced difficulty in

learning disability
Difficulty with academic tasks that is not due to emotional or sensory problems and presumably reflects neurological dysfunction.

school almost from the beginning. Many live with the bewildering sense that something is wrong, though they can't say what. Most feel stupid, though they are not. These adolescents have a learning disability.

DEFINING LEARNING DISABILITIES   Who are these students, and what special problems do they face? Answers focus on three defining features of **learning disabilities**: (1) a discrepancy between expected and actual performance, (2) difficulty with academic tasks that cannot be traced to emotional problems or sensory impairment, and (3) presumed neurological dysfunction.

First, learning-disabled students show a discrepancy between expected and actual performance. Students with a learning disability are of average or above-average intelligence but don't perform at the level one would expect based on their intelligence; they frequently fall at least two grade levels behind their peers in academic skills. Second, their difficulty with academic tasks cannot be traced to emotional or sensory dysfunction. They may experience difficulty in one or more specific areas (for example, reading or math) or in the general skills needed for many areas, such as being able to pay attention or to monitor their performance (such as remembering which subroutines they have completed in a math problem in order to begin the next).

They do not have a learning disability if the source of the difficulty is an emotional problem, problems at home, or a sensory impairment, such as a hearing loss. Finally, students with a learning disability are presumed to have some *neurological dysfunction*, because they are of at least average intelligence and their difficulties are not primarily the result of sensory, emotional, or cultural causes (Pass & Dean, 2008).

ADDRESSING PROBLEMS   Learning-disabled adolescents face problems both inside and outside the classroom. In the classroom, problems can range from difficulty paying attention or following class discussions to failure to turn in written assignments. Learning- disabled students have difficulty keeping up with classmates. A national study of 30,000 10th-graders found that twice as many students with a learning disability as nondisabled students placed in the bottom 25% of their class (Owings & Stocking, 1985). Performance for learning-disabled students is likely to be anywhere from two to four grades below for junior high students and can be even greater for high school students. In addition, most learning-disabled students have poorer study habits, are less likely to do their homework, and, when it comes to demonstrating what they have learned, have poorer test-taking skills. Frequently, nonattendance, incomplete assignments, and failure to turn in homework contribute to their failure in a course as much as their test scores. For a look at the effect of distractions on boys with learning disabilities, see **Box 8.5**.

The problems of learning-disabled adolescents don't end when they leave the classroom. As a group, they have poorer social skills than other students. They are less likely to pick up on another's mood and respond appropriately, and they are less aware of the effect their behavior has on others. Subtle cues can go right by them. The same problems that make it difficult for them to understand what their teachers are saying in class can affect their interactions with friends. They may miss nuances of conversation and respond inappropriately or miss rule changes in a game and feel they've been taken advantage of when the old rules no longer apply. Frequently, they prefer the company of those who are younger, just because they are more compliant.

Learning-disabled students are less likely to be involved in extracurricular activities than other students. Perhaps this fact reflects their general disenchantment with school. Or it may reflect a poorer self-image and expectations of failure in these activities as well. Increasing learning-disabled students' involvement in extracurricular activities such as teams, clubs, and music and

BOX
8.5

Research Focus

Within-Subjects Design and Attention Deficit Disorder: "Can't I Stay Home? I Think I Don't Feel Well."

Robbie hated going to school. He didn't *dislike* going to school. He actually hated it. And Monday mornings were the worst. He hadn't always felt this way. As a matter of fact, he had liked school at first. But things had started to change soon enough. He never could seem to finish his work on time, couldn't concentrate, and was continually distracted by events around him. The least little thing would pull his attention away from what he was doing—someone walking outside the classroom, a fly buzzing overhead, even the sound of someone else's pencil. He had trouble remembering things, too. He would forget assignments or lose the ones he had done. Sometimes he even had difficulty recalling what an assignment had been about. Yes, school made him feel crazy. And it made him feel stupid.

Robbie was anything but stupid. Like 3% to 5% of those in school, Robbie suffered from attention-deficit hyperactivity disorder (ADHD), a learning disability more common among males than females (American Psychiatric Association, 1994). Students with ADHD have difficulty sustaining their attention on the task at hand, are easily distracted by what is going on around them, and often act impulsively, saying or doing whatever comes to mind. Many, though not all, are also hyperactive. ADHD is most likely multiply determined. A number of factors, both genetic and environmental, have been identified as contributing to this disorder. Thus, students identified with ADHD are likely to find that others in their family are also affected. Environmental factors reflect a wide range of experiences, from prenatal exposure to teratogens, or factors that interfere with normal development, to the amount of structure adolescents experience at home or in their classrooms.

Steven Landau, Elizabeth Lorch, and Richard Milich (1992) investigated the effects of one type of structure, the presence or absence of distracters in the room, on ADHD boys' ability to sustain attention to an outgoing task. These investigators reasoned that if boys with ADHD attend significantly less to a task than do other boys when distracters are present but show little difference when they are absent, the difficulties they experience reflect problems not so much in sustaining attention as in selective attention, or screening out distractions. To this end, they had ADHD subjects and control subjects watch two segments from the television show "3-2-1 Contact." While the boys were watching one segment, no distracting toys were present; while they were watching the other, they were available. The researchers measured both the percentage of time boys attended to the programs and how much they remembered of the programs. Finally, each group of boys was divided into younger (6-9 years) and older (10-12 years) subjects.

These investigators used a within-subjects design, in which each subject experienced each of the distraction conditions (toys present, toys absent). This design can be compared with a between-subjects design in which each subject would experience only one condition (see Research Focus Box 10.1 in Chapter 10). Within-subjects designs are *economical*, requiring fewer subjects, because the same subjects react to all conditions. They are also *sensitive*. A design is sensitive to the extent that it can pick up, or detect, differences resulting from the experimental treatment. Within-subjects designs are sensitive because they use the same subjects in all conditions, thus reducing variability due to individual differences.

Despite these important advantages, this type of design has several serious disadvantages. First, there is the risk of *carryover effects*, in which the effect of one treatment is still present when the next is given. In this example, subjects who previously watched the program with attractive toys present in the room may be distracted by thoughts of playing while viewing the subsequent program even though there are no distracters present. Carryover effects are not necessarily symmetrical for each of the orders in which different subjects watch programs under different conditions; watching with no distracters present first might have no effect on subsequent viewing. In addition to carryover effects, there can be *order effects* with this design. These reflect systematic changes in performance over time due to factors such as practice, fatigue, boredom, and so on. Both carryover and order effects introduce the potential for confounding. *Confounding* exists when the difference between treatments can be explained in more than one way,

(continued on next page)

BOX 8.5 continued

that is, when an experiment lacks internal validity (see the Research Focus "Internal and External Validity: Cholas and Gang Girls" on the Web site).

Landau, Lorch, and Milich *counterbalanced* the order in which subjects experienced the two distracter conditions. Counterbalancing presents each condition an equal number of times in each order, thus balancing any effects due to order equally across conditions.

What did they find? First, with respect to attending to the program, the ADHD boys did not differ from the control boys in the percentage of time they attended to the programs when no distracters were present. However, when distracters were present, they spent only half the time attending to the programs that the other boys did. Age was also a factor with respect to length of attention, with older boys paying more attention, but only when distracting toys were present. When there were no distracters in the room, younger boys were as attentive as older ones. With respect to remembering what they had seen, ADHD boys did not differ from controls in their ability to recall aspects of the programs they had watched. Further, having distracters present interfered with recall only for the younger boys. These findings suggest that environmental structure, in the form of removing potential distracters, may be useful in helping students with ADHD attend to the tasks at which they are working. Medication, in the form of stimulants such as Ritalin, has also proven helpful in improving attention (Barkley, 1990). Such treatment, however, is most effective when used in conjunction with programs that teach adolescents how to structure their learning environments so as to support the behaviors they will need to maintain.

Sources: From American Psychiatric Association, 1994, and Landau et al., 1992.

---

mainstreaming
Keeping learning-disabled students in regular classrooms.

special education consultant   A consultant who meets with teachers to discuss ways to meet the needs of learning-disabled students who are mainstreamed.

special education classes
Classes for learning-disabled students that are tailored to the needs of each student.

drama productions might be one of the most important ways to increase their participation and their motivation to stay in school.

SCHOOLING LEARNING-DISABLED ADOLESCENTS   **Mainstreaming** places learning-disabled adolescents in regular classes. The most common accommodation teachers make is to adjust their grades. Perhaps because so little is done to meet the special needs of the learning-disabled in most classrooms, mainstreaming can introduce special problems of attendance. A growing number of schools that mainstream learning-disabled students provide a **special education consultant** who meets with regular teachers to discuss ways of managing the needs of these students. This procedure allows students to attend classes with their peers while receiving materials designed by someone who has specialized in learning disorders.

The other extreme from mainstreaming places learning-disabled students in **special education classes**. The obvious advantages of such an approach are small classes in which materials can be personalized to the needs of students and a teacher who is experienced in the special needs of the learning-disabled. A disadvantage is that special education teachers may not be as well versed in all subjects as regular high school teachers. Association with nondisabled students who might serve as positive role models is limited, and teachers may not hold learning-disabled students to the same standards that are required of other students.

Dropping Out

Dropping out, for most students, is the last step on a path begun years earlier. These students are likely to have experienced more school failure than their classmates, to lack basic skills, to have been held back a grade, to report less satisfaction with school, and to have higher rates of absenteeism. Interviews with adolescents who have dropped out of high school corroborate these findings (Tidwell, 1988). When asked why they dropped out, they mention poor grades, dislike of school, trouble with teachers, and financial problems. Many mention home responsibilities, pregnancy, and marriage. Almost all said they would not recommend dropping out to a friend or sibling.

Relationships within the family are important as well. Adolescents who have poor relationships with their parents are at increased risk of dropping out, as are those with a parent or older sibling who has dropped out. Conversely, those whose parents are supportive and have been involved in their schooling are less likely to drop out even though other risk factors may be present (Englund et al., 2008).

Disproportionate numbers of students who drop out are economically disadvantaged and, in relation to this, are more likely to belong to an ethnic minority, with the exception of Asian American students. Socioeconomic status confers numerous advantages as one moves up the economic ladder. Adolescents from higher income homes have broader cultural experiences, attend better schools, have parents with more time (and skills) to help with homework, and experience lower levels of stress within the family. Not surprisingly, family income level is associated with achievement and staying in school (Englund et al., 2008; Pagani et al., 2008; Tenenbaum et al., 2007).

Parental attitudes toward education are also important. Interviews of African American and Hispanic mothers revealed that they place a high value on getting good grades—often a higher value than does the dominant culture (**Figure 8.5**). In addition to the value placed on education in African American and Hispanic families, these differences may reflect an awareness of the greater need for their children to achieve in order to overcome existing social biases (Stevenson et al., 1990).

EFFECTIVE PROGRAMS   Peter Coleman (1993), at Simon Fraser University, contends that rather than seeing dropouts as a problem within the school system, they are instead a measure of its quality. Because dropouts are part of the system, programs that reach them should benefit all students.

At this point, we have some idea what makes schools more effective. We know, based on Comer's model, described earlier in this chapter, that schools which train students in social skills, involve parents, and establish ties with the community are more successful. Comer invited parents to participate; parents also become involved when schools provide a variety of school-based or refer-

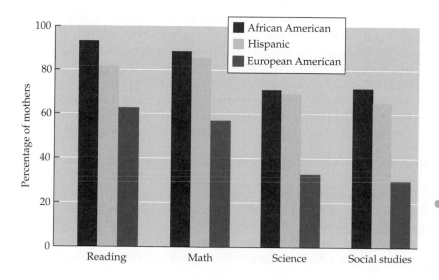

● **Figure 8.5** **Percentage of mothers, by ethnicity, placing high value on academic achievement in various subjects** (After Stevenson et al., 1990.)

computer-assisted instruction (CAI) The use of computers to provide instruction as well as to monitor student progress provides flexibility that helps students continue their education, even when their schedules are erratic.

ral services to students and their families, as they do in full-service schools. Each of these practices makes classroom experiences more relevant to experiences outside the classroom, whether with peers, parents, or the community.

Coleman found, from interviews with several hundred parents, that most of their interactions with schools are not instructionally focused. Yet most parents believe that they could help their children if they were allowed to participate more actively. Coleman points out that because parents' attitudes exert such a strong influence on children's attitudes toward school, reaching out to parents and working collaboratively with them is one of the most effective ways schools can increase students' commitment.

Early childhood intervention programs, particularly those that continue through the second or third grade, both improve academic performance in grade school and increase the likelihood of completing high school. Once again, parents become more involved. They participate more in school activities, volunteer in the classroom, and network with other parents. They're also more likely to monitor their child's activities and know what assignments are due and when (Reynolds & Temple, 1998; Reynolds et al., 2001). Among programs designed specifically for students who drop out, the most effective are those that simultaneously address the many problems these adolescents face at home as well as at school. Many adolescents, especially those from low-income families, need to work to help support themselves and their families. Innovative work-study programs that combine academic coursework with work in job settings for which students also receive academic credit have been successful, as have those that establish for students the connection between finishing high school and making a living. Almost all at-risk students need individual attention.

One program illustrates many of these points with notable success, that of Jefferson County High School in Louisville, Kentucky. This program has enrolled over 5,000 former dropouts, and in its first four years, graduated 1,100 of them. A number of features that are especially important for schooling at-risk adolescents distinguish this high school. The school offers an individualized program to every student, ensuring that they complete each unit of coursework with 70% mastery before moving on to the next. The latter requirement guarantees their success at what they attempt next. Students receive hands-on vocational guidance, in which they complete a battery of tests using manipulative materials. After reaching the end of these, they know what jobs they would like and which ones they would be good at. This high school puts as much emphasis on placing students in the right career track as on getting them ready for college (Gross, 1990;)

Many students who drop out work, and many have children. Schools that allow them to fit their classes into their other schedules minimize the conflicts that might otherwise keep students away from school. Much of Jefferson County High School's flexibility comes from its use of **computer-assisted instruction (CAI)**. CAI provides printouts showing a student's trouble spots, so teachers know where to help. CAI also centralizes bookkeeping so that students can pick up where they left off even after an absence—an important plus for students who need to take time off to complete a job or stay home with a sick child.

Another approach to getting students who drop out back on track utilizes community colleges. The Gateway to College program at Portland Community College in Oregon enables dropouts to earn a high school diploma while accumulating college credits. This program places students first in small learning communities, or cohorts, where they get individualized support and receive concentrated instruction in basic skills. Following this, students meet with a resource specialist who helps them select college courses that will simultaneously satisfy the requirements for their high school degree as well as meet requirements for their community college degree. Courses are offered during the day and evening, providing the flexibility that students need to avoid conflicts with their work or child-care schedules. This program currently is being replicated in other states because of its success (Gateway to College).

Measuring Success

Effective as the above programs are, broad social policy changes are needed to ensure that all students receive a good education. The United States faces a crisis in secondary education—almost a third of students do not graduate high school with a diploma (Barton, 2005). Percentages are even lower for low-income and minority students (**Table 8.3**). The extent of this problem has frequently been obscured since states have been able to report higher than actual graduation rates by using formulas that enable them to count a percentage of students who do not graduate as having transferred to other schools. For instance, California's reported graduation rate of 87% for 2002 was actually closer to 71%. When this figure was broken down for minority students, rates for African Americans (56.6%) and Hispanics (60%) were even lower (Civil Rights Project, 2005). Additionally, there are wide variations in completion rates from state to state, from a high of 88% to a low of 48% (Barton, 2005).

TABLE 8.3 National Graduation Rates by Race and Gender			
RACE/ETHNICITY	NATION (%)	FEMALE (%)	MALE (%)
American Indian/ Alaska Native	51.1	54.4	47.0
Asian/Pacific Islander	76.8	80.0	72.6
Hispanic	53.2	58.5	48.0
Black	50.2	56.2	42.8
White	74.9	77.0	70.8
All Students	68.0	72.0	64.1

Source: Urban Institute, 2005.

Testing and Public Policy

The standards-based educational reform, No Child Left Behind, enacted in 2002, is designed to strengthen academic achievement for all children and to decrease the disparity in achievement that currently exists between children from high- and low-income families and between European American children and those belonging to ethnic minorities. Schools are held accountable for making progress toward meeting higher proficiency levels, and parents are given the option of choosing another school if the one their child attends fails to meet these standards. Critics of this legislation argue that the federal funds which schools receive must go to support increased standardized testing, with little left over for programs that actually change the quality of education—such as teacher training and support, and smaller class sizes. Additionally, in many urban areas, there are not enough high-performing schools for parents to actually have a choice (Urban Institute, 2005).

Solutions to problems in education will need to focus on more than the schools themselves. Schools' successes in graduating more of their students, in the end, must be accompanied by society's success in providing these students with decent-paying jobs. The schools that are in greatest need, with the highest dropout rates, are low-income inner-city schools in neighborhoods with high rates of unemployment. Until programs bring jobs back to inner cities, educational reforms are not likely to succeed (Wilson, 1996).

What will work? Funding for "wraparound" early childhood intervention programs so that children from low-income families are brought up to speed in the skills they need for school; funding for teacher training, basic resources, and improving the physical facilities of schools, especially for impoverished inner city schools; implementing the recommendations of the

Go to the **Adolescence** Companion Website at **www.sinauer.com/cobb** for quizzes, flashcards, summaries, and other study resources.

widely respected Carnegie Council on Adolescent Development (1989), such as establishing small communities for learning and strengthening ties between schools and the community; and giving more local authority to schools to make the changes they need to reach students more effectively.

SUMMARY and KEY TERMS

Educating Adolescents

Structuring the Learning Environment: School districts and teachers face choices as to how to structure classroom learning. The two broad choices include direct instruction, where teachers work with the class as a whole, and the more flexible differentiated instruction, where students work in groups that more closely match their abilities and learning styles.
secondary education ,direct instruction, differentiated instruction, learning styles

Preparing for High School: Middle School or Junior High: Even though junior high schools and middle schools are designed to meet the needs of early adolescents, students' grades tend to drop when they leave elementary school. Difficulties may reflect more impersonal classroom environments and teachers involving students less in classroom decision making, compounded by the onset of puberty and its attendant changes.
middle school, junior high school

What Makes Schools Effective?

Skilled Teachers: Effective schools have skilled teachers who have high expectations for all students, monitor their progress, and make effective use of feedback in guiding students' activities.

Smaller Schools and Smaller Communities for Learning: Smaller schools can overcome differences related to social class and academic background better than large schools; students have more positive interactions, fewer discipline problems, and less absenteeism. But even for large schools, it is possible to create internal smaller communities for learning that can be responsive to students' needs.

School Climate: Effective schools have a supportive school climate that promotes achievement through the way they integrate resources into instruction and emphasize diverse types of achievements.

Full-Service Schools: Effective schools are full-service schools that collaborate with community agencies to provide a variety of health and social services for students and their families.
full-service schools

Parental Involvement: Adolescents whose parents are involved in their schools have more positive attitudes toward school, higher achievement scores, and higher educational aspirations. Parental involvement can include volunteering in the classroom or cafeteria, sitting down with teachers and administrators to discuss educational issues, and participating in parent-teacher organizations.

SUMMARY and KEY TERMS

School Safety

A number of factors are likely to contribute to the presence of violence at school: societal attitudes toward violence, domestic violence, media modeling, poverty and discrimination, and the accessibility of guns.

Bullies and Victims: Many students do not feel safe at school because they are victims of bullying. Adolescents in middle school are more likely to be bullied than those in high school. Intervention programs that involve parents, teachers, and staff, as well as students, have been found to be effective in reducing bullying.
bullying

Teaching Peace: Schools can promote peace through cooperative learning, through training in conflict resolution and constructive controversy, and by establishing conflict resolution centers.
cooperative learning, conflict resolution training, constructive controversy

Education for All

Gender in the Classroom: Though large advances have been made in reducing stereotyping, some gender-role stereotyping still exists in teaching materials. In textbooks, males appear in more diverse occupations and more exciting roles, and the use of male generic language is still prevalent. As a result, students and their teachers' evaluations of the competence of individuals of either sex for different types of work are skewed.
male generic language

Multicultural Education: Jigsaw classrooms, where students work in small groups, each contributing a different part of the lesson, foster cooperation and promote better relations among students from different ethnic backgrounds. Presenting material from several cultural perspectives is also helpful to minority students who may not share the dominant culture perspective. While most intervention programs have focused on problems minority students may experience at the level of the microsystem (that is, in the home and the classroom), problems of poorer achievement and higher dropout rates may have to be addressed at the level of the macrosystem (that is, in the society). The assurance of equal opportunity for jobs may be the most effective form of intervention.
jigsaw classroom

Academic Achievement

Socioeconomic Status: Students from low-income families score lower on achievement tests, get lower grades, and are less likely to finish high school. Home conditions are less conducive to studying, with fewer resources; high rates of unemployment offer less incentive for completing school; and teachers are less likely to be experienced or trained in the subjects they teach. Existing public programs, such as early childhood intervention programs, have been found to be effective in countering the effects of economic adversity on academic achievement.

(continued)

SUMMARY and KEY TERMS *continued*

Addressing Diversity: Academic tracking is a common solution to diverse interests and abilities among students, but tracking may also contribute to differences in achievement and dropout rates among those assigned to college and non-college tracks. Alternatives to tracking include forming small cooperative learning groups in the classroom and involving parents in the educational process. Work-study programs and computer-assisted instruction offer additional alternatives.
academic tracking, parental involvement, work experience

Academic Success: Mastery of basic skills by adolescents in the U.S. has changed little over the last several generations, with the exception of African American and Hispanic adolescents, whose performance has improved significantly. U.S. students place somewhat below students in other industrialized countries in mathematics and science. Spending time with friends, participating in sports, and working are also higher priorities than school for many U.S. adolescents. Not all students believe that doing well in high school is related to their future success. Consequently, they may be motivated more by the fear of failing than by the desire to learn. Academic achievement is strongly correlated with authoritative parenting in terms of involvement, communication, and expectations.

The Power of Positive Thinking: Patterns of Achievement: Adolescents can be distinguished in terms of achievement motivation patterns. Task-oriented adolescents are less likely to be disrupted by initial failure, believing it to result from lack of sufficient effort, while performance-oriented adolescents are likely to withdraw in the face of failure and attribute it to an external cause.
task-mastery orientation, performance-ability orientation, self-handicapping strategies, stereotype threat

Gender Differences and Achievement: Gender differences reveal more adaptive motivational patterns for males. Gender-role stereotypes contribute to the less positive attitudes that affect females' motivation. These differences often do not appear until adolescents enter junior high and encounter work that is challenging enough to prompt defensive withdrawal.

Adolescents at the Edge

Gifted Adolescents: Adolescents who score 130 or above on an intelligence test or who have creative, artistic, leadership, or other special talents are defined as gifted and talented. Educational programs for the gifted either offer enrichment or acceleration.
gifted, enrichment, acceleration

Adolescents with Learning Disabilities: Adolescents with learning disabilities have difficulty in academic tasks that presumably can be traced to a neurological dysfunction. Learning-disabled high school students can fall two or more grade levels behind classmates in some subject areas and generally have poor study habits and test-taking skills. Social skills are also affected for many. Many learning-disabled students are mainstreamed in regular classes with their classmates, while others may be placed in special education classes with specially trained teachers. Each of these options presents advantages and disadvantages.
learning disability, mainstreaming, special education consultant, special education classes

SUMMARY and KEY TERMS

Dropping Out: Dropout rates are related to low socioeconomic status and ethnicity, as well as parents' or siblings' failure to complete high school and family stress. School variables that predict dropping out are a history of difficulty or failure, low self-esteem, assignment to a non-college track, and behavior problems. Early childhood intervention programs improve academic performance in grade school and increase the likelihood of completing high school. Effective programs involve parents, provide individualized counseling, and help students meet their financial as well as academic needs.

computer-assisted instruction

Measuring Success

Broad social policy changes are needed to ensure that all students receive a good education, as nearly a third of U.S. adolescents fail to graduate high school with a diploma. Percentages are even higher for low-income and minority students.

Testing and Public Policy: Standards-based education reform is designed to strengthen academic achievement for all children by holding schools accountable for making progress toward meeting proficiency levels and giving parents the option of placing their children in better schools. Critics argue that federal funding primarily supports assessment, with little for program improvement. Solutions will need to address high rates of unemployment and improve the quality of schools serving low-income inner-city youth.

"**Pass** the pizza, Josh," Sam said, as he deftly maneuvered the box to a space near him. "So what'd he do after you said that?"

"The guy thinks he's impressive—I mean he is big. He leans up against me and breathes in my face…"

"Yeah," added James. "This guy spends his time watching old Rambo movies…jaw muscle twitching, toothpick in his mouth, meaningful stare."

"I said to him, 'You know, Eddie, most people take a step backward if they feel themselves tipping over. You really shouldn't have to lean on others for support.'"

"You got nerve, Josh. That kid's been known to punch someone out just for the exercise," returned Brian, as he surfed the sports channels.

Leisure, Work, and College

"That's not all of it," added Andy. "Our friend's gonna self-destruct one of these days."

"I don't think I want to hear this, but what'd you say next?" Sam asked.

"I just told him that if he wanted to dance, he'd have to ask me nicely."

"Stay outta the locker room for a few days, buddy. That guy's trouble," Brian warned. "Hey, someone move the take-out stuff. I can't see the TV through all this garbage."

"We did some serious damage to our wallets," noted Andy.

"Not to mention our bodies," Brian belched. "Coach says 'lean is mean.' I'm

Chapter Overview

How typical is it for adolescents to spend time the way these boys are? And does it matter whether they spend their time this way instead of doing something more "productive"? In the first section of this chapter, we will look at what adolescents do in their free time and at how this contributes to development. One particular type of leisure activities, those that are organized in some way by adults, contributes notably to development in a number of ways.

Nearly all adolescents spend time watching television, listening to music, and playing video games. Parents and educators, however, voice concerns about the influence of the media, particularly with respect to sex and violence. We will look at the impact of various media on adolescents, and then at the availability of leisure time for adolescents living in different cultures.

Many adolescents have a part-time job while still in high school. Others start full-time jobs after graduating, and still others will work while they go to college. For those who never finish high school, occupational choices are more limited.

Why do individuals choose one type of work and not another? Explanations for vocational choice differ. Social-cognitive theory looks at environmental variables that influence career decisions—such as parents' occupations and the salience of models in different occupations. The developmental theories of Eli Ginzburg and Donald Super identify stages of occupational choice. Ginzburg, for example, believes that realistic decisions occur fairly late in the process, and Super links occupational choice to the development of the self-concept. Finally, John Holland identifies different personality types that are suited to different types of work.

Adolescents in the workforce are considered next. What happens to young workers once they are on the job? Many need additional training beyond high school. Business and industry increasingly find that they must pick up the tab for the education of their newest workers, often having to train them in basic skills such as reading and math. Ironically, many of the nation's newest full-time workers must continue their education on the job.

Many factors affect adolescents' decisions about the type of work they will do. Not least among these are gender and ethnicity. Some adolescents never consider certain jobs because they rarely see individuals of their gender or race in them. Even when adolescents do consider a wide variety of jobs, the opportunity structure all too frequently reflects inequities associated with gender, ethnicity, and socioeconomic level. Intervention programs aimed at changing belief structures about career opportunities have been effective in helping adolescents evaluate the opportunities available to them.

Many adolescents will go to college, some as full-time students and others combining this with work. All will face new experiences; these can change the way they think about themselves, even the way they think about knowledge itself. We will chart different ways of knowing, and examine potential gender differences in each.

How Adolescents Spend Their Time

Most adolescents are out of school by 3:00 p.m., leaving them with roughly the same amount of free time each day as the time they spend in school, about seven hours. Adolescents in the United States typically spend about 20 to 40 minutes a day on chores and another 20 to 40 minutes on homework. Many older adolescents may also have a part-time job, averaging less than an hour a day. The bulk of after-school time, however, is discretionary or leisure time (**Table 9.1**). European adolescents have about the same amount of leisure

TABLE 9.1
How Adolescents Spend Their Free Time

ACTIVITY	NONINDUSTRIAL, UNSCHOOLED POPULATIONS	POSTINDUSTRIAL, SCHOOLED POPULATIONS		
		UNITED STATES	EUROPE	EAST ASIA
Household labor	5–9 hr	20–40 min	20–40 min	10–20 min
Paid labor	0.5–8 hr	40–60 min	10–20 min	0–10 min
Schoolwork	—	3.0–4.5 hr	4.0–5.5 hr	5.5–7.5 hr
Total work time	6–9 hr	4–6 hr	4.5–6.5 hr	6–8 hr
TV viewing	*	1.5–2.5 hr	1.5–2.5 hr	1.5–2.5 hr
Talking	*	2–3 hr	*	45–60 min
Sports	*	30–60 min	20–80 min	0–20 min
Structured voluntary activities	*	10–20 min	1.0–20 min	0–10 min
Total free time	**4–7 hr**	**6.5–8.0 hr**	**5.5–7.5 hr**	**4.0–5.5 hr**

Source: Larson, 2001.

* Insufficient data

Note. The estimates in the table are averaged across a seven-day week, including weekdays and weekends. Time spent in maintenance activities like eating, personal care, and sleeping is not included. The data for nonindustrial, unschooled populations come primarily from rural peasant populations in developing countries.

time as those in the United States, with the exception of spending more time on homework and less in part-time work. In contrast, Asian adolescents have considerably less free time, primarily due to the amount of time they spend on homework (Larson, 2001).

Leisure Time

Leisure activities are, by definition, the things we choose to do when we have time to spend as we please. The types of things adolescents choose to do can be distinguished broadly by whether the activities are organized or unstructured. Many common activities, such as watching TV or hanging out with friends, are unstructured. That is, there are no rules to be followed, as there are in games, nor skills that need to be mastered, such as in playing an instrument, nor is there adult leadership. For the majority of adolescents, most free time involves unstructured activities—hanging out with friends, listening to music, going to the mall or a movie, talking on the phone, and sometimes just doing nothing .

ORGANIZED VOLUNTARY ACTIVITIES   Although adolescents spend the bulk of their time in unstructured activities, most of them also participate in one or more **organized activities** during the week. These activities, just as unstructured ones, are things that adolescents choose to do, but differ in that they're organized by adults. Examples of these are team sports, school clubs, Scouts or 4-H, attending religious youth groups, or being in student government (**Figure 9.1**). Although many of these activities meet only once a week, a few of them, such as sports or being in a school play, can involve long hours of practice. Research consistently finds that participation in organized activities, whether volunteering in a community soup kitchen or playing an instrument in band, promotes healthy development. Adolescents report feeling more positive, have higher self-esteem, are more confident, do better in school, are less likely to drop out, and engage in fewer risky behaviors, to name

organized activities
Leisure activities organized by adults that adolescents choose to engage in.

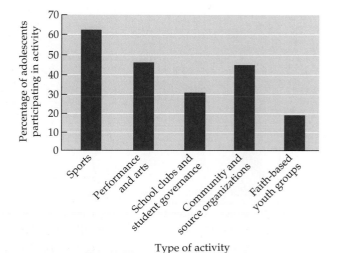

● **Figure 9.1   Percentage of adolescents participating in different types of organized activities**   (After Larson et al., 2006.)

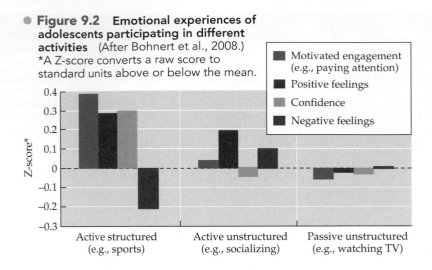

● **Figure 9.2** **Emotional experiences of adolescents participating in different activities** (After Bohnert et al., 2008.) *A Z-score converts a raw score to standard units above or below the mean.

just a few of the developmental benefits (**Figure 9.2**) Additionally, these benefits persist into early adulthood, increasing the likelihood that adolescents will go to college and become active members in their communities as young adults (Bohnert et al., 2008; Eccles & Barber, 1999; Findlay & Bowker, 2009; Fredricks & Eccles, 2008; Gardner et al., 2008; Hansen & Larson, 2007).

Reed Larson (2000), at the University of Illinois, contends that participation in organized activities contributes to positive development in youth by fostering the development of initiative, an important characteristic of self-motivated adults. Activities fostering **initiative** are

initiative A readiness to initiate action, characteristic of self-motivated individuals.

flow The experience of becoming totally absorbed in a challenging activity.

ones that adolescents choose to do because they find them *intrinsically motivating*, that is, these are rewarding in and of themselves. Adolescents also experience these activities as challenging in that they require concentration and effort in order to reach a desired level of mastery. Additionally, because organized activities have well-defined goals, adolescents are able to see how well they are doing and where they need to improve, thus enabling them to evaluate, adjust and reevaluate their performance over the course of time (Larson et al., 2006).

Adolescents find these activities so engrossing that time often just slips by—an hour's practice may seem to last only 10 minutes. This experience of intrinsically rewarding immersion in an ongoing activity is termed **flow**. Episodes of flow occur when adolescents experience a balance between the challenges of a task and their abilities to meet that challenge. That is, the task must be sufficiently demanding to present a challenge, but adolescents must also experience their talents as up to the task. If the task requires less than the available skills, then it will be boring. If skills are not up to the task, then adolescents can experience anxiety (Csikszentmihalyi, 1990).

Larson points out that this combination of intrinsic motivation and concentration is noticeably lacking when adolescents are engaged in schoolwork or even when they are with their friends. While adolescents report that doing schoolwork requires concentration, they also report having little intrinsic interest in this. Just the opposite is true when with their friends, as adolescents find the time they spend this way intrinsically motivating but requiring little concentration (**Figure 9.3**). However, adolescents experience organized activities such as sports, hobbies, or clubs as both intrinsically motivating *and* requiring concentration (**Figure 9.4**).

How much adolescents enjoy what they're doing and their investment in this is generally more important than the particular activities they participate in. Nonetheless, different activities contribute in different ways to development. Being the center on a basketball

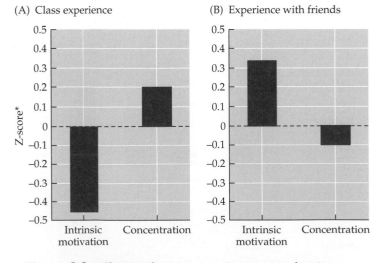

● **Figure 9.3** **Classwork requires concentration, but is not intrinsically motivating, whereas socializing is motivating but requires little concentration** (After Larson, 2000.) *A Z-score converts a raw score to standard units above or below the mean.

team and having a part in a school play, for instance, both promote the development of initiative, however neither of these confers the benefits of adult networking that are afforded by being part of a community-oriented activity such as serving in a food kitchen for the homeless (**Tables 9.2** and **9.3**). Among the different types of activities adolescents engage in, faith-based youth groups stand out for contributing to personal development in numerous ways. The fact that they do should not be surprising. Religion challenges adolescents to reflect on who they are and what their lives are about, while at the same time supporting them through a system of beliefs, and connecting them to a supportive community of peers and adults (Hansen & Larson, 2007; Larson et al., 2006; Linver et al., 2009).

The advantages of participating in organized activities are likely due to many things. Adolescents develop skills and acquire a sense of belonging, whether from being in band, on the yearbook staff, or on the soccer team. These skills in turn enable them to view themselves more positively, leading to improvements in self-confidence and self-esteem. Participating in some activities, particularly sports, also enhances adolescents' prestige with other students. For girls, participation in sports improves their body image and feelings of competence, which together contribute substantially to a sense of well-being (Greenleaf et al., 2009). Also, perhaps because high school sports have traditionally been defined as a masculine domain, female athletes have been found to be more willing to venture into academic domains typically identified as masculine, such as taking a course in physics (Pearson et al., 2009). Extracurricular activities, in general, involve adolescents and their teachers in more supportive and motivating contexts than those of the classroom, increasing their sense of connection to school and, for those at the edge, making it less likely they will drop out. Parents, as well, are more likely to become involved with their adolescents' school through attending the sporting events, musical productions, and plays their children take part in (Erkut & Tracy, 2002; Marsh et al., 2006; McNeal, 1995).

Despite the advantages of participating in organized activities, several concerns exist with respect to adolescents' involvement in sports. Par-

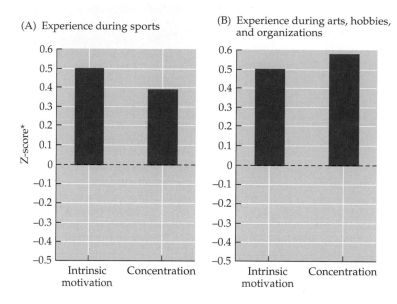

● **Figure 9.4 Participating in organized voluntary activities is both intrinsically motivating and requires concentration** (After Larson, 2000.) *A Z-score converts a raw score to standard units above or below the mean.

TABLE 9.2
Developmental Experiences from Participating in Organized Activities

ACTIVITY	CONTRIBUTION TO DEVELOPMENTAL EXPERIENCES HIGH (Low)
Sports	INITIATIVE
Performance/ fine arts	INITIATIVE Teamwork and social skills
School clubs	Identity work Emotional regulation Teamwork and social skills Positive relationships
Community-oriented activities	ADULT NETWORKS AND SOCIAL CAPITAL
Service activities	POSITIVE RELATIONSHIPS ADULT NETWORKS
Faith-based youth groups	IDENTITY WORK INITIATIVE TEAMWORK AND SOCIAL SKILLS POSITIVE RELATIONSHIPS ADULT NETWORKS AND SOCIAL CAPITAL

Source: Larson et al., 2006.

TABLE 9.3
Percentage of Adolescents in Faith-Based Activities Endorsing Statements About Personal and Interpersonal Development

	TYPE OF ORGANIZED ACTIVITY	
	FAITH-BASED	ALL OTHERS
Identity work		
"This activity got me thinking about who I am"	66	33
Positive relationships		
"We discussed morals and values"	75	24
Adult networks		
"This activity improved my relationship with my parents"	46	21
"Got to know people in the community"	40	20

Source: Larson et al., 2006.

ticipating in high school sports is associated with greater use of alcohol and increased risk of injury. The most common injuries are fractures, although head injuries are an increasing concern for adolescent boys. It is estimated that 20% of the injuries adolescents sustain when playing football involve head injuries, many of which are concussions. The incidence of head injuries is particularly problematic since they are not always recognized and treated. Injury prevention education programs for coaches and athletes, but also for parents, are important, especially given the potentially serious consequences of recurrent injuries (Cobb & Battin, 2004; Gordon, 2006; Mattila et al., 2009; McKeever & Schatz, 2003).

Adolescents and the Media

It's difficult to find a home in the United States that doesn't have a TV set. In fact, in many homes there are more TV sets than people. Most homes also have one or more DVD/VCR players, a number of radios, video game players, and cell phones, not to mention a computer, and access to the Internet. Teens in the United States are more likely than their parents to have a desktop computer, and nearly as likely to have a cell phone. Two-thirds of teenagers also have a TV in their bedroom, as well as their own DVD/VCR player, CDs and tapes, and a radio. About a third have their own computer (**Table 9.4**). Additionally, many of these devices are portable, meaning that teens can take their music, games, and cell phones with them wherever they go (Macgill, 2007; Nielsen Media Research, 2009; Roberts et al., 2005).

What are the developmental implications of living in this electronic "candy land"? What are teenagers downloading, tuning in to, and viewing? And how much time do they spend doing this? Before going any further, recall that teenagers frequently use several media at once. It's common, for instance, for teens to check out a social networking site while listening to music and IMing a friend. Patterns of usage such as this are termed multitasking. As a result, even though adolescents report using media about 6½ hours a day, which is about as much free time as they have on a school day, their total media exposure is closer to 8½ hours. Most of this time is spent watching television and listening to music (**Figure 9.5**). With

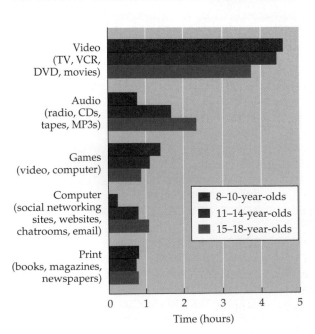

● **Figure 9.5   Amount of daily media use by children and adolescents**   (After Roberts et al., 2005.)

TABLE 9.4
Media Ownership by Children and Adolescents

	8- TO 10-YEAR-OLDS	11- TO 14-YEAR-OLDS	15- TO 18-YEAR-OLDS
Percentage of children and adolescents whose bedroom contains			
TV	69	68	68
VCR/DVD	47	56	56
DVR	8	13	9
Radio	74	85	91
CDs/tapes	75	89	92
Video game	52	52	41
Computer	23	31	37
Cable/satellite TV	32	38	40
Premium channel	16	21	20
Internet	10	21	27
IMing program	9	17	27
Telephone	31	39	50
Percentage of children and adolescents with their own			
Cell phone	21	36	56
Portable CD/tape player	35	65	77
MP3 player	12	20	20
Laptop	13	11	15
Handheld video game	66	60	41
Personal digital assistant	9	14	8
Handheld Xnet device	7	15	17

Source: Roberts et al., 2005.

respect to TV, a majority of adolescents (54%) say there are no rules in their home regarding TV use, however, most of these also say their parents know what they're watching, suggesting some control over what they view. Nearly as many (51%) indicate that the TV is on "most of the time, even when no one is watching" (Roberts et al., 2005).

SEXUAL MESSAGES   Adolescents watch TV at a time when they are developing attitudes toward sex and fitting these into a sense of who they are. And for those who are not sure how to flirt, or even how to start a conversation with someone they're attracted to, television becomes a significant source of information (Kaiser Family Foundation, 2003).

What are adolescents likely to learn from what they see on TV? Dale Kunkel (2007), at the University of Arizona, and his associates randomly sampled nearly 3000 daytime and evening programs on network and cable channels over a period of five years. They found that approximately two-thirds of the shows they sampled included sexual content, with an average of about four scenes per hour either talking about sex or showing some form of sexual behavior, and that most shows devoted more than passing attention to this content. Sitcoms have the highest number of scenes with sexual content (7.8 per hour). In addition, scenes that portrayed, or strongly implied, sexual intercourse occurred almost as frequently (14%) as those showing behaviors such as kissing or intimate touching (18%). With respect to the messages communicated by this sexual content, 25% depicted individuals who were not in a relationship or had just met, and little mention was given to risks or responsibilities attending sexual behavior.

In addition to watching television, adolescents spend considerable amounts of time listening to music, both on the radio as well as on CDs, tapes, and downloaded music. The most popular forms of music are rap and hip-hop, preferred by 65% of adolescents (Roberts et al., 2005). Music contains even more sexual references (40%) than television, and as with television, messages about risks and responsibilities are relatively infrequent (Pardun et al., 2005).

Analyses of other media commonly used by adolescents, such as movies, the Internet, and magazines, reveals patterns similar to those found in TV and music, and suggests that adolescents "live in a sexual media world" (Pardun et al., 2005). Additionally, studies find that the amount of exposure teens have to sexual themes is related to their sexual behavior (Chandra et al., 2008; Pardun et al., 2005). However, this relationship must be viewed with caution since it is not clear whether media exposure to sexual content actually influences adolescents' behavior, or whether adolescents who have already decided to become sexually active are more likely to watch or listen to media containing sexual content (see "Correlational Research" in Chapter 2).

VIOLENCE   Adolescents also are exposed to considerable media violence through television, movies, video games, and the Internet. Roughly 60% of programs on television, for instance, portray violent episodes. Adolescents watching any night during prime-time hours are likely to see from three to five violent acts an hour, a significant percentage of which involve weapons (Johnson et al., 2002; Strasburger & Donnerstein, 1999). Once again, it is reasonable to ask what effect viewing such content might have. Research addressing this question finds that adolescents' viewing habits are significantly associated with aggressive behavior, even after controlling for the presence of other factors related to aggression (Johnson et al., 2002; Ybarra et al., 2008). However, just as with research examining the influence of sexual content in the media, one cannot say that viewing media violence *causes* adolescents to be more aggressive. There is always the possibility that one or more factors, other than those that have been controlled for, is responsible for the association linking media violence to aggressive behavior (Ferguson & Kilburn, 2009).

Spending a lot of time playing violent video games may change the way this adolescent views violence.

Adolescents are exposed to a different type of violence, however, when playing many of the popular video games. This exposure, since it is interactive and involves more than passive viewing, might be expected to impact adolescents more than what they see on television. When playing a video game, for instance, players must consider and choose from a number of strategies, most of which are aggressive, in order to ultimately defeat their enemy and avoid being "killed." Is exposure to this type of media violence related to aggression? Research addressing this question strongly suggests that it is, particularly when players identify with the violent character in a video game (Anderson, 2004; Gentile et al., 2004; Houseman, 2007; Konjin et al., 2007).

How might playing violent video games increase the likelihood of aggressive behavior? One way is by changing how adolescents think about aggression, causing them to see it as more common and acceptable than they would otherwise. In support of this, research finds that adolescents who spend a lot of time playing violent video games have more positive attitudes toward violence and less empathy for a victim (Anderson, 2004; Funk et al., 2004). One could argue, of course, that such a relationship exists only because adolescents who *already* are aggressive prefer violent video games. But additional research suggests otherwise. Ingrid Moller and Barbara Krahe (2009), at the University of Potsdam, followed adolescents over time, assessing the amount of time they played violent video games and their attitudes toward aggression when they were 13 years old and again when they were 15½. Assessing these adolescents at two different ages enabled them to determine that the amount of exposure to violent games when they were 13 predicted both their acceptance of aggression and their aggressive behavior 2½ years later. Conversely, they were also able to see that how aggressive they were at 13 was *unrelated* to their use of video games 2½ years later. In other words, the change in these boys' attitude toward aggression was due to playing violent video games and not to an initial preference for games that are violent (see the Research Focus Box on Path Analysis on the Web site).

Playing violent games may also increase the likelihood of aggression by desensitizing a person to violence; that is, incidents that previously would occasion an emotional reaction no longer do, or do to a lesser extent. Nicholas Carnagey and his associates (2007) tested this possibility by randomly assigning college students to 20 minutes of playing either a violent or non-violent video game, and then showing them footage of graphic violence (e.g., a knifing incident caught on a prison monitor). As expected, those who had played the violent video game showed less physiological arousal when viewing real violence than the others did.

Although desensitization can be adaptive, as in the case of preparing medical interns to do surgery or soldiers to go into combat, it does this by decreasing individuals' sensitivity to another's distress. Brad Bushman and Craig Anderson (2009) also randomly assigned college students to conditions in which they played either a violent or non-violent game, after which they heard a staged fight break out in another room, which ended with the victim groaning in pain and a door slamming as the other said, "I'm outta here." Those who had played the violent game took longer to come to the rescue and also rated the fight as less serious. In case you're doubting that students thought the fight was real, when asked about this, all later agreed that they did. Other research, also with college students, found that those who played a violent sports video game had more aggressive thoughts, emotions, and behavior than those playing an equally competitive but non-violent game, indicating that the violence and not the need to compete resulted in the aggression (Anderson & Carnagey, 2009).

Should parents be worried about teenagers' exposure to violence from playing video games? If the exposure is periodic, probably not. Playing an occasional violent game is no more likely to lead to aggression than having an occasional ice cream sundae is likely to lead to obesity. Something to keep in mind, however, is that violent video games are particularly attractive to adolescent boys. When asked to name their favorite video games, 49% of eighth- and ninth-grade boys named violent ones, more than twice as many as girls their age (Gentile et al., 2004). A second thing to keep in mind is that they're likely to spend about 13 hours a week playing video games, and most of this time will be with the ones they like best—the violent ones.

On a positive note, playing prosocial games makes it less likely that one will see others as hostile, and increases the likelihood of sharing, cooperating, having empathy, and helpful to others (Gentile et al., 2009; Greitemeyer & Osswald, 2009, 2010).

THE MEDIA AND ACADEMIC ACHIEVEMENT   Although amount of media exposure is not reliably related to adolescents' grades in school, trends are in the expected direction, with less media exposure associated with somewhat better grades. With respect to video games, this relationship is more pronounced; adolescents who spend less time playing video games tend to get higher grades. Leaving the world of electronic media and going to the printed page leads us to another expected—and reliable—relationship: adolescents who read more are likely to get better grades (Roberts et al., 2005).

Despite parents expressing concern over the effects of media exposure, surprisingly few attempt to control their children's access. Research reveals, however, that those who do can influence their children's behavior. Simple decisions such as turning the television off during meals, setting limits on how much, and what, can be watched on TV, as well as on the use of other media, and limiting the media their children have personal access to (such as in their bedrooms), can significantly reduce adolescents' media exposure. Decisions such as these are also associated with spending more time reading (Roberts et al., 2005).

Global Comparisons: Child Labor

Teenagers in most industrial societies enjoy nearly as many hours of leisure during the week as they spend in school, and even more free time on weekends. In comparison, children and adolescents in nonindustrial societies have considerably less leisure time. By middle childhood, many will be working for as much as six hours a day. For girls this is likely to include household chores, such as tending younger siblings, and for boys it is likely to involve work outside the home, to bring in additional income. By the time they reach adolescence, many are working the same hours a day as an adult (Larson, 2001).

For many 5- to 17-year-olds in developing nations, this work constitutes child labor (**Figure 9.6**). **Child labor** refers to work done by children and adolescents before they reach the minimum age for work; since this age also typically specifies the end of compulsory education, child labor almost always deprives them of education, and is harmful in one or more ways. UNICEF estimates that in developing countries, one in every six children below the age of 14 is engaged in child labor and, when older adolescents are included, one in 12 is engaged in the "worst forms" of child labor—work that is hazardous and even life threatening (UNICEF, 2009). Child labor has obvious implications for the children and adolescents who are forced to work at an early age. Those who work do so out of necessity, driven by poverty. Many work at repetitive, uninteresting tasks, such as crushing rocks or scrubbing pots, that do not build skills. Since the hours they spend in work are hours they are not in school, this further limits their future options. Frequently, the work they do is physically demanding and, for many, hazardous. Moreover, they are typically paid low wages and are frequently taken advantage of.

child labor   Work done by children and adolescents prior to reaching the minimum age for work, that is harmful in one way or another.

Though child labor is the result of poverty, it also contributes to poverty by diminishing the human capital of a society. It does so by interfering with the education and preparation of a labor force that is able to compete in the global economy (UNICEF, 2005). Paradoxically, globalization may be contributing to child labor in developing countries. As businesses in industrialized nations have moved production sites to developing nations where labor is cheaper, statistics have risen on the numbers of children working on the goods developing nations produce (UNICEF, 2005).

The most successful approaches for combating child labor are multifaceted. In addition to legislation, approaches that raise community awareness of the

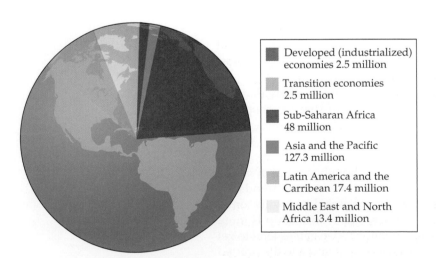

Developed (industrialized) economies 2.5 million

Transition economies 2.5 million

Sub-Saharan Africa 48 million

Asia and the Pacific 127.3 million

Latin America and the Carribean 17.4 million

Middle East and North Africa 13.4 million

● **Figure 9.6   Child labor**   Worldwide, 211 million children under the age of 15 are involved in child labor. Most of these children are engaged in domestic or farm work. (After UNICEF UK, 2005.)

harmful effects of child labor have proven to be effective, particularly if these are accompanied by programs providing an income subsidy to families that is linked to their child's attendance at school. Arranging for flexible school hours to accommodate children who work has also been helpful by enabling children who must work to continue their education (UNICEF, 2006).

Adolescents at Work

Why do we consider some activities as work and others as what we do in our free time? Is it that we find the latter more pleasurable, or does an activity become work when we get paid for it? Ways of thinking about work develop in childhood, and take on a new significance in adolescence.

Attitudes Toward Work over the Lifespan

Attitudes toward work and leisure show surprising continuity through large segments of the lifespan. Many of the attitudes adults hold toward work, for instance, can first be seen by the time children enter adolescence. Adults who are asked to report how they feel about what they are doing at the moment, if asked this while they are at work, are likely to indicate they would rather be doing something else. Yet these same individuals acknowledge that work, more than leisure, contributes significantly to their sense of self and frequently is more deeply satisfying (Csikszentmihalyi, 1997).

In a similar fashion, 10- and 11-year-olds report activities they label as work as being less pleasurable than those they label as play, even though they acknowledge that the former more frequently contribute to feelings of high self-esteem. Adolescents as well, when asked to indicate how they feel while they are working, report they are less happy than if doing something else, even though their feelings of self-esteem are higher when they are working than at other times and even though they are likely to regard what they are doing as important (Csikszentmihalyi, 1997).

Children's chores, as well as adolescents' part-time work, anticipate the gender divisions that characterize work among adults, with girls performing more of the inside chores and boys doing more outside chores. For example, over 80% of boys versus 50% of girls reported having to take the trash out (Entwisle et al., 1999). Thus, not only attitudes toward work but also patterns of work show continuity through the lifespan.

Part-Time Employment

Many high school students have part-time jobs. Predictably, this number increases with age; whereas less than 10% of 15-year-olds are likely to be employed during the school year, nearly 40% of 17-year-olds are likely to be employed. Even more adolescents would be working if they could find jobs. Following the recession which began at the end of 2007, the unemployment rates for all groups of workers rose, reaching 7.6% and 10% for adult women and men, respectively, and 24% for teenagers by mid-2009 (U.S. Bureau of Labor Statistics, 2009a). Unemployment is generally higher among minority adolescents than among European American adolescents; these differences persist into early adulthood, as can be seen in **Figure 9.7**.

SPENDING PATTERNS   Adolescents with jobs spend their money in different ways than they will as adult workers. Most of what they earn they spend on personal items such as a cell phone, clothes, CDs, and entertainment (**Figure 9.8**). Because over half of those who work earn more than $50 a week, adolescents can engage in a fair amount of conspicuous consumption. The price of clothes is high if one buys designer labels—and many adolescents do. Popular name-brand athletic shoes can start at $80. One might imagine that at prices

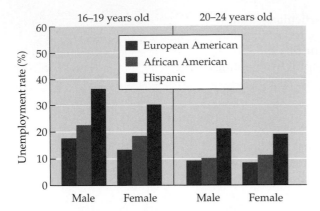

● **Figure 9.7** **Unemployment among European American, Hispanic, and African American Youth** (After Fox et al., 2005.)

such as these, few adolescents would indulge in brand buying, but increasing numbers of adolescents choose to work in order to spend money on personal items such as these. Jeans, a staple wardrobe item for most adolescents, are also expensive, many starting at $50 a pair and more, depending on extras such as acid washes, type of cut, and so on. The cost of an outfit can add up, and we haven't even gotten above the belt in this example.

Adolescents also spend money on entertainment. A simple date, such as a movie and hamburger afterward, can cost $20 or more a person: $6 to $12 for tickets, another $5 to $10 at the concession stand, and a whopping $10 to $15 more for hamburgers and drinks afterward—and this doesn't include the cost of the round-trip gas. Special events, such as rock concerts, can be four to five times as expensive. Even though most adolescents go to concerts infrequently, they go to other events, such as school dances or get-togethers after games, regularly—and these all add up. Just spending an evening with a friend or two can be expensive. When adolescents get together, they eat. Two or three adolescents can polish off several 2-liter bottles of cola in a night and munch through several bags of chips at $2 to $3 a bag.

Many adolescents, however, save their money, as well as spend it. Teen Research Unlimited, a large market research firm, found that over 67% of the adolescents surveyed in a nationally representative sample had savings accounts, 18% had stocks or bonds, and 8% had mutual funds (Teen Research Unlimited, 2001). High school seniors who are planning to attend a four-year college are, predictably, more likely to put more of their money into savings for education than those without plans for college. Some also contribute to their families' expenses (see Figure 9.8).

ADVANTAGES AND DISADVANTAGES OF PART-TIME EMPLOYMENT   Some researchers question whether part-time employment exposes adolescents to an unrealistic standard of living. They point out that most teenagers are allowed to spend what they earn as discretionary income; as we have seen, only a small percentage contribute to family expenses. As a result, few adolescents are prepared for the realities that confront employed adults, such as the costs of housing, food, transportation, and health care. **Figure 9.9** presents a comparison of spending patterns of people under 25 to the spending patterns of all ages.

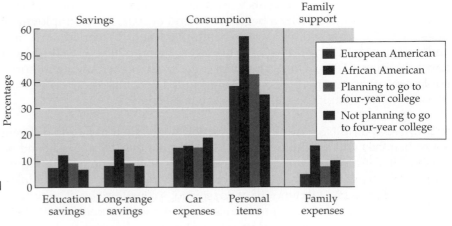

● **Figure 9.8** **How high school seniors spend their money** (After Youth Indicators, 2005.)

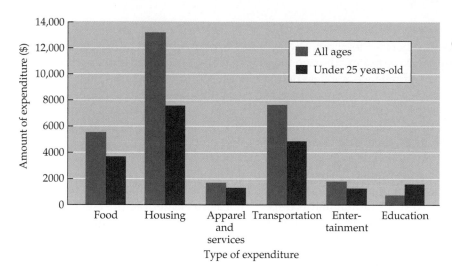

● **Figure 9.9** **Spending patterns of people 25 years of age and under compared with those of all people** (After U.S. Department of Labor, 2001, and Fox et al., 2005.)

Laurence Steinberg, Suzanne Fegley, and Sanford Dornbusch (1993) surveyed 1800 high school sophomores and juniors concerning part-time employment. By following these students over a year's time, they could look for differences that existed prior to their part-time employment, as well as compare adolescents who worked with those who did not. These investigators found that adolescents who work are less invested in school than their peers, even before beginning to work, and that working contributes to their disengagement from school, especially if they work more than 20 hours a week. Conversely, adolescents who work moderate hours and then quit their jobs show improved performance in school.

Jaylen Mortimer and associates (1996) also found that low work hours (versus high work hours) were associated with better performance in school. However, grades for these students were also higher than for those who did not work at all (**Figure 9.10**). It is possible that employment fosters work habits and personal discipline that carry over to their studies. Or, conversely, it may be that students who work accommodate for the demands on their time by taking less rigorous classes (Steinberg et al., 1993). Mortimer and associates (1996), who also studied a large representative sample, did not find evidence of working students taking easier classes, however. Clearly, simple answers concerning the relationship of part-time employment to success in school are not forthcoming.

Nor, for that matter, is the relationship any clearer between part-time employment and measures of mental health. Although part-time employment is related to increased use of alcohol (Mortimer et al., 1996; Steinberg et al., 1993), evidence of its relationship to other criteria of mental health is less con-

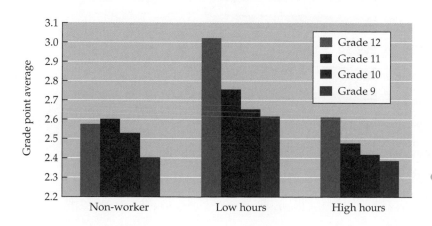

● **Figure 9.10** **Grade-point average by work hours for high school students** (After Mortimer et al., 1996.)

sistent. Whereas Steinberg, Fegley, and Dornbusch found adolescents who do not work to be better adjusted than those who do—having higher self-esteem, greater self-reliance, and less delinquency—Mortimer and associates found no difference in self-esteem or in other measures of adjustment. One factor not addressed in either study is the potential mentoring adolescents may receive from their relationship with an adult at work. Adolescents who report such experiences, saying they learned work skills and acquired values from such an adult not only had higher self-esteem, but were also less likely to use alcohol (Vazsonyi & Snider, 2008).

The types of jobs adolescents fill, in addition to the hours they work, also need to be considered. In this respect, at least, a clearer picture emerges. Most adolescents are employed in high-turnover positions, with little pay, little authority, and relatively little opportunity for advancement. The work is often simple and repetitive and requires little skill or training. Such jobs are associated with negative consequences for workers, whether adolescents or adults (Mortimer et al., 1992).

When adolescents perceive their work as contributing to skills they could later use, however, part-time employment has been found to be associated with a number of measures of well-being (Mortimer et al., 1992). Holding a job can help adolescents develop a sense of responsibility and give them a feeling of being productive. Work can also develop general skills, ranging from interpersonal ones, such as getting along with coworkers, to personal ones, such as managing time. Some jobs may help adolescents discover where their interests lie, even if by exclusion—they may discover, for example, that they would not enjoy the same work in a full-time capacity.

Many adolescents are able to discover more about what they *would* like to do through school-to-work programs that help them step into the work world from the world of school (Legters, 2000). These programs can take a number of forms (**Figure 9.11**). In job shadowing, students spend part of their school day in a work setting, following the activities of one or more workers there, whereas in mentoring, students work with someone who, in addition to overseeing their work and offering advice, serves as a role model. In some schools, students are encouraged to do an internship or apprenticeship in which they spend time working at a job. Cooperative education focuses on making education relevant to jobs in a particular field by enabling students to combine vocational studies with on-the-job experience. Other programs, such as technical preparation and career major, help students define career goals and determine the educational programs necessary for achieving these.

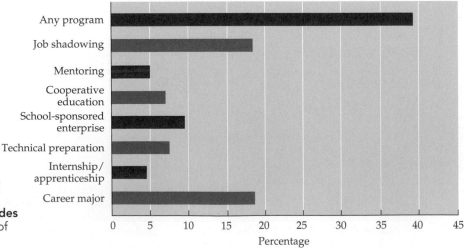

● **Figure 9.11 Percentages of adolescents participating in school-to-work programs, grades 9–12** (After U.S. Department of Labor, 2000.)

Approximately 40% of high school students participate in a school-to-work program (U.S. Department of Labor, 2000).

For some adolescents, such a discovery is a luxury. Adolescents who drop out of high school find it difficult to obtain work even under the best of circumstances. Many cannot afford to be choosy. We turn to this group of workers next.

Dropping Out and Employment

Adolescents who drop out of high school are significantly more likely to be unemployed than those who graduate (Borbely, 2009). Because future jobs will require even more education and preparation, adolescents who fail to complete high school will find it harder to compete for these jobs than in the past. Even when employed, high school dropouts earn less money, are less satisfied with their working conditions, see less opportunity for promotion, and experience less security and permanence in their jobs (Youth Indicators, 2005; Kaufman et al., 2001). Given the importance of finishing high school, one looks for programs that have been successful in working with adolescents at risk of dropping out (see Chapter 8). Several successful programs share a number of features.

First, high schools that are effective in keeping at-risk adolescents in school establish the connection between having a diploma and earning money. Although the actual amount of money earned by high school graduates versus those who drop out is not always large, the likelihood of having a job is significantly greater if one has a diploma. Successful programs offering work opportunities that provide on-the-job experience have been particularly successful. Most also give intensive training in basic skills, increasing the likelihood of success both at school and on the job. Many programs also prepare students to take the GED, a test that, when passed, gives them the equivalent of a high school diploma.

Second, effective programs usually have lower student-teacher ratios, smaller campuses, and an atmosphere that communicates the message that any student who wants to can be successful. Teachers have more time to interact with students. Many schools also provide infant care for adolescent mothers returning to school.

Additionally, many students who fail to graduate have a history of school failure and are demoralized by the time they reach high school. Effective programs integrate computers into their instructional programs, using them for individualized instruction in basic skills. Remedial programs in reading and math help break self-defeating cycles in which students avoid work at which they feel inadequate, causing them to fall even further behind.

Finally, successful schools often involve individuals from the community, such as civic leaders, local businesses and industry, in their programs. In this way, students learn about resources in the community. Parents are an important part of any coalition, and these programs involve parents in the students' progress as well (see Chapter 8). Frequently, too, counseling for emotional problems is available to students who need it.

Successful programs increase the motivation of the students enrolled in them. They also help students set realistic goals. These two benefits are almost surely related. Students' motivation to do well in their courses will increase as they see the

Schools that are effective in reaching potential dropouts communicate to students that they care. These schools typically integrate computers into their instructional programs, and support teacher involvement by reducing class workloads so that teachers can have more time to interact with students.

BOX 9.1

Research Focus

Correlational Research: Hangin' out on a Friday Night

It's Friday night and a group of 16-year-olds are sitting around the television, talking, channel surfing, and working their way through a bag of chips. Periodically, one of them will call the others' attention to something on the screen or mention some event that happened last week at school, but as the evening wears on, the conversation gets more serious. They talk about being friends, about what they've been through together, and what lies ahead for each of them.

Despite their casual appearance, adolescents have a lot on their minds. Mixed in with studying for tests, picking up the latest CD, or hanging out on a Friday night are their concerns about the future—their futures. One of the major tasks facing adolescents is that of identity formation, gaining a sense of themselves that reflects what they value and want to be and, in turn, is valued by those whom they respect (see Chapter 5). One might suspect, as a consequence, that adolescents' aspirations would be related to those of their friends. But are they? Are other factors involved? And how might one go about finding answers to questions such as these?

One would first need to measure both adolescents' and their friends' aspirations, as well as any

other factors one thinks might be related. Then one could look for relationships among these variables. When changes along one variable correspond to changes along another, the variables are said to be *correlated. Correlation coefficients* are statistics that reflect the degree of relationship between variables. Scatterplots show this relationship pictorially. In the **Figure**, the scatterplot on the left illustrates no relationship ($r = 0$); the one on the right shows a strong relationship ($r = +1.00$). One could have an equally strong relationship but in the opposite direction ($r = -1.00$); that is, variables can be either positively or negatively correlated. In the case of positive correlation, increases along one variable match increases along the other. When variables are negatively correlated, increases along one are accompanied by decreases along the other. Let's look at how one team of investigators used this approach to determine whether adolescents' future aspirations are related to various characteristics of their friends, such as their friends' ambitions, beliefs, and use of drugs.

Judith Stein and Michael Newcomb (1999) gave seventh- through ninth-graders a measure of their future aspirations, asking them how well they were doing in school, what their educational aspirations were, and what their ambitions were. They also questioned them about their friends (conventional friends). Specifically, they asked how much they talked with their friends about their homework, what grades their friends got, whether their friends

relationship between their own success and the skills they need for specific jobs. More generally, these programs have an impact on students' self-esteem; when one likes oneself, one does not have to have fantasy-level aspirations about a job—reality does quite well (Bloch, 1989). For a look at the effect of other factors on adolescents' future aspirations, see **Box 9.1**.

Theories of Vocational Development

At-risk students face one problem in common with other students. Almost all adolescents have difficulty discovering the type of work for which they are best suited or would enjoy most. We look first at social-cognitive theory for an explanation of how adolescents select the type of work they will engage in for most of their adult lives, and then at the theories of Eli Ginzburg, Donald Super, and John Holland.

Social-Cognitive Theory

Why do individuals choose the occupations they do? Social-cognitive theory, which emphasizes the role of observational learning and modeling, focuses on

BOX
9.1 *continued*

planned to go to college, and what their parents thought of their friends. In addition, they assessed how conventional adolescents' attitudes were, asking about law abidance, liberalism, and religiosity (social conformity). Finally, they assessed their use of drugs (drug use).

Are adolescents' future aspirations related to characteristics of their friends? Absolutely. These investigators found that adolescents' high future aspirations correlated positively with having conventional friends and with greater social conformity. Conversely, high future aspirations correlated negatively with drug use.

This research is further distinguished by the fact that these investigators followed these same adolescents into adulthood, testing them again 13 years later when they were young adults and again 20 years later when they reached middle adulthood. Tracing the paths of these adolescents into adulthood revealed that those who had positive goals for themselves in adolescence (Positive future aspirations) showed more efficacy and agency as young adults. Further, both efficacy and agency in early adulthood predicted greater fulfillment and satisfaction with life in middle adulthood.

Source: From Stein & Newcomb, 1999.

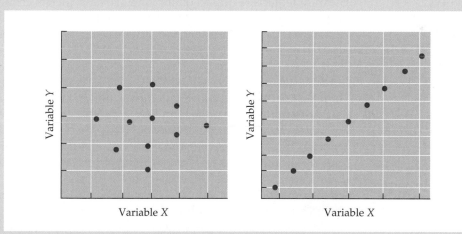

complex interactions between the inborn talents, the environmental conditions in which these are played out (for example, demographic trends affecting the availability of jobs or social policies regulating equal employment opportunities), the unique learning histories of each person, and the skills with which individuals approach their work (see Chapter 2).

Adolescents observe themselves and note how well their skills, interests, and values match the requirements of the situation. These observations have consequences for the types of work they think they might be good at. They are also related to what they are interested in and what they value (Mitchell & Krumboltz, 1990). Let's take a look at how social-cognitive theory puts these various factors together in explaining career choices.

Consider the case of a fictitious adolescent, Carlos, age 17. Carlos grew up in a quiet, ethnically mixed neighborhood; his mother is native-born American, and his father came to this country as a young boy from Mexico. Both parents are hardworking; his father is a contractor and his mother a daycare worker. Carlos was quiet in elementary school and received little attention from his predominantly European American teachers. He often heard his father say that "White teachers think Mexican kids aren't that smart." He began to perceive his teachers as different from himself, and he emotionally shut down when interacting with them. Nothing in elementary school disproved what he had learned from his father.

In junior high, Carlos's English teacher noticed that his creative stories were well written and that he had an unusually large vocabulary for his age. She displayed his work in the classroom. Carlos felt proud, and his classmates often asked him for help. Carlos began to think that not all teachers are alike—some think he is smart.

Carlos tells himself that he might not tell stories as well as his grandma, but he knows he's better than the other kids in his class. Carlos enjoys writing and wonders if he's good enough to get paid for doing it for a living. He also questions whether he would enjoy it more than being a contractor. When he has worked for his father, he has always felt competent. He wonders which occupation would be best for him and decides to take some creative writing courses and talk to his father about a summer job.

Environmental events such as higher interest rates on loans (and a drop-off in construction) or a TV writers' strike can affect vocational decision making. Even though social-cognitive theory emphasizes individual learning experiences, many of which are planned (such as taking a writing course), it acknowledges the impact of unplanned events like an economic recession and its effect on the construction industry, or a screenwriter's strike and national awareness of the importance of writers when faced with only reruns to view (Mitchell & Krumboltz, 1990).

CRITIQUE OF SOCIAL-COGNITIVE THEORY Social-cognitive theory recognizes that people actively attempt to understand the consequences of their actions and use this understanding in ways that change their environments to better meet their needs. Social-cognitive theory also explains the way individuals incorporate social and economic conditions into their decision making. Economic recessions, outsourcing of jobs, a global economy, and consequent competition for jobs all have an impact on career decision making. One shortcoming of this approach is that it does not give us a model of normative behavior at different points in the life cycle, nor does it relate decision making to developmental changes in such important aspects of the self as identity and self-concept (Brown, 1990). For a developmental approach to vocational choice, we turn to the theories of Ginzburg and Super.

fantasy stage Ginzburg's first stage of vocational development, characterized by focus on highly visible aspects of vocations and no assessment of personal qualifications.

Ginzburg: Vocational Stages

Eli Ginzburg (1972) views vocational development as a progressive narrowing of choices that at first reflect only fantasy but with age come to be based on reality. Choosing a career is an adaptive process in which individuals continually seek the best fit between their own goals and the opportunities that actually exist. The process unfolds over three stages: fantasy, tentative, and realistic.

THREE VOCATIONAL STAGES The **fantasy stage** lasts through childhood. During this time, children imagine themselves in the roles of those with whom they identify. These figures can be as real as parents, teachers, even ballerinas or sports heroes, or as fantastic as the cartoon characters they see on television. This stage involves no real assessment of what one might be good at or what the actual

Vocational development can be viewed as a progressive narrowing of choices in the search for the best fit between one's goals and self-concept and the opportunities that actually exist.

requirements of an occupation might be. Children respond to visible aspects of jobs—uniforms, fire trucks, and ballet slippers. Ginzburg (1990) notes that the 5-year-old son of a banker may say he wants to be a policeman when he grows up, because the uniform and activities of a policeman are understandable in a way that those of a banker are not.

In the **tentative stage** (from about age 11 to age 17), career thoughts begin to reflect adolescents' own interests, abilities, and values. At first, however, only their interests are important. One adolescent may plan to be a jockey because she loves horses, or another a musician because he is interested in jazz. With time, adolescents become aware that their interests change and, more importantly, that their interests may not match their abilities. A boy who lives for basketball may fail to make the team at school, or a girl who wants to be a jockey may find that at 12 she is already larger than most professional jockeys. In other words, adolescents discover that interest alone is not enough. Eventually, adolescents think of work in terms of what they value. They question how important it is to make a lot of money, whether their work will contribute to society, or how much they value free time, independence, or security. As they think through the things that are important to them, they let certain choices slide in favor of others that better fit their values and abilities.

Late adolescents enter the **realistic stage** when they explore the tentative choices they have been considering. For college students this means taking courses in a specific field. Some will find these courses interesting and challenging and will go on to major in that field, whereas others may find their coursework not sufficiently interesting or challenging and look for another field in which to concentrate. Similarly, students who start to work after high school will find out whether the jobs remain interesting or whether they need to look for different ones.

Following exploration, adolescents pull together, or crystallize, the many factors bearing upon a career choice: the required training, their own interests and talents, and the actual opportunities that exist. This integration results in commitment to a particular vocational path. College students will complete the required courses in their major; adolescents working at a job will finish the training programs needed for advancement. Finally, individuals specialize within their field. Students preparing to teach, for instance, will decide whether to do so at the elementary or the secondary level; an auto mechanic will decide whether to specialize in foreign or domestic cars.

CRITIQUE OF GINZBURG'S THEORY   Developmental data support Ginzburg's distinctions between fantasy, tentative, and realistic bases for thinking about work. Children understand their world in terms of its visible and tangible properties long before they appreciate its more abstract qualities. Similarly, adolescents begin to think of themselves in terms of their psychological characteristics—interests, abilities, and values—as in Ginzburg's tentative stage; even so, Monica Johnson (2002), at the University of North Carolina, found that adolescents' work values are not nearly as realistic as they will become with time. Finally, the commitment to an occupation that occurs in Ginzburg's realistic stage is an integral part of the identity formation process of late adolescence.

A shortcoming of Ginzburg's theory is that the process responsible for change remains unclear. Also, Ginzburg based his theory on data collected exclusively with males. Although doing so does not necessarily invalidate a theory, limiting one's sample in this way raises the strong possibility that data permitting a better description of the career plans of women were likely to have been missed.

tentative stage   Ginzburg's second stage of vocational development, in which vocational choice is directed more by interests than capacities.

realistic stage   Ginzburg's third stage of vocational development, characterized by exploration of and commitment to a vocational path.

Super: Careers and the Self-Concept

growth stage Super's first stage of vocational development characterized more by discovery about oneself than about vocations.

exploration stage Super's second stage of vocational development, in which one begins to make choices related to one's future work.

establishment stage Super's third stage of vocational development, in which one settles into one's work.

maintenance stage Super's fourth stage of vocational development, in which one maintains one's occupational skills and position.

decline stage Super's fifth stage of vocational development, in which one retires.

Donald Super (1981, 1990) suggests that people choose occupations that are consistent with the way they see themselves, that reflect their interests, values, and strengths. Choosing an occupation means finding a match between the self-perceptions that make up one's self-concept and the actual requirements of the jobs one is considering. This process is made all the more difficult for adolescents because their views of different occupations and of themselves change as they age. An adolescent may have only the vaguest idea of what a psychologist does after speaking with one at school. She may think that all psychologists work in schools testing students. Several years later, that same adolescent may have discovered that some psychologists counsel people with personal problems, that others work in industry, and even others work in laboratories collecting and analyzing data. Meanwhile, this adolescent's sense of herself may have changed from someone who wanted to help others to someone who is more interested in ideas than in people. How suitable she sees psychology as an occupation depends on how her perceptions of the discipline have evolved as she has changed.

FIVE VOCATIONAL STAGES Super describes five stages of vocational development. In the **growth stage**, adolescents discover more about themselves than about an occupation. Super (1990) feels that the major developmental task in this stage is simply to develop a realistic self-concept. At the same time, adolescents are also developing a feeling for what work involves.

In the **exploration stage**, adolescents begin to make choices that relate to their future work. Choosing courses in school is part of this process. This stage unfolds as adolescents move from plans that reflect only their interests (what they would like to be), to those that reflect a growing awareness of their abilities (and how well these match their interests), to a realistic appraisal that includes the availability and accessibility of certain jobs.

For Super, choosing a vocation marks the beginning of a process that typically lasts through early adulthood. In the **establishment stage**, individuals settle into their work. Even if they change jobs, they are likely to find the same form of work in another setting or office.

The years of middle adulthood, from about 45 to 65, are devoted to maintaining one's occupational position, the **maintenance stage**. Super speaks of the developmental task in these years as "holding one's own against competition," whether in the form of others who are involved in the same type of work, or maintaining the same level and quality of work as in the past. Finally, the **decline stage**, which occurs in late adulthood, involves retirement for most workers and the need to find other roles through which to express themselves.

CRITIQUE OF SUPER'S THEORY Super's theory is one of the most widely cited and influential theories of vocational development. It is also one of the most interesting psychologically, in that it traces vocational development through the life cycle by relating it to changes in the self-concept and the roles one fills at different ages. Super's theory enjoys considerable research support (Osipow, 1983).

The process Super uses to account for development is similar to the homeostatic or equilibrium model in other organismic theories, such as Piaget's (see Chapter 2). A match between self perceptions and the requirements of one's work results in vocational stability; this stability is maintained until changes in self-perceptions or work requirements create a mismatch. Mismatches produce instability and the need to repeat elements of the larger cycle until individuals find another type of work that suits them (Super, 1990).

Holland: Personality Types and Work

Picasso once said, "When I work I relax; doing nothing or entertaining visitors makes me tired." Picasso illustrates Holland's explanation for vocational success: His personality type corresponded to the type of work he did. John Holland (1985a) classifies individuals into one of six types. Different work environments either complement or conflict with the qualities that make up any type. As an artist, Picasso excelled; as a banker, he would have been a flop.

SIX PERSONALITY TYPES   **Realistic personality types** are practical and down-to-earth. They prefer problems than can be explicitly defined and that yield to an orderly approach, as opposed to those that require abstract or creative approaches. Their interpersonal skills are weak, and they like work that does not involve them with people. These types prefer occupations such as mechanic, farmer, construction worker, engineer, or surveyor.

Investigative personality types are as curious as realistic types are practical. They delight in situations that call for a creative or analytic approach. They are thinkers rather than doers, and their approach is intellectual and abstract. They enjoy being by themselves and getting caught up in their own world of ideas. Investigative types make good scientists, doctors, computer programmers, and writers.

Artistic personality types are original, imaginative, and creative. They prefer situations that are relatively unstructured and allow them to express their creative talents; they do well as painters, writers, or musicians.

Social personality types are understanding, friendly, and people oriented. They have the verbal and interpersonal skills that allow them to work well with others. They are comfortable with their own and others' feelings, often approaching problems in terms of feelings rather than seeking an intellectual solution. They make good counselors, ministers, teachers, and social workers.

Enterprising personality types are gregarious and dominant. They have strong interpersonal skills and enjoy work that brings them into contact with others in ways that allow them to express their assertiveness. Fields such as real estate, management, law, or sales suit their ambitious temperament.

Conventional personality types are efficient and tidy. They like well-defined tasks in which their conscientious approach is likely to bring success. They are followers—of rules and authority figures—and seek out highly structured environments in which they need not be leaders themselves. Occupations for which they are suited include banking, accounting, and secretarial services.

Holland believes these personality types reflect different learning histories and inborn talents that together shape patterns of success, resulting in preferred approaches to problems or tasks.

CRITIQUE OF HOLLAND'S THEORY   Perhaps the strongest features of Holland's theory are its usefulness and the extent to which it has stimulated research in the field of vocational choice. The Strong-Campbell Interest Inventory (Campbell, 1974) and the Vocational Preference Inventory (Holland, 1985b), both based on Holland's typology, are widely used measures of vocational preference (Donnay & Borgen, 1996). Holland himself considers the usefulness of a theory to be one of its most important features.

Holland's theory, however, gives little consideration to social context variables such as ethnicity and gender. Holland considers personality types to influence the work one chooses, yet for many adolescents vocational choices are limited by variables such as ethnicity, sex, and socioeconomic level. African American and Hispanic males, for instance, are overrepresented (consid-

realistic personality types
In Holland's typology of vocational interests, individuals who prefer situations that are explicitly defined and require few interpersonal skills, for example, a mechanic or computer programmer.

investigative personality types
In Holland's typology of vocational interests, individuals who prefer work requiring intellectual curiosity, for example, a scientist or mathematician.

artistic personality types
In Holland's typology of vocational interests, individuals who prefer work requiring imagination and creativity, for example, a graphic artist or poet.

social personality types
In Holland's typology of vocational interests, individuals who prefer work involving them with people, such as counseling or teaching.

enterprising personality types
In Holland's typology of vocational interests, individuals who prefer work involving interpersonal skills and assertiveness, such as management, law, or sales.

conventional personality types
In Holland's typology of vocational interests, individuals who prefer highly structured environments and well-defined tasks.

Why do some adolescents pursue a career in science versus other fields? A combination of personality type as well as factors such as an inspiring teacher, gender, and ethnicity influences most adolescents' vocational choices.

ering their actual numbers relative to other groups) in low-level realistic jobs and underrepresented in all other types of jobs. All women, regardless of their ethnic background, are overrepresented in conventional and social jobs, and African American and Hispanic women are particularly overrepresented in low-level realistic types of work (Arbona, 1989). Yet the interests of African American and European American high school students are highly similar when assessed with Holland's Vocational Preference Inventory (Ryan et al., 1996).

Differences in the levels of occupation that minority adolescents actually attain versus those in the dominant culture underscore the need for approaches to career counseling developed especially for minority students (Arbona, 1989).

Joining the Workforce

The type of work adolescents feel they are best suited for may not be what they find themselves doing when they get their first real job. A number of additional factors affect their entry into the workforce.

Job Availability

Unemployment among young workers in the United States and other industrialized nations is relatively common, and has been so for several decades. In France, unemployment among youth has been around 20%, and in Italy and Spain around 30% and 40%, respectively. Germany and Japan have been exceptions, employing high percentages of young workers, perhaps due to an apprenticeship system in the former and a cooperative alliance between schools, business, and industry in the latter. However, even in Germany and Japan joblessness among youth has increased to the level of the United States, around 10% (Martin, 2009).

The higher rate of youth unemployment can be traced to a number of factors. Unemployment among workers of all ages has been higher than previously, and young workers are more vulnerable. The risk of being laid off is greater because they have less seniority, and because companies have less invested in them in training. Additionally, younger workers are less likely to have long-term contracts. Even if there is just a slowdown in hiring, young workers face stiff competition against older and more experienced job applicants.

What kinds of jobs await youths who are about to join the workforce? Among the top 10 fastest-growing occupations, over half are related to health care and computers, reflecting our aging population and the growth of technology (Table 9.5) (U.S. Bureau of Labor Statistics, 2007). These figures may be somewhat deceptive, however, because the fastest-growing occupations do not necessarily provide the largest number of jobs. There are far more salesclerks, cashiers, janitors, waiters, and home health aides than there are nurses, systems analysts, and computer engineers.

Creative adolescents are both reflective and spontaneous. They are less likely to conform to accepted practice and more likely to try new ways of doing things than their less creative peers. These adolescents in Miami used their spray cans to transform this concrete wall.

TABLE 9.5
Occupations with the Largest Job Growth, Projections to 2016

OCCUPATION	EMPLOYMENT[a]		PERCENTAGE	POSTSECONDARY EDUCATION	EARNINGS
	2006	2016			
Network systems & data communications analysts	262	402	53.4	Bachelor's degree	$$$$
Personal & home care aides	767	1156	50.6	Short-term on-the-job training	$
Home health aides	797	1171	48.7	Short-term on-the-job training	$
Computer software engineers, applications	507	733	44.6	Bachelor's degree	$$$$
Medical assistants	417	565	35.4	Moderate-term on-the-job training	$
Computer systems analysts	504	650	29.0	Bachelor's degree	$$$$
Customer service representatives	2202	2747	24.8	Moderate-term on-the-job training	$
Registered nurses	2505	3092	23.5	Associate degree	$$$$
Post-secondary teachers	1672	2054	22.9	Doctoral degree	$$$$
Management analysts	678	827	21.9	Bachelor's or higher degree, work experience	$$$$

Source: U.S. Bureau of Labor Statistics, 2007.

[a]Numbers in thousands of jobs

Although most of those entering the workforce will replace workers in existing jobs, the qualifications for jobs are increasing as technology and foreign trade affect the workplace (U.S. Bureau of Labor Statistics, 2005a). Many of the newly created jobs will require more skills than did jobs in the past. Peter Coleman (1993) estimates that approximately 40% of new jobs will require more than 16 years of preparation and training.

Those entering the workforce will be entering a workplace that is increasingly automated and technological. Twenty years ago, an auto mechanic had to master only 5,000 pages of service manuals to work on any car on the road, compared with today, when 465,000 pages of service manuals exist for the hundreds of models sold in this country. Equally demanding changes are present in service sector jobs:

> The secretary who once pecked away at a manual typewriter must now master a word processor, a computer and telecommunications equipment. Even the cashier at the 7-Eleven store has to know how to sell money orders and do minor maintenance jobs on the Slurpee and Big Gulp machines. ("The Forgotten Half," 1989, p. 46)

The upward mobility of entrants to the labor force is limited by the large numbers of baby boomers already there. Shifts in patterns of employment are not likely until these baby boomers reach retirement age, beginning in 2011. The relatively large numbers of middle-aged boomers also cuts down on advancement opportunities for youth who are starting work now, because they will still be in the workforce when the latter are ready to move up to more advanced positions (Toossi, 2004).

Although unemployment among young workers has increased radically since the recession in 2007, this increase has not been uniform across workers of all ages and backgrounds. Many minority youth face significantly higher rates of unemployment than the white majority. Among urban minority youth, unemployment can reach staggering proportions, exceeding 70% in some inner-city areas (U.S. Bureau of Labor Statistics, 2002). These inner-city youth face not only joblessness but also poverty, poorly equipped schools, increased drug use, and high rates of violent crime. Furthermore, many businesses have

More high school students work today than a generation ago. But their jobs are usually for minimum wage and provide few opportunities to move up to more responsible and challenging positions.

left the cities, making employment even less accessible. Job-training programs have offered one of the few opportunities to change the life circumstances of these youth, but federal funding for these programs tends to fluctuate with the political climate. For these youth to begin to realize the promise of the talents within them, they need programs to help not only with jobs, but also with the host of conditions that attend joblessness, both at the individual and community level.

Gender in the Workforce

In past generations, the type of jobs people held could be predicted more easily than today by knowing their sex. The terms *pink collar* and *blue collar* refer to occupations that are female- or male-dominated. Females were more likely to work in service occupations—clerical and salesclerk positions or child care—and males as craftsmen, machine operators, technicians, farmers, or laborers. This is still the case, but the divisions are not as distinct as previously. Occupational planning among high school seniors is less sex-typed. The percentage of high school females planning for professional occupations or thinking of entering male-dominated occupations has increased dramatically, as has the percentage of males entering careers in female-dominated professions such as nursing or teaching.

Despite these changes, the gender gap in pay remains significant. For instance, with the exception of younger workers, who make considerably less irrespective of their sex, women earn approximately 73% of what men earn (U.S. Bureau of Labor Statistics, 2005c). This gap in pay remains even when level of education is equated and even in female-dominant occupations (**Table 9.6**), thus ruling out possible artifacts due to qualifications or to occupational choice (Lips, 2008).

SELF-LIMITING EXPECTATIONS   One of the primary internal barriers adolescent females face when they begin a job is the value they assign to their work. Females place less value on their work than do males; as a consequence, females expect to be paid less—and are. An office worker who sees the importance to a company of maintaining files and records (invoices, shipments, and so on) will value the work she does and expect to be paid accordingly. This person could well argue, with reason, that the company's income depends on how effectively records are kept. Those who consider their work to be important are likely to show initiative and creativity—important for pay increases and advancement to higher positions. Most, if not all, of the self-limiting expectations females have are learned (Major & Forcey, 1985).

A number of factors distinguish females who expect to pursue nontraditional occupations (the ones that also pay more) from those who stay in traditional types of work. The influence of significant others, including role models, is important. So, too, is the anticipated cost of education (Davey & Stoppard, 1993). Information about the availability of jobs and the many types of jobs that exist is also vitally important. But for such information to have an effect, adolescent females must see it as relevant to their own career plans—that

TABLE 9.6
Percentage of Men's Weekly Earnings Earned by Women in 2005 in Female- and Male-Dominated Occupations

	PERCENTAGE OF EMPLOYEES WHO ARE WOMEN	WOMEN'S PERCENTAGE OF MEN'S EARNINGS
Female-dominated occupations		
Secretaries and administrative assistants	97.3	86
Receptionists and information clerks	91.7	92
Registered nurses	91.6	92
Bookkeepers, accounting, and auditing clerks	89.3	95
Teaching assistants	90.8	100
Nursing, psychiatric, and home health aides	88.5	95
Male-dominated occupations		
Computer software engineers	21.2	81
Driver/sales workers and truck drivers	3.7	75
Engineering technicians, except drafters	18.9	85
Supervisors/managers, production and operating workers	19.7	67
Laborers and freight, stock, and material movers, hand	15.2	87
Police and sheriff's patrol officers	14.5	87

Source: Lips, 2008.

is, they must believe that they can be a botanist, beautician, electrician, ship loader, teacher, or business owner.

Many of the problems women face in the workforce are shared by minorities. We turn to a consideration of minorities in the workforce next.

Minorities in the Workforce

Whitney Young, a prominent civil rights leader, once remarked, "The trouble is that blacks are so visible. You hire one secretary and it looks like a whole lot of integration." As Young reminds us, barriers continue to exist to the full range of job opportunities open to minority adolescents. Although the career aspirations of minority youth entering the labor market are as high as those of youth in the dominant culture, they do not face the same career opportunities (Fouad & Byars-Winston, 2005; Kirton, 2009; Lease, 2006).

Many minority youth are likely to encounter social, cultural, and personal barriers to success despite landmark legislation in the 1960s and 1970s that paved the way for equity in employment. **Table 9.7** shows the percentages of minorities and those in the white majority employed in different types of occupations in 2008. One can see, for instance, that African Americans and Hispanic/Latino Americans are underrepresented in management and professional occupations and overrepresented in service ones (U.S. Bureau of Labor Statistics, 2009b).

POVERTY   The relatively high incidence of poverty among minority adolescents is a common link among the factors that affect their future employment. The most important factors are staying in school, receiving quality education, and making informed decisions about their futures. The rate of poverty can be nearly three times as high among some minorities as among adolescents in the dominant culture (**Figure 9.12**; Wright et al., 2010). Low-income students are

TABLE 9.7
Employed Percentage by Occupational Category for European American, African American, Asian American, and Hispanic Workers

OCCUPATIONAL CATEGORY	EUROPEAN AMERICAN	AFRICAN AMERICAN	ASIAN AMERICAN	HISPANIC
Management, professional, and related occupations (e.g., business executives, doctors, nurses, lawyers, teachers, engineers)	37.0	27.4	48.2	18.3
Service occupations (e.g., child-care workers, police officers, firefighters, food service workers, janitors, hairdressers)	15.7	24.4	16.3	24.2
Sales and office occupations (e.g., health technicians, sales representatives, sales clerks, bank tellers, teacher aides)	24.5	25.5	21.5	21.4
Natural resources, construction, and maintenance (e.g., farming, forestry, fishing, mechanics, construction workers)	11.0	6.4	4.1	18.2
Production, transportation, and material moving (e.g., machine operators, truck drivers, bus drivers, freight handlers)	11.9	16.2	9.9	17.8

Source: U.S. Bureau of Labor Statistics, 2009.

significantly more likely to drop out of high school than their upper-income counterparts, and those who remain in school are more likely to be tracked in non-college-preparatory and vocational courses (see Chapter 8).

Poverty is also related to lower academic performance. Low-income students are not as likely to achieve at the same levels as middle- and upper-income students nor, as mentioned, are the educational programs they receive of the same quality as those provided to middle- and upper-income youth. Poverty is unevenly distributed, tending to be centralized in urban and inner-city schools, where minority students make up most of the student body.

Intervention Programs: Strategies for Change

Programs designed to prepare minority and female adolescents to compete for jobs take a number of forms. School counselors play an important role by addressing attitudes that limit opportunity, as well as designing effective intervention programs.

Counselors as Change Agents

Because the opportunity structure for minority adolescents, and for females, is not the same as that for many males in the dominant culture, counselors must become active "change agents" in order to effectively prepare all students for jobs. In doing so they may need to meet with parents, teachers, and local

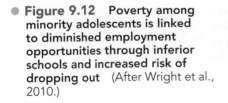
● **Figure 9.12 Poverty among minority adolescents is linked to diminished employment opportunities through inferior schools and increased risk of dropping out** (After Wright et al., 2010.)

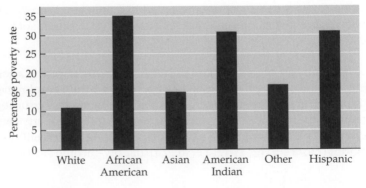

businesses to combat existing inequities, as well as work with teachers and schools to develop effective intervention programs to prepare these youth for the full range of careers open to others.

Before counselors can assume this role, they also need to examine their own biases. A counselor who accepts a talented minority girl's statement that she is interested in working with children as an aide or a helper in a classroom or playground, without suggesting other career opportunities that also involve helping people (such as medicine, psychology, or social work), reveals an insensitivity to the existence of very real gender or culturally based conflicts (Brooks, 1990).

Would it be too intrusive to direct this student to consider other career options? Brooks argues that counselors *must* begin directing minority and female students' attention to areas other than the role-traditional ones in which they might express an initial interest. If any have doubts about the appropriateness of such actions, they might consider what the same counselor would be likely to do if a talented white male with similar interests said he wanted to be a teacher aide or helper (Brooks, 1990).

STEM COURSES   Counselors can also effect change by directing more female and minority students into **STEM courses**. These are courses in science, technology, engineering and math. They are also the courses that provide a gateway to many of the higher level jobs. Female and minority students, with the exception of Asian Americans, take fewer mathematics and science courses in high school, and are less likely to major in science, technology, engineering, and mathematics in college. Yet these fields are the ones preparing students for the high-level jobs of the future.

Many colleges and universities have developed programs that are designed to prepare and mentor minority youth while they are still in high school. California State University, Los Angeles, a university located in the midst of a number of low-income minority neighborhoods, has a number of such programs. In one of these programs, college engineering students serve as mentors to local middle and high school students who have expressed an interest in this field. Another program, with both academic and counseling components, works with local middle schools and secondary schools, encouraging an early interest in science and mathematics. Still another offers summer and weekend workshops in mathematics for talented middle and high school students. Yet another identifies and integrates talented high school students into ongoing research groups at the university for an eight-week summer program (CSULA: Pre-Collegiate Programs).

Until recently, career counselors have focused primarily on external barriers to equal employment—active or passive discrimination. Such barriers will continue until eradicated by social movements. However, internal barriers in the form of self-limiting expectations are also present. An immediate advantage to focusing on these barriers is to place the forces of change in the hands of the individual. Change through broad social movements such as legislation will of course remain important.

Having a teacher or a counselor who believes in them is an important element contributing to the eventual success of many minority adolescents.

STEM courses   Courses in science, technology, engineering, and mathematics that often provide a gateway to higher level jobs.

Irrational Beliefs and Maladaptive Myths

Students frequently approach career decisions with maladaptive beliefs and myths. These can be about themselves ("I'm not very smart"), a profession ("You have to be self-confident to be a nurse"), or the conditions that lead to satisfaction with a career ("I wouldn't be happy in a profession unless I made a lot of money at it") (Krumboltz, 1991). **Box 9.2** identifies types of myths that keep many people from trying interesting careers.

BOX 9.2 In More Depth

Myths That Interfere with Adaptive Career Decision Making

"I have to know exactly what I want to do before I can act."

"Choosing a career involves making just one decision."

"If I change my mind once I've picked a career, I'm a failure."

"If I can only be good in nursing [construction, management, and so on], then I will be content."

"Work satisfies all of a person's needs."

"If I work hard enough, I can be successful at anything."

"How good I am at my job determines my worth as a person."

Source: From Mitchell & Krumboltz, 1987.

cognitive restructuring
A counseling technique that confronts individuals with their irrational beliefs.

attributional retraining
A career counseling technique that focuses on individuals' explanations for anticipated career-related successes or failures.

INTERVENTION TECHNIQUES   One approach to counseling students with career indecision, known as **cognitive restructuring**, recommends confronting them with their irrational beliefs, making more adaptive decision making possible. A young woman, for instance, may think that her parents "would have nothing to do with her" if she didn't become an elementary school teacher. Because she has little interest in teaching, she finds it difficult to plan for college or think about a career.

Intervention in the form of cognitive restructuring would encourage her to look at the evidence supporting the belief that her parents would sever their relationship if she did not become a teacher (she might find little to support this belief). A counselor might then give her the assignment of talking to her parents about her future. She discovers they are concerned only that she will be able to support herself in a secure job. She is also assigned the task of interviewing five women in different professions and asking them the most satisfying and frustrating aspects of their work. She finds that accounting, career guidance, and being a teacher (surprise!) are all attractive alternatives. She decides to apply to college. Cognitive restructuring helps reduce students' anxiety when thinking about career planning, consequently making it easier for them to think about their futures.

A related approach, termed **attributional retraining**, focuses students' attention on the way they explain career-related outcomes. Do they attribute career outcomes to conditions for which they are responsible and over which they have control, conditions that will yield to their efforts? Or do they see career outcomes as being influenced more by circumstances beyond their control, where their efforts will do little to change the situation? The former beliefs are adaptive, whereas the latter are not (Luzzo & Ward, 1995).

Darrell Luzzo, at Auburn University, and Tammy James and Marilyn Luna, at the University of North Alabama, (1996) showed students with maladaptive beliefs an attributional retraining video containing adaptive attributional statements such as the following:

> I realized as I was growing up that anything worthwhile in terms of my career was going to take effort and hard work. I pretty much took control over my career decisions. I've worked hard ... and it has helped me. If I hadn't taken the time and put forth the effort that I did, I wouldn't be doing as well as I am now. (p. 417)

After attributional retraining, these students were significantly more likely to believe that they had control over career decisions, and that the more work they put into these decisions, the more successful they would be. Furthermore, a six-week follow-up showed these differences to persist over time.

BELIEVING IN ONESELF: PERSONAL EFFECTIVENESS   Some of the most important beliefs affecting career decisions are the ones adolescents have about themselves. Feelings of **personal effectiveness** reflect how much control adolescents feel they have in a situation. Adolescents who can anticipate the consequences their actions will have are in a better position to control what happens to them by doing, or not doing, certain things. Those who perceive themselves as effective anticipate positive outcomes. They mentally rehearse adaptive solutions, and these in turn can help them find their way through problems more effectively (Bandura, 1989; Zimmerman et al., 1992).

The type of outcome adolescents anticipate also affects their motivation to engage in an activity. In other words, the goals they set reflect their appraisal of their ability to meet them. Those who doubt themselves are more likely to give up when they face difficulty, whereas adolescents who believe in themselves work harder. Bandura points out that, at times, inaccurate self-assessments can actually help adolescents when making career decisions. Optimistic evaluations of competence—if not too far off the mark—can help. A less optimistic, if truer, judgment can be self-limiting, failing to motivate adolescents to stretch beyond their present circumstances.

Feelings of effectiveness can be either general or quite specific. Poole and Evans (1988) had adolescents rate their competence in several life skill areas (such as use of time, setting goals, making choices, social awareness). They found that adolescents generally see themselves as being competent at the things they value, although not necessarily as much as they might want to be. But important gender differences exist in self-perceptions. These investigators found that females viewed themselves as less competent overall than males and as competent in fewer areas, even though an objective measure that all had completed showed them to have done slightly better than males (Poole & Evans, 1988).

With respect to intervention programs, then, assessing adolescents' self-appraisals is an important step when having them consider the goals they set for themselves with respect to careers.

At present we need much more information about the effectiveness of the many programs that help youth combat the internal and external barriers they face in attaining career goals. What is clear so far is that most teachers, parents, counselors, and students need to expand their thinking beyond role-traditional careers for minorities and females.

personal effectiveness
Perceiving oneself as effective and in control of a situation.

Adolescents and College

The number of students enrolled in college has more than doubled in a single generation, with over 17½ million students attending college in 2006-2007. Female graduates now outnumber male graduates, whereas in their parents' generation, more bachelor's degrees had been awarded to men (Snyder et al., 2009). Additionally, the increase in percentages of minority students earning bachelor's degrees was greater than the increase for students from the dominant culture (Table 9.8). Whereas 22% more white students earned degrees than a decade previously, the increase for minority students was considerably larger: 55% more African Americans, 53% more Asian/Pacific Islanders, 84% Hispanic, and 54% Native American/Alaska

TABLE 9.8 Increases in Percentages of Students Earning a Bachelor's Degree (1997–2007), by Ethnicity	
ETHNICITY	INCREASE
European American	22
African American	55
American Indian/Alaska Native	54
Asian/Pacific Islander	53
Hispanic	84

Source: Snyder et al., 2009.

dialectical thinking
Reasoning that questions the premises on which it is based when tests of the premises are not supported.

Native students graduated from college than had a decade previously (Snyder et al., 2009).

With age, adolescents get better at solving life's problems. We turn next to ways of thinking that enable them to see similarities between the problems they presently face and those they have solved in the past.

New Solutions to Old Problems: Dialectical Thinking

In earlier discussions of intellectual development (see Chapter 4), we saw that adolescents, unlike children even a few years younger, are able to stretch their minds beyond a physical world defined by their senses to a world of possibilities that exists first and foremost in their minds. Piaget referred to this way of thinking as formal thought. However, the capacity for formal thought does not guarantee that the young adolescent will arrive at a satisfactory conclusion. That's because formal thought can only work out the implications of the assumptions with which one has begun. If these assumptions are inappropriate or too narrow, then even perfect logic can lead one to unrealistic conclusions. Such a process can sometimes be seen in the idealistic but extremely impractical ideas of adolescents.

What is needed to get beyond this limitation of formal thought is the ability to go back and question the assumptions with which one began. This development is termed **dialectical thinking**. This more advanced form of reasoning makes it possible for emerging adults to take a more practical approach to problems than the earlier and more narrowly logical way in which adolescents approach them.

Dialectical thinking enables young adults to achieve a kind of cognitive self-awareness, to assume a new perspective that allows them to view the way they have been approaching a problem. By mentally stepping outside their previous perspective, they can discover and change the assumptions that lead them to unrealistic or mistaken conclusions.

FORMAL AND DIALECTICAL THINKING COMPARED   To see how these two ways of reasoning differ, let's consider two fictitious young women as each realizes that even though her parents have always told her that she was free to do or be whatever she wanted, they do not accept her plans for her life. Each has introduced to her parents a young man she intends to marry and has found that they do not approve of her choice.

Connie is upset and confused. She can think of only two explanations for her parents' reaction: Either she is wrong or her parents are wrong. Either her parents *are* willing to accept the choices she makes, but this choice is so outrageous that *no* parent could support it, or her parents have not been telling her the truth—it's not all right with them for her to be anything she wants to be if that means being different from them. She reacts with hurt and anger and can think of nothing to say to them.

Janice recognizes her hurt and anger at her parents and begins to think about the differences in their values and hers. She recognizes that people's values influence their actions, but that in acting, people change events, and these changes frequently lead to new awareness and new values. Her parents' affirmation of her freedom to be herself has allowed her to be the person she is—a person who is quite

Although a job can help older adolescents develop structural analytical thinking and dialectical reasoning, college courses provide more systematic opportunities for cognitive growth, as can discussions with friends outside the classroom.

different from them. Janice knows that because her parents have valued her, they valued her freedom to make her own decisions, and that because of this freedom she has had experiences they never had. She realizes that these experiences have changed her view of the world and allow her to see things in others that her parents are not able to recognize. Although Janice is sad that her parents cannot appreciate the qualities in her fiancé that she values, she is grateful she had the opportunity they gave her to be herself.

Connie and Janice have each dealt with a painful situation in different ways. Connie's approach reflects formal thinking. She believes there are a set of truths that are described by a point of view. She can evaluate situations and events from this point of view but has no way of reconciling differences that may challenge it. Thus, either she or her parents must be wrong. Janice can step outside her beliefs and see how they have evolved from those of her parents. Her ability to see evolution and change as a natural part of people and relationships may help her find ways to establish a new relationship with her parents.

We have discussed the ability to move from one perspective to another, noting differences and finding relationships between them, as an intellectual feat—that is, as dialectical thinking. Yet more than intellect may be involved. The ability to stand back from one's own way of thinking while viewing that of others may reflect one's personality as much as one's intellect—one has to be willing to risk letting one's beliefs be put to the test in this way. We examine the implications of this very personal stance on knowledge in the next section.

How College Can Change the Way Adolescents Think

Given the significant numbers of adolescents attending and graduating from college, it's reasonable to ask what advantages a college education might confer. In particular, how might a college education shape their view of the world and the way they resolve differences between themselves and others?

William Perry (1970), of Harvard University, identified important changes during the college years in the way adolescents think about ideas. These changes reflect their beliefs about the nature of truth as much as their ability to think in general. Perry conducted his observations among college men. However, individuals in any setting should experience similar changes if they let their experiences challenge their ideas. Perry identified three major forms of thought: dualism, relativism, and commitment in relativism.

DUALISM: LOOKING FOR ANSWERS   **Dualistic thinking** is the belief that problems are simply solved by finding the right answer, that is, by discovering the truth. Dualistic thinkers have not yet encountered differences of perspective or belief that are so great they could not be bridged by a single set of answers. They operate, in other words, within a single frame of reference. For them learning is mostly a matter of acquiring the facts; it does not require evaluation of the facts. Adolescents who function at this level tend to view ideas, and people, as right or wrong, as good or bad. Ideas that are familiar—that can be assimilated into their belief system—are accepted as legitimate; those that violate their beliefs are regarded as illegitimate or, at the very least, suspect (Perry, 1970).

Adolescents who function at this level have rarely experienced ways of life that are different from their own. To them, issues are straightforward, and problems yield to discipline and hard work. The following is an adolescent's description of life in his hometown:

> Well I come, I came here from a small town. Midwest, where, well, ah, everyone believed the same things. Everyone's Methodist and everyone's Republican. So, ah, there just wasn't any ... well that's not

dualistic thinking   The first of Perry's three forms of thought: the belief that truth is independent of one's frame of reference.

quite true ... there are some Catholics, two families, and I guess they, I heard they were Democrats, but they weren't really, didn't seem to be in town really, I guess. (Perry, 1970, p. 70)

One of the central experiences of adolescence is the discovery that others have points of view different from one's own. This discovery is pivotal in moving out of the first of Perry's levels. Here is what the same adolescent had to say about diversity:

So in my dorm I, we've been—ah a number of discussions, where, there'll be, well, there's quite a variety in our dorm, Catholic, Protestant, and the rest of them, and a Chinese boy whose parents— ah follow the teachings of Confucianism. He isn't, but his folks are.... And a couple of guys are complete—ah agnostics, agnostics. Of course, some people are quite disturbing, they say they're atheists. But they don't go very far, they say they're atheists, but they're not. And then there are, one fellow who is a deist. And by discussing it— ah, it's the, the sort of thing that, that really—ah awakens you. (p. 70)

RELATIVISM: LOSING ONESELF TO IDEAS   Perry (1970) points out that the steps from dualism to relativism require courage. It's an uncomfortable journey. Instead of accepting simple answers, adolescents must learn to rely on their own judgment and risk their own ideas. Students know that this process is difficult. As one student said, "Every now and again you do....meet people who just give up and try to find 'answers'..." (p. 107).

Relativistic thinking compares ideas instead of looking for the single one that is right. Relativistic thinkers become aware that what they had accepted as facts are actually interpretations that make sense within some frame of reference, whether a theory presented in a class or the perspective offered by the culture. They also know that more than one frame of reference exists and that each represents a legitimate point of view. From Perry's description of these characteristics, it sounds as if students are moving from formal thought, in which they are operating within a single frame of reference, to structural analytical thought, in which they can compare several worldviews or frames of reference. The development of dialectical reasoning may be pivotal to this change, as this would allow students to evaluate their assumptions as they go along.

One student had this to say about the change to relativistic thought:

I think the main thing that was interesting this year was questioning basic assumptions.... It was interesting in anthropology, particularly, which I didn't go into very deeply, but what I saw as the very basic differences, things that never occurred to me to question before, I don't know whether I'm questioning them now, but at least I know that it's possible to question. (p. 117)

Students experience a new freedom in these discoveries: a freedom to see that they can decide for themselves which ideas are best, rather than try to discover what has made most sense to someone else. Learning becomes personally relevant, as they shift their focus from the facts they have been amassing to the process of thinking itself. Relativistic thinking carries a distinct advantage: Students can discover themselves in addition to the concepts and theories they are studying. Looking back on this discovery, one student remembered his first year in college as follows:

I remember my first Christmas vacation home from college. Nobody could say anything about the world that I didn't say was just an hypothesis. My Dad and I argued all the time. He'd say something was an established scientific fact, like gravity or the world being round,

relativistic thinking
The second of Perry's three forms of thought: awareness of more than one frame of reference by which ideas can be evaluated.

or anything else that most people believe, and I would answer that a "fact" is just an hypothesis that hasn't been disproved yet. I know I must have been a pain in the butt to everybody but I had discovered relativism. I "knew" that what people believed to be true, including scientists, was what fit their experience. And since different people had different experiences—and even the same people had new experiences—nothing was true for everybody for all time. I'm a little embarrassed now when I think back to how I must have sounded, but I sure thought that I had found the philosophical answer to everything. (Wapner, 1990)

COMMITMENT IN RELATIVISM: FINDING ONESELF   Erik Erikson (1959) has said that one's sense of identity requires a feeling that what "I" know is also what "I" value. Relativism challenges this equation as students cut themselves adrift from the moorings of ideas and values they once accepted as absolutes. The danger of relativism is the potential loss of identity that adolescents face. If knowledge reflects different contexts, adolescents will experience discontinuity in what they believe and value as they move from one context to the next.

The pathway out of this maze is choice. Adolescents move beyond relativism by making commitments, becoming agents, choosing, investing themselves, and affirming their experiences. Perry notes that choice and **commitment in relativism** create meaning that would not otherwise exist in a relativistic world; reason alone offers little basis for commitment to any particular worldview. Paradoxically, intellectual development lies in going beyond reason, in taking a position despite one's knowledge that reason alone does not justify this position over others. This step, in a very real sense, involves an act of faith, just as the previous one involved courage. Adolescents move from first defining themselves through individual commitments, such as a career or a mate, to the realization that commitment has come to characterize a way of living.

Gender Differences in Approaches to Knowledge

Does the preceding description fit the intellectual journey of college women as well as men? We simply don't know. Perry included a small number of women in his sample, but he referred only to interviews with males in validating his scheme of intellectual development. Although the females he interviewed conformed to this progression, he may have missed other progressions that better describe intellectual transitions in college women. To explore a fuller sample, Mary Belenky, Blythe Clinchy, Nancy Goldberger, and Jill Tarule (1986) conducted a similar study with women.

Unlike Perry, these investigators did not interview a homogeneous sample of students in a university setting. One-third of their sample was composed of mothers facing the real life challenges of parenting. Belenky and her associates point out that it is easiest to see a sequence such as the one Perry observed when the sample is homogeneous and the context in which development takes place does not vary. Only future research will tell us whether females move through a similar intellectual progression. Meanwhile, the comparisons Belenky and her colleagues provide with Perry's data are indeed interesting.

They note, first, that females do not think in ways neatly described by Perry's categories. Differences emerge from the very beginning. Let's look again at the first step males take. Belenky and her associates (1986) note that the adolescent male, once he discovers the multiplicity of truth,

foresees his own future as an authority.... [His] perception of the multiplicity of truth becomes a tool in the process of his separation and differentiation from others. His opinion distinguishes him from all others and he lets them know it. (p. 64)

commitment in relativism
The third of Perry's three forms of thought: committing oneself to a point of view from which one can derive meaning.

subjective knowledge
The first of Belenky and associates' three forms of thought: a covert examination of issues while maintaining a surface conformity to traditional ideas.

procedural knowledge
The second of Belenky and associates' three forms of thought: independent thought that is nonetheless limited to a single frame of reference.

Adolescent females take a different first step. Those who begin the intellectual journey move from subjective knowledge (realizing that truth is relative) to procedural knowledge (assuming responsibility for what they know) to constructive knowledge (being aware that knowledge is constructed by each knower). Not all complete this journey.

SUBJECTIVE KNOWLEDGE: AGREEABLE DISSENT   Adolescent females with **subjective knowledge** appreciate that the multiplicity of truth frees them from traditional authority, but they are cautious about embracing an intellectual position. Unlike males, who have been rewarded for testing the status quo, females have been rewarded for being quiet, predictable, and agreeable. Speaking up, taking a stand, or disagreeing with others is more likely to run counter to what they have learned. Female adolescents repeatedly express concern that, in taking an intellectual stand, they will isolate themselves from others. Thus their relationships constrain them from forming and defending ideas that would distinguish or separate them from other people. They experience few expectations about, and get little support for, this type of intellectual risk taking (Belenky et al., 1986).

Rather than speaking out, many maintain a surface conformity while they covertly examine issues. "They become the polite listeners, the spectators who watch and listen but do not act" (Belenky et al., 1986, p. 66). Belenky and her associates note the intellectual loneliness of these female adolescents:

> The tragedy is that [they] still their public voice and are reluctant to share their private world; ultimately this hinders them from finding mentors who might support their intellectual and emotional growth. [They] can be silently alienated ... knowing somehow that their conformity is a lie and does not reveal the inner truth or potential they have recently come to value. (p. 67)

In speaking up, males lay claim to an intellectual terrain that has been staked out for centuries as theirs. There are few equivalent intellectual domains for females, and few means are identified for their use in defining one. Instead of reason—the ultimate analytic tool—females have been told their strength lies in intuition, which in relation to reason is like a divining rod compared to a surveyor's level. Instead of mapping out ideas, many learn to wait for the gentle tug of mind in an otherwise silent trek across an uncharted terrain.

In becoming skilled listeners to themselves and others, some women come to see the contradictions of their stance. Their observations make it possible for them to develop the more critical thought that characterizes the next step they take.

Many female adolescents maintain a surface conformity, becoming polite listeners and spectators. Rather than asserting their abilities, many experience intellectual loneliness and become silently alienated from the learning process.

PROCEDURAL KNOWLEDGE: STEPPING OUT INTELLECTUALLY   Females who step out intellectually—with **procedural knowledge**—assume responsibility for discovering things for themselves. Some do this by mastering the facts in an area, whether this be political economics, nursing, or managing a home. Others adopt a more subjective approach to what they are learning, approaching ideas for what they have to say about their lives. The understanding these women gain is more intimate and personal than that of the first group. Only the first approach is characteristic of Perry's males. For those who adopt it, doubting becomes an important way of putting ideas on trial, and bull sessions provide a forum in which individuals attack each other's position to hone the cutting edge of their logic. Belenky and her associates (1986) note that

> women find it hard to see doubting as a "game"; they tend to take it personally. Teachers and fathers and boyfriends assure them that arguments are not between persons but between positions, but the women continue to fear that someone may get hurt. (p. 105)

Conversations for females serve the function of bull sessions for males. Belenky and her associates give an example of a young Ethiopian college student who explained in one such conversation with an American friend why her country had adopted communism. They note the following:

> These young women did not engage in metaphysical debate. They did not argue about abstractions or attack or defend positions. No one tried to prove anything or to convert anyone. The Ethiopian articulated her reality, and the American tried to understand it. They did not discuss communism in general, impersonal terms, but in terms of its origins and consequences among a particular group of real people. (p. 114)

Though more advanced than subjective knowledge, procedural knowledge operates within a system of knowledge that cannot examine itself. Females who think in either of these ways

> can criticize a system, but only in the system's terms, only according to the system's standards. Women at this position may be liberals or conservatives, but they cannot be radicals. If, for example, they are feminists, they want equal opportunities for women within the capitalistic structure; they do not question the premises of the structure. When these women speak of "beating the system," they do not mean violating its expectations but rather exceeding them. (Belenky et al., 1986, p. 127)

For females to move beyond these forms of knowing, they need more than formal thought.

CONSTRUCTIVE KNOWLEDGE: EXAMINING THE SELF   Young women who move into constructive knowledge report a period of self-examination in which they experience being out of touch with parts of themselves. "During the transition into a new way of knowing, there is an impetus to allow the self back into the process of knowing, to confront the pieces of the self that may be experienced as fragmented and contradictory" (Belenky et al., 1986, p. 136). These females ask themselves questions such as "Who am I?" and "How will I approach life?"

Questions such as these echo the concerns of Perry's young males who experienced the need for commitment in their relativistic thought. Belenky and her associates note that these females experience a "heightened consciousness and sense of choice" about the ways they examine their world and who they will become. They become aware of the fact that given a different perspective or even a different point in time, they could come up with different answers to the same questions (Belenky et al., 1986). This awareness leads to the central truth of **constructive knowledge**: that knowledge is constructed and hence relative, and the knower is an intrinsic part of the process. This position allows these females to examine a set of beliefs from a perspective outside that system. Something like structural analytical thinking almost surely is present at this point.

Go to the **Adolescence** Companion Website at **www.sinauer.com/cobb** for quizzes, flashcards, summaries, and other study resources.

constructive knowledge
The third of Belenky and associates' three forms of thought: an awareness that knowledge is constructed; the ability to examine one's beliefs.

SUMMARY and KEY TERMS

How Adolescents Spend their Time

Leisure Time: Adolescents enjoy about the same amount of free time (whether unstructured or organized) each day as the time they spend in school. Most adolescents spend most of their leisure time in unstructured activities such as hanging out with friends or watching TV. Participation in organized voluntary activities promotes healthy development, contributing to self-esteem, confidence, academic achievement, and fewer risky behaviors. Students find organized voluntary activities, in contrast with school work, to both be intrinsically motivating and demand concentration.
organized activities, initiative, flow

Adolescents and the Media: Adolescents also spend almost as much time watching television, listening to music, playing video games, and being on the Internet as they spend in school. The TV shows watched, as well as other media commonly used by adolescents routinely include scenes with sexual content.. Although exposure to sexual content has been found to be related to adolescents' sexual behavior, one cannot assume that this exposure is causally related to their behavior, since it's equally possible that adolescents who are already sexually active prefer media with sexual content. A similar objection can be made when inferring that viewing violence leads to aggressive behavior.

Global Comparisons: Child Labor: Although teenagers in most industrial societies have almost as many leisure hours per week as those they spend in school, many children and adolescents in developing nations spend most of their waking hours working. Child labor refers to work by children and adolescents who are below the minimum age for work, and which is often harmful, and usually deprives them of education. Successful approaches to combating child labor are multifaceted, and include raising community awareness, tying family subsidies to the child's school attendance, and flexible school hours— in addition to legislation.
child labor

Adolescents at Work

Attitudes Toward Work over the Lifespan: Attitudes toward work and leisure show much continuity through large segments of the lifespan. Children's chores and adolescents' part-time work still anticipate the gender divisions that characterize work among adults.

Part-Time Employment: Many high school students have part-time jobs, and more want to work than can find jobs. Unemployment among minority adolescents is higher than among youth in the dominant culture. Most adolescents spend their money on personal items such as clothes, entertainment, and cars. Smaller numbers save for education or other long-term plans. Students who work part-time spend less time on schoolwork and with families, but often develop a sense of responsibility and feel productive.

Dropping Out and Employment: Students who drop out of high school are about twice as likely to be unemployed as graduates. Programs that are successful in preventing at-risk students from dropping out communicate the importance of having a degree for making money. These programs create an atmosphere of caring and involvement, provide individualized instruction through computerized programs, and involve the community and parents.

SUMMARY and KEY TERMS

Theories of Vocational Development

Social Cognitive Theory: In explaining vocational choices, social-cognitive theory emphasizes the interrelationships among inborn abilities, one's particular environment and unique learning history, and one's skills.

Ginzburg: Vocational Stages: Developmental theories trace occupational choices over stages. Ginzburg views vocational development as a progressive narrowing of choices that at first reflect only fantasy, then tentative career choices, and, with increasing age, realistic choices.
fantasy stage, tentative stage, realistic stage

Super: Careers and the Self-Concept: Super assumes that people choose occupations that reflect the way they see themselves. Because the self-concept changes with age, so will occupational plans, starting with the growth stage, where adolescents develop a realistic self-concept, and ending with the decline stage, which involves retirement.
growth stage, exploration stage, establishment stage, maintenance stage, decline stage

Holland: Personality Types and Work: Holland classifies individuals into six personality types, and different work environments either complement or oppose the qualities that make up any type. Realistic personality types, for instance, prefer orderly, structured work—occupations that might include mechanic, farmer, or engineer.
realistic personality types, investigative personality types, artistic personality types, social personality types, enterprising personality types, conventional personality types

Joining the Workforce

Job Availability: Unemployment among young workers in the United States and other industrialized nations is relatively common. The high rate of youth unemployment can be traced both to economic recession and to the greater vulnerability of young workers as, for instance, in less seniority. Among the 10 fastest-growing occupations, over half are related to health care and computers, reflecting an aging population and the growth of technology.

Gender in the Workforce: Though more female adolescents plan to work in professional jobs than in the past, sex segregation still exists in the workforce, and advancement opportunities are limited. Female adolescents also have internal, learned barriers to advancement that take the form of lower expectations for pay and lower valuation of their work.

Minorities in the Workforce: Minority adolescents face problems similar to those of females; in addition, for many, poverty contributes heavily to the problems they face. Minority adolescents' career aspirations are as high as those of dominant culture adolescents, but their lower expectations reflect social barriers to equal employment opportunities.

Intervention Programs: Strategies for Change

Counselors as Change Agents: Because of inequities in the opportunity structure for minority adolescents and females, counselors may need to become active change

(continued)

SUMMARY and KEY TERMS *continued*

agents to prepare these students for the full range of jobs that exists. Effective intervention programs work with local businesses, parents, and teachers as well as the students. Counselors often must first address their own biases.
STEM courses

Irrational Beliefs and Maladaptive Myths: Students frequently approach career decisions with maladaptive beliefs and myths. Intervention programs based on cognitive restructuring and on attributional retraining effectively address these as the first step to vocational counseling.
cognitive restructuring, attributional retraining

Adolescents and College

New Solutions to Old Problems: Dialectical Thinking: Structural analytical thinking enables adolescents to find parallels among different views of a problem. Dialectical reasoning is necessary for structural analytical thought, just as propositional reasoning is necessary for formal thought.
personal effectiveness, dialectical thinking

The number of students enrolled in college has more than doubled in a single generation, but with female graduates now outnumbering male graduates. Additionally, the increase in minority students earning bachelor's degrees was greater than the increase for dominant culture students.

How College Can Change the Way Adolescents Think: William Perry identified important changes during college in the way adolescents think about ideas. These changes reflect their beliefs about the nature of truth as much as their ability to think in general. Perry identified three major forms of thought: dualism, relativism, and commitment in relativism.
dualistic thinking, relativistic thinking, commitment in relativism

Gender Differences in Approaches to Knowledge: Female adolescents think in ways other than those captured by Perry's neatly categorized intellectual progressions. Those who begin the intellectual journey move from subjective knowledge to procedural knowledge to constructive knowledge. And not all complete the journey.
subjective knowledge, procedural knowledge, constructive knowledge

"Hey, Raffie," Arnie grinned over the locker door. "You a lucky man this morning, or not?"

"Or not," thought Raffie, as he grabbed his books and gave the door a slam. But he grinned back, "You think you're the only one around here gets lucky?"

"All right!" exclaimed Arnie, giving his friend a "deadarm" and heading for his first class on the run.

Raffie glared at Arnie's back as he disappeared down the hall. What was it with his friends? Did they really have all the sexual adventures they said they had? Was he the only one who was different?

Raffie was 16, and he was worried. Raffie was a virgin.

Now imagine the same scenario between two female adolescents.

"Hey, Rachel," Annie grinned at her friend. "Make anything happen last night, or what?"

"Or what, " thought Rachel, but she grabbed her books and grinned back.

"You think you're the only 'happening' one around?"

"All right!" said Annie, giving her friend an affectionate squeeze. She promised to catch all the details over lunch, then ran off to class.

Rachel stared at her friend as she rushed off. "Am I really that different?" she wondered.

Chapter Overview

Is the second scene harder to imagine than the first? What does the phrase "getting lucky" communicate about a sexual encounter? Are females and males equally likely to think of sex this way? Would Raffie's father have been as embarrassed in his day by sexual inexperience? Is Rachel likely to be? What are the sexual attitudes and practices of adolescents today, and how do these contribute to teenagers' sense of self?

The topic of sexuality raises questions at any age, but especially during adolescence. Sexuality looms large in adolescence, in part because it takes exciting new turns and in part because it contributes so heavily to adolescents' developing sense of themselves. The chapter begins by considering cultural stereotypes of masculinity and femininity, as well as a third alternative of androgyny. We then examine the identity implications of adolescents' sexuality and look at the sexual scripts that guide their behavior.

Sexual decision making brings adolescents several steps closer to adulthood. Some adolescents will limit their experiences to kissing, others will go further. We examine adolescents' sexual attitudes and practices next. For most adolescents, sexual attraction involves someone of the opposite sex; a small percentage discovers they are attracted to those of their own sex. The biological and psychosocial bases of sexual attraction are considered.

The sexual response cycle is strikingly similar for all individuals, despite differences in gender or sexual orientation. Research reveals four phases of response: excitement, plateau, orgasm, and resolution. We examine similarities in sexual response before discussing myths and misconceptions about sexual functioning that are common among adolescents.

Sex means different things to different people. To a lover, it is the stuff of dreams. To a biologist, it is a means of reproduction. Adolescents are better lovers than biologists, and relatively few consistently take care not to reproduce. The chapter moves to a consideration of contraception use before examining some consequences of adolescent sexuality: sexually transmitted diseases and unintended pregnancies. The chapter ends with a discussion of programs aimed at helping adolescents make informed sexual decisions.

Sexual Identity

As we have seen in preceding chapters, adolescents are poised to see themselves in new ways, and one of the most significant of these is in terms of their sexuality. Before going any further, we should be clear that "sexuality" is not equivalent to "sexual behavior." Sexuality refers, in the most general sense, to one's sexual character and embraces general aspects of one's sense of self, such as expressions of one's masculinity or femininity, the social roles one has within a family, and how one is seen in society. In constructing a sexual identity, then, adolescents are integrating sexuality into their sense of self.

Erik Erikson (1968) considered sexuality in this general sense to be one of the domains in which an adult identity is established, the other domains being those in which occupational and ideological preferences and commitments are established. As such, constructing a sexual identity is a healthy developmental process, a normal step taken by adolescents on the path to adulthood. Certainly, it's true that aspects of this sexuality include sexual thoughts and feelings, but as any adolescent might tell us, "It's not just about sex, it's about who I am."

Let's take a look, then, at how adolescents see themselves with respect to this domain of identity.

Gender Stereotypes: The Meaning of Masculine and Feminine

The process of constructing a sexual identity introduces questions of what it means to be masculine or feminine. Adult sex roles, in the form of gender stereotypes, provide cultural answers. **Gender stereotypes** are the cultural expectations concerning which behaviors are appropriate for each sex. These stereotypes play an important role in self-definition as adolescents integrate questions posed by their sexuality into their developing sense of themselves.

THE MASCULINE GENDER ROLE   Attitudes concerning what it is to be masculine and feminine in our society are surprisingly resistant to change, despite significant changes in the roles of men and women both at home and in the workplace (Seem & Clark, 2006). When these attitudes are assessed with well-known measures of sex-role stereotyping, we find that males are expected to be self-reliant, self-sufficient, and able to defend their beliefs, make decisions, take a stand, and be leaders. With respect to sexual decision making, a topic we will consider later in the chapter, the masculine gender stereotype portrays males as the sexual risk takers, the ones to make the moves, to be aggressive, dominant, assertive, and forceful. **Box 10.1** examines an alarming distortion of this gender stereotype.

gender stereotypes   The cultural expectations concerning behaviors that are appropriate for each sex.

BOX 10.1 Research Focus

Between-Subjects Design: Date Rape

It was well past midnight when Carol Ann slipped into the darkened house.

"Is that you, honey?" her mom called out in a sleepy voice.

"Yeah, Mom," she whispered hoarsely as she hurried to the bathroom.

Safe behind the closed door, she tore off her crumpled clothes, turned on the shower, and let the steaming water scald her skin pink.

She felt so dirty. She still didn't know how she had gotten away. She remembered struggling, punching, fighting back. Ugly bruises reddened on her arms and body as she choked back sobs of rage and humiliation. He had tried to rape her!

It had been their third date. He had been so polite and attentive each time before, never out of line. She hadn't been concerned when he suggested a party at a friend's house and turned down a dark road. What could she have said or done to make him think ... ? And why did *she* feel so responsible? So terribly ashamed?

Carol Ann's experience is not that unusual. Judith Vicary, Linda Klingaman, and William Harkness (1995), looking at assault and date rape in high school females, found that 15% had experienced date rape over the four-year period of the study; 60% of acquaintance rapes among college students occur in a dating situation (Koss et al., 1988). What kind of male violates the consent of his date? Is it one whose sex drive is so strong that once aroused, he cannot stop himself? Or

does date rape first start in the mind—with an attitude?

Rape myths are stereotyped perceptions of rapists and victims that minimize rape as a crime by shifting blame to the victim. As the term implies, they represent myth, not fact. Are males who endorse rape myths, such as the statements below, more accepting of violations of consent on a date? Would they be more likely to answer yes than no?

Several examples of these rape myths are:

• If a girl engages in necking or petting and she lets things "get out of hand," it is her fault if her partner forces sex on her.

• Any healthy woman can successfully resist a rapist if she really wants to.

• In the majority of rapes, the victim is promiscuous or has a bad reputation.

• A woman who is stuck up and thinks she is too good to talk to guys on the street deserves to be taught a lesson.

• When women go around braless, or wearing short skirts and tight tops, they are just asking for trouble.

• Many women have an unconscious desire to be raped and may therefore unconsciously set up a situation in which they are likely to be attacked.

• If a woman gets drunk at a party and has intercourse with a man she's just met there, she should be considered fair game to other males at the party who want to have sex with her too, whether she wants to or not.

(continued on next page)

Are beliefs such as these more likely to be held by certain people than by others? What other attitudes are they related to? Do they predict attitudes toward other intimate behaviors such as kissing, petting, or even holding hands? Do attitudes about violations of consent depend on the level of assumed intimacy in the relationship? How could we find out?

Leslie Margolin, Melody Miller, and Patricia Moran (1989) found answers to these and similar questions by having male and female students read a description of a dating situation in which a male tried to kiss a female while they were at a movie together; when she refused, he kissed her anyway. Some of the students read that John and Mary were on a first date, others that they had been going together for two years, and others that they were married. The students were then asked for their reactions to this scenario, and their feelings about some of the rape myth statements listed above. Can you identify the independent variable in this experiment? If you said something like "level of intimacy," you were right. The other variable—gender—is a classification variable, and their reactions constitute the dependent variable (see Research Focus Box 1.1 for definition of terms).

These investigators used a *between-subjects design*. In this type of experiment, each participant experiences only one level of the independent variable. Remember that some of the students read that John and Mary were on a first date, others that they were going together, and still others that they were married. When participants are randomly assigned to one and only one level of

an independent variable, it is a between-subjects design. Why might this matter? Why might we care whether they experienced more than one experimental condition?

A major advantage to this type of design is that investigators need not worry that participants' responses will reflect the effects of another condition that may still be present. In other words, what if participants assigned to the "first date" condition had just previously read of a similar incident involving a couple who was married? Could we safely assume that these individuals would be able to separate their reactions to each situation? In a between-subjects design, one need not worry about such matters. Also, because individuals can be assigned at random to conditions, investigators can be reasonably confident that groups do not initially differ until they impose different treatments. Both assumptions involve the issue of internal validity. To the extent that guarantees exist in experimental research, between-subjects designs offer high guarantees of internal validity.

What did these investigators discover about attitudes toward violations of consent? They found that acceptance of rape myths *is* related to acceptance of violations of consent, regardless of level of intimacy. They also found that males are more accepting of rape myths than are females. Consequently, they were not surprised to find that males also were more supportive of John's right to violate Mary's consent to be kissed.

Sources: After Koss et al., 1988, Margolin et al., 1989, and Vicary et al., 1995.

THE FEMININE GENDER ROLE   Since components of gender stereotypes are often polar opposites of each other, females predictably face a different set of cultural expectations. The feminine gender stereotype portrays females as sensitive to the feelings of others, in touch with their own emotions, understanding, affectionate, warm, and tender. Despite the implicit maturity in such an interpersonal stance, in other respects the cultural stereotype of femininity portrays females as dependent, passive, and childlike. These latter qualities become especially problematic when considered in light of the fact that adolescent females typically assume responsibility for contraception.

Although boys experience more pressure to conform to their gender role than do girls, they are also more satisfied with it, not an unexpected finding given that characteristics regarded as masculine are valued more positively than are those regarded as feminine, and that males enjoy a higher status in society than do females (Leaper & Brown, 2008; Lips, 2008). Additionally, characteristics that are perceived to be masculine are regarded as healthier than feminine characteristics, and by no less than those training to be counselors, a finding that has changed little since first noted some 40 years earlier (Broverman et al., 1970; Seem & Clark, 2006)!

ANDROGYNY   Since stereotypes communicate as much myth as truth, adolescents have some latitude in fashioning their gender roles. Adolescents who are comfortable expressing both masculine and feminine characteristics are **androgynous**. These adolescents, for example, can be both assertive and self-reliant (considered to be masculine characteristics) *and* sensitive to the needs of others and understanding (considered to be characteristically feminine). In a sense, androgyny allows an adolescent to tailor-make a gender role instead of having to select one "off the rack."

Although being typical for one's gender contributes to an adolescent's feelings of self-worth, those who are not typical in this way do not necessarily experience low self-worth. To the extent that their peers accept them for who they are, they generally feel good about themselves and are as well adjusted as those who are gender typical (Smith & Leaper, 2006).

Even so, freedom has its price. The very same loosening of gender-role definition, which allows increasing choice and individuality, can bring with it new ambiguities and conflicts. When role definition is rigid and conformity unanimous, everyone knows what to expect from the other and knows what the other expects as well. Although that may sound unexciting, it certainly simplifies a relationship, especially in its early stages. On the other hand, the greater the freedom and flexibility in the social definition of roles, the more that is left to be decided by the individual or negotiated in the heat of a relationship.

As adolescents begin to integrate sexuality into their identities, one could expect either an increase or a decrease in the flexibility with which they approach gender stereotypes. On the one hand, a decrease in flexibility might occur as they experience the cultural constraints of gender-role expectations at a time when a heightened concern about their sexuality could polarize their attitudes. On the other hand, they are also in a better position to realistically evaluate these gender norms, due to continued intellectual development, making it possible to more flexibly adapt cultural roles to their own needs. Of course, none of these changes occur in a vacuum, and real life contexts in which adolescents work out their sexuality must also be considered.

THE CULTURAL CONTEXT OF GENDER ROLES   Cultures, as well as the company of peers, differ in how flexibly they treat gender roles. Individualistic cultures such as the United States allow adolescents more leeway in defining themselves with respect to the gendered behaviors they adopt than do collectivist cultures, such as Middle Eastern and Latin American societies. In the latter, one's sense of self is defined more strongly through one's roles vis-à-vis others, and few of these are more important than one's gender role. In these societies as well, males have more life options and are freer to engage in life outside the home than are females; these differences are particularly noticeable in rural areas (Dwairy & Menshar, 2006).

Gender Roles in Context

One important real life context is the transition in school settings that brings younger adolescents in daily contact with older ones, the transition that occurs as they move from elementary school into middle school or junior high and then into high school.

Thomas Alfieri, Diane Ruble, and E. Tory Higgins (1996) asked fourth-through ninth-graders to indicate whether each of a number of gender-stereo-

androgynous A personality in which there are both masculine and feminine attributes.

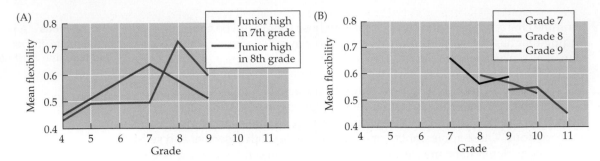

● **Figure 10.1   Gender-role flexibility by grade**   (A) Adolescents show increases in gender-role flexibility until they reach junior high, in either the seventh grade (blue line) or the eighth grade (red line), and then that flexibility decreases. (B) An overall decrease in flexibility in gender roles occurs from seventh grade to 11th grade. (After Alfieri et al., 1996.)

typic adjectives was associated with males, females, or both. A tally of "both" responses was used as their measure of flexibility in gender stereotypes. Some of the early adolescents they studied made the transition to junior high in the seventh grade and some in the eighth grade. As can be seen in **Figure 10.1**, flexibility increases up through the first year of junior high, whether this occurred in the seventh grade or the eighth, but, as these cohort samples were followed over the next two years, flexibility could be seen to decrease dramatically.

Why might gender roles be more flexible early in adolescence than later? These investigators remind us that as early adolescents enter junior high, their status changes from that of being the oldest and wisest to that of being the youngest and most ignorant. Furthermore, their older schoolmates present them with a broader range of gendered behaviors than they have previously encountered. Faced with new challenges to what they have held to be true, it makes sense for early adolescents to put their beliefs on hold as they survey their new surroundings in order to learn more about gender. Decreases in flexibility are to be expected as they consolidate new beliefs and attitudes in the face of increasing pressures to adopt more adult gender roles. The irony to these developments is that adolescents' flexibility is prompted by entering an environment in which the individuals who populate it hold relatively *inflexible* beliefs about gender. Gender stereotypes persist to varying degrees into young adulthood and across the lifespan.

Constructing a Sexual Identity

Most research on sexuality has not examined its identity implications but has focused instead on relatively narrow aspects of adolescents' behavior, such as their attitudes regarding sexual practices. But how do adolescents think of themselves as sexual beings? That is, how do they conceptualize their *sexual selves*? And how does this sense of themselves then relate to their sexual behavior?

Simone Buzwell and Doreen Rosenthal (1996) distinguish several aspects of the sexual self, each of which is thought to contribute to the ways in which adolescents construct a sense of themselves as sexual beings. The constructive perspective, recall, assumes that we actively put together the events to which we respond and, in the process, give meaning to experience. This activity of imposing an order on, and thereby gaining a sense of, our world is not limited to what we take to be external to us, but applies equally to our perception of ourselves. With respect to the sexual self, adolescents are likely to construct self-perceptions along at least three dimensions (**Table 10.1**): their perception

> **TABLE 10.1**
> **Dimensions of the Sexual Self**
>
> **Sexual self-esteem: perception of one's worth as a sexual being**
> Perceptions of one's sexual appeal: "I am confident that males/females find me sexually attractive."
> Feelings concerning one's sexual adequacy: "I know how to behave in a sexual situation."
>
> **Sexual self-efficacy: confidence in one's mastery concerning sexual activities**
> Ability to say no to unwanted sex: "I am confident that I could tell my partner that I do not want to have sex."
> Ability to purchase and use condoms: "I am confident that I could put a condom on an erect penis."
>
> **Sexual self-image: perception of one's sexuality and beliefs about one's sexual needs**
> Perception of openness to sexual experimentation: "I would like to experiment when it comes to sex."
> Commitment to a single sexual partner: "There needs to be commitment before I have sex with someone."

Source: Buzwell & Rosenthal, 1996.

of their worth as sexual beings (*sexual self-esteem*), the control they perceive themselves to have over their sexual experiences (*sexual self-efficacy*), and their beliefs about their sexual needs (*sexual self-image*).

SEXUAL STYLES   Buzwell and Rosenthal (1996) identified five sexual styles, or approaches, taken by adolescents in the construction of their sexual selves. Each style represents a different combination of these dimensions of the sexual self.

Sexually naive adolescents are those who lack confidence in their sexual attractiveness and, with the exception of being able to say no to unwanted sex, feel they have little control over sexual situations. Perhaps not surprisingly, such situations engender more anxiety than desire, and become attractive only in the context of a committed relationship. These adolescents tend to be younger, and most are girls; most also are sexually inexperienced.

A second group of adolescents, the *sexually unassured*, consists primarily of young boys who, although similar to the first group in having low sexual self-esteem and self-efficacy, are interested in exploring their sexuality even though most remain sexually inexperienced.

Sexually competent adolescents are those of either sex who are confident of both their sexual appeal and their ability to control a sexual situation. Predictably, they experience less anxiety in sexual situations than adolescents in either of the other two groups and more interest in exploring their sexuality. These adolescents tend to be older, and most are sexually experienced.

Adolescents in the two remaining groups tend to be highly confident of their sexual attractiveness and of their ability to take charge of their sexual encounters. The *sexually adventurous* are distinguished by high levels of sexual arousal and interest in sexual exploration, in combination with little anxiety and little relationship commitment. Most of the adolescents in this group are older boys who are sexually experienced.

The *sexually driven* are similar to the sexually adventurous with the exception of being unable to say no to sex, whether they consider the partner desirable or not. Most of these adolescents tend to be sexually active boys.

Differences in sexual style are associated not only with sexual experience but also with different patterns of sexual behavior. For instance, adolescents with greater confidence in their sexual attractiveness and in their control over

sexual scripts Learned expectations derived from cultural roles and gender stereotypes that guide behavior in sexual situations.

sexual encounters take greater risks and have more sexual partners. Buzwell and Rosenthal emphasize that sexual behavior is closely tied to adolescents' personal constructions of their sexuality. In other words, adolescents' beliefs about themselves as sexual beings, apart from demographic factors such as ethnicity or social class, are associated with differences in their behavior. In fact, these investigators observed striking differences in sexual behaviors among adolescents who, in other respects, had very similar backgrounds.

Sexual Scripts

Adolescents are not left to themselves to map out a sexual terrain; blueprints exist for them to follow, in the form of sexual scripts. **Sexual scripts** provide a set of guidelines concerning expected patterns of behavior in a sexual situation, informing adolescents not only of what they should do and feel, but also of what the person they are with is likely to do and feel.

These scripts reflect the behaviors that comprise the masculine and feminine gender stereotypes. Stereotypically feminine characteristics, such as tenderness and sensitivity, translate into a sexual script in which females are motivated by a desire for emotional intimacy and love. Conversely, stereotypically masculine characteristics, such as dominance and risk taking, provide a script in which males are motivated by a desire for physical, rather than emotional, satisfaction. Not surprisingly, adolescent females are more likely than males to report being in love as a reason for being sexually active, and males to say they find sex itself exciting. For instance, when asked how they had felt after first having intercourse, many more males (72%) than females (26%) said they felt "thrilled," and many more males (75%) than females (18%) felt "sexually satisfied" (Woody et al., 2000).

With respect to beliefs concerning the causes of sexual desire in others, there is remarkable agreement among adolescents and emerging adults, among females and males alike. Most believe that for males, erotic factors, such as how sexy a woman looks, cause sexual desire, whereas for females, thoughts of love or romance are important. Simply being male, it seems, is reason in itself for causing sexual desire, whereas this is not assumed to be the case if one is female (Crawford & Popp, 2003; Regan & Berscheid, 1995; Woody et al., 2000).

Making Sexual Decisions

Puberty brings new sexual feelings and emotions, and the natural need to integrate these into a sense of oneself. Rather than simply adding new sexual feelings to an old self, adolescents must revise that self so that what they add fits. In other words, adolescents cannot continue to see themselves as children and merely add sexual feelings and behaviors to this self-image. "Sexy children" is a contradiction in terms in most societies—to be sexual is to be adult. To integrate sexuality into their sense of themselves, adolescents must take a big step toward adulthood—and away from childhood. For many, this step is a hard one not so much for what they are stepping into as for what they are leaving behind.

Not surprisingly, adolescents frequently experience conflict when contemplating their own sexuality. Conflict, in itself, isn't bad; but it can interfere with responsible sexual decision making, often leading to avoidance and denial. Translated into the terminology of making sexual decisions, adolescents who experience conflict may deny that they are assuming a stance that is any different from that which they have always taken. Rather than consciously thinking through the consequences of becoming sexually active, these adolescents are likely to engage in sex without planning to do so and without doing so responsibly.

Talking with Parents

Unlike many of the decisions adolescents face, those surrounding sexuality are not likely to be openly discussed, especially with parents (Rosenthal & Feldman, 1999; Troth & Peterson, 2000). In itself, that may not be surprising, but adolescents also find it hard to talk openly about sex even with sexual partners (Troth & Peterson, 2000). Adolescents who talk with their parents about sexual behavior are more likely to delay sexual initiation and to engage in safe sexual practices once they become sexually active than those who do not (Aspy et al., 2007; Buzi et al., 2009; Karofsky et al., 2001; Sneed, 2008). Also, these adolescents are less likely to be influenced by what they believe their peers to be doing than are adolescents whose parents don't talk with them about sex (Whitaker & Miller, 2000). Discussions about sexual behavior are most effective when they involve an open dialogue with adolescents, rather than parents lecturing from a position of authority. Adolescents who experience their mothers as open and understanding when discussing sexual matters, have been found to be more likely to plan on delaying sexual activity than those whose mothers are less responsive (Fasula & Miller, 2006). Similarly, adolescents who can talk openly with their sexual partners engage in sex more responsibly (Darling & Hicks, 1982; Leland & Barth, 1993).

Discussions about sexual behavior are more likely to have an influence on adolescents, both with respect to delaying sexual activity and condom use, if these take place before they become sexually active rather than after. It's easier, that is, to prevent behaviors from developing than to change those that have already become established. Many parents, however, are likely to postpone discussions about sex until they see that their adolescent has become romantically involved, and for some this may take place after the fact (Eisenberg et al., 2006; Rose et al., 2005; Wyckoff et al., 2008).

It's difficult to know how talking with parents contributes to adolescents delaying sexual initiation or avoiding risky behaviors. Perhaps it's what gets said in the course of a conversation; discussions with parents communicate parental values and expectations. But it's also possible that adolescents who can talk with their parents have closer relationships with them, and it is the quality of the relationship that contributes to responsible decision making. Or it may be characteristics of the adolescents themselves, in that those who are able to talk about sex also are able to say "no" to a partner.

When adolescents do talk with their parents, they report talking more with their mothers, perhaps because they regard their mothers as somewhat better at communicating about sexuality than fathers (Feldman & Rosenthal, 2000; Rosenthal et al., 2001). Mothers also are more likely than fathers to talk with their children, and both parents talk more with daughters than with sons (Nolin & Petersen, 1992). As a result, sons have less opportunity than daughters to discuss sexual matters with the same-sex parent. When discussions occur between parents and sons, they are less likely to touch on issues of morality or values than are discussions with daughters. Of course, values can be communicated in many ways, not necessarily just through talking. One important way is by teaching adolescents to be responsible for their actions and to have respect for others. Parents also influence their teenagers' sexual practices by maintaining strong bonds with them, thereby lessening their need for peer approval (DiBlasio & Benda, 1992; Miller & Fox, 1987).

Starting with a kiss, adolescents follow a predictable progression of sexual behavior as they grow older, although the progression varies somewhat among ethnic and racial groups.

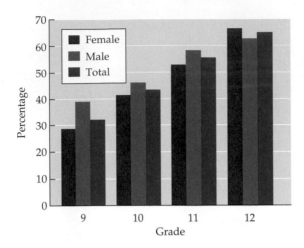

● **Figure 10.2** **Percentage of high school students who indicate they have had sexual intercourse** (After CDC, 2008b.)

Sexual Attitudes and Behaviors

With age, adolescents are increasingly likely to engage in various forms of sexual activity. Most will follow a predictable progression that starts with necking, moves to touching breasts, first over and then under clothing, to touching genitals, once again first over then under clothing, to oral sex, and intercourse (de Graaf et al., 2009; Gowen et al., 2004). By the end of high school, 65% of all adolescents have engaged in sexual intercourse (CDC, 2008b).

With respect to other sexual behaviors, such as touching a partner's genitals, males are likely to be the ones to first touch their partners, perhaps because they experience more permission to be sexually active than do females. In fact, adolescent girls need more commitment in a relationship in order to touch their partners than they do to allow their partners to touch them. This suggests that it may be difficult for most girls to assume an active role in sexual encounters even when most hold positive attitudes about the behaviors in question.

The percentage of adolescents who've had sexual intercourse increases with age (**Figure 10.2**). Approximately one-third of ninth-graders report having had intercourse, whereas close to two-thirds of high school seniors have (CDC, 2008b). A second trend also is apparent in Figure 10.2. As ninth-graders, boys are considerably more likely than girls to be sexually active. However, this difference decreases with age, and by the end of high school, the direction of this difference reverses, with more girls than boys reporting that they have had intercourse. Thus, although boys are more likely to initiate sexual activity earlier than girls, once adolescents reach the 10th grade this difference is substantially reduced. To appreciate the significance of this trend, we need only consider their parents' generation where, by the age of 17, the percentage of boys who were sexually active was still nearly twice that of girls (Hayes, 1987).

A third trend in adolescents' sexual behavior concerns the varieties of sexual activities in which they engage. Attitudes toward oral sex are more positive than in previous generations, and adolescents are significantly more likely to engage in this activity than in the past. In a national survey of 15- to 19-year-olds, over half reported having oral sex, and a tenth having anal sex. Both of these sexual activities were more common among adolescents who were already sexually experienced, with eight in 10 of those surveyed saying they engaged in oral sex within several months of having first engaged in vaginal intercourse. Since sex education courses do not routinely cover these activities, adolescents can be unaware of the risks of sexually transmitted diseases that these—just as vaginal intercourse—pose (Halpern-Felsher, 2008; Lindberg et al., 2008).

SELF-STIMULATION   A sexual practice that evokes considerable concern among adolescents is **self-stimulation**, more commonly referred to as masturbation. Even though most adolescents engage in this practice, most regard it with mixed feelings (Halpern et al., 2000).

Novelist Philip Roth (1969) depicts these concerns in a boy:

> *It was at the end of my freshman year of high school—and freshman year of Masturbating—that I discovered on the underside of my penis, just where the shaft met the head, a little discolored dot that has since been diagnosed as a freckle. Cancer. I had given myself cancer. All that pulling and tugging at my own flesh, all that friction, had*

self-stimulation
Self-stimulation of the genitals (commonly called masturbation).

given me an incurable disease. And not yet fourteen! In bed at night the tears rolled from my eyes. "No!" I sobbed. "I don't want to die. Please—no." But then, because I would shortly be a corpse anyway, I went ahead as usual and jerked off.

Attitudes toward self-stimulation have changed radically. Past generations were taught that masturbation was morally wrong and were warned that excessive masturbation could result in physical deformities or disease. Adolescents today learn that self-stimulation is a normal sexual outlet. Self-stimulation even can help females and males alike learn how their bodies respond sexually. Although most adolescents no longer believe that masturbation is abnormal or dangerous, most still view it with some embarrassment (Strong & DeVault, 2001).

The age at which adolescents become sexually active differs considerably from one ethnic background to another (**Table 10.2**). Among African American and Hispanic adolescents, for instance, males are more likely to be sexually active than females; however, the reverse is true among Caucasian adolescents. Within each sex, as well, differences due to ethnicity are relatively large.

Protective Factors

An adolescent's decision to become sexually active depends on many things. Some of these, such as physical maturation, are biologically based, whereas others reflect the adolescent's values and religious beliefs, and still others the influence of family and friends.

BIOLOGICALLY-BASED FACTORS   As one might expect, adolescents who mature later are less likely to become sexually active at an earlier age (Meschke et al., 2000; Zimmer-Gembeck & Helfand, 2008). As we have seen, gender is also related to the age at which adolescents become sexually active, with girls becoming sexually active later than boys (CDC, 2008b). Perhaps less expectedly, intelligence is also related to the timing of sexual activity, with adolescents of higher intelligence being more likely to delay sexual activity (Halpern et al., 2000).

PSYCHOLOGICAL FACTORS   In addition to biologically-based factors, psychological factors, such as adolescents' religious beliefs, their values and attitudes, and emotional adjustment have been found to influence the timing of sexual activity. Adolescents with strong religious beliefs are less likely to engage in early sexual activity, and more likely to postpone sexual activity (Jones et al., 2005; Rostosky et al., 2004).

Similarly, adolescents' academic interests, as reflected in their day-to-day involvement in school activities and their aspirations for college, are related

TABLE 10.2 Percentage of Sexually Active High School Students				
	EVER HAD SEXUAL INTERCOURSE		CURRENTLY SEXUALLY ACTIVE	
ETHNICITY	FEMALES	MALES	FEMALES	MALES
African American	60.9	72.6	43.5	48.7
Caucasian	43.7	43.6	35.1	30.6
Hispanic	45.8	58.2	35.3	39.6

Source: CDC, 2008b.

to postponing sexual activity (Whitbeck et al., 1999). Conversely, permissive attitudes toward sex and, for boys, placing importance on being popular have been found to be associated with earlier sexual activity (Meschke et al., 2000).

SOCIAL FACTORS   A third domain of influence consists of social factors, such as parents and peers. Families remain a significant influence in adolescents' lives—and adolescents' sexual behavior is no exception. Adolescents who have stable family environments are more likely to delay sexual activity, as are those whose parents provide more supervision, hold higher expectations, and remain emotionally connected to their children (Klein, 2005). Parental monitoring, such as knowing where adolescents are and who they are with, is also effective in delaying sexual activity, at least for younger adolescents (Capaldi et al., 2002). Adolescents whose mothers have strong religious beliefs are more likely to delay sexual intercourse (Whitbeck et al., 1999). With respect to peers, steady dating has been found to increase the likelihood of early sexual activity, especially for girls with older boyfriends (Gowen et al., 2004; Meschke et al., 2000), as has the use of alcohol and associating with delinquent peers (Blinn-Pike et al., 2004; Whitbeck et al., 1999).

Despite the fact that many teenagers are likely to be sexually active today, many of them engage in intercourse infrequently. Some adolescents appear to have had their first sexual experiences for reasons not necessarily sexual but, instead, as a rite of passage or to satisfy their curiosity. Once they have proven themselves or discovered what they wanted to know, they abstain until they become involved in a relationship. Adolescents who decide not to become sexually active mention a number of reasons for remaining abstinent. Common among these are fears of becoming pregnant and of contracting a sexually transmitted disease. Adolescents' values and religious beliefs, as well as waiting for the right person and waiting until they're older, are also reasons frequently given by early adolescents (Blinn-Pike et al., 2004; Edwards et al., 2008).

The most immediate context in which sexual behavior can be studied is the very private world of the human sexual response. Like much else related to sexual functioning, our understanding has been late to develop.

The Sexual Response Cycle

Sputnik had orbited the earth and Neil Armstrong had one foot on the moon before scientists began to unravel the complexities of the human sexual response. William Masters and Virginia Johnson studied actual sexual encounters between men and women, which revealed a sexual response cycle consisting of four phases: excitement, plateau, orgasm, and resolution. Two processes underlie each phase. **Vasocongestion** is an accumulation of blood in the vessels serving the erogenous zones (areas of the body that are particularly sensitive to sexual arousal), and **myotonia** is an increase in muscular tension. The tension is more like a building up of energy in the muscles than a state of feeling tense. At each phase of the cycle, striking similarities exist in the response of females and males.

EXCITEMENT   Vasocongestion is responsible for the first signs of *excitement*, or sexual arousal, in both males and females. In males it causes blood to pour into the spongy tissues in the shaft of the penis, making it erect. Masters, Johnson, and Kolodny (1988) note that because an erection is caused by an increase in fluid pressure, it is essentially a "hydraulic event." Vaginal lubrication, one of the first signs of sexual arousal in females, occurs when blood vessels in the pelvic area swell with blood, pressing fluids into the tissues surrounding the vagina. In both sexes, the nipples harden and muscular tension increases throughout the body (myotonia).

vasocongestion   An accumulation of blood in the vessels serving the erogenous zones (areas of the body that are particularly sensitive to sexual arousal).

myotonia   An increase in muscular tension.

BOX 10.2 In More Depth

Descriptions of the Experience of Orgasm

Research finds that trained judges can't tell which written descriptions of orgasm are given by females and which by males. Can you? (See answers below.)

1. "Like a mild explosion, it left me warm and relaxed after a searing heat that started in my genitals and raced to my toes and head."

2. "Throbbing is the best word to say what it is like. The throbbing starts as a faint vibration, then builds up in wave after wave where time seems to stand still."

3. "When I come it's either like an avalanche of pleasure, tumbling through me, or like a refreshing snack—momentarily satisfying, but then I'm ready for more."

4. "My orgasms feel like pulsating bursts of energy starting in my pelvic area and then engulfing my whole body. Sometimes I feel like I'm in freefall, and sometimes I feel like my body's an entire orchestra playing a grand crescendo."

5. "Some orgasms feel incredibly intense and earth-shattering, but other times orgasms feel like small, compact, self-contained moments."

6. "There is a warm rush from my toes to my head, with a strong, pulsing rhythm. Then everything settles down like a pink sunset."

Source: After Masters et al., 1988.

1. M 2. M 3. F 4. F 5. M 6. M

PLATEAU   Continued vasocongestion during the *plateau* phase causes the erection in males to become harder. Drops of lubricating fluid appear at the opening of the glans. Because this fluid frequently contains live sperm, withdrawal prior to ejaculation—a birth control practice common among teenagers—is not an effective means of preventing pregnancy. In females, continued vasocongestion causes the walls of the vagina to swell, constricting the size of the vagina and making penis size relatively unimportant for stimulation. Because females require more pelvic congestion than males to reach orgasm, the plateau stage lasts longer in females.

ORGASM   The sensations of *orgasm* result from rhythmic muscular contractions and discharge of tensions resulting from vasocongestion and myotonia. Despite similarities in its physiological bases for both sexes, orgasm tends to be a more consistently uniform phenomenon in males than in females; however, individuals of both sexes describe their experience of orgasm in similar ways. **Box 10.2** presents some of these descriptions.

RESOLUTION   In the *resolution* phase, following ejaculation, the penis becomes flaccid, and males experience a *refractory period*, lasting anywhere from several minutes to several hours, during which stimulation will not produce an erection. Resolution lasts much longer in females, because vasocongestion in the pelvic area dissipates slowly, and they can experience *multiple orgasms*.

Sexual Functioning: Myths and Misconceptions

Despite today's relatively open attitudes toward sex, considerable ignorance and myth surround sexual functioning. Interviews with adolescents found that many are surprisingly uninformed about even the basics. A 16-year-old girl remarked, "I wasn't ready for it being so *real*. Because in movies they don't get sweaty and—you know—all this awkward stuff." One boy commented, "I wish sex came with instructions. All the time I was thinking about doing it, I was worrying, *How* do you do it?" Ignorance concerning sexual functioning is by no means limited to adolescents. Countless adults cannot accurately name the parts of their own genitals or those of the opposite sex.

BIGGER IS BETTER   For adolescent boys, concern about the size of their penis is at the top of the list. Many boys don't know what size is normal and are sure theirs is too small. This concern is fueled by large variations from one boy to the next in the timing and rate of growth. Comparisons are inevitable, and a boy's penis almost always looks shorter to him than someone else's simply because his visual perspective (in looking down) foreshortens it (Masters et al., 1988).

Size assumes added importance as a result of the common misconception that penis size is related to sexual adequacy—which is simply untrue. Vaginal constriction corrects for differences in circumference of the penis, and because there are few nerve endings in the upper vagina, length is unimportant. Although one penis can differ noticeably from another in size when flaccid, this difference all but disappears when erect. Masters, Johnson, and Kolodny (1988), in fact, refer to an erection as "the great equalizer."

A common concern among adolescent girls concerns their breasts. Many notice that one breast is slightly larger than the other. Girls may wonder if it's normal for one breast to be smaller than the other (it is) and what they can do about it (nothing short of cosmetic surgery). Boys face a similar concern when they notice that one testicle is higher than the other, which is also quite normal.

CAPACITY FOR SEXUAL PLEASURE   Perhaps the most pervasive cultural myth among adolescents is that males experience more sexual pleasure than females. The fact that females take longer to reach orgasm may contribute to this myth. Once they reach orgasm, however, their capacity to achieve additional orgasms exceeds that of males. Similarities in the phases of the sexual response cycle in either sex, and in the way individuals describe orgasm, suggest similarities in the pleasure each experiences.

NEED FOR ORGASM   A related misconception is that only males need to reach orgasm. Considerable discomfort can result from reaching the plateau phase and not experiencing orgasm. Both males and females experience this discomfort, the result of blood vessels remaining engorged in the pelvic and genital areas. This vasocongestion underlies orgasm in both sexes, and failure to release the accumulated blood and the muscular tension produces discomfort in both males and females.

INTERCOURSE DURING MENSTRUATION   Numerous cultural taboos exist regarding intercourse during menstruation. Some cultures even isolate menstruating females, fearing that they might contaminate the things with which they come into contact. What dangers might befall a male? Misconceptions range from fears of infection to impotence and loss of virility. There is no factual basis for any of these fears.

Current attitudes concerning menstruation are less negative than in previous generations, but reference to it as "the curse" is still common. Cultural messages—for example, advertisements and commercials for pads and tampons—communicate in subtle ways that menstruation is an untidy and unsanitary condition, to be cleaned up by using "sanitary napkins." Similarly, advertisements for tampons communicate that if a female handles things properly, she can go about her business almost as if she were "normal" (Lips, 2008).

INTACT HYMEN AND VIRGINITY   Another common misconception is that the presence of a hymen indicates virginity. The hymen is actually likely to tear in most girls during childhood with active play or curious exploration. Some girls are not even born with a hymen, and in others intercourse only stretches the hymen and does not rupture it.

Sexual Orientation

One of the central tasks of adolescence, particularly late adolescence, involves achieving a personal identity, and a major component of this is one's sexual identity. Although children label themselves as being one sex or the other from the earliest years on, sexual orientation does not become firmly established until adolescence. It is then that sexual experimentation embellishes and confirms, or disconfirms, these earlier labels. Late adolescence brings the additional task of infusing relationships with emotional intimacy.

Sexual orientation refers to the attraction individuals feel for members of the same or the other sex. Those with a **heterosexual** orientation are attracted to people of the opposite sex, those with a **homosexual** orientation are attracted to members of their own sex, and bisexually oriented people are attracted to individuals of both sexes. Heterosexuals are often referred to as *straight*, homosexual men as *gay*, and homosexual women as *lesbian*.

How many adolescents share each of these orientations? Simple answers are not forthcoming, for a number of reasons. Rather than discrete categories into which individuals neatly sort themselves, sexual orientations are more like segments along a continuum (**Figure 10.3**). It is not always clear where one orientation leaves off and another begins. For instance, although many adolescents, particularly males, report having engaged in some form of homosexual sex play at one time or another, relatively few experience feelings of romantic attraction. In a national survey of adolescents, 7.3% of adolescent boys reported such feelings, as did 5% of girls (Russell & Joyner, 2001). Among adults, the percentage of males or females who are exclusively gay or lesbian throughout their adult life is even smaller (Kinsey et al., 1948; Kinsey et al., 1953).

This last point introduces yet another factor that contributes to the fuzziness of these categories. Sexual attraction can change during one's lifetime. An additional complication is that sexuality cannot be reduced simply to behav-

sexual orientation The attraction individuals feel for members of the same and/or the other sex.

heterosexual Sexual attraction toward individuals of the other sex.

homosexual Sexual attraction toward individuals of the same sex.

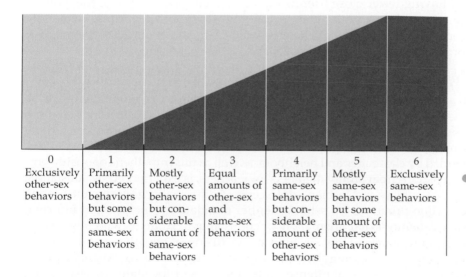

0	1	2	3	4	5	6
Exclusively other-sex behaviors	Primarily other-sex behaviors but some amount of same-sex behaviors	Mostly other-sex behaviors but considerable amount of same-sex behaviors	Equal amounts of other-sex and same-sex behaviors	Primarily same-sex behaviors but considerable amount of other-sex behaviors	Mostly same-sex behaviors but some amount of other-sex behaviors	Exclusively same-sex behaviors

● **Figure 10.3   Kinsey's continuum of sexual orientation** With respect to sexual orientation, individuals can't be neatly sorted into categories; there are gradations of complexity. (After Kinsey et al., 1948.)

Too few gay adolescents are like the young men and women in this group. Most have no one with whom to share concerns and questions about their developing sexual identity, and they must cope by themselves with the social prejudices against homosexuality.

bisexual Sexual attraction toward individuals of both sexes.

ior; it includes attraction and desire as well. One could, in other words, be celibate throughout one's life and still be straight or gay, not to mention those who live a heterosexual lifestyle, even though they are mainly attracted to others of their own sex.

Homosexuality: Gay, Lesbian, and Bisexual Adolescents

How is one to think of homosexuality, if having homosexual experiences does not necessarily mean that one is homosexual? In general, homosexuals are individuals who, for some extended period of their lives, are more attracted sexually to individuals of their own sex than to those of the opposite sex. This definition underscores several points. First, sexual attraction is as important in defining sexual orientation as actual behavior; and second, an isolated sexual experience does not mean one is homosexual: Sexual orientation reflects a prolonged sexual preference. Furthermore, many individuals are neither exclusively heterosexual nor exclusively homosexual.

Establishing a sexual identity is difficult for most adolescents, but especially so for those who wonder whether they're atypical. Many gay, lesbian, and **bisexual** adolescents report experiencing feelings that they recognized as atypical for their gender as early as the age of 10, which prompted a period of sexual questioning even prior to puberty. Even in late childhood, those who question their sexual identity report being more anxious about relationships with peers and are less accepting of themselves (Carver et al., 2004; Egan & Perry, 2001).

Being different is never easy, especially when it places one in a group that is viewed negatively by many segments of society. Sexual-minority adolescents experience more depression, anxiety, and have more suicidal thoughts than their heterosexual peers. Perceived discrimination, bullying, loss of friends, and worries about maintaining existing friendships account for many of the negative emotions experienced by sexual-minority youth. With respect to friendships, although sexual-minority adolescents report losing more friends and having fewer close friends than their heterosexual peers, this pattern changes with age, with older sexual-minority youth reporting more close friends than those who are heterosexual (Almeida et al., 2009; Diamond & Lucas, 2004; Hart & Heimberg, 2001).

Prejudice and Discrimination

At a time when all adolescents, irrespective of their sexual orientation, face the developmental challenges of consolidating an identity, sexual-minority youth experience additional challenges in the form of societal prejudice concerning homosexuality. Bullying, harassment, being verbally or physically assaulted, avoided by classmates and neighbors, as well as unsympathetic or openly hostile reactions from family members, or teachers, is experienced by substantial numbers of gay and lesbian adolescents. Additionally, government-funded education programs for schools neither mandate the inclusion of information related to sexual orientation, or counseling to students who might want to speak to someone, nor prohibit the inclusion of negative material about homosexuality, for example, some even teaching that homosexuality is unacceptable or "a criminal offense under the laws of the state" (Russo, 2006).

These experiences may well account for the greater incidence of substance abuse, thoughts of suicide, and academic problems among sexual-minority youth (Rotheram-Borus et al., 1995; Russell & Joyner, 2001).

School programs to prevent bullying (Chapter 8) can play an important role in establishing a positive climate for all adolescents, one in which homophobic bullying is no more acceptable than any other form of bullying (Birkett et al., 2009).

Biological and Psychosocial Bases of Sexual Attraction

What determines one's sexual orientation? Is sexual orientation biologically based? Can sexual attraction be traced to formative experiences, such as the type of family one is raised in or a first sexual encounter? We will look first at biological explanations and then at psychological ones.

BIOLOGICAL FACTORS   J. Michael Bailey and Richard Pillard (1991) interviewed gay and bisexual men with twin brothers. Twins can be of two types. Identical (monozygotic) twins share the same genetic makeup, having developed from the same cell (zygote). Fraternal (dizygotic) twins develop from separate cells and are no more similar genetically than other siblings. If there is a genetic contribution to sexual orientation, more identical twin brothers should both be homosexual than fraternal twin brothers. This study also included an additional, third group of gay and bisexual men; these men had adoptive brothers, that is, with no shared genetic background but who shared a similar environment. It was expected that the co-incidence of homosexuality would be lowest in this third group.

Bailey and Pillard found that over 50% of the identical twins whose brothers were homosexual were themselves homosexual, whereas only 22% of the fraternal twin brothers were and even fewer, 11%, of the adoptive brothers were.

A similar study of sexual orientation in females revealed comparable findings. Forty-eight percent of identical twin sisters of gay women were also lesbian, in contrast to only 16% of fraternal twin sisters and 6% of adoptive sisters (Bailey et al., 1993).

Overall, these findings strongly suggest a genetic component to sexual orientation. Additional research suggests that the path of genetic transmission, at least for males, is likely to be through the mother. A higher percentage of maternal uncles of gay men, and cousins who are sons of maternal aunts, are gay than the base rate of homosexuals in the population. Higher rates are not found for paternally related males.

The precise means by which genes might influence sexual orientation is still being studied. One possibility is through hormones that are present in differing amounts in males and females. However, studies of gay males and lesbians and of heterosexuals do not find expected differences in the levels of circulating hormones (Money, 1988). Hormones might also affect prenatal brain development. One study found that a node of the hypothalamus, which is related to sexual behavior, is smaller in gay males than in heterosexual males (LeVay, 1991). However, differences in hypothalamic size due to other causes cannot be ruled out.

It is also possible that individuals may be genetically predisposed to homosexuality but nonetheless develop a heterosexual orientation because of the presence or absence of other contributing factors.

PSYCHOLOGICAL FACTORS   Sexual orientation develops within a psychosocial environment. Freud assumed that children are initially bisexual and only gradually develop heterosexual interests through the resolution of the Oedipus or Electra complex in early childhood (see Chapter 2). Other theorists have suggested that homosexuality in males is due to a domineering, overprotective mother and a passive father. However, one would expect such family influences to affect siblings as well, and the incidence of homosexuality among brothers of gay males is no higher than in the population at large, with the exception of twins, as discussed earlier. Similar attempts have been made to trace lesbianism to early traumatic sexual experiences that could turn women away from males as objects of sexual desire. Estimates of the frequency of such experiences, however, are considerably higher than the incidence of lesbianism among females.

Family influences remain important, but not necessarily as theorists would lead us to expect. For instance, adolescents raised by same-sex couples have not been found to differ in either their romantic relationships or other measures of psychosocial adjustment from those raised by opposite-sex couples. Home atmosphere, nonetheless, has been found to be important. It is the closeness of parents' relationships to children, however, that is associated with adjustment, and not their sexual orientation (Anderssen et al., 2002; Fitzgerald, 1999; Vanfraussen et al., 2002; Wainright et al., 2004).

All of this is not to say that psychosocial factors do not contribute to sexual orientation. Recall that even though 50% of the identical twins of gay men were gay, the other half were not. Rather, adolescents' sexual orientation results from a complex mix of environmental and genetic factors that are then shaped and molded to uniquely fit the perceived experiences of each adolescent.

Sexual Health: Risks and Responsibilities

One might think that adolescents' early sexual activity would be accompanied by an equal sophistication concerning contraception, but data suggest this is not the case. Approximately 750,000 adolescent girls (15–19 year olds) become pregnant every year; eighty percent of them do so unintentionally. Additionally, more than nine times that number become infected with a sexually transmitted disease each year (Guttmacher Institute, 2010). Yet adolescents can select from a wide range of contraceptives. Many of these choices all but eliminate the possibility of pregnancy and are highly effective in protecting against sexually transmitted diseases. Why, then, aren't they more effective for teenagers? The obvious answer is that many sexually active teenagers do not consistently use contraceptives.

Contraception

In a national survey of high school students, only 63% of those who were sexually active said they or their partner had used a condom when last having intercourse, with males showing greater use than females, and African Americans showing greater use than Caucasians or Hispanics (Table 10.3) (CDC, 2008b). Why might condom use be sporadic for so many adolescents? A number of reasons exist.

LACK OF INFORMATION   Most adolescents are surprisingly misinformed about their own reproductive capabilities. For instance, many early adolescent girls believe it isn't necessary for them to take any precautions because they are too young to get pregnant, and many boys believe that withdrawal is an effective way to avoid pregnancy. Most adolescents similarly are unaware of the likelihood of becoming infected with a sexually transmitted disease. And some adolescents appear to be so anxious about their sexual activities that they are not able to deal with the associated issues in any practical way.

Most adolescents do not receive much information about reproduction or contraception from their parents. Most are also not likely to disclose their concerns to their parents. How likely adolescents are to talk to their parents depends on the quality of the relationship they have with them and on their parents' willingness to talk when disagreements arise, rather than avoid potential conflict (Papini et al., 1988a; Troth & Peterson, 2000). Talking with parents depends as well on adolescents' levels of self-esteem and individuation (Papini et al., 1988b). This last point suggests that young adolescents especially will have difficulty bringing their sexual concerns to their parents, since they are still in the early stages of individuation (see Chapter 5).

TABLE 10.3 **Percentage of High School Students Who Used a Condom During Last Sexual Intercourse**		
ETHNICITY	FEMALES	MALES
African American	60.1	74.0
Caucasian	53.9	66.4
Hispanic	52.1	69.9

Source: CDC, 2008b.

Many adolescents also do not receive information about contraception at school. For instance, among those attending schools in districts requiring sex education, only half are likely to be given information about various forms of contraception and their effectiveness (Guttmacher Institute, 2006).

Does teaching adolescents about contraception increase the likelihood that they will become sexually active? Research finds just the opposite to be true. Sex education programs that provide adolescents with information about the use of condoms and other forms of contraception have been found to actually delay the initiation of sexual activity and to result in safer sex practices once adolescents become sexually active (Guttmacher Institute, 2004a; Kirby, 2002).

INABILITY TO ACCEPT ONE'S SEXUALITY   First sexual encounters can occasion considerable conflict in many adolescents, especially in girls. A number of reasons exist for this conflict. Sexual behavior is closely tied to religious and moral issues. In some homes, sexual matters are cloaked with secrecy, and discussions of sexual concerns are infrequent or absent entirely. Many adolescents simply are uncomfortable discussing their sexuality, even those who are sexually active. Adolescent girls who *can* accept and talk about their own sexual behavior are more likely to use contraceptives effectively (Tschann & Adler, 1997).

Cause for conflict among many adolescent girls also can be found in current stereotypes of femininity and masculinity. Compare these components of the feminine stereotype—yielding, shy, sensitive to the needs of others, childlike, and compassionate—with those of the masculine stereotype—makes decisions easily and is self-reliant, independent, assertive, and willing to take risks. Who is more likely to make decisions or assertively insist on the use of a condom? Additionally, many females fail to use a contraceptive simply because they think it isn't feminine to plan to have sex or to take precautions against getting pregnant.

COGNITIVE-EMOTIONAL IMMATURITY   One of the hallmarks of cognitive development is the ability to think about things that have not been experienced. Thought that is limited by experience is limited to what has happened before. Most adolescents are just entering a form of thought in which they can consider events that may only exist as possibilities for them. Most have never been pregnant before either.

Despite the emergence of new mental skills that enable adolescents to imagine things they have never experienced, things that exist only as abstractions or possibilities, these skills appear at different times for different individuals.

Some adolescents may be facing sexual decisions while still approaching daily problems in a concrete fashion, their thinking limited to what is immediate and currently apparent (see Chapter 4). Thus a 13-year-old girl flattered by the attentions of an older boy may not have the cognitive maturity, in the pressure of the moment, to consider distant consequences. The concrete problem is "What will make him like me now?" Pregnancy and disease belong to the world of tomorrow, and tomorrow is but dimly represented in concrete thought.

Even among those adolescents who can think more abstractly, the absence of practical experience and accurate information can make imagined consequences hard to evaluate. Many adolescents are able to conceive of problems intellectually yet feel personally immune to them. To these individuals, disease and pregnancy are possible but not real, and it's hard to take dangers seriously if they believe such things only happen to others.

CONFLICTING INTENTIONS   Many adolescents who are aware of the risks and fully *intend* to use condoms nonetheless may not because doing so would conflict with other motives. Laurie Bauman, Alison Karasz, and Adaoha Hamilton (2007), at the Albert Einstein College of Medicine, conducted interviews with adolescents who had completed a program designed to increase their awareness of HIV. All of these adolescents indicated their intention to use condoms, yet when asked if they could think of a situation in which they might not, 24 of the 26 adolescents they interviewed described at least one! Many mentioned situations in which using a condom would conflict with other motives, such as needing to trust the person they were with, or wanting to increase their feelings of intimacy, or believing a condom would diminish their sexual pleasure.

At other times, it is difficult for teenagers to put their intentions into effect when they're actually in a sexual situation. For instance, they may not have expected the situation to arise and not have a condom available, or their ability to carry out their intentions may be compromised by using alcohol or other substances (Bauman et al., 2007).

Sexually Transmitted Diseases

Approximately 9 million adolescents and young adults a year become infected with a **sexually transmitted disease (STD)** (Guttmacher Institute, 2010). Because many STDs are asymptomatic, and because those with symptoms do not always seek treatment, the actual number of adolescents affected is almost surely greater than estimated.

Some STDs, such as syphilis and HIV infection, can be acquired through blood transfusions in addition to sexual contact. They range in seriousness from irritating itches to life-threatening infections. Some are reaching epidemic levels among adolescents. The most serious STDs are HIV infection, syphilis, and gonorrhea. Less serious infections range from genital herpes, for which there is no known cure, to pests such as pubic lice, which can be treated with a prescription shampoo.

Many adolescents mistakenly believe that *other* people get STDs—not them. Well-dressed, neatly groomed teenagers assume they could never get anything like syphilis or gonorrhea, much less AIDS. Assumptions such as these couldn't be further from the truth. STDs are presently as American as apple pie and country music. The facts are simple: Many STDs have reached epidemic proportions, with adolescents accounting for nearly half of all the new cases each year. Those who are sexually active are likely at some point to get a sexually transmitted disease (Guttmacher Institute, 2010).

STDs can be categorized in terms of viral infections, bacterial infections, and infestations. We will begin by looking at the first category of STDs, starting

sexually transitted disease (STD)   An infection that is spread through sexual contact.

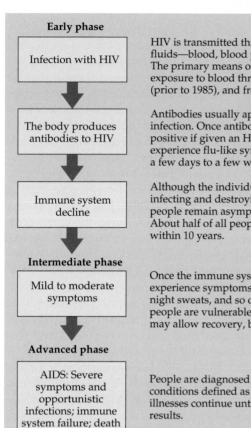

Early phase

Infection with HIV

HIV is transmitted through intimate contact with body fluids—blood, blood products, semen, or vaginal secretions. The primary means of transmission are sexual contact, direct exposure to blood through injection drug use or transfusions (prior to 1985), and from an infected mother to her child.

The body produces antibodies to HIV

Antibodies usually appear two to 12 weeks after the initial infection. Once antibodies appear, an infected person tests positive if given an HIV-antibody test. About 30% of people experience flu-like symptoms during this period, lasting for a few days to a few weeks.

Immune system decline

Although the individual has no symptoms, the virus is infecting and destroying cells of the immune system. Many people remain asymptomatic for three to 10 or more years. About half of all people infected with HIV develop AIDS within 10 years.

Intermediate phase

Mild to moderate symptoms

Once the immune system is damaged, many people begin to experience symptoms such as skin rashes, fatigue, weight loss, night sweats, and so on. When the damage is more severe, people are vulnerable to opportunistic infections. Treatments may allow recovery, but infections often recur.

Advanced phase

AIDS: Severe symptoms and opportunistic infections; immune system failure; death

People are diagnosed with AIDS if they develop one of the conditions defined as a marker for AIDS. Chronic or recurrent illnesses continue until the immune system fails and death results.

Note: The pattern of HIV infection is different for every patient and not everyone infected with HIV will go through all these stages.

● **Figure 10.4   The progressive course of HIV infection**   (After Schwartz, 1992.)

with HIV/AIDS since this is the most serious of the STDs, even though it is the least frequent among adolescents in the United States.[1]

VIRAL INFECTIONS   The risk to adolescents in the United States of infection with **HIV (human immunodeficiency virus)**—the virus that causes **AIDS (acquired immune deficiency syndrome)**—is relatively slight compared with other sexually transmitted diseases. However, HIV remains the riskiest of all STDs because of its life-threatening nature (CDC, 2009c).

Certain ethnic minorities within the United States are disproportionately at risk for HIV infection. More than 50% of those diagnosed with HIV/AIDS are African American, even though they represent only 13% of the population. Similarly, Hispanics are overrepresented among those diagnosed with HIV/AIDS. Rates of infection are also higher among American Indians and Alaska natives, given their proportions within the population; Asians and Pacific Islanders have the lowest rate of infection. Because the incubation period from infection to the appearance of symptoms averages 10 years, it is likely that most adults with AIDS were infected when they were adolescents or young adults (**Figure 10.4**) (CDC, 2009c; National Institute of Allergy and Infectious Diseases, 2005).

HIV   Human immunodeficiency virus: a virus attacking the immune system, leading to AIDS (acquired immune deficiency syndrome).

AIDS   Acquired immune deficiency syndrome: a sexually transmitted disease resulting from a virus that attacks the immune system; can also be transmitted through contaminated blood transfusions or from an infected pregnant woman to her fetus.

---

[1] The Centers for Disease Control classifies HIV, chlamydia, and gonorrhea as discharge diseases because they are transmitted through genital secretions (e.g., semen and vaginal fluids), and in the case of HIV/AIDS also through the blood of infected individuals. Genital herpes and syphilis are classified as genital ulcer diseases, since they are transmitted through contact with sores or ulcers on the skin, or patches that appear normal but are nonetheless infected. Genital warts, or human papilloma virus, can be transmitted either by contact with infected areas of skin or by secretions. Infestations with pests, such as pubic lice, constitute a third type of transmission (CDC, 2009d).

For some adolescents, protecting themselves against HIV infection is not enough; many work for increased awareness and community support of effective intervention programs.

HIV is a virus that attacks the immune system, causing it to break down. This in turn leaves the body defenseless against infection, eventually resulting in death from any of a number of secondary, opportunistic infections. At present, there is no cure for this disease; however, great strides have been made in drug treatments that are effective in combating the development of secondary infections and in prolonging life. HIV infection progresses through several stages, the last of which is AIDS (acquired immune deficiency syndrome). The virus can be transmitted by exposure to infected blood, such as through sharing contaminated needles for injecting drugs or through blood transfusions from an infected person, as well as by sexual contact. However, most adolescent and young adult males become infected through sexual contact with other males, and relatively few through heterosexual contact or contaminated needles. Most females, though, become infected through heterosexual contact (CDC, 2006).

What steps can adolescents take to protect themselves from HIV infection? The first step is simply a mental one, but it is as important as any that follow because adolescents are unlikely to take additional steps unless they begin with the realization that *anyone* can get AIDS, including themselves. Realizing they are at risk is not an easy step for many adolescents. Nancy Leland and Richard Barth (1993) asked 1000 high school students how likely they thought it was for them to "get AIDS." Most adolescents did not think they were likely to be infected, as many as one-third indicating there was "no chance."

For those who can narrow this mental distance, a number of practices can significantly reduce the risk of sexually transmitted HIV infection. Of course, the surest way is to avoid sexual contact of any kind. We have seen earlier in the chapter, however, that a majority of adolescents are sexually active by the end of high school. Furthermore, most will not marry until their mid 20s, resulting in a period of about 10 years during which the risk of acquiring an STD is relatively high (Guttmacher Institute, 2006). The following precautions can significantly reduce the risk of exposure, not only to HIV infection but to other STDs as well.

1. *Use a latex condom.* Latex condoms have been found to be highly effective in protecting against infection since the HIV virus, as well as pathogens causing other STDs, cannot pass through the wall of the condom. Non-latex condoms, however, do not provide the same protection. Additionally, latex condoms are effective only when they are consistently and correctly used (CDC, 2004a).

2. *Avoid the exchange of body fluids.* Although HIV is most highly concentrated in blood and semen, it has also been found in other body fluids, for example, vaginal and pre-ejaculatory secretions. For infection to occur, the virus must enter the body through a break in the skin, usually a cut, tear, or sore, and from there reach the bloodstream. Vaginal intercourse, anal intercourse, and oral-genital sex all carry risk of exposure. Even intercourse without ejaculation carries some risk of infection because, as noted, the virus can be present in pre-ejaculatory and vaginal secretions.

3. *Be discriminating.* Certain practices and lifestyles increase the risk of infection. Individuals who have had numerous sexual partners and those who have used drugs intravenously are more likely to be infected. However, this doesn't mean that someone with a more conservative lifestyle may *not* be infected.

Those who maintain a monogamous sexual relationship with someone are at lowest risk of infection from the HIV virus or any other STD. However, only a blood test can establish whether an individual is free of the virus, since those who are not infected will not have antibodies in their blood. Simply asking someone, even a loving partner, does not guarantee a completely truthful answer.

How likely are adolescents to follow or even understand any of these precautions? A randomly sampled survey of 1773 adolescents age 16 through 19 found that adolescents who have the most sexual partners (more than 10 a year) are least likely to use a condom, and have the highest risk of infection. Even understanding the risk of infection, however, is no guarantee that adolescents will avoid engaging in risky practices. Nearly one-third of adolescents receiving treatment for substance abuse in one study indicated that even though they knew and were worried about the risk of HIV infection, they were likely to go ahead and have unprotected sex anyway (Langer et al., 1998).

All the factors that make it difficult for adolescents to use contraceptives in general apply equally to the precautions they must take against HIV infection. Lack of information among adolescents complicates the problem, even though most adolescents are taught about HIV in school. More than misinformation is at work with adolescents. Almost surely adolescents' cognitive immaturity sets limits on their ability to understand the seriousness of the disease or the precautions that need to be taken. So, too, does adolescents' sense that it couldn't possibly happen to them.

Genital herpes, another common STD, is caused by the herpes simplex virus. There are two types of herpes simplex virus, HSV-1 and HSV-2; genital herpes is most frequently caused by HSV-2. As with other STDs, most adolescents experience few or no symptoms. When symptoms occur, they appear as blisters, usually on the genitals or the rectum. The blisters break after several days, leaving small wet sores that dry up in a week or two. Even though the blisters eventually disappear, the virus remains dormant in the body, and outbreaks can recur at any time. Again, most adolescents may not develop sores or, if they do, these may be mild enough not to be noticed. Although infection can occur through exposure to the sores, a sexual partner with no apparent sores can still transmit the virus. No cure presently exists for herpes, although medication can control outbreaks and may help to reduce the risk of transmission to others (CDC, 2009d).

Genital warts are caused by infection with the human papillomavirus (HPV). This STD is widespread among adolescents (CDC, 2009b). The warts are painless, dry, light-colored outgrowths on the genitals or rectum. HPV actually includes over 100 different strains of the virus, some of which are "high risk" in that they have a known relationship to cervical cancer (CDC, 2009b). Adolescent girls with HPV should have Pap tests at least once a year.

BACTERIAL INFECTIONS **Chlamydia** is one of the most common STDs among adolescents. It is referred to as a "silent" disease since most of those who are infected experience no symptoms and don't even know they are infected; this is especially true for females. Adolescents who do have symptoms may notice a discharge, or a burning feeling when urinating, or itching around the urethral opening.

If untreated in females, the infection can spread through the reproductive tract, causing pelvic inflammatory disease (PID). Inflammation of the tiny tubules of the tract leaves scar tissue and may result in infertility and increased risk of ectopic pregnancy (a pregnancy occurring outside the uterus). Even when chlamydia has spread, many females may remain symptom-free; others can experience abdominal or back pain, nausea, or fever, all symptoms of PID. Immediate treatment should be sought.

genital herpes A sexually transmitted disease characterized by recurring outbreaks of itching or burning blisters; caused by a virus that remains dormant in the body.

genital warts A sexually transmitted disease caused by the human papillomavirus.

chlamydia A sexually transmitted disease, caused by a bacterium, that can affect the reproductive tract, possibly leading to pelvic inflammatory disease.

gonorrhea A sexually transmitted disease caused by a bacterium.

syphilis A sexually transmitted disease, caused by a bacterium, that can also be transmitted through blood transfusions or from a pregnant woman to her fetus; progresses over several stages.

pubic lice Parasitic insects that are usually transmitted sexually; sometimes called "crabs."

Because so many adolescents have no symptoms, and because the consequences of infection are potentially serious, those who are sexually active should be screened for the disease at least once a year, at least until age 25 (CDC, 2009d).

Another common STD, **gonorrhea** can be transmitted by many forms of sexual contact: intercourse, oral-genital sex, or even kissing. Anyone who is sexually active may be at risk for contracting this disease; however, those with the highest rates of infection are adolescents and young adults, because they tend to have more sexual partners and use less protection than adults. Rates of infection are also higher among African Americans (CDC, 2009d). Many adolescents experience either no symptoms or very mild ones. In males, the most noticeable symptom is a watery discharge from the penis, and some may experience swollen testicles; females also may notice a discharge, and both may experience pain when urinating. Left untreated, the disease spreads through the reproductive system, leaving scar tissue that can block the tubules and cause infertility. Untreated cases of gonorrhea can also affect the joints, causing a type of arthritis, and the heart, affecting the valves.

Early adolescent females run a special risk because the immature cervix is especially vulnerable to infection by the bacterium causing gonorrhea. Early coital activity also appears to delay cervical development, as does the use of oral contraceptives. Thus early adolescent females who are using oral contraceptives are at greater risk of infection than those using other forms of birth control. Because the long-term consequences of infection for females include a higher risk of cervical cancer, those who have ever had gonorrhea should routinely get Pap tests (CDC, 2009d).

Both chlamydia and gonorrhea can be treated with antibiotics. Adolescents who discover they are infected should notify all sexual partners who are likely to have been infected or to have passed on the infection. They should also refrain from sexual contact until a checkup indicates that the infection is gone. Both steps are important in preventing the spread of these diseases.

Sexual contact is the most common way **syphilis** is transmitted, although it can also be transmitted through contaminated blood transfusions or passed in utero from an infected pregnant woman to her fetus. Symptoms typically show up from one to three weeks, or even longer, following infection. In the *primary stage* of the disease, a small, usually painless sore, or possibly several, appears on the genitals, rectum, or lips, or in the mouth. These typically heal within several weeks, and unsuspecting adolescents may believe that whatever they had is gone.

If not treated, syphilis progresses to a *secondary stage* marked by symptoms including a rash, fever, headache, and sore throat. These symptoms are easily mistaken for flu, especially as they can come and go for several months. Once these symptoms disappear, the disease enters a *latent stage*. Although adolescents in the latent stage experience no symptoms, the disease continues its course within their bodies. Many who have syphilis remain in this stage and experience no further complications. Others can move into a *tertiary stage* in which damage to the heart, eyes, brain, and spinal cord can occur (CDC, 2009d).

Despite its highly destructive nature, syphilis is easily treated with antibiotics in the primary and secondary stages, and even in later stages is responsive to larger doses over longer periods.

INFESTATIONS Often called "crabs," **pubic lice** are usually spread by sexual contact but can also be transmitted via bedsheets or clothing. Lice live in the pubic hair, causing severe itching as they draw the blood on which they live. Bedding used by an infested person can remain infected for up to a week. A prescription shampoo kills the lice, but because eggs that drop onto bedding and clothing can survive for five or six days, clean sheets and clothing are important to prevent a recurrence.

Risks and Precautions

The risk of acquiring an STD is often greater for an adolescent than it is for an adult because adolescents are likely to have more sexual partners than adults and more likely to have unprotected sex. Additionally, adolescent girls are more susceptible biologically to certain STDs, such as chlamydia and gonorrhea, than are adults, as noted earlier (CDC, 2009d).

KNOWING THE RISKS   One need not be promiscuous to run the risk of contracting an STD. Even adolescents who practice serial monogamy, limiting themselves to one sexual partner before becoming active with another, expose themselves to the sexual history of their partner—as well as the sexual history of each of their partner's partners, and so on. Like standing in a hall of mirrors, the regression is infinite. Because many diseases have no symptoms following the initial infection, adolescents who are infected, even if well intentioned, can pass the disease unknowingly to future partners.

Information concerning how these and other STDs are transmitted, details about symptoms, and what treatments are suggested is available at the Web site for the Centers for Disease Control and Prevention.

TAKING PRECAUTIONS   Symptoms such as a discharge or the appearance of sores should receive immediate medical attention. Most STDs can be treated with an antibiotic if caught before complications develop. Honesty is important, and partners need to be informed so that they can get treatment, too. Routine medical checkups are especially advisable for sexually active females because they are not as likely as males to experience symptoms, and the health complications that arise when infections are left untreated can be considerable.

Adolescents who are sexually active should always use a latex condom. A condom is important even when another form of contraception is used, because it offers protection against STDs as well as pregnancy. Females and males can both assume responsibility here. But as simple as this precaution is, it still is not likely to be consistently followed. Many females feel they can engage in sex only if they are swept away in a moment of passion; pulling a condom out of a purse implies advance planning. Males may fear that stopping to put on a condom will break the mood. Using a condom, however, is the most effective precaution against STDs for sexually active teenagers. Even so, less than two-thirds of high school students indicated they had used one the last time they had sex (CDC, 2008b). Additionally, older adolescents are less likely to use a condom than are younger adolescents, perhaps because they are more likely to be in a steady relationship in which the adolescent girl assumes responsibility for contraception, primarily through the use of birth control pills (**Figure 10.5**). Effective as these may be in preventing pregnancy, they do not offer protection against STDs.

DIFFICULTIES TO CONFRONT   Precautions that are relatively simple for an adult

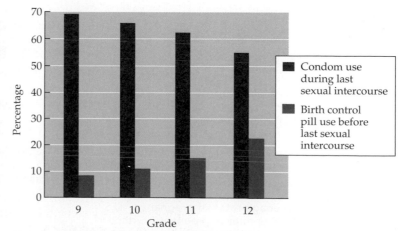

● **Figure 10.5   Condom and birth control pill usage**   The use of condoms among sexually active adolescents decreases with age as the use of birth control pills increases. (After CDC, 2008b.)

may be next to impossible for an adolescent. Many adolescents feel invulnerable to infection and may not take precautions. Others may be too frightened or embarrassed to get medical attention if symptoms do appear. Early adolescents frequently avoid seeking treatment, assuming the problem will go away by itself. Many are afraid their parents will discover their secret problem, and many more don't know how to get treatment or where to go, especially if they do not want their parents to find out. In addition, most don't have enough money to pay for a doctor's visit or for prescription medication. Transportation can be a problem, too, especially for those living in rural areas.

Shame, fear, or anger may prevent adolescents from informing a partner about their own symptoms. And partners who are told may likewise do nothing for the same reasons. Even adolescents who seek treatment will not necessarily comply with the directions they have been given, especially early adolescents who do not yet have an adult's concern about the future. They may fail to take medication as prescribed or discontinue use when symptoms first disappear; similarly, they may fail to abstain from sex or to return for a checkup to make sure they are clear of the infection. Clearly, for preventive programs to be effective, they need to address more than the misinformation and lack of information that currently exists among adolescents.

Teenage Pregnancies

Other countries such as England, Sweden, France, and Canada have rates of sexually active adolescents similar to those in the United States, yet they have lower pregnancy, birth, and abortion rates (**Figure 10.6**) (CDC, 2005g). Why might this be? Lisa Lottes (2002), at the University of Maryland, summarizes a number of key differences.

ATTITUDES TOWARD ADOLESCENT SEXUALITY   These countries have identified teenage *pregnancy*, not teenage sexual activity, as a social problem. In other words, it is believed that adults, not adolescents, should be the ones to have children. Being adult is defined very much as it is in this country: in terms of completing one's education, getting a job, living on one's own, and being in a stable relationship (Darroch et al., 2001). Rather than denying adolescent sexuality, these countries offer programs that teach teenagers to assume responsibility for their sexual activity, and more teenagers in these countries practice contraception effectively. As a consequence, there are far fewer instances of teenage pregnancies, parenting, or abortion, and far fewer adolescents become sexually active at a young age (Darroch et al., 2001).

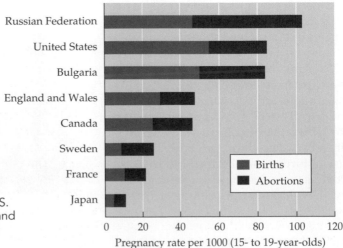

● **Figure 10.6   Teenage rates of pregnancy** U.S. teenagers have higher rates of pregnancy, birth, and abortion than teenagers in most other developed countries. (After Guttmacher Institute, 2004.)

SEX WITHIN COMMITTED RELATIONSHIPS   Sexuality itself tends to be viewed differently in these countries, with sexual activity a healthy expression of one's feelings for another and not as a hedonistic source of pleasurable feelings for oneself. These feelings, in turn, are viewed as developing within the context of a committed and loving relationship. This view of sexuality is explicitly taught in schools (Lottes, 2002). In Sweden, for instance, courses in sex education include the following ethical principles:

> *Nobody is entitled to regard and treat another human being simply as a means of selfish gratification.*

> *Sexuality forming part of a personal relationship has more to offer than casual sex and is therefore worth aspiring to (Swedish National Board of Education, 1986, as cited in Lottes, 2002).*

OPEN DISCUSSION OF SEXUAL RESPONSIBILITY   These countries differ as well in viewing sexual activity as a normal aspect of development. As such, there is no expectation that adolescents will remain abstinent until marriage, and educational programs do not attempt to pressure them to commit to this as a goal. Instead, adolescents learn from adults in their society that when they become sexually active, they are to do so responsibly, protecting themselves and their partner from unintended pregnancies and STDs. Thus, although these countries are more accepting of adolescent sexual activity, they are less accepting of adolescent pregnancy (Guttmacher Institute, 2006).

Research with U.S. adolescents generally finds that those who can talk more freely with parents and sex educators are more likely to delay sexual initiation and be more responsible when they become sexually active (Kirby, 2002; Meschke et al., 2002; Rose et al., 2005).

ACCURATE INFORMATION   European countries provide adolescents with comprehensive sex education through schools and community health centers in which accurate information about effective methods of contraception is made available to them. In contrast, in the United States, contraception is presented as an effective way of preventing pregnancy in only half of the public school districts that require sex education. An additional third of public school districts that mandate sex education require teachers to present abstinence as the only option for unmarried teens, and either do not allow discussion of contraception or allow contraceptives only to be discussed in terms of their possible failure (Guttmacher Institute, 2006).

Although it is true that abstinence is the surest way to avoid STDs and unintended pregnancies, it is not accurate to teach that contraceptives are ineffective. Latex condoms, when consistently and correctly used, are highly effective. Additionally, the use of oral contraceptive pills or injectable contraceptives, which last several months, virtually eliminates unintended pregnancies. Adolescents themselves must be added into the equation when presenting abstinence as a "sure way" to avoid these problems since many do not define abstinence the way federally funded government programs do. Many adolescents believe that one can be abstinent and still engage in oral sex, anal intercourse, or vaginal intercourse without full penetration (Bruckner & Bearman, 2005). Yet STDs can be transmitted through all of these

AN EXTRA SEVEN POUNDS COULD KEEP YOU OFF THE FOOTBALL TEAM.

Become a father before you're ready and you may always wonder what else you could have been.
THE CHILDREN'S DEFENSE FUND

Teenage pregnancies are due partly to a lack of information and partly to a denial of personal responsibility. Adolescents need help in learning how to make decisions about their sexual behaviors, especially those that could alter the course of their lives.

activities, and pregnancy is possible with the latter since live sperm can be present in the lubricating fluid that appears at the opening of the penis.

Abstinence education also teaches that "sexual activity outside of the context of marriage is likely to have harmful psychological and physical effects" (Section 510(b) Title V, 1996). This assertion, again, is not accurate. Nicole Else-Quest, Janet Shibley Hyde, and John Delamater (2005), at the University of Wisconsin, compared the responses of nearly 3500 individuals who either had premarital sex or abstained until marriage, and found no differences with respect to later sexual functioning, feelings of guilt about sex, or their overall physical health. Although those who abstained had fewer STDs, other research has not found such a difference. Hannah Bruckner and Peter Bearman (2005), analyzing data from a large national sample of adolescents and young adults, found that those who had taken pledges to remain virgins until marriage had rates of STDs comparable to non-pledgers. Most likely this is because 88% of pledgers go on to have sex before marriage and are not as likely as non-pledgers to use a condom when they first become sexually active (Bruckner & Bearman, 2005; Rosenbaum, 2009).

ACCESS TO CONTRACEPTIVES AND REPRODUCTIVE HEALTH SERVICES

Adolescents in European countries have better access to health services offering contraceptive counseling and contraceptives than do adolescents in the United States. One of the most effective ways of providing access to adolescents is through school-based health centers located either in the school or close to it. However, centers such as these serve only 2% of students nationally, and most centers are not allowed to provide contraceptive services on-site and can provide these only be referring students to other agencies in the community (**Figure 10.7**) (Santelli et al., 2003).

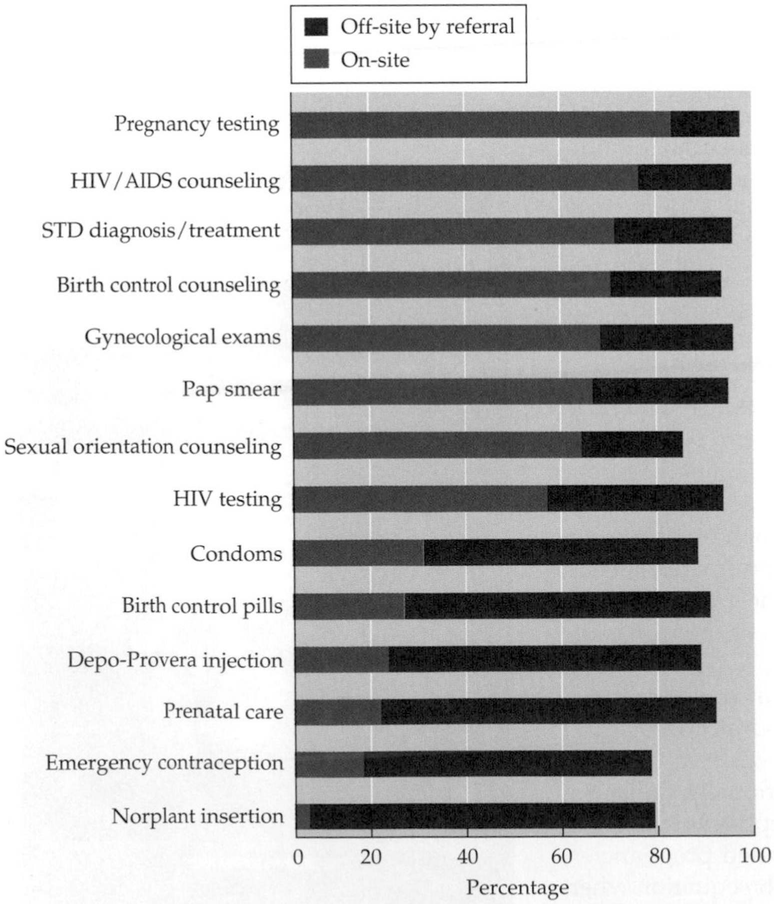

ACCESS TO LOW-COST HEALTH CARE

The absence of a national health plan, similar to the one present in most European countries, that would include contraceptive counseling and services, and be available to all, significantly contributes to unintended pregnancies and STDs among adolescents and adults as well. Not only the present high costs of medical services, but also the accessibility of these, and fears concerning confidentiality prevent adolescents from seeking the reproductive counseling and services they need (Averett et al., 2002; Culwell & Feinglass, 2007).

Better access to clinics, more information, and promotion of contraceptive use are important steps to be taken here at home. Yet teenage pregnancies are likely to remain a problem, especially among poor and low-income adoles-

Figure 10.7   Reproductive health services provided in school-based health centers serving adolescents, 1998–1999   One of the most effective ways of providing reproductive health services is through school-based centers; however, most of these centers are not allowed to provide contraception services on site and must refer students to other agencies in the community. (After Santelli et al. 2003.)

cents for whom the temptation to compromise future options—which may appear doubtful at best—for the immediate gains offered by sex can be hard to resist.

Teenage Parenting

Pregnancy and child rearing present challenges for women of any age, but especially for adolescents. Adolescents are less likely to receive regular prenatal care, and they experience more medical complications during pregnancy. Children born to teenage mothers also experience more complications. The risk of premature birth, low birth weight (which is a general measure of infant health risk), and infant mortality is substantially higher. The children also are at somewhat greater risk for neurological and behavioral problems (Klein, 2005). However, programs that target teenage mothers for prenatal care have been successful in reducing many of these risks (Barnet et al., 2003; Grady & Bloom, 2004). Similarly, interventions following the birth of a child can reduce risks to the infant (Quinlivan et al., 2003). One innovative intervention program involves the use of text messages, in which teenage mothers receive three messages a day—one offering support, one giving information on parenting, and a third sending a message "from the baby" (**Table 10.4**) (Ybarra, 2008).

As might be expected, teenage mothers are less ready for parenting and experience more stress in this role than women who are older. Family support is important, and leads to better parenting (Bunting & McAuley, 2004a; Gee & Rhodes, 2003; Nadeem et al., 2006). Support from the child's father or, in some cases, another male partner is also related to more effective parenting (Bunting & McAuley, 2004a; Krishnakumar & Black, 2003). Despite initial difficulties, most adolescent mothers successfully cope (Oxford et al., 2005).

What do we know of teenage fathers? Contrary to stereotypes casting them as exploitive or uncaring, many remain psychologically involved with the mother through the pregnancy and for some time following the child's birth. Longitudinal research following teenage-mother families finds that most fathers become less involved over time, with only about one-third continuing to remain involved (Gee & Rhodes, 2003; Kalil et al., 2005). Most teenage fathers have less education and lower incomes than do those who postpone parenting, and many find it difficult to provide support for the mother and infant (Bunting & McAuley, 2004b).

Currently, there are few programs to help teenage fathers learn to be better fathers. Those in existence stress the importance of finishing high school and getting a job. Many provide job training as well as parenting classes, enabling teenage fathers to provide financial as well as emotional support.

TABLE 10.4
TXTing 4 Better Parenting[a]

TYPE OF MESSAGE	EXAMPLE
Supportive	"B patient W yrslf. Ur nt solo n ur feelins n dis tym of adjustment wl pass."
Parenting skills	"lrn 2 recogniZ d hunger cry. She may nt B hngry evry tym shes fusy. She may nd burping, a diaper chng, or jst wan2B held."
"From the baby"	"I lk 2 feel warm, +I don't lk heaps of noyZ"

Source: Ybarra, 2008.

[a]Teenage parents receive a parenting skills message, a supportive message, and a message "from the baby" each day in an online intervention to build parenting skills in teenagers.

Adolescents and Abortion

Approximately thirty percent of 15- to 19-year olds end a pregnancy in abortion, with younger adolescents being more likely to do so than older ones. The percentage of adolescents having an abortion has decreased over the last several decades, in large measure due to fewer teens becoming pregnant, which can be attributed primarily to the use of contraception rather than abstaining from sex (Guttmacher Institute, 2006; Santelli et al., 2007).

A number of factors affect the decision to abort or to carry a baby to term. Important among these are family background variables and the influence of peers. Teenagers from middle-class homes are more likely to abort an unintended pregnancy than those living at the poverty level. White adolescents are also more likely to terminate a pregnancy than are African American or Hispanic adolescents (Strauss et al., 2005). Religious beliefs and parents' attitudes are also important in determining a teenage girl's decision to carry a baby to term or to abort. Girls who have strong religious beliefs are less likely to abort a pregnancy, as are those whose parents disapprove of abortion. Peers influence an adolescent's decision, too. Girls with friends who are single teenage parents are more likely to carry the pregnancy to term, whereas those whose friends view abortion positively are more likely to terminate a pregnancy (Benson, 2004; Ellison et al., 2005).

Complicating decisions about abortion for many teenagers is the fact that many do not realize at first that they are pregnant. Young adolescents especially are likely to have irregular menstrual cycles, making it difficult to determine when they have missed a period. Still others may attempt to deny they are pregnant until it is no longer possible to hide from the truth. The difficulties adolescents experience in finding out where to go for health services and arranging transportation compound these problems. As a result, teenagers are somewhat less likely to have an abortion in early pregnancy than are women who are young adults (Strauss et al., 2005).

The issues surrounding abortion are magnified as the result of delay, because the timing of an abortion has both health and moral consequences. Early abortions carry less risk to the adolescent. Similarly, issues concerning the taking of a life are less clear-cut before the fetus becomes viable, or even earlier in the pregnancy, before the appearance of signs, such as brain-wave activity, that are used at the other end of the age spectrum in decisions to terminate life support.

Sex Education: What Adolescents Need to Know

Although many adolescents can talk with their parents about sex, most do not, leaving friends and school-based programs as the most common sources of information about sexuality. School-based programs can differ widely, both in what they cover and in how effective they are (Constantine, 2008; Kirby, 2002). Programs are considered to be effective if they delay the onset of sexual activity among adolescents who are not yet sexually active, and lead to responsible sexual practices among those who are, thereby reducing teenage pregnancy and STDs.

The Effectiveness of School Programs

Programs that teach adolescents assertiveness and decision-making skills offer an attractive supplement to information-based programs. These programs approach sexual decision making by building interpersonal and problem-solving skills. Sex *is* problematic for most adolescents, and it is highly interpersonal. Many adolescents feel pressured into sexual encounters that they would otherwise avoid or postpone if they felt comfortable stating how they felt. These pressures affect adolescents of both sexes. Adolescent males, as well as females, frequently feel pressured into making sexual overtures simply because they assume it's expected of them or that everybody else is having sex. One of the ways in which sex education programs can be effective is to increase adolescents' self-efficacy. The data we have on assertiveness and decision-making programs suggest that these are effective in improving problem-solving and communication skills, as well as knowledge of reproduction; contraception use also improves among adolescents enrolled in such programs (Kirby et al., 2004).

Comprehensive Sex Education Programs

Research evaluating school programs generally finds two types of programs to be effective. These are comprehensive sex education programs (CSE) and CSE programs that include a service learning component (Kirby, 2002). **Comprehensive sex education programs** teach abstinence as a preferred approach, and additionally educate students concerning effective methods of contraception. Despite concerns among supporters of abstinence education that teaching contraception in the same program may be giving students mixed messages, research clearly shows that educating students about contraception does not lead adolescents to engage in sex at an earlier age or have more frequent sexual encounters. To the contrary, these programs are effective in delaying sexual activity, reducing overall sexual activity among adolescents, and reducing unprotected sex (Kirby, 2002; Kohler et al., 2008; Office of the Surgeon General, 2001).

Comprehensive sex education programs that incorporate service learning into the program are even more effective than those utilizing only classroom instruction. **Service learning programs** require students to work as volunteers in the community, doing things such as tutoring in classrooms or helping out in nursing homes. Students are also required to engage in structured reflection on their volunteer work, such as meeting for group discussions or journaling. A meta-review of research on various types of interventions indicates that programs incorporating service learning are the most effective type of sex education program offered in school (Kirby, 2002).

In one such program, low-income seventh- and eighth-graders attending public schools in New York City who participated in service learning along with their classroom instruction in health education were found to be significantly less likely to engage in sexual activity than those who received only the classroom instruction (O'Donnell et al., 1999; O'Donnell et al., 2002). This research was notable in several respects, each of which makes the findings especially significant. Students were assigned at random (by classes) to either of the two conditions, making it unlikely that the findings could be attributed to any preexisting differences. Students were resurveyed, or followed up, two years later to determine the long-term effectiveness of the intervention. Finally, students in the participating schools were from low-income homes, placing them at even greater risk for early sexual activity.

As can be seen in **Figure 10.8**, the longer adolescents had participated in the sex education program that involved them in community service, the more likely they were to delay sexual activity. Additionally, adolescents who already were sexually active were less likely to have engaged in sex during the previous month. The findings of this research are of particular significance because they represent relatively large reductions in sexual activity, and also long-term effects—the data shown in Figure 10.8 were collected two years *after* adolescents had completed the program (O'Donnell et al., 2002).

comprehensive sex education programs Sex education programs that teach abstinence as a preferred approach and educate students concerning effective methods of contraception.

service learning programs Comprehensive education programs that include a community service component, requiring students to do volunteer work.

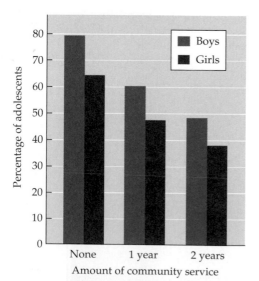

● **Figure 10.8 Reductions in sexual activity among adolescents in a service learning program** Percentage of adolescents initiating sex by the end of the 10th grade after completing a sex education program with no community service, one year of community service, or two years of community service. (After O'Donnell et al., 2002.)

Sex education programs that provide adolescents with information about the use of condoms and other forms of contraception, in addition to teaching abstinence, have been found to actually delay the initiation of sexual activity and to result in safer sex practices once adolescents become sexually active.

How might volunteering for others help adolescents make healthier choices for themselves? Definite answers can't be given. However, it's likely that the caring relationships these adolescents developed through their experiences contributed to their sense of competence and of self-worth.

An after-school program titled the Children's Aid Society Carrera-Model Program (or CAS-Carrera), also has been found to be highly effective in preventing teen pregnancy (Philliber et al., 2001). Participants are recruited for the program when they are 13 to 15 years old and are encouraged to remain in it throughout high school. The approach of the program is holistic, providing not only sex education but also help with such things as schoolwork, finding part-time jobs, and getting into college. In all of this, the aim is to establish close, family-like relationships with the youth. Research evaluating the effectiveness of the program is methodologically sound. Three aspects of the research methodology lend special credence to the findings: Adolescents were randomly assigned to either the experimental program or a regular after-school program offered in their community; the effectiveness of the program was based on long-term assessments; and participants were drawn from high-risk, low-income populations.

The CAS-Carrera after-school program has proved to be extremely effective in reducing teen pregnancy. For instance, girls enrolled in the program have been more than 50% less likely to become pregnant than those in the control group. Girls are also significantly more likely to delay sex and to use condoms or another effective contraceptive when they become sexually active (Kirby, 2002; Philliber et al., 2001).

Abstinence-Only Programs

abstinence-only programs
Sex education programs that teach that abstinence is the only way to avoid pregnancy and the risk of sexually transmitted diseases.

Abstinence-only programs differ from comprehensive sex education programs by teaching that the only effective way for adolescents to avoid pregnancy and the risk of STDs is to abstain from sex. When contraception is discussed, it typically is presented in terms of its failure to protect against pregnancy or disease rather than its effectiveness. However, the chances of becoming pregnant within one year for an adolescent who is sexually active and who does not use contraceptives are 90%—and adolescents who receive abstinence-only education are as likely to be sexually active as those receiving no sex education at all (Guttmacher Institute, 2006; Constantine, 2008; Kohler et al., 2008). Additionally, abstinence programs that pressure teenagers to pledge virginity may place adolescents at greater risk since "pledgers" who subsequently become sexually active are less likely initially to use contraception, increasing the likelihood of pregnancy and contracting an STD (Bruckner & Bearman, 2005).

Federal funding of abstinence-only programs has been substantial despite the absence of research demonstrating the effectiveness of such programs in getting adolescents to delay sex, and in the face of research showing that comprehensive sex education programs *are* effective, both in delaying sexual initiation and in decreasing adolescent pregnancy (Kirby, 2002, 2008; Starkman & Rajani, 2002). The 1996 Welfare Reform Act, for instance, provides federal funds solely for abstinence-only programs. Since states receiving federal funds are required to supply matching funds, state support for comprehensive sex education programs has been decreased. Legislation since 1996 has provided additional federal funds for abstinence-only programs, resulting in an increase in funding for abstinence-only education by almost 3000% between 1996 and 2002 (Starkman & Rajani, 2002).

Yet the majority of parents support comprehensive sex education in the schools, indicating they want adolescents to be given information on contraception as well as abstinence (Eisenberg et al., 2008; Ito et al., 2006).

SUMMARY and KEY TERMS

Sexual Identity

Gender Stereotypes: The Meaning of Masculine and Feminine: Constructing a sexual identity introduces questions of what it means to be masculine or feminine. Adult sex roles, in the form of gender stereotypes, provide cultural answers. These stereotypes play an important role in self-definition as adolescents integrate questions posed by their sexuality into their developing sense of themselves.
gender stereotypes, androgynous

Gender Roles in Context: Cultures differ in how flexibly they treat gender roles; individualistic cultures are more flexible than collectivist cultures in this respect. Schools also are an important context in which adolescents define their gender roles, with younger adolescents looking to those who are older for information relevant to their adult gender roles.

Constructing a Sexual Identity: Sexuality embraces general aspects of one's sense of self, such as expressions of one's masculinity or femininity, the social roles one has within a family, and how one is seen in society. In constructing a sexual identity, adolescents are integrating sexuality into their sense of self.

Sexual Scripts: Sexual scripts inform adolescents not only of what they should do and feel, but also of what the person they are with is likely to do and feel. These scripts reflect masculine and feminine gender stereotypes.
sexual scripts

Making Sexual Decisions

Adolescents must revise their self-concepts to include new sexual feelings and behaviors. This process is problematic for those who experience conflict in leaving their childhood behind them. Adolescents who do not consciously think about the consequences of becoming sexually active may engage in sex without planning to and may do so irresponsibly.

Talking with Parents: Attitudes surrounding sexuality are not likely to be openly discussed by adolescents and their parents. Adolescents who talk with their parents, however, tend to become sexually active later and to engage in sex more responsibly.

Sexual Attitudes and Behaviors: Adolescents move through stages of sexual activity as they grow older. Most start with kissing, progress to touching breasts or genitals, and then engage in oral-genital sex and intercourse. Boys begin their sexual experiences earlier than girls and have more positive feelings about their first intercourse than do girls. Although the number of adolescents who have had sexual intercourse increases with age, the percentage of adolescents who are sexually active has decreased over the past 15 years.
self-stimulation

(continued)

SUMMARY and KEY TERMS *continued*

Protective Factors: A number of protective factors delay the initiation of sexual activity. Biologically based factors include late maturation, being female, and being intelligent. Psychological factors include strong religious beliefs, emotional adjustment, and involvement in school. Social factors include parental monitoring and communication, family religious beliefs, not dating steadily, and not using alcohol or drugs.

The Sexual Response Cycle: The sexual response cycle consists of four phases: excitement, plateau, orgasm, and resolution. Similarities in the sexual response for each gender exist for all phases. Two processes, vasocongestion and myotonia, underlie the changes that occur in each phase.
vasocongestion, myotonia

Sexual Functioning: Myths and Misconceptions: Adolescents have numerous misconceptions about sexual functioning. Many are not aware, for instance, that the size of the male's penis is not important in sexual functioning or that females have the same capacity for sexual pleasure as males. And adolescents frequently do not know that individuals of either sex experience discomfort if orgasm does not follow the plateau phase.

Sexual Orientation

Sexual orientation is the attraction individuals feel for members of the same or the other sex; this does not become firmly established until adolescence. Rather than discrete categories, such as heterosexual, homosexual, or bisexual, sexual orientations lie along a continuum.
sexual orientation, homosexual, heterosexual

Homosexuality: Gay, Lesbian, and Bisexual Adolescents: Gay, lesbian, and bisexual adolescents often go through a period of sexual questioning prior to puberty. Research comparing co-incidence of homosexuality among identical and fraternal twins and adoptive siblings suggests a genetic component to sexual orientation.
bisexual

Prejudice and Discrimination: Sexual-minority youth experience additional challenges in the form of societal prejudice over homosexuality. Bullying, harassment, being verbally or physically assaulted, avoided by classmates and neighbors, as well as unsympathetic or openly hostile reactions from family or teachers, is experienced by substantial numbers of gay and lesbian adolescents.

Biological and Psychosocial Bases of Sexual Attraction: Research findings strongly suggest a genetic component to sexual orientation. Additional research suggests that the path of genetic transmission, at least for males, is likely to be through the mother. While no clear answers have been found with regard to psychological factors affecting sexual orientation, the home atmosphere, and the closeness of parents' relationships to children, is strongly associated with adjustment.

Sexual Health: Risks and Responsibilities

Contraception: Most adolescents do not systematically use contraceptives because they lack adequate information. Many also do not practice responsible sex because they are unable to accept their own sexuality. Many more engage in unprotected sex due to their cognitive and emotional immaturity.

SUMMARY and KEY TERMS

Sexually transmitted diseases: Approximately 9 million adolescents and young adults become infected with a STD each year. STDs can be categorized in terms of viral infections (such as HIV/AIDS), bacterial infections (such as chlamydia), and infestations (such as pubic lice).
sexually transmitted disease (STD), HIV, AIDS, genital herpes, genital warts, chlamydia, gonorrhea, syphilis, pubic lice

Risks and Precautions: Although the rate of teenage sexual activity in some European countries and Canada is similar to that in the United States, the rate of teenage pregnancy is lower because those countries have identified adolescent pregnancy, not sexual activity, as the social problem to be addressed by public policy. These countries also differ in their greater emphasis on the importance of a committed relationship, open discussions of sexual responsibility, and providing accurate information about and access to contraceptives and reproductive services.

Teenage Pregnancies: Pregnancy and child rearing present challenges for women of any age, but especially for adolescents. Adolescents are less likely to receive regular prenatal care, and they experience more medical complications during pregnancy. This is especially true for younger adolescents.

Adolescents and Abortion: Approximately 30% of teenage pregnancies end in abortion. Decisions to abort or carry the pregnancy to term are related to socioeconomic status, race, and personal as well as parents' and friends' attitudes and religious beliefs.

Sex Education: What Adolescents Need to Know

Teenage Parenting: Children born to teenage mothers are more likely to experience complications such as premature birth, low birth weight, and neurological and behavioral problems. However, programs that target teenage mothers for prenatal care can be successful in reducing many of these risks. Most teenage fathers remain psychologically involved with the mother through the pregnancy and for some time following the child's birth. Many fathers have less education and lower income than those who postpone parenting, and find it difficult to provide support for the mother and infant.

The Effectiveness of School Programs: School-based programs differ widely in what they cover and how effective they are. Effective programs delay the onset of sexual activity among adolescents who are not yet sexually active and lead to safer sexual practices among those who already are.

Comprehensive Sex Education Programs: Comprehensive sex education programs have been found to be very effective in delaying sexual activity among adolescents, but service learning programs, which additionally require students to engage in structured reflection on their volunteer service, have met with even higher rates of success.
comprehensive sex education programs, service learning programs

Abstinence-Only Programs: Although federal funding for abstinence-only programs has increased dramatically, these programs have not been found to be effective in delaying sexual initiation and preventing STDs and unintended pregnancies.
abstinence-only programs

White- lipped and shaking, Sarah replaced the receiver with exaggerated care, as if each movement could restore order to her world.

"So what's the word? Are you or aren't you?" asked Gina in a voice tight with urgency.

"I'm not," replied her friend.

"So, then, what's the problem?"

"I'm not sure," began Sarah, "but until now I don't think any of this has been real to me."

"You mean," interrupted Gina, "that a minute ago you weren't afraid you might be pregnant?"

"Hey, I was. I just didn't feel anything. But when I heard that the test was negative, I felt empty...sad...and happy and angry...all at once. It's strange.

Facing The Future:
Values In Transition

When I thought I might be pregnant, I felt nothing, but now that I know I'm
not, I have all these feelings."
Gina looked at her friend with concern. "How could you have taken care of
a baby?"
"I sure can't imagine myself as a mother," agreed Sarah, with a wry look on
her face.
"You would've had to forget about plans for college and working with
abused children."
"That's a laugh!" Sarah answered bitterly. "How can I put those two parts of
myself together—the one that thought about giving the baby away or even
getting an abortion and the other that wants to help children whose parents
hurt them?"
"You have a responsibility to yourself as well," offered Gina.

"Sure, but how do I balance that against my responsibility to someone else? Would it have been responsible to give the baby away if I couldn't have taken care of it properly? Or was it wrong to have even thought of it?"

"Was Eddie any help in thinking about this?" asked Gina.

"We were both too numb to think very clearly," answered Sarah. "But the few times we talked, we seemed to be discussing different problems altogether."

"I can relate to that!" snapped Gina. "At times J.J. doesn't even seem to speak the same language."

"Eddie talked about whether the fetus was a person, and whether it had the same rights that we had. It sounded so impersonal. All I could think of was whether I could take care of it and still take care of myself," Sarah replied quietly, as she broke another toothpick from the dish on the kitchen table and absently added it to the pile in front of her.

Chapter Overview

Many adolescents find themselves face-to-face with problems like Sarah's and Eddie's. In this chapter, we will look at the standards adolescents use in making decisions—decisions that increasingly affect others as well as themselves. Changing roles, untrodden rights, and uncharted responsibilities create a compelling need for a system of values to guide decisions. Beliefs that have worked all through childhood come up again for review in adolescence. Many will withstand close scrutiny; others will not. All will be tested against a developing system of values as adolescents face the challenge of defining themselves.

Self-definition means that adolescents must distinguish values and beliefs that are unique to them from those they acquired from their parents. Many begin by scrutinizing their families' values to see which ones they accept for themselves. Some adolescents forgo this process and continue to live by standards set by others. The development of values is an integral part of one's identity.

What criteria distinguish moral concerns from social convention, or from religious beliefs? Some developmentalists consider early experiences within the family to be pivotal to later moral development, whereas others stress the importance of interactions with peers. Do females and males approach moral issues differently? Are there progressions in religious development as there are in moral development? Developmentalists, as well as the families they study, frequently arrive at different answers to questions such as these. Their answers will structure our discussion of moral development.

The Values of Adolescents

The values of adolescents have changed little over the years. Most adolescents today consider having a good marriage and family life, and being successful in their work to be extremely important, just as their parents did when they were adolescents. They also consider it important to have money and to contribute to society. With respect to the latter, a lot of adolescents put these values into action by doing volunteer work.

Values in Action: Volunteering

Many adolescents are active in community affairs or do volunteer work at least once or twice a month (**Figure 11.1**) (Fox et al., 2005; U.S. Department of Health and Human Services, 2002c). However, it's equally clear from Figure

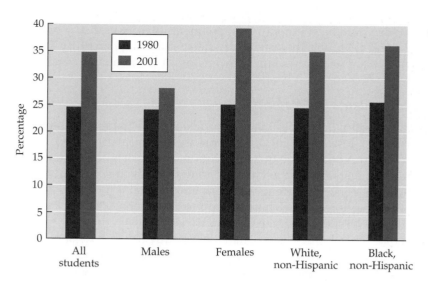

● **Figure 11.1** **Percentage of high school seniors who participated in community affairs or volunteer work at least once a month, by gender and ethnicity, 1980 and 2001** (After Fox et al., 2005.)

11.1 that other adolescents don't become involved. What leads some adolescents to volunteer and others not to? Robert Atkins, Daniel Hart, and Thomas Donnelly (2005), at Rutgers University, asked whether this difference might be due to differences in the personalities of those who volunteer. Using data from a national longitudinal study that followed grade school children into adolescence, they found that **resilient** children who are outgoing, positive, and socially skilled are more likely to volunteer as adolescents than are those who are less socially skilled and less comfortable with others. Of course, one might argue that resilient children are simply more likely to belong to social groups, and thus have more opportunities to volunteer. Even controlling for social opportunities, however, adolescents' personalities remain a better predictor of volunteering than social opportunities (Atkins et al., 2005; Frensch et al., 2007).

Parents also influence the likelihood of adolescents volunteering, both through the values they communicate and in the way they parent. Parents who emphasize the importance of kindness and caring when interacting with others and who engage in authoritative parenting have adolescents who are more likely to volunteer (Frensch et al., 2007; Lawford et al., 2005).

Adolescents' experiences with community service might also be expected to influence later volunteering. Although one might expect that adolescents who have fulfilled a community service requirement in high school would have more positive attitudes toward volunteering in the future, the results have been mixed (Henderson et al., 2007; Hart et al., 2007). The assumption is that by acquainting students with the needs of others, such as through community service, they will feel greater responsibility to help those in need of support. Paradoxically, putting privileged students in touch with the difficulties faced by those struggling to get by may cause them to distance themselves from social issues. Scott Seider (2008), at Boston University, found that affluent high school students who took a course covering social justice issues (e.g., poverty, homelessness, and world hunger), were *less* inclined to agree with statements such as "not right for students in a poorer school system to receive a worse education than students in a wealthier school system" at the end of the

resilient Characterized by attitudes and social skills that enable individuals to function in a variety of settings.

The parents of today's teenagers aren't as different as their children sometimes think. Their attitudes are quite similar with regard to life goals, the value of an education, and the importance of relationships.

course than they had been initially. In subsequent interviews, many of them expressed a fear that they, too, could experience financial hardship, "that it could happen to anyone," revealing an awareness of vulnerability which they previously had lacked.

Values: Adolescents and Parents

Most adolescents hold attitudes that are in substantial agreement with those of their parents. Close to 90% of adolescents and their parents have similar attitudes concerning the value of an education, and nearly 75% agree with parents on big questions such as what to do with one's life. Similarly, high agreement exists concerning religion, work ethic, racial issues, and certain conventional behaviors, such as how to dress (ter Bogt et al., 2005).

This shouldn't be surprising since parents transmit their values to their children in myriad ways, influencing them both explicitly through what they say and implicitly through what they do. With respect to academic achievement, for instance, parents' values have been found to directly predict those of their adolescent children (Jodl et al., 2001). Thus, parents of adolescents who value education and believe their children can succeed academically are more likely to have adolescents who see education as important (for example, "I have to do well in school if I want to be a success in life.") and who have higher educational expectations. These expectations, in turn, are positively linked to adolescents' professional, that is, white-collar, career aspirations for both African American and European American adolescents. Thus, parents appear to influence adolescents' career aspirations by transmitting values concerning the importance of education (Jodl et al., 2001).

Values: Gender and Ethnicity

More similarities than differences also exist in the values held by adolescent females and males. Adolescent females are as likely as males to say that being successful in one's work is "extremely important." Differences appear when it comes to marriage and family and making money: Among high school seniors, females are more likely than males to indicate that marriage and family are important, and males are more likely to place a higher value on having a lot of money. In other respects, the values of each are remarkably similar. (U.S. Department of Health and Human Services, 2002c).

There also are relatively few differences in adolescents' values due to race. Having a good marriage and family life is valued equally by African American and European American adolescents, but the former give greater importance to being successful in their work, having money, and correcting societal inequalities (**Figure 11.2**). With respect to what's necessary for success, parents' beliefs concerning the importance of education affect adolescents' career expectations in similar ways for African American and European American adolescents (Jodl et al., 2001).

Values and Identity

Adolescents' values shape their sense of themselves. Erik Erikson believed values are an important component of our identity. A sense of identity allows us to make countless daily decisions, to take ourselves for granted, as Ruthellen Josselson (1987) puts it. Like much of the way we function, our identity remains largely unavailable for inspection until we hit a snag.

Developmental snags await us all. They take the form of age-related changes in the expectations that we and others hold up to ourselves. Erikson (1956, 1968) refers to these changes as psychosocial crises. Crises arise when physical maturation, together with changing personal and cultural expectations, lead individuals to reexamine their sense of who they are and what they are about.

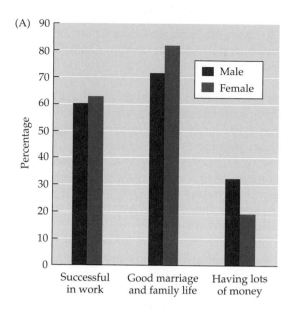

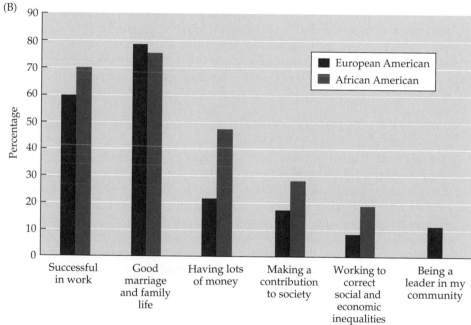

● **Figure 11.2** **Values of high school seniors, by gender and ethnicity** (A) Percentage of male and female high school seniors indicating life goals as "extremely important." (B) Percentage of African American and European American high school seniors indicating life goals as "extremely important." (After U.S. Department of Health and Human Services, 2002.)

"Taking oneself for granted," because it flows from one's identity, is precisely what most adolescents find hardest to do: Most of them are continually revising their sense of themselves (see identity statuses in Chapter 5).

Prior to adolescence, the elements that contribute to identity are ascribed (Josselson, 1987). For example, children have few choices in such matters as where they live, go to school, worship, and so on. Adolescents can begin to explore possibilities that differ from those chosen by their parents. Some will continue to live out the patterns established by their parents. This is still a choice, although adolescents who follow this path may not be aware of making a decision as such. The decision facing all adolescents is whether they will decide things for themselves or live with decisions made by others. Being aware that one has choices, and considering the various possibilities, can make adolescents uncomfortably aware of themselves. Erikson considers this discomfort to be central to one's experience of crisis. By crisis he does not mean that adolescents' lives are in pieces, but simply that until identity decisions are firmly behind them, they cannot "take themselves for granted."

Because identity reflects one's values, the stance toward values taken by adolescents in each of the four identity statuses described in Chapter 5 will differ.

IDENTITY ACHIEVEMENT   Adolescents who have begun to discover the ways in which they differ from their families are more tolerant of differences in others than those who have not experienced a period of crisis. Openness in examining one's own beliefs goes hand in hand with accepting different beliefs in others. Perhaps because of the high value that identity-achieved adolescents place on discovering themselves, even at the risk of displeasing others, they are unwilling to hold others to conventional standards of right or wrong (Marcia, 1988).

Does this description sound too good to be true? Keep in mind that conscientious and principled behavior is not necessarily what most adults label as "good." Adolescents in search of themselves are likely to question and experiment. They may dress flamboyantly, act outrageously, and generally adopt a "show me" attitude. They may not follow in their parents' footsteps or be ready to settle down when others their age have already found their way. The positive side to this picture is that these adolescents develop a sense of who they are and translate that image into effective strategies for living, including close relationships with others. The independence they achieve reflects an internal struggle, one that frees them for change, not an external one in which they must act on all the possibilities they are considering (Cramer, 2000; Schwartz et al., 2000).

IDENTITY FORECLOSURE   Identity-foreclosed adolescents are more rule-bound and authoritarian than identity-achieved adolescents. They have a strong sense of duty and feel that others, just as they, should obey the rules. Their respect for rules and tradition is reflected in the conventional standards they hold for their own and others' behavior. These adolescents tend to be critical of those whose behavior or ideas differ from their own or who are unconventional in other ways (Josselson, 1987).

Foreclosed adolescents derive their feelings of self-esteem from the approval of others. Accordingly, the opinions of others remain important to them; these adolescents are highly sensitive to social cues concerning the appropriateness of their behavior. Actions or beliefs that might cause conflict will be rejected. Security, not independence, is their overriding concern (Cramer, 2000; Marcia, 1980).

MORATORIUM   Moratorium adolescents, like foreclosed adolescents, seek others to complete themselves. However, instead of seeing others as sources of security, they look to them as models. Like identity-achieved adolescents, they realize that their own values are not any more right than those of others, but unlike identity-achieved adolescents, who experiment until they find their own way, moratorium adolescents set out on a "kind of crusade, determined to discover what is 'really right' " (Josselson, 1987). Josselson points out that theirs is an impossible quest, made all the harder because they hold back from experiences that would define them, always leaving a back door open through which to escape if they make a wrong choice. Josselson (1987) writes:

> Often, we unconsciously arrange for someone to function as a kind of savings bank. We deposit our old self in them for safekeeping, trusting them to hold it for us if we decide to come back to claim it. Many of the moratorium women spoke of this process. In describing the ways in which they thought their parents expected them to be,

they were describing old selves, ways they used to be. They could, then, have the luxury of experiencing their growth as an external battle, between themselves and their parents, rather than inside themselves. In addition, they knew that their parents were holding the old selves for them, just in case they ever decided to return, which is exactly what many of them did. (p. 138)

Perhaps because moratorium adolescents live with so much indecision themselves, they are tolerant of differences in others. Their ability to question, and to tolerate the uncertainty of not having all the answers, a characteristic they share with identity-achieved adolescents, allows them to transcend the thinking of the group and move beyond social convention. Adolescents who have not examined their values—foreclosed adolescents—are more likely to live lives of conformity and be bound by the expectations of others (Berzonsky & Kuk, 2000; Josselson, 1987).

Identity-achieved and moratorium adolescents do not automatically define themselves according to convention, and they are tolerant of others who are unconventional.

IDENTITY DIFFUSION   Identity-diffused adolescents, rather than confront issues head-on, tend to avoid them (Berzonsky & Ferrari, 1996; Berzonsky & Kuk, 2000). These adolescents are, in large measure, defined by the absence of strong commitments of their own and by their dismissal of the importance of commitment in others. Their actions, rather than reflecting beliefs or values, are likely to reflect the demands of the situation or the moment. These adolescents are neither rule-bound and authoritarian as are foreclosed adolescents nor truly tolerant as are identity-achieved and moratorium adolescents. Tolerance of differences in both of the latter implies a tension arising out of these differences that is not present in diffused adolescents, because others' ways do not conflict with clear-cut beliefs of their own (Cramer, 2000; Schwartz et al., 2000).

morality   The development of standards of right and wrong.

Morality: What Makes a Thing Right?

Adolescents differ in a number of ways from younger children with respect to how they think about moral issues. As thinking becomes more abstract they are better able to take the intentions of others into consideration when evaluating their actions, whereas children tend to judge actions in terms of their consequences. They are also able to question values; children adopt a fixed standard of right and wrong. Thinking also becomes more systematic, making it possible for adolescents to evaluate individual incidents in terms of general principles. How are we to understand these changes? Answers differ, depending on who is asked. In the sections that follow, we will consider a number of explanations for the development of moral understanding—of **morality**.

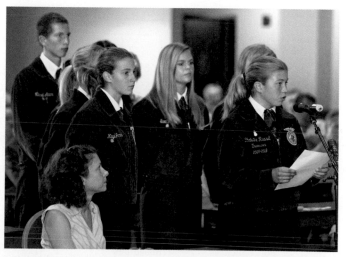

In the course of moral development, adolescents come to see themselves not only as members of the community but also as able to challenge community decisions that they feel are wrong. These high school students are attending a meeting of an agricultural association to protest the sale of the local fairgrounds.

Social-Cognitive Theory and Moral Development

Those who adopt the social-cognitive approach assume that community standards form the basis of self-regulated behavior. It is these standards that determine which behaviors are acceptable and rewarded and which ones are not. In learning the consequences of our behavior, we also acquire the standards of the group.

How does social-cognitive theory explain age-related changes in moral thought? Why might young children fail to consider others' intentions when judging their actions? Social-cognitive theorists are likely to answer that parents' reactions to damage and messes probably contribute to children's literal focus. Most parents become more upset over big messes than small ones, even though both may be equally unintentional. Consider a child who, keeping out of his mother's way as she fixes dinner, attempts to pour himself a glass of milk. His grip slips as he positions the milk carton, and he watches, transfixed, as a stream of milk sends the cup scudding, flooding the countertop with milk. Is this mother likely to comment on his thoughtfulness at not disturbing her? Probably not. This child, like most, will be scolded for making a mess. It makes sense that children fail to understand that intentions can enter into one's evaluation of a situation when theirs are so imperfectly considered.

Social-cognitive theory also explains the questioning of values that occurs in adolescence. Parents and teachers expect adolescents to start thinking for themselves, to evaluate ideas on their merit instead of accepting the endorsement of authorities. Social-cognitive theorists argue that we subtly reward adolescents for questioning the very ideas we taught them to uncritically accept as children. Similarly, the greater variety of learning experiences that occurs with age can explain the relativistic form of thought that emerges in many adolescents as they near their twenties. Exposure to new values challenges them to consider their own values as one of a number of possible belief systems.

TRANSLATING MORALITY INTO ACTION   How likely are adolescents to act in ways that reflect their moral understanding? In part, it depends on the incentives for acting one way or another. Martin Ford and his associates (1989) asked adolescents to indicate how they would respond in a situation involving conflict (for example, giving a friend exam questions versus abiding by the school's honor code) if they could be sure that nothing bad would happen to them if they acted irresponsibly, and then to imagine what they would do if there were negative social consequences (such as getting grounded or peer disapproval). As expected, adolescents were considerably more likely to choose the socially responsible alternative when there would be negative consequences for not doing so (**Figure 11.3**). The emotions motivating their choice reflected both external consequences, like fear of negative sanctions, and internalized ones, such as anticipated guilt and empathic concern. Choices were more likely to be motivated by self-interest or concern with peer approval when negative consequences were not anticipated.

Factors other than incentives also affect the likelihood of action. Adolescents are more likely to imitate the actions of prestigious people than of those whom they don't regard as important. Models who are nurturant are also more likely to be imitated, perhaps because we like them more than less nurturant people and would want to be like them. In the same way, those who are similar to us in one or more ways are also likely to be imitated, again perhaps because we can imagine being like them.

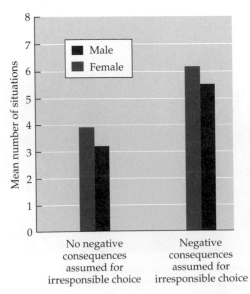

● **Figure 11.3   Mean number of situations in which adolescents choose to act responsibly**   (After Ford et al., 1989.)

MORAL VIRTUES   Although psychology as a discipline has tended to focus more on negative emotions and behaviors than positive ones, especially with respect to adolescents, the recent positive psychology movement (Seligman & Csikszentmihalyi, 2000) has refocused our attention on human virtues such as gratitude, forgiveness, self-control, and hope (Emmons & Paloutzian, 2003). Michael McCullough and his associates (2001), for instance, consider gratitude to be a moral reinforcer, in that individuals are more likely to engage in prosocial behaviors when others express gratitude to them for what they have done. Thus, individuals are likely to choose to act in prosocial ways not only because there may be negative consequences for *not* doing so, but also because their actions are reinforced by others through their expressions of gratitude. These investigators also view gratitude as a motivator, in that individuals who experience gratitude are inspired to act in more positive ways toward others (McCullough et al., 2002).

ACADEMIC CHEATING   How well does this approach explain how adolescents actually act in a moral situation? Let's look at a common behavior among students—academic cheating. High school students report that they frequently cheat even though they consider it wrong to do so, as do college students (Davis et al., 1992; Stephens et al., 2007). Social-cognitive theory reminds us, however, that what people do is not necessarily what they believe is right. Instead, whether adolescents are likely to cheat is influenced by situational factors such as the normative behavior of classmates (Eisenberg, 2004; Vowell & Chen, 2004) and the amount of risk involved (Eisenberg, 2004; Underwood & Szabo, 2003). What is rewarded in the classroom also influences the likelihood of cheating; students are less likely to cheat in classrooms that reward mastery of the material than the grade one gets on a test (Anderman & Midgley, 2004; Murdock et al., 2004). Students' attitudes concerning the seriousness of cheating are also important, with those judging it to be less serious engaging in cheating more often (Jensen et al., 2002).

Little mention has been made about conscience in this discussion. Social-cognitive theory suggests that many internalized controls are not necessarily related to moral values or to conscience; they simply reflect conditioning. Adolescents become helpful or law-abiding in order to avoid the anxiety they associate with doing otherwise. Conscience, when it does apply to behavior, is merely the set of standards one internalizes with the learning process. For social-cognitive theorists, there is no inner voice other than the echo of the voices around them.

Kohlberg: Moral Reasoning

What makes one moral? Is it simply that one internalizes the standards of one's community? Is it ever possible for individuals to function at a higher level than the society in which they live? Where does a sense of justice come from if it is not present in the social order? Lawrence Kohlberg's theory of moral reasoning addresses these questions.

Kohlberg's (1976, 1984) theory bases its assumptions about moral development on the organismic model, stressing the importance of the inner forces that organize development. The most important of these forces is a sense of justice, which underlies the highest forms of moral thought. The development of moral reasoning is prompted by the need to resolve conflict. This conflict arises when one realizes that others view things differently. Individuals gain insight into the perspectives of others through increases in role-taking skills. As they become able to put themselves in the place of another, they can see things as that person does. Cognitive maturity—the ability to think about and balance the competing demands produced by examining several perspectives—also contributes to moral development. Kohlberg assumes that one's

> **TABLE 11.1**
> **Kohlberg's Stages of Moral Reasoning**
>
> **Preconventional level of moral reasoning**
> Moral reasoning is governed by anticipated rewards or punishments
>   rather than by internalized standards or values.
> *Stage 1:* Obedience
> *Stage 2:* Instrumental, or considering intentions
>
> **Conventional level of moral reasoning**
> Moral reasoning is guided by the standards of one's community, in
>   the form of laws and social conventions, which have been internalized.
> *Stage 3:* Conformist, or "good boy, nice girl"
> *Stage 4:* Social accord, or "law and order"
>
> **Postconventional level of moral reasoning**
> Moral reasoning at this level is guided by self-derived principles, which
>   enable individuals to perceive the standards of their communities as
>   relative, in light of universal human principles.
> *Stage 5:* Social contract
> *Stage 6:* Universal principles

level of cognitive development places limits on the sophistication of moral thinking (Kohlberg, 1976, 1984).

Kohlberg traces moral development over three levels of moral reasoning, with two stages at each level (**Table 11.1**). The levels reflect the stance adolescents take in relation to the standards of their community. Not all standards reflect moral issues. Some standards exist as laws, others simply as conventions or customary ways of behaving. It is the law, for example, that one not take another person's life; it is customary that one not giggle when hearing of another's death. Both of these reflect a common value—the sacredness of life. But only when adolescents reach the postconventional level of moral reasoning do they distinguish social convention, whether codified as laws or customs, from the values these conventions reflect. And only then, according to Kohlberg, can they distinguish conventional concerns from moral ones.

PRECONVENTIONAL REASONING

STAGE 1: OBEDIENCE   Individuals at the **preconventional reasoning** stage (usually children) assume that everyone sees things as they do, not realizing that their view of a situation is just one of several possible perspectives. Consequently, they experience little or no conflict in their interactions with others. Their actions reflect only a need to satisfy their own desires, without getting punished for doing so. Stage 1 morality is not reflective; individuals do not take motives and intentions into consideration (they do not understand others' feelings and points of view easily). They judge behavior simply in terms of its consequences. Actions that are rewarded must have been good; those that were punished, bad. Read the dilemma facing a girl named Rachel in **Box 11.1** before continuing, then consider how a Stage 1 adolescent might respond to this situation.

What should Rachel do? Kohlberg reminds us that it is the reasoning rather than the answer itself that reveals the stage at which an adolescent is functioning. Adolescents at Stage 1 might not report Elsie to the school counselor, fearing that the counselor would discover that they, too, had used drugs and that punishment would result. Conversely, they might report her, fearing that they would be punished if they didn't. There is nothing in this reasoning to indicate conflict over which course of action is right; decisions are based on the potential impact the actions have for oneself.

preconventional reasoning
Kohlberg's first level of moral reasoning, characterized by the absence of internalized standards.

BOX **11.1** **In More Depth**

Rachel's Dilemma

Rachel didn't know what to do. Elsie looked so whacked out she could hardly put one foot in front of the other. Was it lack of sleep? (Elsie did party a lot.) Or was she actually on something? They had experimented with marijuana together, and Rachel suspected that Elsie had tried other drugs. Elsie had once started to talk about her friends and the parties they went to. It sounded like they did a lot of drugs. Elsie had gotten nervous when Rachel asked her about this. She'd changed the subject, and Rachel never heard any more about it. Elsie no longer wanted to get together with Rachel and their old friends, even referring to them as "small time" once.

Rachel could see even from here that Elsie's eyes looked funny, like she was having a hard time focusing, even though it was only second-period gym class. She was perspiring, too, and the air conditioning was on. Should she tell her counselor that she thought Elsie was on drugs? Elsie and she had once promised each other they would never betray their confidence about smoking marijuana. And if she reported Elsie, her parents would almost surely find out that she also had experimented with drugs. She could forget about that lifeguard job this summer. They'd never let her out of their sight. Then again, drugs could kill.

STAGE 2: INSTRUMENTAL, OR CONSIDERING INTENTIONS   As adolescents become better able to put themselves in the place of another person, they can see things as the other person would. Adopting the other's perspective gives them two points of view and, in turn, the likelihood that they will experience conflict. Which perspective is right? They can understand the reasons for the other person's actions—their intentions—and know that the other can understand theirs. Adolescents who reason at this level don't have to rely on others' reactions to evaluate behavior. They can look at the motives behind an action. Even though fairness is central to reasoning at this stage, their reasoning is still preconventional because they consider only the actions and intentions of those they are with and not the laws or conventions of the larger group, for example, their school or community.

What would Rachel do? First consider the reasoning that would lead a Stage 2 adolescent to believe Rachel should not report Elsie. This adolescent knows it's the rule to report anyone using drugs. However, Elsie and Rachel had made an agreement never to tell on each other. It's only fair for Rachel to live up to that promise. Besides, if she reported Elsie, she'd almost surely get caught herself. Best to let everyone take care of themselves in this case. The reasoning that might lead an adolescent to say that Rachel should report Elsie is similarly self-serving. Rachel might be rewarded in some way for reporting her friend; even if the authorities found out that she, too, had experimented with drugs, they would not punish her as severely as they would if she didn't indicate her respect for the rules by reporting those who she knew were breaking them.

CONVENTIONAL REASONING: INTERNALIZING STANDARDS

STAGE 3: CONFORMIST, OR "GOOD BOY, NICE GIRL"   The self-reflection that comes with formal thought makes it possible for adolescents to see themselves as they imagine others would. This third-person perspective forms the basis for taking the norms of their group, in the form of concern with what others think of them, into consideration, and here adolescents move into **conventional reasoning**. This concern about the opinions of others adds a new dimension to morality: the need to live up to the expectations of others. Kohl-

conventional reasoning
Kohlberg's second level of moral reasoning, in which moral thinking is guided by internalized social standards.

When they were younger, these skateboarders, along with many roller bladers, probably enjoyed the thrill of skating where they weren't supposed to if they knew they wouldn't be caught. Now, because their moral reasoning is more mature, they are more likely to limit their skateboarding or roller blading to legal sites.

berg believes that Stage 3 reasoning is dominant during adolescence and even common in adulthood (Kohlberg, 1984). The prevalence of Stage 3 reasoning helps to explain adolescents' sensitivity to the approval of peers. Rather than thinking through a situation in terms of the claims of those involved, adolescents are likely to be swayed by the opinions of their friends.

How would Stage 3 adolescents reason about Rachel's dilemma? Reasoning that leads to not reporting Elsie would focus on loyalty among friends—how would Rachel look turning in a friend? Reasoning that leads to reporting her would focus on what her teachers and parents would think of her for not reporting Elsie. The decision turns on which reference group the adolescent considers: that of friends and peers or that of teachers and parents. **Box 11.2** illustrates how cultural values can affect adolescents' evaluations of their own and others' behavior.

STAGE 4: SOCIAL ACCORD, OR "LAW AND ORDER" As the ability to think abstractly increases, adolescents begin to see themselves

---

BOX 11.2 Research Focus

Statistical Tests of Significance: What Do a Huai Haizi, a Warui Ko, and a Bad Kid Have in Common?

None of the students seemed to notice the chatter of birds outside the classroom window, or other signs of spring in Taipei, as they bent over their desks, completing the questionnaire. These Chinese adolescents had been asked to think of someone they knew who was a huai haizi, a "bad kid," and to describe what kind of person that was. In another classroom nearly a thousand miles away, Japanese students were asked to describe a warui ko (bad kid), as were yet other students, American adolescents in Minneapolis, who were similarly asked to describe a "bad kid."

How comparable were the descriptions of these adolescents? To what extent do perceptions of deviance reflect the social values of one's culture? Are the behaviors that American teenagers think of as bad similarly bad in other cultures?

David Crystal and Harold Stevenson (1995), at the University of Michigan, set out to get answers to such questions by asking Chinese, Japanese, and American 11th-graders what a "bad kid" meant to them. After coding their responses to the open-ended questions (see Web box "Coding Descriptive Responses") into 12 types of behavior, they found that 40% of the Chinese students mentioned society-related behaviors, such as "rebels against society," "makes trouble for society," or "is a member of a street gang," whereas only 29% of the American adolescents described a bad kid this way, and even fewer Japanese students did (14%). Other interesting differences emerged. The most frequently mentioned behaviors by Japanese students (84%) made reference to disruptions of interpersonal harmony, such as "hurting other people's feelings," "being argumentative and starting fights," and "speaking badly of other people"; only 50% and 53% of Chinese and American adolescents, respectively, mentioned such behaviors. American adolescents, on the other hand, were most likely to mention behaviors related to self-control, 38% referring to being "weak-willed," childish," or "immature"; in contrast, only 24% of Chinese and Japanese students did so.

as members of an invisible, but nonetheless real, community. As such, they realize the need to evaluate actions by the community's standards. Kohlberg believes that reasoning at the fourth stage is frequently the highest stage that most people reach.

Rachel's dilemma takes on new proportions for adolescents at Stage 4. On the one hand, friendship demands that she not betray Elsie to the authorities; her duty is to be loyal to her friend. On the other hand, Rachel has a duty to live within the law and to see that others do as well. After all, if everyone "did their own thing," the system would break down. Stage 4 reasoning breaks down, however, when laws conflict with human values. When this occurs, adolescents must develop a way to see their society in relation to the needs of others.

POSTCONVENTIONAL REASONING: QUESTIONING VALUES

STAGE 5: SOCIAL CONTRACT   Kohlberg believes that adolescents move into Stage 5 only when they have been exposed to other value systems, usually in late adolescence. Individuals who come to respect others' ways of life find it difficult to continue seeing their own as more valid. Once adolescents recognize that their society's conventions are in some sense arbitrary, they are forced to look beyond the conventions themselves to the function they serve—the level of **postconventional reasoning**. When they do, they discover that laws derive their importance because they represent agreements among people who live together, not because they are right in and of themselves. Members of a society enter into a contract with others in the society in which

postconventional reasoning
Kohlberg's third level of moral reasoning, in which moral thinking is guided by self-derived principles.

random error   Unexplained and unsystematic variability.

test of significance
A statistical procedure for determining whether group differences are due to random error or can be attributed to the variable being studied.

BOX 11.2 *continued*

What are we to make of these differences? Can we conclude that adolescents from each of these cultures differ in what they consider to be bad? How different must their answers be in order to support this conclusion? After all, each adolescent is an individual, and one can always expect slight variances simply as a result of individual differences. Unexplained variability, such as individual differences, that is not due to the variable being investigated is termed **random error**.

To determine whether a difference between two groups is due to random error or whether it reflects the variable being studied, one uses a **test of significance**. Common tests are chi-square, t-tests, and F-tests. If the value obtained is larger than a tabled value for the same number of participants, one can reject the assumption that random error was responsible and attribute the difference to the independent variable. Probability theory tells us that the likelihood that random error is responsible for the difference decreases with increases in the number of participants in each group. Thus, with larger numbers of participants, one needs a smaller difference to reject the assumption that random error was responsible.

Crystal and Stevenson's statistical tests comparing differences in the frequencies with which adolescents from the three cultures mentioned different types of behaviors were significant. Chinese students were significantly more likely to mention society-related behavior than American or Japanese students; Japanese students were significantly more likely to mention interpersonal behavior than were Chinese or American students; and American students were significantly more likely to mention self-control than were Chinese or Japanese students.

Bad kids—unlike roses, which, the poet tells us, would still be a rose by any other name—do not differ in name only. Each culture has its own profile of social values and, although there is considerable overlap from one culture to the next, what is considered to be "bad" differs to the extent that the most prominent values in a culture, but not necessarily those in another, are violated.

Source: Crystal & Stevenson, 1995.

they agree to live within its laws, forgoing some individual freedoms, for the mutual benefit of all.

Stage 5 adolescents might reason that Rachel should not report Elsie because the way she has chosen to live her life reflects her values, and values are relative. They might add that Rachel is obliged to act in a way that protects each person's rights, including Elsie's. Reasons for reporting Elsie would stress that, as members of society, Rachel and Elsie have implicitly agreed to keep the laws of their community and that these laws must be upheld for the greater good of all.

STAGE 6: UNIVERSAL PRINCIPLES This stage provides adolescents with yet another perspective: seeing past the mutual agreements shared by members of a society to the values these agreements reflect. The social contracts we enter into reflect underlying values such as truth, justice, honor, and the value of life itself. The step that late adolescents take in order to gain a perspective on their society removes them from the claims of time and circumstance. Kohlberg asserts that all societies throughout history have recognized these values—that they are, in fact, universal ethical principles. Those who reason at this final stage understand that societal conventions are imperfect reflections of these values and, consequently, individuals must look beyond conventions, and even laws, to their own principles when arriving at moral decisions (Kohlberg, 1984).

Why might Rachel not report Elsie to the counselor? Stage 6 reasoning stresses that honor among friends would require Rachel to keep her promise with Elsie. Conversely, those who reason that Rachel should report Elsie would be likely to mention the value of Elsie's life, which is threatened by her use of drugs. They might add that even if *they* were in Elsie's place, they would hope to be turned in by anyone who cared enough about them to try to help. This last reason illustrates a point that Kohlberg makes about Stage 6 individuals. He describes them as able to imagine themselves in the place of every other person in a situation and to impartially evaluate the rights of each. The image of the Stage 6 person is that of the blindfolded figure of Justice who weighs the claims of each without knowing which person has made which claim. This ability is truly an idealized form of role-taking, and few people function at this level (Kohlberg, 1984).

WHEN JUSTICE MAY NOT BE ENOUGH: FORGIVENESS We know quite a bit about the development of justice in adolescents. But we know relatively little about forgiveness. Justice is a consideration of competing claims among individuals; it weighs them and makes a decision in favor of one or the other. Forgiveness is a decision to release a person from a claim that justice would honor.

How are forgiveness and justice related? Is forgiveness just a special case of justice, one in which the injured person turns over any claims for retribution? If forgiveness is different, does it develop with age and social understanding as Kohlberg assumes justice does? Are these different moralities? To the extent that certain religions, such as Christianity, emphasize the importance of forgiving, will forgiveness be related to the practice of one's faith?

Robert Enright, Maria Santos, and Radhi Al-Mabuk (1989) presented individuals of several ages with situations in which justice or forgiveness were called for. One of these described the dilemma of a man whose wife is dying of cancer. The man unsuccessfully attempts to persuade a druggist who has patented an expensive drug to sell him enough at a reduced price to save his wife's life. The druggist refuses, pointing out that it is through the sale of the drug that he makes his livelihood. In the justice scenario, individuals consider the competing claims of life versus private property. In the forgiveness scenario, the druggist anticipates that the man will try to steal the drug and hides it. The wife dies. Individuals answer questions that reflect stages of forgiveness by the husband ranging from vengeful retribution to unconditional forgiveness based on a principle of love. The degree of religiousness for each individual was also measured.

These investigators found that reasoning about forgiveness, just as about justice, becomes more mature with age. Adolescents find it easiest to be forgiving when they know it's expected of them (expectational forgiveness). Children are more likely to say they can forgive only if they first get back what they lost (restitutional forgiveness). Adults are likely to forgive because it is required by their religion, or to defer to a higher authority (lawful forgiveness). Their forgiveness, like that of adolescents, however, is conditional. With the latter, it depends on encouragement from others, mainly friends, and with the former, from a religious authority. Relatively few instances of unconditional, or principled, forgiveness (based on a principle of loving others) were found, and all of these occurred among adults. Other research as well has found that unconditional forgiveness is most likely to occur among adults, and when it does, it is most likely to be shown by the elderly (Mullet & Girard, 2000).

In addition, religious beliefs and practices appear to contribute to reasoning about forgiveness. Adolescents who practiced their faith, for example, attending church and Bible study groups, had more mature approaches to forgiveness. Although religiosity has been found to be unrelated to forgiveness when the offense has been committed by someone close, such as a family member or friend, when the offense has been committed by a more distant person, such as an employer or a general "other," individuals find they can more easily forgive (Subkoviak et al., 1995).

Research on forgiveness suggests that if adolescents are to learn to forgive, they need the support of friends who encourage them to adopt forgiveness as part of their approach to resolving interpersonal conflicts. Why forgive? Often other strategies of conflict resolution are equally appropriate. Many times, however, these leave the injured person with residual anger and resentment. The decision to release another from obligation, on the other hand, can free the person who has been injured from these feelings and open the way to restoring the relationship.

TRANSLATING REASON INTO ACTION   Kohlberg assumed that older individuals would reason at higher stages than younger ones. Rosemary Jadack, Janet Shibley Hyde, Colleen Moore, and Mary Keller (1995), at the University of Wisconsin, Madison, asked students differing in age to consider dilemmas concerning sexual behavior in which a character must decide whether to tell a partner about the presence of a sexually transmitted disease. These investigators found that older college students (mean age 22 years) generally reasoned at a higher level, as assessed by a scoring system designed for use with Kohlberg's dilemmas, than did younger students (mean age 18 years). Younger students focused more on the likelihood of simply acquiring the disease, whereas older students introduced issues of responsibility and accountability.

Although there is substantial support for Kohlberg's assertion that individuals reason in more principled ways with age (Colby et al., 1983; Gibbs et al., 2007; Rest et al., 1978; Walker et al., 2001), their reasoning does not necessarily correspond to their actions (Gummerum et al., 2008).

Kohlberg's theory, despite the debate it has occasioned, enjoys wide support. His theory has an intrinsic elegance. Each of the six stages is a logical extension of the preceding one, and the progression is systematically related to new role-taking skills and cognitive maturity. But there may be another reason to account for the popularity of this theory: Kohlberg has given us a sympathetic view of human nature. He accounts for our ability to control our

moral domain A form of social understanding concerned with welfare, justice, and rights.

social conventional domain A form of social understanding concerned with the rules and traditions governing social interactions within a group.

personal domain A form of social understanding concerned with activities involving personal choice and prerogative.

behavior in terms of the development of an inner sense of justice, rather than the "carrot and stick" approach of social-cognitive theory.

Social Domain Theory

Social domain theory also derives from the organismic model, and consequently shares a number of features in common with Kohlberg's theory. Both approaches assume that individuals actively construct ways of understanding their world, both recognize the contribution of cognitive development to moral understanding, and both stress the importance of peer interactions to moral development. Social domain theory differs from that of Kohlberg, however, in distinguishing moral understanding and social convention as distinct domains of social understanding rather than viewing these as a developmental progression.

According to social domain theory, each of us engages in qualitatively different types of social interactions throughout the day, and the social understanding we construct from these differs as well, forming separate domains of social knowledge. Some interactions focus on welfare, justice, and rights, such as whether someone has been hurt or a person's rights have been infringed. Concerns of this nature constitute the **moral domain**. Other interactions are governed by the rules and traditions that are agreed upon by members of a group, such as table manners or forms of greeting; these make up the **social conventional domain**. The **personal domain** constitutes a third form of social understanding. This domain encompasses the activities that are taken to be one's prerogative, or personal choice, such as the friends one has or the music one listens to (Nucci, 1981; Turiel, 1983, 2008; Smetana, 2006).

Although both the moral domain and the social conventional domain establish clear rules for behavior, Elliot Turiel (1983), at the University of California, Berkeley, maintains that even very young children distinguish moral issues from conventional ones. Conventional rules reflect accepted ways of doing things. As these ways change, so do the rules. Standards of dress and speech reflect these flexible relationships. The rules relating moral concerns to behavior are inflexible. Moral rules reflect a concern for the well-being of others and do not change with climates of opinion.

Charles Helwig, Carolyn Hildebrandt, and Elliot Turiel (1995) interviewed first-, third-, and fifth-graders and found that children and adolescents alike agreed that moral acts such as pushing someone down would not be all right, even in the context of a game that legitimized such actions. The youngest children, however, were less clear about acts leading to psychological harm, such as name-calling as part of a game. Similarly, Larry Nucci, Cleanice Camino, and Clary Sapiro (1996), interviewing 9- and 15-year-olds in Brazil, found that children as well as adolescents distinguished moral from conventional issues, agreeing that if there were no rules against doing so, it would be all right not to wear a school uniform, but it would not be all right to hit or steal. These findings are consistent with social domain theory, and run counter to Kohlberg's theory in which individuals are thought to make such distinctions only with postconventional reasoning.

To what extent do cultural differences affect social reasoning? For instance, do adolescents in collectivist cultures necessarily consider interpersonal responsibility more important than personal autonomy in situations where these conflict? Or do those in individualistic cultures automatically value individual rights above duties? Kristin Neff and Charles Helwig (2002) found that adolescents from cultures as diverse as the United States, Canada, China, and India evidence concern with individual rights (moral domain) *and* authority (social conventional domain) when asked to evaluate the actions of characters in stories that pitted these issues against each other. Rather than social reasoning being influenced only by their cultural orientations, adolescents can also be seen to evaluate these cultural practices (Neff & Helwig, 2002; Turiel & Wainryb, 2000).

Gilligan: An Ethic of Care

Carol Gilligan's (1982, 1996) understanding of moral development, just as social domain theory, also bears many similarities to that of Kohlberg's. Gilligan notes, however, that Kohlberg based his theory on interviews only with males. Like many developmentalists before him, Kohlberg equated the male perspective with development in general (see Chapter 2). Gilligan, interviewing females, found them to think of morality more personally than Kohlberg's males did. They spoke of morality in terms of their responsibilities to others rather than of the rights of individuals. Their moral decisions were based on compassion as well as reason—an **ethic of care**—stressing care for others as well as fairness.

Because females tend to define themselves in relation to others and males as separate from others, the course of their moral development is different, according to psychologist Carol Gilligan.

Gilligan traces these differences to the way females and males define themselves in relation to others. Whereas males tend to view themselves as separate from others, females are more likely to see themselves in terms of their relationships with others. These themes of separation and connectedness translate into different approaches to morality. The assumption that one is separate from others highlights the need for rules to regulate the actions of each person with respect to the other; the assumption that one is connected to others emphasizes the responsibility each has to the other (Gilligan, 1982).

Gender differences also exist in the way individuals think of responsibility. Males tend to think of responsibility as not doing something that would infringe on the rights of others, such as not hurting them. Females think of responsibility in terms of meeting the needs of others, that is, as something to be done. Both males and females are concerned with not hurting others, yet each sex thinks of this in a different way. Gilligan points out that, given differences such as these, attempts to chart moral development as a single sequence are bound to give us only half the picture.

Gilligan, like Kohlberg, traces moral development in females through three levels, each of which reflects a different resolution to the conflict between responsibility to self and responsibility to others. At the first level, the primary concern is with oneself. Transition to the next level occurs when one sees caring only for oneself as selfish and at odds with responsibility to others. At the second level, females equate morality with goodness and self-sacrifice—caring for others. Transition to the third level occurs when they experience problems in their relationships that result from excluding themselves from their own care. At the third level, they equate morality with care for both themselves and others.

CARING FOR SELF (SURVIVAL)   The primary concerns at this level of moral development are pragmatic: What's best for me? Actions are guided by self-interest and self-preservation. Gilligan (1982) says of this perspective that "the woman focuses on taking care of herself because she feels that she is all alone. From this perspective, *should* is undifferentiated from *would*, and other people influence the decision only through their power to affect its consequences" (p. 75). Gilligan notes that the issue of "rightness" is considered only when

ethic of care Psychologist Carol Gilligan's description of a morality based on responsiveness to and care for others.

one's own needs are in conflict and force the individual to consider which need is more important. Otherwise, there is little conflict over making the right decision.

Why might individuals function at this level? Gilligan believes that a preoccupation with one's needs reflects feelings of helplessness and powerlessness. These feelings have their origin in being emotionally cut off, or disconnected, from others. The young women she interviewed who were at this level had frequently experienced disappointing relationships in which they had been hurt by others. These women often chose to hold themselves apart from others rather than experience further pain. Feeling alone and cut off from others, they were left with the sense that they had to look to their own needs, because no one else would (Gilligan, 1982).

This first level is similar to Kohlberg's preconventional level of moral reasoning. In neither level do individuals consider others except for their possible reactions to what they do, that is, except as potential consequences for their actions. Conflict is also absent in both levels, and self-interest, rather than the need to make the right decision, dictates what one does. Individuals move beyond the first level when they experience a discrepancy between the way they are and the way they feel they ought to be, that is, between self-concern and responsible concern for others. A certain amount of self-worth is needed for this. One must feel sufficiently good about oneself in order to see oneself as having the capacity for good and to be included in the social group (Gilligan, 1982).

CARING FOR OTHERS (GOODNESS) Gilligan assumes that females reason at this level when they internalize social conventions, and equate morality with conventional feminine goodness. This represents a step toward repairing the failed relationships that led to a preoccupation with oneself at the first level, but this equation creates a second imbalance. Since conventional images of feminine goodness center on the care of others, females at this level purchase membership in the larger community at the cost of caring for themselves. The price of membership is costly and introduces tensions that, for some, will prompt movement to the third level, as they realize that excluding themselves from their own care creates as many problems as excluding others had done previously. In other words, goodness can result in hurt just as well as selfishness can for those at the previous level (Gilligan, 1986). Gilligan, like Kohlberg before her, contends that many females do not take this step and do not develop beyond conventional forms of thought.

CARING FOR SELF AND OTHERS (TRUTH) To move beyond the conventional wisdom that tells them to put the needs of others above their own, females must reformulate their definition of care to include themselves as well as others. As they reconsider their relationships with others, they once again must consider their own needs. Questions such as "Is this selfish?" again arise. Because these occur in the context of relationships with others, they also prompt a reexamination of the concept of responsibility. When one moves beyond conventional forms of wisdom, one finds there is no one to turn to for answers but oneself. Females at this level cannot rely on what others might think; they must exercise their own judgment. This judgment requires that they be honest with themselves. Being responsible for themselves, as well as for others, means they must know what their needs actually are. **Box 11.3** highlights similarities in Gilligan's and Kohlberg's approaches to moral reasoning.

Although Gilligan and Kohlberg document developmental sequences that parallel each other in many respects, a critical difference separates these two accounts. Kohlberg believes that his sequence is a path universally trodden by

**BOX
11.3**

In More Depth

Comparison of Kohlberg's and Gilligan's Approaches

Internalizing standards Both Kohlberg and Gilligan assume that initially individuals act primarily out of self-interest, with little thought to how their actions affect others. For Kohlberg, this stance reflects the individual's limited role-taking and cognitive skills; Gilligan attributes it to feelings of being cut off from others, leaving one to take care of one's own needs.

For Kohlberg, the development of abstract thought enables adolescents to imagine how others view their actions; because they are concerned about the opinion of others, they want to live up to the standards of their group. Gilligan assumes that as adolescents feel accepted by and connected to others, they take on the values of their group.

Considering intentions The same cognitive growth by which Kohlberg explains the internalization of group standards is also responsible for considering others' intentions when evaluating their actions. As adolescents become able to take the perspective of others, and understand that others can do the same with respect to their own behavior, motives or intentions become important in evaluating the acceptability of their own and others' actions. For Gilligan, seeing oneself as a member of the social group leads women to evaluate their actions in terms of how "good" they are, with goodness being defined conventionally by taking care of others.

Questioning values Kohlberg believes that exposure to other value systems, usually in high school or at work, gives adolescents a new perspective from which to view their own values and, with this, to examine and question them. Gilligan believes that individuals question conventional definitions of goodness when they begin to experience the tension created by caring for others to the exclusion of caring for oneself.

all individuals as they move into adulthood. He assumes that this sequence takes the form it does because it reflects developments in cognitive maturity that have a strong biological component (see Piaget in Chapter 2). Gilligan is not equally convinced that the sequence she documents in adolescent girls and young women is developmentally *necessary*, being "rooted in childhood," as does Kohlberg. She suggests, instead, that it is a response to a crisis, and that the crisis is adolescence itself (Gilligan, 1989a).

Gilligan proposes that leaving childhood is problematic for girls in ways that it is not for boys. The problem lies with the culture each enters. Adolescence introduces the expectation that children will assume the conventions of their society, whether these be adult gender roles, the knowledge that forms the basis of cultural wisdom, or behaviors that fit prescribed definitions of "goodness" and "rightness." Why should this expectation present more problems for girls?

Gilligan's answer is powerful. The most visible figures populating the landscape of adulthood are males—whether plumbers, politicians, poets, or philosophers—and their collective experiences form its norms. Girls risk losing themselves as they relax the intimate bonds of childhood to embrace a larger world of experience. Gilligan (1989b) writes:

> As the river of a girl's life flows into the sea of Western culture, she is in danger of drowning or disappearing. To take on the problem of her appearance, which is the problem of her development, and to connect her life with history on a cultural scale, she must enter—and by entering disrupt—a tradition in which "human" has for the most part meant male. Thus a struggle often breaks out in girls' lives at the edge of adolescence. (p. 4)

The problem is pervasive because it is woven into the very fabric of cultural thought. Even formal education, Gilligan suggests, presents a challenge to

Individuals, male and female, with a justice orientation are more likely to protest low wages of immigrant workers, whereas those with a care orientation are more likely to express their concern by providing a helping hand.

meta-analysis A statistical procedure for reaching conclusions regarding an area of research by combining the findings from multiple studies.

female identity: "In learning to think in the terms of the disciplines and thus to bring her thoughts and feelings into line with the traditions of Western culture...she also learn[s] to dismiss her own experience" (p. 2).

Gilligan traces the crisis of connection for girls to their ability to find a "voice" with which to speak and a context in which they will be heard. The culture they are entering has not been equally responsive to the voices of women and men, "or at least has not been up to the present. The wind of tradition blowing through women is a chill wind, because it brings a message of exclusion....The message to women is: keep quiet and notice the absence of women and say nothing" (Gilligan, 1989a, p. 26).

TRANSLATING CARE INTO ACTION   What evidence is there for gender differences in moral concerns? Although a **meta-analysis** of research on gender differences in moral reasoning found differences favoring a care orientation for females and a justice orientation for males, differences were small, and there were more similarities than there were differences (Jaffee & Hyde, 2000). In fact, considerable research suggests that individuals of both genders take both care and justice issues into consideration when thinking through moral issues.

In fact, the type of problem individuals are asked to think about appears to be more important than their gender in determining which perspective participants use. Dilemmas that approximate real-life situations, such as those studied by Gilligan, rather than the more impersonal dilemmas of Kohlberg, are more likely to prompt a care perspective. Rosemary Jadack and her associates (1995) found that females and males differed little in the extent to which they adopted a care or a justice orientation in reasoning about real-life types of dilemmas. In fact, individuals of either sex frequently used reasoning characteristic of both approaches, suggesting that these are not competing perspectives. Similarly, Eva Skoe and associates (2002a) have found more care reasoning and more emotional involvement with relational, real-life dilemmas than with non-relational ones (2002b).

It is likely as well that moral reasoning is related not to gender per se, but to one's gender-role orientation, that is, how feminine or masculine one is (Kracher & Marble, 2008). Skoe and her associates (2002a) found that not just women but individuals scoring higher in femininity on a measure of gender-role identity were more likely to engage in care reasoning. A study of Brazilian adolescents also found those with a feminine orientation to be more likely to be sympathetic to another's plight and more likely to assume the other's perspective (Eisenberg et al., 2001).

Freud: Morality and the Superego

For Freud, responsibility for moral behavior resides with the superego, which emerges as the child identifies with the same-sex parent, thus resolving the Oedipus complex (see Chapter 2). Through identification, the child internalizes or appropriates the values and behaviors of the parent. These values form the superego, which includes the conscience, and serve as the basis for an internalized set of standards for behavior.

Prior to the development of the conscience, Freud assumed that children were governed only by the desire to win parental affections and the fear of being rejected for wrongdoing. Like each of the previous theorists, Freud believed that an internalized code or ethic is not present initially.

The final step in moral development occurs in adolescence when puberty threatens the surface tranquility achieved through repression and identification. Freud assumed that adolescents emotionally distance themselves from their parents to defend against newly awakened sexual desires. In doing so, they have to toss out the parental figures they had internalized in childhood. Adolescence becomes a time for reworking the parental standards that were uncritically accepted as part of these figures (Josselson, 1980, 1987). Freud attributed the flexibility that characterizes mature moral thought to the work of the ego in balancing the demands of the id and superego. The ability to evaluate a situation, to develop coping strategies, and to delay gratification of one's impulses are all functions of the ego and characterize mature moral functioning.

CRITIQUE OF FREUD'S THEORY   Freud believed that the absence of castration anxiety in females and the presence, in its stead, of penis envy, resulted in a weaker superego in females and accompanying differences in their moral behavior. Freud (1925b) wrote:

> I cannot evade the notion (though I hesitate to give it expression) that for women the level of what is ethically normal is different from what it is in men. Their superego is never so inexorable, so impersonal, so independent of its emotional origins as we require it to be in men. Character traits which critics of every epoch have brought up against women—that they show less sense of justice than men, that they are less ready to submit it to the great exigencies of life, that they are more often influenced in their judgment by feelings of affection or hostility—all these would be amply accounted for by the modification in the formation of their superego which we have inferred. (pp. 257–258)

These assumptions concerning the basis for gender differences in moral behavior have not received empirical support. Research on the internalization of moral standards does not find males to have stronger superegos than females. Nor do differences in behavior, when they occur, favor males. They are, if anything, as likely to favor females (Ford et al., 1989; Silverman, 2003).

Research has similarly failed to support many of Freud's other assumptions related to the development of morality. For instance, adolescence is not a period of emotional turmoil for most teenagers. Also, surveys of normal adolescents do not find they are preoccupied with sex or with controlling their impulses. Nor do most adolescents have weak egos, nor have they cut emotional ties with their parents (see Chapter 6).

Adolescents' Religious Beliefs

Do adolescents think of God the same way children do? Or do the intellectual developments that occur in adolescence affect their views of God and religion just as they affect their views of so many other things? James Fowler (1981, 2001) suggests that they do. Fowler identifies six stages of religious belief that parallel Kohlberg's stages of moral development discussed earlier (Table 11.2).

Children's views of God reflect the concrete nature of the way they think in general. To them, God is someone with a human form who sits celestially enthroned above them. This figure for children is typically masculine; adolescents, on the other hand, are more likely to have a gender-neutral image of God (Ladd et al., 1998). Children accept the teachings and stories of their religion literally and do not question them, other than to try to fit them into their current ways of understanding, such as wondering how God can be everywhere at the same time. Adolescents subject their views of God to the same questioning they apply to other beliefs (Fowler, 1981).

TABLE 11.2
Fowler's Six Stages of Faith Development

STAGE 1: Intuitive-projective faith (early childhood)
Children's grasp of religious concepts is intuitive and personal, based largely on their own experiences and on narratives of good and evil. Thinking is dominated by imagination and fantasy, and religious beliefs reflect the qualities of Piaget's pre-operational thinking.

STAGE 2: Mythic-literal faith (middle childhood)
As logical thought develops and supplants intuition, children appropriate the religious beliefs of their community. However, religious concepts are interpreted literally, as is characteristic of concrete operational thought.

STAGE 3: Synthetic-conventional faith (early adolescence)
Abstract thought enables adolescents to integrate previously unrelated narratives and beliefs into a single system of beliefs. Since these beliefs are not explored for their personal relevance, faith is largely conformist, reflecting the unexamined tenets of one's religious community. Fowler assumes that many adults do not progress beyond this stage.

STAGE 4: Individuative-reflective faith (emerging adulthood)
As late adolescents and emerging adults assume responsibility for the decisions of life, they take responsibility for their beliefs as well, examining these for their relevance to other life commitments. Commitments in one area have implications for decisions in another, and individuals become aware of tensions in life—for example, individualism versus belonging to a group, or putting oneself first versus putting others first.

STAGE 5: Conjunctive faith (middle adulthood)
Whereas the previous stage is characterized by a need to resolve life tensions, this stage is characterized by an openness to the tensions that result from conflicting claims within different arenas of life. Individuals become able to view their beliefs as one of many belief systems, and they recognize that each of these is incomplete and relative. Fowler believes that few adults reach this stage.

STAGE 6: Universalizing faith (middle or late adulthood)
Individuals at this stage experience themselves as being at one with God and with others; differences in beliefs and practices are no longer seen as important, with the result that previously experienced tensions dissolve. These individuals work for the good of all irrespective of group membership, frequently at risk to their own personal safety.

The ability to think abstractly that comes with adolescence transforms these views, enabling adolescents to appreciate abstract qualities of God, such as righteousness, compassion, and mercy. Bradley Hertel and Michael Donahue (1995) analyzed the responses of fifth- through ninth-graders to nine descriptors of God. Two dimensions emerged. One described God in terms of love, and the second described God in terms of authority. Items related to the first of these, for instance, described God as loving someone irrespective of what that person had done, whereas those related to the second dimension described God in terms of rules and punishing wrongdoers. Of these two dimensions, the image of God that predominated among these youth was overwhelmingly that of a loving God. This was true, by the way, for their parents as well.

These two dimensions suggest parallels to the moral perspectives discussed earlier. In fact, many biblical narratives of conflict between individuals and God lend themselves to either a justice or care interpretation. For instance, one could view the behavior of Adam and Eve from a justice perspective and argue that by eating fruit they had been told not to eat, they broke a rule.

However, one could as easily view the transgression from a care perspective and see their actions as a betrayal of trust in that the fruit had been left within their reach. Similarly, the narrative of the exodus from Egypt, in which the Israelites worshipped a golden calf, might be viewed from either perspective. Worshipping the calf clearly violated the commandment not to worship idols; however, worship is a relational act and, as such, constituted a betrayal of the special relationship the Israelites had with God.

Nancy Cobb, Anthony Ong, and Jerry Tate (2001), at California State University, Los Angeles, examined late adolescents' and early adults' perceptions of biblical and moral wrongdoings in which the characters' actions could be seen to simultaneously violate a rule and betray a trust. When participants were asked to describe the nature of the transgression in each case, they defined the wrongdoing from a justice perspective, speaking of it as breaking a rule. However, when asked what mattered most to the party that had been wronged, they more frequently mentioned the relationship, irrespective of whether this had been God or another person. Given the commonality between religious and moral domains, in that both teach about right and wrong conduct, perhaps these findings should not be that surprising.

Thus, adolescents can engage in sophisticated reasoning about religious, as well as moral, issues. Adolescence is also a time when they may begin to question religious beliefs. "If God is all-powerful, why is there suffering and evil in the world?" The answers adolescents arrive at reflect an increasingly personalized faith much as Kohlberg's and Gilligan's final stages (Fowler, 1981, 2001).

This increasing sophistication is reflected in adolescents' prayers, which include petitions such as to "better understand your holy will" or to "deal better with my anger." Even so, the social identity reflected in adolescents' prayers is, for the most part, limited to family and friends and only occasionally extends beyond these to the larger community (McKinney & McKinney, 1999).

With respect to **religious identity**, one also sees evidence of a clear developmental trend. In a series of studies, David Elkind (1961, 1962, 1963) asked Catholic, Jewish, and Protestant children and adolescents how they could tell whether a person was of the same religion that they were. By middle childhood, children identified members of religious groups in terms of concrete behaviors and characteristics. Thus, one who is Catholic might be identified as someone who goes to Mass every Sunday, or one who is Jewish as a person who goes to temple and attends Hebrew school. Such an understanding, as Elkind points out, highlights the differences between religions. That is, if one is attending Mass, one cannot also be going to temple. One is either one religion or the other, and the two are noticeably different.

Adolescents, however, are able to appreciate the commonalities to different religions, understanding that one can worship God irrespective of whether one does this in a church, a temple, or a mosque. In this stage, adolescents identify their religion in terms of abstract beliefs. Thus, Protestants might describe someone in their faith as "a person who believes in God and Christ and is loving to others," whereas those who are Jewish might describe themselves as "a person who believes in one God and doesn't believe in the New Testament" (Elkind, 1961, 1962, 1963).

How important, one might ask, is religion to one's sense of self? When asked to describe themselves, in other words, how likely are individuals of different ages to mention their religion? Rachel Royle, Martyn Barrett, and Eithne Buchanan-Barrow (1998) asked participants of various ages, religions, and nationalities, all of whom lived in London, to sort cards into either of two boxes, one labeled "Me" and the other "Not Me." Each card identified some single aspect of identity, such as gender, ethnicity, language, age, or religion. Once participants had finished this initial sort, they were asked to go through the "Me" cards again and select the one that was most descriptive of

religious identity An awareness of belonging to a religious group.

For many adolescents, religion is a significant part of their identity.

themselves. This card was removed and they selected the next most descriptive card, continuing in this way until each of the terms had been ranked in order of importance.

Religion emerged as a significant aspect of identity, being among those most likely to be selected as "Me." Furthermore, its importance to a sense of self increased with age. Children were most likely to identify themselves in terms of their gender or their nationality; however, by early adolescence, religion was more important and was mentioned more frequently than sex, age, or nationality. Religion contributed to identity more heavily for some participants than it did for others, possibly reflecting the minority status it conferred on them. A similar trend has been found for ethnicity, in which individuals who are members of a minority are more aware of their ethnicity than those belonging to the majority, the latter frequently not even having a sense of being a member of an ethnic group (Phinney, 1989). So, too, with religion. For Muslims living in London, for instance, religion was more salient than it was for Christians.

Thus, religious beliefs reflect more than adolescents' ability to think in certain ways. The processes of exploration and commitment that are central to identity formation also contribute to differences in religiosity. The ability to think abstractly may make it possible for adolescents to entertain questions such as why God would tolerate suffering, but this ability alone is not enough to determine that they will.

Acceptance of religious tenets has been viewed by some as a means of controlling the ultimate risks of life, risks such as those introduced by disease and natural disaster (Malinowski, 1925). From this perspective, those who reject religious beliefs become the risk takers. However, as we have seen with other aspects of identity exploration, a determination of what is risky cannot be made in any simple way without reference to the particular contexts of an individual's life. In this respect, risk taking in religious beliefs, just as in the vocational and social domains of identity, takes the form of daring the unknown. Thus, it would be equally risky for an adolescent whose parents are avowed atheists to explore a belief in God as it would for an adolescent coming from a deeply religious background to reject those religious beliefs.

The very same willingness to consider the unfamiliar, whether in terms of a career or a lifestyle, is also at the heart of religiosity. Will adolescents give themselves the freedom to explore their religion? Some will; others will not. Adolescents can remain committed to traditional religious beliefs without ever examining them. These adolescents can be said to be foreclosed in their religiosity. Conversely, adolescents can explore their beliefs, asking questions to which they do not have simple or familiar answers, and be identity-achieved (Markstrom-Adams et al., 1994; Markstrom-Adams & Smith, 1996).

One cannot distinguish either type of adolescent simply by looking at their beliefs. It is not so much a question of what adolescents believe as it is the process by which they have gotten to these beliefs. Just as with the broader process of identity formation, the beliefs one ends up with can remain essentially unchanged. It is the believer who has changed. One index of religious exploration, for instance, is switching one's church affiliation due to dissatisfaction with its teachings. Individuals who switch have been found to be more actively involved in their religion subsequent to switching than those whose beliefs have remained unexamined (Hoge et al., 1995).

The extent to which adolescents are involved in their religion also has been found to relate to measures of psychosocial maturity. Carol Markstrom (1999) found that late adolescents who more frequently attended religious services and participated in a Bible study or youth group scored higher on various measures of ego strength, such as hope, will, purpose, fidelity, love, and care, than adolescents who were less involved.

The extent to which adolescents have a strong religious identity is also related to their concern for others (King & Furrow, 2004; Furrow et al., 2004). Michael Kerestes, James Youniss, and Edward Metz (2004), at Catholic University of America, followed students from their sophomore to their senior year of high school and found that those who maintained a strong religious identity were more likely to be involved in prosocial activities, for example, volunteering in the community, demonstrating for causes they believed in, and helping others.

The Importance of Religion

How important is religion in the lives of adolescents? Close to 30% of high school seniors indicate that religion is very important in their lives and attend religious services weekly (Bachman et al., 2009). Additionally, one-quarter of high school seniors have attended a religious youth group for all four years of high school and just under one-third have attended from one to three years (Smith et al., 2002).

The importance of religion in adolescents' lives differs by gender, with religion playing a more significant role in the lives of adolescent females than males. Differences associated with race are even greater. Significantly more African American adolescents attend weekly services than do European American adolescents, and twice as many African American as European American adolescents indicate religion is very important in their lives, 47.4% versus 23.4% (Bachman et al., 2009). As can be seen in **Table 11.3**, religion remains important for significant numbers of adolescents.

Additionally, most of these adolescents put their religious beliefs into action (Youniss et al., 1999). Religious adolescents are nearly three times as likely to be involved in some form of voluntary community service as are adolescents for whom religion is not important. For instance, approximately three-quarters of high school seniors who indicated that religion was important in their lives engaged in volunteer work, either monthly or more frequently. In comparison, only a quarter of those who said that religion was not important volunteered for such work (Youniss et al., 1999).

Are adolescents today as religious as they have been in the past? The answer to that is both "yes" and "no." The percentage of those who attend religious

---

TABLE 11.3
Religious Practices and Beliefs among High School Seniors, 1991 to 2008

	PERCENTAGE OF SENIORS		
	1991	2001	2008
Frequency of Attending Religious Service			
Once a week or more	31.2	32.8	30.1
1–2 times a month	16.8	16.1	15.9
Rarely	37.6	34.2	34.2
Never	14.4	16.9	19.9
Importance of Religion in Life			
Very important	27.7	32.3	28.0
Pretty important	30.0	27.9	27.6
A little important	27.0	24.4	24.9
Not important	15.3	15.5	19.6

Source: Fox et al., 2005 and Bachman et al., 2009.

services, either every week or once or twice a month, has not changed appreciably since the early 1990's. However, among adolescents who don't attend with any regularity, more of these never attend, as opposed to only rarely attend. As might be expected, these trends are reflected in what adolescents have to say about how important religion is in their lives. Even though more adolescents than in the past say that religion is not important to them, the percentage of adolescents for whom religion is either very or pretty important has not changed substantially (Bachman et al., 2009; Fox et al., 2005). Given the importance of religion to so many adolescents, more research on religious beliefs and practices is needed for a fuller understanding of adolescent development.

We have considered in this chapter the ways in which adolescents' values relate to their identity and to a developing system of moral and religious beliefs. In the next chapter, we will look at the crisis of values in adolescents' lives—at alienation, delinquency, violence, and substance abuse.

SUMMARY and KEY TERMS

The Values of Adolescents

Values in Action: Volunteering: Many adolescents routinely do volunteer work in their communities. The likelihood of volunteering is affected by adolescents' personalities and by interactions with their parents.
resilient

Values: Adolescents and Parents: Most adolescents have values that are similar to those of their parents. They place a high value on having a good marriage and family life, and being successful in their work.

Values: Gender and Ethnicity: With respect to gender, more similarities than differences exist in the values held by adolescent females and males. There are also few differences in adolescents' values due to race.

Values and Identity: The way adolescents approach both their own and others' values reflects identity issues. Identity-achieved and moratorium adolescents have explored issues for themselves and are tolerant of similar explorations and differences in others. Foreclosed adolescents tend to be more rule-bound and authoritarian than identity-achieved or moratorium adolescents. They are also more likely to be critical of those who are different from them.

Morality: What Makes a Thing Right?

Social-Cognitive Theory and Moral Development: Social-cognitive theory assumes that community standards form the basis of self-regulated behavior. Age-related changes in considering the intentions of others and questioning values are traced to children's and adolescents' experiences when interacting with others. The experience of gratitude can motivate individuals to act in more positive ways. Adolescents' behavior does not always reflect their moral understanding, and depends on factors such as incentives for responsible behavior and learned internalized controls.
morality

SUMMARY and KEY TERMS

Kohlberg: Moral Reasoning: Kohlberg traces moral development over three levels of moral reasoning, with two stages at each level. The levels reflect the stance adolescents take in relation to the standards of their community. Forgiveness is a decision to release a person from a claim that justice would honor. Reasoning about forgiveness, just as about justice, becomes more mature with age. There is substantial support that individuals reason in more principled ways with age, however their reasoning does not necessarily correspond to their actions. **preconventional reasoning, conventional reasoning, random error, test of significance, postconventional reasoning**

Social Domain Theory: Like Kohlberg's theory, social domain theory assumes that children actively construct ways of understanding their world, recognizes the contribution of cognitive development to moral understanding, and stresses the importance of peer interactions to moral development. Differing from Kohlberg, social domain theory distinguishes moral understanding, and social convention as distinct domains of social understanding, rather than viewing these as a developmental progression, whereas the personal domain constitutes a third form of social understanding.
moral domain, social conventional domain, personal domain

Gilligan: An Ethic of Care: Gilligan assumes females think of morality more personally than do males, emphasizing compassion and a sense of responsibility to others in contrast to a justice orientation, emphasizing reliance on rules and reason. Gilligan traces gender differences in moral reasoning to differences in ways of viewing the self, where females tend to define themselves in relation to others, and males tend to define themselves as separate from others. As such, she describes three levels of moral development in females, each reflecting a different resolution to conflict between responsibilities to themselves and to others. The type of moral dilemma individuals are considering, though, influences their moral reasoning more than their gender. Additionally, moral reasoning is more closely related to gender-role orientation than to gender itself.
ethic of care, meta-analysis

Freud: Morality and the Superego: Freud placed the responsibility for moral behavior in the superego, an aspect of the personality that embraces cultural standards of right and wrong. The superego develops when the young child identifies with the same-sex parent. Freud assumed the superego of females to be weaker than that of males because they are not as motivated to resolve Oedipal tensions. Despite the usefulness of Freud's theory to clinicians, his assumptions concerning gender differences in moral development have not been supported by research.

Adolescents' Religious Beliefs

The Importance of Religion: The intellectual changes that occur in adolescence make it possible for adolescents to view God in new ways and to question beliefs they once accepted uncritically. As with identity status, processes of exploration and commitment determine the form beliefs will take. For more than 60% of adolescents, religion remains very to moderately important in their lives.
religious identity

"No, don't! ..." Abbie bolted upright in a sweat. She sat in the dark, the dream swirled around her, its sharp pain softening with each panting breath.

"Too much!" she cried, slipping her feet over the side of the bed and starting for the bathroom.

As her foot hit the dresser, she hissed angrily, "Why isn't anything where it's supposed to be?" Then, blindly feeling for the light switch and finding nothing, she remembered where she was. This wasn't her room. She was in her

The Problems of Youth

stepsister's bedroom at her father's house. Her mom had thrown her out. She had forgotten the reason for the fight; they had thrown things, said things.

As the heavy reality of her world closed in on her, she slipped to the floor sobbing—the angry words, fists, and ashtrays flying, her friends so far away, her father nervous, on edge, his wife distant and formal—and no place to call her own. She suddenly felt that she could bear none of it anymore.

alienation Indifference where devotion or attachment formerly existed; estrangement.

Chapter Overview

Adolescents face many pressures. Abbie is one of those with more than her share. Most adolescents will cope in one fashion or another; Abbie may, too. Relatively few will fail to cope. In this chapter we will consider first the problems of those for whom coping has become the ultimate test, the alienated and abused, looking at runaway adolescents and those who are maltreated, and at the supports that are available to them and their parents.

Problem behavior in adolescents can be classified in terms of externalizing or internalizing problems according to whether adolescents turn their problems outward, as in antisocial behavior or delinquency, or whether they turn them inward, as in depression, suicide, or eating disorders. We will consider each of these in turn. Substance abuse, covered in a subsequent section, can be either an externalizing or an internalizing problem.

Alienation and the Failure to Cope

Some of the most common stressors in adolescence reflect the *absence* rather than the presence of something. Adolescents frequently feel cut off from themselves and others, emotionally distanced from their world, observers rather than participants in their own reality. Feelings of **alienation**—a sense of estrangement and loss—can be common in adolescence. These feelings are to be expected, given the many changes adolescents experience; however, when alienation becomes the predominant focus of an adolescent's experience, he or she is in trouble.

Loss is central to alienation, and it is always the loss of something important. Reactions to this loss can range from hostility to sadness to indifference—from anger to a defensive "What does it matter anyway?" The alienated who cannot replace their loss with the sense of a competent self, linked to a social order that gives meaning to their lives, surround the void without filling it.

Runaways

For some adolescents, the loss is of something they never had. Upwards of 2 million adolescents, or about 7%, run away from home each year (Sanchez et al., 2006; Tyler & Bersani, 2008). Some run away in the hopes of finding something, but most are running from something (Table 12.1). Despite the uniqueness of individuals when looked full in the face, the profile of runaways is disturbingly similar: low self-esteem, depression, poor interpersonal skills, insecurity, anxiousness, impulsiveness, and little sense of control over life's events. Most do poorly in school, many run into trouble with the law, and 20% attempt suicide (Leslie et al., 2002). Almost all experience conflict within their families, and for many this includes abuse or neglect. Runaways can be from any socio-economic level, although most are from lower income families.

Running away is clearly not the answer to their problems. It is equally clear that these adolescents are unable to face their problems and come up with any reasonable solution at the moment. Running away is almost never well planned. Two-thirds, for example, leave home with little money in their pockets. Many stay with friends or relatives, some seek out youth shelters, and others end up on the street. Most return within a week, and 90% within a month. Most also will run away again in the future (Hammer et al., 2002).

Home life for most runaways is chaotic. The problems from which they are running (and to which almost all will return) have usually existed for years, yet the solutions remain as distant as ever. The dynamics of family life that would offer an answer to these problems are ones that foster personal development. Yet most runaways lack a sense of who they are or what they can become, in large part because the development of their sense of self and of

TABLE 12.1
Percentage of Common Problems Reported by Adolescents in Runaway and Homeless Youth Centers

TYPE OF PROBLEM	TOTAL[a]	FEMALE	MALE
Emotional conflict at home	41	43	39
Parent too strict	21	24	18
Parental physical abuse	20	23	18
Parental neglect	20	19	21
Parent drug or alcohol problems	18	19	17
Family mental health problems	11	12	11
Parental domestic violence	10	10	10
None of the above	16	13	19

Source: Maguire et al., 1993.

[a]Because multiple responses are permitted, totals exceed 100%

their potential has not been supported within their families. Those who do have positive relationships, particularly with their fathers or with a father substitute, are less likely to use drugs or engage in criminal behaviors that typically are a means of survival on the street (Repetti et al., 2002; Stein et al., 2009).

Runaways are in need of programs that give them the interpersonal skills that most do not develop within their families: skills in communicating thoughts and feelings, negotiating conflict, and making responsible decisions (see Chapter 6). Typically, more services are available to abused youth than to runaways, most likely because society tends to see the former as victims and the latter as merely unruly. Runaways also, however, are more likely to have experienced abuse or neglect than their peers. Rather than being the problem itself, running away typically is a symptom of other problems (Dedel, 2006; Kim et al., 2009).

Support for Adolescent Runaways and Parents

Adolescents who do not return home right away face a number of problems. First among these are the basics—finding a safe place to stay, food, and clothing. Life on the streets poses dangers of its own. Runaways, almost by definition, are in a one-down position, having exhausted all other means of coping, and are at risk for victimization. They are exposed to possible physical and sexual assault, are more likely to use and abuse drugs and to trade sex for food or shelter. They are also at high risk for exposure to the HIV virus through drug use and risky sexual practices (Rotheram-Borus et al., 2003; Stein et al., 2009).

The availability of immediate supports varies from one community to the next. Nearly all urban centers, however, have federally and privately funded shelters. Most of these offer short-term help (e.g., 30 days) in the form of meals and a place to stay; some also offer health and counseling services. The Internet is a valuable tool for finding shelters and one with which most adolescents are familiar. For instance, the International Homeless & Homelessness

Adolescent runaways face numerous problems, and the availability of support, in terms of meals and a place to stay, varies from one community to another. The National Runaway Switchboard provides crisis intervention and a message center for adolescents and parents. Rapper and actor Ludacris, pictured in this poster, has helped create public service announcements for the NRS.

maltreatment Instances of harm to children or adolescents that are nonaccidental and avoidable; they can be due to either abuse or neglect.

Directory provides a list of mostly big-city shelters within the United States and in other countries. Additionally, the National Runaway Switchboard, a 24-hour national hotline for adolescent runaways and parents, offers crisis intervention, a message center, and referrals.

Longer term interventions can take the form of counseling and parenting classes, offered by many communities through full-service schools (see Chapter 8, and Chapter 6 for parenting). Skill-focused prevention programs based on social-cognitive theory (see Chapter 2) have been successful in reducing the use of alcohol and drugs and reducing risky sexual behavior among runaways (Rotheram-Borus et al., 2003).

Maltreatment: Abuse and Neglect

Maltreatment refers to instances of harm that are non-accidental and avoidable; these can occur either from abuse or neglect. Abuse can be physical, sexual, or emotional in nature, and often involves some combination of these. Similarly, neglect is distinguished as a failure to provide for an adolescent's physical, educational, or emotional needs. **Box 12.1** distinguishes among these types of maltreatment.

It is difficult to say precisely how many adolescents are maltreated, since not all instances of maltreatment are reported, and of those that are, not all can be substantiated. For children of *all* ages, neglect is the most common form of maltreatment, comprising almost 60% of cases. As can be seen in **Figure 12.1**, older adolescents are less likely to experience maltreatment than are younger adolescents. Boys also are less likely to be maltreated than girls (U.S. Department of Health and Human Services, 2009).

Cases of adolescent abuse and neglect are likely to follow one of three patterns: a continuation of earlier child abuse, a change in the type of punishment used by parents, and neglect related to the onset of adolescence (Doueck et al., 1988).

The maltreatment some adolescents experience continues a pattern of earlier child maltreatment within the family. These adolescents typically come from families with many long-standing problems: violence between parents, alcoholism, financial instability, few social supports, and physical isolation from others. The maltreatment these adolescents suffer is not much different from that experienced when they were younger, and it reflects the inadequate coping skills of the parents and the generally dysfunctional nature of the family.

A second type of maltreatment, physical abuse, involves a change in the type of punishment used. In this instance, parents who have used physical punishment since childhood have increased the intensity of the punishment in an attempt to control adolescent misbehavior. Families in which this form of mistreatment occurs are typified by controlling, rigid parents who become even more controlling, to the point of abuse, when faced with adolescent bids for greater autonomy and independence and the loss of their own control.

A third type of mistreatment is brought about by the onset of adolescence itself. In this type of neglect, parents mistakenly conclude that because children have reached adolescence, they are able to be on their own and care for themselves.

CHARACTERISTICS OF MALTREATING PARENTS   What leads parents to become abusive or neglectful? No simple answers are to be found. Most of these parents love their children and experience genuine remorse for what they do. Simi-

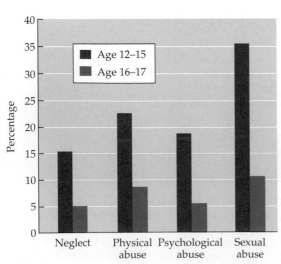

● **Figure 12.1**   **The percentage of victims of different types of maltreatment who are adolescents** (After U.S. Department of Health and Human Services, 2009.)

In More Depth

Types of Maltreatment

ABUSE

- *Physical abuse*: Involves substantial injuries that last for at least 48 hours and often, as in the case of burns, broken bones, or internal injuries, longer. Examples might include bruises or fractures from being hit or punched.

- *Sexual abuse*: Involves exposure, molesting or fondling, or actual penetration. Examples might include a daughter being molested by her mother's live-in boyfriend.

- *Emotional abuse*: Involves behavior that undermines an adolescent's sense of well-being and self-esteem. Examples could include denigrating or derisive remarks ("You stupid brat!").

NEGLECT

- *Physical neglect*: Involves a failure to provide for an adolescent's physical or medical needs, or for adequate supervision. Examples might include failure to provide treatment for a medical condition such as asthma or an abscessed tooth, or not attending to obvious hazards around the home.

- *Educational neglect*: Involves permitting truancy (approximately five unexcused absences from school/month) or keeping an adolescent home to care for other siblings.

- *Emotional neglect*: Differs from emotional abuse in that it is a passive emotional rejection of the adolescent, taking the form of giving little or no emotional support, attention, or affection.

Source: From National Clearinghouse on Child Abuse and Neglect Information, 2005.

---

larly, relatively few would be diagnosed as suffering from a mental illness. Nor could one predict maltreatment simply by knowing their life circumstances. In fact, research on maltreatment has failed to identify any single factor that necessarily leads to maltreatment (Cicchetti & Lynch, 1995). In many ways, maltreating parents are not that different from non-maltreating parents.

In other respects, however, important differences have been found. One difference concerns the way they respond under stress. Parents who engage in maltreatment appear to experience more difficulty coping with stress than do other parents. Not only are they likely to find the normal stresses of life more aversive than other individuals, but they also tend to overreact when they are stressed, experiencing more difficulty controlling their impulses. In addition, maltreating parents are more likely to interpret events as being outside their control, and to react angrily and defensively, than are other parents. Thus, although these parents may behave in ways that are similar to other parents under most circumstances, they are likely to respond differently when stressed (Stith et al., 2008).

Maltreating parents also appear to differ in what might be termed their worldview. They are less likely to have a positive outlook on life, instead seeing the world as a hostile place and life as a struggle, with them on the defensive. This defensive attitude can extend to their interactions with their children, in which they are more likely than are other parents to interpret an adolescent's behavior as intentionally disobedient or otherwise "aimed" at them. With their own feelings so much in the foreground, it also becomes easy for parent-child relationships to undergo a reversal in which the adolescent is expected to be responsive to the parent's feelings and meet the parent's needs. This reversal of roles, in which the child is **parentified**, or functions as a parent, places the burden for caring for the parent's needs on the adolescent. In fact, maltreated adolescents frequently are more nurturing than their parents (Cicchetti & Lynch, 1995).

parentified   A reversal in the parent-child relationship in which the burden of caring for the parent's needs is assumed by the adolescent.

Maltreating parents also tend to hold inappropriate expectations concerning what can reasonably be expected of adolescents. These unrealistic expectations can fuel their tendency to perceive an adolescent's behavior as willfully disobedient rather than as normal for someone of that age. They differ as well in the types of discipline they are likely to use, being less likely to use effective parenting styles. Instead, they are more likely to punish or threaten, and less likely to use reasoning. They are also less consistent in their discipline and less warm and affectionate in general in their relationships (Cicchetti & Lynch, 1995).

Finally, maltreating parents not only are able to bring fewer personal resources to bear when facing stressful life events, but also have fewer interpersonal resources on which they can rely. Perhaps the most important of these for most parents is their relationship with their spouse. Partners of maltreating parents have been found to be less supportive and warm, as well as more aggressive, than those of comparison parents. In general, relationships within the home, whether with a spouse or an adolescent, are less positive and warm than in other homes (Cicchetti & Lynch, 1995; Howes & Cicchetti, 1993; Stith et al., 2008).

None of these characteristics, in themselves, can be regarded as responsible for maltreatment. Maltreatment typically results from a combination of conditions rather than a single factor. Thus, a parent who has difficulty coping with stress may still be able to function adequately unless something untoward happens. The loss of a job, however, or a child entering a "difficult" developmental stage may be enough to precipitate maltreatment. One such condition that places families under significant stress is poverty. Although maltreatment is by no means limited to low-income families, it is unusually high among this group. Life below the poverty line can involve cascading stress on an almost daily basis. A case in point might involve something as simple as an appliance needing repair. A refrigerator breaking down can mean spoiled food. But when money is short, the food that has spoiled may have been purchased with the last of the food stamps. To repair the appliance would leave nothing for groceries; however, without a refrigerator, frequent trips to the market become necessary, taxing the reserves of an already overtaxed parent. Coupled with an unsupportive spouse or inadequate transportation, an event that might have been an ordinary stressor in another family can precipitate maltreatment in an impoverished one (Mersky et al., 2009).

Positive actions for parents to take, information on parenting resources, and hotline numbers are available on the Internet through a Violence Prevention Web site sponsored by the Centers for Disease Control and Prevention (CDC).

Problem Behavior

We've seen with adolescent runaways, as with adolescents in previous chapters, that teenagers at times engage in risky behavior, endangering themselves or others. Then again, so do adults, and with about the same frequency. The majority of teenagers, just as adults, find ways to work through conflicts, manage their emotional ups and downs, and live competent and sensible lives. Only a minority of adolescents experience problems serious enough to attract attention or require treatment. We turn to these adolescents in the sections that follow.

Adolescent problem behavior can be classified into one of two categories depending on how directly it affects others. Behaviors that directly harm others are said to be externalized, and are referred to as **externalized problems**. These include activities such as risky sexual practices, substance abuse, fighting, chronic delinquency, and dangerous driving. As you can see, these are

externalizing problems
Behaviors that directly harm others.

activities that are either explicitly illegal or deemed antisocial. Because such behaviors are, among less troubled individuals, ordinarily inhibited or controlled, when they do occur they are sometimes labeled "acting out" and the adolescents who perform them are referred to as **undercontrolled**.

In contrast to the kinds of behaviors mentioned above, behaviors that are more directly harmful to the adolescent who engages in them are said to be internalized and are referred to as **internalized problems**. These include things such as anxiety, depression, suicidal thoughts, and eating disorders. Individuals evidencing these types of problems are said to be **overcontrolled**. Notice that depression and anxiety are primarily "affective disorders," that is, disturbances of feeling, emotion, and mood. However, in order to come to the attention of others, they must become manifest in behavior. This last point makes clear that the distinction between internalized and externalized problems cannot be pushed too far before the boundary between them becomes fuzzy. Adolescents who are constantly at odds with the law and the people around them are very likely to develop affective disturbances as well. Consequently, an individual who is both chronically delinquent and chronically depressed cannot unambiguously be labeled "externalized" or "internalized." When problem behaviors co-occur in this manner, they are said to be **comorbid**.

Externalizing Problems

Adolescents who exhibit one externalizing problem are likely to engage in a number of other problem behaviors as well. Thus an adolescent who engages in antisocial behavior, such as bullying classmates at school, is likely also to become involved in delinquent activities, such as petty theft, or associated with a gang.

ANTISOCIAL BEHAVIOR   It's important at the outset to make a distinction between two types of adolescents, both of whom engage in antisocial behavior. For some, their antisocial behavior is a disorder that originated in childhood and will continue into adulthood. Terrie Moffitt (2007) classifies their behavior as **life-course persistent antisocial behavior**. For others, antisocial behavior emerges around the time they enter puberty and drops out as they enter early adulthood; their behavior is **adolescence-limited antisocial behavior**. This distinction is important since only the former adolescents can be expected to continue to exhibit problematic behavior in life. The behavior and relationships of the latter adolescents become as normative as those of their peers once they enter early adulthood (Moffitt, 2007).

Terrie Moffitt, affiliated with Duke University and Kings College London, points to different developmental antecedents for each group of adolescents. Adolescents for whom this disorder originated in childhood are likely to have poor impulse control, evidence developmental delays in cognitive and motor development, and have "difficult" temperaments, being more negative in mood and slower to adapt to changes. These risk factors are likely to have been aggravated by environmental risk factors such as poor parenting, exposure to violence, and poverty (Moffitt, 2007; Odgers et al., 2009).

Among adolescence-limited offenders, antisocial behavior first emerges with puberty. Although these adolescents do not persist in delinquent behavior once they reach adulthood, they are nonetheless just as delinquent when adolescents as are persistent offenders. Moffitt traces the emergence of antisocial behavior in this second group to what she calls a "maturity gap," which reflects their impatience with being treated as a child and their resentment of restrictions. Their delinquent behavior becomes a way of exercising autonomy with parents and of affiliating with peers. Delinquent behaviors are appealing to them by making them feel more adult, and because they do not share the

undercontrolled   Adolescents who have difficulty inhibiting and controlling their behavior, frequently resulting in externalizing problems.

internalizing problems
Behaviors that are harmful to the adolescent who engages in them.

overcontrolled   Adolescents who are anxious and inhibited, frequently resulting in internalizing problems.

comorbid   The interrelatedness and co-occurrence of several problem behaviors.

life-course persistent antisocial behavior   Problem behavior that originates in childhood and persists into adulthood.

adolescence-limited antisocial behavior   Problem behavior that originates in adolescence and drops out in early adulthood.

juvenile delinquency   Illegal actions committed by a minor.

index offenses   Actions that are criminal at any age, for example, homicide and burglary.

status offenses   Actions that are illegal when engaged in by minors but legal for adults, for example, truancy and drinking alcohol.

risk factors that characterize life-course persistent offenders, they don't get involved in criminal activities once they reach adulthood.

DELINQUENCY   **Juvenile delinquency** involves illegal acts committed by a minor, someone below the age of 18 or 21 in the United States. These acts can be as serious as homicide or as relatively trivial as shoplifting a candy bar. Some of these acts, such as homicide, rape, or robbery, are illegal at any age; when committed by juveniles, they are termed **index offenses**. Other actions, termed **status offenses**, are behaviors that are illegal when engaged in by minors but perfectly legal for adults. Running away and truancy are status offenses. Adults are free to choose where and with whom they will live and when they will leave. There's no such thing as a 40-year-old runaway—not legally, at least. Similarly, once adolescents reach the legal age of adulthood set by their state, they are no longer considered truant even though they may not attend school.

The types of delinquent acts adolescents engage in vary with age. Many minor forms of delinquency—such as running away, violating curfews, or smoking marijuana—begin in early adolescence but decrease by adulthood. More serious types of crimes—like robbery or violent offenses—are generally more common in adulthood than in adolescence (Puzzanchera, 2009). However, there is little evidence to suggest that minor forms of delinquency predict a shift to more serious crimes later on, even for multiple offenders. The pattern instead suggests a small subgroup of delinquents who start early and account for a relatively high proportion of criminal activity (Henggeler, 1989; Moffitt, 2007).

Gender and Ethnic Differences in Delinquency   Females are less likely to engage in delinquent activities than are males, accounting for only 30% of juvenile arrests (Puzzanchera, 2009). Additionally, the size of the gender difference varies with the type of crime. Females are less likely to commit violent crimes than males, and are more likely to be arrested for running away, sexual offenses, unruly behavior, and theft (Snyder, 2004).

Large differences exist in the numbers of adolescents from different ethnic backgrounds who enter the juvenile justice system. Minority youth are significantly more likely to be arrested than are European Americans (Sickmund, 2004). With the exception of violent crimes, this is true even when each has committed the same offense (Juvenile Justice Evaluation Center, 2004). Custody rates also differ for adolescents of different ethnic backgrounds. The custody rate for African Americans, for instance, is nearly five times that for European Americans and more than twice that for Hispanics (**Figure 12.2**) (Sickmund, 2004). Self-report comparisons for African American and European American high school seniors, however, fail to reveal differences in delinquent activities that would be expected given figures such as these (Sourcebook of Criminal Justice Statistics 2003), strongly suggesting that arrest and detention rates reflect biases within the juvenile justice system (Juvenile Justice Evaluation Center, 2004).

Amendments to the Juvenile Justice and Delinquency Prevention Act of 1974 require states to examine the way minority youth are dealt with, from the

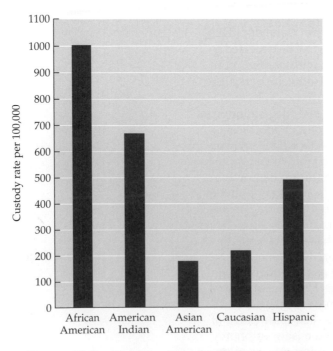

● **Figure 12.2**   **Custody rates of juveniles by ethnicity** (After Sickmund, 2004.)

very first contact up to decisions regarding sentencing, to discover where problems exist in the treatment of minority youth and how these can be corrected (Juvenile Justice Evaluation Center, 2004).

The effects of ethnicity and social class are difficult to separate. Arrest rates for minority adolescents are higher than those for nonminority youth, as are arrests of adolescents from lower income versus middle-income homes. Disproportionate numbers of minority youth come from lower income homes, and factors common to poverty are related to delinquency apart from ethnic status. Unemployment, poorer academic and vocational preparation, and fewer social and family resources are just a few of these factors. In addition, much middle-income delinquency is never reported; families are able to intervene, and youth authorities are more willing to release offenders to their parents' custody.

Even so, some types of delinquent activity vary with social class. Middle-income youth are less likely to commit violent crimes (such as aggravated assault, rape, robbery) or crimes against property (for example, auto theft, burglary) than are lower income youth. Status offenses and minor delinquent acts such as creating a public nuisance, drunkenness, and disorderly conduct are as common among middle-income as lower income adolescents.

Middle- and lower income youth are equally likely to commit status offenses and minor delinquent acts, such as vandalism. Adolescents from lower income homes are more likely, however, to commit violent crimes or major crimes against property, such as auto theft or burglary.

Risk and Protective Factors in Delinquency   We have seen that in some adolescents delinquency can be traced to relatively stable characteristics that increase the likelihood of deviant behavior, such as neurological deficits, impulsivity, and poor self-control (Moffitt, 1997, 2007). Qualities of family life and parenting practices are important as well, particularly as these contribute to children's ability to regulate their emotions (Alink et al., 2009; Repetti et al., 2002). Parents who are warm, supportive, and consistent in their discipline and who monitor their children's activities reduce the risk for delinquency (Ge et al., 2002; Scaramella et al., 2002). Peers, on the other hand, have less direct influence on delinquent behavior. Even though delinquent adolescents are more likely to associate with peers who engage in similar activities, it is also the case that they seek out peers who engage in behaviors similar to their own, rather than being influenced by them (Scaramella et al., 2002).

The quality of children's neighborhoods also affects the likelihood of delinquent behaviors. Children growing up in neighborhoods characterized by high levels of social cohesion, in which neighbors are willing to step forward in support of each other, are less likely to engage in delinquent activities (Odgers et al., 2009).

It is encouraging to find that federally funded early childhood intervention programs, designed initially to give low-income preschoolers the skills necessary to succeed in school, have far-reaching and wide effects, affecting parents as well as children and extending into adolescence. "Wraparound" early childhood intervention programs that continue into the second or third grade, as opposed to ending in kindergarten (see Chapter 8), are associated not only with improved academic performance, but also with preventing juvenile delinquency in adolescence (Reynolds et al., 2004; Smokowski et al., 2004). Children who participate in these programs have better mastery of basic skills and lower rates of grade retention. Important as both of these are, however,

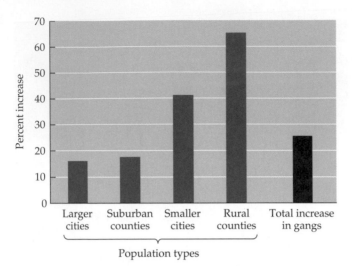

● **Figure 12.3   Increase in estimated number of gangs, from 2002 to 2007**   (After National Youth Gang Center, 2009.)

it is the impact these programs have on parents' involvement in their children's lives that is key to lowering rates of juvenile arrests. The support these programs offer families results in improved parenting practices and greater parental involvement, lessening the likelihood of antisocial behavior (Reynolds et al., 2004).

GANGS   The number of gangs has risen dramatically over the last several generations. In 1960, for instance, only 58 cities reported the presence of gangs. By 2000, gangs were present in all large cities and had spread to 86% of mid-size cities. Recent increases in the number of gangs are due primarily to their presence in smaller cities and rural counties, as can be seen in **Figure 12.3** (National Youth Gang Center, 2009).

Not only the number but also the nature of gangs has changed with time. In previous generations, gangs arose from the spontaneous associations of neighborhood males, and gang activities were primarily oriented toward defending the neighborhood territory or "turf." Membership was almost exclusively limited to males and to those of the same ethnic group. Rumbles with rival gangs defined the territories of each and gave status to gang members. The leader of the gang carried a gun, but most members did not (Kratcoski & Kratcoski, 1986). Since the 1980s, gang members have had access to sophisticated weapons and have used them freely. As one former gang member from Detroit remarked concerning gangs a generation ago,

> When I grew up we had it out with our hands. Maybe we'd steal a car and go for a ride. Now they steal a car and rip somebody off or shoot somebody. I'm afraid to walk down the street at night. I've never seen it like this. (Kratcoski & Kratcoski, 1986)

Gangs are still formed from neighborhood associations, and gang activities still involve defense of turf, but gangs are more likely to be linked with organized crime than in the past, and making money—primarily through the sale of narcotics—is one of their major activities (National Drug Intelligence Center, 2006).

If the purpose of gangs has shifted from defending turf to developing criminal enterprises, what functions do gangs serve in the lives of their members, and how might these have changed? Judy Evans and Jerome Taylor (1995), at the University of Pittsburgh, interviewed 46- to 55-year-old former gang members who participated in gangs prior to 1980 (early gangs) and 15- to 20-year-old gang members who participated in gangs since 1980 (contemporary gangs), asking them why they belonged to a gang and what their role was in the gang. For both early and contemporary gang members, the most frequently given reason for gang membership was social (for example, "I see my homies every day"). However, social reasons were far more important for early gang members than contemporary ones, who also indicated

A drug sale doesn't usually draw attention to itself. Today's gangs are more likely to be linked to organized crime and the sale of drugs than in the past.

TABLE 12.2
Reasons for Staying in Gangs, as Reported by Members of Early (Prior to 1980) and Contemporary (Since 1980) Gangs

REASON	EARLY GANGS (N=18)		CONTEMPORARY GANGS (N=30)	
	N	PERCENTAGE	N	PERCENTAGE
Career	0	0	9	30
Economic	2	11	7	23
Political	2	11	2	7
Social	14	78	12	40

Source: Evans & Taylor, 1995.

career and economic reasons ("It's how I make my money") for belonging to a gang, as shown in **Table 12.2**.

A second difference to emerge between early and contemporary gang members is in the nature of the violence they engage in. For early gang members, violence took the form of fighting, with 56% saying this had something to do with their role in the gang. In stark contrast, none of the contemporary gang members said that fighting had anything to do with what they did as a gang member. Rather, violence for these gang members took the form of shooting, with 26% indicating this as their role within the gang. By way of contrast, none of the early gang members indicated shooting as an activity they engaged in, as shown in **Table 12.3**.

Table 12.3 also reveals another striking difference between early and contemporary gangs. The former had virtually no involvement in drug-related activities, whereas 93% of the activities of contemporary gang members are drug related, 13% being involved in scouting for new members, 53% in dealing, and 27% in shooting. The corresponding percentage for each of these drug-related activities for earlier gang members is 0% (Evans & Taylor, 1995).

What attractions do gangs hold for their members? Gang membership confers a sense of identity, which is of importance in adolescence. Members dress alike and adopt unique identifying behaviors they share with their gang, as in being tattooed with gang insignia. The violence, too, can be an attraction, providing feelings of power and excitement to members. It also has been suggested that gangs serve as surrogate families, offering emotional support, protection, and a sense of belonging (Henggeler, 1989; Vigil, 1988). Research has found, for instance, that families of gang members are less cohesive, and that parents do not monitor their children's activities closely (Henggeler, 1989; Li et al., 2002). Parental absence, in the form of long work hours, family structure,

TABLE 12.3
Distribution of Roles Reported by Members of Early (Prior to 1980) and Contemporary (Since 1980) Gangs

REASON	EARLY GANGS (N=18)		CONTEMPORARY GANGS (N=30)	
	N	PERCENTAGE	N	PERCENTAGE
Fighting	10	56	0	0
Scouting	0	0	4	13
Dealing	0	0	16	53
Robbing	4	22	2	7
Shooting	0	0	8	27
None of the above	4	22	0	0

Source: Evans & Taylor, 1995.

Do violent scenes in the movies and on television desensitize adolescents to violence or make them more likely to act violently? One of the most important factors contributing to lethal violence is the accessibility of firearms.

or simple neglect, is also more common, and positive role models in general are less in evidence.

Relationships within a gang, however, are not likely to provide the support and caring that are afforded by cohesive family relationships. Jean-Marie Lyon, Scott Henggeler, and James Hall (1992) found peer relations among gang members to be less socially mature and more aggressive than those among non-gang members. Indeed, the constant need of gang members to prove themselves to maintain their status within the gang argues against emotional intimacy. Xiaoming Li and associates (2002) found gang members to experience greater levels of distress than their non-gang peers who lived in the same public housing projects, one aspect of which was feeling a lack of belongingness. This finding suggests that membership in a gang itself, given the relative lack of social support provided by its members and the continual need to prove oneself, contributes to symptoms of distress over and above the risk involved in gang activities.

YOUTH AND VIOLENCE Violence is not restricted to inner-city youth or gangs; it extends to the suburbs and to middle-income families. Among high school students, 18% indicate they had carried some type of weapon, such as a knife, club, or gun, during the past 30 days; this was truer for adolescent boys (28.5%) than girls (7.5%). At school, 27.1% reported having something of theirs stolen or deliberately damaged (CDC, 2008b). In their neighborhoods, teenagers are nearly twice as likely to be victims of a violent crime such as assault, robbery, or rape as are young adults 25 to 34 years old (Fox et al., 2005).

Across all ethnic groups, homicide involving a firearm is the second leading cause of death among adolescents. Among those 13 years old or older, 78% are killed with a firearm (CDC, 2005c, 2009; Snyder, 2004). Minority males are most at risk: Native Americans are more than twice as likely to die violently as white males their age, Hispanic males are three to four times more likely, and African American males are nine times more likely than their white counterparts to die violently.

Adolescents in all segments of society risk becoming desensitized to violence. Television programs, video games, and movies model graphic acts of violence as well as provide violent role models with whom adolescents can identify (Browne & Hamilton-Giachritsis, 2005). An anecdote offers an interesting, if chilling, example of the way in which television and the movies contribute to our images of violence. My niece reported she had recently been in a bank when it was held up by two armed men. She noted that on hearing "Everyone down," people knew immediately what to do—lie face down on the floor, not crouch or kneel, and not look at the robbers' faces—because they had all seen this on the screen. However, after the robbers left, no one knew what to do—the TV and movie cameras always cut to the getaway and chase.

One of the most important factors contributing to lethal violence is the accessibility of firearms (**Figure 12.4**). Not only handguns but sophisticated semiautomatic weapons are readily available to those who would have them. The most frequently used weapon in the United States is a gun, accounting for nearly 80% of homicide victims 10 to 24 years of age (CDC,

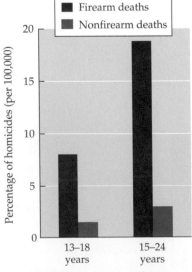

● **Figure 12.4 Rate of firearm and nonfirearm homicides committed by adolescents and young adults** (After CDC, 2005c.)

TABLE 12.4
International Comparisons of Firearms Regulations and Gun Homicides

COUNTRY	LICENSING OF GUN OWNERS	REGISTRATION OF FIREARMS	OTHER	GUN HOMICIDES (PER 100,000)	GUN SUICIDES (PER 100,000)	TOTAL INTENTIONAL GUN DEATH RATE (PER 100,000)
Japan	Yes	Yes	Prohibits handguns with few exceptions	0.03	0.04	0.07
England/ Wales	Yes	Yes	Prohibits handguns	0.07	0.33	0.4
Germany	Yes	Yes		0.21	1.23	1.44
Canada	Yes	Yes		0.60	3.35	3.95
France	Yes	Yes, except sporting rifles		0.55	4.93	5.48
U.S.	In some states	Handguns in some states	Some weapons in some states	6.24	7.23	13.47

Source: Cukier, 2001.

2005c). Studies tracking the relationship between firearms and homicides in the United States find these to be predictably related; the rate of homicides by youth that involve firearms is six times that of those not involving a gun (CDC, 2005c). Further support for the relationship between accessibility of firearms and gun deaths comes from international comparisons of gun homicides in countries with strong firearms regulations with gun homicides in the United States, a country with weak regulations (**Table 12.4**).

Social factors contributing to violence cannot be discounted. The poverty and hopelessness confronting inner-city youth, their daily exposure to community and family violence, and the reality of unemployment and racism for minority adolescents are powerfully related to violence. In the end, however, some adolescents choose violence and others do not. Most who engage in violent crimes have law-abiding siblings with whom they have eaten at the same family table and shared relatives, friends, and life experiences (**Box 12.2**).

Internalizing Problems

The behavior of some adolescents, rather than potentially harming others, more directly affects themselves. When adolescents turn their problems inward, as in depression, suicide, or eating disorders, we speak of internalizing problems, discussed in this section. The abuse of drugs by adolescents can be either an externalizing or an internalizing problem, and is covered in a subsequent section.

DEPRESSION   Emotions color experience and give meaning to life. For most individuals they are anchored in reality, tethered to the situations that prompt them. Some individuals are pulled past these to an inner world of thoughts and feelings that bear little resemblance to the situations that occasion them. These individuals suffer from **affective disorders**, disturbances that affect their mood. Mood is an enduring emotional state that varies along a continuum from **depression** to elation. Individuals who suffer from affective disorders live much of their lives at the extremes of this continuum.

affective disorders   Disorders whose primary symptoms reflect a disturbance of mood, such as depression.

depression   An affective disorder that may take a number of forms, all of which are characterized by a disturbance of mood.

BOX 12.2   In More Depth

Columbine: The Imaginary Audience and a Real Stage

By Michael Wapner

The columbine is a flower. But for many of us the word no longer evokes images of blossoms. Instead, we associate it with students cowering under desks or fleeing for their lives as two of their fellow students hunted them down, eventually killing 12 and a teacher, at Columbine High School in 1999. We have other names that evoke images of violent death—Dallas, Waco, Oklahoma City. But Columbine doesn't belong to that group. Columbine is the name of a school, in Littleton, Colorado, and the images it evokes—of both killers and killed—are those of adolescents. Tragically, Columbine has come to stand for a new collection of events—shootings in which students murder other students at school.

In one sense the image of school as a place of violent death is all out of proportion. Less than 1% of homicides involving school-age children occur in or near school (CDC, 2005d). On the other hand, 1% is an alarming figure given the circumstances that have given rise to it.

How can we begin to understand this rash of deadly violence? Can we even group into a single category the events at Columbine High School in Colorado, and at schools in West Paducah, Kentucky, in Jonesboro, Arkansas, and Springfield, Oregon? A number of elements are certainly common to all, but they seem few indeed, perhaps because of their very ordinariness. The killers were all males, all were teenagers (as were almost all of their victims), all carried out their deadly acts at school, and all used guns to do it. Also common to these events was what was missing: the conditions or characteristics one might expect to find in the lives of violent youth. In none of these cases do we find uncaring or incompetent parents, substance abuse, domestic violence, poverty, or a crime-infested environment. Columbine, like the other shootings, defies easy answers to our questions.

We are unlikely to find a single cause for events such as those that took place at Columbine. Parenting, for instance, is only one of many influences in a child's life and can be expected to interact with many other influences, such as the child's own temperament, the changing developmental challenges faced by a child at different points in life, and the larger culture into which that child steps. This may be especially true for children who by temperament are less easygoing, more nega-

tive in their moods, or less flexible in adapting to change (Garbarino, 1999).

Temperament can similarly interact with another environment, that of school. Examples of friendly, nurturing support among students are to be found everywhere —but so are bullying, teasing, name-calling, and petty exclusiveness. Unfortunately, boys who already feel resentful and unaccepted are much more likely to receive and notice the latter. If one expects to be hurt, there is no place like a schoolyard or cafeteria to have those expectations fulfilled. Adolescents with extremely sensitive temperaments, either violently excessive or coldly deficient, do not easily form friendships or achieve a sense of belonging, making it even more difficult for them to buffer themselves from rejection. But there are other contexts in which such boys may come together—in clubs organized around hate (e.g., neo-Nazi or racist groups), violence (e.g., guns, martial arts), or provocative deviance (e.g., outrageous dress). Or they may find one or two other youths with similar outlooks. The affiliation of several resentful, marginal young men who encourage each other to act out their violent fantasies is particularly dangerous.

Bumper stickers may say that the best revenge is living well. But that's not what Rambo says. And that's not what thousands of movies, television programs, and video games say. Culture is the medium that gives form to feelings. Marginal, hyper-vigilant young men have plenty of feelings. And when the forms provided by the culture feature automatic weapons and high explosives to "blow away" your antagonist, the mix is dangerous. Adolescents are steeped in violence, not only in the commercial images of films, television, and song lyrics, but also in the reality of their lives, from verbal and physical skirmishes at school to nightly statistics on the evening news.

The United States leads other nations in homicides to a staggering degree (see **Figure**). Of all the factors contributing to the lethal nature of violence in this nation, the most important of these is the accessibility of firearms. Individuals are not necessarily more aggressive in the United States than in other countries, but they do have readier access to guns, a difference that can be lethal. A comparison of two demographically similar cities, Seattle and Vancouver, conducted over six years, offers strong support for the position that accessibility of firearms is causally related to the greater incidence of homicide in the United States. Seattle had virtually no restrictions governing gun possession and use, whereas Vancouver had many.

BOX
12.2   *continued*

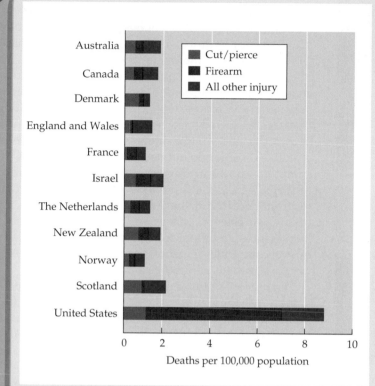

Deaths per 100,000 population

be drawn to their violence, these students may have used the media in an attempt to become celebrities, even going so far as to imagine that famous directors would fight for the chance to make a movie of their story.

If true, this concern with celebrity reflects another quality of adolescent thinking—the tendency to act for an imaginary audience. Adolescents' capacity for abstract thought enables them to think not only about their own thoughts but about the thoughts of others as well. Psychologist and author David Elkind suggests that adolescents frequently lack perspective about what concerns them and what concerns others, leading them to believe that everyone is as interested in them as they are and that others are continually noticing them. The imaginary audience gives adolescents an exaggerated feeling of self-consciousness and self-importance.

What factors contribute to school shootings such as at Columbine? None of the ones we have considered, either separately or in some complex mix, explains why adolescents such as these act as they do while other adolescents, sharing many of their experiences and backgrounds, do not. We frequently think we understand youth violence, at least with respect to those instances in which adolescents come from bad homes or otherwise bad environments. Yet even "predictable" violence such as this leaves us with few explanations when we are asked to consider the many nonviolent youth from those very same homes and neighborhoods who lead caring, disciplined, and considerate lives. The actions of these latter youth are unrecorded, their names absent from police blotters or reports on the evening news. Contributing factors offer no more complete explanation, in other words, for violence that fits the mold than for violence that breaks it. In each case, one is left to explain why a handful of adolescents acted as they did, while others did not.

Despite similar rates of conviction for violent crime in each of the cities, rates of homicide were nearly twice as high in Seattle (Sloan et al., 1988).

A last factor to consider in school shootings involves the characteristics of adolescent thought. In particular, cognitive development enables adolescents to react intellectually and emotionally in new ways. Adolescents' ability to interpret the actions of others enables them to assign more than the obvious meaning to any social encounter. Further, their heightened awareness of themselves makes it likely that they will relate these actions to themselves. As a consequence, adolescents are more likely to experience emotions such as moodiness, depression, or resentfulness than are children or adults.

In the case of Columbine, the motivation seems to have been not just retaliation, but also a desire for celebrity. Why wouldn't students who said they were enraged at athletes who had taunted them place their bombs in the locker room? FBI agent Mark Holstlaw suggests that instead of revenge, they were looking for a way to be famous. This particular shooting may have been influenced by the media, but not in the way typically assumed, which presumes the media to be the cause of the violence. Instead, knowing that the media would

Sources: After Goldstein et al., 1999 and Sloan et al., 1988; Figure after Fingerhut et al., 1998.

Nearly half of all adolescents report experiencing some of the symptoms that characterize depression: sadness, crying spells, pessimism, and feelings of unworthiness.

major depressive disorder
A period of severe depression requiring hospitalization or other treatment.

masked depression
Depression that manifests itself in ways other than depressed mood, for example, agitation, or the inability to sleep.

Feelings of sadness and loneliness become relatively common by mid-adolescence. For some, these feelings can occur frequently enough to be disruptive at times; over one-third of adolescent girls and nearly one-fifth of boys report being bothered by feelings of sadness or hopelessness (CDC, 2008b). A much smaller percentage of adolescents, 4-6%, experience a **major depressive disorder**, an episode of depression which lasts several weeks or more and is characterized by depressed mood as well as cognitive and behavioral symptoms, such as difficulty concentrating, loss of pleasure, slowed speech and movements, sleepiness, loss of appetite, and weight changes (**Table 12.5**). Adolescents with this disorder do not necessarily experience all of these symptoms, however most experience a sizeable proportion of them (APA, 1994; Vitiello, 2009). Adolescents who suffer from depression share with adult depressives feelings of low self-esteem, pervasive sadness, hopelessness, and helplessness. A self-defeating cycle exists in which low self-esteem contributes to depression, which in turn fuels further negative feelings about the self.

Depression is often masked in early adolescence. Several symptoms signal **masked depression**, the most frequent being fatigue, poor concentration, and hypochondriasis (excessive concern with illness or health). Continual fatigue can reflect inner struggles with feelings that adolescents cannot put to rest or talk about with others. Similarly, difficulties in concentration can result from concerns they do not yet feel secure enough to articulate, and preoccupations with their health, or a seeming lack of it, may reflect fears of inadequacy or incompetence.

Each of these symptoms can be mistakenly interpreted as a natural part of adolescence. Fatigue is expected, given the accelerated growth of puberty and the demands of school, friends, and family. Similarly, poor concentration can easily be mistaken for problems with schoolwork ranging from boredom to being overwhelmed, and excessive concern with one's body is natural, given the changes that take place during puberty. Treatments that take into consideration the underlying source of an adolescent's depression will be more effective in combating these symptoms than those that are directed at the symptoms themselves. Irving Weiner (1980) has suggested that adolescents may have difficulty admitting to feelings of inadequacy and still accomplish the developmental tasks they face, such as achieving emotional independence, finding a sense of self, and developing

TABLE 12.5
Symptoms of Adolescents with Major Depressive Disorder
Depressed mood (such as feelings of sadness or emptiness)
Reduced interest in activities that used to be enjoyed
Sleep disturbances (either not being able to sleep well or sleeping too much)
Loss of energy or a significant reduction in energy level
Difficulty concentrating, holding a conversation, paying attention, or making decisions that used to be made fairly easily
Suicidal thoughts or intentions

Source: American Psychiatric Association, 1994.

intimate relationships. Any one of these would be difficult under the best of conditions and can be impossible with feelings of inadequacy. Early adolescents may also be more caught up in doing things than in reflecting about them. In either case, depression, or attempts to keep it at bay, are likely to at first assume a physical form in early adolescence.

Treatment of Depression   Depression in adolescents is commonly treated either with antidepressants, or psychotherapy, or some combination of both. The antidepressants most commonly used with adolescents, as with adults, are a group known as SSRIs (selective serotonin reuptake inhibitors). The most common psychotherapeutic approach is cognitive-behavioral therapy (CBT). This approach has been found to be more effective than others, costing less and achieving results more quickly (Weisz et al., 2009). Cognitive-behavioral therapy, in contrast to psychodynamic approaches, focuses on the present— on the adolescent's behavior. The goal is to alleviate symptoms, and thereby treat the disorder. Adolescents are shown how to become mindful of negative thinking ("I always mess up," "It's never going to change"), and to replace these thoughts with more accurate appraisals of themselves and events. They also learn problem-solving and social skills (Kennard et al., 2009). The use of SSRIs alone has been found to increase the risk of both suicidal thoughts and attempts in adolescents, a risk which *already* is present due to their depression. However, when the use of these antidepressants is combined with cognitive-behavioral therapy, this risk is reduced (Van Voorhees et al., 2008; Vitiello, 2009).

Recent meta-analyses of the effectiveness of antidepressants suggest that a sizeable component of the treatment effect can be attributed to a placebo effect, in which the effect of the medication depends on the patient's belief that it will bring relief (Kirsch et al., 2002; Vitiello, 2009). Furthermore, the effectiveness of antidepressants has been found to vary with the severity of the depression. Although individuals who are severely depressed can benefit substantially from their use, for individuals who are mildly or moderately depressed, antidepressants may have little, or no, more benefit than a placebo (Fournier et al., 2010). Even so, those using an antidepressant should not stop taking the drug, since discontinuing a medication without medical supervision can have serious effects.

SUICIDE   A surprising number of adolescents report thinking about suicide. In a national survey of U.S. high school students, 14% said they had thought seriously about attempting suicide at some point during the past year, 11% even making a plan, and 7% actually attempted suicide. Two percent of these attempts were sufficiently serious to require treatment by a doctor or a nurse (CDC, 2008b). Even though suicide is the third leading cause of death among adolescents, it is not as common as it is among middle-aged adults and the elderly.

Males are more likely than females to complete a suicide, despite the fact that females attempt suicide twice as often as males. In part, this difference can be traced to the different methods chosen by males and females. Males are most likely to use a gun or attempt to hang themselves, both of which are more immediately lethal than ingesting harmful substances, the method most commonly used by females. Among completed suicides, for both sexes, using a gun is the most frequent method. Although at first glance these gender differences would seem to suggest less ambivalence about dying among males, other factors are probably more important. Males, in general, are more impulsive and violent than females, qualities that are reflected in the methods they choose. Impulsivity may be a critical factor in most suicides, and males, because they are likely to choose a violent method, will complete more suicides. Also, females may be able to seek out and use interpersonal supports more easily than males, who typically find it more difficult to reveal neediness or ask for help (CDC, 2008b; Garland & Zigler, 1993).

Ethnic differences exist as well in suicidal thoughts and behavior. White adolescents are less likely to attempt suicide than African Americans, and both groups are less likely to attempt suicide than Hispanic adolescents (CDC, 2008b). Among all ethnic groups, the rate of suicide is highest for Native Americans. However, large differences exist between different tribes. As a rule, tribes that are more traditional tend to have lower suicide rates, perhaps because they provide a greater sense of community and their members experience more support (Wyche et al., 1990).

Warning Signs and Risk Factors Although every case of suicide is unique, a number of common warning signs exist. These include sudden changes in behavior, changes in patterns of sleeping or eating, loss of interest in usual activities or withdrawal from others, experiencing a humiliating event, feelings of guilt or hopelessness, an inability to concentrate, talk of suicide, or giving away one's most important possessions (U.S. Department of Health and Human Services, 2005). The presence of any one of these is a cause for concern; the presence of several is a clear signal that an adolescent may be in danger.

Several factors are associated with an increased risk of suicide. Most of these characterize the person at risk, although some, such as substance abuse or exposure to suicidal behavior, can also involve elements of the family or the larger culture. Even though most suicides are associated with one or more of these risk factors, about one-third of youth suicides are associated with no risk factors at all. Blumenthal and Kupfer (1988) classify risk factors into potentially overlapping domains. As the overlap among domains increases, so does the risk of suicide, as illustrated in **Figure 12.5**. According to this approach,

the breakup of a relationship might be a final humiliating experience that triggers a depressive episode in a young person with a family

● **Figure 12.5** **Factors contributing to suicide** (After Blumenthal & Kupfer, 1988.)

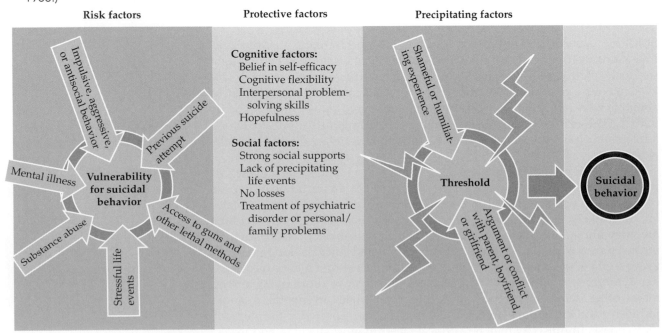

history of affective disorder. Such an individual may also have poor social supports, which interact with the other identified risk factors to increase the individual's vulnerability for suicide. (p. 4)

Adolescents who are alienated, delinquent, depressed, or suicidal follow a different developmental path than most. But all adolescents share the need to be listened to and supported by those who are closest to them.

Cognitive factors that help to protect adolescents from the threat of suicide are feelings of self-efficacy, problem-solving skills, and hopefulness. Similarly, social factors decreasing the risk of suicide are the presence of strong social supports, the lack of precipitating life events, and getting treatment or help for personal or family problems.

Among the most serious risk factors for suicide are depression and having made a prior attempt. Anywhere from 50% to 80% of all completed suicides by adolescents have been preceded by a previous attempt (Shafii et al., 1985). Suicidal remarks or other warning signs among such adolescents assume added significance. In addition to a previous suicide attempt and depression, other significant risk factors are substance abuse, and aggressive or disruptive behaviors (APA, 2005).

A common cultural stereotype of adolescent suicide attempts holds that these are shallow and impulsive bids for attention. Neither assumption is true. Adolescents who are suicidal are in personal pain and have usually sought a number of solutions to their present problems. Suicidal adolescents usually attempt to communicate their distress in a number of ways, and thoughts of suicide are often a last resort. The poem in **Box 12.3** is a poignant illustration of this point.

BOX 12.3 | **In More Depth**

A Poem Written by a 15-Year-Old Boy Two Years Before Committing Suicide

TO SANTA CLAUS AND LITTLE SISTERS

Once…he wrote a poem.
And called it "Chops."
Because that was the name of his dog, and that's what it was all about.
And the teacher gave him an "A"
And a gold star.
And his mother hung it on the kitchen door, and read
it to all his aunts…
Once…he wrote another poem.
And he called it "Question Marked Innocence."
Because that was the name of his grief and that's what it was all about.

And the professor gave him an "A"
And a strange and steady look.
And his mother never hung it on the kitchen door,
because he never let her see it…
Once, at 3 a.m….he tried another poem …
And he called it absolutely nothing, because that's
what it was all about.
And he gave himself an "A"
And a slash on each damp wrist,
And hung it on the bathroom door because he couldn't reach the kitchen.

Source: Lee and Ross, pers. comm.

Adolescents who attempt or commit suicide commonly experience more life stress, more losses, and more changes within the family than those who do not. Frequently a humiliating event precipitates the suicide attempt, such as a crisis or an interpersonal problem involving parents or peers. Family life is more likely to be chaotic, relationships with parents are frequently problematic, and parental strife is more common. Suicidal adolescents generally have fewer social supports and personal resources while facing these added stresses (Blumenthal & Kupfer, 1988).

The availability of lethal methods, particularly firearms, is also a factor affecting suicide rates. Over half of all youth who commit suicide use a firearm (APA, 2005).

Counseling and Prevention   The importance of communication cannot be stressed too much. Caring, open and supportive efforts to address problems on the part of those closest to the adolescent are vital. Yet important as these efforts are, they should never replace professional help.

Frequently suicidal adolescents communicate with their peers. Frequently, too, peers are uninformed concerning warning signs of suicidal intent. Only half of one sample of adolescents knew, for instance, that remarks about wanting to die, seeming worried, or having problems in school or with a relationship might be related to suicidal behavior. Less than 20% knew that adolescents who are suicidal are likely to threaten they will kill themselves. Even more alarming was the finding that over 40% of these adolescents believed that such behaviors were not likely to be related to suicide (Norton et al., 1989).

What advice is there to give to those who fear that an adolescent close to them may be suicidal? Suicidal adolescents communicate their pain to those they are closest to. It is important to pick up on these signals. One should not be afraid to openly ask the adolescent if she or he has thought of self-destructive behavior. Listening to what the adolescent has to say can be painful, but it is vitally important. Attempting to deny the reality of the adolescent's pain through false assurances that everything will be okay only communicates that one has not heard the pain or the hopelessness. Serious thoughts of suicide require professional attention. Loving concern, though important in its own right, is not a substitute. Professional help should be obtained immediately.

The most effective programs help suicidal adolescents face truths in their lives and have these work for them. Sometimes the truth can be as simple as learning how to say something and then make it happen. The approaches that work best are brief, crisis-oriented, and give adolescents skills they can apply in their ongoing relationships (Kerfoot et al., 1995).

To be effective, programs must reach the adolescents who need them. Many adolescents who attempt suicide do not show up for therapy, or they drop out before they complete it. One study found that 20% did not keep any of the appointments they made, another 19% dropped out during the initial assessment sessions, and nearly one-third more discontinued the program before they finished (Trautman & Rotheram, 1986). Given the chaotic home lives of many of these adolescents, completing anything, even breakfast, can be an accomplishment. One program found it helpful to give adolescents who had been hospitalized for a suicide attempt a token that would give them readmission to the hospital on a "no questions asked" basis, should circumstances become intolerable (Cotgrove et al., 1995).

The most effective treatments are highly structured programs that train adolescents in skills they can apply at home and in school. Most also teach adolescents to attribute their successes to their own efforts; they aim at getting them to a place where they can say, "I did that and I did it well."

Usually counselors help adolescents identify problem areas and generate alternative solutions. When adolescents can think of alternative solutions to conflicts and predict the effects of acting one way or another, they can cope more effectively. Even if the other person reacts negatively, being able to predict a response puts adolescents less "at the effect of" the other person. If adolescents can also anticipate their own feelings about negative reactions, they are in an even better place to control these feelings. In a sense, conflict management is a bit like surfing: You need to stay just behind the crest of the wave to keep it from crashing down on you.

Because many suicide attempts are precipitated by conflict with a parent, treatment that includes the family will almost always be the most effective. This type of therapy shifts the focus from the adolescent to family interactions that preceded the suicide attempt. Improving communication within the family is usually an important element to intervention programs (Kerfoot et al., 1995).

EATING DISORDERS   With physical maturation, adolescents experience increases in both height and weight. Some adolescents mistake the natural changes of maturation for unwanted fat; others, perhaps unsure whether they are ready for adulthood, attempt to delay its appearance by literally starving themselves. Still others turn to food when stressed and become obese. We will look at eating disorders next: bulimia, anorexia, and overweight. Anorexia and bulimia are more common among female adolescents than among males; overweight is more common among males (CDC, 2004c).

With respect to the first two disorders, adolescent females today face a standard of beauty that is considerably thinner than in the past. Models of feminine beauty—whether actresses, performers, or individuals advertising products—are thin indeed, compared to their curvaceous counterparts of generations past. The flapper era of the 1920s was the only other time during the past century when the popular images of women were as thin as they are at present. Developmentalists note with some alarm that eating disorders became epidemic among young women then and warn that, with respect to eating disorders, history may be repeating itself.

Bulimia and Anorexia   **Bulimia** is characterized by binge eating, consuming large amounts of food in a short time, usually in less than two hours. Binges are usually accompanied by the fear that one cannot stop oneself and are followed by self-deprecating thoughts and compensatory behaviors to prevent gaining weight, such as self-induced vomiting or the use of laxatives.

Anorexia is a disorder in which individuals severely limit their intake of food, weighing less than 85% of what would be expected for their age and sex, have a distorted perception of their body weight, and are fearful of gaining weight. Severe weight loss has mental and emotional, as well as physical effects, and anorexics can be apathetic and irritable. Due to the loss of body fat, anorexics frequently become amenorrhenic, ceasing to have menstrual periods.

Most bulimics are aware that their eating patterns are abnormal, and most make continued attempts to lose weight through highly restrictive diets, self-induced vomiting, and use of laxatives or diuretics. Anorexics deny that they have any problem and reject help (APA, 2000).

Among high school students, somewhat less than 5% become bulimic (CDC, 2004d; Stice et al., 1998); the percent-

bulimia   An eating disorder characterized by bingeing (excessive or compulsive eating) and then purging (ridding the body of food, such as self-induced vomiting); more common in females.

anorexia   An eating disorder characterized by severely limiting the intake of food; more common in females.

Anorexics severely limit their intake of food; however, they have a distorted body image. Even though they look dangerously emaciated to friends and family, to themselves, they still do not look thin enough.

age of those who are anorexic is even smaller. Whereas anorexia is more common in young adolescents, bulimia is more common in older adolescents and young women.

Although bulimics can be of any weight, they are rarely fat (Ledoux et al., 1993). Usually their weight fluctuates widely, sometimes by as much as 20 to 30 pounds over a relatively brief period. Anorexics are excessively thin, frequently losing up to 25% of their body weight.

Anorexia and bulimia are closely related disorders. Both involve an obsession with food and a morbid fear of being fat. Both also share an obsessive need to be thin. Many anorexics engage in bingeing and purging, and many bulimics start with an initial anorexic phase. Most bulimics usually begin self-induced vomiting a year or two after they start bingeing. Due to the large numbers of calories bulimics consume, they can maintain their weight only by alternating binges with highly restrictive diets or by purging what they have eaten. Anorexics have a distorted body image and are not likely to seek help even when they become emaciated through self-starvation (Stice, 2002). Bulimics are likely to live with the disorder for a number of years before seeking help. During that time they suffer physical as well as emotional symptoms, such as fatigue, weakness, and constipation. Dental caries and erosion of the enamel of the teeth are also common from frequent contact with stomach acids through self-induced vomiting.

Bulimics often have low self-esteem and a history of depression (Ledoux et al., 1993; Zaider et al., 2000). These adolescents are likely to feel self-conscious around others, be sensitive to rejection, and have difficulty expressing their feelings directly. Both bulimics and anorexics are likely to have high standards and expectations for themselves and to be overly critical when they fail to meet them (Polivy & Herman, 2002).

Frequencies of bulimia and anorexia differ with ethnicity, most likely because body type preferences differ among ethnic groups. Anorexia is less common among African American adolescents than among European American adolescents. Bulimia also is less common among African Americans, although not among Hispanic adolescents (Granillo et al., 2005; Mulholland & Mintz, 2001). Both disorders require professional intervention. Each is a serious threat to health and reflects underlying emotional problems that need treatment (Tobias, 1988).

Eating Disorders and Family Conflict   Amy Swarr and Maryse Richards (1996) followed a sample of adolescent girls over a two-year period and found that adolescents who enjoyed close positive relationships with their parents had healthier attitudes both toward their weight and toward eating. Eating disorders, when they occur, hide deeper, underlying problems in which family experiences play an important role. Four characteristics of families that lead to the expression of psychological problems as physical symptoms frequently characterize the families of anorexics and bulimics (Minuchin et al., 1978; Tobias, 1988). Enmeshment exists when boundaries between family members are not clear. In enmeshed families, everyone is involved in everyone else's life, making it difficult to be independent or autonomous. Overprotective families show an inappropriate concern for the welfare of family members. Families characterized by rigidity have a need to maintain the status quo and are unable to face change. These qualities make adolescence, a time of many changes, especially difficult. Finally, families in which there is inadequate conflict resolution avoid conflict, with the result that differences are never cleanly resolved and members continue to impinge on each other. An eating disorder may be the only way in which adolescents from such families can gain a sense of maintaining control over their lives (Tobias, 1988). **Box 12.4** describes research studying the families of girls with eating disorders.

BOX 12.4 Research Focus

Bias and Blind Controls: Eating Disorders

"You always shut yourself off in your room," her mother said, somewhat angrily.

"I just want to be left alone," she pleaded, the hint of a whine in her voice. The teenager was 17, and her dark eyes communicated a sulky resentment.

The research assistant on the other side of the one-way mirror quickly coded the girl's response: "asserting," "appeasing," "separating," and "interdependent."

"Some message!" he thought, as he watched the family in front of him. The girl was trim, neither overweight nor underweight. He couldn't tell from her appearance which type of disorder she suffered from; he only knew that this project was about adolescents with eating disorders. For all he knew, she could be part of the control group.

Why keep this graduate student in the dark about the families he is observing? Why not assume that the more he knows, the better he'll understand and more accurately record their behavior? Investigators have found from painful experience that their expectations all too often influence what they see—sometimes even causing them to read things into a person's behavior that just aren't there. Their expectancies can bias, or systematically alter, the results of the study.

Whenever investigators know the condition of which a subject is part, they can bias the outcome of the research either by unconsciously treating subjects in that condition differently or by interpreting—that is, scoring—their behavior differently. If, for example, this graduate student believed that the parents of girls with a certain type of eating disorder were harsh and demanding, he might read hostility into their remarks even when it wasn't there, or perhaps be less friendly with them when introducing them to the experiment. The latter difference might lead to tensions in family interactions that otherwise would not be present, thus unintentionally confirming initial expectations.

Investigators can eliminate experimenter bias by conducting the experiment "blind." Unlike a single-blind control procedure, in which only the subjects are unaware of which condition they have been exposed to, in a double-blind control, such as the one described here, the experimenter also is ignorant of which condition each subject is in. In this way, the experimenter's expectations cannot contribute to any of the observed differences. Double-blind controls are frequently used in drug studies in which it is necessary to control for the doctor's as well as the patients' expectations that they will get better if they take an experimental medication. In double-blind drug studies, all subjects are given a pill, but half receive a placebo, or sugar pill.

Let's get back to the other side of the one-way mirror. Do families of girls with different eating disorders interact in characteristically different ways? Laura Humphrey (1989) observed 74 adolescent girls with their parents. Sixteen were anorexic, 16 were bulimic, 18 were both bulimic and anorexic, and 24 were normal controls. All of those in the first three categories were patients who had been hospitalized long enough so that one could not distinguish the anorexics by their appearance.

Parents of anorexics were both more nurturing and comforting and more ignoring and neglecting than were those of bulimics or controls. The anorexic girls were the most submissive of the group when they were with their parents. Bulimics and their parents were more likely to engage in mutual grumbling and blaming and to exchange disparaging remarks. Interactions of normal controls and their parents were characterized more by helping, protecting, trusting, and simple enjoyment of each other.

These findings underscore the importance of treating the family as a whole, as well as working individually with the adolescent when treating eating disorders. Most eating disorders are associated with a pattern of disturbed family interactions.

Source: After Humphrey, 1989.

OVERWEIGHT   Physical appearance is perhaps never more important than during adolescence. Body image contributes significantly to self-image for most adolescents. Those who are **overweight** (see Chapter 3) tend to have less positive self-images and lower self-esteem than adolescents of average weight, and also place themselves at risk for chronic health problems (Miller & Downey, 1999; CDC, 2009b). Over one-third of 12- to 19-year-olds in the

overweight   Individuals are considered to be overweight when their weight is at or above the 95th percentile for their body mass index.

U.S. are overweight or obese (Ogden et al., 2009). This increase from previous decades reflects a global trend not only among youth but also adults (Wadden et al., 2002).

A number of factors are most likely responsible for this trend, among the most important being changes in eating habits and in patterns of physical activity (CDC, 2004c; Troiano & Flegal, 1998). With respect to eating habits, a greater reliance on fast foods, which are higher in fats and sugars and lower in dietary fiber, and a tendency to snack more frequently throughout the day have led to an increase in the average daily energy intake. This increase has gone hand in hand with a decrease in physical activity, or in the amount of energy actually expended. As a consequence, the resulting excess energy is stored as fat.

Additionally, the eating patterns of overweight adolescents differ from those who are of average weight. Overweight adolescents are more likely to eat irregularly, missing meals and snacking instead. These habits make it difficult to maintain a balance between hunger and satiation. They are also more likely to eat rapidly, to eat somewhat larger portions, and to eat food that is denser in calories (Wadden et al., 2002). But perhaps the biggest difference between overweight adolescents and those of average weight is in how active they are, not how much they eat. Overweight adolescents are considerably less active than their peers of average weight and thus less likely to burn off the excess calories they take in.

The relationship between overweight and inactivity highlights the importance of exercise in weight reduction programs. Exercise increases the body's metabolism, allowing the body to burn excess calories more rapidly; in moderate amounts, exercise also depresses appetite. Dieting alone can have paradoxical effects, frequently causing a preoccupation with food, which in turn can prompt reactive overeating. Ellen Satter (1988) recommends programs that incorporate procedures to foster a reliance on internal cues rather than on external constraints, such as counting calories and diets. The latter force one to continually think about food and ways of avoiding it.

Adolescents attempting to lose weight often have unrealistic expectations. Many view their weight as central to all of their problems and expect that once they lose weight, their problems will be solved—they will become popular, make the team, and so forth. When their problems do not roll away with the pounds, adolescents can become frustrated and fall off their diets. The most successful programs are multifaceted. The success of a weight control program for adolescents almost always depends on successfully integrating the family into the treatment program (McVey et al., 2002). As with bulimia and anorexia, the condition of being overweight is often a symptom of underlying conflicts within the family.

Adolescents and Drugs

As Ferris Bueller says, "Life moves pretty fast. If you don't stop and look around once in a while, you could miss it." He's right. If anything, it's faster now than ever before: instant messaging, "tweets" and blogs, 24-hour markets, fast foods, and five-lane expressways. Stimulants, tranquilizers, sedatives, and alcohol fit neatly into the pace of our lives—they instantaneously pick us up, settle us down, mellow us out, or just blur the edges.

Today's adolescents expect fast results, and drugs are part of society's response to that expectation. Millions of people in the United States find it impossible to get started in the morning without coffee or a cigarette, or to relax in the evening without a drink. Millions more take medication for pain, pills to sleep, laxatives to correct faulty diets, pills to suppress appetites, and vitamin supplements when they fail to eat enough. Adolescents see quick pick-me-ups and instant remedies modeled everywhere around them. It is little wonder that by their senior year in high school, a majority of adolescents have experimented with drugs. The drugs adolescents most frequently try are the ones most frequently found in their homes—alcohol and cigarettes. Three-quarters of high school seniors have used alcohol and 50% have smoked cigarettes. The only other substance that is tried by a substantial percentage of adolescents by their senior year is marijuana, 38% experimenting with this at least once. Even fewer adolescents, just over one in 10, experiment with any drug other than marijuana (Johnston et al., 2009).

The drugs adolescents are first likely to use are the ones they find at home, such as alcohol with these adolescents.

Adolescents try drugs for many reasons, of course; the prevalence of drugs in society is just one of them. Adolescence itself is a time of experimentation, and many adolescents explore substances as well as roles and ideas. Part of the attraction of legal drugs such as cigarettes and alcohol is that they are used by adults; when adolescents use them, they feel more adult. Also, advertisements make their use look glamorous. Many adolescents experience peer pressure to use substances, and countless other adolescents use substances to boost low self-esteem, dull pain, feel more confident, or compensate for poor social skills. Like any quick remedy, the promise far exceeds the payoff, and with some substances, even casual experimentation carries substantial risk.

Our discussion of drugs follows their pattern of use by adolescents. We will look first at alcohol and cigarettes and then at marijuana—the three most commonly used substances.

What Is Dependence?

Drug addiction and **drug dependence** are interchangeable terms. Both refer to a physical dependence on a substance. Not all drugs lead to dependence; one could take an aspirin a day for months or years with no such effect (although there might be other effects), and many individuals are dependent on prescribed drugs for their health. With respect to substance abuse, however, the drug must be **psychoactive**: one that is self-administered, that alters one's mood, and that comes to control behavior in such a way that one is no longer free not to use it (Surgeon General's Report, 1988). Dependence on a drug always involves developing a tolerance for it; the body requires increased amounts of the drug to achieve the same effect. Dependence also results in withdrawal symptoms whenever use is discontinued. Drug dependence can interfere with school, work, and relationships (**Box 12.5**) (APA, 1994).

Alcohol

Alcohol is typically the first drug adolescents try, and 65% do so before they reach high school (CDC, 2004d). Many people do not think of **alcohol** as a drug because its use is so embedded in the context of everyday life, but it is a powerful central nervous system (CNS) depressant, loosening inhibitions. As a result, adolescents are likely to become more talkative, feel more confident,

drug dependence Physical dependence on a substance, such that one develops a tolerance and experiences withdrawal when use is discontinued; also known as drug addiction.

psychoactive A drug that alters mood.

alcohol A drug that functions as a central nervous system depressant.

In More Depth

Criteria for Drug Dependence

Drug dependence is present when at least three of the following seven criteria are present:

1. Development of tolerance so that more of the substance is needed to achieve the same effect.
2. Physical and/or cognitive withdrawal symptoms if use of the substance is discontinued.
3. Use of the substance in larger amounts or over a longer period than was intended.
4. A persistent desire or unsuccessful attempts to cut down or control substance use.
5. Significant amounts of time devoted to obtaining and using the substance and recovering from its use.
6. Giving up or reducing important social, occupational, or recreational activities because of substance use.
7. Continuing to use the substance in spite of knowing that it contributes to a psychological or physical problem (such as cocaine-induced depression or an ulcer aggravated by alcohol).

Source: After American Psychiatric Association, 1994.

and feel more at ease socially after having a drink. However, as blood alcohol level rises, activities controlled by the central nervous system are increasingly affected; thinking becomes disorganized and reactions slow. Even small amounts of alcohol, depending on the adolescent, can be enough to affect activities requiring coordination and judgment.

Despite, or perhaps because of, its powerful effects, many high school students (47%) drink with some regularity. Just over one-quarter of high school students (26%) are likely to have engaged in heavy drinking, having five or more drinks in a row, within the last month (CDC, 2008b). Adolescents need not be chronic drinkers for alcohol to carry the potential for serious harm to themselves and others. Eighteen percent of high school seniors admit to driving after drinking, and just under 30% say they have ridden with someone who had been drinking (CDC, 2008b). In addition, adolescents who have been drinking, irrespective of their blood alcohol levels, are more likely than drivers of other ages to be involved in an accident (CDC, 2005c).

Cigarettes

Although many drugs carry the potential for great harm, the percentage of adolescents experimenting with them is relatively small, and the numbers of those habitually using these is even smaller. The one substance, however, that a sizable number of adolescents use on a daily basis is cigarettes. Because of this, cigarettes pose one of the most serious, if not *the* most serious, health risks of all drugs to adolescents. Approximately 440,000 people die each year due to smoking or to exposure to cigarette smoke—and most of them started smoking as adolescents (Armour et al., 2004).

Just over half of all adolescents will have tried cigarettes at some point during high school, and by their senior year, 14% smoke on a regular basis. Longitudinal data confirm that smoking is a difficult habit to break, even among adolescents. Half of adolescents who smoke indicate they have tried to quit and have not been able to (CDC, 2008b). This figure is not surprising, given the withdrawal symptoms one experiences when attempting to stop: irritability, nervousness, anxiousness, impatience, difficulty concentrating, increased appetite, and weight gain!

The psychoactive agent in cigarettes is **nicotine**, which is both a stimulant and a depressant. Smokers feel both more alert and more relaxed when they

nicotine The psychoactive substance in cigarettes that is both a stimulant and a depressant.

smoke. These pleasures come with a heavy price tag. Smoking increases heart rate and blood pressure and carries an increased risk of heart disease. It also increases the risk of lung cancer and respiratory diseases, such as emphysema and chronic bronchitis.

Marijuana

By the time they reach the 12th grade, 38% of adolescents have tried **marijuana** at least once and 25% report current occasional use (CDC, 2008b). Marijuana, which comes from the *Cannabis sativa* plant, produces a high characterized by feelings of relaxation and peacefulness, a sense of heightened awareness of one's surroundings and of the increased significance of things. Marijuana can distort perception, affect memory, slow reaction time, and impair motor coordination, especially for unfamiliar or complex tasks. The principal physical effects are an increase in heart rate, reddening of the eyes, and dryness of the mouth. Because marijuana affects perception, reaction time, and coordination, it impairs one's ability to drive. Yet adolescents under the influence of marijuana experience heightened confidence in their abilities, despite their impaired functioning.

Long-term heavy use of marijuana carries a number of potential health risks. The smoke from marijuana causes irritation of the bronchia and can lead to chronic bronchitis. Marijuana smoke also contains considerably more tar than does smoke from even high-tar cigarettes, and 70% more benzopyrene, a known carcinogen, cancer-causing agent.

Age, Ethnicity, and Gender

There are significant age trends as well as ethnic and gender differences with respect to each of these drugs. First, the use of all three substances increases with age. Over one-third of ninth-graders indicate having had a drink within the preceding month in contrast to over one-half of 12th-graders. Similarly, just under 15% of ninth-graders had smoked a cigarette or had marijuana in the preceding month, but over one-quarter of 12th-graders had. This trend is true for all drugs, with the exception of inhalants, which are most likely to be used by younger rather than older adolescents (CDC, 2008b).

There are ethnic differences as well in the use of drugs. African American adolescents are significantly less likely to drink than are European American or Hispanic adolescents, and even less likely to engage in heavy drinking. They are also less likely to have smoked than are European American or Hispanic adolescents; among the latter, European Americans are the more likely to smoke. Only with the use of marijuana do ethnic differences disappear (CDC, 2008b).

Overall, adolescent girls are less likely to smoke or use marijuana than males, but are just as likely to use alcohol, with 45% of all high schoolers having had at least one drink in the past month (CDC, 2008b). Girls also are nearly as likely as boys to engage in binge drinking (i.e. having four or more drinks in a row). Binge drinking, even if done once or twice a month, can damage neural tissue since the brain continues to develop throughout adolescence. For girls, the effects of early heavy drinking are most likely to be seen in processing visual-spatial information, such as recognizing or remembering a complex design. For boys, tasks requiring sustained attention are most likely to reveal the effects of early heavy drinking (Squeglia et al., 2009). Drinking in early adolescence can also be problematic for girls since it has been found to affect pubertal development (see Chapter 3).

Patterns of Drug Use

There is a pattern to the order in which adolescents experiment with different substances. The first drug they are likely to use is alcohol, followed by ciga-

marijuana A mild hallucinogen from the plant *Cannabis sativa*; the primary psychoactive substance is THC (tetrahydrocannabinol).

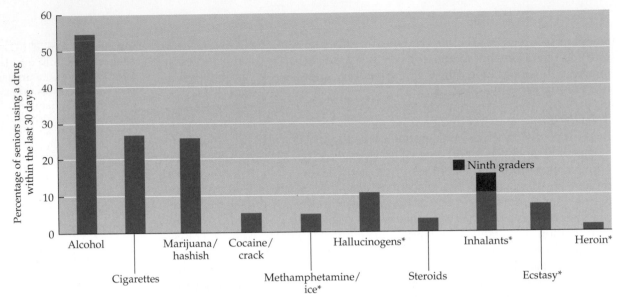

● **Figure 12.6** **Percentages of high school seniors using various drugs within the past month** (*Indicates one or more times during their life) (After CDC, 2008b.)

gateway hypothesis
The assumption that drug use progresses through stages in which the use of one type of drug provides a pathway to the use of other drugs.

rettes, which in turn are followed by marijuana. This pattern has led to the **gateway hypothesis**, which assumes that adolescents' involvement in drugs progresses through a sequence of stages, with the use of one type of drug opening the door to the use of other drugs (Kandel, 1975). Denise Kandel, at Columbia University, states, however, that this theory is often misunderstood. She points out that although using certain drugs precedes the use of other drugs, progression to the next stage isn't inevitable. That is, many adolescents drink without ever smoking; similarly, experimenting with marijuana does not mean that an adolescent will try other illegal drugs; and, in fact, most don't, as can be seen in **Figure 12.6**. Or as a logician might put it, although the use of alcohol and cigarettes might be a necessary condition for progression to the next stage, it is not a sufficient one (Kandel, 2002).

More important than whether adolescents have used a particular drug is how heavily involved they are in its use. Kandel notes that increased involvement with a drug generally precedes progression to a higher stage. For instance, it's not simply the use of alcohol that precedes more advanced drug use; rather, it's excessive drinking (Kandel, 2002). The question of involvement, however, leads us to the issue of risk factors, and protective ones, associated with substance abuse.

Risk and Protective Factors

Risk factors, recall, are the conditions present either as characteristics of adolescents themselves, their families, or communities that place them at risk for substance abuse. In the case of personality characteristics, adolescents at risk for drug abuse tend to be less well-adjusted and more impulsive and to have low self-esteem (Bryant et al., 2003; Shedler & Block, 1990; Siewert et al., 2003). They are also likely to do more poorly at school, experience more problematic relations with their peers, and have friends who use drugs (Bryant et al., 2003; Shedler & Block, 1990; Urberg, 1992).

Families also exert an important influence: Adolescents who are substance abusers are likely to have less nurturing parents and to experience less consistent parenting; they also are more likely to have parents who abuse substances themselves (Chassin et al., 2004). There is evidence of a genetic component, as well, to a number of the problem behaviors seen in adolescent substance abusers (Siewert et al., 2003). Finally, communities in which there is more violence and in which drugs are more available place adolescents at greater risk of drug use (Lambert et al., 2004).

Protective factors are the conditions that provide adolescents with the resources they need for healthy development. These factors, too, can be grouped in terms of characteristics of the adolescents, their families, and their communities that protect against substance abuse. With respect to the first of these, having high self-esteem and good social skills is associated with decreased involvement with drugs, as is involvement in church and religious activities and having friends who do not abuse drugs (Bottvin & Griffin, 2004; Huebner et al., 2005; Oman et al., 2004). Adolescents who maintain good grades in school and feel emotionally connected to their school are also less likely to abuse drugs (Huebner et al., 2005; Marsiglia et al., 2002; Skal et al., 2003).

Parents play a key role in protecting adolescents from drug abuse. Parents who are warm and understanding, with whom adolescents feel they can talk about their problems, are less likely to have adolescents who abuse drugs, as are parents who monitor adolescents' activities, knowing where they are and who they are with. These qualities, you may recall from reading Chapter 6, are characteristic of authoritative parents (Hays et al., 2003; Huebner et al., 2005; Oman et al., 2004; Skal et al., 2003).

Although adolescents continue to try illegal drugs, use among high school seniors has dropped in recent years. Drug education programs are at least partially responsible for having made adolescents more cautious about using drugs. Although the use of many illegal drugs has increased, most adolescents do not use these substances. (These artists are restoring a mural painted in 1986 by the late artist and social activist Keith Haring.)

Finally, media campaigns affecting adolescents' perception of the harmfulness of drugs, at least with respect to marijuana, appear to have had some effect in reducing its use (Johnston et al., 2005). Cigarettes, however, remain a much larger drug problem, being responsible for most substance-related deaths (Allen et al., 2003). Notwithstanding, states have cut spending on preventive programs aimed at tobacco use, whereas the amount spent by the tobacco industry on marketing doubled in 1997 through 2001, presumably in an effort to counteract the effect of public messages (Allen et al., 2003).

Prevention Programs

Efforts to prevent adolescent drug abuse have taken a number of forms, such as controlling adolescents' access to drugs, media campaigns, and school-based educational programs. When it comes to preventing drug abuse among adolescents, however, there is no "silver bullet." For programs to be maximally effective, the combined efforts of parents, schools, the community, and our society become important (Johnston et al., 2005).

Adolescents' access to drugs can be affected in a number of ways. Perhaps the most obvious of these is through stricter enforcement by communities of existing laws prohibiting the sale of alcohol and cigarettes to minors. For instance, 25% of 12th-graders said they purchased cigarettes at a store or gas station, as did 12% of ninth- and 10th-graders (CDC, 2008b). Similarly, access to these drugs can be limited through adolescents' pocketbooks; increases in the price of both cigarettes and alcohol have been accompanied by decreased use of these substances (Johnston et al., 2005).

Media campaigns directed at both adolescents and their parents have been credited with reductions in adolescent drug use (Johnston et al., 2005; Office of National Drug Control Policy, 2005). A federally funded program targeting use of marijuana appears to have been largely responsible for recent declines in the use of marijuana, most likely by increasing adolescents' perception of its harmfulness (Johnston et al., 2005). Antismoking ads are similarly thought to have contributed to decreases in the percentage of adolescents who smoke. Johnston and his colleagues at the University of Michigan's Institute for Social Research note:

> Whether we will see teen smoking continue to decline in the future is likely to depend on what actions society and the tobacco companies take. The fact that a number of states have reduced their allocations of tobacco settlement monies to smoking prevention is likely to have an adverse effect, as is the scheduled decline in funding for the national anti-smoking campaign sponsored by the American Legacy Foundation. (Johnston et al., 2005, p. 3)

The American Legacy Foundation is a public health foundation funded by the settlement agreement with the tobacco industry. There is a downside to the effectiveness of media campaigns, however. Tobacco companies spend $12.7 billion a year in marketing!

A federal mandate requires that all schools have a drug education program, and that the programs schools use have been shown to be effective. Most program evaluations, however, have not examined their long-term effectiveness. When this is done, by looking at the effect they've had a year after the program has ended, there is little evidence that school-based programs, by themselves, have any long-term effect on tobacco use among adolescents (Weiss et al., 2008; West & O'Neal, 2004; Wiehe et al., 2005).

In addition to lacking long-term effectiveness, school-based intervention programs are expensive and draw state funds away from programs that *are* effective (Glantz & Mandel, 2005). An example of such a program is the countermarketing, "Truth" campaign (Mandel et al., 2006). One aspect of this program that makes it so effective is the way it markets its message—giving it the status of a brand, such as "Levi's" or "Pepsi,"—so that adolescents can recognize "truth" messages whenever they see or hear them. Another effective aspect of the program is its use of "edgy," or trend setting, youth that adolescents are likely to identify with, and admire for their independence in the way they challenge the tobacco industry's attempts to influence them. For instance, one "truth" commercial shows youths stacking up body bags, representing those killed by tobacco, in front of the head office of a tobacco company, confronting them with the truth that tobacco kills. The program also uses promotional material, such as T-shirts and bumper stickers, in its "marketing" campaign. This campaign is not only effective in changing adolescents' attitudes about smoking, but is also considerably less expensive than school-based interventions. Matthew Farrelly and his associates point out—in case you hadn't noticed—that the success of the program shouldn't be surprising since it uses the same strategies employed by the tobacco industry to market *its* product to adolescents (Farrelly et al., 2002; Glantz & Mandel, 2005).

A second effective approach is that of comprehensive tobacco control programs (CDC, 2007). For a closer look at one such program, we can look at Oregon's Tobacco Prevention and Education Program (Oregon Statewide Tobacco Control Plan 2005–2010, Ronde et al., 2001).This program was funded by a 1996 ballot initiative that increased the state cigarette tax, and it illustrates the effectiveness of a school-based program when supported by local communities and the media. The program included a statewide media campaign, a "quitline," and a school-based prevention program that was offered in a percentage of schools throughout Oregon. The program was built around guidelines incorporating social-cognitive principles established by the CDC

TABLE 12.6
Policy Recommendations for Comprehensive Tobacco Control Programs at the State and Community Level

1. Pass "Clean Air" legislation prohibiting smoking in indoor public and private workplaces.

2. Increase the sales tax on tobacco products.

3. Implement local and statewide media campaigns.

4. Use "quit lines" offering free counseling and information on effective programs that are available through smokers' health plans.

5. Identify and reduce the sources by which adolescents gain access to tobacco products.

Source: CDC, 2007.

(Table 12.6). The increased tax on cigarettes, by the way, also made these less accessible to adolescents who could not afford the additional cost.

All students throughout Oregon were exposed to the same media campaign and all had access to the quit-line; however, only a portion of the students also participated in the school-based prevention program. Averaged over all schools, students who participated in the school prevention program were 20% less likely to smoke than those who attended schools that did not offer the program. Furthermore, the decline in smoking among participating students was "dose-dependent," being greatest for those whose schools implemented all of the guidelines (42.2%), less when schools implemented fewer guidelines (21.9%), and least when schools implemented the fewest guidelines (6.6%) (CDC, 2001a). Thus, when programs are properly implemented and given local and media support, smoking among teens can be decreased by over 40%!

Most adolescents will experiment with at least some drugs before they reach adulthood. A positive note is that most will not abuse them. However, even casual experimentation with some substances carries substantial risks. How best can society protect adolescents from the potential hazards of experimentation? Is the most effective approach to bombard them with information concerning the dangers of drugs such that they never take that first sip, puff, or pop? Given the pleasurable effects of drugs and the powerful pressures to use them, as well as the excitement of daring the forbidden, scare programs are not likely to keep most adolescents from experimenting. Candid discussions that acknowledge the pleasurable effects of drugs as well as their potential for abuse promise a better safeguard for adolescents. Establishing trust through open communication makes it possible for adolescents to approach adults when they need information or help.

Go to the
Adolescence
Companion Website
at
www.sinauer.com/cobb
for quizzes, flashcards, summaries, and other study resources.

SUMMARY and KEY TERMS

Alienation and the Failure to Cope

Feelings of alienation are common in adolescence. These can be triggered by pubertal changes, identity issues, and feelings of cultural estrangement.
alienation

Runaways: Many alienated adolescents are runaways. These youths are frequently abused or neglected. As a group they suffer from low self-esteem, depression, poor interpersonal skills, insecurity, anxiousness, impulsiveness, and lack of a sense of personal control over their lives. Home life for most is chaotic and characterized by violence.

(continued)

SUMMARY and KEY TERMS *continued*

Support for Adolescent Runaways and Parents: The availability of immediate support for runaways varies from one community to the next. Nearly all urban centers have federally and privately funded shelters. Most of these offer short-term help (e.g., 30 days) in the form of meals and a place to stay; some also offer diagnostic and counseling services. Longer term interventions can take the form of counseling and parenting classes, offered by many communities through full-service schools. The Internet is also a valuable tool for finding shelters and one with which most adolescents are familiar.

Maltreatment: Abuse and Neglect: Three home-life patterns distinguish adolescents who are maltreated. The abuse may be a continuation of abusive patterns that started in childhood, it may reflect a change in the type of discipline used when they reach adolescence, or it may be occasioned by the onset of adolescence itself. Factors that, in combination, characterize maltreating parents include difficulty coping with stress; a negative, defensive worldview; inappropriate expectations of adolescents; less supportive and more aggressive partners; and poverty.
maltreatment, parentified

Problem Behavior

Externalizing Problems: When adolescents turn their problems outward, it shows up in a variety of ways: antisocial behavior, delinquency, participating in gangs, and violence. The type of delinquent act varies with age. There is little evidence suggesting that minor forms of delinquency predict a later shift to more serious crime. The pattern instead suggests a small subgroup of delinquents who start early and account for a relatively large proportion of criminal activity. Gender, ethnic, and social class differences exist in adolescent delinquency. Females are less likely to engage in delinquent activities than are males and are less likely to commit violent crimes. Some ethnic groups are much more likely to enter the juvenile justice system, and although social class differences may be at play, these disparities strongly suggest bias within the juvenile justice system.
externalized problems, undercontrolled, internalized problems, overcontrolled, comorbid

Today, juvenile gangs are more likely to be linked to organized crime than in the past and are associated with more violent crimes and the sale of narcotics. Teenagers are nearly twice as likely to be victims of violent crime as are young adults. Homicide is the second leading cause of death for all young people, and most are killed with a firearm.
life-course persistent antisocial behavior, adolescence-limited antisocial behavior, juvenile delinquency, index offenses, status offenses

Internalizing Problems: When adolescents turn their problems inward, they may become depressed, suicidal, or develop an eating disorder. Adolescents who suffer from depression have feelings of low self-esteem, sadness, hopelessness, and helplessness. Suicide is the third most common cause of death among adolescents. Some of its warning signs include sudden changes in behavior, changes in sleeping or eating patterns, loss of interest in usual activities, withdrawal from others, or talk of suicide. Factors that place adolescents at risk of suicide are depression, a prior suicide attempt, substance abuse, life stresses, and chaotic family lives. The most effective treatment programs work with the family as well as the suicidal adolescent.
affective disorders, depression, major depressive disorder, masked depression

SUMMARY and KEY TERMS

Bulimia and anorexia are closely related eating disorders, and are more likely to occur in adolescents who come from families characterized by enmeshment, overprotectiveness, rigidity, and inadequate conflict resolution. Standards for female attractiveness show thinner models today than in past generations; this trend is problematic in that eating disorders are more common among females. Overweight adolescents are likely to have parents who are overweight. They also eat irregularly, eat food that is denser in calories, and are more inactive than adolescents of average weight. Effective treatments include exercise and involve the family.
bulimia, anorexia, overweight

Adolescents and Drugs

What Is Dependence?: Physical drug dependence occurs with psychoactive substances when they control behavior so that the individual cannot easily discontinue their use. Drug dependence can interfere with school, work, and relationships.
drug dependence, psychoactive

Alcohol: Alcohol loosens inhibitions and makes individuals feel more spontaneous. As blood-alcohol level rises, activities controlled by the central nervous system are increasingly affected. Most high school seniors have tried alcohol and many do so with some regularity.
alcohol

Cigarettes: Cigarettes are the only substance that a sizable number of adolescents use on a daily basis. Because of this, cigarettes pose one of the most serious, if not the most serious, health risks of all drugs to adolescents. Most adolescents who smoke start before they reach high school, and most adolescents who start to smoke have tried unsuccessfully to stop. The use of cigarettes and alcohol is associated with the use of other, illicit substances.
nicotine

Marijuana: Marijuana is a mild hallucinogen that affects thought, perception, reaction time, and coordination. Long-term heavy use carries a number of potential health risks. Of all illicit drugs, marijuana is the most frequently used by adolescents.
marijuana

Age, Ethnicity, and Gender: There are significant age trends with respect to the use of alcohol, cigarettes, and marijuana, with the use of all three increasing with age. There are ethnic differences as well, with African American adolescents being less likely to drink alcohol or smoke cigarettes than European American or Hispanic adolescents. With respect to gender, early adolescent females drink more than males their age; overall, females are as likely to smoke cigarettes but less likely to have used marijuana.

Patterns of Drug Use: There is a pattern to the order in which adolescents experiment with drugs; typically, alcohol is the first drug used, which is followed by cigarettes, which, in turn, is followed by marijuana. Though an adolescent may use a certain drug, progression to the next stage isn't inevitable. A better predictor of whether or not an adolescent will progress down the drug pathway is the extent to which they become involved in a drug's use.
gateway hypothesis

(continued)

SUMMARY and KEY TERMS *continued*

Risk and Protective Factors: Factors that place adolescents at risk for substance abuse are being less well adjusted and impulsive, having low self-esteem, doing poorly in school, having problematic relations with peers, and having friends who use drugs. Adolescents who abuse drugs are likely to have less nurturing parents, to have parents who abuse substances themselves, to live in more violent communities, and to have drugs more available. Protective factors include high self-esteem, good social skills, involvement in religion, friends who do not abuse drugs, and doing well in school. Also important are parents who are warm, communicate well, and monitor their children's activities.

Prevention Programs: Efforts to prevent drug abuse include controlling access to drugs, media campaigns, and school-based educational programs organized around social cognitive principles. Programs using a combination of these approaches are the most effective. Most adolescents will experiment with some drugs before they reach adulthood; most will also not use them frequently. Even casual experimentation with some substances carries substantial risks. Candid discussions that acknowledge the pleasurable effects of drugs as well as their potential dangers promise to be the most effective ways of providing help to adolescents.

What is it that we—as parents, teachers, employers, and members of the community—want of adolescents? What is the cultural agenda awaiting adolescents as they move into adulthood? Do we simply want them to settle down, do well at school, and get to work on time? Or do expectations run deeper than that? What does it take, in other words, for us to consider them "grown up"?

Robert Kegan (1994), at Harvard University, says that it takes a lot. Kegan asserts that we do not simply expect adolescents to change how they behave. We expect them to change how they know, to change the way they understand, or give meaning to, their experiences. Such a change requires adolescents to let go of their current grasp of the way things are, a grasp that includes the way they know themselves.

Consider Sylvia, for instance. Sylvia is 15 and she is having a bad day. She has cut her afternoon classes to go to the mall with her friends. Glancing up from the cosmetics counter where they've been trying on lipsticks, she looks into the

Positive Development in Adolescence:
Meeting the Challenges and Making It Work

face of her mother, who is looking back at her. Her flushed excuse of a short day at school doesn't change the set to her mother's mouth or the look in her eyes, a mixture of hurt and anger.

For her part, Sylvia's mother is wondering why she has bothered for the past five months to pick her daughter up from school when she can so obviously get where she wants to go on her own. Where is the child who used to hold her hand so sweetly whenever they'd leave the house? Not that she wants that in a 15-year-old. No, and as much as she values independence and planning in her children, Sylvia's mother does not feel like congratulating her daughter on the way she has planned her afternoon or gotten to the mall on her own. Not on your life! In fact, she feels like saying, "It's time you started taking your schooling more seriously, sister! You've got a future to think about. You're not a kid anymore. And how do you think I feel knowing you would have met me in the parking lot lying about where you'd been all afternoon!" (Kegan, 1994)

Sylvia's mother was disappointed in her. She expected so much more of her daughter than this. But just what is it that parents expect of their teenagers? Is it simply that they behave better than Sylvia did? Is it that we don't want them to cut class, lie about where they've been, or in other ways deceive us? The answer to that, of course, is yes, but it is also more. What we really want of adolescents has more to do with the reasons behind their actions. We want them to do what they do for the right reasons. Kegan points out, however, that reasons have to do with the way we understand the world. And for Sylvia to behave differently, and do so for the right reasons, she would have to understand her world, understand both herself and others, differently. Sylvia has organized her meaning of self largely in terms of her relationship with her parents. If asked to recount what happened this day, Sylvia would probably talk more about her mother than herself, saying that her mother is always checking up on her or that she doesn't really understand how she feels.

What are we to make of Sylvia? Is she simply thoughtless and "bad," an adolescent with no sense of values? Actually, if you knew a little more about her, you would find her to be quite the opposite, to be affectionate and loving, helpful and polite, and genuinely so. If asked, for instance, about her favorite memories, she would most likely talk about the family holidays, the times when they are all together, the big meals, noisy evenings, and quiet mornings with leftovers for breakfast instead of cereal.

The problem is not as simple as sorting the good kids from the bad kids. If it were, we would all have an easier time of it. Sylvia is, with a few exceptions, a good kid. This does not mean that skipping school or lying to her mother is acceptable or that her mother should let it pass with no consequences. In important ways, however, Sylvia's problem is larger than what happened at the mall. Her problem has to do with how she understands herself.

Sylvia has difficulty separating herself from her parents. For instance, in order for her to see her mother differently, to take her mother's feelings into account, she must come to see herself differently, to distinguish the way she is feeling at the moment from her larger sense of who she is, from her sense of self. Only then will she be able to coordinate her own needs with the needs of others. When adolescents can recognize the needs of others as well as their own and, with this, appreciate the obligations each has toward the other, they can step into relationships characterized by reciprocity and mutuality (Kegan, 1982). And this is a large part of what most of us mean by being "grown up." Mutuality means that one not only does the right things but does them for the right reasons.

A developmental step of this magnitude, even though we expect it of all adolescents, is not an easy one to take. In order for adolescents to move toward greater mutuality in their relationships, to become full members in the adult community, they need the support of that community (Zeldin & Price, 1995). To change the way they know themselves and understand their world, they must let go of themselves enough to grow into new ways of being.

For adolescents to do something as risky as letting go, someone else needs to be there to hold on. In order to "grow up," in other words, adolescents need to experience not only the challenge to grow but the support that makes this possible. The supports that "hold" adolescents as they take these steps toward greater maturity assume a number of forms. Adolescents are held, for instance, by their families. They are also held by their communities—by such things as schools and teachers, activities and clubs, parks, libraries, recreation centers, and places of worship. Adolescents are also sustained, as they construct a new understanding of themselves and their world, by the strengths within them, such as their temperament, attitudes, and religious beliefs.

Chapter Overview

This chapter looks first at the ways in which families provide support through authoritative parenting, the use of supportive adult network structures, and effective use of institutions in the community. From there we move to a consideration of the ways in which community resources promote healthy development before turning to a consideration of the personal strengths of adolescents—such as their outlook on life, competence, and religious beliefs—that sustain healthy development.

Even under the best of conditions, stress is a common part of normal life. We will examine differences in the ways adolescents cope with stress, as well as learn to cope more effectively. The chapter then moves to a consideration of adolescents who are distinguished by their remarkable prosocial behavior, and concludes with an analysis of the types of everyday activities that contribute to the development of initiative.

Protective Factors in Adolescence

Adolescents are supported by many protective factors in their environment. Each of these factors—whether aspects of their homes, schools, or communities—helps adolescents to redefine themselves, to change the way they know themselves, so that the self they bring to their encounters with others will be one that is capable of mutuality and one that can continue to grow.

Families

Among the most important sources of support in adolescents' lives are their relationships within the family, especially with parents (Hillaker et al., 2008). These relationships can be characterized in terms of two broad dimensions: the degree of warmth and supportiveness, or responsiveness, and expectations for mature behavior coupled with consistent discipline, known as demandingness (see Chapter 6). Both of these dimensions of parenting have been found to be related to healthy development (Bogenschneider & Pallock, 2008; Hardy et al., 2008; Hoeve et al., 2009; Laible et al., 2008).

Several longitudinal studies confirm the importance of responsiveness. Kristin Moore and Dana Glei (1995) followed a nationally representative sample of children from the ages of 7 through 11 to the ages of 18 to 22, interviewing both children and parents. These investigators found that adolescents who had warm and emotionally satisfying relationships with their parents in childhood and who experienced fewer family disruptions were more likely to have a greater sense of well-being in adolescence and to avoid serious risk taking, such as dropping out, using cigarettes or other drugs, or engaging in delinquent behavior. Similarly, Kathleen Roche and her associates (2008) found, from interviews of adolescents followed into early adulthood, that warmth and family closeness were associated with fewer problem behaviors in girls, such as dropping out of school or becoming sexually active at an early age. In contrast, boys' behavior was more closely related to parental demandingness—setting limits as to when they had to be home, what friends they could hang out with, or what they could watch on TV. In order for setting limits, or demandingness, to be effective, it must be clear to adolescents what limits have been set. Parental responsiveness, on the other hand, lacks this preciseness, yet contributes to effective parenting even when adolescents' reports of a parent's responsiveness don't always correspond to what the parent might report (Bogenschneider & Pallock, 2008).

Authoritative parenting, or parenting characterized by responsiveness *and* demandingness, contributes to healthy development in a number of ways. Important to many of these is adolescents' ease in listening to their parents'

One of the major steps in growing up is developing a relationship with one's parents that is mutual and reciprocal.

advice when making difficult decisions. Kathleen Mackey, Mary Louise Arnold, and Michael Pratt (2001) interviewed adolescents about decisions in which they'd asked a parent for advice; they also assessed the style of parenting and parental influence on the decision. One adolescent with an authoritative parent had this to say:

At the beginning of the semester, I was thinking of dropping my math class, and we went through that and we (she and mother) talked about all our options....I'm not doing very well, but, we decided I would keep going, and she got a tutor and stuff. She saw how much trouble I was having with it, so she said, "I don't want you to stress yourself out over this, but if you need the course for later on, it's good to keep it." She was just telling me to stick with it...like she would have let me make my own decision....She just told me what she thought, but if I had told her I'm dropping the class, she never would have objected....I decided to stay in the class and get a tutor. It was kind of like it was all my decision, but it was tough....I'm glad I stayed in, but I don't really have much of an interest in it. (p. 251)

We can see both responsiveness and demandingness in this mother. The daughter speaks of her mother as caring and supportive ("She saw how much trouble I was having..."), yet the quality of demandingness is also present in the mother's expectations for responsible behavior ("...if you need the course for later on, it's good to keep it" and "She was just telling me to stick with it"). By supporting her daughter in making this decision ("...she got a tutor and stuff"), she helped her daughter find her own strengths ("...it was tough....I'm glad I stayed..."). Not least among the strengths was the daughter's experience of having made a good decision.

A question not addressed to this point is why parents respond to their children as they do. What made this mother, for instance, more open to letting her daughter feel her way through a decision than an authoritarian parent might have been? In other words, how is one's personality related to the way one parents? Parents that are high in extraversion and agreeableness, two of the five broad dimensions defining differences in personality, tend to be friendlier, more cooperative, and outgoing. It appears that these qualities enable them to feel competent when with others, and it is this sense of competence that underlies their ability to listen openly and to be supportive, without becoming frustrated or needing to control. These findings suggest that the relationship between parents' personalities and their parenting style, then, is mediated at least in part by their sense of competence (de Haan et al., 2009; Prinzie et al., 2009).

Responsiveness is especially important to adolescents exposed to multiple stressors, such as overcrowded living conditions, poverty, and family turmoil. Over time, conditions such as these can have cumulative effects, taking a toll on adolescents both mentally and physically. However, adolescents whose mothers helped them with homework and were available to talk with them when they needed did not show the cumulative effects of stress experienced by others (Evans et al., 2007). Similarly, adolescents who maintain strong emotional ties to their fathers, despite not living with them, benefit uniquely from their relationship with their fathers. Those with fathers who are warm and supportive show fewer externalizing and internalizing problems (see Chapter 12) (King & Sobolewski, 2006).

Robin Jarrett (1995), at Loyola University, summarizes a number of family characteristics—illustrating the dimensions of responsiveness and demandingness—that enhance the development of youth. Although these strategies are ones that have been found effective specifically in counteracting the eroding effects of poverty among African American families, their wisdom cuts across income level and ethnicity, making them applicable in varying degrees to all families. For a look at other strategies used by African American families, see **Box 13.1**.

One of the first characteristics to emerge from the welter of research reviewed by Jarrett, a characteristic illustrating the dimension of responsiveness, involves the use of supportive adult network structures. These networks take the form of additional adults who can be called on to provide care. Adults, such as grandparents, godparents, or neighbors, provide resources that otherwise might not be available to these adolescents. The following excerpt illustrates this type of support:

BOX 13.1 **Research Focus**

Archival Research: Racial Socialization—Survival Tactics in a White Society?

By Michael Wapner

Parents reflect the values of their society and, in doing so, pass them on to their children. Psychologists refer to parents as socialization agents. As "agents" of society, they also communicate the statuses and roles that make up the social order and prepare their children to participate accordingly as adults. So far so good.

So what's the bad part? Minority parents face a special problem when they encounter societal values that can diminish the self-esteem of their children and, if internalized, could prevent them from realizing their potential. How do minority parents prepare their children for entrance into a society that frequently views their group negatively?

In a sense, they become "double agents." In addition to socializing their children into the values of the broader society, minority parents interpret that society's values in ways that shield their children from harm. By explicitly speaking against negative stereotypes, by serving as models themselves, and by exposing their children to cultural experiences that reflect the strengths of their own background, they inculcate feelings of worth and group pride. In African American society, this process is termed *racial socialization*.

The way black parents perceive society, and communicate those perceptions to their children, should reflect their own position in it. Yet we know little about the influence of demographic variables on racial socialization. Frequently, a single study lacks the scope to address such issues. Tapping into existing databases, often collected from national samples, offers a useful alternative. *Archival research* does just that: It uses existing information to obtain answers to research questions.

Archives exist in many forms: examples include vast databases collected from national samples, written records such as books or newspapers, and publicly maintained records. The databases maintained by the U.S. Census Bureau are an obvious source of archival information, illustrating the first of these forms. How might one use books or newspapers to answer research questions? Consider, for example, the question of whether school materials reinforce traditional sex-role stereotypes. To answer, one might sample textbooks and analyze their content for the frequency of female and male characters, their activities, and the settings in which they appear (such as home or work). Is living together prior to marriage more common today than a generation ago? One can look at marriage license applications for common addresses, to determine an answer.

An obvious advantage to archival research is *accessibility*: The data have already been collected. Another advantage is that many archives, such as

(continued on next page)

BOX
13.1 **continued**

the U.S. Census data, are more complete than any data that could be collected in a single research study. A further advantage is that the measures are *unobtrusive*. Subjects do not know they are being studied and therefore do not change their behavior or their answers to questions (as they might, for instance, if asked whether they are living together before marriage). Unobtrusive measures are *nonreactive*: They do not change the behavior they are measuring.

Disadvantages to using archival data also exist. Information may be lost over time. The quality of record keeping can change with time, causing unsuspecting researchers to infer that changes have occurred when in actuality none have. Computers, for example, allow better record keeping by police. As a result, crime may appear to have increased, whereas in actuality it is only being recorded more precisely.

What does archival research tell us about racial socialization? Do most black parents act as double agents to shield their children from harm by the larger society? Michael Thornton, Linda Chatters, Robert Taylor, and Walter Allen (1990), analyzing data from a national survey of African Americans, found that they do. Nearly two-thirds of all black parents engage in some racial socialization. What demographic variables predict racial socialization? These investigators found that sex, age, marital status, and region of the country all predict the likelihood of racial socialization. Mothers are more likely than fathers to prepare their children for the realities of minority status. So, too, are older parents, those who are married (versus never married), and

those who are more educated. Regional differences also predict socialization approaches. Black parents living in the Northeast, more so than those in the South, engage in racial socialization. Other research finds that racial socialization varies with the cultural diversity of the neighborhood. Boys are more likely to receive cultural pride messages when they live in ethnically mixed neighborhoods, whereas the opposite is true for girls, this being more likely when they live in predominantly black neighborhoods (Stevenson et al., 2005).

For most black parents, race is a salient issue in the socialization process. Most feel the need to prepare their children for the minority experience of living in our society. Yet just like jewelers refining a precious metal, they may find that gold appears beneath the surface dross. The dross? Children learn of racially based restrictions, such as job and housing discrimination. And the gold? They learn that they must work hard, get a good education, and, above all, be proud of who they are.

What other groups can you name in which children and adolescents need *corrective socialization*? Can you think of any groups where it is needed but not generally available? Who teaches gay male and lesbian adolescents how to deal with negative stereotypes? Their heterosexual parents? What can mentally handicapped or intellectually gifted adolescents learn from their parents of average intelligence? Who socializes adolescents in more androgynous sex roles? Traditional parents?

Sources: Thornton et al., 1990, and Stevenson et al., 2005.

[Aunt] Ann…paid for [Ben's] class ring, his senior pictures, and his cap and gown. Ann did not see this as unusual behavior as it was exactly what Jean [her sister] had done for her a long time ago. She also pointed out that she had been helping to pay nominal school fees for Jean's children for several years. (Zollar, 1985, p. 79, as cited in Jarrett, 1995)

These successful families also made use of supportive institutions within the community, such as churches and schools. Churches were found not only to undergird these families spiritually but also to offer activities for youth in which they could form friendships and develop new skills. Religious beliefs and activities also foster self-respect, personal discipline, and a concern for others, as well as contribute to improvements academically, particularly for adolescents in low-income neighborhoods (Moore & Glei, 1995; Regnerus & Elder, 2003). Among adolescents girls, frequent attendance at religious services is also related to becoming sexually active at a later age (Jones et al., 2005).

Jarrett found that parental use of schools similarly took a number of forms. Parents collaborated with school personnel, attending parent-teacher meetings, serving on committees, and maintaining close contact with their children's teachers. But parents were also willing to confront school personnel in order to ensure that their children received the attention they needed. As one mother explained, "This lady tells me that the principal doesn't have time to look at everybody's case. So I told that lady, 'that may be the case but this is one that he's going to look at.'…I was going to the Board of Education and everywhere I could think of to see that Marie could go ahead and graduate" (Clark, 1983, p. 41, as cited in Jarrett, 1995).

The effective strategies identified by Jarrett also illustrate the second dimension of family interaction: demandingness. For instance, Jarrett found parents to monitor their adolescents' activities and friendships, setting limits on whom they could associate with, what they could do, and when they were to get home. "Chaperonage" figured centrally in this monitoring, beginning in childhood as parents accompanied their children as they went into the neighborhood, and taking a particularly inventive form in adolescence by having a younger sibling tag along on dates and other activities. Other research, as well, finds that adolescents whose parents monitor their activities by asking where they are going and who they will be with have fewer problem behaviors (Richards et al., 2004; Waizenhofer et al., 2004). This is so even though parents frequently do not know as much as they believe they do (Cottrell et al., 2003; Laird et al., 2003).

Demandingness was also evident in parental expectations that adolescents assume responsibility for helping with the family's needs, whether economic or domestic. Thus, adolescents might be expected to have a part-time job to contribute to the family budget, do chores around the house, or help with younger siblings or an elderly grandparent. Such responsibilities not only contribute to family cohesion but also foster individual competencies and give a feeling of mastery (Jarrett, 1995).

Earlier in the text (see Chapter 5), we discussed several aspects of family interactions that contribute to healthy personality development, specifically, to the development of individuation in adolescence. Harold Grotevant and Catherine Cooper (1986) identified two such dimensions of interaction: connectedness and individuality. The first of these reflects the degree of emotional support within the family, support that takes the form of openness to others' opinions (permeability) and respect for their ideas (mutuality). The dimension of connectedness is similar to the dimension of responsiveness that we discussed earlier in the chapter. The second dimension—individuality—reflects the ability to function as an individual within this supportive context, to see how one differs from others and to express one's own ideas. There is a paradox to these findings, namely, that it is necessary to be "held" in order to be set free. Or, said another way, it is necessary to be supported by one's family in order to find oneself as an individual.

In a sense, these findings should not come as a surprise. Mary Ainsworth (1985; Ainsworth et al., 1978) observed much the same thing in her studies of attachment in infants and toddlers. Infants whose mothers were sensitive and responsive to their needs—qualities, by the way, that are similar to the permeability and mutuality that comprise connectedness—were those who as toddlers were the most independent and curious. These were the ones who would be likely to disappear around a corner to explore, knowing that Mom or Dad would be there in a moment if they should call out. That, after all, is what they had learned: that

Being expected to help with family needs, such as caring for younger siblings, gives adolescents a sense of competence, an important factor in healthy development.

collective efficacy
The willingness of neighbors to intervene in situations that might threaten the well-being of others.

it's safe to venture out on your own, because your parents will be there when you need them. To be held, or supported, by one's family does not create dependency in children. It frees them to develop as individuals.

Communities

Development, for adolescents, is a bit like banking; they need to make daily withdrawals to support healthy growth. And someone needs to make deposits. The neighborhoods they live in, just as their families, fund reserves on which adolescents can draw. Michelle Kegler and her associates (2005) found a number of neighborhood characteristics to contribute to youth assets. Foremost among these were the safety of a neighborhood and the services it provided, such as schools, places to shop, police protection, and sanitation. Neighborhoods with these qualities fostered the development of a number of youth assets. Adolescents in these communities were more likely to report relationships with adult role models who encouraged them and with peers who stayed out of trouble. They were also more likely to participate in organized activities after school and in religious activities.

Neighborhood effects such as these may be attributable directly to community resources like the ones mentioned or may, as well, be due to the operation of more informal social networks and norms (Leventhal & Brooks-Gunn, 2000). An example of one of these neighborhood effects is **collective efficacy**, or the willingness of neighbors to intervene in situations that in some way threaten the well-being of those in the neighborhood (Sampson et al., 2002). Consider, for instance, a woman working in the corner grocery store who sees a young adolescent buying cigarettes. She doesn't know his name or where he lives, but she recognizes him from the neighborhood. Later that week, she mentions this to someone at church, also from the neighborhood, who says, "Oh yeah, that's Molly Beacon's son—she's the one we see at the co-op on Thursdays. Do you think she knows?" Molly is likely to hear that her son is smoking, and not just from one of these women, but from both. Hearing this from them communicates something else as well—their concern and their willingness to step in when they see a problem.

The extent to which adolescents think their neighborhood is a good place to live, and feel safe in it, depends in part on informal social networks such as these. Neighborhoods effects such as those in the preceding example are associated with healthier outcomes, particularly for adolescent boys (Dallago et al., 2009; Drukker et al., 2009).

Dale Blyth and Nancy Leffert (1995), at the Search Institute in Minneapolis, compared over 100 communities in terms of the experiences of the adolescents living in them, to discover the ways in which communities support their youth. The healthiest communities were those in which adolescents were more likely to be "plugged in" to institutions within the community. Adolescents in these communities experienced their schools as caring and supportive and were more likely to attend religious services and to participate in activities within the community. According to Blyth and Leffert, the strong relationship between active participation in religious and other community-based activities and the overall health of the community suggests that such extracurricular activities "may not be extras" after all. Their observation mirrors Robin Jarrett's finding about the way that successful families use institutions within their communities.

Blyth and Leffert note, too, that the adolescents who profit most from living in healthy communities are the ones who are most in need of support and who have the fewest personal resources. Even though similar findings have emerged from comparisons of adolescents from widely differing types of communities, such as inner-city versus suburban youth, Blyth and Leffert point out that they also hold true for communities that, on the surface, have few visible differences.

Schools

Just as with communities, schools contribute to positive development when they enable adolescents to feel safe and supported. That is, adolescents' perceptions of their schools as safe and their teachers as supportive make it possible for them to function more effectively (Colarossi, 2001; Ozer & Weinstein, 2004). Teachers, in addition to parents, offer emotional as well as informational support. In fact, the emotional support adolescents receive from teachers has been found to be importantly related to their achievement (Malecki & Demaray, 2003). This source of support can be especially important for adolescents who have problematic relationships with their parents and for those who are at risk academically (Brewster & Bowen, 2004; Crosnoe & Elder, 2004). It should be noted as well that teachers who are both supportive and demanding—qualities we see in authoritative parents—are most effective, particularly with students from low-income families (Gregory & Weinstein, 2004).

Schools can also change an adolescent's worldview, and with this the potential to realize possibilities not previously imagined. For an adolescent attending a low-performing school in a poor neighborhood, however, this may be possible only when that student is lifted out of his or her neighborhood school by someone who sees this as necessary and understands that neither the student nor the parents realize this to be so. Once again, we're talking about the effects of informal social networks. Melissa Abelev (2009), at Tulane University in New Orleans, conducted life-history interviews with talented African American adults who were educationally at risk as adolescents due to poverty—their own and that of the neighborhoods in which they lived. She notes the frequency with which talented adolescents were identified by middle-class teachers who, because they were familiar with the system and shared the middle-class assumption of entitlement to the benefits good schools have to offer, were able to place these students in high-quality schools which could nurture their talents.

Personal Strengths: Temperament, Competence, and Religion

The personal qualities that adolescents possess also serve as protective factors, qualities such as an easy temperament and a positive outlook on life, intelligence, competence, a sense of self efficacy, and religious beliefs. For instance, adolescents with easy temperaments—that is, those who react positively to new situations and who are sociable and moderate in their activity level—are more likely to ride out the stresses of daily living. Not only does their positive approach equip them to deal with problems better, but their engaging ways endear them to others, thus enabling them to recruit the support they need. Possessing at least average intelligence, being able to communicate well with others, and believing that they are in control of, rather than simply reacting to, the circumstances affecting their life (known also as having an internal locus of control) also serve as important protective factors (Lau & Lau, 1996; Laursen et al., 2002; Werner, 1989).

Attending religious services and having spiritual values are among the protective factors that help adolescents weather the stresses of growing up.

Religious beliefs also are an important factor contributing to healthy development (Donahue & Benson, 1995; Emmons & Paloutzian, 2003; Frank & Kendall, 2001). For instance, Lloyd Wright, Christopher Frost, and Stephen Wisecarver (1993) found that adolescents who attend church frequently and for whom their religion gives their life meaning are also the least likely to suffer from depression. Similarly, Moore and Glei (1995) found that greater religiosity contributes to a sense of well-being in adolescents. Furthermore, religious involvement has been found to help adolescents in low-income neighborhoods stay on track in school (Regnerus & Elder, 2003), and to delay sexual initiation among adolescent girls (Jones et al., 2005). Jarrett (1995), reviewing numerous research studies, found attendance at church and spiritual values to contribute to healthy development, even in the face of the multiple risks associated with poverty. Emily Werner and Ruth Smith (1982, 1992) also noted the importance of a strong religious faith to the healthy development of resilient individuals from infancy to middle adulthood.

Adolescents need all the support they can get. Not only do they face the normative, developmental tasks of adolescence, each of which presses for a new understanding of some aspect of their lives (see Chapter 1), but they must also cope with numerous daily stressors, such as academic pressures and conflicts with parents or peers.

Stress and Coping

Bones mend and cuts heal, but worries fray the edges of the mind. Sometimes it's all one can do to keep from unraveling totally. Adolescence offers no immunity to life's stresses; in fact, the body's response to **stress** is remarkably similar at all ages. The only thing that changes is the way different individuals cope with stress.

Stress is a curious thing. For one thing, it's hard to predict what will be stressful. Trying out for a part in the class play or the debating team and not being picked is stressful, but so is getting the part or making the team. Similarly, losing one's job is an obvious stressor, but so is being promoted. These contrasts tell us something important about the nature of stress. What makes an event stressful is not necessarily the event per se. What is stressful is the need to accommodate, or adapt, to the changes brought about by that event. Generally, the more rapidly we need to adapt, the more stress we experience.

stress The body's response to an event that requires adapting to changes brought about by that event.

In the case of events that demand an immediate response, such as dangerous or threatening ones, chemical messengers ready the body for fight or flight. In other instances, bodily processes remain relatively unchanged (Selye, 1982). Adolescents have the option of interpreting many situations in ways that would make either reaction possible. Consider an example in which someone bumps into a boy's locker, knocking it shut. The adolescent can either swing around ready for a fight or simply ignore the incident. If he chooses to fight, chemical messengers will flood his body with adrenaline, pump blood into his muscles, stop his stomach from digesting his lunch, and heighten his awareness to all incoming stimuli. His blood pressure and heart rate will soar. These adaptations prepare him for a fight if one should occur, but they are also, to use Hans Selye's words, "biologically suicidal" when called upon too frequently.

Adolescents who live in gang-ridden neighborhoods experience a high degree of stress. Some try to cope by looking for solutions to the problem; others try to minimize the emotional damage by joining a gang themselves or by emotionally withdrawing.

Adolescents can also ignore potential stressors. In the above example, doing so would allow other chemical messengers to coordinate the adolescent's reactions, permitting him to reopen the locker, continue a conversation with a friend, and get on with digesting his lunch. The quality of life is determined not simply by the presence or absence of stressors, but by the way adolescents interpret and cope with them. In other words, it's not what happens but how one reacts to what happens that ultimately matters, illustrating again the way in which we construct meaning.

How Adolescents Cope with Stress

The preceding example highlights the distinction between stress and **coping**. A stressor is an event; coping is what one does about it. Adolescents can cope in either of two general ways. **Problem-focused coping** is primarily offensive and attempts to change the stressful situation. **Emotion-focused coping** is primarily defensive and is directed at minimizing the impact of the stress. When adolescents cope in the first of these two ways, they are likely to look for additional information or come up with an alternative, less stressful approach to the problem. The process is an active one in which they evaluate information, make decisions, and confront the problem. Emotion-focused coping is reactive rather than proactive. The focus, as the term suggests, is on minimizing the emotional damage of stress, not on changing the stressor. This approach more frequently takes the form of defensive measures such as wishful thinking, denial, or disengaging from the situation.

The ways adolescents cope reflect more general aspects of their personalities. Adolescents who repress or deny their problems will usually fail to process or deal with negative information. In contrast, those who are hypersensitive will typically focus only on the negative. Neither approach is adaptive, because adolescents need to be not only aware of situations that are potentially threatening but also able to see means of resolving them. Michael Berzonsky (1993; Berzonsky & Ferrari, 1996) distinguishes individuals in terms of their openness to information, whether in coping with stressors or in resolving identity issues (see Chapter 5). Those who seek out experiences that are relevant to the decisions or problems they face (information oriented) are most likely to adopt a problem-focused approach to coping. Conversely, those who are relatively closed to new information, relying instead on the standards of others (normative oriented), are more likely to use emotion-focused approaches, as are individuals who procrastinate and do nothing when faced with stress (avoidant oriented).

Gender and Ethnicity

Females have been found in some studies to be more likely to use emotion-focused coping than males, perhaps because this functions more effectively for them than it does for males (Phelps & Jarvis, 1994; Renk & Creasey, 2003; Wadsworth et al., 2004). Other research, however, finds no gender differences in the types of coping strategies likely to be used or in how successfully either gender copes, instead finding the effectiveness of coping to differ based on personal strengths such as self-esteem and feelings of self-efficacy (Mullis & Chapman, 2000; Phinney & Haas, 2003).

Many of the stressors that adolescents face occur on a daily basis (de Anda et al., 2000). Among the most common sources of stress at school are aggression (whether actual or threatened), bullying, and fear of theft. These safety concerns are considerably higher among African American and Hispanic students than among European American ones, and more of them indicate that at times they have not gone to school because they felt unsafe (CDC, 2008b).

Common among all students, however, are concerns about career goals and grades. Most students set high goals for themselves and most believe they can

coping Strategies for managing stressful situations that tax personal resources.

problem-focused coping Attempts to reduce stress by changing a stressful situation.

emotion-focused coping Attempts to reduce stress by minimizing its emotional impact, for example, denials, wishful thinking.

achieve these (Adwere-Boamah & Curtis, 1993; Phinney et al., 2001). Even so, minority adolescents are more likely to attribute success to hard work than they are to ability. This tendency underscores the importance of interventions in school counseling programs specifically designed to overcome internal barriers and make clear to minority students the many academic and career paths available to them (see Chapter 8).

Despite these similarities in the experience of stress, some important differences exist as well. For instance, many of the situations that nonminority adolescents might find stressful, such as having to take care of younger brothers and sisters, were not perceived as stressful by the minority adolescents. Cultural expectations about extended families and child-care responsibilities rendered these situations normative rather than stressful. On the other hand, adolescents in immigrant families acquire the ways of their new culture more rapidly than their parents do, creating intercultural tensions in addition to the intergenerational tensions that all adolescents experience (Kwak, 2003; Phinney et al., 2005; Phinney et al., 2000).

Learning Effective Coping Strategies

Coping with stress, like most of the activities adolescents engage in, requires skill. As such, we can expect some to be better at it than others. Luckily, as with other skills, adolescents can learn to cope with stress more effectively. Social-cognitive intervention programs teach adolescents alternative ways of viewing potentially stressful situations, making them less stressful and improving the chances of coping successfully (see Chapter 12). In response, adolescents learn to identify and appraise stressful situations, anticipate their own reactions, and manage the resulting emotions (Meichenbaum, 1985).

APPRAISING THE SITUATION   Misinterpretations easily arise from personal blind spots that can cause adolescents to overestimate or underestimate potential stressors. Overestimation can turn a harmless episode into an interpersonal disaster, whereas underestimation can expose adolescents to potential harm. Only by appraising a situation correctly can adolescents predict the most likely set of events. Accurate prediction, therefore, puts them in a place where they can better influence the course of events. Appraisals become more accurate as adolescents learn to think of alternative interpretations for situations.

Adolescents can learn to challenge self-defeating interpretations. This learning requires them to put new intellectual skills to use (see Chapter 4). As adolescents bring these skills to bear on problems, they're better able to revise their reading of ongoing situations and react appropriately; even with these, however, their cognitive appraisals of situations are likely to be less complex than those of adults (Rowley et al., 2005). Frequently the most appropriate step is to get more information to find out which interpretation is the most reasonable. Sometimes this step can be as simple as asking the other person, "Did you really mean...?"

Adolescents, just as individuals of all ages, are likely to make **attributional errors** in which they overestimate the importance of dispositional stressors (presumed traits such as aggressiveness or anger) and underestimate the importance of situational stressors (such as tensions due to relationships or threats of personal violence). A girl who is dissatisfied with one of her friends because she sees her as aggressive and angry (dispositional stressors) may think there is little possibility of improving their relationship. By tracing her friend's anger to situational factors instead—strife at home or hazing at school, for example—it becomes possible for her to think of ways to improve their relationship.

A second error that adolescents frequently commit is to notice only information that confirms their appraisal of a situation—or confirmatory information.

attributional error
An overestimation of the importance of dispositional stressors or an underestimation of the importance of situational ones.

An adolescent who expects a teacher to be unsympathetic or overly demanding is more likely to act in a hostile way toward that teacher, provoking a reaction that confirms the expectation. Instead, adolescents can learn to look for, and even generate, behavior that disconfirms predisposing expectations. The above adolescent might, for example, thank the teacher in advance for her attention and time, thus creating a positive atmosphere in which the teacher will be more likely to listen to the student sympathetically.

RESPONDING TO THE SITUATION   Sometimes the response can be as simple as getting information or advice, or suggesting a talk with a friend. At other times the most effective action can be no action, like not shooting back an angry reply to a friend or parent. In most cases, skills related to assertiveness, communication, negotiation, and compromise are involved. Even adolescents who have these skills don't always think to use them. Under the stress of the moment, they may not use an approach that has worked for them in the past, or they may fail to recognize which skills are called for. Sometimes, too, adolescents fail to respond effectively because other, less adaptive, reactions are more dominant. Nonassertive adolescents might fail to speak up, for instance, simply because of nervousness or shyness.

Difficult school subjects are common stressors for adolescents. Using problem-focused coping, this adolescent heads the stressor off by seeking academic tutoring.

The most effective ways of responding are those that prevent stressful situations from occurring. Individuals create, as well as respond to, their environments. This fact makes preventive actions possible. Adolescents can pick up on social cues that bring out the best in others. Adolescents who develop these skills are more likely to bring out friendly, helpful behavior in others and less likely to cause the hostile or aggressive behaviors that typify stressful interactions.

MANAGING EMOTIONS   Even after successfully handling a stressful encounter, adolescents must still deal with the emotions caused by the situation. Adolescents differ widely in how quickly they get over feelings of anger or frustration. Mentally rehearsing one's successes or failures will either facilitate or interfere with the process of "unwinding." Adolescents who have been trained in a stress-inoculation program involving the above three components (appraising, responding, and managing) have lower anxiety, less anger, and higher self-esteem (Hains & Szyjakowski, 1990).

Most research with adolescents has focused on the problems they face or on the ways in which they have been deficient in responding to these. A newer area of study is that of healthy adolescents who not only cope but make the world better in some way for others as well. Who are these adolescents, and what do we know about them?

Beyond Coping: Caring and Prosocial Behavior

Nearly one-third of adolescents in the United States volunteer in charitable activities, working in after-school programs, food banks, libraries, senior

Adolescents who distinguish themselves for community service and other kinds of prosocial behavior are likely to have experienced caring relationships with their parents or other adults.

centers, and the like (Rudder, 2002). They volunteer for many reasons: They believe they can make a difference in the lives of others; they want to be part of something bigger than themselves, to enrich the lives of others; and some volunteer simply because it's more interesting than anything else they might be doing.

Many of these youth go beyond volunteering to establishing organizations of their own. One adolescent started a program donating hats to cancer patients who were undergoing chemotherapy. It began when he was visiting his grandmother in the cancer ward and noticed many patients had lost their hair; he thought they might appreciate having a hat to wear. He got permission to place boxes in local businesses and schools for people to donate new hats, and then took these to the local hospital each week. In four years time, he had donated hats to more than 160 hospitals around the world, totaling over 40,000 hats (Heavenly Hats, 2005).

In another example, a young woman, after working throughout her adolescence with youth in her community, started a youth program with two friends when she was 21. Their goal, as she put it, "is to help children rescue their dreams deferred and to shape future leaders committed to making their community better for the next generation." They, too, started small, asking those who had just completed the program to volunteer with the next group of kids. As this young woman said, "I have had the pleasure of helping them realize that there is more to life than what they see. Just by showing them a difference and empowering them to make a choice allows them not only to change their world but mine as well" (A Different Side of the Game, Inc., 2005).

Daniel Hart, at Rutgers University, and Suzanne Fegley, at Temple University (1995), were interested in how adolescents who are distinguished by remarkable caring and prosocial behavior understand their world and themselves. These investigators studied a group of urban minority adolescents, African American and Hispanic, in an economically distressed northeastern city. These adolescents were remarkable in one way or another for their involvement in such things as volunteer work or more than the ordinary family responsibilities. (The sample was arrived at by contacting social agencies, church leaders, schools, and youth groups.) A comparison group of adolescents was matched for age, gender, ethnicity, and neighborhood. The latter adolescents were also well adjusted and attended school regularly, and many of them were also involved in volunteer activities, but not to the same degree. All adolescents were interviewed and completed a number of personality measures.

These investigators found, as anticipated, that the "caring" adolescents understood themselves quite differently than did the comparison adolescents. They were more likely to describe themselves in terms of their values and ideals. Also, their parents contributed more heavily to their sense of themselves than was the case for the comparison group, for whom best friends contributed most heavily. Differences between the caring and comparison adolescents, however, did not appear to be due to any single factor, such as overall maturity or sophistication of thought. The former did not, for instance, use more advanced moral reasoning or have more complex or sophisticated perceptions of others. Also, because these adolescents were not followed over time, one cannot say for sure whether the ways in which these remarkable teenagers saw themselves were responsible for the care they extended to others or whether their involvement in the care of others drew them away from friends, thus causing them to see themselves less in terms of their peers and more in terms of idealized figures.

P. Lindsay Chase-Lansdale, Lauren Wakschlag, and Jeanne Brooks-Gunn (1995) point to the importance of the family for the development of caring. The experience of being loved seems to be essential if one is to develop as a caring person. The research on attachment, beginning in infancy but extending throughout the lifespan (Ainsworth, 1985; Ainsworth et al., 1978; Bowlby, 1969), underscores the importance for healthy development of the caregivers' sensitivity to the needs of the child and responsiveness in meeting these needs. Children cared for in this way not only develop a sense of trust in their world but come to believe that others are trustworthy, and perhaps most important of all, that they are worthy of being cared for in this way (Erikson, 1968).

Not all adolescents are born into homes in which they will receive this type of care from their parents. What sort of chances do these adolescents have of developing into competent, caring adults? The research of Emily Werner and her colleagues (Werner, 1989; Werner & Smith, 1982, 1992) indicates that the chances are good—as long as there is at least one caring person in that young person's life, someone such as a grandparent, an aunt or uncle, or a sibling to love him or her (see Chapter 2).

Positive Youth Development

We began this chapter by asking what we want of adolescents—what, that is, do we take to be the markers of positive, healthy development? In asking this, we are speaking of healthy development as more than the absence of problematic behaviors such as those discussed in the previous chapter. Instead, Richard Lerner and his associates (2005) point to the presence of five qualities that together constitute a definition of positive youth development: competence, confidence, connection, character, and caring—or the five Cs (**Table 13.1**).

TABLE 13.1
The Five Cs of Positive Youth Development

FIVE Cs	DEFINITION
Competence	Viewing one's actions positively in different domains: social competence (e.g., resolving conflicts); cognitive competence (e.g., making good decisions); academic competence (e.g., getting good grades); vocational competence (e.g., establishing good work habits)
Confidence	Having an overall sense of self-worth and self-efficacy
Connection	Having positive, mutually rewarding relationships with family members, peers, teachers, and members of the community
Character	Respecting one's community's and society's standards; acting with integrity
Caring	Having understanding and compassion for others

Source: Lerner et al., 2005.

initiative   A readiness to initiate action, characteristic of self-motivated individuals.

intrinsic motivation
Motivation derived from the pleasure one experiences in an activity.

engagement   Concentrated attention, necessary for the performance of complex activities.

temporal arc   The time required for the completion of a project during which skill develops through successive evaluation and adjustment of performance; contributes to initiative.

Reed Larson (2000), at the University of Illinois, believes that characteristics such as caring and prosocial behavior can be traced to the development of **initiative** in adolescents. The concept of initiative is closely related to the construct of agency (see Chapter 5) and describes behavior that is intrinsically motivated, or organized around challenging and personally meaningful goals. Larson considers initiative to be central not only to the development of altruistic behaviors—those directed toward helping others—but also to the development of a vision for one's own life and for the skills needed to realize this. Larson argues, in fact, that in the absence of initiative, adolescents may simply go through the motions without ever becoming invested in what they are doing. He regards the development of initiative, in other words, as essential if adolescents are to become socially competent and responsible adults. Yet Larson's research leads him to believe that the activities at which adolescents spend most of their time afford few opportunities to develop initiative.

The importance of discovering the ingredients to positive youth development became all too clear to Larson and his research associates when they studied the daily emotional states of a representative sample of working- and middle-class adolescents. Adolescents were given pagers to wear and were beeped at random moments throughout the day. When asked what they were doing and how they felt, adolescents indicated feeling bored 27% of the times they were beeped (Larson & Richards, 1991). Larson notes that the "litany of explanations for this boredom—'algebra sucks,' 'I'm always bored on Sunday,' 'there's nothing to do,' 'the *Odyssey* is boring'—reads like a script from Bart Simpson. They communicate an ennui of being trapped in the present, waiting for someone to prove to them that life is worth living" (Larson, 2000, p. 170).

Putting aside for the moment the possibility that algebra or the *Odyssey* may not offer excitement or challenge to all, Larson wondered what would need to be present in order for adolescents to become invested in what they were doing. Worded another way, what components of their ongoing experience would be needed to contribute to the development of initiative?

Larson identifies three conditions that are closely tied to the growth of **initiative**. The first of these is **intrinsic motivation**. Adolescents are most likely to experience initiative when they are able to work at things they find intrinsically motivating, or interesting in their own right. These are activities for which they need no reward other than the pleasure they get from doing them. Important as this type of activity is, however, intrinsic motivation by itself is not enough. A second component that Larson believes essential for the development of initiative is **engagement**, or concentration. Tasks that are sufficiently complex that they demand concentrated attention for their successful completion require adolescents to direct their thoughts and consciously plan what they will do next. These tasks, rather than simple ones, are most likely to engage adolescents. Finally, Larson believes that adolescents develop initiative when they work at projects that can be completed only over an extended period of time, or **temporal arc**, and that require them to evaluate, and then adjust, their performance in order to successfully accomplish what they initially set out to do.

To what extent are these three ingredients present in adolescents' daily experiences? The two contexts that comprise the bulk of adolescents' waking hours are schoolwork and leisure, accounting for 25–30% and 40–50% of their waking hours, respectively. Larson notes, however, that each of these contexts lacks one or more of the elements critical for the development of initiative. When adolescents are paged in the classroom or doing homework, for instance, they typically report feeling challenged but report little intrinsic motivation for what they are doing. They also find it hard to concentrate on the task at hand and, despite being challenged, say they are bored. Conversely, when adolescents are paged during leisure activities, they report relatively high intrinsic motivation for what they are doing but little challenge or concentration. Thus, neither of the two types of activities in which adolescents spend most of their time are likely to promote the development of initiative.

There is a third category of activities, however, that is intrinsically motivating to adolescents and also demands their concentrated attention. Larson refers to these activities as **structured voluntary activities**; examples include extracurricular sports, hobbies, or service learning programs (see Chapter 9). Even though adolescents spend relatively little time at these, the activities afford exposure to the ingredients Larson considers important for the development of initiative. Thus, when adolescents are paged during one of these activities, they report feeling highly motivated as well as needing to pay close attention to what they are doing. Although Larson's data do not directly provide a measure of change over time, other research suggests that this component, that of a temporal arc, is also present in such activities (Larson, 2000; Rogoff et al., 1995).

What changes might we expect to see in adolescents' behavior as they participate in structured voluntary activities? A number of studies suggest that such participation can effect positive changes across a variety of domains in adolescents' lives, from improved grades and educational goals to increases in self-control, independence, and assertiveness (Eccles & Barber, 1999; Hattie et al., 1997; Marsh, 1992). Even adolescents' speech has been found to change over time as they participate in these types of activities. Instead of communicating boredom, passivity, or defensiveness, as Larson and others have noted, adolescents' speech is found to reflect a new sense of agency (Heath, 1993, 1994). Their use of language reveals that they begin to think in terms of the different outcomes that might result from acting in one way or another, and how best to achieve the outcomes they desire. As Larson (2000) comments, "The conditions that make structured youth activities a fertile context for the development of initiative, I believe, also make them a rich context for the development of an array of other positive qualities, from altruism to identity. Children and adolescents come alive in these activities, they become active agents in ways that rarely happen in other parts of their lives. This makes youth activities an invaluable laboratory for the study of processes of positive development, one that deserves much more scientific attention" (p. 178).

Adolescents are more likely to be engaged in tasks that they find interesting and challenging. Playing an instrument in a marching band helps to build initiative because it is intrinsically motivating and requires discipline over a temporal arc.

structured voluntary activities Activities that are intrinsically motivating and challenging that build skills and foster initiative.

Love

Finally, one cannot overestimate the importance of being loved. Even though this is a truth we all live with, it is encouraging to see it find empirical support. Chase-Lansdale, Wakschlag, and Brooks-Gunn (1995) emphasize that just one caring relationship in an adolescent's life can make the difference between developing in a healthy or unhealthy way, even in the face of family conflict, poverty, parental psychopathology, and other formidable factors. Similarly, Werner and Smith (1982, 1992) found that the essential ingredient to healthy development in each of the individuals they studied, who were at risk for one or more reasons, was a "basic, trusting relationship" with someone who cared for them.

Perhaps Urie Bronfenbrenner (1990) summed it all up best when he said what adolescents need most is someone who finds them "somehow special, especially wonderful, and especially precious" (p. 31).

Go to the
Adolescence
Companion Website
at
www.sinauer.com/cobb
for quizzes, flashcards, summaries, and other study resources.

SUMMARY and KEY TERMS

Protective Factors in Adolescence

Families: From their families, and in particular from their parents, adolescents need a combination of care (responsiveness) and discipline (demandingness). Responsiveness can be expressed not only by immediate family members but also by adult network structures and by community institutions. Demandingness is expressed through monitoring adolescents' activities and expecting them to help out with the family's needs. Family interactions that promote both connectedness and individuality also contribute to healthy personality development.

Communities: Neighborhoods that are safe, that offer adequate services, and that provide informal social networks and norms for their residents foster the development of youth assets such as supportive relationships with adult role models, healthy relationships with peers, participation in organized activities after school, and participation in religious activities. The healthiest communities for adolescents are those in which adolescents are more likely to be involved in institutions within the community.
collective efficacy

Schools: Schools contribute to positive development when they enable adolescents to feel safe and when students receive emotional support from their teachers. Teachers who are both supportive and demanding—qualities found in authoritative parents—are most effective.

Personal Strengths: Temperament, Competence, and Religion: In addition to characteristics of families, communities, and schools, the personal qualities of adolescents themselves serve as protective factors. Their temperament, intelligence, competence, sense of self-efficacy, and religious beliefs can help protect them against the stresses of daily life.

Stress and Coping

What makes an event stressful is not necessarily the event per se, but the need to adapt to the changes it brings about. In general, the more rapidly one needs to adapt, the more stress one experiences. Many situations can be interpreted in ways that increase or reduce their stress potential.
stress

How Adolescents Cope with Stress: Adolescents typically cope with stress in either of two general ways: problem-focused coping and emotion-focused coping. Those who seek out experiences that are relevant to the decisions or problems they face (information oriented) are most likely to adopt a problem-focused approach. Those who are relatively closed to new information, relying instead on the standards of others (normative oriented), are more likely to use an emotion-focused approach—as are individuals who procrastinate and do nothing when faced with stress (avoidant oriented).
coping, problem-focused coping, emotion-focused coping

Gender and Ethnicity: Gender differences have been found with respect to methods of coping, with females being more likely to use emotion-focused coping than males. Some research, though, finds no gender differences in types of coping strategies or in how successfully either gender copes, instead finding coping effectiveness to differ based on feelings of self-esteem and self-efficacy. Among the most common sources of stress at school are aggression, bullying, and fear

SUMMARY and KEY TERMS

of theft, with these concerns considerably higher among African American and Hispanic students than among European American ones.

Learning Effective Coping Strategies: Adolescents can learn to cope with stress more effectively. By learning to appraise situations more accurately, adolescents can avoid common errors. Attributional errors, or errors that overestimate the importance of dispositional stressors and underestimate the importance of situational stressors, and errors arising from a tendency to notice only confirming information frequently lead to inaccurate appraisals and less-than-optimal coping strategies. The ways adolescents respond to stress can reduce it or increase it. Skills related to assertiveness, communication, negotiation, and compromise are most effective. Adolescents can also learn to anticipate and manage the emotions prompted by stress.
attributional error

Beyond Coping: Caring and Prosocial Behavior

Nearly one- third of U.S. adolescents volunteer in charitable activities. Many of these youth go beyond volunteering to establishing organizations of their own. Prosocial adolescents are more likely than their peers to describe themselves in terms of their values and ideals; and their sense of themselves is more likely to come from their parents than from their peers. The experience of being loved, of having their needs met by someone in their life, appears to be essential for adolescents to develop into caring people.

Positive Youth Development

The "Five Cs" serve to define positive youth development: competence, confidence, connection, character, and caring. The development of initiative may be critical if adolescents are to develop a vision for their lives and the skills needed to realize them. The daily contexts in which adolescents spend most of their time (schoolwork and leisure) afford few opportunities to develop initiative. Structured voluntary activities incorporate the components thought to contribute to the development of initiative: intrinsic motivation, concentrated attention, and the need to evaluate and adjust one's performance to successfully accomplish a goal.
initiative, intrinsic motivation, engagement, temporal arc, structured voluntary activities

Love: Research shows that just one caring relationship in an adolescent's life can make the difference between developing in a healthy or an unhealthy way.

Glossary

abstinence-only programs Sex education programs that teach that abstinence is the only way to avoid pregnancy and the risk of sexually transmitted diseases.

academic tracking The assignment of students to one of several courses of study in high school on the basis of criteria such as academic interests and goals, past achievement, and ability.

acceleration Allowing gifted adolescents to advance beyond their grade level at a faster than normal rate.

accommodation Piaget's term for the process by which cognitive structures are altered to fit new events or experiences.

acculturation A socialization process by which members of a minority adopt the customs of the dominant group, while maintaining a separate cultural identity.

achieved ethnic identity A stage in ethnic identity formation in which one has a clear sense of one's ethnicity that reflects feelings of belonging and emotional identification.

adolescence A period in life that begins with biological maturation, during which individuals are expected to accomplish certain developmental tasks, and that ends when they achieve a self-sufficient state of adulthood as defined by society.

adolescence-limited antisocial behavior Problem behavior that originates in adolescence and drops out in early adulthood.

adrenal androgens Hormones produced by the adrenal glands, which initiate the initial stage of puberty.

adrenarche The initial phase of puberty, which involves activity of the adrenal androgens.

adult status hypothesis An explanation for the effects of asynchronous development that attributes the result of timing to the status that awaits adolescents of either sex when they become adults.

affective disorders Disorders whose primary symptoms reflect a disturbance of mood, such as depression.

age changes Biological and experiential changes that accompany aging, irrespective of cultural or historical context.

agency An aspect of mature functioning characterized in independent cultures by asserting one's thoughts and feelings, and in interdependent cultures by self-restraint and maintaining harmonious relationships.

AIDS Acquired immune deficiency syndrome: a sexually transmitted disease resulting from a virus that attacks the immune system; can also be transmitted through contaminated blood transfusions or from an infected pregnant woman to her fetus.

alcohol A drug that functions as a central nervous system depressant.

alienation Indifference where devotion or attachment formerly existed; estrangement.

androgens Male sex hormones.

androgynous A personality in which there are both masculine and feminine attributes.

anorexia An eating disorder characterized by severely limiting the intake of food; more common in females.

anovulatory Menstrual cycles that do not include the release of an egg.

anterior pituitary A center within the brain that produces hormones that act on the gonads.

apprenticeship Rogoff's term suggesting that thinking is an activity that is shared with others, guiding practical action.

archival research The use of existing data, such as public records, to provide answers to research questions.

artistic personality types In Holland's typology of vocational interests, individuals who prefer work requiring imagination and creativity, for example, a graphic artist or poet.

assimilation Piaget's term for the process by which new events and experiences are adjusted to fit existing cognitive structures.

asynchrony Differences in the timing of pubertal changes within an adolescent or from one adolescent to the next.

attributional error   An overestimation of the importance of dispositional stressors or an underestimation of the importance of situational ones.

attributional retraining   A career counseling technique that focuses on individuals' explanations for anticipated career-related successes or failures.

authoritarian parenting   Parents who stress obedience, respect for authority, and traditional values.

authoritative parenting   Parents who stress self-reliance and independence, establish clear standards for behavior and give reasons when disciplining.

automaticity   The ability to perform highly practiced cognitive operations without conscious attention.

autonomous   The state of being self-governing and responsible for one's actions.

average adolescents   Adolescents who are moderately popular with their classmates and moderately disliked as well.

bias   Distortion of the effect of a variable due to research design or researcher expectations.

bicultural identity   The process by which minority adolescents identify themselves with respect to the two cultures to which they belong.

bisexual   Sexual attraction toward individuals of both sexes.

body image   An individual's satisfaction or dissatisfaction with the image of their body.

body mass index (BMI)   One's weight in pounds divided by the square of one's height in inches times 703 ({weight in pounds/(height in inches)^2} × 703). Since body fatness varies with age and sex, percentiles for BMI are specific to age and gender.

bulimia   An eating disorder characterized by bingeing (excessive or compulsive eating) and then purging (ridding the body of food, such as self-induced vomiting); more common in females.

bullying   Repeated aggressive behaviors or remarks occurring over an extended period of time that the victim finds difficult to defend against.

carefree diffusion   The resolution of the psychosocial crisis by neither exploring nor committing oneself to life options primarily due to enjoyment of one's present circumstances.

castration anxiety   In Freudian theory, a young boy's fear of being castrated by his father as punishment for the boy's sexual attraction to his mother.

cell proliferation   The overproduction of neurons and their interconnections.

cervix   The opening to the uterus.

child labor   Work done by children and adolescents prior to reaching the minimum age for work, that is harmful in one way or another.

child labor laws   Laws that specify minimum ages for various types of work.

chlamydia   A sexually transmitted disease, caused by a bacterium, that can affect the reproductive tract, possibly leading to pelvic inflammatory disease.

chronosystem   The changing impact of the various environmental systems (micro-, meso-, exo-, macro) at different historical periods.

circumcision   Surgical removal of the prepuce (or foreskin) covering the glans of the penis.

classification variable   A variable, such as age, that cannot be manipulated by randomly assigning participants to levels of the variable.

climacteric   The gradual decline in functioning of the reproductive organs in middle age.

clique   A peer group made up of one's best friends, usually including no more than five or six members.

clitoris   That part of the external genitals in females that is the primary source of sexual stimulation.

cognitive restructuring   A counseling technique that confronts individuals with their irrational beliefs.

cohort differences   Experiential differences between groups of people born at different periods in time; these differences can be confounded with age changes.

cohort group   People born during the same historical period or undergoing the same historical influences.

collective efficacy   The willingness of neighbors to intervene in situations that might threaten the well-being of others.

collectivistic cultures   Cultures that encourage a sense of self in terms of one's rules or status vis-à-vis others.

commitment in relativism   The third of Perry's three forms of thought: committing oneself to a point of view from which one can derive meaning.

commitment   The process of committing oneself to a definite course of action in achieving an identity.

comorbid   The interrelatedness and co-occurrence of several problem behaviors.

comprehensive sex education programs   Sex education programs that teach abstinence as a preferred approach and educate students concerning effective methods of contraception.

compulsory education laws   Legislation making school attendance mandatory for children and adolescents until they graduate or reach a minimum age.

computer-assisted instruction (CAI)   The use of computers to provide instruction as well as to monitor student progress provides flexibility that helps students continue their education, even when their schedules are erratic.

conflict resolution training   Programs designed to teach students to view conflict as a problem to be solved mutually, with a win-win outcome.

conformity   The tendency to go along with the norms and standards of one's group.

confounding   The presence of additional factors other than the variable of interest that can account for observed differences.

connectedness   A quality of family interactions reflecting openness to and respect for others' opinions.

conservation   The realization that something remains the same despite changes in its appearance.

constructive controversy   A technique using controversy to stimulate solutions to problems by having students alternately argue their own and the opposing side of a conflict.

constructive knowledge   The third of Belenky and associates' three forms of thought: an awareness that knowledge is constructed; the ability to examine one's beliefs.

constructive perspective   The view that perception is an active, constructive process in which individuals interpret and give meaning to their experiences.

contextual perspective   The view that development is influenced by one's ethnicity and culture.

controversial adolescents   Adolescents frequently mentioned by classmates as someone they least like and by others as a best friend.

conventional personality types   In Holland's typology of vocational interests, individuals who prefer highly structured environments and well-defined tasks.

conventional reasoning   Kohlberg's second level of moral reasoning, in which moral thinking is guided by internalized social standards.

cooperative learning   Placing students of different ability levels together in small working groups.

coping   Strategies for managing stressful situations that tax personal resources.

correlational research   A procedure in which subjects are assigned to groups on the basis of preexisting characteristics.

cortical gray matter   Regions within the brain consisting of cell bodies, dendrites, and primarily unmyelinated axons.

cross-sectional design   A research design in which several age cohorts are compared at a single time of measurement.

crowd   A peer group formed from several cliques of the same age group.

crush   An idealized fantasy about another person that is rarely reciprocated.

culture   The values, beliefs, and customs that are shared by a group of people and passed from one generation to the next.

culture-fair test   A measure of intelligence that minimizes cultural bias by using materials or requiring skills not likely to be more familiar to one culture over another.

dating   A social activity that typically begins in mid-adolescence.

decline stage   Super's fifth stage of vocational development, in which one retires.

deductive reasoning   Reasoning from the general to the particular.

degrees of freedom   The number of scores in a set that are free to vary given certain constraints, such as a known mean.

demandingness   The degree to which parents expect adolescents to act responsibly, and supervise and monitor their activities.

dependent variable   The measure used to determine the effect of the independent variable in an experiment.

depression   An affective disorder that may take a number of forms, all of which are characterized by a disturbance of mood.

developing countries   Countries that have only recently begun to adopt modern technology, social forms, and means of production. Such countries were previously termed "third world" countries.

developmental tasks   Age-related norms that reflect social expectations for normal development.

dialectical thinking   Reasoning that questions the premises on which it is based when tests of the premises are not supported.

differentiated instruction   Flexible classroom structure providing multiple formats for gaining information.

differentiation   A process by which one distinguishes or perceives differences not previously recognized.

diffuse/avoidant oriented   A style of information processing characterized by procrastinating and avoiding decisions.

direct instruction   Instruction directed toward the mastery of basic skills; all students are involved in the same activities at any given time.

disengaged parenting   Parents who provide little support or supervision.

double-blind controls   A research procedure in which neither the researcher nor the participants know which individuals have been assigned to which experimental conditions.

drug dependence   Physical dependence on a substance, such that one develops a tolerance and experiences withdrawal when use is discontinued; also known as drug addiction.

dualistic thinking   The first of Perry's three forms of thought: the belief that truth is independent of one's frame of reference.

early adolescence   That period of adolescence between the ages of about 11 to 15, marked by the onset of puberty, changing gender roles, more autonomous relationships with parents, and more mature relationships with peers.

early maturation   Pubertal maturation occurring earlier in adolescents than the norm for their sex.

egocentrism   The failure to realize that one's perspective is not shared by others.

Electra complex   A Freudian concept in which the young girl is sexually attracted to her father and regards her mother as her rival.

emerging adulthood   A period between adolescence and adulthood characterized by demographic unpredictability and increased opportunity for identity exploration.

emotion-focused coping   Attempts to reduce stress by minimizing its emotional impact, for example, denials, wishful thinking.

emotional transmission   The transmission of emotions from one person to another within a family.

encoding   The process by which information is transferred from one form to another in memory.

enculturation   Acquiring the norms of one's social group.

engagement   Concentrated attention, necessary for the performance of complex activities.

enrichment   Providing gifted adolescents with additional opportunities and experiences.

enterprising personality types   In Holland's typology of vocational interests, individuals who prefer work involving interpersonal skills and assertiveness, such as management, law, or sales.

environmental model   A set of assumptions in which the environment is taken to be the primary determinant of psychological development.

equilibration   Piaget's term for the process of balancing assimilation and accommodation that is responsible for the growth of thought.

error   Unexplained and unsystematic variability.

establishment stage   Super's third stage of vocational development, in which one settles into one's work.

estradiol   A sex hormone present in higher levels in females than in males; it contributes to breast development, distribution of body fat, and regulation of the menstrual cycle.

estrogens   Female sex hormones.

ethic of care   Psychologist Carol Gilligan's description of a morality based on responsiveness to and care for others.

ethnic identity   An awareness of belonging to an ethnic group that shapes one's thoughts, feelings, and behavior.

ethnic identity search   An intermediate stage in ethnic identity formation involving exploration of the meaning of one's ethnicity.

ethnicity   The cultural group to which an individual belongs.

executive functions   Mental activities, such as decision making, evaluating, and planning, that are regulated by the prefrontal cortex.

exosystem   Contexts occurring at the level of the community, such as types of schools and housing.

experiment   A research procedure in which participants are randomly assigned to groups that are then treated differently.

exploration stage   Super's second stage of vocational development, in which one begins to make choices related to one's future work.

exploration   The process of exploring possibilities and life options in achieving an identity.

external validity   The extent to which a research study's conclusions can be generalized to other populations and contexts.

externalizing problems   Behaviors that directly harm others.

fantasy stage   Ginzburg's first stage of vocational development, characterized by focus on highly visible aspects of vocations and no assessment of personal qualifications.

female genital mutilation (FGM)   The World Health Organization recognizes several forms of FGM, the most severe of which involves cutting out the entire clitoris, along with sewing shut most of the outer labia.

flow   The experience of becoming totally absorbed in a challenging activity.

follicle-stimulating hormone (FSH)   A gonadotropic hormone produced by the anterior pituitary that acts on the gonads.

full-service schools   Schools that provide a variety of health and social services to students and their families in collaboration with the community.

gateway hypothesis   The assumption that drug use progresses through stages in which the use of one type of drug provides a pathway to the use of other drugs.

gender differences   Culturally determined differences in masculinity and femininity.

gender stereotypes   The cultural expectations concerning behaviors that are appropriate for each sex.

gender   The cultural and psychological contributions to being female or male.

genital herpes   A sexually transmitted disease characterized by recurring outbreaks of itching or burning blisters; caused by a virus that remains dormant in the body.

genital warts   A sexually transmitted disease caused by the human papillomavirus.

gifted   Description of students who place above a predetermined cutoff point on intelligence scales or who demonstrate special talents in diverse areas.

glans   The part of the clitoris or penis that is most sensitive to stimulation.

globalization   The process by which expanding international trade, communication, and travel erases national and geographical boundaries.

GnRH pulse generator   Cells within the hypothalamus that pulse out bursts of GnRH.

gonadarche   The second stage of puberty, regulated by the neuroendocrine system.

gonadotropin-releasing hormone (GnRH)   A hormone released by the hypothalamus and involved in regulating the timing of pubertal events.

gonads   The sex glands; the ovaries in females and the testes in males.

gonorrhea   A sexually transmitted disease caused by a bacterium.

gossip   A process by which preadolescents establish group norms.

group identity   A psychosocial task of early adolescence that entails the resolution of issues related to affiliation and belonging.

growth spurt A period of rapid growth that often occurs during puberty.

growth stage Super's first stage of vocational development characterized more by discovery about oneself than about vocations.

habituation Decreased responsiveness to a stimulus with repeated exposure to it.

heterosexual Sexual attraction toward individuals of the other sex.

history effect Any event extraneous to a research project that can affect the results and jeopardize the internal validity of the research.

HIV Human immunodeficiency virus: a virus attacking the immune system, leading to AIDS (acquired immune deficiency syndrome).

homosexual Sexual attraction toward individuals of the same sex.

hormones Chemical messengers that are secreted directly into the bloodstream and regulated by the endocrine system.

hymen A fold of skin partially covering the opening to the vagina.

hypothalamus A center within the brain that governs hormonal activity and regulatory activities such as eating, drinking, and body temperature.

ideal self-image The individual's idealized image of the self, including anticipated as well as actual ways of being.

identity achievement The resolution of the psychosocial crisis of identity by exploring life options and then committing oneself to personally defined goals.

identity diffusion The resolution of the psychosocial crisis without the experience of crisis or commitment over identity issues.

identity foreclosure The resolution of the psychosocial crisis of identity through the assumption of traditional, conventional, or parentally chosen goals and values without the experience of crisis or conflict over identity issues.

identity statuses Resolutions to identity that differ in commitment and exploration of life options.

identity The part of one's personality of which one is aware and is able to see as a meaningful and coherent whole.

imaginary audience The experience of being the focus of attention that emerges with adolescents' ability to think about thinking in others and their confusion of the concerns of others with their own preoccupation with themselves.

independent variable The variable that is manipulated in an experiment, by randomly assigning participants to different levels of the variable.

index offenses Actions that are criminal at any age, for example, homicide and burglary.

individualistic cultures Cultures that encourage a sense of self as independent, self-sufficient, and autonomous.

individuality A quality of family interactions reflecting the ability to express one's ideas and say how one differs from others.

individuation The process of distinguishing one's attitudes and beliefs from those of one's parents.

inductive reasoning Reasoning from the particular to the general.

indulgent parenting Parents who are warm and supportive but provide little supervision.

information oriented A style of information processing characterized by actively searching for and evaluating information.

information processing An approach to cognition that focuses on the processes by which information is encoded, retrieved, and utilized.

initiative A readiness to initiate action, characteristic of self-motivated individuals.

intelligence The ability to profit from experience and adapt to one's surroundings; measured by intelligence tests.

internal validity The extent to which a research study unambiguously answers the questions it was designed to address.

internalizing problems Behaviors that are harmful to the adolescent who engages in them.

intimacy The ability to share oneself with another, characterized by self-disclosure and mutuality.

intrinsic motivation Motivation derived from the pleasure one experiences in an activity.

investigative personality types In Holland's typology of vocational interests, individuals who prefer work requiring intellectual curiosity, for example, a scientist or mathematician.

isolate Adolescents who have few friends, either within a clique or outside it, and who have few links to other adolescents in the social network.

jigsaw classroom A classroom organized into small, ethnically balanced working groups in which each student contributes a different part of the lesson.

junior high school A secondary school that typically includes the seventh through the ninth grades.

juvenile delinquency Illegal actions committed by a minor.

kisspeptin A substance secreted by cells in the hypothalamus that activates the gene GPR54, triggering the pulse generator.

knowledge-acquisition components Cognitive mechanisms—for instance, perception and memory retrieval—that, under the direction of metacomponents, acquire new information as needed.

late adolescence The period of adolescence between the ages of about 16 to 19 that is organized around the central task of achieving an identity, in which adolescents integrate their sexuality into their relationships, prepare for a vocation, and fashion a personal set of beliefs.

late maturation   Pubertal maturation occurring later in adolescents than the norm for their sex.

learning disability   Difficulty with academic tasks that is not due to emotional or sensory problems and presumably reflects neurological dysfunction.

learning styles   Students' preferences concerning various aspects of the learning situation, for example, working individually or in groups, getting information by reading or listening to a class presentation.

leptin   A hormone secreted by fat cells that may play a role in menarche.

liaison   Adolescents who have friends in several cliques but do not themselves belong to any particular clique.

life span perspective   The view that development is characterized by continuity as well as change throughout life.

life-course persistent antisocial behavior   Problem behavior that originates in childhood and persists into adulthood.

limbic system   An area of the brain located beneath the cortex that is involved in processing social and emotional information and evaluating rewards.

longitudinal design   A research design in which a single cohort group is followed over time, tested at several times of measurement.

low-income families   Families with incomes no greater than twice the federal poverty level.

luteinizing hormone (LH)   A gonadotropic hormone produced by the anterior pituitary that acts on the gonads.

macrosystem   The underlying social and political climate at the level of society.

mainstreaming   Keeping learning-disabled students in regular classrooms.

maintenance stage   Super's fourth stage of vocational development, in which one maintains one's occupational skills and position.

major depressive disorder   A period of severe depression requiring hospitalization or other treatment.

male generic language   Use of the pronoun "he" to refer to an individual of either sex, and use of words such as "man" or "mankind" to refer to all people.

maltreatment   Instances of harm to children or adolescents that are nonaccidental and avoidable; they can be due to either abuse or neglect.

marijuana   A mild hallucinogen from the plant *Cannabis sativa*; the primary psychoactive substance is THC (tetrahydrocannabinol).

masked depression   Depression that manifests itself in ways other than depressed mood, for example, agitation, or the inability to sleep.

maturation   A potential confound resulting from systematic changes over time that are not due to the treatment being studied.

maturational deviance hypothesis   An explanation for the effects of asynchronous development that attributes the effects of timing to changing adolescents' status relative to their peers.

menarche   The occurrence of a girl's first menstrual period.

menopause   Cessation of menstrual period in middle age.

mesosystem   Social contexts involving interactions of several microsystems, such as when parents meet teachers.

meta-analysis   A statistical procedure for reaching conclusions regarding an area of research by combining the findings from multiple studies.

metacognition   Awareness of one's thinking, cognitive abilities, and style.

metacomponents   Higher-order cognitive functions that select and monitor lower-order cognitive functions, for example, metacomponents are employed to determine which performance components are required to perform a task.

microsystem   One's immediate social contexts, involving firsthand experiences, such as interactions at home or in the classroom.

middle school   A secondary school that includes the fifth or sixth through the eighth grades.

minority   A social group, distinguished by physical or cultural characteristics, that often receives differential treatment.

model   A set of assumptions about reality in general and human nature in particular from which theories proceed.

moral domain   A form of social understanding concerned with welfare, justice, and rights.

morality   The development of standards of right and wrong.

moratorium   The experience of conflict over the issues of identity formation prior to the establishment of firm goals or long-term commitments.

multiple intelligences   The view that intelligence is comprised of a number of different capacities, each relevant to a different domain—for instance, music, linguistics, mathematics, interpersonal relations. One's ability in each domain is not necessarily highly correlated with ability in other domains.

multitasking   Moving back and forth from one task to another.

myelination   The formation of a fatty sheath surrounding a nerve fiber (axon), which increases the speed of neural conduction.

myotonia   An increase in muscular tension.

naturalistic observation   The observation and recording of participants' behavior in their natural setting.

neglected adolescents   Adolescents who are rarely mentioned by their classmates as someone they most like or as someone they least like.

neuroendrocrine system   The system of the body that includes the glands that produce hormones and those parts of the nervous system that activate, inhibit, and control hormone production.

nicotine   The psychoactive substance in cigarettes that is both a stimulant and a depressant.

nocturnal emission A spontaneous ejaculation of seminal fluid during sleep; sometimes called a wet dream.

normative oriented A style of information processing characterized by reliance on social norms and the expectations of relatives and friends.

Oedipus complex A Freudian concept in which the young boy is sexually attracted to his mother, and regards his father as his rival.

organismic model A set of assumptions in which the unfolding of genetically organized processes is taken to be the primary determinant of psychological development.

organized activities Leisure activities organized by adults that adolescents choose to engage in.

outer labia The outer folds of skin surrounding the opening of the vagina and the clitoris.

ovaries Structures within the female reproductive system flanking the uterus that house the immature eggs and produce female sex hormones.

overcontrolled Adolescents who are anxious and inhibited, frequently resulting in internalizing problems.

overweight Individuals are considered to be overweight when their weight is at or above the 95th percentile for their body mass index.

ovum (plural ova) The female sex cell, also called the egg; the male equivalent is sperm.

parental involvement The involvement of parents in classroom instruction, homework, school governance, and community service.

parental monitoring A practice in which parents monitor their children's behavior when they are not physically present to supervise their activities.

parentified A reversal in the parent-child relationship in which the burden of caring for the parent's needs is assumed by the adolescent.

peer group A group of individuals of the same age; a social group that regulates the pace of socialization.

peer pressure Experienced pressure to think and act like one's friends.

performance components Cognitive mechanisms, selected by metacomponents, that operate directly on the information to be processed.

performance-ability orientation A motivational pattern in which students focus on their own performance, using it as a way to assess their ability.

personal domain A form of social understanding concerned with activities involving personal choice and prerogative.

personal effectiveness Perceiving oneself as effective and in control of a situation.

personal fable The feeling of being special; thought to derive from the imaginary audience.

physical aggression Aggressive actions involving physical contact, such as pushing or hitting.

poor families Families with incomes below the federal poverty level.

popular Adolescents nominated by their classmates as those they most like.

population The entire group of individuals in which an investigator is interested.

possible selves Life options that adolescents imagine for themselves; some are positive, or hoped-for, and others are feared, or negative, possibilities.

postconventional reasoning Kohlberg's third level of moral reasoning, in which moral thinking is guided by self-derived principles.

practical intelligence To be distinguished from "academic intelligence" or intelligence measured by IQ tests, practical intelligence requires the individual, rather than a teacher or an examiner, to define the problem to be solved and decide what constitutes a solution.

preconventional reasoning Kohlberg's first level of moral reasoning, characterized by the absence of internalized standards.

prefrontal cortex Region of the cortex located behind the forehead involved in abstract thought.

prepuce A thin skin covering the glans of the clitoris or penis.

primary sex characteristics Differences between females and males in the reproductive system that develop during puberty.

problem-focused coping Attempts to reduce stress by changing a stressful situation.

procedural knowledge The second of Belenky and associates' three forms of thought: independent thought that is nonetheless limited to a single frame of reference.

progesterone A sex hormone present in higher levels in females than in males; it contributes to regulation of the menstrual cycle.

prosocial behaviors Positive behaviors such as cooperativeness, kindness, and trustworthiness.

psychoactive A drug that alters mood.

psychometric approach An approach that focuses on the measurement of individual differences in abilities contributing to intelligence.

puberty Growth processes, including the skeletal growth spurt and maturation of the reproductive system, that begin in early adolescence and transform children into physically and sexually mature adults.

pubic lice Parasitic insects that are usually transmitted sexually; sometimes called "crabs."

quasi-experimental research A research design in which participants are not randomly assigned to conditions, but in which preexisting groups are used, introducing possible confounding.

random assignment The assignment of participants to groups in such a way that each participant has an equal chance of being assigned to any condition.

random error Unexplained and unsystematic variability.

realistic personality types   In Holland's typology of vocational interests, individuals who prefer situations that are explicitly defined and require few interpersonal skills, for example, a mechanic or computer programmer.

realistic stage   Ginzburg's third stage of vocational development, characterized by exploration of and commitment to a vocational path.

reciprocal determinism   The two-way influence between person and environment; not only does the environment influence behavior but behavior changes the environment.

reinforcement   Any event that when contingent on a behavior increases the probability of that behavior occurring again.

rejected adolescents   Adolescents frequently mentioned by classmates as someone they least like and rarely mentioned as someone they most like.

relational aggression   Aggression achieved by manipulating relationships, such as by excluding someone from a group or spreading rumors.

relativistic thinking   The second of Perry's three forms of thought: awareness of more than one frame of reference by which ideas can be evaluated.

religious identity   An awareness of belonging to a religious group.

resilient   Characterized by attitudes and social skills that enable individuals to function in a variety of settings.

responsiveness   The degree to which parents are sensitive, supportive and involved.

role clarity   Clear under-standing among family members concerning the nature and responsibilities of each person's role.

sample   A subgroup drawn from the population that is the subject of the research.

SAT   The Scholastic Aptitude Test, the most widely used college entrance exam.

scientific method   A method of inquiry in which conclusions are verified empirically by checking them against observations; a methodology for making observations that will support or refute hypotheses.

secondary education   Middle schools, junior high schools, and high schools.

secondary sex characteristics   Differences between females and males in the reproductive system that develop during puberty.

secular trend   The earlier onset of puberty, faster growth, and larger size reached by adolescents today than in the past.

self-concept   The individual's awareness of the self as a person; a theory about the self that explains personal experience.

self-esteem   The individual's overall positive or negative evaluation of herself or himself.

self-handicapping strategies   The adoption of behaviors to account for poor performance in lieu of ability.

self-stimulation   Self-stimulation of the genitals (commonly called masturbation).

self-disclosure   A process by which adolescents understand and define themselves through an intimate sharing of thoughts and feelings.

sequential design   A research design in which several age cohort groups are compared at several times of measurement; essentially, a number of longitudinal studies, each starting with a different age group.

service learning programs   Comprehensive education programs that include a community service component, requiring students to do volunteer work.

sex differences   Biological and physiological differences distinguishing the sexes.

sexual orientation   The attraction individuals feel for members of the same and/or the other sex.

sexual scripts   Learned expectations derived from cultural roles and gender stereotypes that guide behavior in sexual situations.

sexual-minority youth   Adolescents whose sexual orientation is not exclusively heterosexual.

sexually transitted disease (STD)   An infection that is spread through sexual contact.

shaft   The part of the clitoris or penis that becomes erect during sexual stimulation.

social cognition   The ability to assume another's perspective and coordinate this with one's own.

social competence   Skills enabling individuals to accurately assess social situations and respond adaptively.

social conventional domain   A form of social understanding concerned with the rules and traditions governing social interactions within a group.

social personality types   In Holland's typology of vocational interests, individuals who prefer work involving them with people, such as counseling or teaching.

social preference   An index of popularity measuring how much an adolescent is liked by others.

social prestige   An index of popularity measuring how much an adolescent is looked up to by others.

social skills training   A component of social-cognitive intervention programs.

social-cognitive intervention   An intervention program based on social-cognitive learning principles.

special education classes   Classes for learning-disabled students that are tailored to the needs of each student.

special education consultant   A consultant who meets with teachers to discuss ways to meet the needs of learning-disabled students who are mainstreamed.

speed of processing   The rate at which a cognitive operation (e.g., encoding, decoding, retrieval) or a combination of these can be performed.

sperm   The male sex cell; the female equivalent is the ovum.

spermarche   A boy's first ejaculation of seminal fluid.

stage termination hypothesis   An explanation for the effects of early maturation that acknowledges not having as much time as needed to complete the developmental tasks of middle childhood.

statistical regression   A potential confound in quasi-experimental research in which extreme pretest scores drift toward the mean of the posttest distribution.

status offenses   Actions that are illegal when engaged in by minors but legal for adults, for example, truancy and drinking alcohol.

STEM courses   Courses in science, technology, engineering, and mathematics that often provide a gateway to higher level jobs.

stereotype threat   The perceived risk of confirming a negative stereotype.

strategies   Activities that organize cognition so as to improve performance, such as repeating a phone number or categorizing a list of things to be remembered.

stress   The body's response to an event that requires adapting to changes brought about by that event.

structured voluntary activities   Activities that are intrinsically motivating and challenging that build skills and foster initiative.

subject mortality   In longitudinal studies, the loss of participants over time.

subjective knowledge   The first of Belenky and associates' three forms of thought: a covert examination of issues while maintaining a surface conformity to traditional ideas.

superego   The aspect of the personality in Freudian theory that represents the internalized standards and values of society.

synaptic pruning   The selective elimination of brain cells (neurons) and their connections.

syphilis   A sexually transmitted disease, caused by a bacterium, that can also be transmitted through blood transfusions or from a pregnant woman to her fetus; progresses over several stages.

system of juvenile justice   Legislation instituting separate legal proceedings for juveniles and adults.

task-mastery orientation   A motivational pattern in which students focus on the task they are learning and work to increase their mastery and competence.

temporal arc   The time required for the completion of a project during which skill develops through successive evaluation and adjustment of performance; contributes to initiative.

tentative stage   Ginzburg's second stage of vocational development, in which vocational choice is directed more by interests than capacities.

test of significance   A statistical procedure for determining whether group differences are due to random error or can be attributed to the variable being studied.

testes   Structures within the male reproductive system contained in the scrotum that produce sperm and male sex hormones.

testing effect   Knowledge and skills acquired by taking similar tests over the course of a research study; a potential source of confounding.

testosterone   A sex hormone present in higher levels in males than in females.

theory   A set of testable statements derived from the assumptions of a model.

time of measurement differences   Differences due to social conditions, currents of opinion, and historical events that can affect observations in longitudinal research; such differences are confounded with age changes.

traditional cultures   Cultures that have maintained their values and practices over long periods. These cultures often find themselves in conflict with other traditional or more rapidly changing cultures or with internal pressures for change.

undercontrolled   Adolescents who have difficulty inhibiting and controlling their behavior, frequently resulting in externalizing problems.

unexamined ethnic identity   An initial stage in ethnic identity formation that involves a lack of awareness of the issues related to one's ethnicity and a simple internalization of the values of the dominant culture.

uterus   A muscular enclosure at the top of the vagina that holds the fetus during pregnancy.

vagina   The muscular tube in females leading from the labia at its opening to the uterus.

vasocongestion   An accumula-tion of blood in the vessels serving the erogenous zones (areas of the body that are particularly sensitive to sexual arousal).

WAIS–III   An intelligence scale for adolescents and adults.

white matter   Brain areas containing myelinated pathways.

WISC–IV   An intelligence scale for children and adolescents up to 16 years of age.

work experience   Receiving academic credit for work done on a job.

working memory   A brief memory that holds information for less than a minute while further processing occurs.

zone of proximal development   Vygotsky's term for the range of skills which individuals must possess in order to profit from exposure to those who are more skilled.

Illustration Credits

References

A Different Side of the Game, Inc. (2005). *The Foundation Center: Youth in philanthropy*. http://youth.fdncenter.org/youth_stories_kiisha_v.html

Abelev, M. S. (2009). Advancing out of poverty: Social class worldview and its relation to resilience. *Journal of Adolescent Research, 24*(1), 114–141.

Abor, P. A. (2006). Female genital mutilation: Psychological and reproductive health consequences. The case of Kayoro traditional area in Ghana. *Gender & Behavior, 4*(1), 659–684.

Adam, E. K., Snell, E. K., & Pendry, P. (2007). Sleep timing and quantity in ecological and family context: A nationally representative time-diary study. *Journal of Family Psychology, 21*(1), 4–19.

Adams, R. E., Laursen, B., & Wilder, D. (2001). Characteristics of closeness in adolescent romantic relationships. *Journal of Adolescence, 24*, 353–363.

Adams-Price, C., & Greene, A. L. (1990). Secondary attachments and adolescent self-concept. *Sex Roles, 22*, 187–198.

Adelson, J., & Doehrman, M. J. (1980). The psychodynamic approach to adolescence. In J. Adelson (Ed.), *Handbook of adolescence*. New York: Wiley.

Adwere-Boamah, J., & Curtis, D. A. (1993). A confirmatory factor analysis of a four-factor model of adolescent concerns revisited. *Journal of Youth and Adolescence, 22*, 297–312.

African Women's Health Center. (2008). *Table 4. Women living in the United States estimated to be at risk of FGC, by state, 2000*. http://www.brighamandwomens.org/africanwomenscenter/FGCbystate.aspx

Aiken, L. R. (1987). *Assessment of intellectual functioning*. Boston: Allyn & Bacon.

Ainsworth, M. (1985). Attachments across the life-span. *Bulletin of the New York Academy of Medicine, 61*, 791–812.

Ainsworth, M. D. S. (1973). The development of infant–mother attachment. In B. M. Caldwell & H. N. Ricciuti (Eds.), *Review of child development research* (Vol. 3). Chicago: University of Chicago Press.

Ainsworth, M. D. S. (1989). Attachment beyond infancy. *American Psychologist, 44*, 709–716.

Ainsworth, M. D. S. (1993). Attachment as related to mother–infant interaction. In C. Rovee-Collier & L. P. Lipsitt (Eds.), *Advances in infancy research* (Vol. 8). Norwood, NJ: Ablex.

Ainsworth, M., Blehar, M. C., Waters, E., & Wall, S. (1978). *Patterns of attachment: A psychological study of the strange situation*. Hillsdale, NJ: Erlbaum.

Akers, J. F., Jones, R. M., & Coyl, D. D. (1998). Adolescent friendship pairs: Similarities in identity status development, behaviors, attitudes, and intentions. *Journal of Adolescent Research, 13*, 178–201.

Alfieri, T., Ruble, D. N., & Higgins, E. T. (1996). Gender stereotypes during adolescence: Developmental changes and the transition to junior high school. *Developmental Psychology, 32*, 1129–1137.

Ali, M. M., & Dwyer, D. S. (2009). Estimating peer effects in adolescent smoking behavior: A longitudinal analysis. *Journal of Adolescent Health, 45*, 402–408.

Alink, L. R. A., Cicchetti, D., Kim, J., & Rogosch, F. A. (2009). Mediating and moderating processes in the relation between maltreatment and psychopathology: Mother-child relationship quality and emotion regulation. *Journal of Abnormal Child Psychology, 37*, 831–843.

Allen, J. A., Vallone, D., Haviland, M. L., Healton, C., Davis, K. C., Farrelly, M. C., et al. (2003). Tobacco use among middle and high school students-United States, 2002. *Morbidity and Mortality Weekly Reports, 52*, 1096–1098.

Allen, J. P., McElhaney, B., Kuperminc, G. P., & Jodl, K. M. (2004). Stability and change in attachment security across adolescence. *Child Development, 75*, 1792–1805.

Allen, J. P., Porter, M. R., & McFarland, F. C. (2006). Leaders and followers in adolescent close friendships: Susceptibility to peer influence as a predictor of risky behavior, friendship instability, and depression. *Development and Psychopathology, 18*, 155–172.

Allen, J. P., Porter, M. R., & McFarland, F. C. (2006). Leaders and followers in adolescent close friendships: Susceptibility to peer influence as a predictor of risky behavior, friendship instability, and depression. *Development and Psychopathology, 18*(1), 155–172.

Allen, J. P., Weissberg, R. P., & Hawkins, J. A. (1989). The relation between values and social competence in early adolescence. *Developmental Psychology, 25*, 458–464.

Almeida, D. M., Wethington, E., & Chandler, A. L. (1999). Daily transmission of tensions between marital dyads and parent–child dyads. *Journal of Marriage and the Family, 61*, 49–61.

Almeida, J., Johnson, R. M., Corliss, H. L., Molnar, B. E., & Azrael, D. (2009). Emotional distress among LGBT youth: The influence of perceived discrimination based on sexual orientation. *Journal of Youth and Adolescence, 38*(7), 1001–1014.

Alsaker, F. D. (1995). Timing of puberty and reactions to pubertal changes. In M. Rutter (Ed.), *Psychosocial disturbances in young people: Challenges for prevention* (pp. 37–82). Cambridge, England: Cambridge University Press.

Amato, P. R., & Afifi, T. D. (2006). Feeling caught between parents: Adult children's relations with parents and subjective well-being. *Journal of Marriage and Family, 68*, 222–235.

Amaya-Jackson, L., Socolar, R. R. S., Hunter, W., Runyan, D. K., & Colindres, R. (2000). Directly questioning children and adolescents about maltreatment. *Journal of Interpersonal Violence, 15*, 725–759.

American Association of Retired Persons. (1999). *Baby boomers envision their retirement: An AARP segmentation analysis.* http://research.aarp.org/econ/boomecseq_1.html#UNIQEXP/

American Psychiatric Association. (1994). *Diagnostic and statistical manual of mental disorders* (4th ed.). Washington, DC: Author.

American Psychiatric Association. (2000). *Diagnostic and statistical manual of mental disorders* (4th ed., Text rev.). Washington, DC: Author.

Anastasi, A. (1988). *Psychological testing* (6th ed.). New York: Macmillan.

Anderman, E. M., & Midgley, C. (2004). Changes in self-reported academic cheating across the transition from middle school to high school. *Contemporary Educational Psychology, 29*, 499–517.

Anderson, C. A. (2004). An update on the effects of playing violent video games. *Journal of Adolescence, 27*(1), 113–122.

Anderson, C. A., & Carnagey, N. L. (2009). Causal effects of violent sports video games on aggression: Is it competitiveness or violent content? *Journal of Experimental Social Psychology, 45*(4), 731–739.

Anderson, C. A., Duffy, D. L., Martin, N. G., & Visscher, P. M. (2007). Estimation of variance components for age at menarche in twin families. *Behavior Genetics, 37*(5), 668–677.

Anderson, K. J., & Cavallaro, D. (2002). Parents or pop culture? Children's heroes and role models. *Childhood Education*, 161–168.

Anderssen, N., Amlie, C., & Ytterøy, E. A. (2002). Outcomes for children with lesbian or gay parents. A review of studies from 1978 to 2000. *Scandinavian Journal of Psychology, 43*(4), 335–351.

Arbona, C. (1989). Hispanic employment and the Holland typology of work. *Career Development Quarterly, 37*, 257–268.

Archer, S. L. (1985). Career and/or family: The identity process for adolescent girls. *Youth and Society, 16*, 289–314.

Archer, S. L. (1989). Gender differences in identity development: Issues of process, domain, and timing. *Journal of Adolescence, 12*, 117–138.

Archer, S. L. (1992). A feminist's approach to identity research. In G. R. Adams, T. P. Gullotta, & R. Montemayor (Eds.), *Adolescent identity formation.* Newbury Park, CA: Sage.

Archibald, A. B., Graber, J. A., & Brooks-Gunn, J. (2003). Pubertal processes and physiological growth in adolescence. In G. R. Adams & M. D. Berzonsky (Eds.), *Blackwell handbook of adolescence* (pp. 24–47). Malden, MA: Blackwell.

Arehart, D. M., & Smith, P. H. (1990). Identity in adolescence: Influences of dysfunction and psychosocial task issues. *Journal of Youth and Adolescence, 19*, 63–72.

Aries, P. (1962). *Centuries of childhood.* New York: Knopf.

Armistead, L., Wierson, M., & Forehand, R. (1990). Adolescents and maternal employment: Is it harmful for a young adolescent to have an employed mother? *Journal of Early Adolescence, 10*, 260–278.

Armour, B. S., Woollery, T., Malarcher, A., Pechacek, T. F., & Husten, C. (2004). Annual smoking-attributable mortality, years of potential life lost, and productivity losses—United States, 1997–2001. *Morbidity and Mortality Weekly Report, 54*, 625–628.

Arnett, J. J. (2000). Emerging adulthood: A theory of development from the late teens through the twenties. *American Psychologist, 55*, 469–480.

Arnett, J. J. (2001). Conceptions of the transition to adulthood: Perspectives from adolescence to midlife. *Journal of Adult Development, 8*, 133–143.

Arnett, J. J., & Taber, S. (1994). Adolescence terminable and interminable: When does adolescence end? *Journal of Youth and Adolescence, 23*, 517–537.

Aronson, E. (2002). Building empathy, compassion, and achievement in the jigsaw classroom. In J. Aronson (Ed.), *Improving academic achievement: Impact of psychological factors on education* (pp. 209–225). San Diego: Academic Press.

Aronson, E. (2004). Reducing hostility and building compassion: Lessons from the jigsaw classroom. In A. G. Miller (Ed.), *Social psychology of good and evil* (pp. 469–488). New York: Guilford Press.

Arseth, A. K., Kroger, J., Martinussen, M., & Marcia, J. E. (2009). Meta-analytic studies of identity status and the relational issues of attachment and intimacy. *Identity: An International Journal of Theory and Research, 9*, 1–32.

Artman, L., & Cahan, S. (1993). Schooling and the development of transitive inference. *Developmental Psychology, 29*, 753–759.

Asakawa, K., & Csikszentmihalyi, M. (1998). The quality of experience of Asian American adolescents in activities related to future goals. *Journal of Youth and Adolescence, 27*, 141–163.

Ashmore, R. D., Deaux, K., and McLaughlin-Volpe, T. (2004). An organizing framework for collective identity: Articulation and significance of multidimensionality. *Psychological Bulletin, 130*, 80–114.

Aspy, C. B., Vesely, S. K., Oman, R. F., Rodine, S., Marshall, L., & McLeroy, K. (2007). Parental communication and youth sexual behavior. *Journal of Adolescence, 30*(3), 449–466.

Atkins, R., Hart, D., & Donnelly, T. M. (2005). The association of childhood personality type with volunteering during adolescence. *Merrill-Palmer Quarterly, 51*(2), 145–162.

Averett, S. L., Rees, D. I., & Argys, L. M. (2002). The impact of government policies and neighborhood characteristics on teenage sexual activity and contraceptive use. *American Journal of Public Health, 92*, 1773–1778.

Bachman, J. G., Johnston, L. D., & O'Malley, P. M. (2009). *Monitoring the future.* Ann Arbor, MI: Institute for Social Research, The University of Michigan.

Bailey, J. M., & Pillard, R. C. (1991). A genetic study of male sexual orientation. *Archives of General Psychiatry, 48*, 1089–1096.

Bailey, J. M., Pillard, R. C., Neale, M. C., & Agyei, Y. (1993). Heritable factors influence sexual orientation in women. *Archives of General Psychiatry, 50*, 217–223.

Bakan, D. (1966). *The duality of human existence.* Boston: Beacon Press.

Bakan, D. (1971). Adolescence in America: From idea to social fact. *Daedalus, 100*, 979–995.

Baldwin, S. A., & Hoffmann, J. P. (2002). The dynamics of self-esteem: A growth-curve analysis. *Journal of Youth and Adolescence, 31*, 101–113.

Bandini, L. G., Must, A., Naumova, E. N., Anderson, S., Caprio, S., Spadano-Gasbarro, J. I., et al. (2008). Change in leptin, body composition, and other hormones around menarche – a visual representation. *Acta Paediatrica, 97*(10), 1454–1459.

Bandura, A. (1986). *Social foundations of thought and action: A social cognitive theory.* Englewood Cliffs, NJ: Prentice-Hall.

Bandura, A. (1989). Regulation of cognitive processes through perceived self-efficacy. *Developmental Psychology, 25*, 729–735.

Bandura, A. (2004). Model of causality in social learning theory. In A. Freeman, M. J. Mahoney, P. DeVito, & D. Martin (Eds.), *Cognition and psychotherapy* (2nd ed., pp. 25–44). New York: Springer.

Bandura, A., Caprara, G. V., Barbaranelli, C., Pastorelli, C., & Regalia, C. (2001). Sociocognitive self-regulatory mechanisms governing transgressive behavior. *Journal of Personality and Social Psychology, 80,* 125–135.

Bandura, A., Ross, D., & Ross, S. A. (1963). Imitation of film-mediated aggressive models. *Journal of Abnormal and Social Psychology, 66,* 3–11.

Banerjee, I., & Clayton, P. (2007). The genetic basis for the timing of human puberty. *Journal of Neuroendocrinology, 19,* 831–838.

Barber, B. K., & Olsen, J. A. (2004). Assessing the transitions to middle and high school. *Journal of Adolescent Research, 19,* 3–30.

Barkley, R. A. (1990). *Attention deficit hyperactivity disorder: A handbook for diagnosis and treatment.* New York: Guilford Press.

Barkley, T. J., & Procidano, M. E. (1989). College-age children of divorce: Are effects evident in early adulthood? *Journal of College Student Psychotherapy, 4,* 77–87.

Barnet, B., Duggan, A. K., & Devoe, M. (2003). Reduced low birth weight for teenagers receiving prenatal care at a school-based health center: Effect of access and comprehensive care. *Journal of Adolescent Health, 33,* 349–358.

Baron, J. B., & Sternberg, R. J. (1987). *Teaching thinking skills: Theory and practice.* New York: Freeman.

Barth, R. P., Fetro, J. V., Leland, N., & Volkan, K. (1992). Preventing adolescent pregnancy with social and cognitive skills. *Journal of Adolescent Research, 7,* 208–232.

Bartle, S. E., Anderson, S. A., & Sabatelli, R. M. (1989). A model of parenting style, adolescent individuation and adolescent self-esteem: Preliminary findings. *Journal of Adolescent Research, 4,* 283–298.

Barton, P. E. (2005). One third of the nation: Rising dropout rates and declining opportunities. http://www.ets.org/research

Basseches, M. (1984). *Dialectical thinking and adult development.* Norwood, NJ: Ablex.

Bauman, K. E., & Fisher, L. A. (1986). On the measurement of friend behavior in research on friend influence and selection: Findings from longitudinal studies of adolescent smoking and drinking. *Journal of Youth and Adolescence, 15,* 345–353.

Bauman, L. J., Karasz, A., & Hamilton, A. (2007). Understanding failure of condom use intention among adolescents: Completing an intensive preventive intervention. *Journal of Adolescent Research, 22*(3), 248–274.

Baumrind, D. (1967). Child care practices anteceding three patterns of pre-school behavior. *Genetic Psychology Monographs, 75,* 43–88.

Baumrind, D. (1971). Current patterns of parental authority. *Developmental Psychology Monographs, 4,* 1–103.

Baumrind, D. (1986). Sex differences in moral reasoning: Response to Walker's (1984) conclusion that there are none. *Child Development, 57,* 511–521.

Baumrind, D. (1991a). The influence of parenting style on adolescent competence and substance use. *Journal of Early Adolescence, 11,* 56–95.

Baumrind, D. (1991b). Effective parenting during the early adolescent transition. In P. A. Cowan & E. M. Heatherington (Eds.), *Family transitions* (pp. 111–164). Hillsdale, NJ: Erlbaum.

Baumrind, D. (1993). The average expectable environment is not good enough: A response to Scarr. *Child Development, 64,* 1199–1217.

Beausang, C. C., & Razor, A. G. (2000). Young Western women's experiences of menarche and menstruation. *Health Care for Women International, 21,* 517–528.

Bedecarras, P., Gryngarten, M., Ayuso, S., Escobar, M. E., Bergada, C., & Campo, S. (1998). Characterization of serum SHBG isoforms in prepubertal and pubertal girls. *Clinical Endocrinology, 49,* 603–608.

Beentjes, J. W. J., & van der Voort, T. S. A. (1993). Television viewing versus reading: Mental effort, retention, and inferential learning. *Communication Education, 42,* 191–205.

Behrendt, A., & Moritz, S. (2005). Posttraumatic Stress Disorder and memory problems after female genital mutilation. *American Journal of Psychiatry, 162*(5), 1000–1002.

Belenky, M. F., Clinchy, B. M., Goldberger, N. R., & Tarule, J. M. (1986). *Women's ways of knowing.* New York: Basic Books.

Bell, D. C., & Bell, L. G. (1983). Parental validation and support in the development of adolescent daughters. In H. D. Grotevant & C. R. Cooper (Eds.), *Adolescent development in the family.* San Francisco: Jossey-Bass.

Bem, S. L. (1974). The measurement of psychological androgyny. *Journal of Consulting and Clinical Psychology, 42,* 155–162.

Benin, M. H., & Edwards, D. A. (1990). Adolescents' chores: The difference between dual- and single-earner families. *Journal of Marriage and the Family, 52,* 361–373.

Bensley, L. S., Eenwyk, J. V., Spieker, S. J., & Schoder, J. (1999). Self-reported abuse history and adolescent problem behaviors: I. Antisocial and suicidal behaviors. *Journal of Adolescent Health, 24,* 163–172.

Benson, M. J. (2004). After the adolescent pregnancy: Parents, teens, and families. *Child & Adolescent Social Work Journal, 21,* 435–455.

Berg, C. (1989). Knowledge of strategies of dealing with everyday problems from childhood through adolescence. *Developmental Psychology, 25,* 607–618.

Berndt, T. J. (1982). The features and effects of friendships in early adolescence. *Child Development, 53,* 1447–1461.

Berndt, T. J., & Hoyle, S. G. (1985). Stability and change in childhood and adolescent friendships. *Developmental Psychology, 21,* 1007–1015.

Berndt, T. J., Hawkins, J. A., & Jiao, Z. (1999). Influences of friends and friendships on adjustment to junior high school. *Merrill-Palmer Quarterly, 45*(1), 13–41.

Berzonsky, M. D. (1989). Identity style: Conceptualization and measurement. *Journal of Adolescent Research, 4,* 268–282.

Berzonsky, M. D. (1992). A process perspective on identity and stress management. In G. R. Adams, T. P. Gullotta, & R. Montemayor (Eds.), *Adolescent identity formation.* Newbury Park, CA: Sage.

Berzonsky, M. D. (1993). Identity style, gender, and social-cognitive reasoning. *Journal of Adolescent Research, 8,* 289–296.

Berzonsky, M. D. (2004). Identity style, parental authority, and identity commitment. *Journal of Youth and Adolescence, 33,* 213–220.

Berzonsky, M. D., & Ferrari, J. R. (1996). Identity orientation and decisional strategies. *Personality and Individual Differences, 20,* 597–606.

Berzonsky, M. D., & Kuk, L. S. (2000). Identity status, identity processing style, and the transition to university. *Journal of Adolescent Research, 15,* 81–98.

Berzonsky, M. D., & Luyckx, L. (2008). Identity styles, self-reflective cognition, and identity processes: A study of adaptive and maladaptive dimensions of self-analysis. *Identity: An International Journal of Theory and Research, 8,* 205–219.

Betancourt, H., & Lopez, S. R. (1993). The study of culture, ethnicity, and race in American psychology. *American Psychologist, 48,* 629–637.

Bettelheim, B. (1961). The problem of generations. In E. Erikson (Ed.), *The challenge of youth.* New York: Doubleday.

Betz, N. E., Harmon, L. W., & Borgen, F. H. (1996). The relationships of self-efficacy for the Holland themes to gender, occupational group membership, and vocational interests. *Journal of Counseling Psychology, 43,* 90–98.

Beyers, W., Goossens, L., Vansant, I., & Moors, E. (2003). A structural model of autonomy in middle and late adolescence: Connectedness, separation, detachment, and agency. *Journal of Youth and Adolescence, 32*(5), 351–365.

Bieber, L. (1962). *Homosexuality: A psychoanalytic study*. New York: Basic Books.

Bird, G. W., & Kemerait, L. N. (1990). Stress among early adolescents in two-earner families. *Journal of Early Adolescence, 1*, 344–365.

Birkett, M., Espelage, D. L., & Koenig, B. (2009). LGB and questioning students in schools: The moderating effects of homophobic bullying and school climate on negative outcomes. *Journal of Youth and Adolescence, 38*(7), 989–920.

Birndorf, S., Ryan, S., Auinger, P., & Aten, M. (2005). High self-esteem among adolescents: Longitudinal trends, sex differences, and protective factors. *Journal of Adolescent Health, 37*, 194–201.

Bishaw, A., & Stern, S. (2006). Evaluation of poverty estimates: A comparison of the American community survey and the current population survey. *U.S. Census Bureau: Housing and Household Economic Statistics Division*.

Bjorklund, D. F. (1989). *Children's thinking*. Pacific Grove, CA: Brooks/Cole.

Blanchette, I. (2006). The effect of emotion on interpretation and logic in a conditional reasoning task. *Memory & Cognition, 34*, 1112–1125.

Blinn-Pike, L., Berger, T. J., & Hewett, J. (2004). Sexually abstinent adolescents: An 18-month follow-up. *Journal of Adolescent Research, 19*, 495–511.

Bloch, D. P. (1989). Using career information with dropouts and at risk youth. *Career Development Quarterly, 38*, 160–171.

Block, J. H. (1978). Another look at sex differentiation in the socialization behaviors of mothers and fathers. In J. Sherman & F. Denmark (Eds.), *Psychology of women: Future directions of research*. New York: Psychological Dimensions.

Blos, P. (1979). *The adolescent passage*. New York: International Universities Press.

Blumenthal, S. J., & Kupfer, D. J. (1988). Overview of early detection and treatment strategies for suicidal behavior in young people. *Journal of Youth and Adolescence, 17*, 1–23.

Blyth, D. A., & Leffert, N. (1995). Communities as contexts for adolescent development: An empirical analysis. *Journal of Adolescent Research, 10*, 64–87.

Bogenschneider, K., & Pallock, L. (2008). Responsiveness in parent-adolescent relationships: Are influences conditional: Does the reporter matter? *Journal of Marriage and Family, 70*, 1015–1029.

Bohnert, A. M., Richards, M. H., Kolmodin, K. E., & Lakin, B. L. (2008). Young urban African American adolescents' experience of discretionary time activities. *Journal of Research on Adolescence, 18*(3), 517–539.

Bolognini, M., Plancherel, B., Bettschart, W., & Halfon, O. (1996). Self-esteem and mental health in early adolescence: Development and gender differences. *Journal of Adolescence, 19*, 233–245.

Borbely, J. M. (2009). U.S. labor market in 2008: Economy in recession. *Monthly Labor Review, 132*(3), 3–19.

Bosma, H. A., Jackson, S. E., Zijsling, D. H., Zani, B., Cicognani, E., Xerri, M. L., et al. (1996). Who has the final say? Decisions on adolescent behavior within the family. *Journal of Adolescence, 19*, 277–291.

Bottvin, G. J., & Griffin, K. W. (2004). Life Skills Training: Empirical findings and future directions. *Journal of Primary Prevention, 25*, 211–232.

Bowker, A. (2004). Predicting friendship stability during early adolescence. *Journal of Early Adolescence, 24*, 85–112.

Bowlby, J. (1969). Attachment and loss: Vol. 1. *Attachment*. New York: Basic Books.

Bowlby, J. (1980). Attachment and loss: Vol. 3. *Loss*. New York: Basic Books.

Boyes, M. C., & Chandler, M. (1992). Cognitive development, epistemic doubt, and identity formation in adolescence. *Journal of Youth and Adolescence, 21*, 277–304.

Bracey, J. R., Bámaca, M. Y., & Umaña-Taylor, A. J. (2004). Examining ethnic identity and self-esteem among biracial and monoracial adolescents. *Journal of Youth and Adolescence, 33*(2), 123–132.

Bradley, L. A., Flannagan, D., & Fuhrman, R. (2001). Judgment biases and characteristics of friendships of Mexican American and Anglo-American girls and boys. *Journal of Early Adolescence, 21*, 405–424.

Braswell, J. S., Lutkus, A. D., Grigg, W. S., Santapau, S. L., Tay-Lim, B., & Johnson, M. (2001). *The nation's report card: Mathematics 2000 (NCES 2001517)*. National Center for Educational Statistics. http://nces.ed.gov/Pubsearch/pubsinfo.asp?pubid=2001517

Brendgen, M., Markiewicz, D., Doyle, A. B., & Bukowski, W. M. (2001). The relations between friendship quality, ranked-friendship preference, and adolescents' behavior with their friends. *Merrill-Palmer Quarterly, 47*, 395–415.

Brener, N. D., McManus, T., Foti, K., Shanklin, S. L., Hawkins, J., Kann, L., et al. (2009). *School health profiles 2008: Characteristics of health programs among secondary schools*. http://www.cdc.gov/healthyyouth/profiles/2008/profiles_report.pdf

Brewster, A. B., & Bowen, G. L. (2004). Teacher support and the school engagement of Latino middle and high school students at risk of school failure. *Child and Adolescent Social Work Journal, 21*, 47–67.

Brice-Heath, S. (1982). Questioning at home and at school: A comparative study. In G. Spindler (Ed.), *The school achievement of minority children: New perspectives*. Hillsdale, NJ: Erlbaum.

Brody, G. H., Dorsey, S., Forehand, R., & Armistead, L. (2002). Unique and protective contributions of parenting and classroom processes to the adjustment of African American children living in single parent families. *Child Development, 73*, 274–286.

Brody, G. H., Stoneman, Z., & McCoy, J. K. (1994). Forecasting sibling relationships in early adolescence from child temperaments and family processes in middle childhood. *Child Development, 65*, 771–784.

Bronfenbrenner, U. (1979a). Contexts of child rearing. *American Psychologist, 34*, 844–850.

Bronfenbrenner, U. (1979b). *The ecology of human development*. Cambridge, MA: Harvard University Press.

Bronfenbrenner, U. (1990). Discovering what families need. In D. Blankenhorn, S. Bayme, & J. B. Elshtian (Eds.), *Rebuilding the nest* (pp. 27–38). Milwaukee, WI: Family Service American.

Bronfenbrenner, U. (1994). Ecological models of human development. *International Encyclopedia of Education* (2nd ed., Vol. 3, pp. 1643–1647). Oxford: Elsevier.

Brookman, R. R. (1988). Sexually transmitted diseases. In M. D. Levine & E. R. McArney (Eds.), *Early adolescent transitions*. Lexington, MA: D.C. Heath.

Brooks, J. (1999). *The process of parenting* (5th ed.). Mountain View, CA: Mayfield.

Brooks, L. (1990). Counseling special groups: Women and ethnic minorities. In D. Brown, L. Brooks, & Associates (Eds.), *Career choice and development*. San Francisco: Jossey-Bass.

Brooks-Gunn, J., & Ruble, D. N. (1982). The development of menstrual-related beliefs and behaviors during early adolescence. *Child Development, 53*, 1567–1577.

Broverman, I. K., Broverman, D. M., Clarkson, F. E., Rosenkrantz, P. S., & Vogel, S. R. (1970). Sex-role stereotypes and clinical judgments of mental health. *Journal of Consulting and Clinical Psychology, 34*, 1–7.

Brown, B. B., & Lohr, M. J. (1987). Peer group affiliation and adolescent self-esteem: An integration of ego-identity and symbolic interaction theories. *Journal of Personality and Social Psychology, 52,* 47–55.

Brown, D. (1990). Summary, comparison, and critique of major theories. In D. Brown, L. Brooks, & Associates (Eds.), *Career choice and development.* San Francisco: Jossey-Bass.

Brown, L. M., & Gilligan, C. (1992). *Meeting at the crossroads: Women's psychology and girls' development.* Cambridge, MA: Harvard University Press.

Browne, K. D., & Hamilton-Giachritsis, C. (2005). The influence of violent media on children and adolescents: A public-health approach. *Lancet, 365,* 702–710.

Bruckner, H., & Bearman, P. (2005). After the promise: The STD consequences of adolescent virginity pledges. *Journal of Adolescent Health, 36,* 271–278.

Brunquell, D., Crichton, L., & Egeland, B. (1981). Maternal personality and attitude in disturbances of child rearing. *American Journal of Orthopsychiatry, 51,* 680–690.

Bryant, A. L., Schulenberg, J. E., O'Malley, P. M., Bachman, J, G., & Johnston, L. D. (2003). How academic achievement, attitudes, and behaviors relate to the course of substance use during adolescence: A 6-year, multiwave national longitudinal study. *Journal of Research on Adolescence, 13,* 361–397.

Bryk, A. S., & Raudenbush, S. W. (1988). Toward a more appropriate conceptualization of research on school effects: A three level hierarchical linear model. *American Journal of Education, 97,* 65–108.

Buchanan, C. M., Maccoby, E. E., & Dornbusch, S. M. (1992). Adolescents and their families after divorce: Three residential arrangements compared. *Journal of Research on Adolescence, 2,* 261–291.

Buhl, H. M., & Lanz, M. (2009). Emerging adulthood in Europe: Common traits and variability across five European countries. *Journal of Adolescent Research, 22*(5), 439–443.

Buhrmester, D. (1990). Intimacy of friendship, interpersonal competence, and adjustment during preadolescence and adolescence. *Child Development, 61,* 1101–1111.

Buist, K. L., Dekovic, M., Meeus, W., & van Aken, M. A. G. (2002). Developmental patterns in adolescent attachment to mother, father and sibling. *Journal of Youth and Adolescence, 31,* 167–176.

Bukowski, W. M., Newcomb, A. F., & Hoza, B. (1987). Friendship conceptions among early adolescents: A longitudinal study of stability and change. *Journal of Early Adolescence, 7,* 143–152.

Bumpus, M. F., Crouter, A. C., & McHale, S. M. (2001). Parental autonomy granting during adolescence: Exploring gender differences in context. *Developmental Psychology, 37,* 163–173.

Bunge, S. A., & Zelazo, P. D. (2006). A brain-based account of the development of rule use in childhood. *Current Directions in Psychological Science, 15*(3), 118–121.

Bunge, S. A., Dudovic, N. M., Thomason, M. E., Vaidya, C. J., & Gabrieli, J. D. E. (2002). Immature frontal lobe contributions to cognitive control in children: Evidence from fMRI. *Neuron, 33,* 301–311.

Bunting, L., & McAuley, C. (2004a). Teenage pregnancy and motherhood: The contribution of support. *Child & Family Social Work, 9,* 207–215.

Bunting, L., & McAuley, C. (2004b). Research review: Teenage pregnancy and parenthood: The role of fathers. *Child and Family Social Work, 9,* 295–303.

Burns, A. M., & Dunlop, R. K. (2001). "Which basket are your eggs in?" Emotional investments from early adolescence to early adulthood among sons and daughters of divorced and nondivorced parents. *Journal of Family Studies, 7,* 56–71.

Bushman, J. J., & Anderson, C. A. (2009). Comfortably numb: Desensitizing effects of violent media on helping others. *Psychological Science, 20*(3), 273–277.

Buzi, R. S., Smith, P. B., & Weinman, M. L. (2009). Parental communication as a protective factor in increasing condom use among minority adolescents. *International Journal of Adolescent Medicine and Health, 21*(1), 51–59.

Buzwell, S., & Rosenthal, D. (1996). Constructing a sexual self: Adolescents' sexual self-perceptions and sexual risk-taking. *Journal of Research on Adolescence, 6,* 489–513.

Bybee, J., Glick, M., & Zigler, E. (1990). Differences across gender, grade level, and academic track in the content of the ideal self image. *Sex Roles, 22,* 349–358.

Byrnes, J. P., & Takahira, S. (1993). Explaining gender differences on SAT-math items. *Developmental Psychology, 29,* 805–810.

Caird, J. K., Willness, C. R., Steel, P., & Scialfa, C. (2008). A meta-analysis of the effects of cell phones on driver performance. *Accident Analysis & Prevention, 40*(4), 1282–1293.

Caldwell, M. S., Rudolph, K. D., Troop-Gordon, W., & Kim, D.-Y. (2004). Reciprocal influences among relational self-views, social disengagement, and peer stress during early adolescence. *Child Development, 75,* 1140–1154.

Camarena, P. M., Sarigiani, P. A., & Petersen, A. C. (1990). Gender specific pathways to intimacy in early adolescence. *Journal of Youth and Adolescence, 19,* 19–32.

Campbell, B. (2006). Adrenarche and the evolution of human life history. *American Journal of Human Biology, 18,* 569–589.

Campbell, D. (1974). *The Strong-Campbell interest inventory.* Palo Alto, CA: Stanford University Press.

Campione, J. C., & Brown, A. L. (1978). Toward a theory of intelligence: Contributions from research with retarded children. *Intelligence, 2,* 279–304.

Capaldi, D. M., Stoolmiller, M., Clark, S., & Owen, L. D. (2002). Heterosexual risk behaviors in at-risk young men from early adolescence to young adulthood: Prevalence, prediction, and association with STD contraction. *Developmental Psychology, 38,* 394–406.

Carlo, G., Fabes, R. A., Laible, D., & Kupanoff, K. (1999). Early adolescence and prosocial/moral behavior. II: The role of social and contextual influences. *Journal of Early Adolescence, 19,* 133–147.

Carnagey, N. L., Anderson, C. A., & Bushman, B. J. (2007). The effect of video game violence on physiological desensitization to real-life violence. *Journal of Experimental Social Psychology, 43,* 489–496.

Carnegie Council on Adolescent Development. (1989). *Turning points: Preparing American youth for the 21st century.* New York: Carnegie Foundation.

Carr, M., & Jessup, D. L. (1997). Gender differences in first-grade mathematics strategy use: Social and metacognitive influences. *Journal of Educational Psychology, 89,* 318–328.

Carskadon, M. A., Acebo, C., & Jenni, O. G. (2004). Regulation of adolescent sleep: Implications for behavior. *Annals of the New York Academy of Sciences, 1021,* 276–291.

Carskadon, M. A., Harvey, K., Duke, P., Anders, T. F., Litt, I. F., & Dement, W. C. (2002). Pubertal changes in daytime sleepiness. *Sleep, 25*(6), 453–460.

Carver, P. R., Egan, S. K., & Perry D. G. (2004). Children who question their heterosexuality. *Developmental Psychology, 40,* 43–53.

Casas, J. M., Wagenheim, B. R., Banchero, R., & Mendoza-Romero, J. (1994). Hispanic masculinity: Myth or psychological schema meriting clinical consideration? *Hispanic Journal of Behavioral Sciences, 16,* 315–331.

Casazza, K., Goran, M. I., & Gower, B. A. (2008). Associations among insulin, estrogen, and fat mass gain over the pubertal transition in African-American and European-American girls. *The Journal of Clinical Endocrinology and Metabolism, 93*(7), 2610–2615.

Casey, B. J., Getz, S., & Galvan, A. (2008). The adolescent brain. *Developmental Review, 28,* 62–77.

Casey, B. J., Tottenham, N., Liston, C., & Durston, S. (2005). Imaging the developing brain: What have we learned about cognitive development? *Trends in Cognitive Sciences, 9,* 104–110

Casey, M. B. (2001). Spatial-mechanical reasoning skills versus mathematics self-confidence as mediators of gender differences on mathematics subtests using cross-national gender-based items. *Journal for Research in Mathematics Education, 32,* 28–57.

Catsambis, S., Mulkey, L. M., & Crain, R. L. (2001). For better or worse? A nationwide study of the social psychological effects of gender and ability grouping in mathematics. *Social Psychology of Education, 5,* 83–115.

Cauthen, N. K. (2008). *Statement on establishing a modern poverty measure.* National Center for Children in Poverty. http://www.nccp.org/publications/pub_831.html

Cauthen, N. K., & Fass, S. (2008). *Ten important questions about child poverty and family economic hardship.* National Center for Children in Poverty. http://www.nccp.org/publications/pub_829.html

Cavanagh, S. (2004). The sexual debut of girls in early adolescence: The intersection of race, pubertal timing, and friendship group characteristics. *Journal of Research on Adolescence, 14,* 285–312.

Centers for Disease Control and Prevention. (1993). Condom use and sexual identity among men who have sex with men-Dallas, 1991. *Morbidity and Mortality Weekly Report, 42,* 7–17.

Centers for Disease Control and Prevention. (1994). Guidelines for school health programs to prevent tobacco use and addiction. *Morbidity and Mortality Weekly Report, 43,* 1–18.

Centers for Disease Control and Prevention. (1999a). *Intimate partner violence fact sheet.* http://www.cdc.gov/ncipc/dvp/ipvfacts.htm

Centers for Disease Control and Prevention. (1999b). *Prevalence of sedentary leisure-time behavior among adults in the United States.* Hyattsville, MD: National Center for Health Statistics. http://www.cdc.gov/nchswww/products/pubs/pubd/hestats/3and4/sedentary.htm

Centers for Disease Control and Prevention. (2001a). School-based tobacco use prevention programs. *Morbidity and Mortality Weekly Report Highlights, 50*(31). http://www.cdc.gov/tobacco/data_statistics/mmwrs/byyear/2001/mm5031a3/highlights.htm#highlights

Centers for Disease Control and Prevention. (2001b). *Sexually transmitted disease surveillance, 2000.* Atlanta, GA: U.S. Department of Health and Human Services, Centers for Disease Control and Prevention. http://www.cdc.gov/std/stats/TOC2000.htm

Centers for Disease Control and Prevention. (2001c). *Tracking the hidden epidemics: Trends in STDs in the United States 2000.* http://www.cdc.gov/STD/Trends2000/Trends2000.pdf

Centers for Disease Control and Prevention. (2002a). AIDS cases in adolescents and adults under age 25, by sex and exposure category, reported through December 2001, United States. Table 13. *HIV/AIDS surveillance report, 13*(2). http://www.cdc.gov/hiv/topics/surveillance/resources/reports/2001report/default.htm

Centers for Disease Control and Prevention. (2002b). Youth risk behavior surveillance-United States, 2001. *Morbidity and Mortality Weekly Reports, 51* (No. SS-4). http://www.cdc.gov/mmwr/PDF/SS/SS5104.pdf

Centers for Disease Control and Prevention. (2004a). Fact sheet for public health personnel: Male latex condoms and sexually transmitted diseases. http://www.cdc.nchstp/odllatex.htm

Centers for Disease Control and Prevention. (2004b). *Improving the health of adolescents and young adults: A guide for states and communities.* Atlanta, GA: 2004.

Centers for Disease Control and Prevention. (2004c). *Obesity still a major problem, new data show,* [Press release]. http://www.cdc.gov/nchs/pressroom/04facts/obesity.htm

Centers for Disease Control and Prevention. (2004d). Youth risk behavior surveillance-United States, 2003. *Morbidity and Mortality Weekly Reports, 53,* (No. SS-2).

Centers for Disease Control and Prevention. (2005a). *Estimated numbers of cases and rates (per 100,000 population) of HIV/AIDS by race/ethnicity, age category, and sex, 2004.* HIV/AIDS Surveillance Report, 2004, Vol. 16. Atlanta, GA: U.S. Department of Health and Human Services, Centers for Disease Control and Prevention: 14. http://www.cdc.gov/hiv/topics/surveillance/resources/reports/2004report/table5b.htm

Centers for Disease Control and Prevention. (2005b). Injury & violence: Slide presentation. *Healthy Youth.* http://www.cdc.gov/healthyYouth/injury/slides/slides/14.htm

Centers for Disease Control and Prevention. (2005c). National Center for Injury Prevention and Control. WISQARS [Web-based Injury Statistics Query and Reporting System]. http://webappa.cdc.gov/sasweb/ncip/mortrate10_sy.html

Centers for Disease Control and Prevention. (2005d). *Healthy youth! Physical activity.* http://www.cdc.gov/HealthyYouth/PhysicalActivity/

Centers for Disease Control and Prevention. (2005e). *Prevalence of overweight among children and adolescents: United States, 1999–2002.* http://www.cdc.gov/nchs/data/hestat/overwght99.htm

Centers for Disease Control and Prevention. (2005f). Trends in reportable sexually transmitted diseases in the United States, 2004. *STD Surveillance 2004.* http://www.cdc.gov/std/stats04/trends2004.htm

Centers for Disease Control and Prevention. (2005g). *Unintended and teen pregnancy prevention: Teen pregnancy.* http://www.cdc.gov/reproductivehealth/UnintendedPregnancy/Teen.htm

Centers for Disease Control and Prevention. (2006). Racial/ethnic disparities in diagnoses of HIV/AIDS—33 states, 2001–2004. *Morbidity and Mortality Weekly Reports, 55,* 121–125.

Centers for Disease Control and Prevention. (2007). *Best practices for comprehensive tobacco control programs—2007.* http://www.cdc.gov/tobacco

Centers for Disease Control and Prevention. (2008a). Asthma. *Healthy youth!* http://www.cdc.gov/HealthyYouth/asthma/

Centers for Disease Control and Prevention. (2008b). *Teen drivers: Fact sheet.* www.cdc.gov/ncipc/factsheets/teenmvh.htm

Centers for Disease Control and Prevention. (2008c). Youth risk behavior surveillance—United States, 2007. *Morbidity & Mortality Weekly Report, 57*(SS–4), 1–131.

Centers for Disease Control and Prevention. (2009a). *Obesity and overweight.* http://www.cdc.gov/nccdphp/dnpa/obesity/

Centers for Disease Control and Prevention. (2009b). *Scientific data, surveillance, and injury statistics – NCIPC.* http://www.cdc.gov/injury/wisqars/LeadingCauses.html

Centers for Disease Control and Prevention. (2009c). *Sexual and reproductive health of persons aged 10–24 years—United States, 2002–2007.* http://ww.cdc.gov/mmwr/preview/mmwrhtml/ss5806a1.htm

Centers for Disease Control and Prevention. (2009d). *Sexually transmitted diseases surveillance, 2007.* http://www.cdc.gov/STD/stats07/main.htm

Chandra, A., Martino, S. C., Collins, R. L., Elliott, M. N., Berry, S. H., Kanouse, D. E., et al. (2008). Does watching sex on television predict teen pregnancy? Findings from a National Longitudinal Survey of Youth. *Pediatrics, 122*(5), 1047–1054.

Chao, R. K. (1994). Beyond parental control and authoritarian parenting style: Understanding Chinese parenting through the cultural notion of training. *Child Development, 65,* 1111–1119.

Chao, R. K. (2001). Extending research on the consequences of parenting style for Chinese Americans and Europeans Americans. *Child Development, 72*(6), 1832–1843.

Chase-Lansdale, P. L., Wakschlag, L. S., & Brooks-Gunn, J. (1995). A psychological perspective on the development of caring in children and youth: The role of the family. *Journal of Adolescence, 18,* 515–556.

Chassin, L., Flora, D. B., & King, K. M. (2004). Trajectories of alcohol and drug use and dependence from adolescence to adulthood: The effects of familial alcoholism and personality. *Journal of Abnormal Psychology, 113,* 483–498.

Cheek, D. B. (1974). Body composition, hormones, nutrition, and adolescent growth. In M. M. Grumbach, G. D. Grave, & F. E. Mayer (Eds.), *Control of the onset of puberty.* New York: Wiley.

Chen, E., Langer, D. A., Raphaelson, Y. E., & Matthews, K. A. (2004). Socioeconomic status and health in adolescents: The role of stress interpretations. *Child Development, 75,* 1039–1052.

Chen, L., Baker, S. P., Braver, E. R., & Li, G. (2000). Carrying passengers as a risk factor for crashes fatal to 16- to 17-year-old drivers. *JAMA, 283*(12), 1578–1582.

Cheng, L. C. Y., Maffulli, N., Leung, S. S. S. F., Lee, W. T. K., Lau, J. T. F., & Chan, K. M. (1999). Axial and peripheral bone mineral acquisition: A 3-year longitudinal study in Chinese adolescents. *European Journal of Pediatrics, 156,* 506–512.

Cheng, T. L., Savageau, J. A., Sattler, A. L., & DeWitt, T. G. (1993). Confidentiality in health care: A survey of knowledge, perceptions, and attitudes among high school students. *JAMA, 268,* 1404.

Cheung, C. C., Thornton, J. E., Nurani, S. D., Clifton, D. K., & Steiner, R. A. (2001). A reassessment of leptin's role in triggering the onset of puberty in the rat and mouse. *Neuroendocrinology, 74,* 12–21.

Children's Defense Fund. (2005). *Students outreach programs.* http://www.childrensdefense.org

Children's Defense Fund. (2008). *Data: Uninsured children in the states.* http://www.childrensdefense.org/child-research-data-publications/data/data-uninsured-children-by-state.html

Children's Defense Fund. (2008). *The state of America's children 2008.* http://www.childrensdefense.org/stateofamericaschildren

Chiu, D., Beru, Y., Watley, E., Wubu, S., Simson, E., Kessinger, R., et al. (2008). Influences of math tracking on seventh-grade students' self-beliefs and social comparisons. *Journal of Educational Research, 102*(2), 125–135.

Chiu, M. L., Feldman, S. S., & Rosenthal, D. A. (1992). The influence of immigration on parental behavior and adolescent distress in Chinese families residing in two Western nations. *Journal of Research on Adolescence, 2,* 205–239.

Chodorow, N. (1978). *The reproduction of mothering.* Los Angeles: University of California Press.

Chodorow, N. (2004). Psychoanalysis and women: A personal thirty-five-year retrospect. In J. A. Willer, W. W. Anderson, & C. C. Kieffer (Eds.), *Psychoanalysis and women* (pp. 101–129). Hillsdale, NJ: Analytic Press.

Chomsky, N. (1957). *Syntactic structures.* The Hague: Mouton.

Cicchetti, D., & Lynch, M. (1995). Failures in the expectable environment and their impact on individual development: The case of child maltreatment. In D. Cicchetti & D. L. Cohen (Eds.), *Developmental psychopathology: Vol. 2. Risk, disorder, and adaptation* (pp. 32–71). New York: Wiley.

Cillessen, A. H. N., & Mayeux, L. (2004). From censure to reinforcement: Developmental changes in the association between aggression and social status. *Child Development, 75,* 147–163.

Civil Rights Project. (2005). Confronting the graduation rate crisis in California. http://www.civilrightsproject.ucla.edu/research/dropouts/dropouts05.pdf

Claes, M. (1998). Adolescents' closeness with parents, siblings, and friends in three countries: Canada, Belgium, and Italy. *Journal of Youth and Adolescence, 27,* 165–184.

Clark, B. (1988). *Growing up gifted* (3rd ed.). New York: Macmillan.

Clark, L., & Tiggemann, M. (2008). Sociocultural and individual psychological predictors of body image in young girls: A prospective study. *Developmental Psychology, 44*(4), 1124–1134.

Clasen, D. R., & Brown, B. B. (1985). The multidimensionality of peer pressure in adolescence. *Journal of Youth and Adolescence, 14,* 451–468.

Clay, D., Vignoles, V. L., & Dittmar, H. (2005). Body image and self-esteem among adolescent girls: Testing the influence of sociocultural factors. *Journal of Research on Adolescence, 15*(4), 451–477.

Clayton, P. E., & Trueman, J. A. (2000). Leptin and puberty. *Archives of Disease in Children, 83,* 1–3.

Clayton, P. E., Gill, M. S., Hall, C. M., Tillmann, V., Whatmore, A. J., & Price, D. A. (1997). Serum leptin through childhood and adolescence. *Clinical Endocrinology, 46,* 727–733.

Cleary, T. L., & Zimmerman, B. J. (2004). Self-regulation empowerment program: A school-based program to enhance self-regulated and self-motivated cycles of student learning. *Psychology in the Schools, 41,* 537–550.

Cleveland, H. H., Wiebe, R. P., & Rowe, D. C. (2005). Sources of exposure to smoking and drinking friends among adolescents: A behavioral-genetic evaluation. *Journal of Genetic Psychology, 166,* 153–169.

Cleveland, M. J., Feinberg, M. E., & Greenberg, M. T. (2010). Protective families in high- and low-risk environments: Implications for adolescent substance use. *Journal of Youth and Adolescence, 39,* 114–126.

Cobb, N. L., Ong, A. D., & Tate, J. (2001). Reason-based evaluations of wrongdoing in religious and moral narratives. *International Journal for the Psychology of Religion, 11,* 259–276.

Cobb, S., & Battin, B. (2004). Second-impact syndrome. *The Journal of School Nursing, 20*(5), 262–267.

Cohen, R. J., & Swerdlik, M. E. (1999). *Psychological testing and assessment* (4th ed.). Mountain View, CA: Mayfield.

Cohen, R. J., & Swerdlik, M. E. (2001). *Psychological testing and assessment* (5th ed.). New York: McGraw-Hill.

Colarossi, L. G. (2001). Adolescent gender differences in social support: Structure, function and provider type. *Social Work Research, 25,* 233–241.

Colarossi, L. G., & Eccles, J. S. (2000). A prospective study of adolescents' peer support: Gender differences and the influence of parental relationships. *Journal of Youth and Adolescence, 29,* 661–678.

Colby, A., Kohlberg, L., Gibbs, J., & Lieberman, M. (1983). A longitudinal study of moral judgment. *Monographs of the Society for Research in Child Development, 48*(200).

Cole, D. A., Martin, J. M., Peeke, L. A., Seroczynski, A. D., & Fier, J. (1999). Children's over- and underestimation of academic competence: A longitudinal study of gender differences, depression, and anxiety. *Child Development, 70,* 459–473.

Cole, T. J. (2003). The secular trend in human physical growth: A biological view. *Economics and Human Biology, 1*(2), 161–168.

Coleman, J. (1961). *The adolescent society.* Glencoe, IL: Free Press.

Coleman, P. (1993). Testing the school system: Dropouts, accountability, and social policy. *Curriculum Inquiry, 23,* 329–342.

Coles, Robert. (1970). *Erik Erikson: The growth of his work.* Boston: Little, Brown.

Coley, R. L., & Chase-Lansdale, P. L. (1998). Adolescent pregnancy and parenthood: Recent evidence and future directions. *American Psychologist, 53,* 152–166.

Collins, W. A., & Luebker, C. (1994). Parent and adolescent expectancies: Individual and relational significance. In J. G.

Smetana (Ed.), *New directions for child development: Beliefs about parenting* (pp. 65–80). San Francisco: Jossey-Bass.

Colom, R., Escorial, S., & Rebollo, L. (2004). Sex differences on the Progressive Matrices are influenced by sex differences on spatial ability. *Personality and Individual Differences, 37,* 1289–1293.

Colom, R., Lluis-Font, J. M., & Andres-Pueyo, A. (2005). The generational intelligence gains are caused by decreasing variance in the lower half of the distribution: Supporting evidence for the nutrition hypothesis. *Intelligence, 33,* 83–91.

Comer, J. P. (1985). The Yale-New Haven Primary Prevention Project: A follow-up study. *Journal of the American Academy of Child Psychiatry, 24,* 154–160.

Comer, J. P. (1988). Educating poor minority children. *Scientific American, 259*(5), 42–48.

Comer, J. P. (2008). Promoting well-being among at-risk children: Restoring a sense of community and support for development. In K. K. Kline (Ed.), *The Scientific case for nurturing the whole child* (pp. 305–321). New York: Springer Science & Behavior Media.

Comer, J. P., & Joyner, E. T. (2006). Translating theory and research into practice through the Yale Child Study Center School Development Program. In M. A. Constas & R. J. Sternberg (Eds.), *Translating theory and research into educational practice: Developments in content domains, large scale reform, and intellectual capacity* (pp. 151–171). New York: Routledge.

Comer, J. P., Haynes, N. M., Joyner, E. T., & Ben-Avie, M. (Eds.). (1996). *Rallying the whole village: The Comer process for reforming education.* New York: Teachers College Press.

Commons, M. L., & Richards, F. A. (1982). A general model of stage theory. In M. L. Commons, F. A. Richards, & S. Armon (Eds.), *Beyond formal operations: Late adolescent and adult cognitive development.* New York: Praeger.

Condry, J. C., & Ross, D. F. (1985). Sex and aggression: The influence of gender label on the perception of aggression in children. *Child Development, 56,* 225–233.

Connell, C. M., & Janevic, M. R. (2003). Health and human development. In I. B. Weiner (Ed.), *Handbook of psychology* (Vol. 6, pp. 579–600). Hoboken, NJ: Wiley.

Connell, J. P., Halpern-Felsher, B. L., Clifford, E., Crichlow, W., & Usinger, P. (1995). Hanging in there: Behavioral, psychological, and contextual factors affecting whether African American adolescents stay in high school. *Journal of Adolescent Research, 10,* 41–63.

Connolly, J., Craig, W., Goldberg, A., & Pepler, D. (2004). Mixed gender groups, dating, and romantic relationships in early adolescence. *Journal of Research on Adolescence, 14,* 185–207.

Constantine, N. A. (2008). Converging evidence leaves policy behind: Sex education in the United States. *Journal of Adolescent Health, 42,* 324–326.

Constantinople, A. (1973). Masculinity-femininity: An exception to a famous dictum? *Psychological Bulletin, 80,* 389–407.

Cooper, C. R., Grotevant, H. D., & Condon, S. M. (1983). Individuality and connectedness in the family as a context for adolescent identity formation and role-taking skill. In H. D. Grotevant & C. R. Cooper (Eds.), *Adolescent development in the family.* San Francisco: Jossey-Bass.

Corville-Smith, J., Ryan, B. A., Adams, G. R., & Delicandro, T. (1998). Distinguishing absentee students from regular attenders: The combined influence of personal, family, and school factors. *Journal of Youth and Adolescence, 27,* 626–641.

Costanzo, P. R. (1970). Conformity development as a function of self-blame. *Journal of Personality and Social Psychology, 14,* 366–374.

Costos, D., Ackerman, R., & Paradis, L. (2002). Recollections of menarche: Communication between mothers and daughters regarding menstruation. *Sex Roles, 46,* 49–59.

Cota-Robles, S., Neiss, M., & Rowe, D. C. (2002). The role of puberty in violent and nonviolent delinquency among Anglo American, Mexican American, and African American boys. *Journal of Adolescent Research, 17,* 364–376.

Côté, J. E., & Schwartz, S. J. (2002). Comparing psychological and sociological approaches to identity: Identity status, identity capital, and the individualization process. *Journal of Adolescence, 25,* 571–586.

Cotgrove, A., Zirinsky, L., Black, D., & Weston, D. (1995). Secondary prevention of attempted suicide in adolescence. *Journal of Adolescence, 18,* 569–577.

Cottrell, L., Lli, X., Harris, C., D'Alessandri, D., Atkins, M., Richardson, B., et al. (2003). Parent and adolescent perceptions of parental monitoring and adolescent risk involvement. *Parenting: Science and Practice, 3,* 179–195.

Courtney, M. L., & Cohen, R (1996). Behavior segmentation by boys as a function of aggressiveness and prior information. *Child Development, 67,* 1034–1047.

Covington, M. V. (1983). Strategic thinking and the fear of failure. In S. F. Chipman, J. Segal, & R. Glaser (Eds.), *Thinking and learning skills: Current research and open questions* (Vol. 2). Hillsdale, NJ: Erlbaum.

Craig, W. M., Pepler, D., Connolly, J., & Henderson, K. (2001). Developmental context of peer harassment in early adolescence. In J. Juvonen & S. Graham (Eds.), *Peer harassment in school: The plight of the vulnerable and victimized* (pp. 242–261). New York: Guilford Press.

Cramer, P. (1998). Freshman to senior year: A follow-up of identity, narcissism, and defense mechanisms. *Journal of Research in Personality, 32,* 156–172.

Cramer, P. (2000). Development of identity: Gender makes a difference. *Journal of Research in Personality, 34,* 42–72.

Crawford, M., & Popp, D. (2003). Sexual double standards: A review and methodological critique of two decades of research. *Journal of Sex Research, 40,* 13–26.

Crockett, D. (2003). Critical issues children face in the 2000s. *School Psychology Quarterly, 18,* 446–453.

Crone, E. A., Donohue, S. E., Honomichl, R., Wendelken, C., & Bunge, S. A. (2006). Brain regions mediating flexible rule use during development. *The Journal of Neuroscience, 26*(4), 11239–11247.

Crosnoe, R., & Elder, G. H., Jr. (2004). Family dynamics, supportive relationships, and educational resilience during adolescence. *Journal of Family Issues, 25,* 571–602.

Crosnoe, R., & Needham, B. (2004). Holism, contextual variability, and the study of friendships in adolescent development. *Child Development, 75,* 264–279.

Cross, W. E., Jr. (1980). Models of psychological nigrescence: A literature review. In R. L. Jones (Ed.), *Black psychology.* New York: Harper & Row.

Cross, W. E., Jr. (2005). Ethnicity, race, and identity. In T. S. Weisner (Ed.), *Discovering successful pathways in children's development: Mixed methods in the study of childhood and family life* (pp. 171–182). Chicago: University of Chicago Press.

Crouter, A. C., & Crowley, M. S. (1990). School-age children's time alone with fathers in single- and dual-earner families: Implications for the father-child relationship. *Journal of Early Adolescence, 10,* 296–312.

Crowley, S. J., Acebo, C., & Carskadon, M. A. (2006). Sleep, circadian rhythms, and delayed phase in adolescence. *Sleep Medicine, 8*(6), 602–612.

Crowley, S. J., Acebo, C., Fallone, G., & Carskadon, M. A. (2006). Estimating dim light melatonin onset (DLMO) phase in adolescents using summer or school-year sleep/wake schedules. *Journal of Sleep and Sleep Disorders Research, 29*(12), 1632–1641.

Crystal, D. S., & Stevenson, H. W. (1995). What is a bad kid? Answers of adolescents and their mothers in three cultures. *Journal of Research on Adolescence, 5,* 71–91.

Csikszentmihalyi, M. (1990). *Flow: The psychology of optimal experience.* New York: Harper & Row.

Csikszentmihalyi, M. (1997). *Finding flow.* New York: Basic Books.

CSULA Pre-collegiate programs. http://www.calstatela.edu/academic/sem_ed/precol-list.htm

Cukier, W. (2001). Firearms regulation: Canada in the international context. *Chronic Diseases in Canada.*

Culwell, K. R., Feinglass, J. (2007). The association of health insurance with use of prescription contraceptives. *Perspectives on Sexual and Reproductive Health, 39*(4), 226–230.

Daddis, C. (2008). Similarity between early and middle adolescent close friends' beliefs about personal jurisdiction. *Social Development, 17*(4), 1019–1038.

Dallago, L., Perkins, D. D., Santinello, M., Boyce, W., Molcho, M., & Morgan, A. (2009). Adolescent place attachment, social capital, and perceived safety: A comparison of 13 countries. *American Journal of Community Psychology, 44,* 148–160.

Darling, C. A., & Hicks, M. W. (1982). Parental influence on adolescent sexuality: Implications for parents as educators. *Journal of Youth and Adolescence, 11,* 231–245.

Darling, N. (2008). Putting conflict in context. *Monographs of the Society for Research in Child Development, 73*(2), 169–175.

Darling, N., Cumsille, P., Caldwell, L. L., & Dowdy, B. (2006). Predictors of adolescents' disclosure to parents and perceived parental knowledge: Between- and within-person differences. *Journal of Youth and Adolescence, 35*(4), 667–678.

Darroch, J. E., Frost, J. J., Singh, S., et al. (2001). *Teenage sexual and reproductive behavior in developed countries: Can more progress be made?* New York: Alan Guttmacher Institute.

Davey, F. H., & Stoppard, J. M. (1993). Some factors affecting the occupational expectations of female adolescents. *Journal of Vocational Behavior, 43,* 235–250.

Davidson, M. D., Lawrence, A. J., & Casey, B. J. (2006). Predicting cognitive control from preschool to late adolescence and young adulthood. *Psychological Science, 17,* 478–484.

Davies, P. T., & Windle, M. (2001). Interparental discord and adolescent adjustment trajectories: The potentiating and protective role of intrapersonal attributes. *Child Development, 72,* 1163–1178.

Davis, S. F., Grover, C. A., Becker, A. H., & McGregor, L. N. (1992). Academic dishonesty: Prevalence, determinants, techniques, and punishments. *Teaching of Psychology, 19,* 16–20.

Davison, K. K., & Susman, E. J. (2001). Are hormone levels and cognitive ability related during early adolescence? *International Journal of Behavioral Development, 25,* 416–428.

de Anda, D., Baroni, S., Boskin, L., Buchwald, L., Morgan, J., Ow, J., et al. (2000). Stress, stressors and coping among high school students. *Children and Youth Services Review, 22,* 441–463.

de Graaf, H., Vanwesenbeeck, I., Meijer, S., Woertman, L., & Meeus, W. (2009). Sexual trajectories during adolescence: Relation to demographic characteristics and sexual risk. *Archives of Sexual Behavior, 38*(2), 276–282.

de Haan, A. D., Prinzie, P., & Dekovic, M. (2009). Mothers' and fathers' personality and parenting: The mediating role of sense of competence. *Developmental Psychology, 45*(6), 1695–1707.

De Roux, N., Genin, E., Carel, J. C., Matsuda, F., & Chaussain, J. L. (2003). Hypogonadotropic hypogonadism due to loss of function of the KiSS1-derived peptide receptor GPR54. *Proceedings of the National Academy of Sciences, 100,* 10972–10976.

Deci, E. L., & Ryan, R. M. (2000). The "what" and "why" of goal pursuits: Human needs and the self-determination of behavior. *Psychological Inquiry, 11,* 319–338.

Dedel, K. (2006). Juvenile Runaways. *Office of Community Oriented Policing Services. Problem-Specific Guide Series, 37.* Washington, DC: U.S. Department of Justice. http://www.cops.usdoj.gov

Dees, W. L., Dissen, G. A., Hiney, J. K., Lara, F., & Ojeda, S. R. (2000). Alcohol injection inhibits the increased secretion of puberty related hormones in the developing female rhesus monkey. *Endocrinology, 141,* 1325–1331.

Dees, W. L., Srivastava, V. K., & Hiney, J. K. (2001). Alcohol and female puberty: The role of intraovarian systems. *Alcohol Research and Health, 25,* 271–275.

Deutsch, M. (1993). Educating for a peaceful world. *American Psychologist, 48,* 510–517.

Diamond, L. M., & Lucas, S. (2004). Sexual-minority and heterosexual youths' peer relationships: Experiences, expectations, and implications for well-being. *Journal of Research on Adolescence, 14,* 313–340.

DiBlasio, F. A., & Benda, B. B. (1992). Gender differences in theories of adolescent sexual activity. *Sex Roles, 27,* 221–236.

Dick, D. M., Rose, R. J., Pulkkinen, L., & Kaprio, J. (2001). Measuring puberty and understanding its impact: A longitudinal study of adolescent twins. *Journal of Youth and Adolescence, 30,* 385–399.

DiClemente, R. J. (1998). Preventing sexually transmitted infections among adolescents: A clash of ideology and science. *JAMA, 279,* 1574–1575.

Diener, M. L., & Lucas, R. E. (2004). Adults' desires for children's emotions across 48 countries: Associations with individual and national characteristics. *Journal of Cross-Cultural Psychology, 35,* 525–547.

Digest of Education Statistics. (1993). U.S. Department of Education. Washington, DC: U.S. Government Printing Office.

Digest of Education Statistics. (1996). U.S. Department of Education. Washington, DC: U.S. Government Printing Office.

Dillard, A. (1974). *Pilgrim at Tinker Creek.* New York: Harper's Magazine Press.

Dixon, S. V., Graber, J. A., & Brooks-Gunn, J. (2008). The roles of respect for parental authority and parenting practices in parent-child conflict among African American, Latino, and European American families. *Journal of Family Psychology, 22*(1), 1–10.

Dmitrieva, J., Chen, C., Greenberger, E., & Gil-Rivas, V. (2004). Family relationships and adolescent psychosocial outcomes: Converging findings from Eastern and Western cultures. *Journal of Research on Adolescence, 14,* 425–447.

Dodge, K. A. (1983). Behavioral antecedents of peer social status. *Child Development, 54,* 1386–1399.

Donahue, M. J., & Benson, P. L. (1995). Religion and the well-being of adolescents. *Journal of Social Issues, 51,* 145–160.

Donnay, D. A. C., & Borgen, F. H. (1996). Validity, structure, and content of the 1994 Strong Interest Inventory. *Journal of Counseling Psychology, 43,* 275–291.

Dornbusch, S. M., Carlsmith, L., Gross, R. T., Martin, J. A., Jenning, D., Rosenberg, A., et al. (1981). Sexual development, age, and dating: A comparison of biological and sociological influences upon the set of behaviors. *Child Development, 52,* 179–185.

Dornbusch, S. M., Ritter, P. L., Leiderman, P. H., Roberts, D. F., & Fraleigh, M. J. (1987). The relation of parenting style to adolescent school performance. *Child Development, 58,* 1244–1257.

Dotterer, A. M., McHale, S. M., & Crouter, A. C. (2009). The development and correlates of academic interests from childhood through adolescence. *Journal of Educational Psychology, 101*(2), 509–519.

Doueck, H. J., Ishisaka, A. H., & Greenaway, K. D. (1988). The role of normative development in adolescent abuse and neglect. *Family Relations, 37,* 135–139.

Douglas-Hall, A., & Chau, M. (2009). *Basic facts about low-income adolescents.* National Center for Children in Poverty, Columbia University: Mailman School of Public Health. http://www.nccp.org/publications/pdf/text_872.pdf

Douglas-Hall, A., & Koball, H. (2003). *Parental employment in low-income families.* National Center for Children in Poverty. http://www.nccp.org/pub_pe104.html

Douvan, E., & Adelson, J. (1966). *The adolescent experience.* New York: Wiley.

Dovidio, J., & Gaertner, S. (1986). *Prejudice, discrimination, and racism.* Orlando, FL: Academic Press.

Dowdy, B. B., & Kliewer, W. (1998). Dating, parent-adolescent conflict, and behavioral autonomy. *Journal of Youth and Adolescence, 27,* 473–492.

Downey, G., Purdie, V., & Schaffer-Neitz, R. (1999). Anger transmission from mother to child: A comparison of mothers in chronic pain and well mothers. *Journal of Marriage and the Family, 61,* 62–73.

Doyle, J. M., & Kao, G. (2007). Are racial identities of multiracials stable? Changing self-identification among single and multiple race individuals. *Social Psychology Quarterly, 70*(4), 405–423.

Driscoll, A. K., Russell, S. T., & Crockett, L. J. (2008). Parenting styles and youth well-being across immigrant generations. *Journal of Family Issues, 29*(2), 185–209.

Drukker, M., Feron, F. J. M., Mengelers, R., & Os, J. V. (2009). Neighborhood socioeconomic and social factors and school achievement in boys and girls. *Journal of Early Adolescence, 29*(2), 285–306.

Drumm, P., & Jackson, D. W. (1996). Developmental changes in questioning strategies during adolescence. *Journal of Adolescent Research, 11,* 285–305.

Dryfoos, J., & Maguire, S. (2002). *Inside full-service community schools.* Thousand Oaks, CA: Corwin Press.

DuBois, D. L., & Hirsch, B. J. (1990). School and neighborhood friendship patterns of Blacks and Whites in early adolescence. *Child Development, 61,* 524–536.

DuBois, D. L., Felner, R. D., Brand, S., Phillips, R. S. C., & Lease, A. M. (1996). Early adolescent self-esteem: A developmental-ecological framework and assessment strategy. *Journal of Research on Adolescence, 6,* 543–579.

Dubow, E. F., Arnett, M., Smith, K., & Ippolito, M. R. (2001). Predictors of future expectations of inner-city children: A 9-month prospective study. *Journal of Early Adolescence, 21,* 5–28.

Ducharme, J., Doyle, A. B., & Markiewicz, D. (2002). Attachment security with mother and father: Associations with adolescents' reports of interpersonal behavior with parents and peers. *Journal of Social and Personal Relationships, 19,* 203–231.

Duckworth, A. L., & Seligman, M. E. P. (2005). Self-discipline outdoes IQ in predicting academic performance of adolescents. *Psychological Science, 16,* 939–944.

Dumalska, I., Wu, M., Morozova, E., Liu, R., van den Pol, A., & Alreha, M. (2008). Excitatory effects of the puberty-initiating peptide Kisspeptin and Group I metabotropic glutamate receptor agonists differentiate two distinct subpopulations of gonadotropin-releasing hormone neurons. *The Journal of Neuroscience, 28,* 8003–8013.

Dunkel, C. S. (2000). Possible selves as a mechanism for identity exploration. *Journal of Adolescence, 23,* 519–529.

Dunkel, C. S., & Anthis, K. S. (2001). The role of possible selves in identity formation: A short-term longitudinal study. *Journal of Adolescence, 24,* 765–776.

Dunlop, R., Burns, A., & Bermingham, S. (2001). Parent-child relations and adolescent self-image following divorce: A 10-year study. *Journal of Youth and Adolescence, 30,* 117–134.

Dunn, R., & Dunn, K. (1993). *Teaching secondary students through their individual learning styles: Practical approaches for grades 7–12.* Boston: Allyn & Bacon.

Dunphy, D. (1963). The social structure of urban adolescent peer groups. *Sociometry, 26,* 230–246.

Dusek, J. B., & McIntyre, J. G. (2003). Self-concept and self-esteem development. In G. R. Adams & M. D. Berzonsky (Eds.), *Blackwell handbook of adolescence* (pp. 291–309). Malden, MA: Blackwell.

Dwairy, M. (2002). Foundations of a psycho-social dynamic personality theory of collective people. *Clinical Psychology Review, 22,* 343–360.

Dwairy, M. A. (2008). Parental inconsistency versus parental authoritarianism: Associations with symptoms of psychological disorders. *Journal of Youth and Adolescence, 37,* 616–626.

Dwairy, M., & Menshar, K. E. (2006). Parenting style, individuation, and mental health of Egyptian adolescents. *Journal of Adolescence, 29*(1), 103–117.

Dwairy, M., Achoui, M., Abouserie, R., & Farah, A. (2006a). Adolescent-family connectedness among Arabs: A second cross-regional research study. *Journal of Cross-Cultural Psychology, 37*(3), 248–261.

Dwairy, M., Achoui, M., Abouserie, R., & Farah, A. (2006b). Parenting styles, individuation, and mental health of Arab adolescents: A third cross-regional research study. *Journal of Cross-Cultural Psychology, 37*(3), 262–272.

Dwairy, M., Achoui, M., Abouserie, R., Farah, A., Sakhleh, A. A., Fayad, M., et al. (2006). Parenting styles in Arab societies: A first cross-regional research study. *Journal of Cross-Cultural Psychology, 37*(3), 230–247.

Dweck, C. S. (1986). Motivational processes affecting learning. *American Psychologist, 41,* 1040–1048.

Dweck, C. S. (1989). Motivation. In A. Lesgold & R. Glaser (Eds.), *Foundations for a psychology of education.* Hillsdale, NJ: Erlbaum.

Dweck, C. S. (1999). *Self-theories: Their role in motivation, personality and development.* Philadelphia: Psychology Press.

Dweck, C. S. (2002). Beliefs that make smart people dumb. In R. J. Sternberg (Ed.), *Why smart people can be so stupid* (pp. 24–41). New Haven, CT: Yale University Press.

Dweck, C. S. (2002). Messages that motivate: How praise molds students' beliefs, motivation, and performance (in surprising ways). In J. Aronson (Ed.), *Improving academic achievement: Impact of psychological factors on education* (pp. 37–60). Elsevier Science.

Dweck, C. S., & Molden, D. C. (2005). Self-theories: Their impact on competence motivation and acquisition. In A. J. Elliot & C. S. Dweck (Eds.), *Handbook of competence and motivation* (pp. 122–140). New York: Guilford Press.

Dweck, C. S., & Reppucci, N. D. (1973). Learned helplessness and reinforcement responsibility in children. *Journal of Personality and Social Psychology, 25,* 109–116.

Dyk, P. H., & Adams, G. R. (1990). Identity and intimacy: An initial investigation of three theoretical models using cross-lag panel correlations. *Journal of Youth and Adolescence, 19,* 91–110.

Eaves, L., Silberg, J., Foley, D., Bulik, C., Maes, H., Erkanli, A., et al. (2004). Genetic and environmental influences on the relative timing of pubertal change. *Twin Research, 7,* 471–481.

Eberly, M. B., & Montemayor, R. (1999). Adolescent affection and helpfulness toward parents: A 2-year follow-up. *Journal of Early Adolescence, 19,* 226–248.

Eccles, J. S. (2004). Schools, academic motivation, and stage-environment fit. In R. Lerner and L. Steinberg (Eds.), *Handbook of adolescent psychology*. New York: Wiley.

Eccles, J. S., & Barber, B. L. (1999). Student council, volunteering, basketball, or marching band: What kind of extracurricular involvement matters? *Journal of Adolescent Research, 14,* 10–43.

Eccles, J. S., Buchanan, C. M., Midgley, C., Fuligni, A. J., & Flanagan, C. (1991). Individuation reconsidered: Autonomy and control during early adolescence. *Journal of Social Issues, 47,* 53–68.

Eccles, J., & Barber, B. (1999). Student council, volunteering, basketball, or marching-band: What kind of extracurricular involvement matters. *Journal of Adolescent Research, 14,* 10–43.

Edwards, L. M., Fehring, R. J., Jarrett, K. M., & Haglund, K. A. (2008). The influence of religiosity, gender, and language preference acculturation on sexual activity among Latino/a adolescents. *Hispanic Journal of Behavioral Sciences, 30*(4), 447–462.

Egan, S. K., & Perry, D. G. (2001). Gender identity: A multidimensional analysis with implications for psychosocial adjustment. *Developmental Psychology, 37,* 451–463.

Egley, A., Jr. (2002). National youth gang survey trends from 1996 to 2000. *OJJDP Fact Sheet.* http://www.ncjrs.gov/pdffiles1/ojjdp/fs200203.pdf

Eisenberg, J. (2004). To cheat or not to cheat: Effects of moral perspective and situational variables on students' attitudes. *Journal of Moral Education, 33,* 163–178.

Eisenberg, M. E., Bernat, D. H., Bearinger, L. H., & Resnick, M. D. (2008). Support for comprehensive sexuality education: Perspectives from parents of school-age youth. *Journal of Adolescent Health, 42,* 352–359.

Eisenberg, M. E., Sieving, R. E., Bearinger, L. H., Swain, C., & Resnick, M. D. (2006). Parents' communication with adolescents about sexual behavior: A missed opportunity for prevention? *Journal of Youth and Adolescence, 35,* 893–902.

Eisenberg, N., Hofer, C., Spinrad, T. L., Gershoff, E. T., Valiente, C., Losoya, S. H., et al. (2008). Understanding mother-adolescent conflict discussions: Concurrent and across-time prediction from youths' dispositions and parenting. *Monographs of the Society for Research in Child Development, 73*(2), 1–160.

Eisenberg, N., Zhou, Q., & Koller, S. (2001). Brazilian adolescents' prosocial moral judgment and behavior: Relations to sympathy, perspective taking, gender-role orientation, and demographic characteristics. *Child Development, 72,* 518–534.

Eisert, D. C., & Kahle, L. R. (1986). The development of social attributions: An integration of probability and logic. *Human Development, 29,* 61–81.

Elkind, D. (1961). The child's conception of his religious denomination: I. The Jewish child. *Journal of Genetic Psychology, 99,* 209–225.

Elkind, D. (1962). The child's conception of his religious denomination: II. The Catholic child. *Journal of Genetic Psychology, 101,* 185–193.

Elkind, D. (1963). The child's conception of his religious denomination: III. The Protestant child. *Journal of Genetic Psychology, 103,* 291–304.

Elkind, D. (1967). Egocentrism in adolescence. *Child Development, 38,* 1025–1034.

Elkind, D. (1978). *A sympathetic understanding of the child: Birth to sixteen* (2nd ed.). Boston: Allyn & Bacon.

Elkind, D. (1980). Strategic interactions in early adolescence. In J. Adelson (Ed.), *Handbook of adolescence.* New York: Wiley.

Elliott, B. A., & Larson, J. T. (2004). Adolescents in mid-sized and rural communities: Forgone care, perceived barriers, and risk factors. *Journal of Adolescent Health, 35,* 303–309.

Ellis, B. J. (2004). Timing of pubertal maturation in girls: An integrated life history approach. *Psychological Bulletin, 130*(6), 920–958.

Ellis, B. J., McFadyen-Ketchum, S., Dodge, K. A., Pettit, G. A., & Bates, J. E. (1999). Quality of early family relationships and individual differences in the timing of pubertal maturation in girls: A longitudinal test of an evolutionary model. *Journal of Personality and Social Psychology, 77,* 387–401.

Ellison, C. G., Echevarria, S., & Smith, B. (2005). Religion and abortion attitudes among U.S. Hispanics: Findings from the 1990 Latino National Political Survey. *Social Science Quarterly, 86,* 192–208.

Else-Quest, N. M., Hyde, J. S., & DeLamater, J. D. (2005). Context counts: Long-term sequelae of premarital intercourse or abstinence. *Journal of Sex Research, 42,* 102–112.

Emmons, R. A., & Paloutzian, R. F. (2003). The psychology of religion. *Annual Review of Psychology, 54,* 1–26.

Engels, R. C. M. E., Dekovi, M., & Meeus, W. (2002). Parenting practices, social skills and peer relationships in adolescence. *Social Behavior and Personality, 30,* 3–18.

Englund, M. M., Egeland, B., & Collins, W. A. (2008). Exceptions to high school dropout predictions in a low-income sample: Do adults make a difference? *Journal of Social Issues, 64*(1), 77–93.

Ennett, S. T., & Bauman, K. E. (1996). Adolescent social networks: School, demographic, and longitudinal considerations. *Journal of Adolescent Research, 11,* 194–215.

Enright, R. D., Santos, M. J., & Al-Mabuk, R. (1989). The adolescent as a forgiver. *Journal of Adolescence, 12,* 95–110.

Entwisle, D. R., & Alexander, K. L. (1990). Beginning school math competence: Minority and majority comparisons. *Child Development, 61,* 454–471.

Entwisle, D. R., Alexander, K. L., Olson, L. S., & Ross, K. (1999). Paid work in early adolescence: Developmental and ethnic patterns. *Journal of Early Adolescence, 19,* 363–388.

Epstein, J. (1990). What matters in the middle grades—Grade span or practices? *Phi Delta Kappan, 71,* 438–444.

Epstein, L. H. (1994). Ten-year outcome of behavioral family-based treatment for childhood obesity. *Health Psychology, 13,* 373–383.

Erikson, E. H. (1950). *Childhood and society.* New York: Norton.

Erikson, E. H. (1954). Problems of infancy and early childhood. In G. Murphy & A. J. Bachrach (Eds.), *An outline of abnormal psychology.* New York: Modern Library.

Erikson, E. H. (1956). The problem of ego identity. *Journal of the American Psychoanalytic Association, 4,* 56–121.

Erikson, E. H. (1959). Identity and the life cycle: Selected papers. *Psychological Issues Monograph, Series 1, No.1.* New York: International Universities Press.

Erikson, E. H. (1963). *Childhood and society* (2nd ed.). New York: Norton.

Erikson, E. H. (1968). *Identity, youth and crisis.* New York: Norton.

Erkut, S., & Tracy, S. J. (2002). Predicting adolescent self-esteem from participation in school sports among Latino subgroups. *Hispanic Journal of Behavioral Sciences, 24*(4), 409–429.

Euling, S. Y., Selevan, S. G., Pescovitz, O. H., & Skakkebaek, N. E. (2008). Role of environmental factors in the timing of puberty. *Pediatrics, 121,* S167–171.

Evans, G. W. (2004). The environment of childhood poverty. *American Psychologist, 59,* 77–92.

Evans, G. W., Kim, P., Ting, A. H., Tesher, H. B., & Shannis, D. (2007). Cumulative risk, maternal responsiveness, and allostatic load among young adolescents. *Developmental Psychology, 43*(2), 341–351.

Evans, J. P., & Taylor, J. (1995). Understanding violence in contemporary and earlier gangs: An exploratory application of the theory of reasoned action. *Journal of Black Psychology, 21,* 71–81.

Falk, G. (2009). The potential role of the Temporary Assistance for Needy Families (TANF) Block Grant in the recession. Congressional Research Service. http://www.crs.gov

Fan, X. T., & Chen, M. (2001). Parental involvement and students' academic achievement: A meta-analysis. *Educational Psychology Review, 13*, 1–22.

Farah, M. J., Shera, D. M., Savage, J. H., Betancourt, L., Giannetta, J. M., Brodsky, N. L., et al. (2006). Childhood poverty: Specific associations with neurocognitive development. *Brain Research, 1110*(1), 166–174.

Farber, E. (1987). The adolescent who runs. In B. S. Brown & A. R. Mills (Eds.), *Youth at high risk.* (DHHS Publication No. ADM 87–1537). Washington, DC: U.S. Government Printing Office.

Farrell, M. C., Healton, C. G., Davis, K. C., Messeri, P., Hersey, J. C., & Haviland, L. (2002). Getting to the truth: Evaluating national tobacco countermarketing campaigns. *American Journal of Public Health, 92*(6), 901–907.

Farver, J. A. M., Narang, S. K., & Bhadha, B. R. (2002). East meets West: Ethnic identity, acculturation, and conflict in Asian Indian families. *Journal of Family Psychology, 16*, 338–350.

Fasula, A. M., & Miller, K. S. (2006). African-American and Hispanic adolescents' intentions to delay first intercourse: Parental communication as a buffer for sexually active peers. *Journal of Adolescent Health, 38*, 193–200.

Fauber, R., Forehand, R., Thomas, A. M., & Wierson, M. (1990). A mediational model of the impact of marital conflict on adolescent adjustment in intact and divorced families. *Child Development, 61*, 1112–1123.

Fechner, P. Y. (2003). The biology of puberty: New developments in sex differences. In C. Hayward (Ed.), *Gender differences at puberty* (pp. 17–28). New York: Cambridge University Press.

Feiring, C., & Lewis, M. (1991). The transition from middle childhood to early adolescence: Sex differences in the social network and perceived self-competence. *Sex Roles, 24*, 489–509.

Feiring, C., & Lewis, M. (1993). Do mothers know their teenagers' friends? Implications for individuation in early adolescence. *Journal of Youth and Adolescence, 22*, 337–354.

Feldman, C. F., Stone, A., & Renderer, B. (1990). Stage, transfer, and academic achievement in dialect-speaking Hawaiian adolescents. *Child Development, 61*, 472–484.

Feldman, S. S., & Rosenthal, D. A. (2000). The effect of communication characteristics on family members' perceptions of parents as sex educators. *Journal of Research on Adolescence, 10*, 119–150.

Feldman, S. S., Mont-Reynaud, R., & Rosenthal, D. A. (1992). When East moves West: The acculturation of values of Chinese adolescents in the U.S. and Australia. *Journal of Research on Adolescence, 2*, 147–173.

Felner, R. D., Brand, S., DuBois, D. L., Adam, A. M., Mulhall, P. F., & Evans, E. G. (1995). Socioeconomic disadvantage, proximal environmental experiences, and socioemotional and academic adjustment in early adolescence: Investigation of a mediated effects model. *Child Development, 66*, 774–792.

Fennema, E. (2000). *Gender and mathematics: What is known and what do I wish was known?* Prepared for the Fifth Annual Forum of the National Institute for Science Education, May 22–23, 2000. Detroit, MI. http://www.wcer.wisc.edu/archive/nise/News_Activities/Forums/Fennemapaper.htm

Fennema, E., Carpenter, T. P., Jacobs, V. R., Franke, M. L., & Levi, L. W. (1998). A longitudinal study of gender differences in young children's mathematical thinking. *Educational Researcher, 27*, 6–11.

Ferguson, C. J., & Kilburn, J. (2009). The public health risks of media violence: A meta-analytic review. *The Journal of Pediatrics, 154*(5), 759–763.

Field, A. E., Camargo, C. A., Taylor, C. B., Berkey, C. S., Frazier, L., & Gillman, M. W. (1999). Overweight, weight concerns, and bulimic behaviors among girls and boys. *Journal of the American Academy of Child and Adolescent Psychiatry, 38*, 754–760.

Field, A. E., Cheung, L., Wolf, A. M., Herzog, D. B., Gortmaker, S. L., & Colditz, G. A. (1999). Exposure to the mass media and weight concerns among girls. *Pediatrics, 103*, E36.

Findlay, L. C., & Bowker, A. (2009). The link between competitive sport participation and self-concept in early adolescence: A consideration of gender and sport orientation. *Journal of Youth and Adolescence, 38*(1), 29–40.

Fingerhut, L. A., Cox, C. S., & Warner, M. (1998). International comparative analysis of injury mortality: Findings from the ICE on injury statistics. *Advance data from vital and health statistics, 303*. Hyattsville, MD: National Center for Health Statistics.

Finkenauer, C., Engels, R. C. M. E., & Meeus, W. (2002). Keeping secrets from parents: Advantages and disadvantages of secrecy in adolescence. *Journal of Youth and Adolescence, 31*, 123–136.

Fischer, F. M., Nagai, R., & Teiseira, L. R. (2008). Explaining sleep duration in adolescents: The impact of socio-demographic and lifestyle factors and working status. *Chronobiology International, 25*(2–3), 359–372.

Fischhoff, B. (2008). Assessing adolescent decision-making competence. *Developmental Review, 28*, 12–28.

Fisk, W. R. (1985). Responses to "neutral" pronoun presentations and the development of sex-biased responding. *Developmental Psychology, 21*, 481–485.

Fitzgerald, F. (1999). Children of lesbian and gay parents: A review of the literature. *Marriage & Family Review, 29*(1), 57–75.

Flavell, J. H. (1963). *The developmental psychology of Jean Piaget.* Princeton, NJ: Van Nostrand.

Flavell, J. H., Miller, P. H., & Miller, S. A. (1993). *Cognitive development* (3rd ed.). Englewood Cliffs, NJ: Prentice-Hall.

Fletcher, A. C., Darling, N. E., Steinberg, L., & Dornbusch, S. M. (1995). The company they keep: Relation of adolescents' adjustment and behavior to their friends' perceptions of authoritative parenting in the social network. *Developmental Psychology, 31*, 300–310.

Fletcher, A., Steinberg, L., & Williams-Wheeler, M. (2004). Parental influences on adolescent problem-behavior: Revisiting Stattin and Kerr. *Child Development, 75*, 781–796.

Flynn, J. R. (1984). The mean IQ of Americans: Massive gains 1932 to 1978. *Psychological Bulletin, 95*, 29–51.

Fondacaro, M. R, Dunkle, M. E., & Pathak, M. K. (1998). Procedural justice in resolving family disputes: A psychological analysis of individual and family functioning in late adolescence. *Journal of Youth and Adolescence, 27*, 101–119.

Ford, M. E., Wentzel, K. R., Wood, D., Stevens, E., & Siesfeld, G. A. (1989). Processes associated with integrative social competence: Emotional and contextual influences on adolescent social responsibility. *Journal of Adolescent Research, 4*, 405–425.

Fouad, N. A., & Byars-Winston, A. M. (2005). Cultural context of career choice: Meta-analysis of race/ethnicity differences. *The Career Development Quarterly, 53*, 223–233.

Fournier, J. C., DeRubeis, R. J., Hollon, S. D., Dimidjian, S., Amsterdam, J. D., Shelton, R. C., et al. (2010). Antidepressant drug effects and depression severity: A patient-level meta-analysis. *JAMA, 303*(1), 47–53.

Fouts, G., & Burggraf, K. (2000). Television situation comedies: Female weight, male negative comments and audience reactions. *Sex Roles, 42*, 925–935.

Fowler, J. W. (1981). *Stages of faith: The psychology of human development and the quest for meaning.* San Francisco: Harper & Row.

Fowler, J. W. (2001). Faith development theory and the postmodern challenges. *International Journal for the Psychology of Religion, 11*, 159–172.

Fox, M. A., Connolly, B. A., & Snyder, T. D. (2005). *Youth indicators 2005: Trends in the well-being of American youth* (NCES 2005-050). U.S. Department of Education, National Center for Education Statistics. Washington, DC: U.S. Government Printing Office.

Frabutt, J. M., Walker, A. M., & MacKinnon-Lewis, C. (2002). Racial socialization messages and the quality of mother/child interactions in African American families. *Journal of Early Adolescence, 22*, 200–217.

Frank, N. C., & Kendall, S. J. (2001). Religion, risk prevention and health promotion in adolescents: A community-based approach. *Mental Health, Religion and Culture, 4*, 133–148.

Frankel, K. A. (1990). Girls' perceptions of peer relationship support and stress. *Journal of Early Adolescence, 10*, 69–88.

Frankel, L. (2002). "I've never thought about it": Contradictions and taboos surrounding American males' experiences of first ejaculation (semenarche). *The Journal of Men's Studies, 11*(1), 37–54.

Franklin, A. J. (1985). The social context and socialization variables as factors in thinking and learning. In S. F. Chipman, J. W. Segal, & R. Glaser (Eds.), *Thinking and learning skills* (Vol. 2). Hillsdale, NJ: Erlbaum.

Fredricks, J. A., & Eccles, J. S. (2002). Children's competence and value beliefs from childhood through adolescence: Growth trajectories in two male-sex-typed domains. *Developmental Psychology, 38*, 519–533.

Fredricks, J. A., & Eccles, J. S. (2008). Participation in extracurricular activities in the middle school years: Are there developmental benefits for African American and European American youth? *Journal of Youth and Adolescence, 37*, 1029–1043.

Frensch, K. M., Pratt, M. W., & Norris, J. E. (2007). Foundations of generativity: Personal and family correlates of emerging adults' generative life-story themes. *Journal of Research in Personality, 41*, 45–62.

Freud, A. (1969). Adolescence as a developmental disturbance. In G. Caplan & S. Lebovici (Eds.), *Adolescence*. New York: Basic Books.

Freud, S. (1925a). The dissolution of the Oedipal complex. In J. Strachey (Ed.), *The standard edition of the complete psychological works of Sigmund Freud* (Vol. 19). London: Hogarth Press, 1961.

Freud, S. (1925b). Some psychical consequences of the anatomical distinction between the sexes. In J. Strachey (Ed.), *The standard edition of the complete psychological works of Sigmund Freud* (Vol. 19). London: Hogarth Press, 1961.

Freud, S. (1954). *Collected works, standard edition*. London: Hogarth Press.

Frey, C. U., & Rothlisberger, C. (1996). Social support in healthy adolescents. *Journal of Youth and Adolescence, 25*, 17–31.

Friman, P. C., Woods, D. W., Freeman, K. A., Gilman, R., Short, M., McGrath, A. M., et al. (2004). Relationships between tattling, likeability, and social classification: A preliminary investigation of adolescents in residential care. *Behavior Modification, 28*, 331–348.

Frisch, R. E. (1984). Body fat, puberty, and fertility. *Biological Reviews of the Cambridge Philosophical Society, 59*, 161–188.

Frisco, M. L., Muller, C., & Dodson, K. (2004). Participation in voluntary youth-serving associations and early adult voting behavior. *Social Science Quarterly, 85*, 660–676.

Fuligni, A. J. (1998). Authority, autonomy, and parent-adolescent conflict and cohesion: A study of adolescents from Mexican, Chinese, Filipino, and European backgrounds. *Developmental Psychology, 34*(4), 782–792.

Fuligni, A. J., & Eccles, J. S. (1993). Perceived parent-child relationships and early adolescents' orientation toward peers. *Developmental Psychology, 29*, 622–632.

Fuligni, A. J., & Hardway, C. (2006). Daily variations in adolescents' sleep, activities, and psychological well-bring. *Journal of Research on Adolescence, 16*, 353–378.

Fuligni, A. J., Yip, T., & Tseng, V. (2002). The impact of family obligation on the daily activities and psychological well-being of Chinese American adolescents. *Child Development, 73*, 302–314.

Funk, J. B., Baldacci, H. B., Pasold, T., & Baumgardner, J. (2004). Violence exposure in real-life, video games, television, movies, and the internet: Is there desensitization? *Journal of Adolescence, 27*, 23–29.

Furman, W., & Buhrmester, D. (1985). Children's perceptions of the personal relationships in their social networks. *Developmental Psychology, 21*(6), 1016–1024.

Furman, W., & Buhrmester, D. (1992). Age and sex differences in perceptions of networks of personal relationships. *Child Development, 63*, 103–115.

Furrow, J. L., King, P. E., & White, K. (2004). Religion and positive youth development: Identity, meaning, and prosocial concerns. *Applied Developmental Science, 8*, 17–26.

Furstenberg, F. F., Jr., Brooks-Gunn, J., & Morgan, S. P. (1987). *Adolescent mothers in later life*. New York: Cambridge University Press.

Gaddis, A., & Brooks-Gunn, J. (1985). The male experience of pubertal change. *Journal of Youth and Adolescence, 14*, 61–69.

Galambos, N. L., & Maggs, J. L. (1990). Putting mothers' work-related stress in perspective: Mothers and adolescents in dual-earner families. *Journal of Early Adolescence, 10*, 313–328.

Galambos, N. L., Sears, H. A., Almeida, D. M., & Kolaric, G. C. (1995). Parents' work overload and problem behavior in young adolescents. *Journal of Research on Adolescence, 5*, 201–223.

Gallagher, A. M., & De Lisi, R. (1994). Gender differences in Scholastic Aptitude Test: Mathematics problem solving among high-ability students. *Journal of Educational Psychology, 86*, 204–211.

Gallagher, A. M., De Lisi, R., Holst, P. C., McGillicuddy-De Lisi, A. V., Morely, M., & Cahalan, C. (2000). Gender differences in advanced mathematical problem solving. *Journal of Experimental Child Psychology, 75*, 165–190.

Garbarino, J. (1980). Some thoughts on school size and its effects on adolescent development. *Journal of Youth and Adolescence, 9*, 19–31.

Garbarino, J. (1999). *Lost boys*. New York: Free Press.

Garber, J., Robinson, N. S., & Valentiner, D. (1997). The relation between parenting and adolescent depression: Self-worth as a mediator. *Journal of Adolescent Research, 12*, 12–33.

Garcia, J. (1993). The changing image of ethnic groups in textbooks. *Phi Delta Kappan, 75*, 29–35.

Gardner, H. (1983). *Frames of mind*. New York: Basic Books.

Gardner, H. (1999). *Intelligence reframed: Multiple intelligences for the 21st century*. New York: Basic Books.

Gardner, H. (2006). *Multiple intelligences: New horizons in theory and practice*. New York: Basic Books.

Gardner, M., & Steinberg, L. (2005). Peer influence on risk taking, risk preference, and risky decision making in adolescence and adulthood: An experimental study. *Developmental Psychology, 41*(4), 625–635.

Gardner, M., Roth, J., & Brooks-Gunn, J. (2008). Adolescents' participation in organized activities and developmental success 2 and 8 years after high school: Do sponsorship, duration, and intensity matter? *Developmental Psychology, 44*(3), 814–830.

Garland, A. F., & Zigler, E. (1993). Adolescent suicide prevention: Current research and social policy implications. *American Psychologist, 48,* 169–182.

Garlick, D. (2002). Understanding the nature of the general factor in intelligence: The role of individual differences in neural plasticity as an explanatory mechanism. *Psychological Review, 109,* 116–136.

Gateway to College. (2005). http://www.gatewaytocollege.org

Gathercole, S. E., Pickering, S. J., Ambridge, B., & Wearing, H. (2004). The structure of working memory from 4 to 15 years of age. *Developmental Psychology, 40,* 177–190.

Gavin, L. A., & Furman, W. (1989). Age differences in adolescents' perceptions of their peer groups. *Developmental Psychology, 25,* 827–834.

Gavin, L. A., & Furman, W. (1996). Adolescent girls' relationships with mothers and best friends. *Child Development, 67,* 375–386.

Gazelle, H., & Rudolph, K. D. (2004). Moving toward and away from the world: Social approach and avoidance trajectories in anxious solitary youth. *Child Development, 75,* 829–849.

Ge, X., Brody, G. H., Conger, R. D., & Simons, R. L. (2006). Pubertal maturation and African American children's internalizing and externalizing symptoms. *Journal of Youth and Adolescence, 35*(4), 531–540.

Ge, X., Brody, G. H., Conger, R D., Simons, R. L., & Murry, V. M. (2002). Contextual amplification of pubertal transition effects on deviant peer affiliation and externalizing behavior among African American children. *Developmental Psychology, 38,* 42–54.

Ge, X., Conger, R. D., & Elder, G. H. (1996). Coming of age too early: Pubertal influences on girls' vulnerability to psychological distress. *Child Development, 67,* 3386–3400.

Ge, X., Conger, R. D., & Elder, G. H., Jr. (2001a). Pubertal transition, stressful life events, and the emergence of gender differences in adolescent depressive symptoms. *Developmental Psychology, 37,* 404–417.

Ge, X., Conger, R. D., & Elder, G. H., Jr. (2001b). The relation between puberty and psychological distress in adolescent boys. *Journal of Research on Adolescence, 11,* 49–70.

Ge, X., Conger, R. D., Lorenz, F. O., Elder, G. H., Montague, R. B., & Simons, R. L. (1992). Linking family economic hardship to adolescent distress. *Journal of Research on Adolescence, 2,* 351–378.

Ge, X., Natsuaki, M. N., & Conger, R. D. (2006). Trajectories of depressive symptoms and stressful life events among male and female adolescents in divorced and nondivorced families. *Development and Psychopathology, 18,* 253–273.

Gee, C. B., & Rhodes, L. E. (2003). Adolescent mothers' relationship with their children's biological fathers: Social support, social strain and relationship continuity. *Journal of Family Psychology, 17,* 370–383.

Geller, L. G. (1985). *Word play and language learning for children.* Urbana, IL: National Council of Teachers of English.

General Accounting Office. (2003). *Youth illicit drug use prevention: DARE long-term evaluations and federal efforts to identify effective programs.* http://www.gpoaccess.gov/gaoreports/index.html

Gentile, D. A., Anderson, C. A., Yukawa, S., Ihori, N., Saleem, M., Ming, L. K., et al. (2009). The effects of prosocial video games on prosocial behaviors: International evidence from correlational, longitudinal, and experimental studies. *Personality and Social Psychology Bulletin, 35*(6), 752–763.

Gentile, D. A., Lynch, P. J., Linder, J. R., & Walsh, D. A. (2004). The effects of violent video game habits on adolescent hostility, aggressive behaviors, and school performance. *Journal of Adolescence, 27*(1), 5–22.

Georgas, J., Mylonas, K., Bafiti, T., Poortinga, Y. H., Christakopoulou, S., Kagitcibasi, C., et al. (2001). Functional relationships in the nuclear and extended family: A 16-culture study. *International Journal of Psychology, 36*(5), 289–300.

Geuzaine, C., Debry, M., & Liesens, V. (2000). Separation from parents in late adolescence: The same for boys and girls? *Journal of Youth and Adolescence, 29,* 79–91.

Gibbs, J. C., Basinger, K. S., Grime, R. L., & Snarey, J. R. (2007). Moral judgment development across cultures: Revisiting Kohlberg's universality claims. *Developmental Review, 27*(4), 443–500.

Gibbs, J. T (1989). Black American adolescents. In J. T. Gibbs, L. N. Huang, & Associates (Eds.), *Children of color.* San Francisco: Jossey-Bass.

Giles-Sims, J., & Crosbie-Burnett, M. (1989a). Stepfamily research: Implications for policy, clinical interventions, and further research. *Family Relations, 38,* 19–23.

Giles-Sims, J., & Crosbie-Burnett, M. (1989b). Adolescent power in stepfather families: A test of normative-resource theory. *Journal of Marriage and the Family, 51,* 1065–1078.

Gilliam, M. L., Warden, M. W., & Tapia, B. (2004). Young Latinas recall contraceptive use before and after pregnancy: A focus group study. *Journal of Pediatric Adolescent Gynecology, 17,* 279–287.

Gilligan, C. (1982). *In a different voice: Psychological theory and women's development.* Cambridge, MA: Harvard University Press.

Gilligan, C. (1986). Exit-voice dilemmas in adolescent development. In A. Foxley, M. S. McPherson, & G. O'Donnell (Eds.), *Development, democracy, and the art of trespassing: Essays in honor of Albert O. Hirschman.* Notre Dame, IN: University of Notre Dame Press.

Gilligan, C. (1988b). Exit-voice dilemmas in adolescent development. In C. Gilligan, J. V. Ward, J. M. Taylor, & B. Bardige (Eds.), *Mapping the moral domain.* Cambridge, MA: Harvard University Press.

Gilligan, C. (1989a). Preface: Teaching Shakespeare's sister. In C. Gilligan, N. P. Lyons, & T. J. Hanmer (Eds.), *Making connections: The relational worlds of adolescent girls at Emma Willard School.* Cambridge, MA: Harvard University Press.

Gilligan, C. (1989b). Prologue. In C. Gilligan, N. P. Lyons, & T. J. Hanmer (Eds.), *Making connections: The relational worlds of adolescent girls at Emma Willard School.* Cambridge, MA: Harvard University Press.

Gilligan, C. (1996). The centrality of relationships in psychological development: A puzzle, some evidence, and a theory. In G. G. Noam & K. W. Fischer (Eds.), *Development and vulnerability in close relationships* (pp. 237–261). Hillside, NJ: Erlbaum.

Gilligan, C. (2004). Recovering Psyche: Reflections on life-history and history. In J. A. Winer, W. W. Anderson, and C. C. Kieffer (Eds.), *Psychoanalysis and women* (pp. 131–147). Hillsdale, NJ: Analytic Press.

Gilligan, C., & Attanucci, J. (1988). Two moral orientations: Gender differences and similarities. *Merrill-Palmer Quarterly, 34,* 223–237.

Gilligan, C., Lyons, N. P., & Hanmer, T. L. (Eds.). (1989). *Making connections.* Troy, NY: Emma Willard School.

Ginsburg, H., & Opper, S. (1988). *Piaget's theory of intellectual development* (3rd ed.). Englewood Cliffs, NJ: Prentice-Hall.

Ginzburg, E. (1972). Toward a theory of occupational choice: A restatement. *Vocational Guidance Quarterly, 20,* 169–176.

Ginzburg, E. (1990). Career development. In D. Brown, L. Brooks, & Associates (Eds.), *Career choice and development.* San Francisco: Jossey-Bass.

Glantz, S. A., & Mandel, L. L. (2005). Since school-based tobacco prevention programs do not work, what should we do? *Journal of Adolescent Health, 36,* 157–159.

Goldsmith, H. H., Buss, A. H., Plomin, R., Rothbart, M. K., Thomas, A., Chess, S., et al. (1987). Roundtable: What is temperament? Four approaches. *Child Development, 58,* 505–529.

Goldstein, A., Harrington, M., & Woodbury, R. (1999, December 20). The Columbine tapes: In final secret videos they recorded before the massacre, the killers reveal their hatred—and their lust for fame. *Time, 40.*

Goldstein, B. (1976). *Introduction to human sexuality.* Belmont, CA: Star.

Goldstein, S. E., Davis-Kean, P. E., & Eccles, J. S. (2005). Parents, peers, and problem behavior: A longitudinal investigation of the impact of relationship perceptions and characteristics on the development of adolescent problem behavior. *Developmental Psychology, 41,* 401–413.

Goodwin, R. D., Pine, D. S., and Hoven, C. W (2003). Asthma and panic attacks among youth in the community. *Journal of Asthma, 40,* 139–145.

Goossens, L. (2001). Global versus domain-specific statuses in identity research: A comparison of two self- report measures. *Journal of Adolescence, 24,* 681–699.

Gootman, E. (2009, June 5). Next test: Value of $125,000-a-year teachers. *New York Times.*

Gordon, K. E. (2006). Pediatric minor traumatic brain injury. *Seminars in Pediatric Neurology, 13*(4), 243–255.

Gottfredson, G. D., Gottfredson, D. C., Payne, A. A., & Gottfredson, N. C. (2005). School climate predictors of school disorder: Results from a national study of delinquency prevention in schools. *Journal of Research in Crime and Delinquency, 42,* 412–444.

Gottfried, A. E., Gottfried, A. W., & Bathurst, K. (2002). Maternal and dual-earner employment status and parenting. In M. H. Bornstein (Ed.), *Handbook of parenting: Vol. 2. Biology and ecology of parenting* (2nd ed., pp. 207–229). Mahwah, NJ: Erlbaum.

Gowen, L. K., Feldman, S. S., Diaz, R., & Yisrael, D. S. (2004). A comparison of the sexual behaviors and attitudes of adolescent girls with older vs. similar-aged boyfriends. *Journal of Youth and Adolescence, 33,* 167–175.

Graber, J. A. (2003). Puberty in context. In C. Hayward (Ed.), *Gender differences at puberty* (pp. 307–325). New York: Cambridge University Press.

Graber, J. A., & Brooks-Gunn, J. (2002). Adolescent girls' sexual development. In G. M. Wmgood & R. J. DiClemente (Eds.), *Handbook of women's sexual and reproductive health* (pp. 21–42). New York: Kluwer Academic/Plenum.

Graber, J. A., Lewinsohn, P. M., Seeley, J. R., & Brooks-Gunn, J. (1997). Is psychopathology associated with the timing of pubertal development? *Journal of the American Academy of Child and Adolescent Psychiatry, 36,* 1768–1776.

Graber, J. A., Seeley, L. R., Brooks-Gunn, J., & Lewinsohn, P. M. (2004). Is pubertal timing associated with psychopathology in young adulthood? *Journal of the American Academy of Child and Adolescent Psychiatry, 43,* 718–726.

Grady, M. A., & Bloom, K. S. (2004). Pregnancy outcomes of adolescents enrolled in a centering pregnancy program. *Journal of Midwifery and Women's Health, 49,* 412–420.

Graham, S., & Juvonen, J. (2002). Ethnicity, peer harassment, and adjustment in middle school: An exploratory study. *Journal of Early Adolescence, 22,* 173–199.

Granillo, T., Jones-Rodriguez, G., & Carvajal, S. C. (2005). Prevalence of eating disorders in Latina adolescents: Associations with substance use and other correlates. *Journal of Adolescent Health, 36,* 214–220.

Grant, H., & Dweck, C. S. (2003). Clarifying achievement goals and their impact. *Journal of Personality and Social Psychology, 85,* 541–553.

Gray, N. J., Klein, J. D., Noyce, P. R., Sesselberg, T. S., & Cantrill, J. A. (2005). Health information-seeking behaviour in adolescence: The place of the Internet. *Social Science and Medicine, 60,* 1467–1478.

Greenleaf, C., Boyer, E. M., & Petrie, T. A. (2009). High school sport participation and subsequent psychological well-being and physical activity: The mediating influences of body image, physical competence, and instrumentality. *Sex Roles, 61,* 714–726.

Greenough, W. T., Black, J. E., & Wallace, C. S. (1987). Experience and brain development. *Child Development, 58,* 539–559.

Gregory, A., & Weinstein, R. S. (2004). Connection and regulation at home and in school: Predicting growth in achievement for adolescents. *Journal of Adolescent Research, 19,* 405–427.

Greif, G. L., & DeMaris, A. (1990). Single fathers with custody. *Families in Society, 71,* 259–266.

Greitemeyer, T., & Osswald, S. (2009). Prosocial video games reduce aggressive cognitions. *Journal of Experimental Social Psychology, 45*(4), 896–900.

Greitemeyer, T., & Osswald, S. (2010). Effects of prosocial video games on prosocial behavior. *Journal of Personality and Social Psychology, 98*(2), 211–221.

Griffiths, M. (1999). Violent video games and aggression: A review of the literature. *Aggression and Violent Behavior, 4*(2), 203–212.

Gross, B. (1990). Here dropouts drop in-and stay! *Phi Delta Kappan, 71,* 625–627.

Gross, E. F. (2004). Adolescent Internet use: What we expect, what teens report. *Applied Developmental Psychology, 25,* 633–649.

Grotevant, H. D., & Cooper, C. R. (1986). Individuation in family relationships. *Human Development, 29,* 82–100.

Gummerum, M., & Keller, M. (2008). Affection, virtue, pleasure, and profit: Developing an understanding of friendship closeness and intimacy in western and Asian societies. *International Journal of Behavioral Development, 32*(3), 218–231.

Gummerum, M., Keller, M., Takezawa, M., & Mata, J. (2008). To give or not to give: Children's and adolescents' sharing and moral negotiations in economic decision situations. *Child Development, 79*(3), 562–576.

Gunnoe, M. L., & Hetherington, E. M. (2004). Stepchildren's perceptions of noncustodial mothers and noncustodial fathers: Differences in socioemotional involvement and associations with adolescent adjustment problems. *Journal of Family Psychology, 18,* 555–563.

Gunter, K., Baxter-Jones, A. D., Mirwald, R. L., Almstedt, H., Fuller, A., Durski, et al. (2008). Jump starting skeletal health: A 4-year longitudinal study assessing the effects of jumping on skeletal development in pre and circum pubertal children. *Bone, 42,* 710–718.

Guttmacher Institute. (1999). *Facts in brief: Teen sex and pregnancy.* http://www.agi-usa.org/pubs/fb_teen_sex.html

Guttmacher Institute. (2004a). *Sex education: Needs, programs and policies.* http://www.guttmacher.org/presentations/sex_ed.pdf

Guttmacher Institute. (2004b). *U.S. teenage pregnancy statistics: Overall trends, trends by race and ethnicity and state-by-state information.* http://www.guttmacher.org

Guttmacher Institute. (2006). *Sex Education: Needs, Programs and Policies.* http://www.guttmacher.org/presentations/sex_ed.pdf

Guttmacher Institute. (2010). *Facts on American teens' sexual and reproductive health.* http://www.guttmacher.org/pubs/FB-ATSRH.html

Haffner, D. W., & Wagoner, J. (1999). Vast majority of Americans support sexuality education. *SIECUS Report,* August/September.

Hains, A. A., & Szyjakowski, M. (1990). A cognitive stress-reduction intervention program for adolescents. *Journal of Counseling Psychology, 37,* 79–84.

Hall, C. S. (1999). *A primer of Freudian psychology.* New York: Meridian Books.

Hall, T. (2002). *Differentiated instruction*. Wakefield, MA: National Center on Acccessing the General Curriculum. http://www.cast.org/publications/ncac/ncac_diffinstruc.html

Hallinan, M. T., & Teixeira, R. A. (1987). Opportunities and constraints: Black-white differences in the formation of interracial friendships. *Child Development, 58*, 1358–1371.

Halpern, C. J. T., Udry, J. R., Suchindran, C., & Campbell, B. (2000). Adolescent males' willingness to report masturbation. *Journal of Sex Research, 37*, 327–335.

Halpern, C. T., Udry, J. R., Campbell, B., & Suchindran, C. (1999). Effects of body fat on weight concerns, dating, and sexual activity: A longitudinal analysis of black and white adolescent girls. *Developmental Psychology, 35*, 721–736.

Halpern, D. W., Joyner, K., Udry, J. R., & Suchindran, C. (2000). Smart teens don't have sex (or kiss much either). *Journal of Adolescent Health, 26*, 213–225.

Halpern-Felsher, B. (2008). Oral sexual behavior: Harm reduction or gateway behavior? *Journal of Adolescent Health, 43*(3), 207–208.

Hamer, D. H., Hu, S., Magnuson, V.-L., Hu, N., & Pattatucci, A. M. L. (1993). A linkage between DNA markers on the X-chromosome and male sexual orientation. *Science, 261*, 321–326.

Hamm, J. (2000). Do birds of a feather flock together? The variable bases for African American, Asian American, and European American adolescents' selection of similar friends. *Developmental Psychology, 36*, 209–219.

Hammer, H., Finkelhor, D., & Sedlak, A. J. (2002). *Runaway/throwaway children: National Estimates and Characteristics*. Washington, DC: Office of Juvenile Justice and Delinquency Prevention.

Hansen, D. M., & Larson, R. W. (2007). Amplifiers of developmental and negative experiences in organized activities: Dosage, motivation, lead roles, and adult-youth ratios. *Journal of Applied Developmental Psychology, 28*, 360–374.

Hardway, C., & Fuligni, A. J. (2006). Dimensions of family connectedness among adolescents with Mexican, Chinese, and European backgrounds. *Developmental Psychology, 42*(6), 1246–1258.

Hardy, C. L., Bukowski, W. M., & Sippola, L. K. (2002). Stability and change in peer relationships during the transition to middle-level school. *Journal of Early Adolescence, 22*, 117–142.

Hardy, S. A., Padilla-Walker, L. M., & Carlo, G. (2008). Parenting dimensions and adolescents' internalization of moral values. *Journal of Moral Education, 37*(2), 205–223.

Harris, D. R., and Sim, J. J. (2002). Who is multiracial? Assessing the complexity of lived race. *American Sociological Review, 67*, 614–627.

Hart, D., & Fegley, S. (1995). Prosocial behavior and caring in adolescence: Relations to self-understanding and social judgment. *Child Development, 66*, 1346–1359.

Hart, D., Donnelly, T., Youniss, J., & Atkins, R. (2007). High school community service as a predictor of adult voting and volunteering. *American Educational Research Journal, 44*, 197–219.

Hart, T. A., & Heimberg, R. G. (2001). Presenting problems among treatment-seeking gay, lesbian, and bisexual youth. *Journal of Clinical Psychology, 57*, 615–627.

Hartup, W. W. (1993). Adolescents and their friends. In B. Laursen (Ed.), *New directions for child development* (pp. 3–22). San Francisco: Jossey-Bass.

Harvey, O. J., & Rutherford, J. (1980). Status in the informal group. *Child Development, 31*, 377–385.

Hatcher, R., Hatcher, S., Berlin, M., Okla, K., & Richards, J. (1990). Psychological mindedness and abstract reasoning in late childhood and adolescence: An exploration using new instruments. *Journal of Youth and Adolescence, 19*, 307–326.

Hatchett, S. J., & Jackson, J. S. (1993). African American extended kin systems: An assessment. In H. P. McAdoo (Ed.), *Family ethnicity: Strength in diversity* (pp. 90–107). Newbury Park, CA: Sage.

Hattie, J., Marsh, H. W., Neill, J. T., & Richards, G. E. (1997). Adventure education and Outward Bound: Out-of-class experiences that make a lasting difference. *Review of Educational Research, 67*, 43–87.

Hauser, S. T., Borman, E. H., Jacobson, A. M., Powers, S. I., & Noam, G. G. (1991). Understanding family contexts of adolescent coping: A study of parental ego development and adolescent coping strategies. *Journal of Early Adolescence, 11*, 96–124.

Hausmann, M., Slabbekoorn, D., Van Goozen, S. H. M., Cohen-Kettenis, P. T., & Guentuerkuen, O. (2000). Sex hormones affect spatial abilities during the menstrual cycle. *Behavioral Neuroscience, 114*, 1245–1250.

Havighurst, R. J. (1952). *Developmental tasks and education*. New York: Longman.

Havighurst, R. J. (1972). *Developmental tasks and education*. New York: David McKay.

Hayes, C. D. (Ed.). (1987). *Risking the future: Adolescent sexuality, pregnancy, and childbearing* (Vol. 1). Washington, DC: National Academy Press.

Haynie, D. L., Nansel, T., Eitel, P., Crump, A. D., Saylor, K., Yu, K., & Simons-Morton, B. (2001). Bullies, victims, and bully/victims: Distinct groups of at-risk youth. *Journal of Early Adolescence, 21*, 29–49.

Hays, S. P., Hays, C. E., & Mulhall, P. F. (2003). Community risk and protective factors and adolescent substance use. *Journal of Primary Prevention, 24*, 125–142.

Health Access Survey. (2003). *Minnesota's uninsured: Findings from the 2001 Health Access Survey*. http://www.health.state.mn.us/divs/hpsc/hep/publications/coverage/hhsrvrpt.pdf

Heath, S. B. (1993). Inner city life through drama: Imagining the language classroom. *TESOL Quarterly, 27*, 177–192.

Heath, S. B. (1994). The project of learning from the inner-city youth perspective. In F. A. Villarruel & R. M. Lerner (Eds.), *Promoting community-based programs for socialization and learning: New directions for child development* (pp. 25–34). San Francisco: Jossey-Bass.

Heavenly Hats. (2005). *The Foundation Center: Youth in philanthropy* http://youth.fdncenter.org/youth_stories_anthony_leanna.html.

Hedges, L. V., & Nowell, A. (1995). Sex differences in mental test scores, variability, and numbers of high-scoring individuals. *Science, 269*, 41–45.

Hedley, A. A., Ogden, C. L., Johnson, C. L., Carroll, M. D., Curtin, L. R., & Flegal, K. M. (2004). Prevalence of overweight and obesity among U.S. children, adolescents, and adults, 1999–2002. *JAMA, 291*, 2847–2850.

Helwig, C. C., & Kim, S. (1999). Children's evaluations of decision making procedures in peer, family, and school contexts. *Child Development, 70*, 502–512.

Helwig, C. C., Hildebrandt, C., & Turiel, E. (1995). Children's judgments about psychological harm in social context. *Child Development, 66*, 1680–1693.

Henderson, A., Brown, S. D., Pancer, S. M., Ellis-Hale, K. (2007). Mandated community service in high school and subsequent civic engagement: The case of the 'double cohort' in Ontario, Canada. *Journal of Youth and Adolescence, 36*(7), 849–860.

Hendry, L. B., Glendinning, A., & Shucksmith, J. (1996). Adolescent focal theories: Age-trends in developmental transitions. *Journal of Adolescence, 19*, 307–320.

Henggeler, S. W. (1989). *Delinquency in adolescence*. Newbury Park, CA: Sage.

Henry, K. L., Oetting, E. R., & Slater, M. D. (2009). The role of attachment to family, school, and peers in adolescents' use of alcohol: A longitudinal study of within-person and between-person effects. *Journal of Counseling Psychology, 56*(4), 564–572.

Henry, K. L., Slater, M. D., & Oetting, E. R. (2005). Alcohol use in early adolescence: the effect of changes in risk taking, perceived harm and friends' alcohol use. *Journal of Studies on Alcohol, 66,* 275–283.

Herbert, J., & Stipek, J. (2005). The emergence of gender differences in children's perceptions of their academic competence. *Journal of Applied Developmental Psychology, 26,* 276–295.

Herlihy, C. M., & Kemple, J. J. (2005). The Talent Development middle school model: The 2002–2003 school year; an update to the December 2004 report. http://www.mdrc.org

Herman, M. (2004). Forced to choose: Some determinants of racial identification in multiracial adolescents. *Child Development, 75,* 730–748.

Herrera, R. S., & DelCampo, R. L. (1995). Beyond the superwoman syndrome: Work satisfaction and family functioning among working-class, Mexican-American women. *Hispanic Journal of Behavioral Sciences, 17,* 49–60.

Herrlinger, B., & Raisor, P. (1999). *Jefferson County High School.* http://www.jefferson.k12.ky.us/Schools/High/JCHS/jchs.htm

Hertel, B. R., & Donahue, M. J. (1995). Parental influences on God images among children: Testing Durkheim's metaphoric parallelism. *Journal for the Scientific Study of Religion, 34,* 186–199.

Hetherington, E. M. (1989). Coping with family transitions: Winners, losers, and survivors. *Child Development, 60,* 1–14.

Hetherington, E. M., & Kelly, J. (2002). *For better or worse: Divorce reconsidered.* New York: Norton.

Hetherington, E. M., & Stanley-Hagan, M. (2002). Parenting in divorced and remarried families. In M. Bornstein (Ed.), *Handbook of parenting: Vol 3. Being and becoming a parent* (2nd ed.). Mahwah, NJ: Erlbaum.

Hetherington, E. M., Cox, M., & Cox, R. (1982). Effects of divorce on children and parents. In M. E. Lamb (Ed.), *Nontraditional families.* Hillsdale, NJ: Erlbaum.

Hetherington, E. M., Hagan, M. S., & Anderson, E. R. (1989). Marital transitions: A child's perspective. *American Psychologist, 44,* 303–312.

Heyman, G. D., & Giles, J. W. (2004). Valence effects in reasoning about evaluative traits. *Merrill-Palmer Quarterly, 50,* 86–109.

Hill, N. E., & Tyson, D. F. (2009). Parental involvement in middle school: A meta-analytic assessment of the strategies that promote achievement. *Developmental Psychology, 45*(3), 740–763.

Hill, N. E., Castellino, D. R., Lansford, J. E., Nowlin, P., Dodge, K. A., Bates, J. E., et al. (2004). Parent academic involvement as related to school behavior, achievement, and aspirations: Demographic variations across adolescence. *Child Development, 75,* 1491–1509.

Hillaker, B. D., Brophy-Herb, H. E., Villarruel, F. A., & Haas, B. E. (2008). The contributions of parenting to social competencies and positive values in middle school youth: Positive family communication, maintaining standards, and supportive family relationships. *Family Relations, 57,* 591–601.

Hiller-Sturmhofel, S., & Bartke, A (1998). The endocrine system: A review. *Alcohol Health and Research World, 22,* 153–164.

Hind, K., & Burrows, M. (2007). Weight-bearing exercise and bone mineral accrual in children and adolescents: a review of controlled trials. *Bone, 40,* 14–27.

Hingson, R. W., Strunin, L., Berlin, B., & Heeren, T. (1990). Beliefs about AIDS, use of alcohol and drugs, and unprotected sex among Massachusetts adolescents. *American Journal of Public Health, 80,* 295–299.

Hoerster, K. D., Chrisler, J. C., & Rose, J. G. (2003). Attitudes toward and experience with menstruation in the U.S. and India. *Women & Health, 38,* 77–95.

Hoeve, M., Dubas, J. S., Eichelsheim, V. I., van der Laan, P. H., Smeenk, W., & Gerris, J. R. M. (2009). The relationship between parenting and delinquency: A meta-analysis. *Journal of Abnormal Child Psychology, 37*(6), 749–775.

Hof, P. R., Trapp, B. D., deVellis, J., Claudio, L., & Colman, D. R. (1999). The cellular components of nervous tissue. In M. J. Zigmond, F. E. Bloom, S. C. Landis, J. L. Roberts, & L. R. Squire (Eds.), *Fundamental neuroscience* (pp. 41–70). San Diego: Academic Press.

Hoffman, M. L. (1980). Moral development in adolescence. In J. Adelson (Ed.), *Handbook of adolescent psychology.* New York: Wiley.

Hoffman, M. L. (1988). Moral development. In M. H. Bornstein & M. E. Lamb (Eds.), *Developmental psychology: An advanced textbook.* Hillsdale, NJ: Erlbaum.

Hogan, R. (1980). The gifted adolescent. In J. Adelson (Ed.), *Handbook of adolescence.* New York: Wiley.

Hogan, R., & Weiss, D. (1974). Personality correlates of superior academic achievement. *Journal of Counseling Psychology, 21,* 144–149.

Hogan, R., Viernstein, M. C., McGinn, P. V., Daurio, S., & Bohannon, W. (1977). Verbal giftedness and sociopolitical intelligence. *Journal of Educational Psychology, 50,* 135–142.

Hoge, D. R., Johnson, B., & Luidens, D. A. (1995). Types of denominational switching among Protestant young adults. *Journal for the Scientific Study of Religion, 34,* 253–258.

Hogue, A., & Steinberg, L. (1995). Homophily of internalized distress in adolescent peer groups. *Developmental Psychology, 31,* 897–906.

Holland, J. L. (1961). Creative and academic performance among talented adolescents. *Journal of Educational Psychology, 52,* 136–147.

Holland, J. L. (1985a). *Making vocational choices: A theory of vocational personalities and work environments* (2nd ed.). Englewood Cliffs, NJ: Prentice-Hall.

Holland, J. L. (1985b). *Manual for the Vocational Preference Inventory.* Odessa, FL: Psychological Assessment Resources.

Holland, J. L. (1987). Current status of Holland's theory of careers: Another perspective. *Career Development Quarterly, 36,* 24–30.

Hooper, C. J., Luciana, M., Conklin, H. M., & Yarger, R. S. (2004). Adolescents' performance on the Iowa Gambling Task: Implications for the development of decision making and ventromedial prefrontal cortex. *Developmental Psychology, 40,* 1148–1158.

Hopmeyer Gorman, A., Kim, J., & Schimmelbusch, A. (2002). The attributes adolescents associate with peer popularity and teacher preference. *Journal of School Psychology, 40,* 143–165.

Horney, K. (1937). *The neurotic personality of our time.* New York: Norton.

Horney, K. (1967). *Feminine psychology.* New York: Norton.

Horowitz, F. D., & O'Brien, M. (1986). Gifted and talented children. *American Psychologist, 41,* 1147–1152.

Horrey, W. J., & Wickens, C. D. (2006). Examining the impact of cell phone conversations on driving using meta-analytic techniques. *Human Factors, 48*(1), 196–205.

Houseman, L. R. (2007). The impact of electronic media violence: Scientific theory and research. *Journal of Adolescent Health, 41,* S6–S13.

Howes, P., & Cicchetti, D. (1993). A family/relational perspective on maltreating families: Parallel processes across systems and social policy implications. In D. Cicchetti & S. L. Toth (Eds.), *Child abuse, child development, and social policy* (pp. 399–438). Norwood, NJ: Ablex.

Hoyert, D. L., Kochanek, K. D., & Murphy, S. L. (1999). Deaths: Final Data for 1997. *National Vital Statistics Reports, 47*(19). Hyattsville, MD: National Center for Health Statistics. http://www.cdc.gov/nchs/data/nvsr/nvsr47/nvs47_19.pdf

Hu-DeHart, E. (1993). The history, development, and future of ethnic studies. *Phi Delta Kappan, 74,* 718–721.

Huebner, A. J., & Mancini, J. A. (2003). Shaping structured out-of school time use among youth: The effects of self, family, and friend systems. *Journal of Youth and Adolescence, 32,* 453–463.

Huebner, A. J., Shettler, L., Matheson, J. L., Meszaros, P. S., Piercy, F. P., & Davis, S. D. (2005). Factors associated with former smokers among female adolescents in rural Virginia. *Addictive Behaviors, 30,* 167–173.

Huff, C. R. (1996). The criminal behavior of gang members and non-gang, at-risk youth. In C. R. Huff (Ed.), *Gangs in America* (2nd ed.). Thousand Oaks, CA: Sage.

Huff, C. R., & Trump, K. S. (1996). Youth violence and gangs: School safety initiatives in urban and suburban school districts. *Education and Urban Society, 28,* 492–503.

Huizenga, H. M., Crone, E. A., & Jansen, B. J. (2007). Decision-making in healthy children, adolescents and adults explained by the use of increasingly complex propositional reasoning rules. *Developmental Science, 10*(6), 814–825.

Humphrey, L. L. (1989). Observed family interactions among subtypes of eating disorders using structural analysis of social behavior. *Journal of Consulting and Clinical Psychology, 57,* 206–214.

Hunt, J. M. (1961). *Intelligence and experience.* New York: Ronald Press.

Hur, Y., & Bouchard, T. J., Jr. (1995). Genetic influences on perceptions of childhood family environment: A reared apart twin study. *Child Development, 66,* 330–345.

Huston, A., McLoyd, V., & Garcia Coll, C. (1994). Children and poverty: Issues in contemporary research. *Child Development, 65,* 275–282.

Huttenlocher, P. R. (1990). Morphometric study of human cerebral cortex development. *Neuropsychologia, 28,* 517–527.

Hyde, J. S. (1984). Children's understanding of sexist language. *Developmental Psychology, 20,* 697–706.

Hyde, J. S. (1991). *Understanding human sexuality* (4th ed.). New York: McGraw-Hill.

Hyde, J. S. (2005). The gender similarities hypothesis. *American Psychologist, 60*(6), 581–592.

Hyde, J. S., & Durik, A. M. (2005). Gender, competence, and motivation. In A. J. Elliott & C. S. Dweck (Eds.), *Handbook of competence and motivation* (pp. 375–391). New York: Guilford Press.

Hyde, J. S., & Kling, K. C. (2001). Women, motivation, and achievement. *Psychology of Women Quarterly, 25,* 364–378.

Imamo lu, E. O., & Karakitapo lu-Aygün, Z. (2007). Relatedness of identities and emotional closeness with parents across and within cultures. *Asian Journal of Social Psychology, 10,* 145–161.

Imbimbo, P. V. (1995). Sex differences in the identity formation of college students from divorced families. *Journal of Youth and Adolescence, 24,* 745–761.

Impett, E. A., Sorsoli, L., Schooler, D., Henson, J. M., & Tolman, D. L. (2008). Girls' relationship authenticity and self-esteem across adolescence. *Developmental Psychology, 44*(3), 722–733.

Inhelder, B., & Piaget, J. (1958). *The growth of logical thinking from childhood to adolescence.* New York: Basic Books.

Irwin, C. E., Jr. (2004). Eating and physical activity during adolescence: Does it make a difference in adult health status? *Journal of Adolescent Health, 34,* 459–460.

Ito, K. E., Gizlice, Z., Owen-O'Dowd, J., Foust, E., Leone, P. A., & Miller, W. C. (2006). Parent opinion of sexuality education in a state with mandated abstinence education: Does policy match parental preference? *Journal of Adolescent Health, 39*(5), 634–641.

Jackson, J. F. (1993). Human behavioral genetics, Scarr's theory, and her views on interventions: A critical review and commentary on their implications for African American children. *Child Development, 64,* 1318–1332.

Jackson, R., & Howe, N. (2008). *The graying of the great powers: Demography and geopolitics in the 21st century.* Center for Strategic and International Studies, Washington, D.C. http://csis.org/files/media/csis/pubs/080630_gai_majorfindings.pdf

Jacobson, K. C. (2000). Parental monitoring and adolescent adjustment: An ecological perspective. *Journal of Research on Adolescence, 10,* 65–97.

Jadack, R. A., Hyde, L. S., Moore, C. F., & Keller, M. L. (1995). Moral reasoning about sexually transmitted diseases. *Child Development, 66,* 167–177.

Jaffee, S., & Hyde, J. S. (2000). Gender difference in moral orientation: A meta-analysis. *Psychological Bulletin, 126,* 703–726.

Jarrett, R. L. (1995). Growing up poor: The family experiences of socially mobile youth in low-income African American neighborhoods. *Journal of Adolescent Research, 10,* 111–134.

Jenni, O. G., & Carskadon, M. A. (2004). Spectral analysis of the sleep electroencephalogram during adolescence. *Sleep, 27*(4), 774–783.

Jensen, L. A., Arnett, J. J., Feldman, S. S., & Cauffman, E. (2002). It's wrong, but everybody does it: Academic dishonesty among high school and college students. *Contemporary Educational Psychology, 27,* 209–228.

Jensen, L. A., Arnett, J. L., Feldman, S. S., & Caaffman, E. (2004). The right to do wrong: Lying to parents among adolescents and emerging adults. *Journal of Youth and Adolescence, 33,* 101–112.

Jensen-Campbell, L. A., Adams, R., Perry, D. G., Workman, K. A., Furdella, J. Q., & Egan, S. K. (2002). Agreeableness, extraversion, and peer relations in early adolescence: Winning friends and deflecting aggression. *Journal of Research in Personality, 36,* 224–251.

Jodl, K. M., Michael, A., Malanchuk, O., Eccles, J. S., & Sameroff, A. (2001). Parents' roles in shaping early adolescents' occupational aspirations. *Child Development, 72,* 1247–1265.

Joebgen, A. M., & Richards, M. H. (1990). Maternal education and employment: Mediating maternal and adolescent emotional adjustment. *Journal of Early Adolescence, 10,* 329–343.

Johns, M., Schmader, T., & Martins, A. (2005). Knowing is half the battle: Teaching stereotype threat as a means of improving women's math performance. *Psychological Science, 16,* 175–179.

Johnson, B. M., Shulman, S., & Collins, W. A. (1991). Systematic patterns of parenting as reported by adolescents: Developmental differences and implications for psychosocial outcomes. *Journal of Adolescent Research, 6,* 235–252.

Johnson, J. G., Cohen, P. Smailes, E. M., Kasen, S., & Brook, J. S. Television viewing and aggressive behavior during adolescence and adulthood. (2002). *Science, 5564,* 2468–2471.

Johnson, M. K. (2002). Social origins, adolescent experiences, and work value trajectories during the transition to adulthood. *Social Forces, 80,* 1307–1341.

Johnston, L. D., O'Malley, P. M., & Bachman, J. G. (1989). *Drug use, drinking, and smoking: National survey results from high school, college, and young adult populations, 1975–1988* (DHHS Publication No. ADM 89–1638). Washington, DC: U.S. Government Printing Office.

Johnston, L. D., O'Malley, P. M., Bachman, J. G., & Schulenberg, J. E. (2005). *Monitoring the Future national results on adolescent drug use: Overview of key findings, 2004.* http://www.monitoringthefuture.org

Johnston, L. D., O'Malley, P. M., Bachman, J. G., & Schulenberg, J. E. (2009). *Monitoring the future.* Ann Arbor, MI: Institute for Social Research.

Jones, M. C. (1965). Psychological correlates of somatic development. *Child Development, 36,* 899–911.

Jones, M. C., & Bayley, N. (1950). Psychological maturing among boys as related to behavior. *Journal of Educational Psychology, 41,* 129–148.

Jones, R. K., Darroch, J. E., & Singh, S. (2005). Religious differentials in the sexual and reproductive behaviors of young women in the United States. *Journal of Adolescent Health, 36,* 279–288.

Jones, S. D., Ehiri, J., & Anyanwu, E. (2004). Female genital mutilation in developing countries: An agenda for public health response. *European Journal of Obstetrics & Gynecology and Reproductive Biology, 116,* 144–151.

Jonson-Reid, M. (2002). After a child abuse report: Early adolescents and the child welfare system. *Journal of Early Adolescence, 22,* 24–48.

Josselson, R. L. (1980). Ego development in adolescence. In J. Adelson (Ed.), *Handbook of adolescent psychology.* New York: Wiley.

Josselson, R. L. (1982). Personality structure and identity status in women as viewed through early memories. *Journal of Youth and Adolescence, 11,* 293–299.

Josselson, R. L. (1987). *Finding herself: Pathways to identity development in women.* San Francisco: Jossey-Bass.

Josselson, R. L. (1988). The embedded self: I and thou revisited. In D. K. Lapsley & F. C. Power (Eds.), *Self, ego, and identity.* New York: Springer-Verlag.

Josselson, R. L. (1992). *The space between us.* San Francisco: Jossey-Bass.

Joussemet, M., Landry, R., Koestner, R. (2008). A self-determination theory perspective on parenting. *Canadian Psychology, 49*(3), 194–200.

Juan-Espinosa, M., Garcia, L., Colam, R., & Abad, F. J. (2000). Testing the age related differentiation hypothesis through the Wechsler's scales. *Personality and Individual Differences, 29,* 1069–1075.

Juvenile Justice Evaluation Center. (2004). *Disproportionate Minority Contact (DMC).* http://www.jrsa.org/jjec/

Kaiser Family Foundation (2003). *National survey of adolescents and young adults: Sexual health knowledge, attitudes and experiences.* Menlo Park, CA: Kaiser Family Foundation.

Kalil, A., Ziol-Guest, K. M., & Coley, R. L. (2005). Perceptions of father involvement patterns in teenage-mother families: Predictors and links to mothers' psychological adjustment. *Family Relations: Interdisciplinary Journal of Applied Family Studies, 54,* 197–211.

Kandel, D. B. (1975). Stages in adolescent involvement in drug use. *Science, 190,* 912–914.

Kandel, D. B. (1978). Similarity in real-life adolescent friendship pairs. *Journal of Personality and Social Psychology, 36,* 306–312.

Kandel, D. B. (1996). The parental and peer contexts of adolescent deviance: An algebra of interpersonal influences. *Journal of Drug Issues, 26,* 289–315.

Kandel, D. B. (2002). Examining the gateway hypothesis. In D. B. Kandel (Ed.), *Stages and pathways of drug involvement: Examining the gateway hypothesis* (pp. 3–15). New York: Cambridge University Press.

Kaplowitz, P. B. (2008). Link between body fat and the timing of puberty. *Pediatrics, 121,* S208–217.

Karofsky, P. S., Zeng, L., & Kosorok, M. R. (2001). Relationship between adolescent-parental communication and initiation of first intercourse by adolescents. *Journal of Adolescent Health, 28,* 41–45.

Kass, S. J., Cole, K. S., & Stanny, C. J. (2007). Effects of distraction and experience on situation awareness and simulated driving. *Transportation Research Part F, 10*(4), 321–329.

Kaufman, P., Alt, M. N., & Chapman, C. D. (2001). *Dropout rates in the United States: 2000* (NCES 2002-114). Washington, DC: U.S. Department of Education, National Center for Education Statistics.

Keefe, K., & Berndt, T. J. (1996). Relations of friendship quality to self-esteem in early adolescence. *Journal of Early Adolescence, 16,* 110–129.

Kegan, R. (1982). *The evolving self.* Cambridge, MA: Harvard University Press.

Kegan, R. (1994). *In over our heads.* Cambridge, MA: Harvard University Press.

Kegler, M. C., Oman, R. F., Vesely, S. K., McLeroy, K. R., Aspy, C. B., Rodine, S., & Marshall, L. (2005). Relationships among youth assets and neighborhood and community resources. *Health Education and Behavior, 32,* 380–397.

Keith, J. G., Nelson, C. S., Schlaback, J. H., & Thompson, C. J. (1990). The relationship between parental employment and three measures of early adolescent responsibility: Family-related, personal and social. *Journal of Early Adolescence, 10,* 399–415.

Keller, M., & Wood, P. (1989). Development of friendship reasoning: A study of interindividual differences in intraindividual change. *Developmental Psychology, 25,* 820–826.

Kelly, A. M., Wall, M., Eisenberg, M. E., Story, M., & Neumark-Sztainer, D. (2005). Adolescent girls with high body satisfaction: Who are they and what can they teach us? *Journal of Adolescent Health, 37,* 391–396.

Kennard, B. D., Weersing, V. R., Asarnow, J. R., Shamseddeen, W., Porta, G., Berk, M., et al. (2009). Effective components of TORDIA cognitive-behavioral therapy for adolescent depression: Preliminary findings. *Journal of Consulting Psychology, 77*(6), 1033–1041.

Kennison, S. M., & Trofe, J. L. (2003). Comprehending pronouns: A role for word-specific gender stereotype information. *Journal of Psycholinguistic Research, 32,* 355–378.

Kenny, M. E., & Gallagher, L. A. (2002). Instrumental and social/relational correlates of perceived maternal and paternal attachment in adolescence. *Journal of Adolescence, 25,* 203–219.

Kerestes, M., Youniss, J., & Metz, E. (2004). Longitudinal patterns of religious perspective and civic integration. *Applied Developmental Science, 8,* 39–46.

Kerfoot, M., Harrington, R., & Dyer, E. (1995). Brief home-based intervention with young suicide attempters and their families. *Journal of Adolescence, 18,* 557–568.

Kernan, C. L., & Greenfield, P. M. (2005). Becoming a team: Individualism, collectivism, ethnicity, and group socialization in Los Angeles girls' basketball. *Ethos, 33,* 542–566.

Keselman, A. (2003). Supporting inquiry learning by promoting normative understanding of multivariable causality. *Journal of Research in Science Teaching, 40,* 898–921.

Kett, J. F. (1977). *Rites of passage.* New York: Basic Books.

Khanlou, N. (2004). Influences on adolescent self-esteem in multicultural Canadian secondary schools. *Public Health Nursing, 21,* 404–411.

Kiang, L., & Fuligni, A. J. (2009). Ethnic identity and family processes among adolescents from Latin American, Asian, and European backgrounds. *Journal of Youth and Adolescence, 38,* 228–241.

Kilpatrick, D. G., Acierno, R., Saunders, B., Resnick, H. S., Best, C. L., & Schnurr, P. P. (2000). Risk factors for adolescent substance abuse and dependence: Data from a national sample. *Journal of Consulting and Clinical Psychology, 68,* 19–30.

Kim, M. J., Tajima, E. A., Herrenkohl, T. I., & Huang, B. (2009). Early child maltreatment, runaway youths, and risk of delinquency and victimization in adolescence: A meditational model. *Social Work Research, 33*(1), 19–28.

King, P. E., & Furrow, J. L. (2004). Religion as a resource for positive youth development: Religion, social capital, and moral outcomes. *Developmental Psychology, 40*, 703–713.

King, V. (2006). The antecedents and consequences of adolescents' relationships with stepfathers and nonresident fathers. *Journal of Marriage & the Family, 68*(4), 910–928.

King, V. (2007). When children have two mothers: Relationships with nonresident mothers, stepmothers, and fathers. *Journal of Marriage and Family, 69*(5), 1178–1193.

King, V., & Sobolewski, J. M. (2006). Nonresident fathers' contributions to adolescent well-being. *Journal of Marriage and Family, 68*, 537–557.

Kingston, M. H. (1977). *The woman warrior*. New York: Vintage Books.

Kinsey, A. C., Pomeroy, W. B., & Martin, C. E. (1948). *Sexual behavior in the human male*. Philadelphia: Saunders.

Kinsey, A. C., Pomeroy, W. B., Martin, C. E., & Gebhard, P. H. (1953). *Sexual behavior in the human female*. Philadelphia: Saunders.

Kirby, D. (2002). Effective approaches to reducing adolescent unprotected sex, pregnancy, and childbearing. *The Journal of Sex Research, 39*, 51–57.

Kirby, D. B., Baumler, E., Coyle, K. K, Base-Engquist, K., Parcel, S. S., Harrist, R., et al. (2004). The "Safer Choices" intervention: Its impact on the sexual behaviors of different subgroups of high school students. *Journal of Adolescent Health, 35*, 442–452.

Kirsch, I., Moore, T. J., Scoboria, A., & Nicholls, S. S. (2002). The emperor's new drugs: An analysis of antidepressant medication data submitted to the U.S. Food and Drug Administration. *Prevention & Treatment, 5*(23), 1–11.

Kirton, G. (2009). Career plans and aspirations of recent Black and minority ethnic business graduates. *Work, Employment and Society, 23*(1), 12–29.

Klebanov, P. K., & Brooks-Gunn, J. (1992). Impact of maternal attitudes, girls' adjustment, and cognitive skills upon academic performance in middle and high school. *Journal of Research on Adolescence, 2*, 81–102.

Klein, J. D. (2005). Adolescent pregnancy: Current trends and issues. *Pediatrics, 116*, 281–286.

Klein, M. W. (1995). *The American street gang*. New York: Oxford University Press.

Klein, S. S. (1985). *Handbook for achieving sex equity through education*. Baltimore, MD: Johns Hopkins University Press.

Kling, K. C., Hyde, J. S., Showers, C. J., & Buswell, B. N. (1999). Gender differences in self-esteem: A meta-analysis. *Psychological Bulletin, 125*, 470–500.

Klomsten, A. T., Shaalvik, E. M., & Espnes, G. A. (2004). Physical self-concept and sports: Do gender differences still exists? *Sex Roles, 50*, 119–127.

Knox, M., Funk, J., Elliott, R., & Bush, E. G. (2000). Gender differences in adolescents' possible selves. *Youth and Society, 31*, 287–309.

Kochman, T. (1987). The ethnic component in black language and culture. In M. J. Rotheram & J. S. Phinney (Eds.), *Children's ethnic socialization: Pluralism and development* (pp. 219–238). Beverly Hills, CA: Sage.

Koff, E., & Rierdan, J. (1995). Preparing girls for menstruation: Recommendations from adolescent girls. *Adolescence, 30*, 795–811.

Kohlberg, L. (1976). Moral stages and moralization: The cognitive developmental approach. In T. Lickona (Ed.), *Moral development and behavior*. New York: Holt, Rinehart & Winston.

Kohlberg, L. (1984). *The psychology of moral development*. New York: Harper & Row.

Kohlberg, L., & Kramer, R. (1969). Continuities and discontinuities in childhood and adult moral development. *Human Development, 12*, 93–120.

Kohler, P. K., Manhart, L. E., & Lafferty, W. E. (2008). Abstinence-only and comprehensive sex education and the initiation of sexual activity and teen pregnancy. *Journal of Adolescent Health, 42*, 344–351.

Kohut, S., Jr. (1988). *The middle school: A bridge between elementary and high schools* (2nd ed.). Washington, DC: National Education Association.

Konjin, E. A., Nije Bijvank, M., & Bushman, B. J. (2007). I wish I were a warrior: The role of wishful identification in the effects of violent video games on aggression in adolescent boys. *Developmental Psychology, 43*(4), 1038–1044.

Koss, M. P., Dinero, T. E., Seibel, C. A., & Cox, S. L. (1988). Stranger and acquaintance rape: Are there differences in the victim's experience? *Psychology of Women Quarterly, 12*, 1–24.

Kracher, B., & Marble, R. P. (2008). The significance of gender in predicting the cognitive moral development of business practitioners using the Sociomoral Reflection Objective Measure. *Journal of Business Ethics, 78*(4), 503–526.

Kratcoski, P. C., & Kratcoski, L. D. (1986). *Juvenile delinquency*. Englewood Cliffs, NJ: Prentice-Hall.

Kreider, R. M., & Elliott, D. B. (2009). America's families and living arrangements: 2007. *Current Population Reports*, P20–561. Washington, DC: U.S. Census Bureau. http://www.census.gov/prod/2009pubs/p20-561.pdf

Krieger, N., & Fee, E. (1994). Social class: The missing link in U.S. health data. *International Journal of Health Services, 24*, 25–44.

Krishnakumar, A., & Black, M. M. (2003). Family processes within three-generation households and adolescent mothers' satisfaction with father involvement. *Journal of Family Psychology, 17*, 488–498.

Kristjansson, A. L., Sigfusdotter, I. D., James, J. E., Allegrante, J. P., & Helgason, A. R. (2010). Perceived parental reactions and peer respect as predictors of adolescent cigarette smoking and alcohol use. *Addictive Behaviors, 35*, 256–259.

Kroger, J. (1988). A longitudinal study of ego identity status interview domains. *Journal of Adolescence, 11*, 49–64.

Kroger, J. (1992). Intrapsychic dimensions of identity during late adolescence. In G. R. Adams, T. P. Gullotta, & R. Montemayor (Eds.), *Adolescent identity formation*. Newbury Park, CA: Sage.

Kroger, J. (1995). The differentiation of "firm" and "developmental" foreclosure identity statuses: A longitudinal study. *Journal of Adolescent Research, 10*, 317–337.

Kroger, J. (2000). Ego identity status research in the new millennium. *International Journal of Behavioral Development, 24*, 145–148.

Kroger, J. (2003). Identity development during adolescence. In G. R. Adams & M. D. Berzonsky (Eds.), *Blackwell handbook of adolescence* (pp. 205–226). Malden, MA: Blackwell.

Kroger, J. (2007). Why is identity achievement so elusive? *Identity: An International Journal of Theory and Research, 7*(4), 331–348.

Kronenberger, W. G., Mathews, V. P., Dunn, D. W., Wood, E. A., Rembusch, M. E., Giauque, A. L., et al. (2005). Media violence exposure in aggressive and control adolescents: Differences in self- and parent-reported exposure to violence on television and in video games. *Aggressive Behavior, 31*(3), 201–216.

Krumboltz, J. D. (1991). *Career beliefs inventory*. Palo Alto, CA: Consulting Psychologists Press.

Kulin, H. E. (1991a). Puberty, hypothalamic-pituitary changes of. In R. M. Lerner, A. C. Petersen, & J. Brooks-Gunn (Eds.), *Encyclopedia of adolescence* (Vol. 2, pp. 900–907). New York: Garland.

Kulin, H. E. (1991b). Puberty, endocrine changes at. In R. M. Lerner, A. C. Petersen, & J. Brooks-Gunn (Eds.), *Encyclopedia of adolescence* (Vol. 2, pp. 897–899). New York: Garland.

Kunkel, D., Eyal, K., Donnerstein, E., Farrar, K. M., Eiely, E., & Rideout, V. (2007). Sexual socialization messages on entertainment television: Comparing content trends 1997-2002. *Media Psychology, 9*, 595–622.

Kuperminc, G. P., Blatt, S. J., Shahar, G., Henrich, C., & Leadbeater, B. J. (2004). Cultural equivalence and cultural variance in longitudinal associations of young adolescent self-definition and interpersonal relatedness to psychological and school adjustment. *Journal of Youth and Adolescence, 33*, 13–30.

Kurdek, L. A., & Fine, M. A. (1994). Family acceptance and family control as predictors of adjustment in young adolescents: Linear, curvilinear, or interactive effects? *Child Development, 65*, 1137–1146.

Kuttler, A. F., & La Greca, A. M. (2004). Linkages among adolescent girls' romantic relationships, best friendships, and peer networks. *Journal of Adolescence, 27*, 395–414.

Kuttler, A. F., Parker, J. G., & La Greca, A. M. (2002). Developmental and gender differences in preadolescents' judgments of the veracity of gossip. *Merrill-Palmer Quarterly, 48*, 105–132.

Kwak, K. (2003). Adolescents and their parents: A review of intergenerational family relations for immigrant and non-immigrant families. *Human Development, 46*, 15–136.

Labouvie-Vief, G. (1990). Modes of knowledge and the organization of development. In M. L. Commons, J. D. Sinnott, F. A. Richards, & C. Armon (Eds.), *Models and methods in the study of adolescent and adult thought* (pp. 43–62). New York: Springer.

Lacombe, A. C., & Gay, J. (1998). The role of gender in adolescent identity and intimacy decisions. *Journal of Youth and Adolescence, 27*, 795–802.

Ladd, K. L., McIntosh, D. N., & Spilka, B. (1998). Children's God concepts: Influences of denomination, age, and gender. *International Journal for the Psychology of Religion, 8*, 49–56.

LaFromboise, T. D., & Low, K. G. (1989). American Indian children and adolescents. In J. T. Gibbs, L. N. Huang, & Associates (Eds.), *Children of color*. San Francisco: Jossey-Bass.

Laible, D., Eye, J., & Carlo, G. (2008). Dimensions of conscience in mid-adolescence: Links with social behavior, parenting, and temperament. *Journal of Youth and Adolescence, 37*(7), 875–887.

Laird, R. D., Pettit, G. S., Bates, J. E., & Dodge, K. A. (2003). Parents' monitoring-relevant knowledge and adolescents' delinquent behavior: Evidence of correlated developmental changes and reciprocal influences. *Child Development, 74*, 752–768.

Lam, T. H., Stewart, S. M., Leung, G. M., Lee, P. W. H., Wong, J. P. S., & Ho, L. M. (2004). Depressive symptoms among Hong Kong adolescents: Relation to atypical sexual feelings and behaviors, gender dissatisfaction, pubertal timing, and family and peer relationships. *Archives of Sexual Behavior, 33*, 487–496.

Lambert, S. F., Brown, T. L., Phillips, C. M., & Ialongo, N. S. (2004). The relationship between perceptions of neighborhood characteristics and substance use among urban African American adolescents. *American Journal of Community Psychology, 34*, 205–218.

Lamborn, S. D., Dornbusch, S. M., & Steinberg, L. (1996). Ethnicity and community context as moderators of the relations between family decision making and adolescent adjustment. *Child Development, 67*, 283–301.

Landau, S., Lorch, E. P., & Milich, R. (1992). Visual attention to and comprehension of television in attention-deficit hyperactivity disordered and normal boys. *Child Development, 63*, 928–937.

Langer, L. M., Tubman, J. G., & Duncan, S. (1998). Anticipated mortality, HIV vulnerability, and psychological distress among adolescents and young adults at higher and lower risk for HIV infection. *Journal of Youth and Adolescence, 27*, 513–538.

Lapsley, D. K., FitzGerald, D. P., Rice, K. G., & Jackson, S. (1989). Separation-individuation and the "new look" at the imaginary audience and personal fable: A test of an integrative model. *Journal of Adolescent Research, 4*, 483–505.

Larson, R. (2001). How U.S. children and adolescents spend time: What it does (and doesn't) tell us about their development. *Current Directions in Psychological Science, 10*(5), 160–164.

Larson, R., & Richards, M. H. (1994). *Divergent realities*. New York: Basic Books.

Larson, R., Dworkin, J., & Gillman, S. (2001). Facilitating adolescents' constructive use of time in one-parent families. *Applied Developmental Science, 5*(3), 143–157.

Larson, R. W. (2000). Toward a psychology of positive youth development. *American Psychologist, 55*, 170–183.

Larson, R. W. (2002). Globalization, societal change, and new technologies: What they mean for the future of adolescence. *Journal of Research on Adolescence, 12*, 1–30.

Larson, R. W., & Almeida, D. M. (1999). Emotional transmission in the daily lives of families: A new paradigm for studying family process. *Journal of Marriage and the Family, 61*, 30–37.

Larson, R. W., & Gilman, S. (1999). Transmission of emotions in the daily interactions of single-mother families. *Journal of Marriage and the Family, 61*, 21–37.

Larson, R. W., & Richards, M. H. (1991). Boredom in the middle school years: Blaming schools versus blaming students. *American Journal of Education, 99*, 418–443.

Larson, R. W., & Wilson, S. (2004). Adolescence across place and time: Globalization and the changing pathways to adulthood. In R. Lerner & L. Steinberg (Eds.), *Handbook of adolescent psychology*. New York: Wiley.

Larson, R. W., Hansen, D. M., & Moneta, G. (2006). Differing profiles of developmental experiences across types of organized youth activities. *Developmental Psychology 42*(5), 849–863.

Larson, R. W., Richards, M. H., Moneta, G., Holmbeck, G., & Duckett, E. (1996). Changes in adolescents' daily interactions with their families from ages 10 to 18: Disengagement and transformation. *Developmental Psychology, 32*, 744–754.

Larson, R. W., Richards, M. H., Sims, B., & Dworkin, J. (2001). How urban African American young adolescents spend their time: Time budgets for locations, activities, and companionship. *American Journal of Community Psychology, 29*(4), 565–597.

Lassek, W. D., & Gaulin, S. J. (2008). Brief communication: menarche is related to fat distribution. *American Journal of Physical Anthropology, 133*(4), 1147–1151.

Lau, S., & Lau, W. (1996). Outlook on life: How adolescents and children view the life-style of parents, adults and self. *Journal of Adolescence, 19*, 293–296.

Laursen, B., Coy, K. C., & Collins, W. A. (1998). Reconsidering changes in parent-child conflict across adolescence: A meta-analysis. *Child Development, 69*, 817–832.

Laursen, B., Pulkkinen, L., & Adams, R. (2002). The antecedents and correlates of agreeableness in adulthood. *Developmental Psychology, 38*, 591–603.

Lawford, H., Pratt, M. W., Hunsberger, B., & Pancer, S. M. (2005). Adolescent generativity: A longitudinal study of two possible contexts for learning concern for future generations. *Journal of Research on Adolescence, 15*(3), 261–273.

Leaper, C., & Brown, C. S. (2008). Perceived experiences with sexism among adolescent girls. *Child Development, 79*(3), 685–704.

Lease, S. H. (2006). Factors predictive of the range of occupations considered by African American juniors and seniors in high school. *Journal of Career Development, 32*(4), 333–350.

Ledoux, S., Choquet, M., & Manfredi, R. (1993). Associated factors for self-reported binge eating among male and female adolescents. *Journal of Adolescence, 16*, 75–91.

Lee, A. R., M. D. Director of Family Therapy Training, Pacific Medical Center, San Francisco, CA, and Contra Costa, CA, Mental Health Services.

Lee, J. (2008). 'A Kotex and a smile': Mothers and daughters at menarche. *Journal of Family Issues, 29*(10), 1325–1347.

Lee, J. H., Miele, M. E., Hicks, D. J., Phillips, K. K., Trent, J. M., Weissman, B. E., et al. (1996). KiSS-1, a novel human malignant melanoma metastis-suppressor gene. *Journal of the National Cancer Institute, 88*, 1731–1736.

Legters, N. E. (2000). Small learning communities meet school-to-work: Whole school restructuring for urban comprehensive high schools. In M. G. Sanders (Ed.), *Schooling students placed at risk: Research, policy, and practice in the education of poor and minority adolescents* (pp. 309–337). Mahwah, NJ: Erlbaum.

Lehr, S. T., Dilorio, C., Dudley, W. N., & Lipana, J. A. (2000). The relationship between parent-adolescent communication and safer sex behaviors in college students. *Journal of Family Nursing, 6*, 180–196.

Leland, N. L., & Barth, R. P. (1993). Characteristics of adolescents who have attempted to avoid HIV and who have communicated with parents about sex. *Journal of Adolescent Research, 8*, 58–76.

Lempers, J. D., & Clark-Lempers, D. S. (1992). Young, middle, and late adolescents' comparisons of the functional importance of five significant relationships. *Journal of Youth and Adolescence, 21*, 53–96.

Lempers, J. D., & Clark-Lempers, D. S. (1993). A functional comparison of same-sex and opposite-sex friendships during adolescence. *Journal of Adolescent Research, 8*, 89–108.

Lenhart, A., & Madden, M. (2007). Teens, privacy & online social networks: How teens manage their online identities and personal information in the age of MySpace. Washington, DC: *Pew Internet & American Life Project.*

Lenhart, A., Madden, M., Rankin Macgill, A., & Smith, A. (2007). Teens and social media: The use of social media gains a greater foothold in teen life as email continues to lose its luster. Washington, DC: *Pew Internet & American Life Project.*

Lenroot, R. K., & Giedd, J. N. (2006). Brain development in children and adolescents: Insights from anatomical magnetic resonance imaging. *Neuroscience and Biobehavioral Reviews, 30*, 718–729.

Lenroot, R. K., Gogtay, N., Greenstein, D. K., Wells, E. M., Wallace, G. L., Clasen, L. S., et al. (2007). Sexual dimorphism of brain developmental trajectories during childhood and adolescence. *NeuroImage, 36*(4), 1065–1073.

Lenton, A. P., Sedikides, C., & Bruder, M. (2009). A latent semantic analysis of gender stereotype-consistency and narrowness in American English. *Sex Roles, 60*, 269–278.

Lerner, R. M. (2002). *Concepts and theories of human development* (3rd ed.). Mahwah, NJ: Erlbaum.

Lerner, R. M., Anderson, P. M., Balsano, A. B., Dowling, E. M., & Bobek, D. L. (2003). Applied developmental science of positive human development. In R. M. Lerner, A. A. Easterbrooks, & J. Mistry (Eds.), *Handbook of psychology: Vol. 6. Developmental psychology* (pp. 535–558). Hoboken, NJ: Wiley.

Lerner, R. M., Fisher, C. B., & Weinberg, R. A. (2000). Toward a science for and of the people: Promoting civil society through the application of developmental science. *Child Development, 71*, 11–20.

Lerner, R. M., Lerner, J. V., Almerigi, J. B., Theokas, C., Phelps, E., Gestsdottir, S., et al. (2005). Positive youth development, participation in community youth development programs, and community contributions of fifth grade adolescents: Findings from the first wave of the 4-H study of positive youth development. *Journal of Early Adolescence, 25*, 17–71.

Leslie, M. B., Stein, J. A., & Rotheram-Borus, M. J. (2002). Sex-specific predictors of suicidality among runaway youth. *Journal of Clinical Child and Adolescent Psychology, 31*, 27–40.

LeVay, S. (1991). A difference in hypothalamic structure between heterosexual and homosexual men. *Science, 253*, 1034–1037.

Leventhal, T., & Brooks-Gunn, J. (2000). The neighborhoods they live in: The effects of neighborhood residence on child and adolescent outcomes. *Psychological Bulletin, 126*, 309–337.

Lever, J. (1976). Sex differences in the games children play. *Social Problems, 23*, 478–487.

Lever, J. (1978). Sex differences in the complexity of children's play and games. *American Sociological Review, 43*, 471–483.

Levinson, D. J. (1978). *The seasons of a man's life.* New York: Ballantine Books.

Levitt, M. J., Guacci-Franco, N., & Levitt, J. L. (1993). Convoys of social support in childhood and early adolescence: Structure and function. *Developmental Psychology, 29*, 811–818.

Levitt, R.A. (1981). *Physiological psychology.* New York: Holt, Rinehart & Winston.

Leye, E., Powell, R. A., Nienhuis, G., Claeys, P., & Temmerman, M. (2006). Health care in Europe for women with genital mutilation. *Health Care for Women International, 27*(4), 362–378.

Li, X., Sano, H., & Merwin, J. C. (1996). Perception and reasoning abilities among American, Japanese, and Chinese adolescents. *Journal of Adolescent Research, 11*, 173–193.

Li, X., Stanton, B., Pack, R., Harris, C., Cottrell, L., & Burns, J. (2002). Risk and protective factors associated with gang involvement among urban African American adolescents. *Youth & Society, 34*(2), 172–194.

Liben, L. S., Bigler, R. S., & Krogh, H. R. (2002). Language at work: Children's gendered interpretations of occupational titles. *Child Development, 73*, 810–828.

Liben, L. S., Susman, E. J., Finkelstein, J. W., Chinchilli, V. M., Kunselman, S., Schwab, J., et al. (2002). The effects of sex steroids on spatial performance: A review and an experimental clinical investigation. *Developmental Psychology, 38*, 236–253.

Licht, B. G., Linden, T. A., Brown, D. A., & Sexton, M. A. (1984). *Sex differences in achievement orientation: An "A" student phenomenon?* Paper presented at the meeting of the American Psychological Association, Toronto, Canada.

Life Skills Training Program. www.lifeskillstraining.com/

Lindberg, L. D., Jones, R., & Santelli, J. S. (2008). Noncoital sexual activities among adolescents. *Journal of Adolescent Health Care, 43*(3), 231–238.

Ling, P. M., & Glantz, S. A. (2002). Using tobacco-industry marketing research to design more effective tobacco-control campaigns. *Journal of the American Medical Association, 287*, 2983–2989.

Link, B. G., Phelan, J. C., Meich, R., & Westin, E. L. (2008). The resources that matter: Fundamental social causes of health disparities and the challenge of intelligence. *Journal of Health and Social Behavior, 49*(1), 72–91.

Linver, M. R., Roth, J. L., & Brooks-Gunn, J. (2009). Patterns of adolescents' participation in organized activities: Are sports best when combined with other activities? *Developmental Psychology, 45*, 354–367.

Lips, H. M. (1997). *Sex and gender: An introduction* (3rd ed.). Mountain View, CA: Mayfield.

Lips, H. M. (2003). The gender pay gap: Concrete indicator of women's progress toward equality. *Analysis of Social Issues and Public Policy, 3*, 87–109.

Lips, H. M. (2005). *Sex and gender: An introduction* (5th ed.). New York: McGraw-Hill.

Lips, H. M. (2008). *Sex and gender: An introduction* (6th ed.). New York: McGraw-Hill.

Lipsitz, J. (1984). *Successful schools for young adolescents.* New Brunswick, NJ: Transaction Books.

LoSciuto, L., Rajala, A. K., Townsend, T. N., & Taylor, A. S. (1996). An outcome evaluation of Across Ages: An intergenerational mentoring approach to drug prevention. *Journal of Adolescent Research, 11,* 116–129.

Lottes, L. L. (2002). Sexual health policies in other industrialized countries: Are there lessons for the United States? *Journal of Sex Research, 39,* 79–83.

Loukas, A., & Robinson, S. (2004). Examining the moderating role of perceived school climate in early adolescent adjustment. *Journal of Research on Adolescence, 14,* 209–233.

Lovelace, M. K. (2005). Meta-analysis of experimental research based on the Dunn and Dunn model. *Journal of Educational Research, 98,* 176–183.

Lovitt, T. C. (1989). *Introduction to learning disabilities.* Boston: Allyn & Bacon.

Lowry, R., Galuska, D. A., Fulton, J. E., Burgeson, C. R., & Kann, L. (2005). Weight management goals and use of exercise for weight control among U.S. high school students, 1991–2001. *Journal of Adolescent Health, 36,* 320–326.

Lucas, B. (1988). Family patterns and their relationship to obesity. In K. L. Clark, R. B. Parr, & W. P. Castelli (Eds.), *Evaluation and management of eating disorders.* Champaign, IL: Life Enhancement Publications.

Luna, B., Garver, K. E., Urban, T. A., Lazar, N. A., & Sweeney, J. A. (2004). Maturation of cognitive processes from late childhood to adulthood. *Child Development, 75,* 1357–1372.

Luyckx, L., Goossens, L., Soenens, B., Beyers, W., & Vansteenkiste, M. (2005). Identity statuses based on 4 rather than 2 identity dimensions: Extending and refining Marcia's paradigm. *Journal of Youth and Adolescence, 34*(6), 605–618.

Luzzo, D. A., & Ward, B. E. (1995). The relative contributions of self-efficacy and locus of control to the prediction of vocational congruence. *Journal of Career Development, 21,* 307–317.

Luzzo, D. A., Funk, D., & Strang, J. (1996). Attributional retraining increases career decision-making self-efficacy. *Career Development Quarterly, 44,* 378–386.

Luzzo, D. A., James, T., & Luna, M. (1996). Effects of attributional retraining on the career beliefs and career exploration behavior of college students. *Journal of Counseling Psychology, 43,* 415–422.

Lynn, R., & Irwing, P. (2004a). Sex differences on the advanced progressive matrices in college students. *Personality and Individual Differences, 37,* 219–223.

Lynn, R., & Irwing, P. (2004b). Sex differences on the progressive matrices: A meta-analysis. *Intelligence, 32,* 481–498.

Lyon, J. M., Henggeler, S., & Hall, J. A. (1992). The family relations, peer relations, and criminal activities of Caucasian and Hispanic-American gang members. *Journal of Abnormal Child Psychology, 20,* 439–449.

Macgill, A. R. (2007). *Parent and teen internet use.* http://www.pewinternet.org

Machin, S., & Pekkarinen, T. (2008). Global sex differences in test score variability. *Science, 322,* 1331–1332.

MacKay, A. P., & Duran, C. (2007). Adolescent health in the United States, 2007. *DHHS Publication No. (PHS) 2008–1034.* Centers for Disease Control and Prevention.

MacKay, A. P., Fingerhut, L. A., & Duran, C. R. (2000). *Adolescent Health Chartbook. Health, United States, 2000.* Hyattsville, MD: National Center for Health Statistics.

Mackey, K., Arnold, M. L., & Pratt, M. W. (2001). Adolescents' stories of decision making in more and less authoritative families: Representing the voices of parents in narrative. *Journal of Adolescent Research, 16,* 243–268.

MacKinnon, J. L., & Marcia, J. E. (2002). Concurring patterns of women's identity status styles, and understanding of children's development. *International Journal of Behavioral Development, 26,* 70–80.

Madsen, S. D. (2008). Parents' management of adolescents' romantic relationships through dating rules: Gender variations and correlates of relationship qualities. *Journal of Youth and Adolescence, 37,* 1044–1058.

Magarey, A. M., Boulton, T. J. C., Chatterton, B. E., Schultz, C., Nordin, B. E. C., & Cockington, R. A. (1999). Bone growth from 11 to 17 years: Relationship to growth, gender, and changes with pubertal status including timing of menarche. *Acta Paediatrica, 88,* 139–146.

Maguire, K., Pastore, A. L., & Flanagan, T. J. (1993). *Sourcebook of criminal justice statistics 1992.* U.S. Department of Justice, Bureau of Justice Statistics. Washington, DC: U.S. Government Printing Office.

Major, B., & Forcey, B. (1985). Social comparisons and pay evaluations: Preferences for same sex and same-job wage comparisons. *Journal of Experimental Social Psychology, 21,* 393–405.

Malecki, C. K., & Demaray, M. K. (2003). What type of support do they need? Investigating student adjustment as related to emotional, informational, appraisal, and instrumental support. *School Psychology Quarterly, 18,* 231–252.

Malinowski, B. (1925). Magic, science, and religion. In J. Needham (Ed.), *Science, religion and reality* (pp. 18–94). New York: Macmillan.

Mandel, L. L., Bialous, S. A., & Glantz, S. A. (2006). Avoiding "truth": Tobacco industry promotion of Life Skills Training. *Journal of Adolescent Health, 39,* 868–879.

Mann, L., Harmoni, R., & Power, C. (1989). Adolescent decision-making: The development of competence. *Journal of Adolescence, 12,* 265–278.

Marcia, J. E. (1966). Development and validation of ego identity status. *Journal of Personality and Social Psychology, 3,* 551–558.

Marcia, J. E. (1976). Identity six years after: A follow-up study. *Journal of Youth and Adolescence, 5,* 145–150.

Marcia, J. E. (1980). Identity in adolescence. In J. Adelson (Ed.), *Handbook of adolescent psychology.* New York: Wiley.

Marcia, J. E. (1988). Common processes underlying ego identity, cognitive/moral development, and individuation. In D. K. Lapsley & F. C. Power (Eds.), *Self, ego and identity: Integrative approaches.* New York: Springer-Verlag.

Marcia, J. E. (2002). Adolescence, identity, and the Bernardone family. *Identity, 2,* 199–209.

Margolin, L., Miller, M., & Moran, P. B. (1989). When a kiss is not just a kiss: Relating violations of consent in kissing to rape myth acceptance. *Sex Roles, 20,* 231–243.

Marin, K. A., Bohanek, J. G., & Fivush, R. (2008). Positive effects of talking about the negative: Family narratives of negative experiences and preadolescents' perceived competence. *Journal of Research on Adolescence, 18*(3), 573–593.

Markstrom, C. A. (1999). Religious involvement and adolescent psychosocial development. *Journal of Adolescence, 22,* 205–221.

Markstrom-Adams, C., & Smith, M. (1996). Identity formation and religious orientation among high school students from the United States and Canada. *Journal of Adolescence, 19,* 247–261.

Markstrom-Adams, C., Hofstra, G., & Dougher, K. (1994). The ego-virtue of fidelity: A case for the study of religion and identity formation in adolescence. *Journal of Youth and Adolescence, 23,* 453–469.

Markus, H. R., & Kitayama, S. (1991). Culture and the self: Implications for cognition, emotion, and motivation. *Psychological Review, 98*(2), 224–253.

Markus, H. R., & Kitayama, S. (1998). The cultural psychology of personality. *Journal of Cross-Cultural Psychology, 29*(1), 63–87.

Marsh, H. W. (1992). Extracurricular activities: Beneficial extension of the traditional curriculum or subversion of academic goals? *Journal of Educational Psychology, 84,* 553–562.

Marsh, H. W., Chanal, J. P., & Sarrazin, P. G. (2006). Self-belief does make a difference: A reciprocal effects model of the causal ordering of physical self-concept and gymnastics performance. *Journal of Sports Sciences, 24*(1), 101–111.

Marsiglia, F. F., Miles, B. W., Dustman, P., & Sills, S. (2002). Ties that protect: An ecological perspective on Latino/a urban pre-adolescent drug use. *Journal of Ethnic and Cultural Diversity in Social Work, 11*, 191–220.

Martin, G. (2009). A portrait of the youth labor market in 13 countries, 1980–2007. *Monthly Labor Review*, 3–21.

Martinez, I., & Garcia, J. F. (2008). Internalization of values and self-esteem among Brazilian teenagers from authoritative, indulgent, authoritarian, and neglectful homes. *Family Therapy, 35*(1), 43–59.

Martorano, S. C. (1977). A developmental analysis of performance on Piaget's formal operations tasks. *Developmental Psychology, 13*, 666–672.

Marvan, M. L., Morales, C., & Cortes-Iniestra, S. (2006). Emotional reactions to menarche among Mexican women of different generations. *Sex Roles, 54*(5–6), 323–330.

Masters, W. H., Johnson, V. E., & Kolodny, R. C. (1988). *Human sexuality* (3rd ed.). Boston: Little, Brown.

Matchock, R. L., Dorn, L. D., & Susman, E. J. (2007). Diurnal and seasonal cortisol, testosterone, and DHEA rhythms in boys and girls during puberty. *Chronobiology International, 24*(5), 969–990.

Matjasko, J. L., & Feldman, A. F. (2006). Bringing work home: The emotional experiences of mothers and fathers. *Journal of Family Psychology, 20*(1), 47–55.

Matkovic, V., Ilich, J. Z., Skugor, M., Badenhop, N. E., Goel, P., Clairmont, A., et al. (1997). Leptin is inversely related to age at menarche in human females. *Journal of Clinical Endocrinology and Metabolism, 82*, 3239–3245.

Mattila, V. M., Parkkari, J., Kannus, P., & Rimpela, A. (2009). Participation in sports clubs is a strong predictor of injury hospitalization: A prospective cohort study. *Scandinavian Journal of Medicine & Science in Sports, 19*(2), 267–273.

Maynard, R. A., Trenhold, C., Devaney, B., Johnson, A., Clark, M. A., Homrighausen, J., et al. (2005). First-year impacts of four Title V, Section 510 abstinence education programs. http://aspe.hhs.gov/hsp/05/abstinence/

Maynard, R. C. (1990, August 5). An example of how Afro-American parents socialize children. *Oakland Tribune*.

Mayr, E. (1982). *Growth of biological thought: Diversity, evolution, and inheritance*. Cambridge, MA: Harvard University Press.

Mazor, A., & Enright, R. D. (1988). The development of the individuation process from a social-cognitive perspective. *Journal of Adolescence, 11*, 29–47.

McComb, C. (2003). *Teens and social service: Who volunteers?* The Gallup Organization. http://www.gallup.com/poll/8500/Teens-Social-Service-Who-Volunteers.aspx

McCullough, M. E., Emmons, R. A., & Tsang, J. (2002). The grateful disposition: A conceptual and empirical topography. *Journal of Personality and Social Psychology, 82*, 112–127.

McCullough, M. E., Kilpatrick, S. D., Emmons, R. A., & Larson, D. B. (2001). Is gratitude a moral affect? *Psychological Bulletin, 127*, 249–266.

McDowell, M. A., Brody, D. J., & Hughes, J. P. (2007). Has age at menarche changed? Results from the National Health and Nutrition Examination Survey (NHANES) 1999-2004. *Journal of Adolescent Health, 40*, 227–231.

McElhaney, K. B., & Allen, J. P. (2001). Autonomy and adolescent social functioning: The moderating effect of risk. *Child Development, 72*, 220–235.

McElhaney, K. B., Porter, M. R., Thompson, L. W., & Allen, J. P. (2008). Apples and oranges: Divergent meanings of parents' and adolescents' perceptions of parental influence. *Journal of Early Adolescence, 28*(2), 206–229.

McFarlane, A. H., Bellissimo, A., Norman, G. R., & Lange, P. (1994). Adolescent depression in a school-based community sample: Preliminary findings on contributing social factors. *Journal of Youth and Adolescence, 23*, 601–620.

McGrory, K. (2009, March 8). Principal strives to remake Miami Central High. *Miami Herald*. http://www.miamiherald.com/centralhigh/story/1061149.html

McGue, M., Elkins, I., Walden, B., & Iacono, W. G. (2005). Perceptions of the parent-adolescent relationship: A longitudinal investigation. *Developmental Psychology, 41*(6), 971–984.

McGue, M., Sharma, A., & Benson, P. (1996). The effect of common rearing on adolescent adjustment: Evidence from a U.S. adoption cohort. *Developmental Psychology, 32*, 604–613.

McKeever, C. K., & Schatz, P. (2003). Current issues in the identification, assessment, and management of concussions in sports-related injuries. *Applied Neuropsychology, 10*(1), 4–11.

McKinney, C., & Renk, K. (2008). Differential parenting between mothers and fathers: Implications for late adolescents. *Journal of Family Issues, 29*(6), 806–827.

McKinney, J. P., & McKinney, K. G. (1999). Prayer in the lives of late adolescents. *Journal of Adolescence, 22*, 279–290.

McLanahan, S. S., & Booth, K. (1989). Mother-only families: Problems, prospects, and politics. *Journal of Marriage and the Family, 51*, 557–580.

McLanahan, S. S., Astone, N. M., & Marks, N. (1988). *The role of mother-only families in reproducing poverty*. Paper presented at the Conference on Poverty and Children, Lawrence, KS.

McLoyd, V. C. (1998). Socioeconomic disadvantage and child development. *American Psychologist, 53*, 185–204.

McNeal, R. B. (1995). Extracurricular activities and high school dropouts. *Journal of Educational Sociology, 68*(1), 62–80.

McNelles, L. R., & Connolly, J. A. (1999). Intimacy between adolescent friends: Age and gender differences in intimate affect and intimate behaviors. *Journal of Research on Adolescence, 9*, 143–159.

McVey, G. L., Pepler, D., Davis, R., Flett, G. L., & Abdolell, M. (2002). Risk and protective factors associated with disordered eating during early adolescence. *Journal of Early Adolescence, 22*, 75–95.

Mechanic, D., & Hansell, S. (1989). Divorce, family conflict, and adolescents' well-being. *Journal of Health and Social Behavior, 30*, 105–116.

Meeus, W., & Dekovic, M. (1995). Identity development, parental and peer support in adolescence: Results of a national Dutch survey. *Adolescence, 30*, 931–944.

Meeus, W., Iedema, J., Maassen, G., & Engels, R. (2005). Separation-individuation revisited: On the interplay of parent-adolescent relations, identity and emotional adjustment in adolescence. *Journal of Adolescence, 28*, 89–106.

Meichenbaum, D. H. (1985). *Stress inoculation training*. New York: Pergamon.

Mersky, J. P., Berger, L. M., Reynolds, A. J., & Gromoske, A. N. (2009). Risk factors for child and adolescent maltreatment: A longitudinal investigation of a cohort of inner-city youth. *Child Maltreatment, 14*(1), 73–88.

Meschke, L. L., Bartholomae, S., & Zentall, S. R. (2002). Adolescent sexuality and parent-adolescent processes: Promoting healthy teen choices. *Journal of Adolescent Health, 31*, 264–279.

Meschke, L. L., Zweig, J. M., Barber, B. L., & Eccles, J. S. (2000). Demographic, biological, psychological, and social predictors of the timing of first intercourse. *Journal of Research on Adolescence, 10*, 315–338.

MetLife. (2009). *The 2009 MetLife study of the American dream*. http://www.metlife.com/dream

Michael, A., & Eccles, J. S. (2003). When coming of age means coming undone: Links between puberty and psychosocial adjustment among European American and African American girls. In C. Hayward (Ed.), *Gender differences at puberty* (pp. 277–303). New York: Cambridge University Press.

Michel, A. (1986). *Down with stereotypes? Eliminating sexism from children's literature and school textbooks*. Washington, DC: UNESCO.

Midgley, C., Arunkumar, R., & Urdan, T. C. (1996). "If I don't do well tomorrow, there's a reason": Predictors of adolescents' use of academic self-handicapping strategies. *Journal of Educational Psychology, 88*, 423–434.

Milevsky, A., Schlechter, M., Klem, L., & Kehl, R. (2008). Contellations of maternal and paternal parenting styles in adolescence: Congruity and well-being. *Marriage & Family Review, 44*(1), 81–98.

Miller, B. C., & Fox, G. L. (1987). Theories of adolescent heterosexual behavior. *Adolescent Research, 2*, 269–282.

Miller, C. T., & Downey, K. T. (1999). A meta-analysis of heavyweight and self-esteem. *Personality and Social Psychology Review, 3*, 68–84.

Miller, G. A., Galanter, E., & Pribram, K. H. (1960). *Plans and the structure of behavior*. New York: Holt, Rinehart & Winston.

Miller, J. (Ed.). (1973). *Psychoanalysis and women*. New York: Brunner/Mazel.

Miller, J. (1976). *Toward a new psychology of women*. Boston: Beacon Press.

Miller, J. G., & Bersoff, D. M. (1989). When do American children and adults reason in social conventional terms? *Developmental Psychology, 24*, 366–375.

Miller, K. E. (1990). Adolescents' same-sex and opposite-sex peer relations: Sex differences in popularity, perceived social competence, and social cognitive skills. *Journal of Adolescent Research, 5*, 222–241.

Miller, R. L. (1989). Desegregation experiences of minority students: Adolescent coping strategies in five Connecticut high schools. *Journal of Adolescent Research, 4*, 173–189.

Miller-Johnson, S., Costanzo, P. R., Coie, J. D., Rose, M. R., Browne, D. C., & Johnson, C. (2003). Peer social structure and risk-taking behaviors among African American early adolescents. *Journal of Youth and Adolescence, 32*, 375–384.

Millman, R. P. (2005). Excessive sleepiness in adolescents and young adults: Causes, consequences, and treatment strategies. *Pediatrics, 115*(6), 1774–1786.

Minuchin, S., Rosman, B., & Baker, L. (1978). *Psychosomatic families: Anorexia nervosa in context*. Cambridge, MA: Harvard University Press.

Mischel, W., & Mischel, H. N. (1976). A cognitive social-learning approach to morality and self-regulation. In T. Lickona (Ed.), *Moral development and behavior: Theory, research, and social issues*. New York: Holt, Rinehart & Winston.

Mitchell, L. K., & Krumboltz, J. D. (1987). The effects of cognitive restructuring and decision-making training on career indecision. *Journal of Counseling and Development, 66*, 171–174.

Mitchell, L. K., & Krumboltz, J. D. (1990). Social learning approach to career decision making: Krumboltz's theory. In D. Brown, L. Brooks, & Associates (Eds.), *Career choice and development*. San Francisco: Jossey-Bass.

Mizell, M. H. (1999). *Thirty and Counting*. Remarks at the middle grades education conference sponsored by the Southern Regional Education Board, Atlanta, GA.

Moffitt, T. E. (1997). Adolescent-limited and life-course-persistent offending: A complementary pair of developmental theories. In T. P. Thornberry (Ed.), *Developmental theories of crime and delinquency* (pp. 11–54). New Brunswick, NJ: Transaction Books.

Moffitt, T. E. (2007). A review of research on the taxonomy of life-course persistent versus adolescence-limited antisocial behavior. In D. J. Flannery, A. T. Alexander, & I. D. Waldman (Eds.), *The Cambridge handbook of violent behavior and aggression* (pp. 49–74). New York: Cambridge University Press.

Molina, B. S. G., & Chassin, L. (1996). The parent-adolescent relationship at puberty: Hispanic ethnicity and parent alcoholism as moderators. *Developmental Psychology, 32*, 675–686.

Moller, I., & Krahe, B. (2009). Exposure to violent video games and aggression in German adolescents: A longitudinal analysis. *Aggressive Behavior, 35*(1), 75–89.

Money, J. (1988). Commentary: Current status of sex research. *Journal of Psychology and Human Sexuality, 1*, 5–16.

Montemayor, R., & Van Komer, R. (1985). The development of sex differences in friendship patterns and peer group structure during adolescence. *Journal of Early Adolescence, 5*, 285–294.

Montgomery, M. J. (2005). Psychosocial intimacy and identity: From early adolescence to emerging adulthood. *Journal of Adolescent Research, 20*, 346–374.

Moore, K. A., & Glei, D. (1995). Taking the plunge: An examination of positive youth development. *Journal of Adolescent Research, 10*, 15–40.

Moore, M., & Meltzer, L. J. (2008). The sleepy adolescent: Causes and consequences of sleepiness in teens. *Paediatric Respiratory Reviews, 9*(2), 114–120.

Moore, S., & Cartwright, C. (2005). Adolescents' and young adults' expectations of parental responsibilities in stepfamilies. *Journal of Divorce and Remarriage, 43*, 109–127.

Morelli, A., Marini, M., Mancina, R., Luconi, M., Vignozzi, L., Fibbi, B., et al. (2007). Sex steroids and leptin regulate the "First Kiss" (KiSS 1/G-protein-coupled receptor 54 system) in human gonadotropin-releasing-hormone-secreting neuroblasts. *The Journal of Sexual Medicine, 5*, 1097–1113.

Morin, R., & Taylor, P. (2009). *Luxury or necessity? The public makes a U-turn*. Pew Research Center Publications. http://pewresearch.org/pubs/1199/more-items-seen-as-luxury-not-necessity

Mortimer, J. T., Finch, M. D., Ryu, S., Shanahan, M. J., & Call, K. T. (1996). The effects of work intensity on adolescent mental health, achievement, and behavioral adjustment: New evidence from a prospective study. *Child Development, 67*, 1243–1261.

Mortimer, J. T., Finch, M., Shanahan, M., & Ryu, S. (1992). Work experience, mental health, and behavioral adjustment in adolescence. *Journal of Research on Adolescence, 2*, 25–57.

Mosher, F. A., & J. R. Hornsby, J. R. (1966). On asking questions. In J. Bruner, R. R. Olver, & R. Greenfield (Eds.), *Studies in cognitive growth*. New York: Wiley.

Mounts, N. S. (2001). Young adolescents' perceptions of parental management of peer relationships. *Journal of Early Adolescence, 21*, 92–122.

Mounts, N. S., & Steinberg, L. (1995). An ecological analysis of peer influence on adolescent grade point average and drug use. *Developmental Psychology, 31*, 915–922.

Mukherjee, P., Miller, J. H., Shimony, J. S., Philip, J., Nehra, D., Snyder, A. Z., et al. (2002). Diffusion tensor MR imaging of gray and white matter development during normal human brain maturation. *American Journal of Neuroradiology, 23*, 1445–1456.

Mulholland, A. M., & Mintz, L. B. (2001). Prevalence of eating disorders among African American women. *Journal of Counseling Psychology, 48*, 111–116.

Muller, U., Overton, W. F., & Reene, K. (2001). Development of conditional reasoning: A longitudinal study. *Journal of Cognition and Development, 2*(1), 27–49.

Mullet, E., & Girard, M. (2000). Developmental and cognitive points of view on forgiveness. In M. E. McCullough, K. I. Pargament, & C. E. Thoresen (Eds.), *Forgiveness: Theory, research, and practice* (pp. 111–132). New York: Guilford Press.

Mullis, R. L., & Chapman, P. (2000). Age, gender, and self-esteem differences in adolescent coping styles. *Journal of Social Psychology, 140,* 539–541.

Munroe, R. (1955). *Schools of psychoanalytic thought.* New York: Dryden Press.

Munson, M. L., & Sutton, P. D. (2005). Births, marriages, divorces, and deaths: Provisional data for 2004. *National Vital Statistics Reports, 53*(21). Hyattsville, MD: National Center for Health Statistics.

Muntner, P., He, J., Cutler, J. A., Wildman, R. P., & Whelton, P. K. (2004). Trends in blood pressure among children and adolescents. *JAMA, 291,* 2107–2113.

Murdock, T. B., Miller, A., & Kohlhardt, J. (2004). Effects of classroom context variables on high school students' judgments of the acceptability and likelihood of cheating. *Journal of Education Psychology, 96,* 765–777.

Muuss, R. E. (1975). Adolescent development and the secular trend. In R. E. Muuss (Ed.), *Adolescent behavior and society: A book of readings.* New York: Random House.

Muuss, R. E. (1990). *Adolescent behavior and society* (4th ed.). New York: Random House.

Nadeem, E., Whaley, S. E., & Anthony, S. (2006). Characterizing low-income Latina adolescent mothers: Living arrangements, psychological adjustment, and use of services. *Journal of Adolescent Health, 38,* 68–71.

Nansel, T. R., Overpeck, M., Pilla, R. S., Ruan, W. J., Simons-Morton, B., & Scheidt, P. (2001). Bullying behaviors among U.S. youth: Prevalence and association with psychosocial adjustment. *JAMA, 285,* 2094–2100.

National Assembly of Health and Human Service Organizations. (1999). *Runaway and homeless youth.* http://web.archive.org/web/20000603023529/http://www.nassembly.org/html/runhome.html

National Center for Children in Poverty. (2003). *Low-income children in the United States.* http://web.archive.org/web/20040517215959/http://www.nccp.org/pub_cpf04.html

National Center for Children in Poverty. (2009). *Ten important questions about child poverty and family economic hardship.* http://www.nccp.org/topics/childpoverty.html

National Center for Education Statistics. (1995). *The condition of education, 1995.* Washington, DC: U.S. Department of Education.

National Center for Education Statistics. (2003). *Condition of education 2003.* Washington, DC: U.S. Department of Education.

National Center for Health Statistics. (2004). *Health, United States, 2004 with chartbook on trends in the health of Americans.* Hyattsville, MD: U.S. Department of Education.

National Clearinghouse on Child Abuse and Neglect Information. (2005). Washington, DC: U.S. Department of Health and Human Services.

National Drug Intelligence Center. (2006). *Organized gangs and drug trafficking.* http://www.justice.gov/ndic/pubs11/18862/gangs.htm

National Institute of Allergy and Infectious Diseases. (2005). *HIV infection in adolescents and young adults in the U.S.* http://www3.niaid.nih.gov/topics/HIVAIDS/Understanding/Population+Specific+Information/hivadolescent.htm

National Runaway Switchboard. (2004). http://www.nrscrisisline.org

National School Safety Center. (1998). *Total school-associated violent death count: July 1992 to Present.* http://www.nccsl.org

National Youth Gang Center. (2009). *National Youth Gang Survey Analysis.* http://www.nationalgangcenter.gov/Survey-Analysis

Needle, R. H., Su, S. S., & Doherty, W. J. (1990). Divorce, remarriage, and adolescent substance use: A prospective longitudinal study. *Journal of Marriage and the Family, 52,* 157–169.

Neff, K. D., & Helwig, C. C. (2002). A constructivist approach to understanding the development of reasoning about rights and authority within cultural contexts. *Cognitive Development, 17,* 1429–1450.

Neisser, U. (1967). *Cognitive psychology.* New York: Appleton-Century-Crofts.

Neisser, U. (1976). *Cognition and reality.* San Francisco: Freeman.

Neisser, U., Boodoo, G., Bouchard, T. J., Jr., Boykin, A. W., Brody, N., Ceci, S. J. et al. (1996). Intelligence: Knowns and unknowns. *American Psychologist, 51,* 77–101.

Nelson, L. J., and Barry, C. M. (2005). Distinguishing features of emerging adulthood: The role of self-classification as an adult. *Journal of Adolescent Research, 20,* 242–262.

Nelson, M. R. (1988). Issues of access to knowledge: Dropping out of school. In L. N. Tanner (Ed.), *Critical issues in curriculum, 87th yearbook of the National Society for the Study of Education.* Chicago: University of Chicago Press.

Newhouse, P., Newhouse, C., & Astur, R. S. (2007). Sex differences in visual-spatial learning using a virtual water maze in pre-pubertal children. *Behavioral Brain Research, 183*(1), 1–7.

Newman, B. M., & Newman, P. R. (2001). Group identity and alienation: Giving the We its due. *Journal of Youth and Adolescence, 30,* 515–538.

Newman, D. L. (2005). Ego development and ethnic identity formation in rural American Indian adolescents. *Child Development, 76,* 734–746.

Newman, J. (1985). Adolescents: Why they can be so obnoxious. *Adolescence, 20,* 635–645.

Nielsen Media Research (2009). *Television Audience Report, 2008.* http://www.nielsenmedia.com

Nishina, A., Ammon, N., Bellmore, A. D., & Graham, S. (2006). Body dissatisfaction and physical development among ethnic minority adolescents. *Journal of Youth and Adolescence, 35*(2), 189–201.

Nitz, K., Ketterlinus, R. D., & Brandt, L. J. (1995). The role of stress, social support, and family environment in adolescent mothers' parenting. *Journal of Adolescent Research, 10,* 358–382.

Nolin, M. J., & Petersen, K. K. (1992). Gender differences in parent–child communication about sexuality. *Journal of Adolescent Research, 7,* 59–79.

Nomagushi, K. M. (2008). Gender, gamily structure, and adolescents' primary confidants. *Journal of Marriage and Family, 70*(5), 1213–1227.

Noom, M. J., Dekovic, M., & Meeus, W. (2001). Conceptual analysis and measurement of adolescent autonomy. *Journal of Youth and Adolescence, 30,* 577–595.

Norton, E. M., Durlak, J. A., & Richards, M. H. (1989). Peer knowledge of and reactions to adolescent suicide. *Journal of Youth and Adolescence, 18,* 427–437.

Nosek, B. A., Banaji, M. R., & Greenwald, A. G. (2002). Math = male, me = female, therefore math ≠ me. *Journal of Personality and Social Psychology, 83,* 44–49.

Nottelmann, E. D., Susman, E. J., Blue, J. H., Inoff-Germain, C., Dorn, L. D., Loriaux, D. L., et al. (1987). Gonadal and adrenal hormone correlates of adjustment in early adolescence. In R. M. Lerner & T. T. Foch (Eds.), *Biological-psychological interactions in early adolescence.* Hillsdale, NJ: Erlbaum.

Nucci, L. P. (1981). The development of personal concepts: A domain distinct from moral or social concepts. *Child Development, 52,* 114–121.

Nucci, L., Camino, C., & Sapiro, C. M. (1996). Social class effects on northeastern Brazilian children's conceptions of areas of personal choice and social regulation. *Child Development, 67,* 1223–1242.

Nye, B., Hedges, L. V., & Konstantopoulos, S. (2001). The long-term effects of small classes in early grades: Lasting benefits in mathematics achievement at grade 9. *Journal of Experimental Education, 69,* 245–257.

O'Brien, S. F., & Bierman, K. L. (1988). Conceptions and perceived influence of peer groups: Interviews with preadolescents and adolescents. *Child Development, 59,* 1360–1365.

O'Donnell, L., Stueve, A., O'Donnell, C., Duran, R., San Doval, A., Wilson, R. F., et al. (2002). Long-term reductions in sexual initiation and sexual activity among urban middle schoolers in the Reach for Health service learning program. *Journal of Adolescent Health, 31,* 93–100.

O'Donnell, L., Stueve, A., San Doval, A., Duran, R., Haber, D., Atnafou, R., et al. (1999). The effectiveness of the Reach for Health community youth service learning program in reducing early and unprotected sex among urban middle school students. *American Journal of Public Health, 89,* 176–181.

Odgers, C. L., Moffitt, T. E., Tach, L. M., Taylor, A., Matthews, C. L., & Sampson, R. J. (2009). The protective effects of neighborhood collective efficacy on British children growing up in deprivation: A developmental analysis. *Developmental Psychology, 45*(4), 942–957.

OECD. (2008). Executive summary. *PISA 2006: Science competences for tomorrow's world.*

OECD/UNESCO. (2003). *Literacy skills for the world of tomorrow: Further results from PISA 2000.* Paris, France: Authors.

Offer, D., Ostrov, E., & Howard, K. I. (1981). *The adolescent.* New York: Basic Books.

Office of Juvenile Justice and Delinquency Prevention. (2002). *Statistical briefing book.* http://ojjdp.ncjrs.gov/ojstatbb/publications/statbb.asp?ID=T35

Office of National Drug Control Policy. (2005). *Media campaign: New report shows that teens who receive anti-drug messages are less likely to use drugs.* http://www.newsforparents.org/expert_anti_drug_messages_teens.html

Office of the Surgeon General. (2001). The Surgeon General's call to action to promote sexual health and responsible sexual behavior. Rockville, MD: Author.

Ogbu, J. U. (1981). Black education: A cultural-ecological perspective. In H. P. McAdoo (Ed.), *Black families.* Beverly Hills: Sage.

Ogbu, J. U. (1992). Understanding cultural diversity and learning. *Educational Researcher, 21,* 5–14.

Ogden, C. L., Carroll, M. D., & Flegal, K. M. (2008). High Body Mass Index for age among US children and adolescents, 2003–2006. *JAMA, 299*(20), 2401–2405.

Okun, M. A., & Sasfy, J. H. (1977). Adolescence, the self-image and formal operations. *Adolescence, 12,* 373–379.

Olweus, D. (1978). *Aggression in the schools: Bullies and whipping boys.* Washington, DC: Hemisphere Press (Wiley).

Olweus, D. (1993). *Bullying at school: What we know and what we can do.* Cambridge, MA: Blackwell.

Olweus, D. (1999). Norway. In P. K. Smith, Y. Morita, J. Junger-Tas, D. Olweus, R. Catalano, & P. Slee (Eds.), *The nature of school bullying: A cross-national perspective* (pp. 28–48). New York: Routledge.

Olweus, D. (2001). Peer harassment: A critical analysis and some important issues. In J. Juvonen & S. Graham (Eds.), *Peer harassment in school: The plight of the vulnerable and victimized* (pp. 3–20). New York: Guilford Press.

Oman, R. F., Vesely, S., Aspy, C. B., McLeroy, K. R., Rodine, S., & Marshall, L. (2004). The potential protective effect of youth assets on adolescent alcohol and drug use. *American Journal of Public Health, 94,* 1425–1430.

Oregon Statewide Tobacco Control Plan 2005–2010. http:Oregon.gov/DHS/ph/tobacco/plan05-10.shtml

Orlofsky, J., & Frank, M. (1986). Personality structure as viewed through early memories and identity status in college men and women. *Journal of Personality and Social Psychology, 5,* 580–586.

Osherson, D. N., & Markman, E. M. (1975). Language and the ability to evaluate contradictions and tautologies. *Cognition, 3,* 213–226.

Osipow, S. H. (1983). *Theories of career development* (3rd ed.). Englewood Cliffs, NJ: Prentice-Hall.

Owings, J., & Stocking, C. (1985). *High school and beyond: Characteristics of high school students who identify themselves as handicapped.* Washington, DC: National Center for Education Statistics, U.S. Department of Education.

Oxford, M. L., Gilchrist, L. D., Lohr, M. J., Gillmore, M. R., Morrison, D. M., & Spieker, S. J. (2005). Life course heterogeneity in the transition from adolescence to adulthood among adolescent mothers. *Journal of Research on Adolescence, 15,* 479–504.

Oyserman, D., Coon, H. M., & Kemmelmeier, M. (2002). Rethinking individualism and collectivism: Evaluation of theoretical assumptions and meta-analyses. *Psychological Bulletin, 128,* 3–72.

Ozawa, M. N. (2004). Social welfare spending on family benefits in the United States and Sweden: A comparative study. *Family Relations, 53,* 301–309.

Ozer, E. J., & Weinstein, R. S. (2004). Urban adolescents' exposure to community violence: The role of support, school safety, and social constraints in a school-based sample of boys and girls. *Journal of Clinical Child and Adolescent Psychology, 33,* 463–476.

Pagani, L. S., Vitaro, F., Tremblay, R. E., McDuff, P., Japel, C., & Larose, S. (2008). When predictions fail: The case of unexpected pathways toward high school dropout. *Journal of Social Issues, 64*(1), 175–193.

Pahl, K., & Way, N. (2006). Longitudinal trajectories of ethnic identity among urban Black and Latino adolescents. *Child Development, 77*(5), 1403–1415.

Pakaslahti, L., Karjalainen, A., & Keltikangas-Jarvinen, L. (2002). Relationships between adolescent prosocial problem-solving strategies, prosocial behaviour, and social acceptance. (2002). *International Journal of Behavioral Development, 26,* 137–144.

Palinscar, A. S., & Brown, A. L. (1984). Reciprocal teaching of comprehension-monitoring activities. *Cognition and Instruction, 1,* 117–175.

Panel on High-Risk Youth. Commission on Behavioral and Social Sciences and Education, National Research Council. (1993). *Losing generations: Adolescents in high-risk settings.* Washington, DC: National Academy Press.

Papini, D. R., Farmer, F. L., Clark, S. M., & Snell, W. E., Jr. (1988). An evaluation of adolescent patterns of sexual self-disclosure to parents and friends. *Journal of Adolescent Research, 3,* 387–401.

Papini, D. R., Snell, W. E., Belk, S. S., & Clark, S. (1988). *Developmental correlates of women's and men's sexual self-disclosures.* Paper presented at the meeting of the Southwestern Psychological Association, Tulsa, OK.

Pardun, C. J., L'Engle, K. L., & Brown, J. D. (2005). Linking exposure to outcomes: Early adolescents' consumption of sexual content in six media. *Mass Communication & Society, 8*(2), 75–91.

Parker, J. G., & Gottman, J. M. (1989). Social and emotional development in a relational context. In T. J. Berndt & G. W. Ladd (Eds.), *Peer relationships in child development.* New York: Wiley.

Parker, J. G., Low, C. M., Walker, A. R., & Gamm, B. K. (2005). Friendship jealousy in young adolescents: Individual differences and links to sex, self-esteem, aggression, and social adjustment. *Developmental Psychology, 41*(1), 235–250.

Parker, S., Nichter, M., Nichter, M., Vuckovic, N., Sims, C., & Ritenbaugh, C. (1995). Body image and weight concern among Afro American and White adolescent females: Differences that make a difference. *Human Organization, 54,* 103–115.

Pasley, B. K., & Ihenger-Tallman, M. (1989). Boundary ambiguity in remarriage: Does ambiguity differentiate degree of marital adjustment and integration? *Family Relations, 38,* 46–52.

Pass, L. A., & Dean, R. S. (2008). Neuropsychology and RTI: LD policy, diagnosis, and interventions. In E. Fletcher-Janzen & C. R. Reynolds (Eds.), *Neuropsychological perspectives on learning disabilities in the era of RTI: Recommendations for diagnosis and intervention* (pp. 238–246). Hoboken, NJ: Wiley.

Passel, J. S., & Cohn, D. (2008). *U.S. population projections: 2005–2050.* Pew Research Center. http://www.pewresearch.org

Paterson, J. E., Field, J., & Pryor, J. (1994). Adolescents' perceptions of their attachment relationships with their mothers, fathers, and friends. *Journal of Youth and Adolescence, 23,* 579–600.

Patrikakou, E. N. (1996). Investigating the academic achievement of adolescents with learning disabilities: A structural modeling approach. *Journal of Educational Psychology, 88,* 435–450.

Patterson, S. J., Sochting, I., & Marcia, J. E. (1992). The inner space and beyond: Women and identity. In G. R. Adams, T. P. Gullotta, & R. Montemayor (Eds.), *Adolescent identity formation.* Newbury Park, CA: Sage.

Paus, T. (2005). Mapping brain maturation and cognitive development during adolescence. *Trends in Cognitive Sciences, 9*(2), 60–68.

Paus, T., Zijdenbos, A., Worsley, K., Collins, D. L., Blumenthal, J., Giedd, J. N., Rapoport, J. L., & Evans, A. C. (1999). Structural maturation of neural pathways in children and adolescents: In vivo study. *Science, 283,* 1908–1911.

Pearl, R., Bryan, T., & Herzog, A. (1990). Resisting or acquiescing to peer pressure to engage in misconduct: Adolescents' expectations of probable consequences. *Journal of Youth and Adolescence, 19,* 43–55.

Pearson, J., Crissey, S. R., & Riegle-Crumb, C. (2009). Gendered fields: Sports and advanced course taking in high school. *Sex Roles, 61,* 519–535.

Pellegrini, A. D., & Long, J. D. (2002). A longitudinal study of bullying, dominance, and victimization during the transition from primary school through secondary school. *British Journal of Developmental Psychology, 20,* 259–280.

Perkins, D. N. (1987). Knowledge as design: Teaching thinking through content. In J. B. Baron & R. J. Sternberg (Eds.), *Teaching thinking skills: Theory and practice.* New York: Freeman.

Perry, W. G. (1970). *Forms of intellectual and ethical development in the college years.* San Francisco: Holt, Rinehart & Winston.

Petersen, A. C., Compas, B. E., Brooks-Gunn, J., Stemmler, M., Ey, S., & Grant, K. (1993). Depression in adolescence. *American Psychologist, 48,* 155–168.

Pettit, G. S., Bates, J. E., Dodge, K. A., & Meece, D. W. (1999). The impact of after-school peer contact on early adolescent externalizing problems is moderated by parental monitoring, perceived neighborhood safety, and prior adjustment. *Child Development, 70,* 768–778.

Pew Internet & American Life Project. (2007). *Teens and social media.* http://www.pewinternet.org

Pew Internet and American Life Project. (2001). http://www.pewinternet.org

Pham, M. T. (2007). Emotion and rationality: A critical review and interpretation of empirical evidence. *Review of General Psychology, 11*(2), 155–178.

Phelps, S. B., & Jarvis, P. A. (1994). Coping in adolescence: Empirical evidence for a theoretically based approach to assessing coping. *Journal of Youth and Adolescence, 23,* 359–371.

Philliber, S., Kaye, J., & Herrling, S. (2001). The national evaluation of the Children's Aid Society Carrera-Model Program to prevent teen pregnancy. Children's Aid Society. http://www.childrensaidsociety.org/files/cas-full_12-site_report1.pdf

Phinney, J. (1989). Stages of ethnic identity development in minority group adolescents. *Journal of Early Adolescence, 9,* 34–49.

Phinney, J. (1990). Ethnic identity in adolescents and adults: Review of research. *Psychological Bulletin, 108,* 499–514.

Phinney, J. (1993). A three-stage model of ethnic identity development. In M. Bernal & G. Knight (Eds.), *Ethnic identity: Formation and transmission among Hispanics and other minorities* (pp. 61–79). Albany: State University of New York Press.

Phinney, J. (1996). When we talk about American ethnic groups, what do we mean? *American Psychologist, 51,* 918–927.

Phinney, J. S. (2005). Ethnic identity in late modern times: A response to Rattansi and Phoenix. *Identity, 5,* 187–194.

Phinney, J. S., & Cobb, N. J. (1996). Reasoning about intergroup relations among Hispanic and Euro-American adolescents. *Journal of Adolescent Research, 11,* 306–324.

Phinney, J. S., & Devich-Navarro, M. (1997). Variations in bicultural identification among African American and Mexican American adolescents. *Journal of Research on Adolescence, 7,* 3–32.

Phinney, J. S., & Haas, K. (2003). The process of coping among ethnic minority first-generation college freshmen: A narrative approach. *Journal of Social Psychology, 143,* 707–726.

Phinney, J. S., & Rotheram, M. J. (1987). Children's ethnic socialization: Themes and implications. In M. J. Rotheram & J. S. Phinney (Eds.), *Children's ethnic socialization: Pluralism and development.* Beverly Hills: Sage.

Phinney, J. S., Baumann, K., & Blanton, S. (2001). Life goals and attributions for expected outcomes among adolescents from five ethnic groups. *Hispanic Journal of Behavioral Sciences, 23,* 363–377.

Phinney, J. S., Cantu, C. L., & Kurtz, D. A. (1997). Ethnic and American identity as predictors of self-esteem among African-American, Latino, and White adolescents. *Journal of Youth and Adolescence, 26,* 165–185.

Phinney, J. S., Ferguson, D. L., & Tate, J. D. (1997). Intergroup attitudes among ethnic adolescents: A causal model. *Child Development, 68,* 955–969.

Phinney, J. S., Jacoby, B., & Silva, C. (2007). Positive intergroup attitudes: The role of ethnic identity. *International Journal of Behavioral Development, 31*(5), 478–490.

Phinney, J. S., Kim-Jo, T., Osorio, S., & Vilhjalmsdottir, P. (2005). Autonomy and relatedness in adolescent-parent disagreements: Ethnic and developmental factors. *Journal of Adolescent Research, 20*(1), 8–39.

Phinney, J. S., Ong, A., & Madden, T. (2000). Cultural values and intergenerational value discrepancies in immigrant and nonimmigrant families. *Child Development, 71,* 528–539.

Phinney, J., & Kohatsu, E. (1997). Ethnic and racial identity and mental health. In J. Schulenberg, J. Maggs, & K. Hurrelmann (Eds.), *Health risks and developmental transitions during adolescence.* New York: Cambridge University Press.

Phinney, J., & Rosenthal, D. A. (1992). Ethnic identity in adolescence: Process, context, and outcome. In G. Adams, R. Montemayor, & T. Gulotta (Eds.), *Advances in adolescent development* (Vol. 4). Newbury Park, CA: Sage.

Phinney, J., & Tarver, S. (1988). Ethnic identity search and commitment in black and white eighth graders. *Journal of Early Adolescence, 8,* 265–277.

Piaget, J. (1952a). *The child's conception of number.* New York: Humanities Press.

Piaget, J. (1952b). *The origins of intelligence in children.* New York: International Universities Press.

Piaget, J. (1954). *The construction of reality in the child.* New York: Basic Books.

Piaget, J. (1965). *The moral judgment of the child.* New York: Free Press.

Piaget, J. (1971). *Biology and knowledge.* Chicago: University of Chicago Press.

Pikas, A. (2002). New developments of the Shared Concern Model. *School Psychology International, 23,* 307–326.

Pinquart, M., & Silbereisen, R. K. (2002). Changes in adolescents' and mothers' autonomy and connectedness in conflict discussions: An observational study. *Journal of Adolescence, 25,* 509–522.

Pinquart, M., Silbereisen, R. K., & Wiesner, M. (2004). Changes in discrepancies between desired and present states of developmental tasks in adolescence: A 4-process model. *Journal of Youth and Adolescence, 33,* 467–477.

Place, D. M. (1975). The dating experience for adolescent girls. *Adolescence, 10,* 157–174.

Plant, T. M. (2006). The role of KiSS-1 in the regulation of puberty in higher primates. *European Journal of Endocrinology, 155,* S11–S16.

Plant, T. M. (2008). Hypothalamic control of the pituitary-gonadal axis in higher primates: key advances over the last two decades. *Journal of Neuroendocrinology, 20,* 719–726.

Planty, M., Hussar, W., Snyder, T., Kena, G., KewalRamani, A., Kemp, J., et al. (2009). *The Condition of Education 2009* (NCES 2009–081). Washington, D.C.: National Center for Education Statistics, Institute of Education Sciences, U.S. Department of Education.

Plomin, R., & Daniels, D. (1987). Why are children in the same family so different from one another? *Behavioral and Brain Sciences, 10,* 1–60.

Plomin, R., Reiss, D., Hetherington, E. M., & Howe, G. W (1994). Nature and nurture: Genetic contributions to measures of the family environment. *Developmental Psychology, 30,* 32–43.

Polivy, J., & Herman, C. P. (2002). Causes of eating disorders. *Annual Review of Psychology, 53,* 187–213.

Pollack, S., & Gilligan, C. (1982). Images of violence in Thematic Apperception Test stories. *Journal of Personality and Social Psychology, 42,* 159–167.

Poole, M. E., & Evans, G. T. (1988). Adolescents' self-perceptions of competence in life skill areas. *Journal of Youth and Adolescence, 18,* 147–173.

Postman, N. (1982). *The disappearance of childhood.* New York: Delacorte.

Powell, G. J. (1985). Self-concepts among Afro-American students in racially isolated minority schools: Some regional differences. *Journal of the American Academy of Child Psychiatry, 24,* 142–149.

Powers, S. I., Hauser, S. T., Schwartz, J. M., Noam, G. G., & Jacobson, A. M. (1983). Adolescent ego development and family interaction: A structural-developmental perspective. In H. D. Grotevant & C. R. Cooper (Eds.), *Adolescent development in the family.* San Francisco: Jossey-Bass.

Pratt, M. W., Arnold, M. L., Pratt, A. T., & Diessner, R. (1999). Predicting adolescent moral reasoning from family climate: A longitudinal study. *Journal of Early Adolescence, 19,* 148–175.

Pratt, M. W., Norris, J. E., van de Hoef, S., & Arnold, M. L. (2001). Stories of hope: Parental optimism in narratives about adolescent children. *Journal of Social and Personal Relationships, 18,* 603–623.

Pratt, M. W., Hunsberger, B., Pancer, S. M., & Alisat, S. (2003). A longitudinal analysis of personal values socialization: Correlates of a moral self-ideal in late adolescence. *Social Development, 12,* 563–585.

Prinzie, P., Stams, G. J., Dekovi, M., Reijntes, A. H., & Belsky, J. (2009). The relations between parents' Big Five personality factors and parenting: A meta-analytic review. (2009). *Journal of Personality and Social Psychology, 97*(2), 351–362.

Pulkkinen, L., & Kokko, K. (2000). Identity development in adulthood: A longitudinal study. *Journal of Research in Personality, 34,* 445–470.

Purcell, P., & Stewart, L. (1990). Dick and Jane in 1989. *Sex Roles, 22,* 177–185.

Purves, D., Brannon, E. M., Cabeza, R., Huettel, S. A., LaBar, K. S., Platt, M. L., et al. (2008). *Principles of cognitive neuroscience.* Sunderland, MA: Sinauer Associates, Inc.

Putallaz, M. (1983). Predicting children's sociometric status from their behavior. *Child Development, 54,* 1417–1426.

Puzzanchera, C. (2009). Juvenile arrests 2008. *Juvenile Justice Bulletin, December.* Washington, DC: U.S. Department of Justice, Office of Juvenile Justice and Delinquency Prevention. www.ojp.usdoj.gov/ojjdp

Quatman, T., & Watson, C. M. (2001). Gender differences in adolescent self-esteem: An exploration of domains. *Journal of Genetic Psychology, 162,* 93–117.

Quatman, T., Sokolik, E., & Smith, K. (2000). Adolescent perception of peer success: A gendered perspective over time. *Sex Roles, 43,* 61–84.

Quinlivan, J. A., Box, H., & Evans, S. F. (2003). Postnatal home visits in teenage mothers: A randomised controlled trial. *The Lancet, 361,* 893–900.

Quinlivan, J. A., Luehr, B., & Evans, S. F. (2004). Teenage mothers' predictions of their support levels before and actual support levels after having a child. *Journal of Pediatric Adolescent Gynecology, 17,* 273–278.

Raja, S. N., McGee, R., & Stanton, W. R. (1992). Perceived attachments to parents and peers and psychological well-being in adolescence. *Journal of Youth and Adolescence, 21,* 471–485.

Rakic, P. (1995). Corticogenesis in human and nonhuman primates. In M. S. Gazzaniga (Ed.), *The cognitive neurosciences* (pp. 127–145). Cambridge, MA: MIT Press.

Ramirez, O. (1989). Mexican American children and adolescents. In J. T. Gibbs, L. N. Huang, & Associates (Eds.), *Children of color.* San Francisco: Jossey-Bass.

Raudenbush, S. W., Rowan, B., & Cheong, Y. F. (1993). Higher order instructional goals in secondary schools: Class, teacher, and school influences. *American Educational Research Journal, 30,* 523–553.

Reese, H. W., & Overton, W. F. (1970). Models of development and theories of development. In L. R. Goulet & P. B. Baltes (Eds.), *Lifespan developmental psychology: Research and theory.* New York: Academic Press.

Regan, P. C., & Berscheid, E. (1995). Gender differences in beliefs about the causes of male and female sexual desire. *Personal Relationships, 2,* 345–358.

Regnerus, M. D., & Elder, G. H., Jr. (2003). Staying on track in school: Religious influences in high- and low-risk settings. *Journal for the Scientific Study of Religion, 42,* 633–649.

Reid, M., Landesman, S., Treder, R., & Jaccard, J. (1989). "My family and friends": Six- to twelve-year-old children's perceptions of social support. *Child Development, 60,* 896–910.

Reiss, A. L., Abrams, M. T., Singer, H. S., Ross, J. L., & Denckla, M. B. (1996). Brain development, gender and IQ in children: A volumetric imaging study. *Brain, 119*, 1763–1774.

Rembeck, G. I., & Gunnarsson, R. K. (2004). Improving pre- and post-menarcheal 12-year-old girls' attitudes toward menstruation. *Health Care for Women International, 25*, 680–698.

Renk, K., & Creasey, G. (2003). The relationship of gender, gender identity and coping strategies in late adolescence. *Journal of Adolescence, 26*, 159–168.

Repetti, R. L. (1994). Short-term and long-term processes linking job stressors to father-child interaction. *Social Development, 3*, 1–15.

Repetti, R. L., Taylor, S. E., & Seeman, T. E. (2002). Risky families: Family social environments and the mental and physical health of offspring. *Psychological Bulletin, 128*, 330–366.

Resnick, M., Harris, L., & Blum, R. (1993). The impact of caring and connectedness on adolescent health and well-being. *Journal of Pediatrics and Child Health, 29* (Suppl. 1), 3–9.

Rest, J. R., Davison, M. L., & Robbins, S. (1978). Age trends in judging moral issues: A review of cross-sectional, longitudinal, and sequential studies of the Defining Issues Test. *Child Development, 49*(1), 263–279.

Restak, R. (1984). Master clock of the brain and body. *Science Digest*, pp. 54–104.

Reyes, O., & Jason, L. A. (1993). Pilot study examining factors associated with academic success for Hispanic high school students. *Journal of Youth and Adolescence, 22*, 57–71.

Reynolds, A. J., & Temple, J. A. (1998). Extended early childhood intervention and school achievement: Age thirteen findings from the Chicago Longitudinal Study. *Child Development, 69*, 231–246.

Reynolds, A. J., Ou, S., & Topitzes, J. W. (2004). Paths of effects of early childhood intervention on educational attainment and delinquency: A confirmatory analysis of the Chicago Child–Parent Centers. *Child Development, 75*, 1299–1328.

Reynolds, A. J., Temple, J. A., Robertson, D. L., & Mann, E. A. (2001). Long-term effects of an early childhood intervention on educational achievement and juvenile arrest: A 15-year follow-up of low-income children in public schools. *JAMA, 285*, 2339–2346.

Rice, K. G., & Mulkeen, P. (1995). Relationships with parents and peers: A longitudinal study of adolescent intimacy. *Journal of Adolescent Research, 10*, 338–357.

Richards, M. H., Miller, B. V., O'Donnell, P. C., Wasserman, M. S., & Colder, C. (2004). Parental monitoring mediates the effects of age and sex on problem behaviors among African American urban young adolescents. *Journal of Youth and Adolescence, 33*, 221–233.

Rideout, V. (2001). *Generation Rx.com: How young people use the Internet for health information.* Menlo Park, CA: Kaiser Family Foundation.

Riegel, K. F. (1973). *Dialectic operations: The final period of cognitive development.* Princeton, NJ: Educational Testing Service.

Rigby, K. (2001). Health consequences of bullying and its prevention in schools. In J. Juvonen & S. Graham (Eds.), *Peer harassment in school: The plight of the vulnerable and victimized* (pp. 310–331). New York: Guilford Press.

Roa, J., Aguilar, E., Dieguez, C., Pinilla, L., & Tena-Sempere, M. (2008). New frontiers in kisspeptin/GPR54 physiology as fundamental gatekeepers of reproductive function. *Frontiers in Neuroendocrinology, 29*, 48–69.

Roberts, D. F., Foehr, U. G., & Rideout, V. (2005). *Generation M: Media in the lives of 8-18 year-olds.* http://www.kff.org/entmedia/upload/Generation-M-Media-in-the-Lives-of-8-18-Year-olds-Report.pdf

Roche, K. M., Ahmed, S., & Blum, R. W. (2008). Enduring consequences of parenting for risk behaviors from adolescence into early adulthood. *Social Science & Medicine, 66*(9), 2023–2034.

Rodriguez, R. (1982). *Hunger of memory: The education of Richard Rodriguez.* New York: Bantam Dell.

Rogoff, B. (1990). *Apprenticeship in thinking: Cognitive development in social context.* New York: Oxford University Press.

Rogoff, B. (2003). *The cultural nature of human development.* New York: Oxford University Press.

Rogoff, B., Paradise, R., Arauz, R. M., Correa-Chavez, M., & Angelillo, C. (2003). Firsthand learning through intent participation. *Annual Review of Psychology, 54*, 175–203.

Rogoff, E., Baker-Sennett, J., Lacasa, P., & Goldsmith, D. (1995). Development through participation in sociocultural activity. *New Directions for Child Development, 67*, 45–65.

Roisman, G. I., Masten, J. S., Coatsworth, J. D., and Tellegen, A. (2004). Salient and emerging developmental tasks in the transition to adulthood. *Child Development, 75*, 123–133.

Romero, A. J. (2005). Low-income neighborhood barriers and resources for adolescents' physical activity. *Journal of Adolescent Health, 36*, 253–259.

Ronde, K., Pizacani, B., Stark, M., Pietrukowicz, M., Mosbaek, C., Romoli, C., et al. (2001). Effectiveness of school-based programs as a component of a statewide tobacco control initiative—Oregon, 1999–2000. *Morbidity and Mortality Weekly Report, 50*, 663–666.

Rose, A. J., & Asher, S. R. (2004). Children's strategies and goals in response to help-giving and help-seeking tasks within a friendship. *Child Development, 75*, 749–763.

Rose, A. J., Swenson, L. P., & Waller, E. M. (2004). Overt and relational aggression and perceived popularity: Developmental differences in concurrent and prospective relations. *Developmental Psychology, 40*, 378–387.

Rose, A., Koo, H. P., Bhaskar, B., Anderson, K., White, G., & Jenkins, R. R. (2005). The influence of primary caregivers on the sexual behavior of early adolescents. *Journal of Adolescent Health, 37*(2), 135–144.

Rosenbaum, J. E. (2009). Patient teenagers? A comparison of the sexual behavior of virginity pledgers and matched nonpledgers. *Pediatrics, 123*(1), e110–120.

Rosenblum, G. D., & Lewis, M. (1999). The relations among body image, physical attractiveness, and body mass in adolescence. *Child Development, 70*, 50–64.

Rosenthal, D. A., & Feldman, S. S. (1992). The nature and stability of ethnic identity in Chinese youth: Effects of length of residence in two cultural contexts. *Journal of Cross-Cultural Psychology, 23*, 213–227.

Rosenthal, D. A., & Feldman, S. S. (1999). The importance of importance: Adolescents' perceptions of parental communication about sexuality. *Journal of Adolescence, 22*, 835–852.

Rosenthal, D. A., & Hrynevich, C. (1985). Ethnicity and ethnic identity: A comparative study of Greek-, Italian-, and Anglo-Australian adolescents. *International Journal of Psychology, 20*, 723–742.

Rosenthal, D. A., Senserrick, T., & Feldman, S. S. (2001). A typology approach to describing parents as communicators about sexuality. *Archives of Sexual Behavior, 30*, 463–482.

Rostosky, S. S., Wilcox, B. L., Wright, M. L. C., & Randall, B. A. (2004). The impact of religiosity on adolescent sexual behavior: A review of the evidence. *Journal of Adolescent Research, 19*, 677–697.

Roth, M. A., & Parker, J. G. (2001). Affective and behavioral responses to friends who neglect their friends for dating partners: Influences of gender, jealousy and perspective. *Journal of Adolescence, 24*, 281–296.

Roth, P. (1969). *Portnoy's complaint.* New York: Random House.

Rotheram, M. J., & Phinney, J. S. (1983). *Intercultural attitudes and behaviors of children.* Paper presented at the meeting of the Society for Intercultural Evaluation, Training and Research, San Gemignano, Italy.

Rotheram, M. J., & Phinney, J. S. (1987). Ethnic behavior patterns as an aspect of identity. In J. Phinney & M. Rotheram (Eds.), *Children's ethnic socialization: Pluralism and development*. Beverly Hills: Sage.

Rotheram-Borus, M. J., & Phinney, J. S. (1990). Patterns of social expectations among black and Mexican-American children. *Child Development, 61*, 542–556.

Rotheram-Borus, M. J., Song, J., Gwadz, M., Lee, M., Van Rossem, R., & Koopman, C. (2003). Reductions in HIV risk among runaway youth. *Prevention Science, 4*, 173–187.

Rotheram-Borus, M., Rosario, M., Van Rossem, R., Reid, H., & Gillis, R. (1995). Prevalence, course, and predictors of multiple problem behaviors among gay and bisexual male adolescents. *Developmental Psychology, 31*, 75–85.

Rowley, A. A., Roesch, S. C., Jurica, B. J., & Vaughn, A. A. (2005). Developing and validating a stress appraisal measure for minority adolescents. *Journal of Adolescence, 28*, 547–557.

Royle, R., Barrett, M., & Buchanan-Barrow, E. (1998). *"Religion is the opiate of the masses" (Marx, 1876): An investigation of the salience of religion for children*. Paper presented at the XVth Biennial Meeting of the International Society for the Study of Behavioural Development, Berne, Switzerland.

Ruangkanchanasetr, S., Plitponkarnpim, A., Hetrakul, P., & Kongsakon, R. (2005). Youth risk behavior survey: Bangkok, Thailand. *Journal of Adolescent Health Care, 36*(3), 227–235.

Rubin, K. H., Dwyer, K. M., Booth-LaForce, C., Kim, A. H., Burgess, K. B., Rose-Krasnor, L. (2004). Attachment, friendship, and psychosocial functioning in early adolescence. *Journal of Early Adolescence, 24*, 326–356.

Ruble, D. N., & Brooks-Gunn, J. (1982). The experience of menarche. *Child Development, 53*, 1557–1566.

Ruck, M. D., Peterson-Badali, M., & Day, D. M. (2002). Adolescents' and mothers' understanding of children's rights in the home. *Journal of Research on Adolescence, 12*, 373–398.

Rudder, T. (2002). *Teen volunteerism: A model for America*. The Gallup Organization. http://www.gallup.com/poll/5695/Teen-Volunteerism-Model-America.aspx

Russell, S. T., & Joyner, K. (2001). Adolescent sexual orientation and suicide risk: Evidence from a national study. *American Journal of Public Health, 91*, 1276–1283.

Russo, R. G. (2006). The extent of public education nondiscrimination policy protections for lesbian, gay, bisexual, and transgender students: A national study. *Urban Education, 41*, 115–150.

Ryan, J. M., Tracey, T. J. G., & Rounds, J. (1996). Generalizability of Holland's structure of vocational interests across ethnicity, gender, and socioeconomic status. *Journal of Counseling Psychology, 43*, 330–337.

Ryan, K. E., & Ryan, A. M. (2005). Psychological processes underlying stereotype threat and standardized math test performance. *Educational Psychologist, 40*, 53–63.

Salmivalli, C. (2001). Group view on victimization: Empirical findings and their implications. In J. Juvonen & S. Graham (Eds.), *Peer harassment in school: The plight of the vulnerable and victimized* (pp. 398–419). New York: Guilford Press.

Samargia, L. A., Saewyc, E. M., & Elliott, B. A. (2006). Foregone mental health care and self-reported access barriers among adolescents. *The Journal of School Nursing, 22*(1), 17–24.

Sampson, R. J., Morenoff, J. D., & Gannon-Rowley, T. (2002). Assessing 'neighborhood effects': Social processes and new directions in research. *Annual Review of Sociology, 28*, 443–478.

Sanchez, R. P., Waller, M. W., & Greene, J. M. (2006). Who runs: A demographic profile of runaway youth in the United States. *Journal of Adolescent Health, 39*, 778–781.

Sanders, G., Sjodin, M., & de Chastelaine, M. (2002). On the elusive nature of sex differences in cognition: Hormonal influences contributing to within-sex variation. *Archives of Sexual Behavior, 31*, 145–152.

Santelli, J. S., Nystrom, R. J., Brindis, C., Juszczak, L., Klein, J. D., Bearss, N., et al. (2003). Reproductive health in school-based health centers: Findings from the 1998–99 census of school-based health centers. *Journal of Adolescent Health, 32*, 443–451.

Sapru, S. (2006). Parenting and adolescent identity: A study of Indian families in New Delhi and Geneva. *Journal of Adolescent Research, 21*(5), 484–513.

Satter, E. (1988). Should the obese child diet? In K. Clark, R. Parr, & W. Castelli (Eds.), *Evaluation and management of eating disorders*. Champaign, IL: Life Enhancement Publications.

Scaramella, L. V., Conger, R. D., Spoth, R., & Simons, R. L. (2002). Evaluation of a social contextual model of delinquency: A cross-study replication. *Child Development, 73*, 175–195.

Scarr, S. (1992). Developmental theories for the 1990s: Development and individual differences. *Child Development, 63*, 1–19.

Scarr, S. (1993). Biological and cultural diversity: The legacy of Darwin for development. *Child Development, 64*, 1333–1353.

Schaie, K. W. (1965). A general model for the study of development problems. *Psychological Bulletin, 64*, 92–107.

Schiedel, D. G., & Marcia, J. E. (1985). Ego identity, intimacy, sex role orientation, and gender. *Developmental Psychology, 21*, 149–160.

Schleyer-Lindenmann, A. (2006). Developmental tasks of adolescents of native or foreign origin in France and Germany. *Journal of Cross-Cultural Psychology, 37*(1), 85–99.

Schonert-Reichl, K. A. (1999). Relations of peer acceptance, friendship adjustment, and social behavior to moral reasoning during early adolescence. *Journal of Early Adolescence, 19*, 249–279.

Schooler, D. (2008). Real women have curves: A longitudinal investigation of TV and the body image development of Latina adolescents. *Journal of Adolescent Research, 23*(2), 132–153.

Schoon, I., Parsons, S., & Sacker, A. (2004). Socioeconomic adversity, educational resilience, and subsequent levels of adult adaptation. *Journal of Adolescent Research, 19*, 383–404.

Schreiber, J. B. (2002). Institutional and student factors and their influence on advanced mathematics achievement. *Journal of Educational Research, 95*, 247–255.

Schultz, P. W., Gouveia, V. V., Cameron, L. D., Tankha, G., Schmuck, P., & Franek, M. (2005). Values and their relationship to environmental concern and conservation behavior. *Journal of Cross-Cultural Psychology, 36*, 457–475.

Schwartz, R. (1992). AIDS medical guide. *HIV Infection and AIDS: Are you at risk?* San Francisco: San Francisco AIDS Foundation and Centers for Disease Control (1991).

Schwartz, S. J., & Montgomery, M. J. (2002). Similarities or differences in identity development? The impact of acculturation and gender on identity process and outcome. *Journal of Youth and Adolescence, 31*, 359–372.

Schwartz, S. J., Mullis, R. L., Waterman, A. S., & Dunham, R. M. (2000). Ego identity status, identity style, and personal expressiveness: An empirical investigation of three convergent constructs. *Journal of Adolescent Research, 15*, 504–521.

Schwartzberg, N. S., & Dytell, R. S. (1996). Dual-earner families: The importance of work stress and family stress for psychological wellbeing. *Journal of Occupational Health Psychology, 1*, 211–223.

Schweder, R. A., Mahapatra, M., & Miller, J. (1987). Culture and development. In J. Kagan (Ed.), *The emergence of moral concepts in young children*. Chicago: University of Chicago Press.

Scott, M. E., Booth, A., King, V., & Johnson, D. R. (2007). Postdivorce father-adolescent closeness. *Journal of Marriage & the Family, 69*(5), 1194–1209.

Sedikides, C., Gaertner, L., & Vevea, J. L. (2005). Pancultural self-enhancement reloaded: A meta-analytic reply to Heine (2005). *Journal of Personality and Social Psychology, 89*, 539–551.

Seem, S. R., & Clark, M. D. (2006). Healthy women, healthy men, and healthy adults: An evaluation of gender role stereotypes in the twenty-first century. *Sex Roles, 55,* 247–258.

Seginer, R. (1998). Adolescents' perceptions of relationships with older siblings in the context of other close relationships. *Journal of Research on Adolescence, 8,* 287–308.

Seiber, J. E. (1980). A social learning approach to morality. In M. Windmiller, N. Lambert, & E. Turiel (Eds.), *Moral development and socialization.* Boston: Allyn & Bacon.

Seider, S. (2008). "Bad things could happen" How fear impedes social responsibility in privileged adolescents. *Journal of Adolescent Research, 23*(6), 647–666.

Seixas, P. (1993). Historical understanding among adolescents in a multicultural setting. *Curriculum Inquiry, 23,* 301–327.

Seligman, M. E. P., & Csikszentmihalyi, M. (2000). Positive psychology: An introduction. *American Psychologist, 55,* 5–14.

Selman, R. L. (1980). *The growth of interpersonal understanding.* New York: Academic Press.

Selye, H. (1982). Stress: Eustress, distress, and human perspectives. In S. B. Day (Ed.), *Life stress* (Vol. 3). New York: Van Nostrand Reinhold.

Seminara, S. B. (2005). We all remember our first kiss: Kisspeptin and the male gonadal axis. *The Journal of Clinical Endocrinology & Metabolism, 90*(12), 6738–6740.

Seminara, S. B. (2006). Mechanisms of Disease: The first kiss-a crucial role for kisspeptin-1 and its receptor, G-protein-coupled receptor 54, in puberty and reproduction. *Nature clinical practice. Endocrinology & metabolism, 2*(6), 328-334.

Seminara, S. B., Messager, S., Chatzidaki, E. E., Thresher, R. R., Acierno, J. S., Shagoury, J. K., et al. (2003). The GPR54 gene as a regulator of puberty. *New England Journal of Medicine, 349,* 1614–1627.

Sessa, F. M., & Steinberg, L. (1991). Family structure and the development of autonomy during adolescence. *Journal of Early Adolescence, 11,* 38–55.

Shafii, M., Carrigan, S., Whittinghill, J. R., & Derrick, A. (1985). Psychological autopsy of completed suicide in children and adolescents. *American Journal of Psychiatry, 142,* 1061–1064.

Shahab, M., Mastronardi, C., Seminara, S. B., Crowley, W. F., Ojeda, S. R., & Plant, T. M. (2005). Increased hypothalamic GPR54 signaling: A potential mechanism for initiation of puberty in primates. *Proceedings of the National Academy of Sciences, 102,* 2129–2134.

Shalitin, S., & Phillip, M. (2003). The role of obesity and leptin in the pubertal process and pubertal growth—a review. *International Journal of Obesity and Related Metabolic Disorders, 27,* 869–874.

Shedler, J., & Block, J. (1990). Adolescent drug use and psychological health: A longitudinal inquiry. *American Psychologist, 45,* 612–630.

Sheley, J. F., Zhang, J., Brody, C. J., & Wright, J. D. (1995). Gang organization, gang criminal activity, and individual gang members' criminal behavior. *Social Science Quarterly, 76,* 53–69.

Shifflett-Simpson, K., & Cummings, E. M. (1996). Mixed message resolution and children's responses to interadult conflict. *Child Development, 67,* 437–448.

Sickmond, M. (2004). Juveniles in corrections. *National Report Series Bulletin.* Office of Juvenile Justice and Delinquency Prevention, U.S. Department of Justice. www.ojjdp.ncjrs.gov

SIECUS. (2001). *Toward a sexually healthy America.* Washington, DC. Author.

Siegler, R. S., & Alibali, M. W. (2004). *Children's thinking* (4th ed.). Upper Saddle River, NJ: Prentice-Hall.

Siewert, E. A., Stallings, M. C., & Hewitt, J. K. (2003). Genetic and environmental analysis of behavioral risk factors for adolescent drug use in a community twin sample. *Twin Research, 6,* 490–496.

Silverberg, S. B., & Steinberg, L. (1990). Psychological well-being of parents with early adolescent children. *Developmental Psychology, 26,* 658–666.

Silverman, I. W. (2003). Gender differences in resistance to temptation: Theories and evidence. *Developmental Review, 23,* 219–259.

Silverstein, B., Perdue, L., Peterson, B., & Kelly, E. (1986). The role of the mass media in promoting a thin standard of bodily attractiveness for women. *Sex Roles, 14,* 519–532.

Simmons, R. G., & Blyth, D. A. (1987). *Moving into adolescence.* New York: Aldine de Gruyter.

Simons, L. G., & Conger, R. D. (2007). Linking mother-father differences in parenting to a typology of family parenting styles and adolescent outcomes. *Journal of Family Issues, 28*(2), 212–241.

Simpson, G. E., & Yinger, J. M. (1985). *Racial and cultural minorities* (5th ed.). New York: Plenum Press.

Sionean, C., DiClemente, R. J., Wingood, G. M., Crosby, R., Cobb, B. K., Harrington, K., et al. (2002). Psychosocial and behavioral correlates of refusing unwanted sex among African-American adolescent females. *Journal of Adolescent Health, 30,* 55–63.

Sisk, C. L., & Zehr, J. L. (2005). Pubertal hormones organize the adolescent brain and behavior. *Frontiers in Neuroendocrinology, 26,* 163–174.

Skal, P., Ireland, M., & Borowsky, I. W. (2003). Smoking among American adolescents: A risk and protective factor analysis. *Journal of Community Health, 28,* 79–97.

Skinner, B. F. (1938). *The behavior of organisms: An experimental analysis.* New York: Appleton-Century-Crofts.

Skinner, B. F. (1953). *Science and human behavior.* New York: Macmillan.

Skinner, B. F. (1961). *Cumulative record* (rev. ed.). New York: Appleton-Century-Crofts.

Skoe, E. E., Cumberland, A., Eisenberg, N., Hansen, K., & Perry, J. (2002a). The influences of sex and gender-role identity on moral cognition and prosocial personality traits. *Sex Roles, 46,* 295–309.

Skoe, E. E., Eisenberg, N., & Cumberland, A. (2002b). The role of reported emotion in real-life and hypothetical moral dilemmas. *Personality and Social Psychology Bulletin, 28,* 962–973.

Slaughter-Defoe, D. T., Nakagawa, K., Takanishi, R., & Johnson, D. J. (1990). Toward cultural/ecological perspectives on schooling and achievement in African- and Asian-American children. *Child Development, 61,* 363–383.

Slavin, R. E. (1985). Cooperative learning: Applying contact theory in desegregated schools. *Journal of Social Issues, 41,* 45–62.

Slavin, R. E., Hurley, E. A., & Chamberlin, A. (2003). Cooperative learning and achievement: Theory and research. In W. M. Reynolds & G. E. Miller (Eds.), *Handbook of psychology* (Vol. 7, pp. 177–198). New York: Wiley.

Slicker, E. K. (1998). Relationship of parenting style to behavioral adjustment in graduating high school seniors. *Journal of Youth and Adolescence, 27,* 345–372.

Sloan, J., Kellermann, A., Reay, D., Ferris, J., Koepsell, T., Rivara, F., et al. (1988). Handgun regulation, crime, assaults, and homicides. *New England Journal of Medicine, 319,* 1256–1262.

Smetana, J. (1988). Concepts of self and social convention: Adolescents' and parents' reasoning about hypothetical and actual family conflicts. In M. R. Gunnar (Ed.), *21st Minnesota Symposium on Child Psychology.* Hillsdale, NJ: Erlbaum.

Smetana, J. G. (2000). Middle-class African American adolescents' and parents' conceptions of parental authority and parenting practices: A longitudinal investigation. *Child Development, 71,* 1672–1686.

Smetana, J. G. (2005). Adolescent-parent conflict: Resistance and subversion as developmental process. In L. Nucci (Ed.), *Conflict, contradiction, and contrarian elements in moral development and education* (pp. 69–91). Mahwah, NJ: Erlbaum.

Smetana, J. G. (2006). Social domain theory: Consistencies and variations in children's moral and social judgments. In M. Killen and J. G. Smetana (Eds.), *Handbook of moral development* (pp. 119–153). Mahwah, NJ: Erlbaum.

Smetana, J. G., & Asquith, P. (1994). Adolescents' and parents' conceptions of parental authority and personal autonomy. *Child Development, 65,* 1147–1162.

Smetana, J. G., & Berent, R. (1993). Adolescents' and mothers' evaluations of justifications for disputes. *Journal of Adolescent Research, 8,* 252–273.

Smetana, J. G., & Chuang, S. (2001). Middle-class African American parents' conceptions of parenting in the transition to adolescence. *Journal of Research on Adolescence, 11,* 177–198.

Smetana, J. G., & Daddis, C. (2002). Domain-specific antecedents of parental psychological control and monitoring: The role of parenting beliefs and practices. *Child Development, 73*(2), 563–580.

Smetana, J. G., Braeges, J. L., & Yau, J. (1991). Doing what you say and saying what you do: Reasoning about adolescent–parent conflict in interviews and interactions. *Journal of Adolescent Research, 6,* 276–295.

Smetana, J. G., Campione-Barr, N., & Daddis, C. (2004). Longitudinal development of family decision making: Defining healthy behavioral autonomy for middle-class African American adolescents. *Child Development, 75,* 1418–1434.

Smetana, J. G., Daddis, C., & Chuang, S. S. (2003). "Clean your room!" A longitudinal investigation of adolescent-parent conflict and conflict resolution in middle-class African American families. *Journal of Adolescent Research, 18*(6), 631–650.

Smetana, J. G., Metzger, A., & Campione-Barr, N. (2004). African American late adolescents' relationships with parents: Developmental transitions and longitudinal patterns. *Child Developement, 75*(3), 932–947.

Smetana, J. G., Metzger, A., Gettman, D. C., & Campione-Barr, N. (2006). Disclosure and secrecy in adolescent-parent relationships. *Child Development, 77*(1), 201–217.

Smetana, J. G., Tasopoulos-Chan, M., Gettman, D. C., Villalobos, M., Campione-Barr, N., & Metzger, A. (2009). Adolescents' and parents' evaluations of helping versus fulfilling personal desires in family situations. *Child Development, 80*(1), 280–294.

Smith, A. (2000). The inter-ethnic friendships of adolescent students: A Canadian study. *International Journal of Intercultural Relations, 24,* 247–258.

Smith, C., Denton, M. L., Faris, R., & Regnerus, M. (2002). Mapping American adolescent religious participation. *Journal for the Scientific Study of Religion, 41,* 597–612.

Smith, M. K. (2004). *"Full-service schooling," the encyclopedia of informal education.* http://www.infed.org/schooling/f-serv.htm

Smith, T. E. (1990). Parental separation and the academic self-concepts of adolescents: An effort to solve the puzzle of separation effects. *Journal of Marriage and the Family, 52,* 107–118.

Smith, T. E., & Leaper, C. (2006). Self-perceived gender typicality and the peer context during adolescence. *Journal of Research on Adolescence, 16*(1), 91–103.

Smokowski, P. R., Mann, E. A., Reynolds, A. J., & Fraser, M. W. (2004). Childhood risk and protective factors and late adolescent adjustment in inner-city minority youth. *Children and Youth Services Review, 26,* 63–91.

Snarey, J. R. (1985). Cross-cultural universality of social-moral development: A critical review of Kohlbergian research. *Psychological Bulletin, 97,* 202–232.

Sneed, C. D. (2008). Parent-adolescent communication about sex: The impact of content and comfort on adolescent sexual behavior. *Journal of HIV/AIDS Prevention in Children & Youth, 9*(1), 70–83.

Snow, R. E. (1986). Individual differences and the design of educational programs. *American Psychologist, 41,* 1029–1039.

Snowden, C. T., & Ziegler, T. E. (2000). Reproductive hormones. In J. T. Cacioppo, L. G. Tassinary, & G. Berntson (Eds.), *Handbook of psychophysiology* (2nd ed., pp. 368–396). New York: Cambridge University Press.

Snyder, H. N. (2004). Juvenile arrests 2002. *Juvenile Justice Bulletin.* Office of Juvenile Justice and Delinquency Prevention, U.S. Department of Justice Web site: http://www.ojp.usdoj.gov/ojjdp

Snyder, T. C., & Hoffman, C. M. (2002). *Digest of education statistics, 2001* (NCES 2002-130). Washington, DC: U.S. Department of Education, National Center for Education Statistics.

Snyder, T. D., & Tan, A. G. (2005). *Digest of Education Statistics.* Department of Education, National Center for Education Statistics. http://nces.ed.gov/programs/digest/d04

Snyder, T. D., Dillow, S. A., & Hoffman, C. M. (2009). *Digest of Education Statistics 2008.* (NCES 2009–020). Washington, DC: National Center for Education Statistics, Institute of Education Sciences, U.S. Department of Education.

Soenens, B., Vansteenkiste, M., Lens, W., Luyckx, K., Goossens, L., Beyers, W., et al. (2007). Conceptualizing parental autonomy support: Adolescent perceptions of promotion of independence versus promotion of volitional functioning. *Developmental Psychology, 43*(3), 633–646.

Soenens, B., Vansteenkiste, M., Luyckx, K., & Goossens, L. (2006). Parenting and adolescent problem behavior: An integrated model with adolescent self-disclosure and perceived parental knowledge as intervening variables. *Developmental Psychology 42*(2), 305–318.

Sokolov, E. M. (1963). Higher nervous functions: The orienting reflex. *Annual Review of Physiology, 25,* 545–580.

Solomon, G. (1990). Using technology to reach at-risk students. *Electronic Learning, 9,* 14–15.

Sommer, K., Whitman, T. L., Borkowski, J. G., Schellenbach, C., Maxwell, S., & Keogh, D. (1993). Cognitive readiness and adolescent parenting. *Developmental Psychology, 29,* 389–398.

Sorkhabi, N. (2005). Applicability of Baumrind's parent typology to collective cultures: Analysis of cultural explanations of parent socialization effects. *International Journal of Behavioral Development, 29,* 552–563.

Sourcebook of Criminal Justice Statistics 2003. http://www.albany.edu/sourcebook/pdf/t345.pdf

Sowell, E. R., Thompson, P. M., Tessner, K. D., & Toga, A. W. (2001). Mapping continued brain growth and gray matter density reduction in dorsal frontal cortex: Inverse relationships during postadolescent brain maturation. *Journal of Neuroscience, 21,* 8819–8829.

Sowell, T. (1978). Race and IQ reconsidered. In T. Sowell (Ed.), *American ethnic groups.* The Urban Institute.

Spence, S. H. (2003). Social skills training with children and young people: Theory, evidence and practice. *Child and Adolescent Mental Health, 8,* 84–96.

Spencer, M. B. (1985). Racial variations in achievement prediction: The school as a conduit for macrostructural cultural tension. In H. McAdoo & J. McAdoo (Eds.), *Black children: Social, educational, and parental environments.* Beverly Hills, CA: Sage.

Spiel, C., Glück, J., & Gössler, H. (2001). Stability and change of unidimensionality: The sample case of deductive reasoning. *Journal of Adolescent Research, 16,* 150–168.

Spinazzola, J., Wilson, H.W., & Stocking, V. B. (2002). Dimensions of silencing and resistance in adolescent girls: Development of a narrative method for research and prevention. In L. H. Collins, M. R. Dunlap, & J. C. Chrisler (Eds.), *Charting a new course for feminist psychology* (pp. 111–138). Westport, CT: Praeger/Greenwood.

Spires, H. A., Gallini, J., & Riggsbee, J. (1992). Effects of schema-based and text structure-based cues on expository prose comprehension in fourth graders. *Journal of Experimental Education, 60*, 307–320.

Spreen, O. (1988). *Learning disabled children growing up*. New York: Oxford University Press.

Squeglia, L. M., Spadoni, A. D., Infante, M. A., Myers, M. G., & Tapert, S. F. (2009). Initiating moderate to heavy alcohol use predicts changes in neuropsychological functioning for adolescent girls and boys. *Psychology of Addictive Behaviors, 23*(4), 715–722.

Sroufe, L. A. (1989). Relationships, self and individual adaptation. In A. J. Sameroff & R. N. Emde (Eds.), *Relationship disturbances in early childhood: A developmental approach* (pp. 70–94). New York: Basic Books.

Stams, G.-J., Juffer, F., & van Jzendoorn, M. H. (2002). Maternal sensitivity, infant attachment, and temperament in early childhood predict adjustment in middle childhood: The case of adopted children and their biologically unrelated parents. *Developmental Psychology, 38*, 806–821.

Starkman, N., & Rajani, N. (2002). The case for comprehensive sex education. *AIDS Patient Care and STDs, 16*, 313–318.

Stavrinos, D., Byington, K. W., & Schwebel, D. C. (2009). Effect of cell phone distraction on pediatric pedestrian injury risk. *Pediatrics, 123*(2), 179–185.

Steele, C. M. (1992). Race and the schooling of Black Americans. *The Atlantic Monthly, 269*, pp. 68–78.

Steele, C. M., & Aronson, J. (1995). Stereotype threat and the intellectual test performance of African Americans. *Journal of Personality and Social Psychology, 5*, 797–811.

Steele, J., James, J. B., & Barnett, R. C. (2002). Learning in a man's world: Examining the perceptions of undergraduate women in male-dominated academic areas. *Psychology of Women Quarterly, 26*, 46–50.

Stein, J. A., & Newcomb, M. D. (1999). Adult outcomes of adolescent conventional and agentic orientations: A 20-year longitudinal study. *Journal of Early Adolescence, 19*, 39–65.

Stein, J. A., Norweeta, G. M., Zane, J. I., & Rotheram-Borus, M. J. (2009). Paternal and maternal influences on problem behaviors among homeless and runaway youth. *American Journal of Orthopsychiatry, 79*(1), 39–50.

Stein, J. H., & Reiser, L. W. (1994). A study of white middle-class adolescent boys' responses to "semenarche" (the first ejaculation). *Journal of Youth and Adolescence, 23*, 373–384.

Steinberg, L. (1987). The impact of puberty on family relations: Effects of pubertal status and pubertal timing. *Developmental Psychology, 23*, 451–460.

Steinberg, L. (2001). We know some things: Parent–adolescent relationships in retrospect and prospect. *Journal of Research on Adolescence, 11*, 1–19.

Steinberg, L. (2008). A social neuroscience perspective on adolescent risk-taking. *Developmental Review, 28*, 78–106.

Steinberg, L., Brown, B. B., & Dornbusch, S. M. (1996). *Beyond the classroom*. New York: Simon & Schuster.

Steinberg, L., Fegley, S., & Dornbusch, S. (1993). Negative impact of part-time work on adolescent adjustment: Evidence from a longitudinal study. *Developmental Psychology, 29*, 171–180.

Steinberg, L., Lamborn, S. D., Darling, N., Mounts, N. S., & Dornbusch, S. M. (1994). Over-time changes in adjustment and competence among adolescents from authoritative, authoritarian, indulgent, and neglectful families. *Child Development, 65*, 754–770.

Stephens, J. M., Young, M. F., & Calabrese, T. (2007). Does moral judgment go offline when students are online? A comparative analysis of undergraduates' beliefs and behaviors relates to conventional and digital cheating. *Ethics & Behavior, 17*(3), 233–254.

Sternberg, R. J. (1981). Intelligence and nonentrenchment. *Journal of Educational Psychology, 73*, 1–16.

Sternberg, R. J. (1984). Mechanisms of cognitive development: A componential approach. In R. J. Sternberg (Ed.), *Mechanisms of cognitive development*. New York: Freeman.

Sternberg, R. J. (1985). *Beyond I.Q.: A triarchic theory of human intelligence*. New York: Cambridge University Press.

Sternberg, R. J. (2004). Culture and intelligence. *American Psychologist, 59*(5), 325–338.

Sternberg, R. J., & Rifkin, B. (1979). The development of analogical reasoning processes. *Journal of Experimental Child Psychology, 27*, 195–232.

Sternberg, R. J., Forsythe, G. B., Hedlund, J., Horvath, J., Snook S., Williams, W. M., et al. (2000). *Practical intelligence in everyday life*. New York: Cambridge University Press.

Stevens-Long, J., & Commons, M. L. (1992). *Adult life: Developmental processes* (4th ed.). Mountain View, CA: Mayfield.

Stevenson, H. C., McNeil, J. D., Herrero-Taylor, T., & Davis, G. Y. (2005). Influence of perceived neighborhood diversity and racism experience on the racial socialization of Black youth. *Journal of Black Psychology, 31*, 273–290.

Stevenson, H. W., Chen, C., & Uttal, D. H. (1990). Beliefs and achievement: A study of black, white, and Hispanic children. *Child Development, 61*, 508–523.

Stice, E. (2002). Risk and maintenance factors for eating pathology: A meta-analytic review. *Psychological Bulletin, 128*, 825–848.

Stice, E., Killen, J. D., Hayward, C., & Taylor, C. B. (1998). Age of onset for binge eating and purging during late adolescence: A 4-year survival analysis. *Journal of Abnormal Psychology, 107*, 671–675.

Stigler, J. W., & Stevenson, H. W. (1991). How Asian teachers polish each lesson to perfection. *American Educator, 15*(1), 12–20, 43–47.

Stith, S. M., Liu, T., Davies, L. C., Boykin, E. L., Alder, M. C., Harris, J. M., et al. (2008). Risk factors in child maltreatment: A meta-analytic review of the literature. *Aggression and Violent Behavior, 14*, 13–29.

Stone, M. R., Barber, B. L., & Eccles, J. S. (2008). We knew them when: Sixth grade characteristics that predict adolescent high school social identities. *Journal of Early Adolescence, 28*(2), 304–328.

Strasburger, V., & Donnerstein, E. (1999). Children, adolescents, and the media: Issues and solutions. *Pediatrics, 103*, 129–139.

Strauss, L. T., Herndon, J., Chang, J., Parker, W. Y., Bowens, S. V., & Berg, C. J. (2005). Abortion surveillance-United States, 2002. *Morbidity and Mortality Weekly Reports, 54*, 1–31.

Strayer, D. L., Drews, F. A., & Crouch, D. J. (2006). A comparison of the cell-phone driver and the drunk driver. *Human Factors, 48*, 381–391.

Strong, B., & DeVault, C. (2001). *Human sexuality* (4th ed.). New York: McGraw-Hill.

Subkoviak, M. J., Enright, R. D., Wu, C., Gassin, E. A., Freedman, S., Olson, L. M., & Sarinopoulos, I. (1995). Measuring interpersonal forgiveness in late adolescence and middle adulthood. *Journal of Adolescence, 18*, 641–655.

Subrahmanyam, K., & Greenfield, P. M. (2004). Constructing sexuality and identity in an Internet teen chatroom. *Journal of Applied Developmental Psychology, 25*, 651–666.

Sue, S. (1991). Ethnicity and culture in psychological research and practice. In J. Goodchilds (Ed.), *Psychological perspectives on human diversity in America* (pp. 51–85). Washington, DC: American Psychological Association.

Sukhodolsky, D. G., Kassinove, H., & Gorman, B. S. (2004). Cognitive-behavioral therapy for anger in children and adolescents: A meta-analysis. *Aggression and Violent Behavior, 9*, 247–269.

Summers-Effler, E. (2004). Little girls in women's bodies: Social interaction and the strategizing of early breast development. *Sex Roles, 51*, 29–44.

Sumter, S. R., Bokhorst, C. L., Steinberg, L., & Westenberg, P. M. (2009). The developmental pattern of resistance to peer influence in adolescence: Will the teenager ever be able to resist? *Journal of Adolescence, 32*, 1009–1021.

Sun, P., Unger, J. B., Palmer, P. H., Gallaher, P., Chou, C. P., Baezcone-Garbanati, L., et al. (2005). Internet accessibility and usage among urban adolescents in Southern California: Implications for Web-based health research. *CyberPsychology & Behavior, 5*, 441–453.

Sun, Y. (2001). Family environment and adolescents' well-being before and after parents' marital disruption: A longitudinal analysis. *Journal of Marriage and the Family, 63*, 697–713.

Sundet, J. M., Barlaug, D. G., & Torjussen, T. M. (2004). The end of the Flynn effect? A study of secular trends in mean intelligence test scores of Norwegian conscripts during half a century. *Intelligence, 32*, 349–362.

Super, D. E. (1981). A developmental theory: Implementing a self concept. In D. H. Montross & C. J. Shinkman (Eds.), *Career development in the 1980s: Theory and practice.* Springfield, IL: Thomas.

Super, D. E. (1990). A life-span, life-space approach to career development. In D. Brown, L. Brooks, & Associates (Eds.), *Career choice and development* (2nd ed., pp. 197–261). San Francisco: Jossey-Bass.

Surgeon General's Report. (1988). *The health consequences of smoking: Nicotine addiction.* U.S. Department of Health and Human Services. Washington, DC: U.S. Government Printing Office.

Susman, E. J., Dorn, L. D., & Schiefelbein, V. L. (2003). Puberty, sexuality, and health. In I. B. Weiner (Ed.), *Handbook of psychology* (Vol. 6, pp. 295–324). Hoboken, NJ: Wiley.

Suzuki, L. K., & Calzo, J. P. (2004). The search for peer advice in cyberspace: An examination of online teen bulletin boards about health and sexuality. *Applied Developmental Psychology, 25*, 685–698.

Swarr, A. E., & Richards, M. H. (1996). Longitudinal effects of adolescent girls' pubertal development, perceptions of pubertal timing, and parental relations on eating problems. *Developmental Psychology, 32*, 636–646.

Switzer, J. Y. (1990). The impact of generic word choices: An empirical investigation of age- and sex-related differences. *Sex Roles, 22*, 69–82.

Syed, M., & Azmitia, M. (2008). A narrative approach to ethnic identity in emerging adulthood: Bringing life to the identity status model. *Developmental Psychology, 44*(4), 1012–1027.

Tanner, J. M. (1968). Earlier maturation in man. *Scientific American, 218*(1), 21–27.

Tanner, J. M. (1972). Sequence, tempo and individual variation in growth and development of boys and girls aged twelve to sixteen. In J. Kagan & R. Coles (Eds.), *Twelve to sixteen: Early adolescence.* New York: Norton.

Tanner, J. M. (1991). Menarche, secular trend in age of. In R. M. Lerner, A. C. Petersen, & J. Brooks-Gunn (Eds.), *Encyclopedia of adolescence* (Vol. 2, pp. 637–641). New York: Garland.

Tasopoulos-Chan, M., Smetana, J. G., & Yau, J. P. (2009). How much do I tell thee? Strategies for managing information to parents among American adolescents from Chinese, Mexican, and European backgrounds. *Journal of Family Psychology, 23*(3), 364–374.

Tavris, C., & Wade, C. (1984). *The longest war: Sex differences in perspective* (2nd ed.). San Diego, CA: Harcourt Brace Jovanovich.

Taylor, D. J., Jenni, O. G., Acebo, C., & Carskadon, M. A. (2005). Sleep tendency during extended wakefulness: insights into adolescent sleep regulation and behavior. *Journal of Sleep Research, 14*, 239–244.

Taylor, R. D. (1996). Adolescents' perceptions of kinship support and family management practices: Association with adolescent adjustment in African American families. *Developmental Psychology, 32*, 687–695.

Teddlie, C., Kirby, P. C., & Stringfield, S. (1989). Effective vs. ineffective schools: Observable differences in the classroom. *American Journal of Education, 97*, 221–236.

Teen Research Unlimited. (2001). *Teens spend $155 billion in 2000.* http://www.tru-insight.com/pressrelease.cfm?page_id=75

Teitelman, A. M. (2004). Adolescent girls' perspectives of family interactions related to menarche and sexual health. *Qualitative Health Research, 14*, 1292–1308.

Tena-Sempere, M. (2006). KiSS-1 and reproduction: Focus on its role in the metabolic regulation of fertility. *Neuroendocrinology, 83*, 275–281.

Tena-Sempere, M. (2006a). GPR54 and kisspeptin in reproduction. (2006). *Human Reproduction Update, 12*, 631–639.

Tenenbaum, H. R., & Leaper, C. (2003). Parent-child conversations about science: The socialization of gender inequities? *Developmental Psychology, 39*, 34–47.

Tenenbaum, H. R., Porche, M. V., Snow, C. E., Tabors, P., & Ross, S. (2007). Maternal and child predictors of low-income children's educational attainment. *Journal of Applied Developmental Psychology, 28*(3), 227–238.

ter Bogt, T., Raaijmakers, Q., & van Wel, F. (2005). Socialization and development of the work ethic among adolescents and young adults. *Journal of Vocational Behavior, 66*, 420–437.

Terman, L. M. (1925). *Genetic studies of genius: Vol. 1. Mental and physical traits of a thousand gifted children.* Stanford, CA: Stanford University Press.

The forgotten half. (1989, June 26). *U.S. News and World Report,* pp.45–53.

Thomas, J. J., & Daubman, K. A (2001). The relationship between friendship quality and self-esteem in adolescent girls and boys. *Sex Roles, 45*, 53–65.

Thompson, S. H., Corwin, S. J., Rogan, T. J., & Sargent, R. G. (1999). Body-size beliefs and weight concerns among mothers and their adolescent children. *Journal of Child and Family Studies, 7*, 91–108.

Thornberry, T. P., Krohn, M. D., Lizotte, A. J., & Chard-Wierschem, D. (1993). The role of juvenile gangs in facilitating delinquent behavior. *Journal of Research in Crime and Delinquency, 30*, 55–87.

Thornton, M. C., Chatters, L. M., Taylor, R. J., & Allen, W. R. (1990). Sociodemographic and environmental correlates of racial socialization by black parents. *Child Development, 61*, 401–409.

Tidwell, R. (1988). Dropouts speak out: Qualitative data on early school departures. *Adolescence, 23*, 939–954.

Tittle, C. K. (1986). Gender research and education. *American Psychologist, 41*, 1161–1168.

Tobias, A. L. (1988). Bulimia: An overview. In K. Clark, R. Parr, & W. Castelli (Eds.), *Evaluation and management of eating disorders.* Champaign, IL: Life Enhancement Publications.

Toch, T. (1993). Violence in schools. *U.S. News and World Report, 115*, 31–37.

Tolson, J. M., & Urberg, K. A. (1993). Similarity between adolescent best friends. *Journal of Adolescent Research, 8*, 274–288.

Toossi, M. (2004). Labor force projections to 2012: The graying of the U.S. workforce. *Monthly Labor Review, 127*, 37–57. http://www.bls.gov/opub/ted/

Toubia, N. (1994). Female circumcision as a public health issue. *New England Journal of Medicine, 331*, 712–716.

Trautman, P. D., & Rotheram, M. J. (1986). Specific treatment modalities for adolescent suicide attempters. In *Report of the Secretary's Task Force (Vol. 3.): Prevention and Interventions in Youth Suicide.* Washington, DC: U.S. Government Printing Office.

Treboux, D., & Busch-Rossnagel, N. A. (1990). Social network influences on adolescent sexual attitudes and behaviors. *Journal of Adolescent Research, 5*, 175–189.

Triandis, H. C. (1988). Collectivism vs. individualism: A reconceptualization of a basic concept in cross-cultural psychology. In G. Verma & C. Bagley (Eds.), *Cross-cultural studies of personality, attitudes and cognition* (pp. 60–95). London: Macmillan.

Troiano, R. P., & Flegal, K. M. (1998). Overweight children and adolescents: Description, epidemiology, and demographics. *Pediatrics, 101*, 497–504.

Troth, A., & Peterson, C. C. (2000). Factors predicting safe-sex talk and condom use in early sexual relationships. *Health Communication, 12*, 195–218.

Tschann, J. M., & Adler, N. E. (1997). Sexual self-acceptance, communication with partner, and contraceptive use among adolescent females: A longitudinal study. *Journal of Research on Adolescence, 7*, 413–430.

Tschirgi, J. E. (1980). Sensible reasoning: A hypothesis about hypotheses. *Child Development, 51*, 1–10.

Tucker, C. J., Updegraff, K. A, McHale, S. M., & Crouter, A. C. (1999). Older siblings as socializers of younger siblings' empathy. *Journal of Early Adolescence, 19*, 176–198.

Turiel, E. (1983). *The development of social knowledge: Morality and convention.* Cambridge, England: Cambridge University Press.

Turiel, E. (2008). The development of children's orientations toward moral, social, and personal orders: More than a sequence of development. *Human Development, 51*, 21–39.

Turiel, E., & Wainryb, C. (2000). Social life in cultures: Judgments, conflict, and subversion. *Child Development, 71*(1), 250–256.

Turillazzi, E., & Fineschi, V. (2007). Femal genital mutilation: The ethical impact of the new Italian law. *Journal of Medical Ethics, 33*(2), 98–101.

Turnage, B. F. (2004). African American mother–daughter relationships mediating daughters' self-esteem. *Child and Adolescent Social Work Journal, 21*, 155–173.

Turner, H. A., & Kopiec, K. (2006). Exposure to interparental conflict and psychological disorder among young adults. *Journal of Family Issues, 27*, 131-158.

Twenge, J. M., & Crocker, J. (2002). Race and self-esteem: Meta-analyses comparing Whites, Blacks, Hispanics, Asians, and American Indians and Comment on Gray-Little and Hafdahl (2000). *Psychological Bulletin, 128*, 371-408.

Tyler, K. A., & Bersani, B. E. (2008). A longitudinal study of early adolescent precursors to running away. *Journal of Early Adolescence, 28*(2), 230–251.

U.S. Bureau of Labor Statistics. (2002). *Occupational outlook handbook, 2002–2003 edition.* http://www.bls.gov/oco/oco2003.htm

U.S. Bureau of Labor Statistics. (2005a). *Employment projections.* http://www.bls.gov/emp/emptab4.htm

U.S. Bureau of Labor Statistics. (2005b). *Occupational outlook handbook, 2004 edition.* http://www.bls.gov/oco/

U.S. Bureau of Labor Statistics. (2005c). Differences in earnings by age and sex in 2004. *Monthly Labor Review.* http://www.bls.gov/opub/ted/

U.S. Bureau of Labor Statistics (2007). *Employment projections.* http://www.bls.gov/emp/emptab3.htm

U.S. Bureau of Labor Statistics. (2009a). *The employment situation: June 2009.* http://www.bls.gov/news.release/pdf/metro.pdf

U.S. Bureau of Labor Statistics. (2009b). Household data annual averages: Employed persons by occupation, race, Hispanic or Latino ethnicity, and sex. http://www.bls.gov/cps/cpsaat10.pdf

U.S. Census Bureau. (1996a). In E. Baugher, & L. Lamison-White, *Current population reports, Series P60–194, Poverty in the United States: 1995.* Washington, DC: U.S. Government Printing Office.

U.S. Census Bureau. (1996b). In J. C. Day, *Current population reports, Series P25–1130, Population projections of the United States by age, sex, race, and Hispanic origin: 1995 to 2050.* Washington, DC: U.S. Government Printing Office.

U.S. Census Bureau. (1998a). Current population reports, Series P25, Marital status and living arrangements: March 1998 (update). Washington, DC: U.S. Government Printing Office.

U.S. Census Bureau. (1998b). *Current population reports, Series P20–500.* Washington, DC: U.S. Government Printing Office.

U.S. Census Bureau. (1999a). http://www.census/gov/population/socdemo/school/report98/tab0.1txt

U.S. Census Bureau. (1999b). *Current population reports, Series P60, Consumer income.* Washington, DC: U.S. Government Printing Office.

U.S. Census Bureau. (2000). *Projections of the total resident population by 5-year age groups, and sex with special age categories: Middle series, 2075 to 2100 (NP-T3-H).* http://www.census.gov/population/projections/nation/summary/np-t3-h.txt

U.S. Census Bureau. (2001a). *Statistical abstract of the United States* (121st ed.). http://www.census.gov/prod/2002pubs/01statab/stat-ab01.html

U.S. Census Bureau. (2001b). *Population by age, sex, race, and Hispanic or Latino origin for the United States: 2000 (PHC-T-9).* Table 1. http://www.census.gov/population/cen2000/phc-t9/tab01.pdf

U.S. Census Bureau. (2002). From birth to seventeen: The living arrangements of children, 2000. In *The population profile of the United States: 2000 (Internet release)* (pt. 2). http://www.census.gov/population/pop-profile/2000/chap06.pdf

U.S. Census Bureau. (2004). *U.S. interim projections by age, sex, race, and Hispanic origin.* http://www.census.gov/ipc/www/usinterimproj/

U.S. Census Bureau. (2005a). *America's families and living arrangements: 2004.* http://www.census/gov/population/www/socdemo/hh-fam/cps2004.html

U.S. Census Bureau. (2005b). Poverty thresholds 2004. *The 2004 Health and Human Services Policy Guidelines.* U.S. Department of Health and Human Services. http://aspe.hhs.gov/poverty/04poverty.shtml

U.S. Census Bureau. (2007). Single-parent households showed little variation since 1994. *Census Bureau reports.* http://www.census.gov/Press-Release/www/releases/archives/families_households/009842

U.S. Census Bureau. (2008a). *An older and more diverse nation by midcentury.* http://www.census.gov/Press-Release/www/releases/archives/population/012496.html

U.S. Census Bureau. (2008b). *Income, Poverty, and Health Insurance Coverage in the United States: 2007.* Report P60 (235), 53.

U.S. Department of Education. (1988). *Ninth annual report to Congress on the implementation of the Education of the Handicapped Act.* Washington, DC: OSERS.

U.S. Department of Education. (1996). *Digest of educational statistics 1996, NCES 96-133.* Washington, DC: U.S. Government Printing Office.

U.S. Department of Education. (1998). *The condition of education, 1998: Indicator 37: Homework and television viewing.* National Center for Education Statistics. http://nces.ed.gov/pubs98/98013.pdf

U.S. Department of Health and Human Services, Children's Bureau. (1998). *Child Maltreatment 1996: Reports from the States to the National Child Abuse and Neglect Data System.* Washington, DC: U.S. Government Printing Office.

U.S. Department of Health and Human Services, Office of the Assistant Secretary for Planning and Evaluation. (2002a). Population, family, and neighborhood. In *Trends in the well-being of America's children & youth, 2001* (sect. 1). http://aspe.hhs.gov/hsp/01trends/contents.htm

U.S. Department of Health and Human Services, Office of the Assistant Secretary for Planning and Evaluation. (2002b). Economic security. In *Trends in the well-being of America's children & youth, 2001* (sect. 2). http://aspe.hhs.gov/hsp/01trends/contents.htm

U.S. Department of Health and Human Services, Office of the Assistant Secretary for Planning and Evaluation. (2002c). Social development and behavioral health. In *Trends in the well-being of America's children & youth, 2001* (sect. 4). http://aspe.hhs.gov/hsp/01trends/contents.htm

U.S. Department of Health and Human Services, Office of the Assistant Secretary for Planning and Evaluation. (2005). *Suicide warning signs.* http://mentalhealth.samhsa.gov/publications/allpubs/walletcard/_pdf/nsple.pdf

U.S. Department of Health and Human Services, Office of the Assistant Secretary for Planning and Evaluation. (2006). *The 2006 HHS poverty guidelines.* http://aspe.hhs.gov/poverty/06poverty.shtml

U.S. Department of Health and Human Services. (2009). Administration on Children, Youth and Families. *Child Maltreatment 2007.* Washington, DC: U.S. Government Printing Office.

U.S. Department of Human Services (2005). *Female genital cutting.* http://www.womenshealth.gov/faq/female-genital-cutting.

U.S. Department of Justice, Bureau of Justice Statistics. (1995). *School crime supplement to the national crime victimization survey, Spring.* Washington, DC: Bureau of Justice Statistics.

U.S. Department of Labor, Bureau of Labor Statistics. (2001) *Consumer expenditure survey: Integrated survey, 2001.*

U.S. Department of Labor. (2000). *Report on the youth labor force.* http://www.bls.gov/opub/rylf/rylfhome.htm

Underwood, J., & Szabo, A. (2003). Academic offenses and e-learning: Individual propensities in cheating. *British Journal of Educational Technology, 34,* 467–477.

UNICEF UK. (2005). *End child exploitation: Child labor today.* http://www.unicef.org.uk/publications/pdf/ECECHILD2_a4.pdf

UNICEF. (2006). *Child protection information sheet: Child labor.* http://www.unicef.org/protection/files/Child_Labour.pdf

UNICEF. (2009). Statistics by Area: Child Protection. In *Childinfo: Monitoring the situation of children and women.* http://www.childinfo.org/labour.html

Urban Institute. (2005). *Education in the age of accountability.* http://web.archive.org/web/20050310013056/ http://www.urban.org/content/IssuesInFocus/EducationintheAgeofAccountability/Education.htm

Urberg, K. A. (1992). Locus of peer influence: Social crowd and best friend. *Journal of Youth and Adolescence, 21,* 439–450.

Urberg, K. A., Degirmencioglu, S. M., Tolson, J. M., & Halliday-Scher, K. (1995). The structure of adolescent peer networks. *Developmental Psychology, 31,* 540–547.

Valkenburg, P. M., & Peter, J. (2008). Adolescents' identity experiments on the internet: Consequences for social competence and self-concept unity. *Communication Research, 35*(2), 208–231.

Valkenburg, P. M., Schouten, A. P., & Peter, J. (2005). Adolescents' identity experiments on the internet. *New Media & Society, 7*(3), 383–402.

Van den Berg, S. M., & Boomsma, D. I. (2007). The familial clustering of age at menarche in extended twin families. *Behavior Genetics, 37,* 661–667.

van der Sluis, S., Posthuma, D., Dolan, C. V., de Geus, E. J. C., Colum, R., & Boomsma, D. I. (2006). Sex differences on the Dutch WAIS–III. *Intelligence, 34*(3), 273–289.

van Manen, T. G., Prins, P. J. M., & Emmelkamp, P. M. G. (2004). Reducing aggressive behavior in boys with a social cognitive group treatment: Results of a randomized controlled trial. *Journal of the American Academy of Child and Adolescent Psychiatry, 43,* 1478–1487.

Van Voorhees, B. W., Smith, S., & Ewigman, B. (2008). Treat depressed teens with medication *and* psychotherapy. *The Journal of Family Practice, 57*(11), 735–739.

van Wel, F., Linssen, H., & Abma, R. (2000). The parental bond and the well-being of adolescents and young adults. *Journal of Youth and Adolescence, 29,* 307–318.

Vanfraussen, K., Ponjaert-Kristoffersen, I., & Brewaeys, A. (2002). What does it mean for youngsters to grow up in a lesbian family created by means of donor insemination? *Journal of Reproductive & Infant Psychology, 20*(4), 237–252.

Vazsonyi, A. T., & Snider, J. B. (2008). Mentoring, competencies, and adjustment in adolescents: American part-time employment and European apprenticeships. *International Journal of Behavioral Development, 32*(1), 46–55.

Vazsonyi, A. T., Hibbert, J. R., & Snyder, J. B. (2003). Exotic enterprise no more? Adolescent reports of family and parenting processes from youth in four countries. *Journal of Research on Adolescence, 13,* 129–160.

Ventura, S. J., Mathews, T. J., & Curtin, S. C. (2000). Declines in teenage birth rates, 1991–98: Update of national and state trends. *National Vital Statistics Reports, 47,* 1–9.

Verma, S., & Saraswathi, T. S. (2002). Adolescents in India: Street urchins or Silicon Valley millionaires? In B. B. Brown, R. Larson, & T. S. Saraswathi (Eds.), *The World's Youth: Adolescence in Eight Regions of the Globe* (pp. 105–140). New York: Cambridge University Press.

Vicary, J. R., Klingaman, L. R., & Harkness, W. L. (1995). Risk factors associated with date rape and sexual assault of adolescent girls. *Journal of Adolescence, 18,* 289–306.

Vigil, J. D. (1988). *Barrio gangs.* Austin: University of Texas Press.

Vitiello, B. (2009). Treatment of adolescent depression: What we have come to know. *Depression and Anxiety, 26,* 393–395.

Vosniadou, S., & Brewer, W. F. (1992). Mental models of the earth: A study of conceptual change in childhood. *Cognitive Psychology, 24,* 535–585.

Vowell, P. R., & Chen, J. (2004). Predicting academic misconduct: A comparative test of four sociological explanations. *Sociological Inquiry, 74,* 226–249.

Voyer, D. (1996). The relation between mathematical achievement and gender differences in spatial abilities: A suppression effect. *Journal of Educational Psychology, 88,* 563–571.

Vuchinich, S., Angelelli, J., & Gatherum, A. (1996). Context and development in family problem solving with preadolescent children. *Child Development, 67,* 1276–1288.

Vygotsky, L. (1978). *Mind in society.* Cambridge, MA: Harvard University Press.

Vygotsky, L. S. (1978). *Mind in society: The development of higher psychological processes.* Cambridge, MA: Harvard University Press.

Wadden, T. A., Brownell, K. D., & Foster, G. D. (2002). Obesity: Responding to the global epidemic. *Journal of Consulting and Clinical Psychology, 70,* 510–525.

Wadsworth, M. E., Gudmundsen, G. R., Raviv, T., Ahlkvist, J. A., McIntosh, D. N., Kline, G. H., et al. (2004). Coping with terrorism: Age and gender differences in effortful and involuntary responses to September 11th. *Applied Developmental Science, 8,* 143–157.

Wagner, B. M., Cohen, P., & Brook, J. S. (1996). Parent/adolescent relationships: Moderators of the effects of stressful life events. *Journal of Adolescent Research, 11,* 347–374.

Wagner, R. K., & Sternberg, R. J. (1986). Tacit knowledge and intelligence in the everyday world. In R. J. Sternberg & R. K. Wagner (Eds.), *Practical intelligence: Nature and origins of competence in the everyday world.* New York: Cambridge University Press.

Wahlstrom, K. L. (2002). Changing times: Findings from the first longitudinal study of later high school start times. *Sleep, 86,* 3–21.

Wainright, J. L., Russell, S. T., & Patterson, C. J. (2004). Psychosocial adjustment, school outcomes, and romantic relationships of adolescents with same-sex parents. *Child Development, 75,* 1886–1898.

Waizenhofer, R. N., Buchanan, C. M., & Jackson-Newsom, J. (2004). Mothers' and fathers' knowledge of adolescents' daily activities: Its sources and its links with adolescent adjustment. *Journal of Family Psychology, 18,* 348–360.

Waldinger, R. J., Diguer, L., Guastella, F., Lefebvre, R., Allen, J. P., Luborsky, L., et al. (2002). The same old song: Stability and change in relationship schemas from adolescence to young adulthood. *Journal of Youth and Adolescence, 31,* 17–29.

Walker, L. J., Gustafson, P., & Hennig, K. H. (2001). The consolidation/transition model in moral reasoning development. *Developmental Psychology, 37*(2), 187–197.

Wallerstein, J., & Lewis, J. M. (2004). The unexpected legacy of Divorce: Report of a 25-year study. *Psychoanalytic Psychology, 21*(3), 353–370.

Wallerstein, J. S., Lewis, J. M., & Blakeslee, S. (2000). *The unexpected legacy of divorce: A 25-year landmark study.* New York: Hyperion.

Walters, J. M., & Gardner, H. (1986). The theory of multiple intelligences: Some issues and answers. In R. J. Sternberg & R. K. Wagner (Eds.), *Practical intelligence: Nature and origins of competence in the everyday world.* New York: Cambridge University Press.

Wang, J., Simons-Morton, B. G., Farhart, T., & Luk, J. W. (2009). Socio-demographic variability in adolescent substance use: Mediation by parents and peers. *Prevention Science, 10*(4), 387–396.

Wang, Q., Pomerantz, E. M., & Chen, H. (2007). The role of parents' control in early adolescents' psychological functioning: A longitudinal investigation in the United States and China. *Child Development, 78*(5), 1592–1610.

Wapner, M. L. (1980). Personal communication.

Wapner, M. L. (1990). Personal communication.

Ward, L. M. (2002). Does television exposure affect emerging adults' attitudes and assumptions about sexual relationships? Correlational and experimental confirmation. *Journal of Youth and Adolescence, 31,* 1–15.

Ward, S. L., & Overton, W. F. (1990). Semantic familiarity, relevance, and the development of deductive reasoning. *Developmental Psychology, 26,* 488–493.

Warren, M. P. (1983). Physical and biological aspects of puberty. In J. Brooks-Gunn & A. C. Petersen (Eds.), *Girls at puberty: Biological and psychosocial perspectives.* New York: Plenum Press.

Wason, P. C., & Johnson-Laird, P. N. (1972). *Psychology of reasoning: Structure and content.* Cambridge, MA: Harvard University Press.

Waters, A. (2005a). *Slow food, slow schools: Transforming education through a school lunch program.* http://www.edibleschoolyard.org/homepage.html

Waters, A. (2005b). On making school lunch an academic subject. (Personal communication.)

Way, N., & Greene, M. L. (2006). Trajectories of perceived friendship quality during adolescence: The patterns and contextual predictors. *Journal of Research on Adolescence, 16*(2), 293–320.

Webster, C. (1994). Effects of Hispanic ethnic identification on marital roles in the purchase decision process. *Journal of Consumer Research, 21,* 319–331.

Wechsler, D. (1981). *WAIS–R Manual: Wechsler Adult Intelligence Scale—Revised.* San Antonio, TX: Psychological Corporation.

Weersing, V. R., Rozenman, M., & Gonzalez, A. (2009). Core components of therapy in youth: Do we know what to disseminate? *Behavior Modification, 33*(1), 24–47.

Weimann, E. (2002). Gender-related differences in elite gymnasts: The female athlete triad. *Journal of Applied Physiology, 92,* 2146–2152.

Weiner, I. B. (1980). Psychopathology in adolescence. In J. Adelson (Ed.), *Handbook of adolescent psychology.* New York: Wiley.

Weiss, C. H., Murphy-Graham, E., Petrosino, A., & Gandhi, A. G. (2008). The fairy godmother—and her warts: Making the dream of evidence-based policy come true. *American Journal of Evaluation, 29*(1), 29–47.

Weisz, J. R., Southam-Gerow, M. A., Gordis, E. B., Connor-Smith, J. K., Chu, B. C., Langer, D. A., et al. (2009). Cognitive–behavioral therapy versus usual clinical care for youth depression: An initial test of transportability to community clinics and clinicians. *Journal of Consulting and Clinical Psychology, 77*(3), 383–396.

Wellman, B., Smith, A., Wells, A., & Kennedy, T. (2008). *Networked families.* http://www.pewinternet.org/Reports/2008/Networked-Families

Wells, J. C. (2007). Sexual dimorphism of body composition. *Best Practice & Research : Clinical Endocrinology & Metabolism, 21*(3), 415–430.

Wentzel, K. R. (2002). Are effective teachers like good parents? Teaching styles and student adjustment in early adolescence. *Child Development, 73,* 287–301.

Werner, E. (1989). Children of the garden island. *Scientific American, 260*(4), 106–111.

Werner, E. (1989). High-risk children in young adulthood: A longitudinal study from birth to 32 years. *American Journal of Orthopsychiatry, 59,* 72–81.

Werner, E., & Smith, R. (1982). *Vulnerable but invincible: A longitudinal study of resilient children and youth.* New York: McGraw-Hill.

Werner, E., & Smith, R. (1992). *Overcoming the odds: High-risk children from birth to adulthood.* Ithaca, NY: Cornell University Press.

West, S. L., & O'Neal, K. K. (2004). Project D.A.R.E. outcome effectiveness revisited. *American Journal of Public Health, 94*(6), 1027–1029.

Whitaker, D. J., & Miller, K. S. (2000). Parent-adolescent discussions about sex and condoms: Impact on peer influences of sexual risk behavior. *Journal of Adolescent Research, 15*(2), 251–273.

Whitbeck, L. B., Yoder, K. A., Hoyt, D. R., & Conger, R. D. (1999). Early adolescent sexual activity: A developmental study. *Journal of Marriage and the Family, 61,* 934–946.

White, F. A., & Matawie, K. M. (2004). Parental morality and family processes as predictors of adolescent morality. *Journal of Child & Family Studies, 13,* 219–233.

White, K. L., Speisman, J. C., & Costos, D. (1983). Young adults and their parents: Individuation to mutuality. In H. D. Grotevant & C. R. Cooper (Eds.), *Adolescent development in the family.* San Francisco: Jossey-Bass.

Wicherts, J. M., Dolan, C. V., Hessen, D. J., Oosterveld, P., van Baal, G. C. M., Boomsma, D. I., et al. (2004). Are intelligence tests measurement invariant over time? Investigating the nature of the Flynn effect. *Intelligence, 32,* 509–537.

Wiehe, S. E., Garrison, M. M., Christakis, D. A., Ebel, B. E., & Rivera, F. P. (2005). A systematic review of school-based smoking prevention trials with long-term follow-up. *Journal of Adolescent Health, 36*, 162–169.

Williams, J. M., & Currie, C. (2002). Self-esteem and physical development in early adolescence: Pubertal timing and body image. *Journal of Early Adolescence, 20*, 129–149.

Williams, J. M., & White, K. A. (1983). Adolescent status systems for males and females at three age levels. *Adolescence, 18*, 381–389.

Wilson, W. J. (1996). *When work disappears: The world of the new urban poor.* New York: Knopf.

Wintre, M. G., Hicks, R., McVey, G., & Fox, J. (1988). Age and sex differences in choice of consultant for various types of problems. *Child Development, 59*, 1046–1055.

Wirth, L. (1945). The problem of minority groups. In R. Linton (Ed.), *The science of man in the world crisis.* New York: Columbia University Press.

Wolfson, A. R., Spaulding, N. L., Dandrow, C., & Baroni, E. M. (2007). Middle school start times: The importance of a good night's sleep for young adolescents. *Behavioral Sleep Medicine, 5*, 194–209.

Women on Words and Images. (1975). *Dick and Jane as victims: Sex stereotyping in children's readers* (Expanded ed.). Princeton, NJ: Author.

Woody, J. D., Russel, R., D'Souza, H. J., & Woody, J. K. (2000). Adolescent non-coital sexual activity: Comparisons of virgins and non-virgins. *Journal of Sex Education and Therapy, 25*, 261–268.

World Health Organization. (2008). *Media centre, Fact sheet No 241: Female genital mutilation.* http://www.who.int/mediacentre/factsheets/fs241/en/

Wright, L. S., Frost, C. J., & Wisecarver, S. J. (1993). Church attendance, meaningfulness of religion, and depressive symptomatology among adolescents. *Journal of Youth and Adolescence, 22*, 559–568.

Wright, S. M., Matlen, B. J., Baym, C. L., Ferrer, E., & Bunge, S. A. (2008). Neural correlates of fluid reasoning in children and adults. *Frontiers in Human Neuroscience, 1*, 1662–5161.

Wright, V. R., Chau, V., & Aratani, Y. (2010). *Who are America's poor children?* National Center for Children in Poverty. http://www.nccp.org/publications/pub_912.html

Wyche, K., Obolensky, N., & Glood, E. (1990). American Indian, Black American, and Hispanic American youth. In M. J. Rotheram-Borus, J. Bradley, & N. Obolensky (Eds.), *Planning to live: Evaluating and treating suicidal teens in community settings* (pp. 355–389). Tulsa: University of Oklahoma Press.

Wyckoff, S. C., Miller, K. S., Forehand, R., Bau, J. J., Fasula, A., & Long, N. (2008). Patterns of sexuality communication between preadolescents and their mothers and fathers. *Journal of Child and Family Studies, 17*(5), 649–662.

Xie, H., Cairns, R. B., & Cairns, B. D. (2002). The development of social aggression and physical aggression: A narrative analysis of interpersonal conflicts. *Aggressive Behavior, 28*, 341–355.

Xiong, Z. B., Eliason, P. A., Detzner, D. S., & Cleveland, M. J. (2005). Southeast Asian immigrants' perceptions of good adolescents and good parents. *Journal of Psychology, 139*, 159–175.

Yasui, M., Dorham, C. L., & Dishion, T. J. (2004). Ethnic identity and psychological adjustment: A validity analysis for European American and African American adolescents. *Journal of Adolescent Research, 19*, 807–825.

Yau, J., & Smetana, J. (2003). Adolescent-parent conflict in Hong Kong and Shenzhen: A comparison of youth in two cultural contexts. *International Journal of Behavioral Development, 27*(3), 201–211.

Yau, J., & Smetana, J. G. (1993). Chinese-American adolescents' reasoning about cultural conflicts. *Journal of Adolescent Research, 8*, 419–438.

Yau, J., & Smetana, J. G. (1996). Adolescent-parent conflict among Chinese adolescents in Hong Kong. *Child Development, 67*, 1262–1275.

Ybarra, M. (2008). *Texting 4 health 2008: Using text messaging to affect teen health.* http://www.texting4health.org/slides/Ybarra%20ISK%20T4H%2002%2029%202008.pdf

Ybarra, M. L., Diener-West, M., Markow, D., Leaf, P. J., Hamburger, M., & Boxer, P. (2008). Linkages between Internet and other media violence with seriously violent behavior by youth. *Pediatrics, 122*(5), 929–937.

Yeung, D. Y. L., Tang, C. S., & Lee, A. (2005). Psychosocial and cultural factors influencing expectations of menarche: A study on Chinese premenarcheal teenage girls. *Journal of Adolescent Research, 20*, 118–135.

Ying, Y. (1994). Chinese American adults' relationship with their parents. *International Journal of Social Psychology, 40*, 35–45.

Yoder, J. D., & Kahn, A. S. (1993). Working toward an inclusive psychology of women. *American Psychologist, 48*, 846–850.

Youniss, J. (1980). *Parents and peers in social development.* Chicago: University of Chicago Press.

Youniss, J., & Smollar, J. (1989). Adolescents' interpersonal relationships in social context. In T. J. Berndt & G. W. Ladd (Eds.), *Peer relationships in child development.* New York: Wiley.

Youniss, J., McLellan, J. A., & Yates, M. (1999). Religion, community service, and identity in American youth. *Journal of Adolescence, 22*, 243–253.

Youniss, J., McLellan, J. A., Su, Y., & Yates, M. (1999). The role of community service in identity development: Normative, unconventional, and deviant orientations. *Journal of Adolescent Research, 14*, 248–261.

Youth Indicators. (2005). *Trends in the well-being of American youth.* U.S. Department of Education, National Center for Education Statistics. Washington, DC: U.S. Government Printing Office.

Youth Service California. (2005). *Why youth service matters.* http://web.archive.org/web/20050222104928/http://yscal.org/ysmatters/stats.html

Yurgelun-Todd, D. (2007). Emotional and cognitive changes during adolescence. *Current Opinion in Neurobiology, 17*, 251–257.

Zaider, T. I., Johnson, J. G., & Cockell, S. J. (2000). Psychiatric comorbidity associated with eating disorder symptomatology among adolescents in the community. *International Journal of Eating Disorders, 28*, 58–67.

Zeldin, S., & Price, L. A. (1995). Creating supportive communities for adolescent development: Challenges to scholars. *Journal of Adolescent Research, 10*, 6–14.

Zhang, W., & Fuligni, A. J. (2006). Authority, autonomy, and family relationships among adolescents in urban and rural China. *Journal of Research on Adolescence, 16*(4), 527–537.

Zimmer-Gembeck, M. J., & Helfand, M. (2008). Ten years of longitudinal research on U.S. adolescent sexual behavior: Developmental correlates of sexual intercourse, and the importance of age, gender, and ethnic background. *Developmental Review, 28*, 153–224.

Zimmermann, B. J. (2000). Attaining self-regulation: A social-cognitive perspective. In M. Boekaerts, P. Pintrich, & M. Seidner (Eds.), *Self-regulation: Theory, research, and applications* (pp. 13–39). Orlando, FL: Academic Press.

Zimmermann, B. J., Bandura, A., & Martinez-Pons, M. (1992). Self-motivation for academic attainment: The role of self-efficacy beliefs and personal goal-setting. *American Educational Research Journal, 29*, 663–676.

Zimmermann, P., & Becker-Stoll, F. (2002). Stability of attachment representations during adolescence: The influence of ego-identity status. *Journal of Adolescence, 25*, 107–124.

Author Index

Subject Index